Business Law Today, Standard Edition

Smeal College of Business | Penn State University

University Park Campus | B LAW 346

Miller | Jentz

CENGAGE Learning™

Australia • Brazil • Japan • Korea • Mexico • Singapore • Spain • United Kingdom • United States

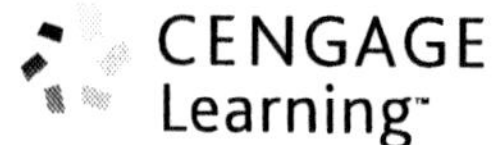

Business Law Today, Standard Edition: Smeal College of Business | Penn State University | University Park Campus | B LAW 346

Business Law Today, Standard Edition, 9th Edition
Roger LeRoy Miller | Gaylord A. Jentz

Study Guide to Accompany Business Law Today, Standard Edition, 9th Edition
Roger LeRoy Miller | Gaylord A. Jentz

Executive Editors:
Maureen Staudt
Michael Stranz

Senior Project Development Manager:
Linda deStefano

Marketing Specialist:
Courtney Sheldon

Senior Production/Manufacturing Manager:
Donna M. Brown

PreMedia Manager:
Joel Brennecke

Sr. Rights Acquisition Account Manager:
Todd Osborne

Cover Image:
Getty Images*

*Unless otherwise noted, all cover images used by Custom Solutions, a part of Cengage Learning, have been supplied courtesy of Getty Images with the exception of the Earthview cover image, which has been supplied by the National Aeronautics and Space Administration (NASA).

ISBN-13: 978-1-111-77491-2

ISBN-10: 1-111-77491-9

Cengage Learning
5191 Natorp Boulevard
Mason, Ohio 45040
USA

Cengage Learning is a leading provider of customized learning solutions with office locations around the globe, including Singapore, the United Kingdom, Australia, Mexico, Brazil, and Japan. Locate your local office at: **international.cengage.com/region.**
Cengage Learning products are represented in Canada by Nelson Education, Ltd.
For your lifelong learning solutions, visit **www.cengage.com/custom.**
Visit our corporate website at **www.cengage.com.**

Printed in the United States of America

BRIEF CONTENTS

From *Business Law Today, 9th Edition*

CHAPTER 23	AGENCY RELATIONSHIP IN BUSINESS	580
CHAPTER 24	EMPLOYMENT, IMMIGRATION, AND LABOR LAW	606
CHAPTER 25	EMPLOYMENT DISCRIMINATION	638
CHAPTER 26	SOLE PROPRIETORSHIPS AND PRIVATE FRANCHISES	668
CHAPTER 27	ALL FORMS OF PARTNERSHIP	683
CHAPTER 28	LIMITED LIABILITY COMPANIES AND SPECIAL BUSINESS FORMS	706
CHAPTER 29	CORPORATE FORMATION, MERGER, AND TERMINATION	722
CHAPTER 30	CORPORATE DIRECTORS, OFFICERS, AND SHAREHOLDERS	753
CHAPTER 31	INVESTOR PROTECTION, INSIDER TRADING, AND CORPORATE GOVERNANCE	778
CHAPTER 33	CONSUMER AND ENVIRONMENTAL LAW	835
CHAPTER 34	LIABILITY OF ACCOUNTANTS AND OTHER PROFESSIONALS	860
APPENDIX A	HOW TO BRIEF CASES AND ANALYZE CASE PROBLEMS	A-1
APPENDIX E	SAMPLE ANSWERS FOR END-OF-CHAPTER *HYPOTHETICAL QUESTIONS WITH SAMPLE ANSWER*	A-126
APPENDIX F	CASE EXCERPTS FOR *CASE ANALYSIS QUESTIONS*	A-132
	GLOSSARY	G-1
	INDEX	I-1

From *Study Guide for Business Law Today, 9th Edition*

CHAPTER 23	AGENCY RELATIONSHIP IN BUSINESS	191
CHAPTER 24	EMPLOYMENT, IMMIGRATION, AND LABOR LAW	199
CHAPTER 25	EMPLOYMENT DISCRIMINATION	209
CHAPTER 26	SOLE PROPRIETORSHIPS AND PRIVATE FRANCHISES	219
CHAPTER 27	ALL FORMS OF PARTNERSHIP	225
CHAPTER 28	LIMITED LIABILITY COMPANIES AND SPECIAL BUSINESS FORMS	233
CHAPTER 29	CORPORATE FORMATION, MERGER, AND TERMINATION	239
CHAPTER 30	CORPORATE DIRECTORS, OFFICERS, AND SHAREHOLDERS	249
CHAPTER 31	INVESTOR PROTECTION, INSIDER TRADING, AND CORPORATE GOVERNANCE	257
CHAPTER 33	CONSUMER AND ENVIRONMENTAL LAW	277
CHAPTER 34	LIABILITY OF ACCOUNTANTS AND OTHER PROFESSIONALS	287

Unit Four

Agency and Employment Law

Unit Contents

23 Agency Relationships in Business

24 Employment, Immigration, and Labor Law

25 Employment Discrimination

Chapter 23

Agency Relationships in Business

Chapter Outline

- Agency Relationships
- How Agency Relationships Are Formed
- Duties of Agents and Principals
- Agent's Authority
- Liability in Agency Relationships
- How Agency Relationships Are Terminated

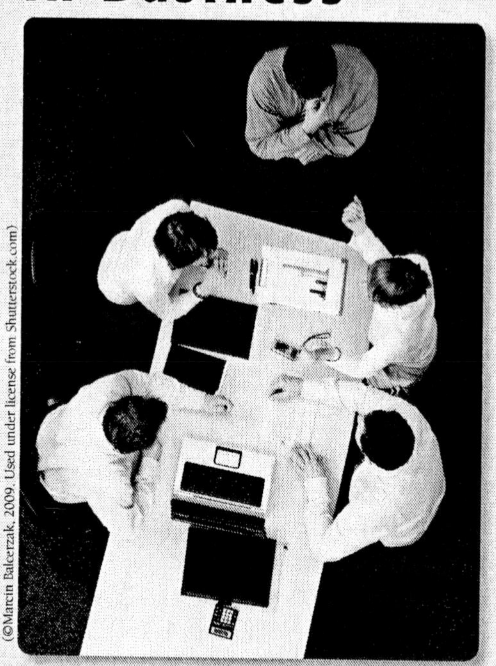

(©Marcin Balcerzak, 2009. Used under license from Shutterstock.com)

"[It] is a universal principle in the law of agency, that the powers of the agent are to be exercised for the benefits of the principal only, and not of the agent or of third parties."

—Joseph Story, 1779–1845
(Associate justice of the United States Supreme Court, 1811–1844)

Learning Objectives

After reading this chapter, you should be able to answer the following questions:

1. What is the difference between an employee and an independent contractor?
2. How do agency relationships arise?
3. What duties do agents and principals owe to each other?
4. When is a principal liable for the agent's actions with respect to third parties? When is the agent liable?
5. What are some of the ways in which an agency relationship can be terminated?

Agency A relationship between two parties in which one party (the agent) agrees to represent or act for the other (the principal).

One of the most common, important, and pervasive legal relationships is that of **agency**. In an agency relationship between two parties, one of the parties, called the *agent,* agrees to represent or act for the other, called the *principal.* The principal has the right to control the agent's conduct in matters entrusted to the agent, and the agent must exercise his or her powers "for the benefit of the principal only," as Justice Joseph Story indicated in the chapter-opening quotation. By using agents, a principal can conduct multiple business operations simultaneously in various locations. Thus, for example, contracts that bind the principal can be made at different places with different persons at the same time.

Agency relationships permeate the business world. Indeed, agency law is essential to the existence and operation of a corporate entity, because only through its agents can a corporation function and enter into contracts. A familiar example of an agent is a corporate officer who serves in a representative capacity for the owners of the corporation. In this capacity, the officer has the authority to bind the principal (the corporation) to a contract.

Agency Relationships

Section 1(1) of the *Restatement (Second) of Agency*[1] defines agency as "the fiduciary relation which results from the manifestation of consent by one person to another that the other shall act in his [or her] behalf and subject to his [or her] control, and consent by the other so to act." In other words, in a principal-agent relationship, the parties have agreed that the agent will act *on behalf and instead of* the principal in negotiating and transacting business with third parties.

Fiduciary As a noun, a person having a duty created by his or her undertaking to act primarily for another's benefit in matters connected with the undertaking. As an adjective, a relationship founded on trust and confidence.

The term **fiduciary** is at the heart of agency law. The term can be used both as a noun and as an adjective. When used as a noun, it refers to a person having a duty created by her or his undertaking to act primarily for another's benefit in matters connected with the undertaking. When used as an adjective, as in "fiduciary relationship," it means that the relationship involves trust and confidence.

Agency relationships commonly exist between employers and employees. Agency relationships may sometimes also exist between employers and independent contractors who are hired to perform special tasks or services.

Employer-Employee Relationships

ON THE WEB For information on the *Restatements of the Law,* including planned revisions, go to the American Law Institute's Web site at www.ali.org.

Normally, all employees who deal with third parties are deemed to be agents. A salesperson in a department store, for instance, is an agent of the store's owner (the principal) and acts on the owner's behalf. Any sale of goods made by the salesperson to a customer is binding on the principal. Similarly, most representations of fact made by the salesperson with respect to the goods sold are binding on the principal.

Because employees who deal with third parties are generally deemed to be agents of their employers, agency law and employment law overlap considerably. Agency relationships, though, as will become apparent, can exist outside an employer-employee relationship and thus have a broader reach than employment laws do. Additionally, bear in mind that agency law is based on the common law. In the employment realm, many common law doctrines have been displaced by statutory law and government regulations relating to employment relationships.

Employment laws (state and federal) apply only to the employer-employee relationship. Statutes governing Social Security, withholding taxes, workers' compensation, unemployment compensation, workplace safety, employment discrimination, and the like (see Chapters 24 and 25) are applicable only if employer-employee status exists. *These laws do not apply to an independent contractor.*

(Greg Younger/Creative Commons)

An independent contractor communicates from a building site. What are some significant differences between employees and independent contractors?

Employer–Independent Contractor Relationships

Independent contractors are not employees because, by definition, those who hire them have no control over the details of their physical performance. Section 2 of the *Restatement (Second) of Agency* defines an **independent contractor** as follows:

Independent Contractor One who works for, and receives payment from, an employer but whose working conditions and methods are not controlled by the employer. An independent contractor is not an employee but may be an agent.

> [An independent contractor is] a person who contracts with another to do something for him [or her] but who is not controlled by the other nor subject to the other's right to control with respect to his [or her] physical conduct in the performance of the undertaking. *He [or she] may or may not be an agent.* [Emphasis added.]

1. The *Restatement (Second) of Agency* is an authoritative summary of the law of agency and is often referred to by judges and other legal professionals.

"Keep up the good work, whatever it is, whoever you are."

Building contractors and subcontractors are independent contractors; a property owner does not control the acts of either of these professionals. Truck drivers who own their equipment and hire themselves out on a per-job basis are independent contractors, but truck drivers who drive company trucks on a regular basis are usually employees.

The relationship between a person or firm and an independent contractor may or may not involve an agency relationship. To illustrate: An owner of real estate who hires a real estate broker to negotiate a sale of his or her property not only has contracted with an independent contractor (the real estate broker) but also has established an agency relationship for the specific purpose of assisting in the sale of the property. Another example is an insurance agent, who is both an independent contractor and an agent of the insurance company for which she or he sells policies. (Note that an insurance *broker,* in contrast, normally is an agent of the person obtaining insurance and not of the insurance company.)

Determining Employee Status

The courts are frequently asked to determine whether a particular worker is an employee or an independent contractor. How a court decides this issue can have a significant effect on the rights and liabilities of the parties. Employers are required to pay certain taxes, such as Social Security and unemployment taxes, for employees but not for independent contractors.

Criteria Used by the Courts In determining whether a worker has the status of an employee or an independent contractor, the courts often consider the following questions:

1. How much control can the employer exercise over the details of the work? (If an employer can exercise considerable control over the details of the work, this would indicate employee status. This is perhaps the most important factor weighed by the courts in determining employee status.)
2. Is the worker engaged in an occupation or business distinct from that of the employer? (If so, this points to independent-contractor status, not employee status.)
3. Is the work usually done under the employer's direction or by a specialist without supervision? (If the work is usually done under the employer's direction, this would indicate employee status.)
4. Does the employer supply the tools at the place of work? (If so, this would indicate employee status.)
5. For how long is the person employed? (If the person is employed for a long period of time, this would indicate employee status.)
6. What is the method of payment—by time period or at the completion of the job? (Payment by time period, such as once every two weeks or once a month, would indicate employee status.)
7. What degree of skill is required of the worker? (If little skill is required, this may indicate employee status.)

Sometimes, workers may benefit from having employee status—for tax purposes and to be protected under certain employment laws, for example. As mentioned earlier, federal statutes governing employment discrimination apply only when an employer-employee relationship exists. Protection under employment-discrimination statutes provides significant incentive for workers to claim that they are employees rather than independent contractors.

CASE EXAMPLE 23.1 A Puerto Rican television station, WIPR, contracted with a woman to co-host a television show profiling cities in Puerto Rico. The woman signed a new contract for each episode, each of which required her to work a certain number of days. She was under no other commitment to work for WIPR and was free to pursue other opportunities during the weeks between filming. WIPR did not withhold any taxes from the lump-sum amount it paid her for each contract. When the woman became pregnant, WIPR stopped contracting with her. She filed a lawsuit claiming that WIPR was discriminating against her in violation of federal employment-discrimination laws, but the court found in favor of WIPR. Because the parties had structured their relationship through the use of repeated fixed-length contracts and had described the woman as an independent contractor on tax documents, she could not maintain an employment-discrimination suit.[2] ●

Whether a worker is an employee or an independent contractor can also affect the employer's liability for the worker's actions. In the following case, the court had to determine the status of a taxi driver whose passengers were injured in a collision.

Case 23.1 Lopez v. El Palmar Taxi, Inc.

Court of Appeals of Georgia, 297 Ga.App. 121, 676 S.E.2d 460 (2009).

Is a taxi driver who is not subject to the control of the taxi company an independent contractor or an employee?

FACTS El Palmar Taxi, Inc., requires its drivers to supply their own cabs, which must display El Palmar's logo. The drivers pay gas, maintenance, and insurance costs, and a fee to El Palmar. They are expected to follow certain rules–dress neatly, for example–and to comply with the law, including licensing regulations, but they can work when they want for as long as they want. El Palmar might dispatch a driver to pick up a fare, or the driver can look for a fare. Mario Julaju drove a taxi under a contract with El Palmar that described him as an independent contractor. El Palmar sent Julaju to pick up Maria Lopez and her children. During the ride, Julaju's cab collided with a truck. To recover for their injuries, the Lopezes filed a suit in a Georgia state court against El Palmar. The employer argued that it was not liable because Julaju was an independent contractor. The court ruled in El Palmar's favor. The plaintiffs appealed.

ISSUE Is a taxi driver who is not subject to the control of the taxi company considered an independent contractor?

DECISION Yes. A state intermediate appellate court affirmed this part of the lower court's decision. (But the appellate court reversed the judgment in El Palmar's favor on other grounds and remanded the case for trial.)

REASON An employer normally is not responsible for the actions of an independent contractor with whom the employer contracts. The test to determine if a worker is an independent contractor is whether the employer has the right to control the time, manner, and method of the work. In this case, the only restriction imposed on Julaju was to comply with the law. El Palmar did not own the cab that Julaju was driving at the time of the collision, nor did it exercise control over the time, manner, or method of his work. Julaju could work any time for as long as he wanted. He was not required to accept fares from the company. The cab displayed the El Palmar logo and El Palmar might dispatch him to pick up a passenger, but these factors alone do not create an employer-employee relationship.

WHY IS THIS CASE IMPORTANT? *When an employment contract clearly designates one party as an independent contractor, the relationship between the parties is presumed to be that of employer and independent contractor. But this is only a presumption. Evidence can be introduced to show that the employer exercised sufficient control to establish the other party as an employee. Or, as this case makes clear, the evidence can underscore that the parties' relationship is that of employer and independent contractor.*

CRITERIA USED BY THE IRS The Internal Revenue Service (IRS) has established its own criteria for determining whether a worker is an independent contractor or an employee. Although the IRS once considered twenty factors in determining a worker's status, guidelines that took effect in 1997 encourage IRS examiners to focus on just one of those factors—the degree of control the business exercises over the worker.

2. *Alberty-Vélez v. Corporación de Puerto Rico para la Difusión Pública*, 361 F.3d 1 (1st Cir. 2004).

The IRS tends to closely scrutinize a firm's classification of its workers because, as mentioned, employers can avoid certain tax liabilities by hiring independent contractors instead of employees. Even when a firm classifies a worker as an independent contractor, the IRS may decide that the worker is actually an employee. In that situation, the employer will be responsible for paying any applicable Social Security, withholding, and unemployment taxes. Microsoft Corporation, for example, was once ordered to pay back payroll taxes for hundreds of workers that the IRS determined had been misclassified as independent contractors.[3] (The *Business Application* feature at the end of the chapter offers suggestions on using independent contractors.)

EMPLOYEE STATUS AND "WORKS FOR HIRE" Under the Copyright Act of 1976, any copyrighted work created by an employee within the scope of her or his employment at the request of the employer is a "work for hire," and the *employer* owns the copyright to the work. When an employer hires an independent contractor—a freelance artist, writer, or computer programmer, for example—the independent contractor owns the copyright *unless* the parties agree in writing that the work is a "work for hire" and the work falls into one of nine specific categories, including audiovisual and other works.

EXAMPLE 23.2 Gabe, who marketed DVDs containing compilations of software programs, hired Katlin to create a file-retrieval program that would allow users to access the software on the DVDs. Katlin built into the final version of the program a notice stating that she was the author of the program and owned the copyright. Gabe removed the notice, claiming that Katlin's file-retrieval program was a "work for hire" and that he owned the copyright to the program. In this situation, however, because Katlin was a skilled computer programmer who controlled the manner and method of her work, she was an independent contractor and not an employee for hire. Thus, Katlin owned the copyright to the file-retrieval program. ●

How Agency Relationships Are Formed

Agency relationships normally are consensual; that is, they come about by voluntary consent and agreement between the parties. Generally, the agreement need not be in writing,[4] and consideration is not required.

ON THE WEB An excellent source for information on agency, including court cases involving agency concepts, is the Legal Information Institute (LII) at Cornell University. You can access the LII's Web page on this topic at www.law.cornell.edu/wex/index.php/Agency.

A person must have contractual capacity to be a principal.[5] Those who cannot legally enter into contracts directly should not be allowed to do so indirectly through an agent. Any person can be an agent, though, regardless of whether he or she has the capacity to enter a contract (including minors).

An agency relationship can be created for any legal purpose. An agency relationship that is created for an illegal purpose or that is contrary to public policy is unenforceable. **EXAMPLE 23.3** Sharp (as principal) contracts with McKenzie (as agent) to sell illegal narcotics. This agency relationship is unenforceable because selling illegal narcotics is a felony and is contrary to public policy. ● It is also illegal for physicians and other licensed professionals to employ unlicensed agents to perform professional actions.

Generally, an agency relationship can arise in four ways: by agreement of the parties, by ratification, by estoppel, or by operation of law.

3. See *Vizcaino v. U.S. District Court for the Western District of Washington*, 173 F.3d 713 (9th Cir. 1999).

4. The following are two main exceptions to the statement that agency agreements need not be in writing: (1) Whenever agency authority empowers the agent to enter into a contract that the Statute of Frauds requires to be in writing, the agent's authority from the principal must likewise be in writing (this is called the *equal dignity rule*, to be discussed later in this chapter). (2) A power of attorney, which confers authority to an agent, must be in writing.

5. Note that some states allow a minor to be a principal, but any resulting contracts will be voidable by the minor.

(©Max Bukovski, 2009. Used under license from Shutterstock.com)

Sometimes, a homeowner asks a lawn-care specialist to contract with others for the care of the homeowner's lawn on a regular basis. What type of relationship is established between the homeowner and the lawn-care specialist?

Agency by Agreement

Most agency relationships are based on an express or implied agreement that the agent will act for the principal and that the principal agrees to have the agent so act. An agency agreement can take the form of an express written contract or be created by an oral agreement. **EXAMPLE 23.4** Reese asks Cary, a gardener, to contract with others for the care of his lawn on a regular basis. Cary agrees. An agency relationship is established between Reese and Cary for the lawn care. •

An agency agreement can also be implied by conduct. **EXAMPLE 23.5** A hotel expressly allows only Boris Koontz to park cars, but Boris has no employment contract there. The hotel's manager tells Boris when to work, as well as where and how to park the cars. The hotel's conduct amounts to a manifestation of its willingness to have Boris park its customers' cars, and Boris can infer from the hotel's conduct that he has authority to act as a parking valet. It can be inferred that Boris is an agent-employee for the hotel, his purpose being to provide valet parking services for hotel guests. •

Agency by Ratification

On occasion, a person who is in fact not an agent (or who is an agent acting outside the scope of her or his authority) may make a contract on behalf of another (a principal). If the principal approves or affirms that contract by word or by action, an agency relationship is created by **ratification.** Ratification involves a question of intent, and intent can be expressed by either words or conduct. The basic requirements for ratification will be discussed later in this chapter.

Ratification The act of accepting and giving legal force to an obligation that previously was not enforceable.

Agency by Estoppel

When a principal causes a third person to believe that another person is his or her agent, and the third person deals with the supposed agent, the principal is "estopped to deny" the agency relationship. In such a situation, the principal's actions create the *appearance* of an agency that does not in fact exist. The third person must prove that she or he *reasonably* believed that an agency relationship existed, though.[6] Facts and circumstances must show that an ordinary, prudent person familiar with business practice and custom would have been justified in concluding that the agent had authority.

CASE EXAMPLE 23.6 Marsha and Jerry Wiedmaier owned Wiedmaier, Inc., a corporation that operated a truck stop. Their son, Michael, did not own any interest in the corporation but had worked at the truck stop as a fuel operator. Michael decided to form his own business called Extreme Diecast, LLC. To obtain a line of credit with Motorsport Marketing, Inc., a company that sells racing memorabilia, Michael asked his mother to sign the credit application form. After Marsha had signed as "Secretary-Owner" of Wiedmaier, Inc., Michael added his name to the list of corporate owners and faxed it to Motorsport. Later, when Michael stopped making payments on the merchandise he had ordered, Motorsport sued Wiedmaier for the unpaid balance. The court ruled that Michael was an apparent agent of Wiedmaier, Inc., because the credit application had caused Motorsport to reasonably believe that Michael was acting as Wiedmaier's agent in ordering merchandise.[7] •

Note that the acts or declarations of a purported *agent* in and of themselves do not create an agency by estoppel. Rather, it is the deeds or statements *of the principal* that create

6. These concepts also apply when a person who is in fact an agent undertakes an action that is beyond the scope of her or his authority, as will be discussed later in this chapter.

7. *Motorsport Marketing, Inc. v. Wiedmaier, Inc.*, 195 S.W.3d 492 (Mo.App. 2006).

an agency by estoppel. In other words, in Case Example 23.6, if Marsha Wiedmaier had not signed the credit application on behalf of the principal-corporation, then Motorsport would not have been reasonable in believing that Michael was Wiedmaier's agent.

Agency by Operation of Law

The courts may find an agency relationship in the absence of a formal agreement in other situations as well. This can occur in family relationships, such as when one spouse purchases certain basic necessaries and charges them to the other spouse's charge account, for example. The courts will often rule that a spouse is liable to pay for the necessaries, either because of a social policy of promoting the general welfare of the spouse or because of a legal duty to supply necessaries to family members.

Agency by operation of law may also occur in emergency situations, when the agent's failure to act outside the scope of his or her authority would cause the principal substantial loss. If the agent is unable to contact the principal, the courts will often grant this emergency power. For instance, a railroad engineer may contract on behalf of her or his employer for medical care for an injured motorist hit by the train. The *Concept Summary* below reviews the various ways that agencies are formed.

Duties of Agents and Principals

Once the principal-agent relationship has been created, both parties have duties that govern their conduct. As discussed previously, an agency relationship is *fiduciary*—one of trust. In a fiduciary relationship, each party owes the other the duty to act with the utmost good faith. We now examine the various duties of agents and principals.

"If God had an agent, the world wouldn't be built yet. It'd only be about Thursday."
Jerry Reynolds, 1940–present
(National Basketball Association executive)

In general, for every duty of the principal, the agent has a corresponding right, and vice versa. When one party to the agency relationship violates his or her duty to the other party, the remedies available to the nonbreaching party arise out of contract and tort law. These remedies include monetary damages, termination of the agency relationship, an injunction, and required accountings.

Agent's Duties to the Principal

Generally, the agent owes the principal five duties—performance, notification, loyalty, obedience, and accounting.

PERFORMANCE An implied condition in every agency contract is the agent's agreement to use reasonable diligence and skill in performing the work. When an agent fails entirely

Concept Summary How Agency Relationships Are Formed

METHOD OF FORMATION	DESCRIPTION
By Agreement	The agency relationship is formed through express consent (oral or written) or implied by conduct.
By Ratification	The principal either by act or by agreement ratifies the conduct of a person who is not in fact an agent.
By Estoppel	The principal causes a third person to believe that another person is the principal's agent, and the third person acts to his or her detriment in reasonable reliance on that belief.
By Operation of Law	The agency relationship is based on a social duty (such as the need to support family members) or formed in emergency situations when the agent is unable to contact the principal and failure to act outside the scope of the agent's authority would cause the principal substantial loss.

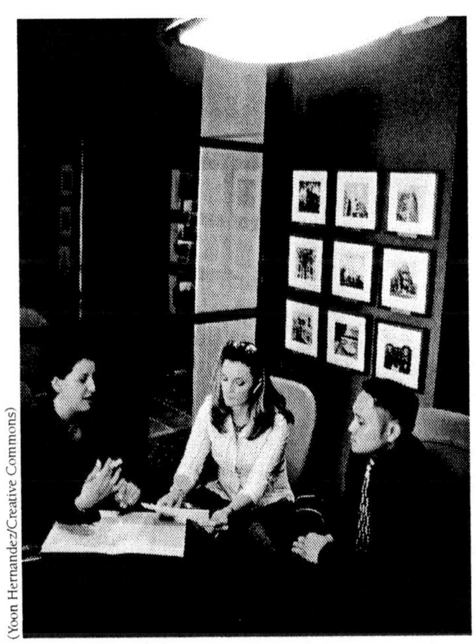
(Yoon Hernandez/Creative Commons)

A real estate agent meets with clients in her office. Suppose that the agent knows a buyer who is willing to pay more than the asking price for a property. What duty would the agent breach if she bought the property from the seller and sold it at a profit to that buyer?

to perform her or his duties, liability for breach of contract normally will result. The degree of skill or care required of an agent is usually that expected of a reasonable person under similar circumstances. Generally, this is interpreted to mean ordinary care. If an agent has represented himself or herself as possessing special skills, however, the agent is expected to exercise the degree of skill or skills claimed. Failure to do so constitutes a breach of the agent's duty.

Not all agency relationships are based on contract. In some situations, an agent acts gratuitously—that is, not for monetary compensation. A gratuitous agent cannot be liable for breach of contract, as there is no contract; he or she is subject only to tort liability. Once a gratuitous agent has begun to act in an agency capacity, he or she has the duty to continue to perform in that capacity in an acceptable manner and is subject to the same standards of care and duty to perform as other agents.

NOTIFICATION An agent is required to notify the principal of all matters that come to her or his attention concerning the subject matter of the agency. This is the duty of notification, or the duty to inform. **EXAMPLE 23.7** Lang, an artist, is about to negotiate a contract to sell a series of paintings to Barber's Art Gallery for $25,000. Lang's agent learns that Barber is insolvent and will be unable to pay for the paintings. The agent has a duty to inform Lang of this fact because it is relevant to the subject matter of the agency—the sale of Lang's paintings. ● Generally, the law assumes that the principal knows of any information acquired by the agent that is relevant to the agency—regardless of whether the agent actually passes on this information to the principal. It is a basic tenet of agency law that notice to the agent is notice to the principal.

BE AWARE An agent's disclosure of confidential information could constitute the business tort of misappropriation of trade secrets.

LOYALTY Loyalty is one of the most fundamental duties in a fiduciary relationship. Basically, the agent has the duty to act *solely for the benefit of his or her principal* and not in the interest of the agent or a third party. For example, an agent cannot represent two principals in the same transaction unless both know of the dual capacity and consent to it. The duty of loyalty also means that any information or knowledge acquired through the agency relationship is considered confidential. It would be a breach of loyalty to disclose such information either during the agency relationship or after its termination. Typical examples of confidential information are trade secrets and customer lists compiled by the principal.

In short, the agent's loyalty must be undivided. The agent's actions must be strictly for the benefit of the principal and must not result in any secret profit for the agent. **CASE EXAMPLE 23.8** Don Cousins contracts with Leo Hodgins, a real estate agent, to negotiate the purchase of an office building as an investment. While working for Cousins, Hodgins discovers that the property owner will sell the building only as a package deal with another parcel. If Hodgins then forms a new company with his brother to buy the two properties and resell the building to Cousins, he has breached his fiduciary duties. As a real estate agent, Hodgins has a duty to communicate all offers to his principal and not to secretly purchase the property and then resell it to his principal. Hodgins is required to act in Cousins's best interests and can become the purchaser in this situation only with Cousins's knowledge and approval.[8] ●

OBEDIENCE When acting on behalf of a principal, an agent has a duty to follow all lawful and clearly stated instructions of the principal. Any deviation from such instructions is a violation of this duty. During emergency situations, however, when the principal cannot be consulted, the agent may deviate from the instructions without violating this

8. *Cousins v. Realty Ventures, Inc.*, 844 So.2d 860 (La.App. 5 Cir. 2003).

duty. Whenever instructions are not clearly stated, the agent can fulfill the duty of obedience by acting in good faith and in a manner reasonable under the circumstances.

ACCOUNTING Unless an agent and a principal agree otherwise, the agent has the duty to keep and make available to the principal an account of all property and funds received and paid out on behalf of the principal. This includes gifts from third parties in connection with the agency. For example, a gift from a customer to a salesperson for prompt deliveries made by the salesperson's firm, in the absence of a company policy to the contrary, belongs to the firm. The agent has a duty to maintain separate accounts for the principal's funds and for the agent's personal funds, and the agent must not intermingle these accounts.

Principal's Duties to the Agent

The principal also owes certain duties to the agent. These duties relate to compensation, reimbursement and indemnification, cooperation, and safe working conditions.

COMPENSATION In general, when a principal requests certain services from an agent, the agent reasonably expects payment. The principal therefore has a duty to pay the agent for services rendered. For example, when an accountant or an attorney is asked to act as an agent, an agreement to compensate the agent for such service is implied. The principal also has a duty to pay that compensation in a timely manner. Except in a gratuitous agency relationship, in which an agent does not act for payment in return, the principal must pay the agreed-on value for an agent's services. If no amount has been expressly agreed on, the principal owes the agent the customary compensation for such services.

Preventing Legal Disputes

Many disputes arise because the principal and agent did not specify how much the agent would be paid. To avoid such disputes, always state in advance, and in writing, the amount or rate of compensation that you will pay your agents. Even when dealing with salespersons, such as real estate agents, who customarily are paid a percentage of the value of the sale, it is best to explicitly state the rate of compensation.

REMEMBER An agent who signs a negotiable instrument on behalf of a principal may be personally liable on the instrument. Liability depends, in part, on whether the identity of the principal is disclosed and whether the parties intend the agent to be bound by her or his signature.

REIMBURSEMENT AND INDEMNIFICATION Whenever an agent disburses funds to fulfill the request of the principal or to pay for necessary expenses in the course of reasonable performance of his or her agency duties, the principal has the duty to reimburse the agent for these payments. Agents cannot recover for expenses incurred through their own misconduct or negligence, though.

Subject to the terms of the agency agreement, the principal has the duty to compensate, or *indemnify,* an agent for liabilities incurred because of authorized and lawful acts and transactions. For instance, if the principal fails to perform a contract formed by the agent with a third party and the third party then sues the agent, the principal is obligated to compensate the agent for any costs incurred in defending against the lawsuit.

Additionally, the principal must indemnify (pay) the agent for the value of benefits that the agent confers on the principal. The amount of indemnification is usually specified in the agency contract. If it is not, the courts will look to the nature of the business and the type of loss to determine the amount. Note that this rule applies to acts by gratuitous agents as well. If the finder of a dog that becomes sick takes the dog to a veterinarian and pays the required fees for the veterinarian's services, the (gratuitous) agent is entitled to be reimbursed by the dog's owner for those fees.

COOPERATION A principal has a duty to cooperate with the agent and to assist the agent in performing her or his duties. The principal must do nothing to prevent such performance.

When a principal grants an agent an exclusive territory, for example, the principal creates an *exclusive agency* and cannot compete with the agent or appoint or allow another agent to so compete. If the principal does so, she or he will be exposed to liability for the agent's lost sales or profits. **EXAMPLE 23.9** Akers (the principal) creates an exclusive agency by granting Johnson (the agent) an exclusive territory within which Johnson may sell Akers's products. If Akers begins to sell the products himself within Johnson's territory or permits another agent to do so, Akers has violated the exclusive agency and can be held liable for Johnson's lost sales or profits. ●

SAFE WORKING CONDITIONS Under the common law, a principal is required to provide safe working premises, equipment, and conditions for all agents and employees. The principal has a duty to inspect the working conditions and to warn agents and employees about any unsafe areas. When the agent is an employee, the employer's liability is frequently covered by state workers' compensation insurance, and federal and state statutes often require the employer to meet certain safety standards (to be discussed in Chapter 24).

Agent's Authority

An agent's authority to act can be either *actual* (express or implied) or *apparent*. If an agent contracts outside the scope of his or her authority, the principal may still become liable by ratifying the contract.

Actual Authority

As indicated, an agent's actual authority can be express or implied. We look here at both of these forms of actual authority.

Equal Dignity Rule In most states, a rule stating that express authority given to an agent must be in writing if the contract to be made on behalf of the principal is required to be in writing.

EXPRESS AUTHORITY *Express authority* is authority declared in clear, direct, and definite terms. Express authority can be given orally or in writing. In most states, the **equal dignity rule** requires that if the contract being executed is or must be in writing, then the agent's authority must also be in writing. Failure to comply with the equal dignity rule can make a contract voidable *at the option of the principal*. The law regards the contract at that point as a mere offer. If the principal decides to accept the offer, acceptance must be ratified, or affirmed, in writing.

EXAMPLE 23.10 Lee (the principal) orally asks Parkinson (the agent) to sell a ranch that Lee owns. Parkinson finds a buyer and signs a sales contract (a contract for an interest in realty must be in writing) on behalf of Lee to sell the ranch. The buyer cannot enforce the contract unless Lee subsequently ratifies Parkinson's agency status *in writing*. Once Parkinson's agency status is ratified, either party can enforce rights under the contract. ●

Modern business practice allows an exception to the equal dignity rule. An executive officer of a corporation normally is not required to obtain written authority from the corporation to conduct *ordinary* business transactions. The equal dignity rule does not apply when an agent acts in the presence of a principal or when the agent's act of signing is merely perfunctory (automatic). Thus, if Dickens (the principal) negotiates a contract but is called out of town the day it is to be signed and orally authorizes Santini to sign the contract, the oral authorization is sufficient.

Power of Attorney A written document, which is usually notarized, authorizing another to act as one's agent; can be special (permitting the agent to do specified acts only) or general (permitting the agent to transact all business for the principal).

POWER OF ATTORNEY Giving an agent a **power of attorney** confers express authority.[9] The power of attorney normally is a written document and is usually notarized. (A

9. An agent who holds the power of attorney is called an *attorney-in-fact* for the principal. The holder does not have to be an attorney-at-law (and often is not).

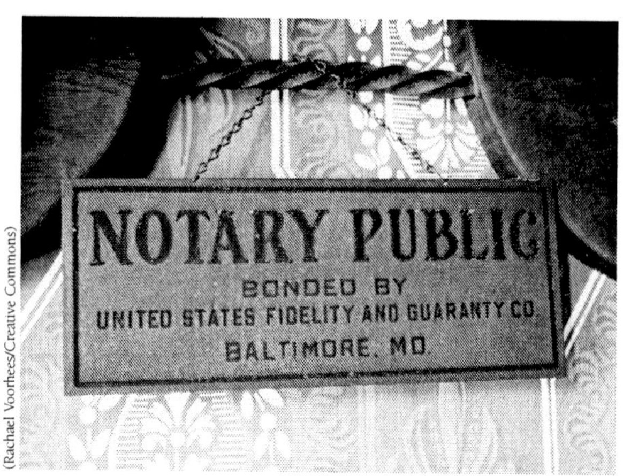

(Rachael Voorhees/Creative Commons)

Notary publics are those who are authorized by a state to attest to the authenticity of signatures. In most states, there are few restrictions on who can become a notary public.

Notary Public A public official authorized to attest to the authenticity of signatures.

document is notarized when a **notary public**—a public official authorized to attest to the authenticity of signatures—signs and dates the document and imprints it with his or her seal of authority.) Most states have statutory provisions for creating a power of attorney. A power of attorney can be special (permitting the agent to do specified acts only), or it can be general (permitting the agent to transact all business for the principal). Because a general power of attorney grants extensive authority to an agent to act on behalf of the principal in many ways, it should be used with great caution. Ordinarily, a power of attorney terminates on the incapacity or death of the person giving the power.[10]

Implied Authority An agent has the *implied authority* to do what is reasonably necessary to carry out express authority and accomplish the objectives of the agency. Authority can also be implied by custom or inferred from the position the agent occupies. **EXAMPLE 23.11** Mueller is employed by Al's Supermarket to manage one of its stores. Al's has not expressly stated that Mueller has authority to contract with third persons. In this situation, though, authority to manage a business implies authority to do what is reasonably required (as is customary or can be inferred from a manager's position) to operate the business. This includes forming contracts to hire employees, to buy merchandise and equipment, and to advertise the products sold in the store. ●

Ethical Issue

Does an agent's breach of loyalty terminate the agent's authority? Suppose that an employee-agent who is authorized to access company trade secrets contained in computer files takes those secrets to a competitor for whom the employee is about to begin working. Clearly, the agent has violated the ethical—and legal—duty of loyalty to the principal. Does this breach of loyalty mean that the employee's act of accessing the trade secrets was unauthorized? The question has significant implications because if the act was unauthorized, the employee will be subject to state and federal laws prohibiting unauthorized access to computer information and data. If the act was authorized, the laws will not apply.

Although a few courts have found that an employee's authority as an agent terminated the moment the employee accessed trade secrets for the purpose of divulging them to a competitor,[11] most courts hold that an agent's authority continues. For example, when Jeff Gast became an employee of Shamrock Foods Company, he signed a confidentiality agreement promising not to disclose trade secrets. In January 2008, Gast e-mailed numerous documents containing Shamrock's confidential proprietary information to himself at his personal e-mail account. That same month, Gast quit his job at Shamrock and went to work for Sysco, a competitor. Shamrock filed a lawsuit in a federal court in Arizona against Gast for violating the Computer Fraud and Abuse Act (CFAA, discussed in Chapter 4). The court held that the phrase "without authorization" in the CFAA was meant to refer to outsiders rather than to agents who had a principal's authority to access the computer information. Gast was initially authorized to access the computer he used at Shamrock and to view the specific files containing the information. Therefore, the court concluded that Gast did not access the information at issue "without authorization" or in a manner that "exceeded authorized access." Although Gast had behaved unethically, the court found that his activity was not actionable under the CFAA and dismissed the lawsuit.[12]

10. A *durable* power of attorney, however, continues to be effective despite the principal's incapacity. An elderly person, for example, might grant a durable power of attorney to provide for the handling of property and investments or specific health-care needs should she or he become incompetent.

11. See, for example, *International Airport Centers, LLC v. Citrin*, 440 F.3d 418 (7th Cir. 2006); and *ViChip Corp. v. Lee*, 438 F.Supp.2d 1087 (N.D.Cal. 2006).

12. *Shamrock Foods Co. v. Gast*, 535 F.Supp.2d 962 (D.Ariz. 2008). For a case involving three employee-agents who stole confidential data from their employer-principal, see *Lockheed Martin Corp. v. Speed*, 2006 WL 2683058 (M.D.Fla. 2006).

Apparent Authority

Apparent Authority Authority that is only apparent, not real. In agency law, a person may be deemed to have had the power to act as an agent for another party if the other party's manifestations to a third party led the third party to believe that an agency existed when, in fact, it did not.

Actual authority (express or implied) arises from what the principal manifests *to the agent.* An agent has **apparent authority** when the principal, by either words or actions, causes a *third party* reasonably to believe that an agent has authority to act, even though the agent has no express or implied authority. If the third party changes her or his position in reliance on the principal's representations, the principal may be *estopped* (prevented) from denying that the agent had authority.

Apparent authority usually comes into existence through a principal's pattern of conduct over time. **EXAMPLE 23.12** Bailey is a traveling salesperson with the authority to solicit orders for a principal's goods. Because she does not carry any goods with her, she normally would not have the implied authority to collect payments from customers on behalf of the principal. Suppose that she does accept payments from Corgley Enterprises, however, and submits them to the principal's accounting department for processing. If the principal does nothing to stop Bailey from continuing this practice, a pattern develops over time, and the principal confers apparent authority on Bailey to accept payments from Corgley. ●

At issue in the following case was a question of apparent authority or, as the court referred to it, "ostensible [apparent] agency."

Case 23.2 Ermoian v. Desert Hospital

Court of Appeal of California, Fourth District, 152 Cal.App.4th 475, 61 Cal.Rptr.3d 754 (2007).

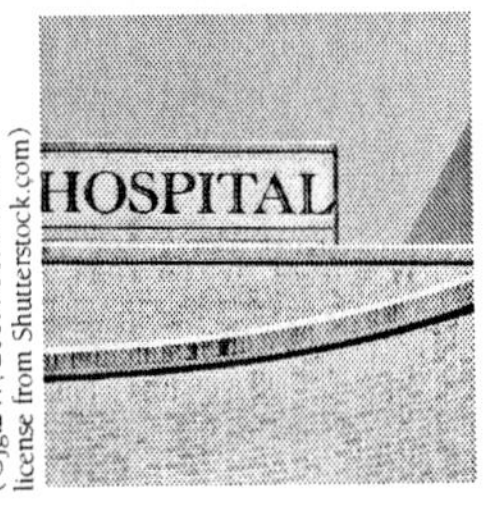

(©jgl247, 2009. Used under license from Shutterstock.com)

Did clinic physicians have apparent authority to act for the hospital in a negligence claim?

FACTS In 1990, Desert Hospital in California established a comprehensive perinatal services program (CPSP) to provide obstetrical care to women who were uninsured (*perinatal* is often defined as relating to the period from about the twenty-eighth week of pregnancy to around one month after birth). The CPSP was set up in an office suite across from the hospital and named "Desert Hospital Outpatient Maternity Services Clinic." The hospital contracted with a corporation controlled by Dr. Morton Gubin, which employed Dr. Masami Ogata, to provide obstetrical services. In January 1994, Jackie Shahan went to the hospital's emergency room because of cramping and other symptoms. The emergency room physician told Shahan that she was pregnant and referred her to the clinic. Shahan visited the clinic throughout her pregnancy. On May 15, Shahan's baby, Amanda Ermoian, was born with brain abnormalities that left her severely mentally retarded and unable to care for herself. Her conditions could not have been prevented, treated, or cured *in utero.* Through a guardian, Amanda filed a suit in a California state court against the hospital and others, alleging "wrongful life." She claimed that the defendants negligently failed to inform her mother of her abnormalities before her birth, depriving her mother of the opportunity to make an informed choice to terminate the pregnancy. The court ruled in the defendants' favor, holding, among other things, that the hospital was not liable because Drs. Gubin and Ogata were not its employees. Amanda appealed to a state intermediate appellate court, contending, in part, that the physicians were the hospital's "ostensible [apparent] agents."

ISSUE Did the physicians who were working at the clinic during Shahan's pregnancy have apparent authority to act for the hospital?

DECISION Yes. The state intermediate appellate court decided that, contrary to the lower court's finding, the physicians, Gubin and Ogata, were "ostensible [apparent] agents of the Hospital." The appellate court affirmed the lower court's ruling on Amanda's "wrongful life" claim, however, concluding that the physicians were not negligent in failing to advise Shahan to have an elective abortion.

REASON The court pointed out that ostensible agency (apparent agency) can be implied when a principal "by his acts has led others to believe that he has conferred authority upon an agent." Liability for an act of an ostensible agent rests on a doctrine of estoppel. The court noted that a person dealing with an agent must believe in the agent's authority. In this case, the hospital "held out the clinic and the personnel in the clinic as part of the hospital." The clinic used the same name as the hospital and labeled itself as an outpatient clinic. Moreover, personnel in the hospital's emergency room referred Shahan specifically to Dr. Gubin. When Shahan called the hospital, the receptionist told her "that she was calling the Hospital outpatient clinic which was the clinic of Dr. Gubin." The appellate court ruled that the hospital, and those associated with it, created the appearance to Shahan that the hospital was the provider of obstetrical care.

FOR CRITICAL ANALYSIS—Ethical Consideration *Does a principal have an ethical responsibility to inform an unaware third party that an apparent (ostensible) agent does not in fact have authority to act on the principal's behalf?*

Ratification

BE AWARE An agent who exceeds his or her authority and enters into a contract that the principal does not ratify may be liable to the third party on the ground of misrepresentation.

As already mentioned, ratification occurs when the principal affirms an agent's *unauthorized* act. When ratification occurs, the principal is bound to the agent's act, and the act is treated as if it had been authorized by the principal *from the outset.* Ratification can be either express or implied.

If the principal does not ratify the contract, the principal is not bound, and the third party's agreement with the agent is viewed as merely an unaccepted offer. Because the third party's agreement is an unaccepted offer, the third party can revoke the offer at any time, without liability, before the principal ratifies the contract.

The requirements for ratification can be summarized as follows:

1. The agent must have acted on behalf of an identified principal who subsequently ratifies the action.
2. The principal must know of all material facts involved in the transaction. If a principal ratifies a contract without knowing all of the facts, the principal can rescind (cancel) the contract.
3. The principal must affirm the agent's act in its entirety.
4. The principal must have the legal capacity to authorize the transaction at the time the agent engages in the act and at the time the principal ratifies. The third party must also have the legal capacity to engage in the transaction.
5. The principal's affirmation must occur before the third party withdraws from the transaction.
6. The principal must observe the same formalities when approving the act done by the agent as would have been required to authorize it initially.

Liability in Agency Relationships

Frequently, a question arises as to which party, the principal or the agent, should be held liable for contracts formed by the agent or for torts or crimes committed by the agent. We look here at these aspects of agency law.

Liability for Contracts

Liability for contracts formed by an agent depends on how the principal is classified and on whether the actions of the agent were authorized or unauthorized. Principals are classified as disclosed, partially disclosed, or undisclosed.[13]

Disclosed Principal A principal whose identity is known to a third party at the time the agent makes a contract with the third party.

Partially Disclosed Principal A principal whose identity is unknown by a third party, but the third party knows that the agent is or may be acting for a principal at the time the agent and the third party form a contract.

Undisclosed Principal A principal whose identity is unknown by a third person, and the third person has no knowledge that the agent is acting for a principal at the time the agent and the third person form a contract.

A **disclosed principal** is a principal whose identity is known by the third party at the time the contract is made by the agent. A **partially disclosed principal** is a principal whose identity is not known by the third party, but the third party knows that the agent is or may be acting for a principal at the time the contract is made. **EXAMPLE 23.13** Sarah has contracted with a real estate agent to sell certain property. She wishes to keep her identity a secret, but the agent makes it perfectly clear to potential buyers of the property that the agent is acting in an agency capacity. In this situation, Sarah is a partially disclosed principal. ● An **undisclosed principal** is a principal whose identity is totally unknown by the third party, and the third party has no knowledge that the agent is acting in an agency capacity at the time the contract is made.

AUTHORIZED ACTS If an agent acts within the scope of her or his authority, normally the principal is obligated to perform the contract regardless of whether the principal was disclosed, partially disclosed, or undisclosed. Whether the agent may also be held liable

13. *Restatement (Second) of Agency,* Section 4.

under the contract, however, depends on the disclosed, partially disclosed, or undisclosed status of the principal.

Disclosed or Partially Disclosed Principal. A disclosed or partially disclosed principal is liable to a third party for a contract made by an agent who is acting within the scope of her or his authority. If the principal is disclosed, an agent has no contractual liability for the nonperformance of the principal or the third party. If the principal is partially disclosed, in most states the agent is also treated as a party to the contract, and the third party can hold the agent liable for contractual nonperformance.[14]

CASE EXAMPLE 23.14 Walgreens leased commercial property to operate a drugstore at a mall owned by Kedzie Plaza Associates. A property management company, Taxman Corporation, signed the lease on behalf of the principal, Kedzie. The lease required the landlord to keep the sidewalks free of snow and ice, so Taxman, on behalf of Kedzie, contracted with another company to remove ice and snow from the sidewalks surrounding the Walgreens store. When a Walgreens employee slipped on ice outside the store and was injured, she sued Walgreens, Kedzie, and Taxman for negligence and ended up settling her claims with the other defendants except Taxman. Because the principal's identity (Kedzie) was fully disclosed in the snow-removal contract, however, the Illinois court ruled that the agent, Taxman, could not be held liable. Taxman did not assume a contractual obligation to remove the snow but merely retained a contractor to do so on behalf of the owner.[15] ●

"Let every eye negotiate for itself and trust no agent."
William Shakespeare, 1564–1616
(English dramatist and poet)

Undisclosed Principal. When neither the fact of agency nor the identity of the principal is disclosed, the undisclosed principal is bound to perform just as if the principal had been fully disclosed at the time the contract was made. The agent is also liable as a party to the contract.

When a principal's identity is undisclosed and the agent is forced to pay the third party, the agent is entitled to be indemnified (compensated) by the principal. The principal had a duty to perform, even though his or her identity was undisclosed, and failure to do so will make the principal ultimately liable. Once the undisclosed principal's identity is revealed, the third party generally can elect to hold either the principal or the agent liable on the contract. Conversely, the undisclosed principal can require the third party to fulfill the contract, *unless* (1) the undisclosed principal was expressly excluded as a party in the contract; (2) the contract is a negotiable instrument signed by the agent with no indication of signing in a representative capacity; or (3) the performance of the agent is personal to the contract, allowing the third party to refuse the principal's performance.

UNAUTHORIZED ACTS If an agent has no authority but nevertheless contracts with a third party, the principal cannot be held liable on the contract. It does not matter whether the principal was disclosed, partially disclosed, or undisclosed. The *agent* is liable, however. **EXAMPLE 23.15** Scranton signs a contract for the purchase of a truck, purportedly acting as an agent under authority granted by Johnson. In fact, Johnson has not given Scranton any such authority. Johnson refuses to pay for the truck, claiming that Scranton had no authority to purchase it. The seller of the truck is entitled to hold Scranton liable for payment. ●

If the principal is disclosed or partially disclosed, the agent is liable to the third party as long as the third party relied on the agency status. The agent's liability here is based on the breach of an *implied warranty of authority* (an agent impliedly warrants that he or she has the authority to enter a contract on behalf of the principal), not on breach of the contract itself.[16] If the third party knows at the time the contract is made that the agent does

14. *Restatement (Second) of Agency,* Section 321.
15. *McBride v. Taxman Corp.,* 327 Ill.App.3d 992, 765 N.E.2d 51 (2002).
16. The agent is not liable on the contract because the agent was never intended personally to be a party to the contract.

not have authority—or if the agent expresses to the third party *uncertainty* as to the extent of her or his authority—then the agent is not personally liable.

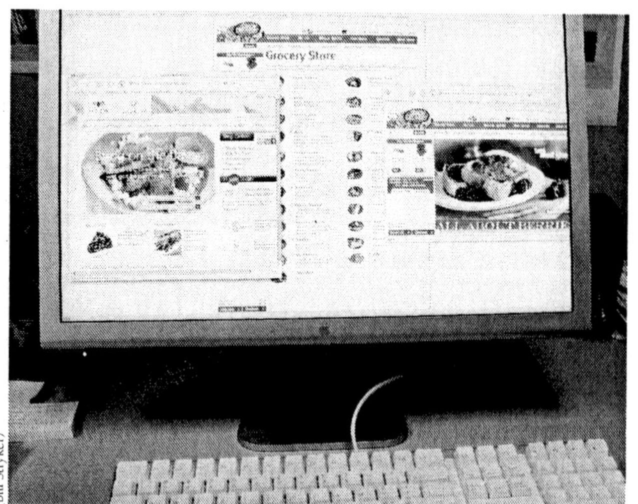
(Bill Stryker)

Today, one can buy an array of products, including groceries, online. What act has taken steps to apply traditional agency principles to online transactions?

Liability for E-Agents Although in the past standard agency principles applied only to *human* agents, today these same principles are being applied to electronic agents. An electronic agent, or **e-agent,** is a semiautonomous computer program that is capable of executing specific tasks. E-agents used in e-commerce include software that can search through many databases and retrieve only information that is relevant for the user.

The Uniform Electronic Transactions Act (UETA), which was discussed in Chapter 10 and has been adopted by most states, contains several provisions relating to the principal's liability for the actions of e-agents. Section 15 of the UETA states that e-agents may enter into binding agreements on behalf of their principals. Presumably, then—at least in those states that have adopted the act—the principal will be bound by the terms in a contract entered into by an e-agent. Thus, when you place an order over the Internet, the company (principal) whose system took the order via an e-agent cannot claim that it did not receive your order.

E-Agent A computer program that by electronic or other automated means can independently initiate an action or respond to electronic messages or data without review by an individual.

The UETA also stipulates that if an e-agent does not provide an opportunity to prevent errors at the time of the transaction, the other party to the transaction can avoid the transaction. For instance, if an e-agent fails to provide an on-screen confirmation of a purchase or sale, the other party can avoid the effect of any errors.

Liability for Torts and Crimes

Obviously, any person, including an agent, is liable for her or his own torts and crimes. Whether a principal can also be held liable for an agent's torts and crimes depends on several factors, which we examine here. In some situations, a principal may be held liable not only for the torts of an agent but also for the torts committed by an independent contractor.

A serious ski accident occurs under the supervised instruction of a ski resort employee. Are there any circumstances under which the principal (the resort) will not be liable?

(Rob Lee/Creative Commons)

Principal's Tortious Conduct A principal conducting an activity through an agent may be liable for harm resulting from the principal's own negligence or recklessness. Thus, a principal may be liable for giving improper instructions, authorizing the use of improper materials or tools, or establishing improper rules that resulted in the agent's committing a tort. **EXAMPLE 23.16** Jack knows that Suki cannot drive but nevertheless tells her to use the company truck to deliver some equipment to a customer. If someone is injured as a result, Jack (the principal) will be liable for his own negligence in giving improper instructions telling Suki to drive. ●

Principal's Authorization of Agent's Tortious Conduct A principal who authorizes an agent to commit a tort may be liable to persons or property injured thereby, because the act is considered to be the principal's. **EXAMPLE 23.17** Selkow directs his agent, Warren, to cut the corn on specific acreage, which neither of them has the right to do. The harvest is therefore a trespass (a tort), and Selkow is liable to the owner of the corn. ●

Note also that an agent acting at the principal's direction can be liable as a *tortfeasor* (one who commits a wrong, or tort), along with the principal, for committing the tortious act even if the agent was unaware of the wrongfulness of the act. Assume in the above example that Warren, the agent, did not know that Selkow had no right to harvest the corn. Warren can be held liable to the owner of the field for damages, along with Selkow, the principal.

LIABILITY FOR AGENT'S MISREPRESENTATION A principal is exposed to tort liability whenever a third person sustains a loss due to the agent's misrepresentation. The principal's liability depends on whether the agent was actually or apparently authorized to make representations and whether the representations were made within the scope of the agency. The principal is always directly responsible for an agent's misrepresentation made within the scope of the agent's authority. **EXAMPLE 23.18** Bassett is a demonstrator for Moore's products. Moore sends Bassett to a home show to demonstrate the products and to answer questions from consumers. Moore has given Bassett authority to make statements about the products. If Bassett makes only true representations, all is fine; but if he makes false claims, Moore will be liable for any injuries or damages sustained by third parties in reliance on Bassett's false representations. •

Respondeat Superior Latin for "let the master respond." A doctrine under which a principal or an employer is held liable for the wrongful acts committed by agents or employees while acting within the course and scope of their agency or employment.

Vicarious Liability Legal responsibility placed on one person for the acts of another; indirect liability imposed on a supervisory party (such as an employer) for the actions of a subordinate (such as an employee) because of the relationship between the two parties.

LIABILITY FOR AGENT'S NEGLIGENCE As mentioned, an agent is liable for his or her own torts. A principal may also be liable for harm an agent caused to a third party under the doctrine of ***respondeat superior***,[17] a Latin term meaning "let the master respond." This doctrine, which is discussed in this chapter's *Landmark in the Law* feature on page 597, is similar to the theory of strict liability discussed in Chapters 4 and 17. It imposes **vicarious liability**, or indirect liability, on the employer—that is, liability without regard to the personal fault of the employer for torts committed by an employee in the course or scope of employment.

When an agent commits a negligent act, can the agent, as well as the principal, be held liable? That was the issue in the following case.

17. Pronounced ree-*spahn*-dee-uht soo-*peer*-ee-your.

Case 23.3 Warner v. Southwest Desert Images, LLC

Court of Appeals of Arizona, 218 Ariz. 121, 180 P.3d 986 (2008).

(Jerry/Creative Commons)

Can an employee-agent, as well as the employer, be held liable for negligence in the use of a herbicide?

FACTS Aegis Communications hired Southwest Desert Images (SDI) to provide landscaping services for its property. SDI employee David Hoggatt was spraying an herbicide to control weeds around the Aegis building one day when he was told that the spray was being sucked into the building by the air-conditioning system and making people sick. The building was evacuated, and employees were treated for breathing problems and itchy eyes. Aegis employee Catherine Warner, who had previously suffered two heart attacks, was taken to the hospital. It was determined that she had suffered a heart attack. She continued experiencing health complications that she blamed on exposure to the spray. Warner sued SDI and Hoggatt for negligence. The trial judge dismissed the suit against Hoggatt. The jury found that SDI was solely liable for Warner's injuries. She was awarded $3,825 in damages. She appealed the decision.

ISSUE Can Hoggatt, the employee-agent who negligently sprayed the herbicide, be held liable for damages in addition to his employer-principal, SDI?

DECISION Yes. The appeals court held that Hoggatt should not have been dismissed from the lawsuit.

REASON The fact that Hoggatt was an agent-employee of SDI did not excuse him from liability for his negligence in spraying. The court reasoned

Case 23.3—Continues next page

Case 23.3–Continued

that there was evidence that Hoggatt had ignored instructions provided by the company that sold SDI the spray. In doing so, he was negligent. An agent (Hoggatt) is not excused from responsibility for tortious conduct just because he is working for a principal (SDI). Although the jury found SDI completely responsible, the dismissal of the suit against Hoggatt denied Warner the right to collect from him as a joint tortfeasor. The appeals court held that Warner should be able to collect from Hoggatt as well.

FOR CRITICAL ANALYSIS—Legal Consideration *How could SDI reduce the likelihood of similar lawsuits occurring in the future?*

Determining the Scope of Employment. The key to determining whether a principal may be liable for the torts of an agent under the doctrine of *respondeat superior* is whether the torts are committed within the scope of the agency or employment. The *Restatement (Second) of Agency*, Section 229, indicates the factors that today's courts will consider in determining whether a particular act occurred within the course and scope of employment. These factors are as follows:

1. Whether the employee's act was authorized by the employer.
2. The time, place, and purpose of the act.
3. Whether the act was one commonly performed by employees on behalf of their employers.
4. The extent to which the employer's interest was advanced by the act.
5. The extent to which the private interests of the employee were involved.
6. Whether the employer furnished the means or instrumentality (for example, a truck or a machine) by which the injury was inflicted.
7. Whether the employer had reason to know that the employee would do the act in question and whether the employee had ever done it before.
8. Whether the act involved the commission of a serious crime.

(Evelynshere/Creative Commons)

Suppose that the driver of the bus in this photo caused a traffic accident that resulted in property damages and personal injuries. If the driver's employer (the principal) learns that the driver had been drinking alcohol during a break right before the incident, can the principal avoid liability? Why or why not?

The Distinction between a "Detour" and a "Frolic." A useful insight into the "scope of employment" concept may be gained from the judge's classic distinction between a "detour" and a "frolic" in the case of *Joel v. Morison*.[18] In this case, the English court held that if a servant merely took a detour from his master's business, the master will be responsible. If, however, the servant was on a "frolic of his own" and not in any way "on his master's business," the master will not be liable.

EXAMPLE 23.19 Mandel, a traveling salesperson, while driving his employer's vehicle to call on a customer, decides to stop at the post office—which is one block off his route—to mail a personal letter. As Mandel approaches the post office, he negligently runs into a parked vehicle owned by Chan. In this situation, because Mandel's detour from the employer's business is not substantial, he is still acting within the scope of employment, and the employer is liable. The result would be different, though, if Mandel had decided to pick up a few friends for cocktails in another city and in the process had negligently run into Chan's vehicle. In that circumstance, the departure from the employer's business would be substantial, and the employer normally would not be liable to Chan for damages. Mandel would be considered to have been on a "frolic" of his own. ●

18. 6 Car. & P. 501, 172 Eng. Reprint 1338 (1834).

Landmark in the Law The Doctrine of *Respondeat Superior*

The idea that a master (employer) must respond to third persons for losses negligently caused by the master's servant (employee) first appeared in Lord Holt's opinion in *Jones v. Hart* (1698).[a] By the early nineteenth century, this maxim had been adopted by most courts and was referred to as the doctrine of *respondeat superior.*

Theories of Liability The vicarious (indirect) liability of the master for the acts of the servant has been supported primarily by two theories. The first theory rests on the issue of *control,* or *fault:* the master has control over the acts of the servant and is thus responsible for injuries arising out of such service. The second theory is economic in nature: because the master takes the benefits or profits of the servant's service, he or she should also suffer the losses; moreover, the master is better able than the servant to absorb such losses.

The *control* theory is clearly recognized in the *Restatement (Second) of Agency,* which defines a master as "a principal who employs an agent to perform service in his [or her] affairs and who controls, or has the right to control, the physical conduct of the other in the performance of the service." Accordingly, a servant is defined as "an agent employed by a master to perform service in his [or her] affairs whose physical conduct in his [or her] performance of the service is controlled, or is subject to control, by the master."

a. K.B. 642, 90 Eng. Reprint 1255 (1698).

Limitations on the Employer's Liability There are limitations on the master's liability for the acts of the servant, however. An employer (master) is responsible only for the wrongful conduct of an employee (servant) that occurs in "the scope of employment." The criteria used by the courts in determining whether an employee is acting within the scope of employment are set forth in the *Restatement (Second) of Agency* and discussed in the text. Generally, the act must be of a kind the servant was employed to do; must have occurred within "authorized time and space limits"; and must have been "activated, at least in part, by a purpose to serve the master."

• **Application to Today's World** *The courts have accepted the doctrine of* respondeat superior *for nearly two centuries. This theory of vicarious liability is laden with practical implications in all situations in which a principal-agent (master-servant, employer-employee) relationship exists. Today, the small-town grocer with one clerk and the multinational corporation with thousands of employees are equally subject to the doctrinal demand of "let the master respond." (For a further discussion of employers' liability for wrongs committed by their employees, including wrongs committed in the online employment environment, see Chapter 24.)*

• **Relevant Web Sites** To locate information on the Web concerning the doctrine of *respondeat superior,* go to this text's Web site at www.cengage.com/blaw/blt, select "Chapter 23," and click on "URLs for Landmarks."

NOTE An agent-employee going to or from work or meals usually is not considered to be within the scope of employment. An agent-employee whose job requires travel, however, is considered to be within the scope of employment for the entire trip, including the return.

Employee Travel Time. An employee going to and from work or to and from meals is usually considered outside the scope of employment. If travel is part of a person's position, however, such as a traveling salesperson or a regional representative of a company, then travel time is normally considered within the scope of employment. Thus, the duration of the business trip, including the return trip home, is within the scope of employment unless there is a significant departure from the employer's business.

Notice of Dangerous Conditions. The employer is charged with knowledge of any dangerous conditions discovered by an employee and pertinent to the employment situation. **EXAMPLE 23.20** Chad, a maintenance employee in Martin's apartment building, notices a lead pipe protruding from the ground in the building's courtyard. The employee neglects either to fix the pipe or to inform the employer of the danger. John falls on the pipe and is injured. The employer is charged with knowledge of the dangerous condition regardless of whether or not Chad actually informed the employer. That knowledge is imputed to the employer by virtue of the employment relationship. •

LIABILITY FOR AGENT'S INTENTIONAL TORTS Most intentional torts that employees commit have no relation to their employment; thus, their employers will not be held liable. Nevertheless, under the doctrine of *respondeat superior,* the employer can be liable for intentional torts of the employee that are committed within the course and scope of employment, just as the employer is liable for negligence. For instance, an employer is liable when an employee (such as a "bouncer" at a nightclub or a security guard at a department store) commits the tort of assault and battery or false imprisonment while acting within the scope of employment.

In addition, an employer who knows or should know that an employee has a propensity for committing tortious acts is liable for the employee's acts even if they would not ordinarily be considered within the scope of employment. For example, if the employer hires a bouncer knowing that he has a history of arrests for assault and battery, the employer may be liable if the employee viciously attacks a patron in the parking lot after hours.

An employer may also be liable for permitting an employee to engage in reckless actions that can injure others. **EXAMPLE 23.21** An employer observes an employee smoking while filling containerized trucks with highly flammable liquids. Failure to stop the employee will cause the employer to be liable for any injuries that result if a truck explodes. ● (See this chapter's *Beyond Our Borders* feature for a discussion of another approach to an employer's liability for an employee's acts.)

Liability for Independent Contractor's Torts Generally, an employer is not liable for physical harm caused to a third person by the negligent act of an independent contractor in the performance of the contract. This is because the employer does not have the right to control the details of an independent contractor's performance. Exceptions to this rule are made in certain situations, though, such as when unusually hazardous activities are involved. Typical examples of such activities include blasting operations, the transportation of highly volatile chemicals, or the use of poisonous gases. In these situations, an employer cannot be shielded from liability merely by using an independent contractor. Strict liability is imposed on the employer-principal as a matter of law. Also, in some states, strict liability may be imposed by statute.

Liability for Agent's Crimes An agent is liable for his or her own crimes. A principal or employer is not liable for an agent's crime even if the crime was committed within the scope of authority or employment—unless the principal participated by conspiracy or other action. In some jurisdictions, under specific statutes, a principal may be liable for an agent's violation, in the course and scope of employment, of regulations, such as those governing sanitation, prices, weights, and the sale of liquor.

How Agency Relationships Are Terminated

Agency law is similar to contract law in that both an agency and a contract can be terminated by an act of the parties or by operation of law. Once the relationship between the principal and the agent has ended, the agent no longer has the right (*actual* authority) to bind the principal. For an agent's *apparent* authority to be terminated, though, third persons may also need to be notified that the agency has been terminated.

Termination by Act of the Parties

An agency may be terminated by act of the parties in any of the following ways:

1. *Lapse of time.* When an agency agreement specifies the time period during which the agency relationship will exist, the agency ends when that time period expires. If no definite time is stated, then the agency continues for a reasonable time and can be terminated at will by either party. What constitutes a "reasonable time" depends, of course, on the circumstances and the nature of the agency relationship.

Beyond Our Borders — Islamic Law and *Respondeat Superior*

The doctrine of *respondeat superior* is well established in the legal systems of the United States and most Western countries. As you have already read, under this doctrine employers can be held liable for the acts of their agents, including employees. The doctrine of *respondeat superior* is not universal, however. Most Middle Eastern countries, for example, do not follow this doctrine. Islamic law, as codified in the *sharia*, holds to a strict belief that responsibility for human actions lies with the individual and cannot be vicariously extended to others. This belief and other concepts of Islamic law are based on the writings of Muhammad, the seventh-century prophet whose revelations form the basis of the Islamic religion and, by extension, the *sharia*. Muhammad's prophecies are documented in the Koran (Qur'an), which is the principal source of the *sharia*.

• For Critical Analysis

How would U.S. society be affected if employers could not be held vicariously liable for their employees' torts?

2. *Purpose achieved.* If an agent is employed to accomplish a particular objective, such as the purchase of stock for a cattle rancher, the agency automatically ends after the cattle have been purchased. If more than one agent is employed to accomplish the same purpose, such as the sale of real estate, the first agent to complete the sale automatically terminates the agency relationship for all the others.
3. *Occurrence of a specific event.* When an agency relationship is to terminate on the happening of a certain event, the agency automatically ends when the event occurs. If Posner appoints Rubik to handle her business affairs while she is away, the agency terminates when Posner returns.
4. *Mutual agreement.* The parties to an agency can cancel (rescind) their contract by mutually agreeing to terminate the agency relationship, whether the agency contract is in writing or whether it is for a specific duration.
5. *Termination by one party.* As a general rule, either party can terminate the agency relationship (the act of termination is called *revocation* if done by the principal and *renunciation* if done by the agent). Although both parties have the *power* to terminate the agency, they may not possess the *right*. Wrongful termination can subject the canceling party to a suit for breach of contract. **EXAMPLE 23.22** Rawlins has a one-year employment contract with Munro to act as an agent in return for $65,000. Although Munro has the *power* to discharge Rawlins before the contract period expires, if he does so, he can be sued for breaching the contract because he had no *right* to terminate the agency. •

When an agency has been terminated by act of the parties, it is the principal's duty to inform any third parties who know of the existence of the agency that it has been terminated (although notice of the termination may be given by others). Although an agent's actual authority ends when the agency is terminated, an agent's *apparent authority* continues until the third party receives notice (from any source) that such authority has been terminated. If the principal knows that a third party has dealt with the agent, the principal is expected to notify that person *directly*. For third parties who have heard about the agency but have not yet dealt with the agent, *constructive notice* is sufficient.[19]

No particular form is required for notice of agency termination to be effective. The principal can personally notify the agent, or the agent can learn of the termination through some other means. **EXAMPLE 23.23** Manning bids on a shipment of steel, and Stone is hired as an agent to arrange transportation of the shipment. When Stone learns that Manning has lost the bid, Stone's authority to make the transportation arrangement terminates. • If the agent's authority is written, however, it normally must be revoked in writing.

19. *Constructive notice* is information or knowledge of a fact imputed by law to a person if he or she could have discovered the fact by proper diligence. Constructive notice is often accomplished by newspaper publication.

Termination by Operation of Law

Termination of an agency by operation of law occurs in the circumstances discussed here. Note that when an agency terminates by operation of law, there is no duty to notify third persons.

1. *Death or insanity.* The general rule is that the death or mental incompetence of either the principal or the agent automatically and immediately terminates an ordinary agency relationship. Knowledge of the death is not required. **EXAMPLE 23.24** Geer sends Pyron to China to purchase a rare painting. Before Pyron makes the purchase, Geer dies. Pyron's agent status is terminated at the moment of Geer's death, even though Pyron does not know that Geer has died. ● Some states, however, have enacted statutes changing this common law rule to make knowledge of the principal's death a requirement for agency termination.
2. *Impossibility.* When the specific subject matter of an agency is destroyed or lost, the agency terminates. **EXAMPLE 23.25** Bullard employs Gonzalez to sell Bullard's house. Prior to any sale, the house is destroyed by fire. In this situation, Gonzalez's agency and authority to sell Bullard's house terminate. ● Similarly, when it is impossible for the agent to perform the agency lawfully because of a change in the law, the agency terminates.
3. *Changed circumstances.* When an event occurs that has such an unusual effect on the subject matter of the agency that the agent can reasonably infer that the principal will not want the agency to continue, the agency terminates. **EXAMPLE 23.26** Roberts hires Mullen to sell a tract of land for $20,000. Subsequently, Mullen learns that there is oil under the land and that the land is worth $1 million. The agency and Mullen's authority to sell the land for $20,000 are terminated. ●
4. *Bankruptcy.* If either the principal or the agent petitions for bankruptcy, the agency is *usually* terminated. In certain circumstances, as when the agent's financial status is irrelevant to the purpose of the agency, the agency relationship may continue. Insolvency (defined as the inability to pay debts when they become due or when liabilities exceed assets), as distinguished from bankruptcy, does not necessarily terminate the relationship.
5. *War.* When the principal's country and the agent's country are at war with each other, the agency is terminated. In this situation, the agency is automatically suspended or terminated because there is no way to enforce the legal rights and obligations of the parties.

Reviewing . . . Agency Relationships in Business

Lynne Meyer, on her way to a business meeting and in a hurry, stopped by a Buy-Mart store for a new pair of nylons to wear to the meeting. There was a long line at one of the checkout counters, but a cashier, Valerie Watts, opened another counter and began loading the cash drawer. Meyer told Watts that she was in a hurry and asked Watts to work faster. Watts, however, only slowed her pace. At this point, Meyer hit Watts. It is not clear from the record whether Meyer hit Watts intentionally or, in an attempt to retrieve the nylons, hit her inadvertently. In response, Watts grabbed Meyer by the hair and hit her repeatedly in the back of the head, while Meyer screamed for help. Management personnel separated the two women and questioned them about the incident. Watts was immediately fired for violating the store's no-fighting policy. Meyer subsequently sued Buy-Mart, alleging that the store was liable for the tort (assault and battery) committed by its employee. Using the information presented in the chapter, answer the following questions.

1. Under what doctrine discussed in this chapter might Buy-Mart be held liable for the tort committed by Watts?
2. What is the key factor in determining whether Buy-Mart is liable under this doctrine?
3. How is Buy-Mart's potential liability affected depending on whether Watts's behavior constituted an intentional tort or a tort of negligence?
4. Suppose that when Watts applied for the job at Buy-Mart, she disclosed in her application that she had previously been convicted of felony assault and battery. Nevertheless, Buy-Mart hired Watts as a cashier. How might this fact affect Buy-Mart's liability for Watts's actions?

Business Application

How Can an Employer Use Independent Contractors?*

As an employer, you may at some time consider hiring an independent contractor. Hiring workers as independent contractors instead of as employees may help you reduce both your potential tort liability and your tax liability.

Minimizing Potential Tort Liability

One reason for using an independent contractor is that employers usually are not liable for torts that an independent contractor commits against third parties. Nevertheless, there are exceptions. If an employer exercises significant control over the activities of the independent contractor, for example, the contractor may be considered an employee, and the employer can then be liable for the contractor's torts.

To minimize even the possibility of being liable for the negligence of an independent contractor, you should check the contractor's qualifications before hiring him or her. The degree to which you should investigate depends, of course, on the nature of the work. For example, hiring an independent contractor to maintain the landscaping around your building should require less investigation than employing an independent contractor to install the electrical systems that you sell. Also, a more thorough investigation is necessary when the contractor's activities present a potential danger to the public (as in delivering explosives).

Generally, it is a good idea to have the independent contractor assume, in a written contract, liability for harms caused to third parties by the contractor's negligence. You should also require that the independent contractor purchase liability insurance to cover the costs of potential lawsuits for harms caused to third persons by the contractor's hazardous activities or negligence.

Reducing Tax Liability and Other Costs

Another reason for hiring independent contractors is that you do not need to pay or withhold Social Security, income, or unemployment taxes on their behalf. The independent contractor is responsible for paying these taxes. Additionally, the independent contractor is not eligible for any retirement or medical plans or other fringe benefits that you provide for yourself and your employees, and this is a cost saving to you. Make sure that your contract with an independent contractor spells out that the contractor is responsible for paying taxes and is not entitled to any employment benefits.

A word of caution, though: simply designating a person as an independent contractor does not make her or him one. The Internal Revenue Service (IRS) will reclassify individuals as employees if it determines that they are "in fact" employees, regardless of how you have designated them. Keep proper documentation of the independent contractor's business identification number, business cards, and letterhead so that you can show the IRS that the contractor works independently.

If you improperly designate an employee as an independent contractor, the penalty may be high. Usually, you will be liable for back Social Security and unemployment taxes, plus interest and penalties. When in doubt, seek professional assistance in such matters.

CHECKLIST FOR THE EMPLOYER

1. **Check the qualifications of any independent contractor you plan to use to reduce the possibility that you might be legally liable for the contractor's negligence.**
2. **Require in any contract with an independent contractor that the contractor assume liability for harm to a third person caused by the contractor's negligence.**
3. **Require that independent contractors carry liability insurance. Examine the policy to make sure that it is current, particularly when the contractor will be undertaking actions that are more than normally hazardous to the public.**
4. **Do not do anything that would lead a third person to believe that an independent contractor is your employee, and do not allow independent contractors to represent themselves as your employees.**
5. **Regularly inspect the work of the independent contractor to make sure that it is being performed in accordance with contract specifications. Such supervision on your part will not change the worker's status as an independent contractor.**

* This *Business Application* is not meant to substitute for the services of an attorney who is licensed to practice law in your state.

Key Terms

agency 580
apparent authority 591
disclosed principal 592
e-agent 594
equal dignity rule 589
fiduciary 581
independent contractor 581
notary public 590
partially disclosed principal 592
power of attorney 589
ratification 585
***respondeat superior* 595**
undisclosed principal 592
vicarious liability 595

Chapter Summary: Agency Relationships in Business

Agency Relationships (See pages 581–584.)	In a *principal-agent* relationship, an agent acts on behalf of and instead of the principal in dealing with third parties. An employee who deals with third parties is normally an agent. An independent contractor is not an employee, and the employer has no control over the details of physical performance. An independent contractor may or may not be an agent.
How Agency Relationships Are Formed (See pages 584–586.)	Agency relationships may be formed by agreement, by ratification, by estoppel, and by operation of law—see the *Concept Summary* on page 586.
Duties of Agents and Principals (See pages 586–589.)	1. *Duties of the agent*— a. Performance—The agent must use reasonable diligence and skill in performing her or his duties or use the special skills that the agent has represented to the principal that the agent possesses. b. Notification—The agent is required to notify the principal of all matters that come to his or her attention concerning the subject matter of the agency. c. Loyalty—The agent has a duty to act solely for the benefit of the principal and not in the interest of the agent or a third party. d. Obedience—The agent must follow all lawful and clearly stated instructions of the principal. e. Accounting—The agent has a duty to make available to the principal records of all property and funds received and paid out on behalf of the principal. 2. *Duties of the principal*— a. Compensation—Except in a gratuitous agency relationship, the principal must pay the agreed-on value (or reasonable value) for an agent's services. b. Reimbursement and indemnification—The principal must reimburse the agent for all funds disbursed at the request of the principal and for all funds that the agent disburses for necessary expenses in the course of reasonable performance of his or her agency duties. c. Cooperation—A principal must cooperate with and assist an agent in performing her or his duties. d. Safe working conditions—A principal must provide safe working conditions for the agent-employee.
Agent's Authority (See pages 589–592.)	1. *Express authority*—Can be oral or in writing. Authorization must be in writing if the agent is to execute a contract that must be in writing. 2. *Implied authority*—Authority customarily associated with the position of the agent or authority that is deemed necessary for the agent to carry out expressly authorized tasks. 3. *Apparent authority*—Exists when the principal, by word or action, causes a third party reasonably to believe that an agent has authority to act, even though the agent has no express or implied authority. 4. *Ratification*—The affirmation by the principal of an agent's unauthorized action or promise. For the ratification to be effective, the principal must be aware of all material facts.
Liability in Agency Relationships (See pages 592–598.)	1. *Liability for contracts*—If the principal's identity is disclosed or partially disclosed at the time the agent forms a contract with a third party, the principal is liable to the third party under the contract if the agent acted within the scope of his or her authority. If the principal's identity is undisclosed at the time of contract formation, the agent is personally liable to the third party, but if the agent acted within the scope of his or her authority, the principal is also bound by the contract. 2. *Liability for agent's negligence*—Under the doctrine of *respondeat superior,* the principal is liable for any harm caused to another through the agent's torts if the agent was acting within the scope of her or his employment at the time the harmful act occurred. 3. *Liability for agent's intentional torts*—Usually, employers are not liable for the intentional torts that their agents commit, *unless:* a. The acts are committed within the scope of employment, and thus the doctrine of *respondeat superior* applies. b. The employer knows or should know that the employee has a propensity for committing tortious acts. c. The employer allowed an employee to engage in reckless acts that caused injury to another. 4. *Liability for independent contractor's torts*—A principal is not liable for harm caused by an independent contractor's negligence, unless hazardous activities are involved (in this situation, the principal is strictly liable for any resulting harm) or other exceptions apply.

Chapter Summary: Agency Relationships in Business—Continued

Liability in Agency Relationships —Continued	5. *Liability for agent's crimes*—An agent is responsible for his or her own crimes, even if the crimes were committed while the agent was acting within the scope of authority or employment. A principal will be liable for an agent's crime only if the principal participated by conspiracy or other action or (in some jurisdictions) if the agent violated certain government regulations in the course of employment.
How Agency Relationships Are Terminated (See pages 598–600.)	1. *By act of the parties*— Notice to third parties is required when an agency is terminated by act of the parties. Direct notice is required for those who have previously dealt with the agency; constructive notice will suffice for all other third parties. See pages 598–599 for a list of the ways that an agency may be terminated by act of the parties. 2. *By operation of law*— Notice to third parties is not required when an agency is terminated by operation of law. See page 600 for a list of the ways that an agency can be terminated by operation of law.

ExamPrep

ISSUE SPOTTERS

1 Vivian, owner of Wonder Goods Company, employs Xena as an administrative assistant. In Vivian's absence, and without authority, Xena represents herself as Vivian and signs a promissory note in Vivian's name. In what circumstance is Vivian liable on the note?

2 Davis contracts with Estee to buy a certain horse on her behalf. Estee asks Davis not to reveal her identity. Davis makes a deal with Farmland Stables, the owner of the horse, and makes a down payment. Estee does not pay the rest of the price. Farmland Stables sues Davis for breach of contract. Can Davis hold Estee liable for whatever damages he has to pay? Why or why not?

BEFORE THE TEST

Check your answers to the Issue Spotters, and at the same time, take the interactive quiz for this chapter. Go to www.cengage.com/blaw/blt and click on "Chapter 23." First, click on "Answers to Issue Spotters" to check your answers. Next, click on "Interactive Quiz" to assess your mastery of the concepts in this chapter. Then click on "Flashcards" to review this chapter's Key Term definitions.

For Review

Answers for the even-numbered questions in this **For Review** *section can be found on this text's accompanying Web site at* www.cengage.com/blaw/blt. *Select "Chapter 23" and click on "For Review."*

1 What is the difference between an employee and an independent contractor?
2 How do agency relationships arise?
3 What duties do agents and principals owe to each other?
4 When is a principal liable for the agent's actions with respect to third parties? When is the agent liable?
5 What are some of the ways in which an agency relationship can be terminated?

Hypothetical Scenarios and Case Problems

23–1 **Ratification by Principal.** Springer was a political candidate running for Congress. He was operating on a tight budget and instructed his campaign staff not to purchase any campaign materials without his explicit authorization. In spite of these instructions, one of his campaign workers ordered Dubychek Printing Co. to print some promotional materials for Springer's campaign. When the printed materials arrived, Springer did not return them but instead used them during his campaign. When Springer failed to pay for the materials, Dubychek sued for recovery of the price. Springer contended that he was not liable on the sales contract because he had not authorized his agent to purchase the printing services.

Dubychek argued that the campaign worker was Springer's agent and that the worker had authority to make the printing contract. Additionally, Dubychek claimed that even if the purchase was unauthorized, Springer's use of the materials constituted ratification of his agent's unauthorized purchase. Is Dubychek correct? Explain.

23-2 **Hypothetical Question with Sample Answer** Paul Gett is a well-known, wealthy financial expert living in the city of Torris. Adam Wade, Gett's friend, tells Timothy Brown that he is Gett's agent for the purchase of rare coins. Wade even shows Brown a local newspaper clipping mentioning Gett's interest in coin collecting. Brown, knowing of Wade's friendship with Gett, contracts with Wade to sell a rare coin valued at $25,000 to Gett. Wade takes the coin and disappears with it. On the payment due date, Brown seeks to collect from Gett, claiming that Wade's agency made Gett liable. Gett does not deny that Wade was a friend, but he claims that Wade was never his agent. Discuss fully whether an agency was in existence at the time the contract for the rare coin was made.

—**For a sample answer to Question 23–2, go to Appendix E at the end of this text.**

23-3 **Employee versus Independent Contractor.** Stephen Hemmerling was a driver for the Happy Cab Co. Hemmerling paid certain fixed expenses and abided by a variety of rules relating to the use of the cab, the hours that could be worked, and the solicitation of fares, among other things. Rates were set by the state. Happy Cab did not withhold taxes from Hemmerling's pay. While driving the cab, Hemmerling was injured in an accident and filed a claim against Happy Cab in a Nebraska state court for workers' compensation benefits. Such benefits are not available to independent contractors. On what basis might the court hold that Hemmerling is an employee? Explain.

23-4 **Liability for Independent Contractor's Torts.** Dean Brothers Corp. owns and operates a steel drum manufacturing plant. Lowell Wyden, the plant superintendent, hired Best Security Patrol, Inc. (BSP), a security company, to guard Dean property and "deter thieves and vandals." Some BSP security guards, as Wyden knew, carried firearms. Pete Sidell, a BSP security guard, was not certified as an armed guard but nevertheless took his gun, in a briefcase, to work. While working at the Dean plant on October 31, 2010, Sidell fired his gun at Tyrone Gaines, in the belief that Gaines was an intruder. The bullet struck and killed Gaines. Gaines's mother filed a lawsuit claiming that her son's death was the result of BSP's negligence, for which Dean was responsible. What is the plaintiff's best argument that Dean is responsible for BSP's actions? What is Dean's best defense? Explain.

23-5 **Case Problem with Sample Answer** Su Ru Chen owned the Lucky Duck Fortune Cookie Factory in Everett, Massachusetts, which made Chinese-style fortune cookies for restaurants. In November 2001, Chen listed the business for sale with Bob Sun, a real estate broker, for $35,000. Sun's daughter Frances and her fiancé, Chiu Chung Chan, decided that Chan would buy the business. Acting as a broker on Chen's (the seller's) behalf, Frances asked about the Lucky Duck's finances. Chen said that each month the business sold at least 1,000 boxes of cookies at a $2,000 profit. Frances negotiated a price of $23,000, which Chan (her fiancé) paid. When Chan began to operate the Lucky Duck, it became clear that the demand for the cookies was actually about 500 boxes per month—a rate at which the business would suffer losses. Less than two months later, the factory closed. Chan filed a suit in a Massachusetts state court against Chen, alleging fraud, among other things. Chan's proof included Frances's testimony as to what Chen had said to her. Chen objected to the admission of this testimony. What is the basis for this objection? Should the court admit the testimony? Why or why not? [*Chan v. Chen,* 70 Mass.App.Ct. 79, 872 N.E.2d 1153 (2007)]

—**After you have answered Problem 23–5, compare your answer with the sample answer given on the Web site that accompanies this text. Go to www.cengage.com/blaw/blt, select "Chapter 23," and click on "Case Problem with Sample Answer."**

23-6 **Apparent Authority.** Lee Dennegar and Mark Knutson lived in Dennegar's house in Raritan, New Jersey. Dennegar paid the mortgage and other household expenses. With Dennegar's consent, Knutson managed their household's financial affairs and the "general office functions concerned with maintaining the house." Dennegar allowed Knutson to handle the mail and "to do with it as he chose." Knutson wrote checks for Dennegar to sign, although Knutson signed Dennegar's name to many of the checks with Dennegar's consent. AT & T Universal issued a credit card in Dennegar's name in February 2001. Monthly statements were mailed to Dennegar's house, and payments were sometimes made on those statements. Knutson died in June 2003. The unpaid charges on the card of $14,752.93 were assigned to New Century Financial Services, Inc. New Century filed a suit in a New Jersey state court against Dennegar to collect the unpaid amount. Dennegar claimed that he never applied for or used the card and knew nothing about it. Under what theory could Dennegar be liable for the charges? Explain. [*New Century Financial Services, Inc. v. Dennegar,* 394 N.J.Super. 595, 928 A.2d 48 (A.D. 2007)]

23-7 **Undisclosed Principal.** Homeowners Jim and Lisa Criss hired Kevin and Cathie Pappas, doing business as Outside Creations, to undertake a landscaping project. Kevin signed the parties' contract as "Outside Creations Rep." The Crisses' payments on the contract were by checks payable to Kevin, who deposited them in his personal account—there was no Outside Creations account. Later, alleging breach, the Crisses filed a suit in a Georgia state court against the Pappases. The defendants contended that they could not be liable because the contract was not with them personally. They claimed that they were the agents of Forever Green Landscaping and Irrigation, Inc., which had been operating under the name "Outside Creations" at the time of the contract and had since filed for bankruptcy. The Crisses pointed out that the name "Forever Green" was not in the contract. Can the Pappases be liable on this contract? Why or why not? [*Pappas v. Criss,* 296 Ga.App. 803, 676 S.E.2d 21 (2009)]

23-8 **A Question of Ethics** *Emergency One, Inc. (EO), makes fire and rescue vehicles. Western Fire Truck, Inc., contracted with EO to be its exclusive dealer in Colorado and Wyoming through December 2003. James Costello, a Western salesperson, was authorized to order EO vehicles for his customers. Without informing Western, Costello e-mailed EO about Western's difficulties in obtaining cash to fund its operations. He asked about the viability of Western's contract and his possible employment with EO. On EO's request, and in disregard of Western's instructions, Costello sent some payments for EO vehicles directly to EO. In addition, Costello, with EO's help, sent a competing bid to a potential Western customer. EO's representative e-mailed Costello, "You have my permission to kick [Western's] ass." In April 2002, EO terminated its contract with Western, which, after reviewing Costello's e-mail, fired Costello. Western filed a suit in a Colorado state court against Costello and EO, alleging, among other things, that Costello breached his duty as an agent and that EO aided and abetted the breach.* [Western Fire Truck, Inc. v. Emergency One, Inc., *134 P.3d 570 (Colo.App. 2006)*]

1. Was there an agency relationship between Western and Costello? Western required monthly reports from its sales staff, but Costello did not report regularly. Does this indicate that Costello was *not* Western's agent? In determining whether an agency relationship exists, is the *right* to control or the *fact* of control more important? Explain.
2. Did Costello owe Western a duty? If so, what was the duty? Did Costello breach it? How?
3. A Colorado state statute allows a court to award punitive damages in "circumstances of fraud, malice, or willful and wanton conduct." Did any of these circumstances exist in this case? Should punitive damages be assessed against either defendant? Why or why not?

Critical Thinking and Writing Assignments

23-9 **Critical Legal Thinking.** What policy is served by the law that employers do not have copyright ownership in works created by independent contractors (unless there is a written "work for hire" agreement)?

Practical Internet Exercises

Go to this text's Web site at www.cengage.com/blaw/blt, select "Chapter 23," and click on "Practical Internet Exercises." There you will find the following Internet research exercises that you can perform to learn more about the topics covered in this chapter.

Practical Internet Exercise 23-1: LEGAL PERSPECTIVE—**Employees or Independent Contractors?**
Practical Internet Exercise 23-2: MANAGEMENT PERSPECTIVE—**Liability in Agency Relationships**

Chapter 24

Employment, Immigration, and Labor Law

"The employer generally gets the employees he deserves."

—Sir Walter Gilbey, 1831–1914
(English merchant)

Chapter Outline

- Employment at Will
- Wage and Hour Laws
- Layoffs
- Family and Medical Leave
- Worker Health and Safety
- Income Security
- Employee Privacy Rights
- Immigration Law
- Labor Unions

(©Photosani, 2009. Used under license from Shutterstock.com)

Learning Objectives

After reading this chapter, you should be able to answer the following questions:

1. What is the employment-at-will doctrine? When and why are exceptions to this doctrine made?
2. What federal statute governs working hours and wages?
3. Under the Family and Medical Leave Act of 1993, in what circumstances may an employee take family or medical leave?
4. What are the two most important federal statutes governing immigration and employment today?
5. What federal statute gave employees the right to organize unions and engage in collective bargaining?

Until the early 1900s, most employer-employee relationships were governed by the common law. Even today, under the common law *employment-at-will doctrine,* private employers generally are free to hire and fire workers at will, unless doing so violates an employee's contractual or statutory rights. (This is one reason why employers generally get the employees they deserve, as the chapter-opening quotation observed.) Now, however, there are numerous statutes and administrative agency regulations that regulate the workplace. Common law doctrines have thus been displaced to a large extent by statutory law.

In this chapter, we look at the most significant laws regulating employment relationships. We will deal with other important laws regulating the workplace—those that prohibit employment discrimination—in the next chapter.

Employment at Will

Employment at Will A common law doctrine under which either party may terminate an employment relationship at any time for any reason, unless a contract specifies otherwise.

Traditionally, employment relationships have generally been governed by the common law doctrine of **employment at will.** Under the employment-at-will doctrine, either party may terminate the employment relationship at any time and for any reason, unless doing so would violate the provisions of an employment contract. The majority of U.S. workers continue to have the legal status of "employees at will." In other words, this common law doctrine is still in widespread use, and only one state (Montana) does not apply the doctrine.

Nonetheless, as mentioned in the chapter introduction, federal and state statutes governing employment relationships prevent this doctrine from being applied in a number of circumstances. Today, an employer is not permitted to fire an employee if doing so would violate a federal or state employment statute, such as one prohibiting employment termination for discriminatory reasons (see Chapter 25). Note that the distinction made under agency law (discussed in Chapter 23) between employee status and independent-contractor status is important here. The employment laws that are discussed in this chapter and in Chapter 25 apply only to the employer-employee relationship; they do not apply to independent contractors.

Exceptions to the Employment-at-Will Doctrine

Under the employment-at-will doctrine, as mentioned, an employer may hire and fire employees at will (regardless of the employees' performance) without liability, unless doing so violates the terms of an employment contract or statutory law. Because of the harsh effects of the employment-at-will doctrine for employees, the courts have carved out various exceptions to the doctrine. These exceptions are based on contract theory, tort theory, and public policy.

REMEMBER **An implied contract may exist if a party furnishes a service expecting to be paid, and the other party, who knows (or should know) of this expectation, has a chance to reject the service and does not.**

Exceptions Based on Contract Theory Some courts have held that an *implied* employment contract exists between an employer and an employee. If an employee is fired outside the terms of the implied contract, he or she may succeed in an action for breach of contract even though no written employment contract exists. **EXAMPLE 24.1** BDI Enterprise's employment manual and personnel bulletin both state that, as a matter of policy, workers will be dismissed only for good cause. If an employee reasonably expects BDI to follow this policy, a court may find that there is an implied contract based on the terms stated in the manual and bulletin.[1] ● Generally, the key factor in determining whether an employment manual creates an implied contractual obligation is the employee's reasonable expectations.

An employer's oral promises to employees regarding discharge policy may also be considered part of an implied contract. If the employer fires a worker in a manner contrary to what was promised, a court may hold that the employer has violated the implied contract and is liable for damages. Most state courts will judge a claim of breach of an implied employment contract by traditional contract standards.

Courts in a few states have gone further and held that all employment contracts contain an implied covenant of good faith. This means that both sides promise to abide by the contract in good faith. If an employer fires an employee for an arbitrary or unjustified reason, the employee can claim that the covenant of good faith was breached and the contract violated.

Exceptions Based on Tort Theory In a few situations, the discharge of an employee may give rise to an action for wrongful discharge under tort theories. Abusive discharge procedures may result in a suit for intentional infliction of emotional distress or defamation. In addition, some courts have permitted workers to sue their employers under the tort theory of fraud. **EXAMPLE 24.2** Goldfinch, Inc., induces a prospective employee to leave a lucrative job and move to another state by offering "a long-term job with a thriving business." In fact, Goldfinch is not only having significant financial problems but is also planning a merger that will result in the elimination of the position offered to the prospective employee. If the employee takes the job in reliance on Goldfinch's representations and

1. See, for example, *Ross v. May Co.*, 377 Ill.App.3d 387, 880 N.E.2d 210 (1 Dist. 2007).

(Katy Batdorff/Grand Rapids Press/Landov)

This mother is spending time with her two small children and one of their friends. Working mothers face numerous challenges in attempting to balance family and income-earning activities. The federal Family and Medical Leave Act (FMLA) requires that employees be given up to twelve weeks of unpaid family medical care per year. In some situations, employees are not covered by the FMLA. What is a major limitation on who is covered by the FMLA?

is fired shortly thereafter, the employee may be able to bring an action against the employer for fraud. ●

EXCEPTIONS BASED ON PUBLIC POLICY The most common exception to the employment-at-will doctrine is made on the basis of public policy. Courts may apply this exception when an employer fires a worker for reasons that violate a fundamental public policy of the jurisdiction. Generally, the public policy involved must be expressed clearly in the statutory law governing the jurisdiction.

EXAMPLE 24.3 As you will read later in this chapter, employers with fifty or more employees are required by the Family and Medical Leave Act (FMLA) to give employees up to twelve weeks of unpaid family or medical leave per year. Mila's employer, however, has only forty employees and thus is not covered by the federal law. Nonetheless, if Mila is fired from her job because she takes three weeks of unpaid family leave to help her son through a difficult surgery, a court may deem that the employer's actions violated the public policy expressed in the FMLA. ●

Whistleblowing An employee's disclosure to government authorities, upper-level managers, or the media that the employer is engaged in unsafe or illegal activities.

An exception may also be made when an employee "blows the whistle" on an employer's wrongdoing. **Whistleblowing** occurs when an employee tells government authorities, upper-level managers, or the media that her or his employer is engaged in some unsafe or illegal activity. Whistleblowers on occasion have been protected from wrongful discharge for reasons of public policy. **CASE EXAMPLE 24.4** Rebecca Wendeln was the staff coordinator at a nursing home in Nebraska. One of the patients at the home was wheelchair-bound and could be moved only by two persons using a special belt. When Wendeln discovered that the patient had been improperly moved and was injured as a result, she reported the incident to state authorities, as she was required to do by state law. Wendeln's supervisor angrily confronted her about the report, and she was fired shortly after that. Wendeln filed a lawsuit. The court held that although Wendeln was an employee at will, she was protected in this instance from retaliatory firing because a very clear mandate of public policy had been violated.[2] ● Normally, however, whistleblowers seek protection from retaliatory discharge under federal and state statutory laws, such as the Whistleblower Protection Act of 1989.[3]

Wrongful Discharge

Wrongful Discharge An employer's termination of an employee's employment in violation of the law.

Whenever an employer discharges an employee in violation of an employment contract or a statute protecting employees, the employee may bring an action for **wrongful discharge.** Even if an employer's actions do not violate any provisions in an employment contract or a statute, the employer may still be subject to liability under a common law doctrine, such as a tort theory or agency. Note that in today's business world, an employment contract may be established or modified via e-mail exchanges, as discussed in this chapter's *Adapting the Law to the Online Environment* feature.

"All I've ever wanted was an honest week's pay for an honest day's work."
Steve Martin, 1945–present
(American actor and comedian)

Wage and Hour Laws

In the 1930s, Congress enacted several laws regulating the wages and working hours of employees. In 1931, Congress passed the Davis-Bacon Act,[4] which requires contractors and subcontractors working on federal government construction projects to pay "prevailing

2. *Wendeln v. The Beatrice Manor, Inc.*, 271 Neb. 373, 712 N.W.2d 226 (2006).
3. 5 U.S.C. Section 1201.
4. 40 U.S.C. Sections 276a–276a-5.

Adapting the Law to the Online Environment

Can Parties Create and Modify Employment Contracts via E-Mail?

E-mail is used in nearly every aspect of the employment environment—from workplace communications to contracts with employees. As you learned in Chapter 12, under the one-year rule of the Statute of Frauds, most employment contracts must be in writing. But electronic communications, including e-mail, instant messages, text messages, and even Twitter, can be used as evidence to show that a contract existed or that the parties modified their contract.

Moreover, although many employment contracts include traditional integration clauses stating that the contract can be modified only by a signed writing, such a clause may not necessarily prevent e-mail modifications. Under the federal E-Sign Act and the Uniform Electronic Transactions Act (both discussed in Chapter 10), what constitutes a signed writing has changed. A court cannot refuse to enforce a contract solely because it is contained in an electronic record, and a name typed at the end of an e-mail can be a signature.

E-Mail Evidence That an Employment Contract Existed

For example, Robert Moroni negotiated a deal to provide consulting services for Medco Health Solutions, Inc., a third party administrator of prescription-drug plans. Medco's agent, Brian Griffin, sent Moroni an e-mail setting forth the details of the parties' agreement. Moroni e-mailed a counteroffer suggesting that he would work on Medco's projects two days a week for thirteen months, in exchange for $17,000 a month ($204,000 annually), plus travel expenses. Medco accepted via e-mail, and Moroni began performing the contract, but Medco refused to pay him. Moroni sued for breach of contract. Medco argued that no enforceable contract existed and that the e-mail showed only an agreement to agree. The court, however, ruled that the e-mail amounted to an agreement to the essential terms of an employment contract.[a]

E-Mail Modifications of Employment Contracts

In another case, Arthur Stevens sold his public relations firm in New York to Publicis, S.A., a French global communications company. (*S.A.* are the initials for *Société Anonyme*, which is the French equivalent to a corporation in the United States.) The sale involved two contracts: a stock purchase agreement (SPA) and an employment contract. Stevens received an initial payment of more than $3 million under the SPA and stood to receive additional payments of up to $4 million over the next three years, depending on the new company's earnings. The employment contract allowed Stevens to stay on as chief executive officer (CEO) of the new company for three years and contained an integration clause requiring any modification to be in a signed writing.

Within six months of the sale, however, the new company had lost $900,000 and was not meeting revenue and profit targets. Stevens was removed as CEO and given the option of leaving the firm or staying to develop new business. An agent of Publicis, Bob Bloom, then e-mailed Stevens another option, giving him specific information on the responsibilities he could assume. Within a day, Stevens e-mailed a response, "I accept your proposal with total enthusiasm and excitement," and said that he was "psyched" about his new position. Nevertheless, Stevens later sued Publicis, claiming that it had breached the terms of his original employment contract by not keeping him on as CEO. The court, however, held that in the e-mail exchanges, Stevens had accepted the proposed modification of his employment contract in a signed writing. Because the e-mail modification was binding, Stevens could not sue Publicis.[b]

FOR CRITICAL ANALYSIS

Suppose that an employer sends an e-mail to an employee stating that the employee will not be terminated without good cause, but later discharges that employee for no reason. Would that e-mail be sufficient to establish the existence of an employment contract that would allow the employee to sue for damages? Why or why not?

a. *Moroni v. Medco Health Solutions, Inc.*, 2008 WL 3539476 (E.D.Mich. 2008).

b. *Stevens v. Publicis, S.A.*, 50 A.D.3d 253, 854 N.Y.S.2d 690 (1 Dept. 2008).

wages" to their employees. In 1936, the Walsh-Healey Act[5] was passed. This act requires that a minimum wage, as well as overtime pay at 1.5 times regular pay rates, be paid to employees of manufacturers or suppliers entering into contracts with agencies of the federal government.

In 1938, Congress passed the Fair Labor Standards Act[6] (FLSA). This act extended wage and hour requirements to cover all employers engaged in interstate commerce or in the production of goods for interstate commerce, plus selected types of other businesses. Here, we examine the FLSA's provisions in regard to child labor, maximum hours, and minimum wages.

5. 41 U.S.C. Sections 35–45.

6. 29 U.S.C. Sections 201–260.

Child Labor

The FLSA prohibits oppressive child labor. Children under fourteen years of age are allowed to do certain types of work, such as deliver newspapers, work for their parents, and work in the entertainment and (with some exceptions) agricultural areas. Children who are fourteen or fifteen years of age are allowed to work, but not in hazardous occupations. There are also numerous restrictions on how many hours per day (particularly on school days) and per week they can work.

Working times and hours are not restricted for persons between the ages of sixteen and eighteen, but they cannot be employed in hazardous jobs or in jobs detrimental to their health and well-being. None of these restrictions apply to persons over the age of eighteen.

Wages and Hours

Minimum Wage The lowest wage, either by government regulation or union contract, that an employer may pay an hourly worker.

The FLSA provides that a **minimum wage** of a specified amount ($7.25 per hour in 2009) must be paid to employees in covered industries. Congress periodically revises this minimum wage.[7] Under the FLSA, employers who customarily furnish food or lodging to employees can deduct the reasonable cost of those services from the employees' wages.

Under the FLSA, employees who work more than forty hours per week normally must be paid 1.5 times their regular pay for all hours over forty. Note that the FLSA overtime provisions apply only after an employee has worked more than forty hours per *week*. Thus, employees who work for ten hours a day, four days per week, are not entitled to overtime pay because they do not work more than forty hours per week.

Overtime Exemptions

Certain employees—usually executive, administrative, and professional employees, as well as outside salespersons and computer programmers—are exempt from the FLSA's overtime provisions. Employers are not required to pay overtime wages to exempt employees. Employers can voluntarily pay overtime to ineligible employees but cannot waive or reduce the overtime requirements of the FLSA.

"By working faithfully eight hours a day, you may eventually get to be a boss and work twelve hours a day."
Robert Frost, 1875–1963
(American poet)

An executive employee is one whose primary duty is management. An employee's primary duty is determined by what he or she does that is of principal value to the employer, not by how much time the employee spends doing particular tasks. An employer cannot deny overtime wages to an employee based only on the employee's job title, however, and must be able to show that the employee's primary duty qualifies her or him for an exemption.[8]

CASE EXAMPLE 24.5 Starbucks hired Kevin Keevican as a barista (someone who waits on customers, operates the cash register, makes drinks, and cleans and maintains the equipment). Over time, he was promoted to shift supervisor, assistant manager, and then manager. As a manager, Keevican worked 70 hours a week for $650 to $800, a 10 to 20 percent bonus, and fringe benefits, such as paid sick leave, that were not available to baristas. Eventually, Keevican quit and, along with several other former managers, filed a claim against Starbucks for unpaid overtime and other amounts. The plaintiffs admitted that they performed many managerial tasks, but argued that they spent 70 to 80 percent of their time on barista chores and thus were not executive employees. The court, however, found that each plaintiff was "the single highest-ranking employee in his [or her] particular store and was responsible on site for that store's day-to-day overall operations." Therefore, the court

ON THE WEB For more details about the regulations concerning overtime, go to the Web site of the U.S. Department of Labor at www.dol.gov.

7. Note that many state and local governments also have minimum-wage laws; these laws can provide for higher minimum-wage rates than required by the federal government.
8. See, for example, *Slusser v. Vantage Builders, Inc.*, 576 F.Supp.2d 1207 (D.N.M. 2008).

concluded that each plaintiff's primary duty was management regardless of any other tasks and that Starbucks was not required to pay them overtime.[9] ●

The exemptions to the overtime-pay requirement do not apply to manual laborers or to police, firefighters, licensed nurses, and other public-safety workers. White-collar workers who earn more than $100,000 per year, computer programmers, dental hygienists, and insurance adjusters are typically exempt—though they must also meet certain other criteria.

Should workers get overtime pay for using their BlackBerrys after work hours? **Some workers are claiming that they should be paid overtime for the time they spend staying connected to work through their BlackBerrys or other handheld electronic devices. Indeed, many employers require that their employees carry a BlackBerry, iPhone or other smart phone, or PDA (personal digital assistant) to keep in contact. Checking e-mail, responding to text messages, and using other employment-related applications of these handheld devices can be considered work. If employees who are not exempt under the overtime regulations are required to use these devices after office hours, the workers may have a valid claim to overtime wages. In 2009, for example, a maintenance worker in Wisconsin filed a lawsuit against his employer, CB Richard Ellis (CBRE), a property management company. CBRE requires all of its hourly employees to carry BlackBerrys during off hours. The worker is seeking back overtime pay for himself and all the other CBRE employees who are required to carry the device.**[10]

Layoffs

During the latest economic recession in the United States, hundreds of thousands of workers lost their jobs as many businesses disappeared. Other companies struggling to keep afloat reduced costs by restructuring their operations and downsizing their workforces, which meant layoffs.

ON THE WEB **For more information and statistics on employee layoffs in the United States, go to the Mass Layoff Statistics page at the U.S. Bureau of Labor Statistics' Web site at www.bls.gov/mls.**

Mass layoffs of U.S. workers resulted in high unemployment rates. Later in this chapter, we will discuss unemployment insurance, which helps some workers manage financially until they can find another job. In this section, we discuss the laws pertaining to employee layoffs—an area that is increasingly the subject of litigation.

The Worker Adjustment and Retraining Notification (WARN) Act

Since 1988, federal law has required large employers to provide sixty days' notice before implementing a mass layoff or closing a plant that employs more than fifty full-time workers. The Worker Adjustment and Retraining Notification Act,[11] or WARN Act, applies to employers with at least one hundred full-time employees. It is intended to give workers advance notice so that they can start looking for a new job while they are still employed and to alert state agencies so that they can provide training and other resources for displaced workers.

The WARN Act defines the term *mass layoff* as a reduction in the workforce that, during any thirty-day period, results in an employment loss of either:

1. At least 33 percent of the full-time employees at a single job site *and* at least fifty employees; or
2. At least five hundred full-time employees.

An *employment loss* is defined as a layoff that exceeds six months or a reduction in hours of work of more than 50 percent during each month of any six-month period.

9. *Mims v. Starbucks Corp.*, 2007 WL 10369 (S.D.Tex. 2007).
10. "Employee Seeks Class Action in Unpaid Overtime Lawsuit," *The Business Journal of Milwaukee*, March 18, 2009.
11. 29 U.S.C. Sections 2101 *et seq.*

The WARN Act requires that advance notice of the layoff be sent to the affected workers *or* their representative (if the workers are members of a labor union), as well as to state and local government authorities. The state and local authorities are notified so that they can provide resources, such as job training, to displaced workers. Employers must also provide notice to part-time and seasonal employees who are being laid off, even though these workers do not count in determining whether the act's provisions are triggered. Note also that even companies who anticipate filing for bankruptcy normally must provide notice under the WARN Act before implementing a mass layoff.

Criticisms and Compliance Issues Critics claim that the WARN Act protects too few employees and contains loopholes. Although the U.S. Department of Labor considers a mass layoff to be one that affects fifty or more employees, enforcing the WARN Act rules is not easy. Because the rules depend on the percentage of full-time workers affected at a particular site, employers can avoid the WARN requirements by staggering layoffs over many months or at various locations. Sometimes, employers lay off dozens or even hundreds of workers without having to provide WARN notice. Small employers, of course, never have to provide WARN notice.

Remedies for WARN Act Violations If sued, an employer who orders a mass layoff or plant closing in violation of the WARN Act can be fined up to $500 for each day of the violation. Employees can recover back pay for each day of the violation (up to sixty days), plus reasonable attorneys' fees. An employee can also recover benefits under an employee benefit plan, including the cost of medical expenses that would have been covered and were not. Employees who are laid off may also claim that the layoff was in violation of employment discrimination laws (see Chapter 25), if it disproportionately affects members of a protected class, such as minorities, older persons, or women.

"I stopped carrying a briefcase. I don't like to flaunt my employment."

State Laws May Also Require Layoff Notices

Many states also have statutes requiring employers to provide notice before initiating mass layoffs, and these laws may have different and even stricter requirements than the WARN Act. In New York, for instance, companies with fifty or more employees must provide ninety days' notice before any layoff that affects twenty-five or more full-time employees. The law in Illinois applies to companies with seventy-five or more employees and requires sixty days' advance notice of any layoff that affects twenty-five or more full-time employees at one plant or 250 employees.

Family and Medical Leave

In 1993, Congress passed the Family and Medical Leave Act (FMLA)[12] to allow employees to take time off from work for family or medical reasons. A majority of the states also have legislation allowing for a leave from employment for family or medical reasons, and many employers maintain private family-leave plans for their workers. Significant changes to the FMLA regulations that became effective in 2009 created new categories of leave for military caregivers and for qualifying exigencies that arise due to military service.

Coverage and Applicability of the FMLA

The FMLA requires employers who have fifty or more employees to provide employees with up to twelve weeks of unpaid family or medical leave during any twelve-month period. The FMLA expressly covers private and public (government) employees who have worked for

12. 29 U.S.C. Sections 2601, 2611–2619, 2651–2654.

(PhotoDisc Red)

A boy leans against his pregnant mother. The mother hopes to take time off from her full-time corporate job when the baby is born. What is required for the Family and Medical Leave Act (FMLA) to apply to her employer? If the employer is covered by the FMLA, how much family leave does the act authorize?

their employers for at least a year.[13] An employee may take *family leave* to care for a newborn baby, an adopted child, or a foster child.[14] An employee can take *medical leave* when the employee or the employee's spouse, child, or parent has a "serious health condition" requiring care.

In addition, an employee caring for a family member with a serious injury or illness incurred as a result of military duty can now take up to *twenty-six weeks of military caregiver leave* within a twelve-month period.[15] Also, an employee can take up to twelve weeks of *qualifying exigency leave* to handle specified *nonmedical* emergencies when a spouse, parent, or child is in, or called to, active military duty.[16] For instance, when a spouse is deployed to Afghanistan, an employee may take exigency leave to arrange for child care or to deal with financial or legal matters.

Benefits and Protections

When an employee takes FMLA leave, the employer must continue the worker's health-care coverage on the same terms as if the employee had continued to work. On returning from FMLA leave, most employees must be restored to their original position or to a comparable position (with nearly equivalent pay and benefits, for example). An important exception allows the employer to avoid reinstating a *key employee*—defined as an employee whose pay falls within the top 10 percent of the firm's workforce.

Employees suffering from addiction to drugs and alcohol pose a special problem under the FMLA. Under what circumstances do days off resulting from the addiction, as opposed to days off for medical treatment in a medical facility, count as part of protected leave? That issue was addressed in the following case.

13. Note that changes to the FMLA rules allow employees who have taken a break from their employment to qualify for FMLA leave if they worked a total of twelve months during the previous seven years. See 29 C.F.R. Section 825.110(b)(1-2).
14. The foster care must be state sanctioned before such an arrangement falls within the coverage of the FMLA.
15. 29 C.F.R. Section 825.200.
16. 29 C.F.R. Section 825.126.

Case 24.1 Darst v. Interstate Brands Corp.

United States Court of Appeals, Seventh Circuit, 512 F.3d 903 (2008).

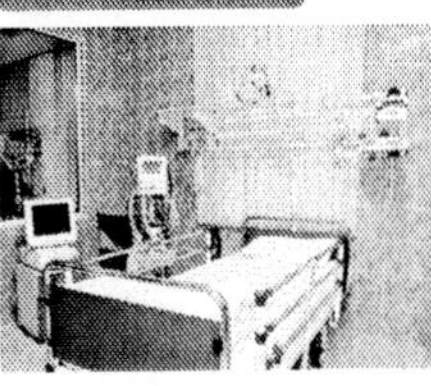

(©Orkhan Aslanov, 2009. Used under license from Shutterstock.com)

Can FMLA leave for hospitalization mitigate excessive absences that led to the termination of an employee?

FACTS Krzysztof Chalimoniuk worked for Interstate Brands Corporation (IBC) for fifteen years before he was fired for excessive absenteeism. Chalimoniuk, an alcoholic, sought treatment for his condition. He requested leave under the Family and Medical Leave Act (FMLA) from July 29 to August 14, 2000, to deal with the problem. From August 4 to 11, he was hospitalized for treatment of alcohol dependence and withdrawal. When he failed to return to work on August 15, he was fired for being absent. IBC noted that he was also absent from July 29 to August 3, when he was not hospitalized, and those days were counted as improper absences because he was already over the limit for the number of days he could miss under the company's leave policy. Chalimoniuk sued, contending that IBC had violated his FMLA rights. During the course of litigation, Chalimoniuk filed for bankruptcy, and his claim against IBC became part of the bankruptcy estate. Richard Darst, as trustee for the estate, continued to prosecute the claim. The district court granted summary judgment in favor of IBC. Darst appealed.

ISSUE Was Chalimoniuk entitled to FMLA leave from July 29 through August 3, before he was hospitalized for treatment of alcoholism?

DECISION No. The appeals court affirmed the lower court's ruling. IBC had not violated Chalimoniuk's rights under the FMLA by firing him for excessive absences. FMLA leave covered the days he was receiving medical treatment, but not the days he missed work before and after treatment.

REASON Chalimoniuk was entitled to FMLA leave to obtain treatment for alcoholism, but not because he was incapacitated by his condition and could not, or would not, come to work. Treatment for a serious

Case 24.1—Continues next page

Case 24.1—Continued

health condition qualifies for FMLA leave, but absence from work because of the employee's abuse of a substance does not. Furthermore, contrary to Chalimoniuk's assertion, IBC had the right to determine the dates during which Chalimoniuk was to receive treatment for alcoholism. The employer is allowed this right unless it interferes with or denies the worker's exercise of his or her rights under the FMLA.

FOR CRITICAL ANALYSIS—Ethical Consideration *Did IBC take unfair advantage of the "letter of the law" by not granting Chalimoniuk a little more leave time, given that he was dealing with his problem? Explain your answer.*

Violations of the FMLA

ON THE WEB An excellent Web site for information on employee benefits—including the full text of relevant statutes, such as the FMLA and COBRA, as well as case law and current articles—is BenefitsLink. Go to www.benefitslink.com/index.shtml.

An employer that violates the FMLA can be required to provide various remedies, including (1) damages to compensate an employee for lost benefits, denied compensation, and actual monetary losses (such as the cost of providing for care of the family member) up to an amount equivalent to the employee's wages for twelve weeks (twenty-six weeks for military caregiver leave); (2) job reinstatement; and (3) promotion, if a promotion has been denied. A successful plaintiff is entitled to court costs; attorneys' fees; and, in cases involving bad faith on the part of the employer, two times the amount of damages awarded by a judge or jury. Supervisors can also be held personally liable, as employers, for violations of the act.

Employers generally are required to notify employees when an absence will be counted against leave authorized under the act. If an employer fails to provide such notice, and the employee consequently suffers an injury because he or she did not receive notice, the employer may be sanctioned.[17]

Worker Health and Safety

Under the common law, employees who were injured on the job had to file lawsuits against their employers to obtain recovery. Today, numerous state and federal statutes protect employees and their families from the risk of accidental injury, death, or disease resulting from their employment. This section discusses the primary federal statute governing health and safety in the workplace, along with state workers' compensation laws.

The Occupational Safety and Health Act

At the federal level, the primary legislation protecting employees' health and safety is the Occupational Safety and Health Act of 1970,[18] which is administered by the Occupational Safety and Health Administration (OSHA). Congress passed this act in an attempt to ensure safe and healthful working conditions for practically every employee in the country. The act imposes on employers a general duty to keep workplaces safe. To this end, OSHA has established specific safety standards that employers must follow depending on the industry. For instance, OSHA regulations require the use of safety guards on certain mechanical equipment and set maximum exposure levels to substances in the workplace that may be harmful to a worker's health.

The act also imposes record-keeping and reporting requirements and requires that employers post certain notices in the workplace. OSHA compliance officers may enter and

17. *Ragsdale v. Wolverine World Wide, Inc.*, 535 U.S. 81, 122 S.Ct. 1155, 152 L.Ed.2d 167 (2002).
18. 29 U.S.C. Sections 553, 651–678.

inspect facilities of any establishment covered by the Occupational Safety and Health Act.[19] Employees may also file complaints of violations and cannot be fired by their employers for doing so. Employers with eleven or more employees are required to keep occupational injury and illness records for each employee. Each record must be made available for inspection when requested by an OSHA inspector.

ON THE WEB A good source for information relating to workplace health and safety is OSHA's Web site. Go to www.osha.gov.

Whenever a work-related injury or disease occurs, employers must make reports directly to OSHA. If an employee dies or five or more employees are hospitalized, the employer must notify the U.S. Department of Labor within forty-eight hours. A company that fails to do so will be fined. Following the accident, a complete inspection of the premises is mandatory. Criminal penalties for willful violation of the Occupational Safety and Health Act are limited. Employers may also be prosecuted under state laws, however. In other words, the act does not preempt state and local criminal laws.[20]

State Workers' Compensation Laws

Workers' Compensation Laws State statutes establishing an administrative procedure for compensating workers for injuries that arise out of—or in the course of—their employment, regardless of fault.

State **workers' compensation laws** establish an administrative procedure for compensating workers injured on the job. Instead of suing, an injured worker files a claim with the administrative agency or board that administers local workers' compensation claims.

Most workers' compensation statutes are similar. No state covers all employees. Typically, domestic workers, agricultural workers, temporary employees, and employees of common carriers (companies that provide transportation services to the public) are excluded, but minors are covered. Usually, the statutes allow employers to purchase insurance from a private insurer or a state fund to pay workers' compensation benefits in the event of a claim. Most states also allow employers to be self-insured—that is, employers that show an ability to pay claims do not need to buy insurance.

(AP Photo/Austin Daily Herald/Eric Johnson)

This former employee of Quality Pork Processors believed that she had contracted a neurological illness while working at the processing plant, and she filed a workers' compensation claim. Her claim was approved. What are the requirements for receiving workers' compensation benefits?

REQUIREMENTS FOR RECEIVING WORKERS' COMPENSATION In general, the only requirements to recover benefits under state workers' compensation laws are:

1. The existence of an employment relationship; and
2. An *accidental* injury that *occurred on the job or in the course of employment*, regardless of fault. (If an injury occurs while an employee is commuting to or from work, it usually will not be considered to have occurred on the job or in the course of employment and hence will not be covered.)

An injured employee must notify her or his employer promptly (usually within thirty days of the accident). Generally, an employee must also file a workers' compensation claim with the appropriate state agency or board within a certain period (sixty days to two years) from the time the injury is first noticed, rather than from the time of the accident.

WORKERS' COMPENSATION VERSUS LITIGATION An employee's acceptance of workers' compensation benefits bars the employee from suing for injuries caused by the employer's negligence. By barring lawsuits for negligence, workers' compensation laws also

19. Initially, warrantless inspections were conducted. In 1978, however, the United States Supreme Court held that warrantless inspections violated the warrant clause of the Fourth Amendment to the U.S. Constitution. See *Marshall v. Barlow's, Inc.*, 436 U.S. 307, 98 S.Ct. 1816, 56 L.Ed.2d 305 (1978).

20. *Pedraza v. Shell Oil Co.*, 942 F.2d 48 (1st Cir. 1991); *cert.* denied, *Shell Oil Co. v. Pedraza*, 502 U.S. 1082, 112 S.Ct. 993, 117 L.Ed.2d 154 (1992).

prevent employers from raising common law defenses to negligence, such as contributory negligence, assumption of risk, or injury caused by a "fellow servant" (another employee). A worker may sue an employer who *intentionally* injures the worker, however.

Income Security

Federal and state governments participate in insurance programs designed to protect employees and their families by covering the financial impact of retirement, disability, death, hospitalization, and unemployment. The key federal law on this subject is the Social Security Act of 1935.[21]

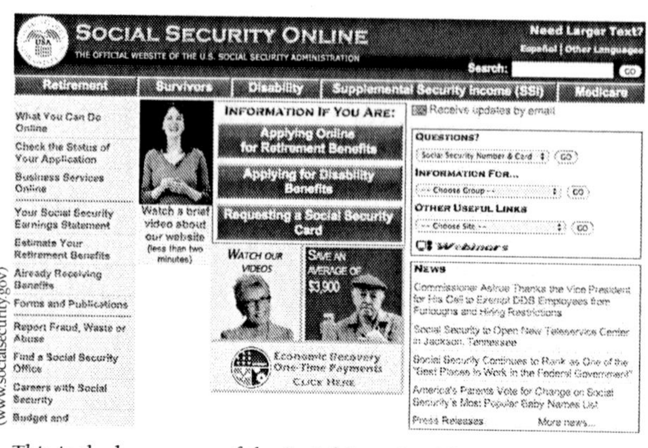

This is the home page of the Social Security Administration. Who might wish to consult this Web site?

NOTE **Social Security covers almost all jobs in the United States. Nine out of ten workers "contribute" to this protection for themselves and their families.**

Social Security

The Social Security Act provides for old-age (retirement), survivors', and disability insurance. The act is therefore often referred to as OASDI. Both employers and employees must "contribute" under the Federal Insurance Contributions Act (FICA)[22] to help pay for benefits that will partially make up for the employees' loss of income on retirement.

The basis for the employee's and the employer's contributions is the employee's annual wage base—the maximum amount of the employee's wages that are subject to the tax. The employer withholds the employee's FICA contribution from the employee's wages and then matches this contribution. (In 2009, employers were required to withhold 6.2 percent of each employee's wages, up to a maximum wage base of $106,800, and to match this contribution.)

Retired workers are then eligible to receive monthly payments from the Social Security Administration, which administers the Social Security Act. Social Security benefits are fixed by statute but increase automatically with increases in the cost of living.

Medicare

Medicare, a federal government health-insurance program, is administered by the Social Security Administration for people sixty-five years of age and older and for some under the age of sixty-five who are disabled. It originally had two parts, one pertaining to hospital costs and the other to nonhospital medical costs, such as visits to physicians' offices. Medicare now offers additional coverage options and a prescription-drug plan. People who have Medicare hospital insurance can also obtain additional federal medical insurance if they pay small monthly premiums, which increase as the cost of medical care increases.

As with Social Security contributions, both the employer and the employee "contribute" to Medicare, but unlike Social Security, there is no cap on the amount of wages subject to the Medicare tax. In 2009, both the employer and the employee were required to pay 1.45 percent of *all* wages and salaries to finance Medicare. Thus, for Social Security and Medicare together, in 2009 the employer and the employee each paid 7.65 percent of the first $106,800 of income (6.2 percent for Social Security + 1.45 percent for Medicare) for a combined total of 15.3 percent. In addition, all wages and salaries above $106,800 were taxed at a combined (employer and employee) rate of 2.9 percent for Medicare. Self-employed persons pay both the employer and the employee portions of the Social Security

21. 42 U.S.C. Sections 301–1397e.

22. 26 U.S.C. Sections 3101–3125.

and Medicare taxes (15.3 percent of income up to $106,800 and 2.9 percent of income above that amount in 2009).

Private Pension Plans

The major federal act regulating employee retirement plans is the Employee Retirement Income Security Act (ERISA) of 1974.[23] This act empowers a branch of the U.S. Department of Labor to enforce its provisions governing employers who have private pension funds for their employees. ERISA created the Pension Benefit Guaranty Corporation (PBGC), an independent federal agency, to provide timely and uninterrupted payment of voluntary private pension benefits. The pension plans pay annual insurance premiums (at set rates adjusted for inflation) to the PBGC, which then pays benefits to participants in the event that a plan is unable to do so. Under the Pension Protection Act of 2006,[24] the director of the PBGC is appointed by the president and confirmed by the U.S. Senate.

ERISA does not require an employer to establish a pension plan. When a plan exists, however, ERISA specifies standards for its management. A key provision of ERISA concerns vesting. **Vesting** gives an employee a legal right to receive pension benefits at some future date when he or she stops working. Before ERISA was enacted, some employees who had worked for companies for as long as thirty years received no pension benefits when their employment terminated, because those benefits had not vested. ERISA establishes complex vesting rules. Generally, however, all employee contributions to pension plans vest immediately, and employee rights to employer contributions to a plan vest after five years of employment.

Vesting The creation of an absolute or unconditional right or power.

In an attempt to prevent mismanagement of pension funds, ERISA has established rules on how they must be invested. Pension managers must be cautious in choosing investments and must diversify the plan's investments to minimize the risk of large losses. ERISA also imposes detailed record-keeping and reporting requirements.

Unemployment Insurance

Long lines of those searching for employment are often seen in front of so-called job fairs throughout the country. When they become unemployed, do the formerly employed workers receive payments from the federal government or the state government?

(AP Photo/Richard Drew)

To ease the financial impact of unemployment, the United States has a system of unemployment insurance. The Federal Unemployment Tax Act (FUTA) of 1935[25] created a state-administered system that provides unemployment compensation to eligible individuals. Under this system, employers pay into a fund, and the proceeds are paid out to qualified unemployed workers. The FUTA and state laws require employers that fall under the provisions of the act to pay unemployment taxes at regular intervals.

To be eligible for unemployment compensation, a worker must be willing and able to work. Workers who have been fired for misconduct or who have voluntarily left their jobs are not eligible for benefits. In the past, workers had to be actively seeking employment to continue receiving benefits. Due to the high unemployment rates in 2009, however, President Barack Obama announced new measures that allow jobless persons

23. 29 U.S.C. Sections 1001 *et seq.*
24. The Pension Protection Act amended 26 U.S.C. Sections 430–432, 436, 4966, 4967, 6039I, 6050U, 6050V, 6695A, 6720B, 7443B; and 29 U.S.C. Sections 1082–1085, 1202a.
25. 26 U.S.C. Sections 3301–3310.

WATCH OUT If an employer does not pay unemployment taxes, a state government can place a lien (claim) on the business's property to secure the debt. (Liens were discussed in Chapter 21.)

to retain their unemployment benefits while pursuing additional education and training (rather than seeking employment).

COBRA

For workers whose jobs have been terminated—and who are thus no longer eligible for group health-insurance plans—federal law also provides a right to continue their health-care coverage. The Consolidated Omnibus Budget Reconciliation Act (COBRA) of 1985[26] prohibits an employer from eliminating a worker's medical, optical, or dental insurance on the voluntary or involuntary termination of the worker's employment. Employers, with some exceptions, must inform an employee of COBRA's provisions when that worker faces termination or a reduction of hours that would affect his or her eligibility for coverage under the plan. Only workers fired for gross misconduct are excluded from protection.

PROCEDURES A worker has sixty days (beginning with the date that the group coverage would stop) to decide whether to continue with the employer's group insurance plan. If the worker chooses to discontinue the coverage, the employer has no further obligation. If the worker chooses to continue coverage, though, the employer is obligated to keep the policy active for up to eighteen months (or twenty-nine months if the worker is disabled). The coverage provided must be the same as that enjoyed by the worker prior to the termination or reduction of work. If family members were originally included, for instance, COBRA prohibits their exclusion.

PAYMENT The worker does not receive the insurance coverage for free, however. Generally, an employer can require the employee to pay all of the premiums, plus a 2 percent administrative charge. In 2009, however, the law was changed to provide for certain workers who involuntarily lost their jobs between September 2008 and December 2009.[27] For these employees, the employer can only require the worker to pay up to 35 percent of the premiums. The employer is reimbursed for the remaining 65 percent of the premiums through a tax credit.

If the worker fails to pay the required amount of the premiums (or if the employer completely eliminates its group benefit plan), the employer is relieved of further responsibility. An employer that does not comply with COBRA risks substantial penalties, such as a tax of up to 10 percent of the annual cost of the group plan or $500,000, whichever is less.

Employer-Sponsored Group Health Plans

The Health Insurance Portability and Accountability Act (HIPAA),[28] which was discussed in Chapter 2 in the context of privacy protections, contains provisions that affect employer-sponsored group health plans. HIPAA does not require employers to provide health insurance, but it does establish requirements for those that do provide such coverage. For instance, HIPAA strictly limits an employer's ability to exclude coverage for *preexisting conditions*, except pregnancy.

In addition, HIPAA restricts the manner in which covered employers collect, use, and disclose the health information of employees and their families. Employers must train employees, designate privacy officials, and distribute privacy notices to ensure that employees' health information is not disclosed to unauthorized parties. Failure to comply with HIPAA regulations can result in civil penalties of up to $100 per person per violation (with

26. 29 U.S.C. Sections 1161–1169.

27. These changes were made by the American Recovery and Reinvestment Act (ARRA) of 2009, Pub. L. No. 111-5, 123 Stat. 115 (February 17, 2009).

28. 29 U.S.C.A. Sections 1181 *et seq.*

a cap of $25,000 per year). The employer is also subject to criminal prosecution for certain types of HIPAA violations and can face up to $250,000 in criminal fines and imprisonment for up to ten years if convicted.

Employee Privacy Rights

In the last thirty years, concerns about the privacy rights of employees have arisen in response to the sometimes invasive tactics used by employers to monitor and screen workers. Perhaps the greatest privacy concern in today's employment arena has to do with electronic performance monitoring.

Electronic Monitoring in the Workplace

According to a survey by the American Management Association, more than half of employers engage in some form of surveillance of their employees. Types of monitoring include reviewing employees' e-mail, blogs, instant messages, Twitters, Internet use, and computer files; video recording of employee job performance; and recording and reviewing telephone conversations, voice mail, and text messages. (See the *Business Application* feature at the end of this chapter for a discussion of how employers should develop an Internet policy for the workplace.)

Employers are increasingly using sophisticated surveillance systems to monitor their employees' conduct in the workplace. What legitimate interests might employers have for using surveillance cameras?

("Redjar"/Creative Commons)

Various specially designed software products have made it easier for employers to track employees' Internet use, including the specific Web sites visited and the time spent surfing the Web. Indeed, inappropriate Web surfing seems to be a primary concern for employers. More than 75 percent of them are monitoring workers' Web connections. Filtering software, which was discussed in Chapter 2, is also being used to prevent employees from accessing certain Web sites, such as sites containing pornographic or sexually explicit images. Private employers generally are free to use filtering software to block access to certain Web sites because the First Amendment's protection of free speech prevents only *government employers* from restraining speech by blocking Web sites.

Employee Privacy Rights under Constitutional and Tort Law

Recall from Chapter 2 that the U.S. Constitution does not contain a provision that explicitly guarantees a right to privacy. A personal right to privacy, however, has been inferred from other constitutional guarantees provided by the First, Third, Fourth, Fifth, and Ninth Amendments to the Constitution. Tort law (see Chapter 4), state constitutions, and a number of state and federal statutes also provide for privacy rights.

When determining whether an employer should be held liable for violating an employee's privacy rights, the courts generally weigh the employer's interests against the employee's reasonable expectation of privacy. Normally, if employees have been informed that their communications are being monitored, they cannot reasonably expect those communications to be private. If employees are not informed that certain communications are being monitored, however, the employer may be held liable for invading their privacy. For this reason, most employers notify their employees about electronic monitoring.

ON THE WEB **The American Civil Liberties Union (ACLU) has a page on its Web site devoted to employee privacy rights with respect to electronic monitoring. Go to www.aclu.org/privacy/workplace/index.html.**

Nevertheless, establishing general policies or notifying employees about e-mail monitoring may not sufficiently protect an employer who monitors text messages or other forms of communications not specifically mentioned. (For an example of a situation in which a general e-mail policy did not protect the employer, see Case Example 24.6 on the next page.)

THE ELECTRONIC COMMUNICATIONS PRIVACY ACT Employers must comply with the Electronic Communications Privacy Act (ECPA) of 1986.[29] This act amended existing federal wiretapping law to cover electronic forms of communications, such as communications via cell phones or e-mail. The ECPA prohibits the intentional interception of any wire or electronic communication and the intentional disclosure or use of the information obtained by the interception. Excluded from coverage, however, are any electronic communications through devices that are "furnished to the subscriber or user by a provider of wire or electronic communication service" and that are being used by the subscriber or user, or by the provider of the service, "in the ordinary course of its business."

This "business-extension exception" to the ECPA permits employers to monitor employees' electronic communications made in the ordinary course of business. It does not, however, permit employers to monitor employees' personal communications. Under another exception to the ECPA, however, an employer may avoid liability under the act if the employees consent to having their electronic communications intercepted by the employer. Thus, an employer may be able to avoid liability under the ECPA by requiring employees to sign forms indicating that they consent to the monitoring of personal as well as business communications.

"We are rapidly entering the age of no privacy, where everyone is open to surveillance at all times; where there are no secrets."

William O. Douglas, 1898–1980
(Associate justice of the United States Supreme Court, 1939–1975)

STORED COMMUNICATIONS Part of the ECPA is known as the Stored Communications Act (SCA).[30] The SCA prohibits intentional and unauthorized access to *stored* electronic communications and sets forth criminal and civil sanctions for violators. A person can violate the SCA by intentionally accessing a stored electronic communication or by intentionally exceeding the authorization given to access the communication.

CASE EXAMPLE 24.6 Arch Wireless Operating Company contracted with the city of Ontario, California, to provide wireless text-messaging services via two-way alphanumeric pagers. The city distributed the pagers to its employees, including Police Sergeant Jeff Quon. The city had a general policy concerning the use of computers, Internet, and e-mail, which stated that these should not be used for personal matters and that any communications were not confidential. The policy did not expressly mention the pagers or text messaging, however.

Under the city's contract with Arch Wireless, each pager was allotted 25,000 characters, after which the city was required to pay overage charges. If an employee exceeded the character limit, the city asked the employee to pay the overage charges. Quon had exceeded the limit on several occasions and had paid overage charges for text messaging on his pager. Without Quon's knowledge, his supervisors requested transcripts of his stored text messages from Arch Wireless and read them to determine whether the texts were exclusively work related or personal. When Quon found out that the city had read his personal (and sexually explicit) text messages to his wife, he filed a lawsuit against the city and Arch Wireless for violating his privacy rights. Although the lower court found in the defendants' favor, Quon won on appeal. The federal appellate court ruled that Quon had a reasonable expectation of privacy with regard to text messages that were temporarily stored by Arch Wireless, a third party provider. Quon's text messages were protected from the employer, and Arch Wireless should not have accessed them and provided transcripts to the city without his authorization.[31] •

29. 18 U.S.C. Sections 2510–2521.
30. 18 U.S.C. Sections 2701–2711.
31. *Quon v. Arch Wireless Operating Co.*, 529 F.3d 892 (9th Cir. 2008); rehearing denied, 554 F.3d 769 (9th Cir. 2009).

Preventing Legal Disputes

To avoid legal disputes, exercise caution when monitoring employees and make sure that any monitoring is conducted in a reasonable place and manner. Establish written policies that include all types of electronic devices used by your employees, and notify employees of how and when they may be monitored on these devices. Consider informing employees of the reasons for the monitoring. Explain what the concern is, what job repercussions could result, and what recourse employees have in the event that a negative action is taken against them. By providing more privacy protection to employees than is legally required, you can both avoid potential privacy complaints and give employees a sense that they retain some degree of privacy in their workplace, which can lead to greater job satisfaction.

Other Types of Monitoring

In addition to monitoring their employees' online activities, employers also engage in other types of employee screening and monitoring. These practices, which have included lie-detector tests, drug tests, genetic testing, and employment screening, have often been subject to challenge as violations of employee privacy rights.

LIE-DETECTOR TESTS At one time, many employers required employees or job applicants to take lie-detector (polygraph) tests in connection with their employment. In 1988, Congress passed the Employee Polygraph Protection Act,[32] which generally prohibits employers from requiring or causing employees or job applicants to take lie-detector tests or suggesting or requesting that they do so. The act also restricts employers' ability to use or ask about the results of any lie-detector test or to take any negative employment action based on the results.

Employers excepted from these prohibitions include federal, state, and local government employers; certain security service firms; and companies manufacturing and distributing controlled substances. Other employers may use lie-detector tests when investigating losses attributable to theft, including embezzlement and the theft of trade secrets.

(U.S. Navy/Jim Watson)

Workers at a toxicology lab place employees' urine samples in barcoded test tubes before screening the samples for drugs. Many private employers today routinely require their employees to submit to drug testing. What recourse, if any, does an employee who does not consent to a drug test have against the employer?

DRUG TESTING In the interests of public safety, many employers, including the government, require their employees to submit to drug testing. Government (public) employers are constrained in drug testing by the Fourth Amendment to the U.S. Constitution, which prohibits unreasonable searches and seizures (see Chapter 6). Drug testing of public employees is allowed by statute for transportation workers and is normally upheld by the courts when drug use in a particular job may threaten public safety. Also, when there is a reasonable basis for suspecting government employees of using drugs, courts often find that drug testing does not violate the Fourth Amendment.

The Fourth Amendment does not apply to drug testing conducted by private employers. Hence, the privacy rights and drug testing of private-sector employees are governed by state law, which varies widely. Many states have statutes that allow drug testing by private employers but place restrictions on when and how the testing may be performed. A collective bargaining agreement may also provide protection against drug testing (or authorize drug testing under certain conditions). The permissibility of a private employer's drug tests typically hinges

32. 29 U.S.C. Sections 2001 *et seq.*

on the determination of whether the testing was reasonable. Random drug tests and even "zero-tolerance" policies (that deny a "second chance" to employees who test positive for drugs) have been held to be reasonable.[33]

GENETIC TESTING A serious privacy issue arose when some employers began conducting genetic testing of employees or prospective employees in an effort to identify individuals who might develop significant health problems in the future. To date, however, only a few cases involving this issue have come before the courts. **CASE EXAMPLE 24.7** Lawrence Berkeley Laboratory screened prospective employees for the gene that causes sickle-cell anemia, although the applicants were not informed of this. In a lawsuit subsequently brought by the prospective employees, a federal appellate court held that they had a cause of action for violation of their privacy rights.[34] The case was later settled for $2.2 million. ●

To prevent the improper use of genetic information in employment and health insurance, in 2008 Congress passed the Genetic Information Nondiscrimination Act (GINA).[35] Under GINA, employers cannot make decisions about hiring, firing, job placement, or promotion based on the results of genetic testing. GINA also prohibits group health plans and insurers from denying coverage or charging higher premiums based solely on a genetic predisposition to developing a specific disease in the future.

SCREENING PROCEDURES Preemployment screening procedures are another area of concern to potential employees. What kinds of questions are permissible on an employment application or a preemployment test? What kinds of questions go too far in invading the applicant's privacy? Is it an invasion of privacy, for example, to ask questions about the prospective employee's sexual orientation or religious convictions? Generally, questions on an employment application must have a reasonable nexus, or connection, with the job for which the person is applying.

KEEP IN MIND An employer may act on the basis of any professionally developed test, provided the test relates to the employment and does not violate the law.

Another issue that has arisen with employment screening involves health-risk-assessment and wellness programs. Many employers today, mindful of the rising cost of health care, are assessing their employees' overall health and instituting mandatory wellness programs at the workplace. Some of these programs require health exams and record employees' weight, blood sugar, blood pressure, cholesterol levels, and tobacco use. Other programs require employees to participate in health-risk assessments to get health-insurance coverage or charge them higher premiums if they refuse to take part in health-risk assessments. Some employers have banned tobacco use both on and off the job, and test their employees for nicotine.

Employers clearly have an economic interest in having their employees maintain healthful lifestyles and implementing mandatory wellness and health assessment programs. These efforts can be legally problematic, however, particularly if they penalize employees who fail to meet health goals. Employees can claim that these programs violate their privacy rights.[36] Although the courts have not yet decided many cases alleging privacy violations from health screening, litigation in this area is expected to increase. These programs may also violate the Americans with Disabilities Act (ADA, which will be discussed in Chapter 25) if employers discriminate against persons with, say, diabetes or obesity. In addition, a number of states have passed lifestyle discrimination laws that prohibit employers from taking adverse employment action against employees for lawful conduct outside of work.

---

33. See, for example, *CITGO Asphalt Refining Co. v. Paper, Allied-Industrial, Chemical, and Energy Workers International Union Local No. 2-991*, 385 F.3d 809 (3d Cir. 2004).
34. *Norman-Bloodsaw v. Lawrence Berkeley Laboratory*, 135 F.3d 1260 (9th Cir. 1998).
35. 26 U.S.C. Section 9834; 42 U.S.C. Sections 300gg-53, 1320d-9, 2000ff-1 to 2000ff-11.
36. See, for example, *Anderson v. City of Taylor*, 2006 WL 1984104 (E.D.Mich. 2006).

Immigration Law

"Immigration is the sincerest form of flattery."

Jack Paar, 1918–2004
(American entertainer)

The United States had no laws restricting immigration until the late nineteenth century. Today, the most important laws governing immigration and employment are the Immigration Reform and Control Act (IRCA) of 1986[37] and the Immigration Act of 1990.[38] The IRCA provided amnesty to certain groups of illegal aliens then living in the United States and also established a system that sanctions employers who hire illegal immigrants lacking work authorization. As immigration has grown in recent years, an understanding of the related legal requirements for business has become increasingly important. Employers must take steps to avoid hiring illegal immigrants or face serious penalties.

(AP Photo/Elaine Thompson)

There are an estimated 11 to 12 million illegal immigrants living and usually working in the United States today. Some of these Latino workers in Washington State, shown here, are in the United States legally, and others are not. What to do about illegal immigrants is a political hot potato. Some believe that all illegal immigrants should be given amnesty and a chance to become citizens. Others believe that they should all be arrested and returned to their countries of origin. What are the roadblocks against the latter solution?

Immigration Reform and Control Act (IRCA)

An estimated 11 to 12 million illegal immigrants live in the United States today and are the subject of considerable controversy. The IRCA makes it illegal to hire, recruit, or refer for a fee someone not authorized to work in this country. The federal government—through Immigration and Customs Enforcement officers—conducts random compliance audits and engages in enforcement actions against employers who hire illegal immigrants. This section sets out the compliance requirements for employers.

I-9 Verification A process that all employers in the United States must perform within three business days of hiring a new worker to verify the employment eligibility and identity of the worker by completing an I-9 Employment Eligibility Verification form.

I-9 EMPLOYMENT VERIFICATION To comply with current law (based on the 1986 act), an employer must perform **I-9 verifications** for new hires, including those hired as "contractors" or "day workers" if they work under the employer's direct supervision. Form I-9, Employment Eligibility Verification, which is available from U.S. Citizenship and Immigration Services,[39] must be completed within three days of a worker's commencement of employment. The three-day period is to allow the employer to check the form's accuracy and to review and verify documents establishing the prospective worker's identity and eligibility for employment in the United States.

The employer must attest, under penalty of perjury, that an employee produced documents establishing his or her identity and legal employability. Acceptable documents include a U.S. passport establishing the person's citizenship or a document authorizing a foreign citizen to work in the United States, such as a Permanent Resident Card or an Alien Registration Receipt (discussed on page 625).

Note that most legal actions alleging violations of I-9 rules are brought against employees. An employee must state that she or he is a U.S. citizen or otherwise authorized to work in the United States. If the employee enters false information on an I-9 form or presents false documentation, the employer can fire the worker, who then may be subject to deportation.

37. 29 U.S.C. Section 1802.
38. This act amended various provisions of the Immigration and Nationality Act of 1952, 8 U.S.C. Sections 1101 *et seq*.
39. U.S. Citizenship and Immigration Services is a federal agency that is part of the U.S. Department of Homeland Security.

The IRCA prohibits "knowing" violations, including situations in which an employer "should have known" that the worker was unauthorized. Good faith is a defense under the statute, and employers are legally entitled to rely on a document authorizing a person to work that reasonably appears on its face to be genuine, even if it is later established to be counterfeit.

ENFORCEMENT U.S. Immigration and Customs Enforcement (ICE) was established in 2003 as the largest investigative arm of the U.S. Department of Homeland Security. ICE has a general inspection program that conducts random compliance audits. Other audits may occur if the agency receives a written complaint alleging an employer's violations. Government inspections include a review of an employer's file of I-9 forms. The government does not need a subpoena or a warrant to conduct such an inspection.

If an investigation reveals a possible violation, ICE will bring an administrative action and issue a Notice of Intent to Fine, which sets out the charges against the employer. The employer has a right to a hearing on the enforcement action if it files a request within thirty days. This hearing is conducted before an *administrative law judge* (see Chapter 1), and the employer has a right to counsel and to *discovery* (see Chapter 3). The typical defense in such actions is good faith or substantial compliance with the documentation provisions. As Exhibit 24–1 indicates, the federal government increased its enforcement efforts significantly during the Bush administration. In fiscal year 2008, ICE made more than 5,100 administrative arrests and 1,100 criminal arrests. In 2009, however, the Obama administration announced that its focus would shift from conducting enforcement actions to reforming immigration laws.

PENALTIES An employer who violates the law by hiring an unauthorized alien is subject to substantial penalties. The employer may be fined up to $2,200 for each unauthorized employee for a first offense, $5,000 per employee for a second offense, and up to $11,000 for subsequent offenses. Criminal penalties, including additional fines and imprisonment for up to ten years, apply to employers who have engaged in a "pattern or practice of violations." A company may also be barred from future government contracts for violations. In determining the penalty, ICE considers the seriousness of the violation (such as intentional falsification of documents) and the employer's past compliance. ICE regulations also

Exhibit 24–1 Worksite Enforcement Arrests by U.S. Immigration and Customs Enforcement

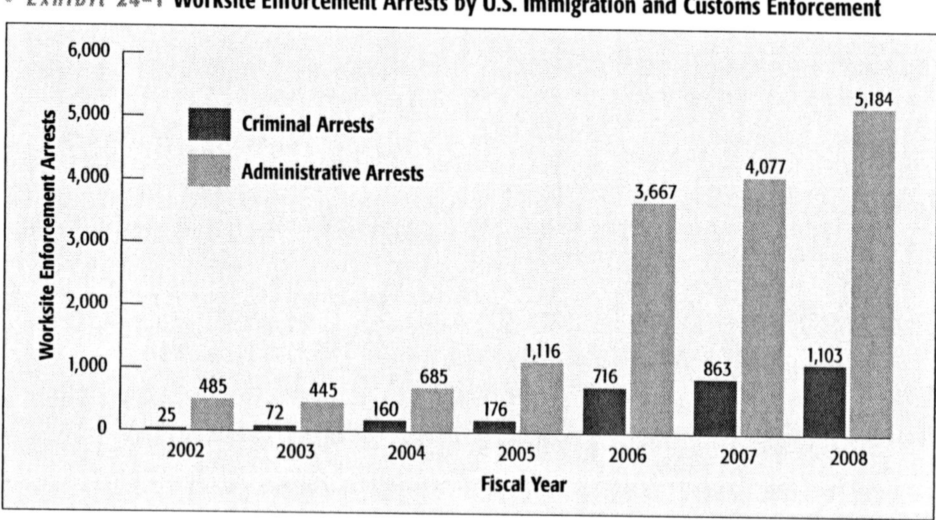

provide for mitigation or aggravation of the penalty under certain circumstances, such as whether the employer cooperated in the investigation or is a small business.

The Immigration Act

Often, U.S. businesses find that they cannot hire sufficient domestic workers with specialized skills. For this reason, U.S. immigration laws have long made provisions for businesses to hire especially qualified foreign workers. The Immigration Act of 1990 placed caps on the number of visas (entry permits) that can be issued to immigrants each year.

Most temporary visas are set aside for workers who can be characterized as "persons of extraordinary ability," members of the professions holding advanced degrees, or other skilled workers and professionals. To hire these individuals, employers must submit a petition to Citizenship and Immigration Services, which determines whether the job candidate meets the legal standards. Each visa is for a specific job, and there are legal limits on the employee's ability to switch jobs once in the United States.

I-551 Alien Registration Receipt A document, commonly known as a "green card," that shows that a foreign-born individual has been lawfully admitted for permanent residency in the United States. Persons seeking employment can prove to prospective employers that they are legally within the United States by showing this receipt.

I-551 Alien Registration Receipts A company seeking to hire a noncitizen worker may do so if the worker is self-authorized. This means that the worker either is a lawful permanent resident or has a valid temporary Employment Authorization Document. A lawful permanent resident can prove his or her status to an employer by presenting an **I-551 Alien Registration Receipt,** known as a "green card," or a properly stamped foreign passport. Many immigrant workers are not already self-authorized, and employers may obtain labor certification, or green cards, for those immigrants whom they wish to hire. Approximately fifty thousand new green cards are issued each year. A green card can be obtained only for a person who is being hired for a permanent, full-time position. (A separate authorization system provides for the temporary entry and hiring of nonimmigrant visa workers.)

To gain authorization for hiring a foreign worker, the employer must show that no U.S. worker is qualified, willing, and able to take the job. The employer must advertise the job opening in suitable newspapers or professional journals within six months of the hiring action. The government has detailed regulations governing this advertising requirement as well as the certification process.[40] Any U.S. applicants who meet the stated job qualifications must be interviewed for the position. The employer must also be able to show that the qualifications required for the job are a business necessity. A panel of administrative law judges rejected one company's notice for hiring kitchen supervisors because the company required that the applicants speak Spanish.[41]

The H-1B Visa Program The most common and controversial visa program today is the H-1B visa system. Individuals with H-1B visas can stay in the United States for three to six years and can work only for the sponsoring employer. The recipients of these visas include many high-tech workers, such as computer programmers and electronics specialists. Sixty-five thousand H-1B visas are set aside each year for new immigrants. In recent years, the total allotment of H-1B visas has been filled within the first few weeks of the year, leaving no slots available for the remaining eleven months. Consequently, many businesses, such as Microsoft, have lobbied Congress to expand the number of H-1B visas available to immigrants.

To obtain an H-1B visa, the potential employee must be qualified in a "specialty occupation," which is defined as involving highly specialized knowledge and the attainment of a bachelor's or higher degree or its equivalent. In one 2006 ruling, ICE found that the

40. The most relevant regulations can be found at 20 C.F.R. Section 655 (for temporary employment) and 20 C.F.R. Section 656 (for permanent employment).

41. *In the Matter of Malnati Organization, Inc.*, 2007-INA-00035 (Bd. Alien Lab. Cert. App. 2007).

position of "accountant" did not qualify as a specialty occupation because the American Council for Accountancy and Taxation did not require a degree for an individual to have this credential.

Labor Certification Before an employer can submit an H-1B application, it must file a Labor Certification application on a form known as ETA 9035. The employer must agree to provide a wage level at least equal to the wages offered to other individuals with similar experience and qualifications and attest that the hiring will not adversely affect other workers similarly employed. The employer must inform U.S. workers of the intent to hire a foreign worker by posting the form. The U.S. Department of Labor reviews the applications and may reject them for omissions or inaccuracies. **EXAMPLE 24.8** In 2002, a former employee of Sun Microsystems complained to the U.S. Justice Department that the company was discriminating against U.S. workers in favor of H-1B visa holders. Sun had laid off nearly four thousand domestic workers while applying for thousands of temporary visa employees. A court ultimately found that Sun had violated minor technical requirements and ordered it only to change its posting practices for applicants for open positions. ●

H-2, O, L, and E Visas Other specialty temporary visas are available for other categories of employees. H-2 visas provide for workers performing agricultural labor of a seasonal nature. O visas provide entry for persons who have "extraordinary ability in the sciences, arts, education, business or athletics which has been demonstrated by sustained national or international acclaim." L visas allow a company's foreign managers or executives to work inside the United States. E visas permit the entry of certain foreign investors or entrepreneurs.

H-2B visas are available for temporary foreign guest workers in housekeeping, maintenance, and hotel-clerk positions. Are guest workers or their employers liable for the workers' recruitment, transportation, and visa expenses? That was the question in the following case.

Case 24.2 Castellanos-Contreras v. Decatur Hotels, LLC

United States Court of Appeals, Fifth Circuit, 559 F.3d 332 (2009).
www.ca5.uscourts.gov[a]

HISTORICAL AND ENVIRONMENTAL SETTING *According to the National Hurricane Center, Hurricane Katrina, which struck in August 2005, was "one of the most devastating natural disasters" in history. With maximum winds extending across a thirty-mile radius and spawning forty-three tornadoes, the storm swept across Florida and the Gulf Coast states, causing $81 billion in damage and more than 1,800 deaths, including 1,577 in Louisiana. A storm surge of up to twenty-eight feet in a twenty-mile-wide swath flooded parts of Mississippi and Alabama, and burst through levees surrounding the city of New Orleans. More than one million people were evacuated from the afflicted area.*

FACTS Decatur Hotels, LLC, operates luxury hotels in New Orleans. After Hurricane Katrina, Decatur lost 85 percent of its staff. Unable to recruit local residents, Decatur accepted the offer of Accent Personnel Services, Inc., to guide the hotelier through the H-2B visa process to hire temporary foreign workers. Accent sold the information about Decatur's positions—for $900 per job—to recruitment companies representing foreign workers. Each worker paid a recruitment company $1,700 to $2,000 to guide him or her through the H-2B visa process and arrange transportation to the United States. The workers also paid the related fees and expenses for an added $1,000 to $3,000. Decatur paid its guest workers between $6.02 and $7.79 per hour but did not reimburse their recruitment, transportation, or visa expenses. Daniel Castellanos-Contreras and other workers filed a suit in a federal district court against Decatur to recover these costs. The court denied the hotelier's motion for summary judgment. Decatur appealed.

(Jerry/Creative Commons)

In the aftermath of Hurricane Katrina, a company that operates several luxury hotels in New Orleans needed to hire temporary foreign workers. Who should pay for their recruitment and travel expenses?

ISSUE Are guest workers liable for their own recruitment, transportation, and visa expenses if these are incurred without their employer's knowledge?

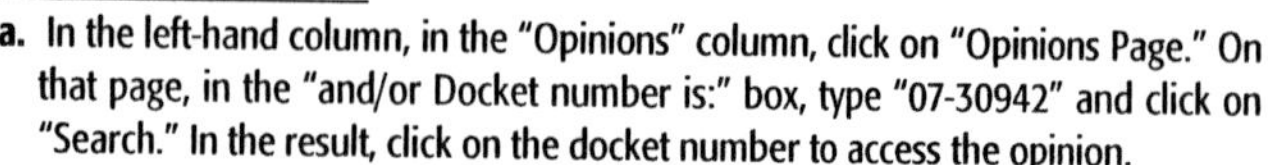

a. In the left-hand column, in the "Opinions" column, click on "Opinions Page." On that page, in the "and/or Docket number is:" box, type "07-30942" and click on "Search." In the result, click on the docket number to access the opinion.

Case 24.2–Continued

DECISION Yes. The U.S. Court of Appeals for the Fifth Circuit held that these fees did not constitute business expenses of the employer, who was therefore not required to reimburse the workers. The court reversed the lower court's ruling and remanded the case to be dismissed.

REASON Decatur did not know about the foreign recruitment companies or that the companies charged each worker a fee to receive an offer of employment. For these fees—which were most likely incurred before the workers knew about Decatur—applicants received the recruitment companies' guidance in applying for H-2B visas and arranging transportation. The workers may not have known of any other way to obtain jobs with Decatur other than to apply through the recruitment companies, and in fact there may not have been any other way. But Decatur did not require or approve the payment by a guest worker of any fee to anyone as a condition of an H-2B job offer or employment. "Furthermore, the expenses were not business expenses of Decatur's by custom or practice of Decatur's industry."

FOR CRITICAL ANALYSIS—Global Consideration *Could the guest workers have circumvented the fees by applying directly to Decatur or Accent for the positions? Discuss.*

Labor Unions

In the 1930s, in addition to wage-hour laws, the government also enacted the first of several labor laws. These laws protect employees' rights to join labor unions, to bargain with management over the terms and conditions of employment, and to conduct strikes.

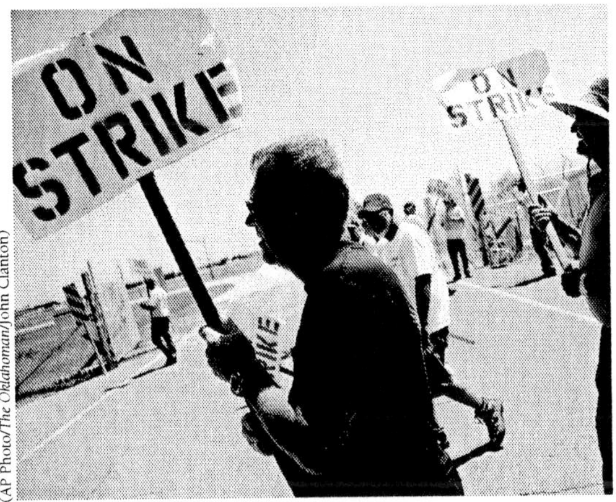

(AP Photo/The Oklahoman/John Clanton)

These aircraft mechanics are on strike in Enid, Oklahoma. They walked off the job after negotiators could not reach an agreement on a new contract. Under what circumstances does it make sense for union employees to go on strike? What are the costs of going on strike?

Federal Labor Laws

Federal labor laws governing union-employer relations have developed considerably since the first law was enacted in 1932. Initially, the laws were concerned with protecting the rights and interests of workers. Subsequent legislation placed some restraints on unions and granted rights to employers. We look here at four major federal statutes regulating union-employer relations.

NORRIS-LAGUARDIA ACT In 1932, Congress protected peaceful strikes, picketing, and boycotts in the Norris-LaGuardia Act.[42] The statute restricted the power of federal courts to issue injunctions against unions engaged in peaceful strikes. In effect, this act established a national policy permitting employees to organize.

NATIONAL LABOR RELATIONS ACT One of the foremost statutes regulating labor is the National Labor Relations Act (NLRA) of 1935.[43] This act established the rights of employees to engage in collective bargaining and to strike. The act also specifically defined a number of employer practices as unfair to labor:

1. Interference with the efforts of employees to form, join, or assist labor organizations or with the efforts of employees to engage in concerted activities for their mutual aid or protection.
2. An employer's domination of a labor organization or contribution of financial or other support to it.
3. Discrimination in the hiring or awarding of tenure to employees based on union affiliation.

---

42. 29 U.S.C. Sections 101–110, 113–115.
43. 20 U.S.C. Section 151.

4. Discrimination against employees for filing charges under the act or giving testimony under the act.
5. Refusal to bargain collectively with the duly designated representative of the employees.

The National Labor Relations Board (NLRB). The NLRA also created the National Labor Relations Board to oversee union elections and to prevent employers from engaging in unfair and illegal union activities and unfair labor practices. The NLRB has the authority to investigate employees' charges of unfair labor practices and to file complaints against employers in response to these charges. When violations are found, the NLRB may also issue a cease-and-desist order compelling the employer to stop engaging in the unfair practices. Cease-and-desist orders can be enforced by a federal appellate court if necessary. After the NLRB rules on claims of unfair labor practices, its decision may be appealed to a federal court.

Under the NLRA, employers and unions have a duty to bargain in good faith. Bargaining over certain subjects is mandatory, and a party's refusal to bargain over these subjects is an unfair labor practice that can be reported to the NLRB. In one case, for example, an employer was required to bargain with the union over the use of hidden video surveillance cameras.[44]

Workers Protected by the NLRA. To be protected under the NLRA, an individual must be an *employee,* as that term is defined in the statute. Courts have long held that job applicants fall within the definition (otherwise, the NLRA's ban on discrimination in hiring would mean nothing). Additionally, the United States Supreme Court has held that individuals who are hired by a union to organize a company are to be considered employees of the company for NLRA purposes.[45]

Closed Shop A firm that requires union membership by its workers as a condition of employment. The closed shop was made illegal by the Labor-Management Relations Act of 1947.

Union Shop A firm that requires all workers, once employed, to become union members within a specified period of time as a condition of their continued employment.

Right-to-Work Law A state law providing that employees may not be required to join a union as a condition of retaining employment.

LABOR-MANAGEMENT RELATIONS ACT The Labor-Management Relations Act (LMRA) of 1947[46] was passed to proscribe certain unfair union practices, such as the *closed shop.* A **closed shop** requires union membership by its workers as a condition of employment. Although the act made the closed shop illegal, it preserved the legality of the union shop. A **union shop** does not require membership as a prerequisite for employment but can, and usually does, require that workers join the union after a specified amount of time on the job.

The LMRA also prohibited unions from refusing to bargain with employers, engaging in certain types of picketing, and *featherbedding*—causing employers to hire more employees than necessary. The act also allowed individual states to pass their own **right-to-work laws,** which make it illegal for union membership to be required for *continued* employment in any establishment. Thus, union shops are technically illegal in the twenty-three states that have right-to-work laws.

LABOR-MANAGEMENT REPORTING AND DISCLOSURE ACT In 1959, Congress enacted the Labor-Management Reporting and Disclosure Act (LMRDA).[47] The act established an employee bill of rights and reporting requirements for union activities. The act strictly regulates unions' internal business procedures, including union elections. For example, the LMRDA requires a union to hold regularly scheduled elections of officers using secret ballots. Ex-convicts are prohibited from holding union office. Moreover, union officials are

44. *National Steel Corp. v. NLRB,* 324 F.3d 928 (7th Cir. 2003).
45. *NLRB v. Town & Country Electric, Inc.,* 516 U.S. 85, 116 S.Ct. 450, 133 L.Ed.2d 371 (1995).
46. 29 U.S.C. Sections 141 *et seq.*
47. 29 U.S.C. Sections 401 *et seq.*

accountable for union property and funds. Members have the right to attend and to participate in union meetings, to nominate officers, and to vote in most union proceedings.

The act also outlawed **hot-cargo agreements,** in which employers voluntarily agree with unions not to handle, use, or deal in goods produced by nonunion employees working for other employers. The act made all such boycotts (called **secondary boycotts**) illegal.

Hot-Cargo Agreement An agreement in which employers voluntarily agree with unions not to handle, use, or deal in other employers' goods that were not produced by union employees; a type of secondary boycott explicitly prohibited by the Labor-Management Reporting and Disclosure Act of 1959.

Secondary Boycott A union's refusal to work for, purchase from, or handle the products of a secondary employer, with whom the union has no dispute, in order to force that employer to stop doing business with the primary employer, with whom the union has a labor dispute.

Authorization Card A card signed by an employee that gives a union permission to act on his or her behalf in negotiations with management.

Union Organization

Typically, the first step in organizing a union at a particular firm is to have the workers sign authorization cards. An **authorization card** usually states that the worker desires to have a certain union, such as the United Auto Workers, represent the workforce. If a majority of the workers sign authorization cards, the union organizers (unionizers) present the cards to the employer and ask for formal recognition of the union. The employer is not required to recognize the union at this point in the process, but it may do so voluntarily on a showing of majority support. (Under legislation that was proposed in 2007 and reintroduced in the U.S. Congress in 2009, the employer would be required to recognize the union as soon as a majority of the workers had signed authorization cards—without holding an election, as described next.)[48]

Union Elections

If the employer refuses to voluntarily recognize the union after a majority of the workers sign authorization cards—or if fewer than 50 percent of the workers sign authorization cards—the union organizers present the cards to the NLRB with a petition for an election. For an election to be held, the unionizers must demonstrate that at least 30 percent of the workers to be represented support a union or an election on unionization. The proposed union must also represent an *appropriate bargaining unit.* Not every group of workers can form a single union. One key requirement of an appropriate bargaining unit is a *mutuality of interest* among all the workers to be represented by the union. Factors considered in determining whether there is a mutuality of interest include the *similarity of the jobs* of all the workers to be unionized and their physical location.

If all of these requirements are met, an election is held. The NLRB supervises the election and ensures secret voting and voter eligibility. If the proposed union receives majority support in a fair election, the NLRB certifies the union as the bargaining representative for the employees.

Union Election Campaigns

Many disputes between labor and management arise during union election campaigns. Generally, the employer has control over unionizing activities that take place on company property during working hours. Employers may thus limit the campaign activities of union supporters as long as the employer has a legitimate business reason for doing so. The employer may also reasonably limit the times and places that union solicitation occurs so long as the employer is not discriminating against the union.

EXAMPLE 24.9 A union is seeking to organize clerks at a department store owned by Amanti Enterprises. Amanti can prohibit all union solicitation in areas of the store open to the public because that activity could seriously interfere with the store's business. If Amanti allows solicitation for charitable causes in the workplace, however, it may not prohibit union solicitation. ●

An employer may campaign among its workers against the union, but the NLRB carefully monitors and regulates the tactics used by management. Otherwise, management might use its economic power to coerce the workers into voting against unionization. If the employer issued threats ("If the union wins, you'll all be fired") or engaged in other unfair

48. If the proposed Employee Free Choice Act becomes law, some of the information stated here may change.

labor practices, the NLRB may certify the union even though it lost the election. Alternatively, the NLRB may ask a court to order a new election.

In the following case, the question was whether managers' brief interruptions of unionizing activities constituted illegal surveillance in violation of the National Labor Relations Act.

Case 24.3 Local Joint Executive Board of Las Vegas v. National Labor Relations Board

United States Court of Appeals, Ninth Circuit, 515 F.3d 942 (2008).

(Smneale/Creative Commons)

Were managers at the Aladdin casino engaged in "illegal surveillance" of union-organizing activities?

FACTS Aladdin Gaming, LLC, operates a hotel and casino in Las Vegas, Nevada. On May 30, 2003, Local Joint Executive Board of Las Vegas and two other unions (the Unions) began an open campaign to organize Aladdin's housekeeping, food, and beverage departments. On two occasions during this campaign, human resources managers at Aladdin (Tracy Sapien and Stacey Briand) approached union organizers who were discussing unionization with employees in an employee dining room during a lunch break. Sapien and Briand interrupted the organizers while they were obtaining signatures on authorization cards and asked whether the employees were fully informed of the facts before signing. The Unions filed a complaint with the National Labor Relations Board (NLRB) claiming that the managers' actions were illegal surveillance in violation of the National Labor Relations Act (NLRA). The NLRB ruled in favor of Aladdin, and the Unions appealed.

ISSUE Did the managers' conduct violate the NLRA?

DECISION No. The federal appellate court denied the Unions' petition for review, concluding that the managers' brief interruptions of organizing activity did not constitute illegal surveillance.

REASON The NLRA states that an observation of union activity becomes unlawful when that surveillance "goes beyond casual and becomes unduly intrusive." The court found no evidence that Sapien and Briand used threats or other blatant, coercive means to strip union organizers of their rights under the act. The court noted that in both instances Sapien and Briand only attempted to give workers additional information to consider before signing the union cards. Once they were finished speaking to the employees, they left the area.

WHAT IF THE FACTS WERE DIFFERENT? *If management employees had interrupted union-organizing activities twenty-five times rather than just twice, would the outcome of this case have been different? Why or why not?*

Collective Bargaining

Collective Bargaining The process by which labor and management negotiate the terms and conditions of employment, including working hours and workplace conditions.

If the NLRB certifies the union, the union becomes the *exclusive bargaining representative* of the workers. The central legal right of a union is to engage in collective bargaining on the members' behalf. **Collective bargaining** is the process by which labor and management negotiate the terms and conditions of employment, including wages, benefits, working conditions, and other matters. Collective bargaining allows union representatives elected by union members to speak on behalf of the members at the bargaining table.

When a union is officially recognized, it may demand to bargain with the employer and negotiate new terms or conditions of employment. In collective bargaining, as in most other business negotiations, each side uses its economic power to pressure or persuade the other side to grant concessions.

Bargaining does not mean that one side must give in to the other or that compromises must be made. It does mean that a demand to bargain with the employer must be taken seriously and that both sides must bargain in "good faith." Good faith bargaining means that management, for instance, must be willing to meet with union representatives and consider the union's wishes when negotiating a contract. Examples of bad faith bargaining on the part of management include engaging in a campaign to undermine the union among workers, constantly shifting positions on disputed contract terms, and sending bargainers who lack authority to commit the company to a contract. If an employer (or a union) refuses to bargain in good faith without justification, it has committed an unfair labor practice, and the other party may petition the NLRB for an order requiring good faith bargaining.

Strikes

Even when labor and management have bargained in good faith, they may be unable to reach a final agreement. When extensive collective bargaining has been conducted and an impasse results, the union may call a strike against the employer to pressure it into making concessions. In a **strike,** the unionized workers leave their jobs and refuse to work. The workers also typically picket the workplace, standing outside the facility with signs stating their complaints.

Strike An action undertaken by unionized workers when collective bargaining fails; the workers leave their jobs, refuse to work, and (typically) picket the employer's workplace.

A strike is an extreme action. Striking workers lose their rights to be paid, and management loses production and may lose customers when orders cannot be filled. Labor law regulates the circumstances and conduct of strikes. Most strikes take the form of "economic strikes," which are initiated because the union wants a better contract. **EXAMPLE 24.10** In 2007, the United Auto Workers engaged in an economic strike when General Motors (GM) proposed that its workers accept wage cuts and pay much higher monthly premiums for health care. Approximately 73,000 GM employees walked off the job, shutting down several plants in the United States and Canada. Although the strike was settled quickly, it nevertheless resulted in lost production and profits for the company, its suppliers, and its contractors, as well as lost wages for the strikers. •

"Show me the country in which there are no strikes, and I'll show you the country in which there is no liberty."

Samuel Gompers 1850–1924
(American labor leader)

The Right to Strike The right to strike is guaranteed by the NLRA, within limits, and strike activities, such as picketing, are protected by the free speech guarantee of the First Amendment to the U.S. Constitution. Nonworkers have a right to participate in picketing an employer. The NLRA also gives workers the right to refuse to cross a picket line of fellow workers who are engaged in a lawful strike. Employers are permitted to hire replacement workers to substitute for the workers who are on strike.

The Rights of Strikers after a Strike Ends An important issue concerns the rights of strikers after the strike ends. In a typical economic strike over working conditions, the employer has a right to hire permanent replacements during the strike and need not terminate the replacement workers when the economic strikers seek to return to work. In other words, striking workers are not guaranteed the right to return to their jobs after the strike if satisfactory replacement workers have been found.

If the employer has not hired replacement workers to fill the strikers' positions, however, then the employer must rehire the economic strikers to fill any vacancies. Employers may not discriminate against former economic strikers, and those who are rehired retain their seniority rights. Different rules apply when a union strikes because the employer has engaged in unfair labor practices. In this situation, the employer may still hire replacements but must give the strikers back their jobs once the strike is over.

Reviewing . . . Employment, Immigration, and Labor Law

Rick Saldona began working as a traveling salesperson for Aimer Winery in 1987. Sales constituted 90 percent of Saldona's work time. Saldona worked an average of fifty hours per week but received no overtime pay. In June 2010, Saldona's new supervisor, Caesar Braxton, claimed that Saldona had been inflating his reported sales calls and required Saldona to submit to a polygraph test. Saldona reported Braxton to the U.S. Department of Labor, which prohibited Aimer from requiring Saldona to take a polygraph test for this purpose. In August 2010, Saldona's wife, Venita, fell from a ladder and sustained a head injury while employed as a full-time agricultural harvester. Saldona delivered to Aimer's human resources department a letter from his wife's physician indicating that she would need daily care for several months, and Saldona took leave until December 2010. Aimer had sixty-three employees at that time. When Saldona returned to Aimer, he was informed that his position had been eliminated because his sales territory had been combined with an adjacent territory. Using the information presented in the chapter, answer the following questions.

1. Would Saldona have been legally entitled to receive overtime pay at a higher rate? Why or why not?
2. What is the maximum length of time Saldona would have been allowed to take leave to care for his injured spouse?
3. Under what circumstances would Aimer have been allowed to require an employee to take a lie-detector test?
4. Would Aimer likely be able to avoid reinstating Saldona under the *key employee* exception? Why or why not?

Business Application

How to Develop an Employee Internet Policy*

Most businesses provide their employees with access to computer systems and other electronic devices. Employers that make electronic communications systems (such as access to the Internet and e-mail) available to their employees face some obvious risks, though. An employee could use e-mail to harass other employees or subject the employer to liability by reproducing, without authorization, copyright-protected materials found on the Internet. Another risk is that an outside party might intercept confidential information contained in e-mail messages transmitted via the Internet. Finally, by monitoring employees' Internet use and e-mail in an attempt to avoid these problems, the employer may risk being held liable for violating the employees' privacy rights. If you are an employer and find it prudent to monitor employees' Internet use, you should take certain precautions.

Remember that a small company can be bankrupted by just one successful lawsuit against it. Even if your company wins the suit, the legal fees incurred to defend against the claim could be devastating for your profits.

Inform Your Employees of the Monitoring and Obtain Their Consent

First, you should notify your employees that you will be monitoring their Internet communications, including their e-mail. Second, you should ask your employees to consent, in writing, to such actions. Generally, as discussed earlier in this chapter, if employees consent to employer monitoring, they cannot claim that the employer has invaded their privacy rights. You will find it easier to obtain employees' consent to monitoring if you explain why it is necessary or desirable and let them know what methods will be used to monitor Internet communications. As a rule, when employees are told the reasons for monitoring and clearly understand their rights and duties with respect to the company's communications system, they are less offended by the surveillance.

Spell Out Permissible and Impermissible Internet Uses

Employees should be told which uses of the firm's communications system are permissible and which uses are prohibited. To make sure that employees understand your policy, develop a comprehensive statement setting forth your standards for Internet use and provide specific examples of impermissible activities. It is also important to let employees know what will happen if they violate the policy. The policy might state, for example, that any employee who violates the policy will be subject to disciplinary actions, including termination.

CHECKLIST FOR THE EMPLOYER

1. **Inform employees that their Internet communications will be monitored, explain why monitoring is necessary or desirable, and indicate how it will be conducted.**
2. **Obtain employees' written consent to having their electronic communications monitored.**
3. **Develop a comprehensive policy statement that explains how Internet communications should and should not be used and indicates the consequences of misusing the firm's communications system.**

* This *Business Application* is not meant to substitute for the services of an attorney who is licensed to practice law in your state.

Key Terms

authorization card 629
closed shop 628
collective bargaining 630
employment at will 606
hot-cargo agreement 629
I-9 verification 623
I-551 Alien Registration Receipt 625
minimum wage 610
right-to-work law 628
secondary boycott 629
strike 631
union shop 628
vesting 617
whistleblowing 608
workers' compensation laws 615
wrongful discharge 608

Chapter Summary: Employment, Immigration, and Labor Law

Employment at Will (See pages 606–608.)	1. *Employment-at-will doctrine*—Under this common law doctrine, either party may terminate the employment relationship at any time and for any reason ("at will"). This doctrine is still in widespread use throughout the United States, although federal and state statutes prevent it from being applied in certain circumstances. 2. *Exceptions to the employment-at-will doctrine*—To protect employees from some of the harsh results of the employment-at-will doctrine, courts have made exceptions to the doctrine on the basis of contract theory, tort theory, and public policy. Whistleblowers have occasionally received protection under the common law for reasons of public policy. 3. *Wrongful discharge*—Whenever an employer discharges an employee in violation of an employment contract or statutory law protecting employees, the employee may bring a suit for wrongful discharge.
Wage and Hour Laws (See pages 608–611.)	1. *Davis-Bacon Act (1931)*—Requires contractors and subcontractors working on federal government construction projects to pay their employees "prevailing wages." 2. *Walsh-Healey Act (1936)*—Requires firms that contract with federal agencies to pay their employees a minimum wage and overtime pay. 3. *Fair Labor Standards Act (1938)*—Extended wage and hour requirements to cover all employers whose activities affect interstate commerce plus certain other businesses. The act has specific requirements in regard to child labor, maximum hours, and minimum wages.
Layoffs (See pages 611–612.)	1. *The Worker Adjustment and Retraining Notification (WARN) Act*—Applies to employers with at least one hundred full-time employees and requires that sixty days' advance notice of mass layoffs (defined on page 611) be given to affected employees or their representative (if workers are in a labor union). Employers who violate the WARN Act can be fined up to $500 for each day of the violation and may also have to pay damages and attorneys' fees to the laid-off employees affected by the failure to warn. 2. *State layoff notice requirements*—Many states have statutes requiring employers to provide notice before initiating mass layoffs, and these laws may have different and even stricter requirements than the WARN Act.
Family and Medical Leave (See pages 612–614.)	The Family and Medical Leave Act (FMLA) requires employers with fifty or more employees to provide their employees with up to twelve weeks of unpaid leave (twenty-six weeks for military caregiver leave) during any twelve-month period. The FMLA authorizes leave for the following reasons: 1. *Family leave*—May be taken to care for a newborn baby, an adopted child, or a foster child. 2. *Medical leave*—May be taken when the employee or the employee's spouse, child, or parent has a serious health condition requiring care. 3. *Military caregiver leave*—May be taken when the employee is caring for a family member with a serious injury or illness incurred as a result of military duty. 4. *Qualifying exigency leave*—May be taken by an employee to handle specified nonmedical emergencies when a spouse, parent, or child is in, or is called to, active military duty.
Worker Health and Safety (See pages 614–616.)	1. *Occupational Safety and Health Act (1970)*—Requires employers to meet specific safety and health standards that are established and enforced by the Occupational Safety and Health Administration (OSHA). 2. *State workers' compensation laws*—Establish an administrative procedure for compensating workers who are injured in accidents that occur on the job, regardless of fault.
Income Security (See pages 616–619.)	1. *Social Security and Medicare*—The Social Security Act of 1935 provides for old-age (retirement), survivors', and disability insurance. Both employers and employees must make contributions under the Federal Insurance Contributions Act (FICA) to help pay for benefits that will partially make up for the employees' loss of income on retirement. The Social Security Administration also administers Medicare, a health-insurance program for older or disabled persons. 2. *Private pension plans*—The federal Employee Retirement Income Security Act (ERISA) of 1974 establishes standards for the management of employer-provided pension plans. 3. *Unemployment insurance*—The Federal Unemployment Tax Act of 1935 created a system that provides unemployment compensation to eligible individuals. Covered employers are taxed to help defray the costs of unemployment compensation. 4. *COBRA*—The Consolidated Omnibus Budget Reconciliation Act (COBRA) of 1985 requires employers to give employees, on termination of employment, the option of continuing their medical, optical, or dental insurance coverage for a certain period.

Continued

Chapter Summary: Employment, Immigration, and Labor Law—Continued

Income Security—Continued	5. *HIPAA*—The Health Insurance Portability and Accountability Act (HIPAA) establishes certain requirements for employer-sponsored health insurance. Employers must comply with a number of administrative, technical, and procedural safeguards to ensure the privacy of employees' health information.
Employee Privacy Rights (See pages 619–622.)	A right to privacy has been inferred from guarantees provided by the First, Third, Fourth, Fifth, and Ninth Amendments to the U.S. Constitution. State laws may also provide for privacy rights. Employer practices that are often challenged by employees as invasive of their privacy rights include electronic performance monitoring, lie-detector tests, drug testing, genetic testing, and screening procedures.
Immigration Law (See pages 623–627.)	1. *Immigration Reform and Control Act (1986)*—Prohibits employers from hiring illegal immigrants; administered by U.S. Citizenship and Immigration Services. Compliance audits and enforcement actions are conducted by U.S. Immigration and Customs Enforcement. 2. *Immigration Act (1990)*—Limits the number of legal immigrants entering the United States by capping the number of visas (entry permits) that are issued each year.
Labor Unions (See pages 627–631.)	1. *Federal labor laws*— a. Norris-LaGuardia Act (1932)—Protects peaceful strikes, picketing, and primary boycotts. b. National Labor Relations Act (1935)—Established the rights of employees to engage in collective bargaining and to strike; also defined specific employer practices as unfair to labor. The National Labor Relations Board (NLRB) was created to administer and enforce the act. c. Labor-Management Relations Act (1947)—Proscribes certain unfair union practices, such as the closed shop. d. Labor-Management Reporting and Disclosure Act (1959)—Established an employee bill of rights and reporting requirements for union activities. 2. *Union organization*—Union campaign activities and elections must comply with the requirements established by federal labor laws and the NLRB. 3. *Collective bargaining*—The process by which labor and management negotiate the terms and conditions of employment (such as wages, benefits, and working conditions). The central legal right of a labor union is to engage in collective bargaining on the members' behalf. 4. *Strikes*—When collective bargaining reaches an impasse, union members may use their ultimate weapon in labor-management struggles—the strike. A strike occurs when unionized workers leave their jobs and refuse to work.

ExamPrep

ISSUE SPOTTERS

1 Erin, an employee of Fine Print Shop, is injured on the job. For Erin to obtain workers' compensation, does her injury have to have been caused by Fine Print's negligence? Does it matter whether the action causing the injury was intentional? Explain.

2 Onyx applies for work with Precision Design Company, which tells her that it requires union membership as a condition of employment. She applies for work with Quality Engineering, Inc., which does not require union membership as a condition of employment but requires employees to join a union after six months on the job. Are these conditions legal? Why or why not?

BEFORE THE TEST

Check your answers to the Issue Spotters, and at the same time, take the interactive quiz for this chapter. Go to www.cengage.com/blaw/blt and click on "Chapter 24." First, click on "Answers to Issue Spotters" to check your answers. Next, click on "Interactive Quiz" to assess your mastery of the concepts in this chapter. Then click on "Flashcards" to review this chapter's Key Term definitions.

For Review

Answers for the even-numbered questions in this For Review *section can be found on this text's accompanying Web site at* www.cengage.com/blaw/blt. *Select "Chapter 24" and click on "For Review."*

1 What is the employment-at-will doctrine? When and why are exceptions to this doctrine made?
2 What federal statute governs working hours and wages?
3 Under the Family and Medical Leave Act of 1993, in what circumstances may an employee take family or medical leave?
4 What are the two most important federal statutes governing immigration and employment today?
5 What federal statute gave employees the right to organize unions and engage in collective bargaining?

Hypothetical Scenarios and Case Problems

24–1 Wages and Hours. Calzoni Boating Co. is an interstate business engaged in manufacturing and selling boats. The company has five hundred nonunion employees. Representatives of these employees are requesting a four-day, ten-hours-per-day workweek, and Calzoni is concerned that this would require paying time and a half after eight hours per day. Which federal act is Calzoni thinking of that might require this? Will the act in fact require paying time and a half for all hours worked over eight hours per day if the employees' proposal is accepted? Explain.

24–2 Hypothetical Question with Sample Answer Denton and Carlo were employed at an appliance plant. Their job required them to do occasional maintenance work while standing on a wire mesh twenty feet above the plant floor. Other employees had fallen through the mesh; one was killed by the fall. When Denton and Carlo were asked by their supervisor to do work that would likely require them to walk on the mesh, they refused due to their fear of bodily harm or death. Because of their refusal to do the requested work, the two employees were fired from their jobs. Was their discharge wrongful? If so, under what federal employment law? To what federal agency or department should they turn for assistance?
—For a sample answer to Question 24–2, go to Appendix E at the end of this text.

24–3 Collective Bargaining. Visco, Inc., provides Internet services. Visco and the Internet Workers of America (IWA) have entered into a collective bargaining agreement covering installation and maintenance employees. At one time, Visco supported annual blood drives and worked with IWA and charitable organizations to jointly set dates, arrange appointments, and adjust work schedules for the drives. For each drive, about a thousand employees, including managers, spent up to four hours traveling to a donor site, giving blood, recovering, and returning to their jobs. Employees received full pay for the time. In 2010, Visco told IWA that due to economic conditions, it would no longer allow employees to participate in the drives "on Company time." IWA filed a complaint with the National Labor Relations Board (NLRB), asking that Visco be ordered to bargain over the decision. Did Visco commit an unfair labor practice? Should the NLRB grant IWA's request? Why or why not? [*Visco New York, Inc. v. National Labor Relations Board*, 360 F.3d 206 (D.C.Cir. 2004)]

24–4 FMLA. Jennifer Willis worked for Coca-Cola Enterprises, Inc. (CCE), in Louisiana as a senior account manager. On a Monday in May 2003, Willis called her supervisor to tell him that she was sick and would not be able to work that day. She also said that she was pregnant, but she did not say she was sick *because* of the pregnancy. On Tuesday, she called to ask where to report to work and was told that she could not return without a doctor's release. She said that she had a doctor's appointment on "Wednesday," which her supervisor understood to be the next day. Willis meant the *following* Wednesday. More than a week later, during which time Willis did not contact CCE, she was told that she had violated CCE's "No Call/No Show" policy. Under this policy "an employee absent from work for three consecutive days without notifying the supervisor during that period will be considered to have voluntarily resigned." She was fired. Willis filed a suit in a federal district court against CCE under the Family and Medical Leave Act (FMLA). To be eligible for FMLA leave, an employee must inform the employer of the reason for the leave. Did Willis meet this requirement? Did CCE's response to Willis's absence violate the FMLA? Explain. [*Willis v. Coca-Cola Enterprises, Inc.*, 445 F.3d 413 (5th Cir. 2006)]

24–5 Unemployment Insurance. Mary Garas, a chemist, sought work in Missouri through Kelly Services, Inc. Kelly is a staffing agency that places individuals in jobs of varying duration with other companies. Through Kelly, Garas worked at Merial Co. from April 2005 to February 2006. After the assignment ended, Garas asked Kelly for more work. Meanwhile, she filed a claim for unemployment benefits with the Missouri Division of Employment Security (DES). In March, Kelly recruiter Rebecca Cockrum told Garas about a temporary assignment with Celsis Laboratory. Garas said that she would prefer a "more stable position," but later asked Cockrum to submit her résumé to Celsis. Before the employer responded, Kelly told the DES that Garas had refused suitable work. Under a Missouri state statute, a claim for unemployment benefits must be denied if "the claimant failed without good cause . . . to accept suitable work when offered the claimant . . . by an employer by whom the individual was formerly employed." The DES denied Garas's claim for benefits. She filed an appeal with a state court. Was the DES's denial right or wrong? Why? [*Garas v. Kelly Services, Inc.*, 211 S.W.3d 149 (Mo.App.E.D. 2007)]

24-6 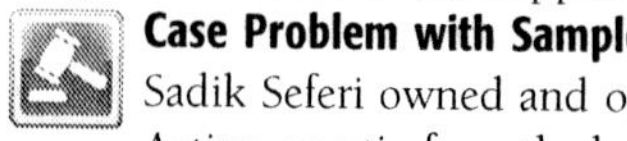 **Case Problem with Sample Answer** Nicole Tipton and Sadik Seferi owned and operated a restaurant in Iowa. Acting on a tip from the local police, agents of Immigration and Customs Enforcement executed search warrants at the restaurant and at an apartment where some restaurant workers lived. The agents discovered six undocumented aliens working at the restaurant and living together. When the I-9 forms for the restaurant's employees were reviewed, none were found for the six aliens. They were paid in cash while other employees were paid by check. The jury found Tipton and Seferi guilty of hiring and harboring illegal aliens. Both were given prison terms. The defendants challenged the conviction, contending that they did not violate the law because they did not know that the workers were unauthorized aliens. Was that argument credible? Why or why not? [*United States v. Tipton*, 518 F.3d 591 (8th Cir. 2008)]

—After you have answered Problem 24–6, compare your answer with the sample answer given on the Web site that accompanies this text. Go to www.cengage.com/blaw/blt, select "Chapter 24," and click on "Case Problem with Sample Answer."

24-7 **Immigration Work Status.** Mohammad Hashmi, a citizen of Pakistan, entered the United States in 2002 on a student visa. Two years later, when he applied for a job at CompuCredit, he completed an I-9 form and checked the box to indicate that he was "a citizen or national of the United States." Soon after submitting that form, he married a U.S. citizen. Several months later, the federal immigration services claimed that he had misrepresented himself as a U.S. citizen. Hashmi contended that he had not misrepresented himself. At an administrative hearing, he testified that when he filled out the I-9 form he believed that he was a "national of the United States" because he was legally in the country under a student visa and was going to marry a U.S. citizen. He requested that his immigration status be adjusted to account for the fact that he was employed and married to an American. The immigration judge rejected that request and found that Hashmi had made a false claim on the I-9 form. He ruled that Hashmi was "inadmissible" to the United States and that his legal status in the country could not be amended because of his marriage or employment. Hashmi appealed. Do you think it was reasonable for Hashmi to think he was a U.S. national? Should his visa status be changed because of his marriage and employment? Why or why not? [*Hashmi v. Mukasey*, 533 F.3d 700 (8th Cir. 2008)]

24-8 **Vesting.** The United Auto Workers (UAW) represents workers at Caterpillar, Inc., and negotiates labor contracts on their behalf. A 1988 labor agreement provided lifetime no-cost medical benefits for retirees but did not state when the employees' rights to those benefits vested. This agreement expired in 1991. Caterpillar and the UAW did not reach a new agreement until 1998. Under the new agreement, retiree medical benefits were subject to certain limits, and retirees were to be responsible for paying some of the costs. Workers who retired during the period when no agreement was in force filed a suit in a federal district court to obtain benefits under the 1988 agreement. Review the Employee Retirement Income Security Act vesting rules for private pension plans on page 617. What is the most plausible application of those rules by analogy to these facts? Discuss. [*Winnett v. Caterpillar, Inc.*, 553 F.3d 1000 (6th Cir. 2009)]

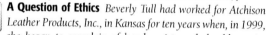

24-9 **A Question of Ethics** *Beverly Tull had worked for Atchison Leather Products, Inc., in Kansas for ten years when, in 1999, she began to complain of hand, wrist, and shoulder pain. Atchison recommended that she contact a certain physician, who in April 2000 diagnosed the condition as carpal tunnel syndrome "severe enough" for surgery. In August, Tull filed a claim with the state workers' compensation board. Because Atchison changed workers' compensation insurance companies every year, a dispute arose as to which company should pay Tull's claim. Fearing liability, no insurer would authorize treatment, and Tull was forced to delay surgery until December. The board granted her temporary total disability benefits for the subsequent six weeks that she missed work. On April 23, 2002, Berger Co. bought Atchison. The new employer adjusted Tull's work to be less demanding and stressful, but she continued to suffer pain. In July, a physician diagnosed her condition as permanent. The board granted her permanent partial disability benefits. By May 2005, the bickering over the financial responsibility for Tull's claim involved five insurers—four of which had each covered Atchison for a single year and one of which covered Berger. [*Tull v. Atchison Leather Products, Inc.*, *37 Kan.App.2d 87, 150 P.3d 316 (2007)]*

1 When an injured employee files a claim for workers' compensation, there is a proceeding to assess the injury and determine the amount of compensation. Should a dispute between insurers over the payment of the claim be resolved in the same proceeding? Why or why not?

2 The board designated April 23, 2002, as the date of Tull's injury. What is the reason for determining the date of a worker's injury? Should the board in this case have selected this date or a different date? Why?

3 How should the board assess liability for the payment of Tull's medical expenses and disability benefits? Would it be appropriate to impose joint and several liability on the insurers, or should the individual liability of each of them be determined? Explain.

Critical Thinking and Writing Assignments

24–10 **Critical Legal Thinking.** Employees have a right to privacy, but employers also have a right to create and maintain an efficient and safe workplace. Do you think that existing laws strike an appropriate balance between employers' rights and employees' rights? Why or why not?

24–11 **Video Question** Go to this text's Web site at www.cengage.com/blaw/blt and select "Chapter 24." Click on "Video Questions" and view the video titled *Employment at Will*. Then answer the following questions.

1. In the video, Laura asserts that she can fire Ray "For any reason. For no reason." Is this true? Explain your answer.
2. What exceptions to the employment-at-will doctrine are discussed in the chapter? Does Ray's situation fit into any of these exceptions?
3. Would Ray be protected from wrongful discharge under whistleblowing statutes? Why or why not?
4. Assume that you are the employer in this scenario. What arguments can you make that Ray should not be able to sue for wrongful discharge in this situation?

Practical Internet Exercises

Go to this text's Web site at www.cengage.com/blaw/blt, select "Chapter 24," and click on "Practical Internet Exercises." There you will find the following Internet research exercises that you can perform to learn more about the topics covered in this chapter.

Practical Internet Exercise 24–1: LEGAL PERSPECTIVE—**Workers' Compensation**
Practical Internet Exercise 24–2: MANAGEMENT PERSPECTIVE—**Workplace Monitoring and Surveillance**
Practical Internet Exercise 24–3: HISTORICAL PERSPECTIVE—**Labor Unions and Labor Law**

Chapter 25

Employment Discrimination

"Equal rights for all, special privileges for none."

—Thomas Jefferson, 1743–1826 (Third president of the United States, 1801–1809)

Chapter Outline

- Title VII of the Civil Rights Act of 1964
- Discrimination Based on Age
- Discrimination Based on Disability
- Defenses to Employment Discrimination
- Affirmative Action
- State Statutes

(Getty Images)

Learning Objectives

After reading this chapter, you should be able to answer the following questions:

1. Generally, what kind of conduct is prohibited by Title VII of the Civil Rights Act of 1964, as amended?
2. What is the difference between disparate-treatment discrimination and disparate-impact discrimination?
3. What remedies are available under Title VII of the 1964 Civil Rights Act, as amended?
4. What federal acts prohibit discrimination based on age and discrimination based on disability?
5. What are three defenses to claims of employment discrimination?

Out of the 1960s civil rights movement to end racial and other forms of discrimination grew a body of law protecting employees against discrimination in the workplace. This protective legislation further eroded the employment-at-will doctrine, which was discussed in the previous chapter. In the past several decades, judicial decisions, administrative agency actions, and legislation have restricted the ability of both employers and unions to discriminate against workers on the basis of race, color, religion, national origin, gender, age, or disability. A class of persons defined by one or more of these criteria is known as a **protected class.** The laws designed to protect these individuals embody the sentiment expressed by Thomas Jefferson in the chapter-opening quotation.

Protected Class A group of persons protected by specific laws because of the group's defining characteristics. Under laws prohibiting employment discrimination, these characteristics include race, color, religion, national origin, gender, age, and disability.

Several federal statutes prohibit **employment discrimination** against members of protected classes. The most important statute is Title VII of the Civil Rights Act of 1964.[1] Title VII prohibits discrimination on the basis of race, color, religion, national origin, or gender at any stage of employment. The Age Discrimination in Employment Act of 1967[2] and the Americans with Disabilities Act of 1990[3] prohibit discrimination on the basis of age and disability, respectively.

Employment Discrimination Treating employees or job applicants unequally on the basis of race, color, national origin, religion, gender, age, or disability; prohibited by federal statutes.

1. 42 U.S.C. Sections 2000e–2000e-17.
2. 29 U.S.C. Sections 621–634.
3. 42 U.S.C. Sections 12102–12118.

This chapter focuses on the kinds of discrimination prohibited by these federal statutes. Note, though, that discrimination against employees on the basis of any of these criteria may also violate state human rights statutes or other state laws or public policies prohibiting discrimination.

Title VII of the Civil Rights Act of 1964

Title VII of the Civil Rights Act of 1964 and its amendments prohibit job discrimination against employees, applicants, and union members on the basis of race, color, national origin, religion, or gender at any stage of employment. Title VII applies to employers with fifteen or more employees, labor unions with fifteen or more members, labor unions that operate hiring halls (to which members go regularly to be rationed jobs as they become available), employment agencies, and state and local governing units or agencies. The United States Supreme Court has also ruled that an employer with fewer than fifteen employees is not automatically shielded from a lawsuit filed under Title VII.[4] A special section of the act prohibits discrimination in most federal government employment.

The Equal Employment Opportunity Commission

ON THE WEB You can find the complete text of Title VII and information about the activities of the EEOC at that agency's Web site. Go to www.eeoc.gov.

Compliance with Title VII is monitored by the Equal Employment Opportunity Commission (EEOC). A victim of alleged discrimination must file a claim with the EEOC before bringing a suit against the employer. The EEOC may investigate the dispute and attempt to obtain the parties' voluntary consent to an out-of-court settlement. If a voluntary agreement cannot be reached, the EEOC may then file a suit against the employer on the employee's behalf. If the EEOC decides not to investigate the claim, the victim may bring her or his own lawsuit against the employer.

The EEOC does not investigate every claim of employment discrimination, regardless of the merits of the claim. Generally, it investigates only "priority cases," such as cases involving retaliatory discharge (firing an employee in retaliation for submitting a claim to the EEOC) and cases involving types of discrimination that are of particular concern to the EEOC.

Disparate-Treatment Discrimination A form of employment discrimination that results when an employer intentionally discriminates against employees who are members of protected classes.

Intentional and Unintentional Discrimination

Lyndon B. Johnson signs the Civil Rights Act of 1964. Among the guests behind him is Martin Luther King, Jr.

(Lyndon Baines Johnson Presidential Library and Museum)

Title VII prohibits both intentional and unintentional discrimination.

INTENTIONAL DISCRIMINATION Intentional discrimination by an employer against an employee is known as **disparate-treatment discrimination.** Because intent may sometimes be difficult to prove, courts have established certain procedures for resolving disparate-treatment cases. **EXAMPLE 25.1** A woman applies for employment with a construction firm and is rejected. If she sues on the basis of disparate-treatment discrimination in hiring, she must show that (1) she is a member of a protected class, (2) she applied and was qualified for the job in question, (3) she was rejected by the employer, and (4) the employer continued to seek applicants for the position or filled the position with a person not in a protected class. ●

4. *Arbaugh v. Y&H Corp.*, 546 U.S. 500, 126 S.Ct. 1235, 163 L.Ed.2d 1097 (2006).

***Prima Facie* Case** A case in which the plaintiff has produced sufficient evidence of his or her claim that the case can go to a jury; a case in which the evidence compels a decision for the plaintiff if the defendant produces no affirmative defense or evidence to disprove the plaintiff's assertion.

If the woman can meet these relatively easy requirements, she has made out a ***prima facie* case** of illegal discrimination. *Prima facie* is Latin for "at first sight." Legally, it refers to a fact that is presumed to be true unless contradicted by evidence. Making out a *prima facie* case of discrimination means that the plaintiff has met her initial burden of proof and will win in the absence of a legally acceptable employer defense. (Defenses will be discussed later in this chapter.) The burden then shifts to the employer-defendant, who must articulate a legal reason for not hiring the plaintiff. To prevail, the plaintiff must then show that the employer's reason is a *pretext* (not the true reason) and that discriminatory intent actually motivated the employer's decision.

UNINTENTIONAL DISCRIMINATION Employers often use interviews and testing procedures to choose from among a large number of applicants for job openings. Minimum educational requirements are also common. These practices and procedures may have an unintended discriminatory impact on a protected class. (For tips on how human resources managers can prevent these types of discrimination claims, see the *Linking the Law to Management* feature on pages 658 and 659.)

Disparate-Impact Discrimination A form of employment discrimination that results from certain employer practices or procedures that, although not discriminatory on their face, have a discriminatory effect.

Disparate-impact discrimination occurs when a protected group of people is adversely affected by an employer's practices, procedures, or tests, even though they do not appear to be discriminatory. In a disparate-impact discrimination case, the complaining party must first show statistically that the employer's practices, procedures, or tests are discriminatory in effect. Once the plaintiff has made out a *prima facie* case, the burden of proof shifts to the employer to show that the practices or procedures in question were justified. There are two ways of proving that disparate-impact discrimination exists, as discussed next.

Pool of Applicants. A plaintiff can prove a disparate impact by comparing the employer's workforce to the pool of qualified individuals available in the local labor market. The plaintiff must show that as a result of educational or other job requirements or hiring procedures, the percentage of nonwhites, women, or members of other protected classes in the employer's workforce does not reflect the percentage of that group in the pool of qualified applicants. If a person challenging an employment practice can show a connection between the practice and the disparity, he or she has made out a *prima facie* case and need not provide evidence of discriminatory intent.

Rate of Hiring. A plaintiff can prove disparate-impact discrimination by comparing the selection rates of whites and nonwhites (or members of another protected class), regardless of the racial balance in the employer's workforce. When an educational or other job requirement or hiring procedure excludes members of a protected class from an employer's workforce at a substantially higher rate than nonmembers, discrimination occurs.

The EEOC has devised a test, called the "four-fifths rule," to determine whether an employment examination is discriminatory on its face. Under this rule, a selection rate for protected classes that is less than four-fifths, or 80 percent, of the rate for the group with the highest rate will generally be regarded as evidence of disparate impact. **EXAMPLE 25.2** One hundred white applicants take an employment test, and fifty pass the test and are hired. One hundred minority applicants take the test, and twenty pass the test and are hired. Because twenty is less than four-fifths (80 percent) of fifty, the test would be considered discriminatory under the EEOC guidelines. ●

Discrimination Based on Race, Color, and National Origin

Title VII prohibits employers from discriminating against employees or job applicants on the basis of race, color, or national origin. If an employer's standards or policies for selecting or promoting employees have a discriminatory effect on employees or job applicants in these protected classes, then a presumption of illegal discrimination arises. To avoid liability, the employer must then show that its standards or policies have a substantial, demonstrable relationship to realistic qualifications for the job in question.

EXAMPLE 25.3 Silver City fires Cheng Mai, a Chinese American, who has worked in the city's planning department for two years. Mai claims that he was fired because of his national origin and presents evidence that the city's "residents only" policy has a discriminatory effect on Chinese Americans. The policy requires that all city employees become residents of the city within a reasonable time after being hired. Cheng Mai has not moved to the city but instead has continued to live with his wife and children in a nearby town where a number of other Chinese Americans live. Although residency requirements sometimes violate antidiscrimination laws, if the city can show that its residency requirement has a substantial, demonstrable relationship to realistic qualifications for the job in question, then it normally will not be illegal. ●

REVERSE DISCRIMINATION Note that discrimination based on race can also take the form of *reverse discrimination*, or discrimination against "majority" individuals, such as white males. **CASE EXAMPLE 25.4** An African American woman fired four white men from their management positions at a school district. The men filed a lawsuit for racial discrimination, alleging that the woman was trying to eliminate white males from the department. The woman claimed that the terminations were part of a reorganization plan to cut costs in the department. The jury sided with the men and awarded them nearly $3 million in damages. The verdict was upheld on appeal (though the damages award was reduced slightly).[5] ●

In 2009, the United States Supreme Court issued a decision that will have a significant impact on disparate-impact discrimination litigation. **CASE EXAMPLE 25.5** The fire department in New Haven, Connecticut, administered a test to determine which firefighters were eligible for promotions. No African Americans and only two Hispanic firefighters passed the test. Fearing that it would be sued for racial discrimination if it used the test results for promotions, the city refused to certify (and basically discarded) the results. The white firefighters (and one Hispanic) who had passed the test then sued the city, claiming reverse discrimination. The lower courts found in favor of the city, but the United States Supreme Court reversed.

The Court held that an employer can engage in intentional discrimination to remedy an unintentional disparate-impact only if the employer has "a strong basis in evidence" to believe that it will be successfully sued for disparate-impact discrimination "if it fails to take the race-conscious, discriminatory action." In this case, said the Court, mere fear of litigation was not a sufficient reason for the city to discard its test results.[6] ● The Court's ruling has been criticized as confusing for employers because although the New Haven officials tried to avoid discrimination, the Court found that throwing out the test was discriminatory.

POTENTIAL "SECTION 1981" CLAIMS Victims of racial or ethnic discrimination may also have a cause of action under 42 U.S.C. Section 1981. This section, which was enacted as part of the Civil Rights Act of 1866 to protect the rights of freed slaves, prohibits discrimination on the basis of race or ethnicity in the formation or enforcement of contracts. Because employment is often a contractual relationship, Section 1981 can provide an alternative basis for a plaintiff's action and is potentially advantageous because it does not place a cap on damages.[7]

Discrimination Based on Religion

Title VII of the Civil Rights Act of 1964 also prohibits government employers, private employers, and unions from discriminating against persons because of their religion.

5. *Johnston v. School District of Philadelphia*, ___ F.Supp.2d ___ (E.D.Pa. 2006).
6. *Ricci v. DeStefano*, ___ U.S. ___, 129 S.Ct. 2658, ___ L.Ed.2d ___ (2009).
7. See, for example, *EEOC v. Sephora USA, LLC*, 419 F.Supp.2d 408 (S.D.N.Y. 2005).

(AP Photo/The Tennessean/Eric Parsons)

Two Muslims, originally from Somalia, perform religious acts in the evening in Nashville, Tennessee. Under Title VII of the Civil Rights Act, do employers have to accommodate the religious practices of their employees?

Employers cannot treat their employees more or less favorably based on their religious beliefs or practices and cannot require employees to participate in any religious activity (or forbid them from participating in one). **EXAMPLE 25.6** Three fifty-year-old men were dismissed from their jobs at a Florida car dealership. The men filed a complaint with the EEOC alleging religious, as well as age, discrimination. They claimed that the employer targeted them for not attending the weekly prayer meetings of dealership employees. If the dealership did require its employees to attend prayer gatherings and fired the men for not attending, they will have a valid case of religious discrimination.[8] ●

An employer must "reasonably accommodate" the religious practices of its employees, unless to do so would cause undue hardship to the employer's business. If an employee's religion prohibits him or her from working on a certain day of the week or at a certain type of job, for instance, the employer must make a reasonable attempt to accommodate these religious requirements. Employers must reasonably accommodate an employee's religious belief even if the belief is not based on the doctrines of a traditionally recognized religion, such as Christianity or Judaism, or a denomination, such as Baptist. The only requirement is that the belief be sincerely held by the employee.

Discrimination Based on Gender

"A sign that says 'men only' looks very different on a bathroom door than a courthouse door."

Thurgood Marshall, 1908–1993
(Associate justice of the United States Supreme Court, 1967–1991)

Under Title VII, as well as other federal acts (including the Equal Pay Act of 1963, which we also discuss here), employers are forbidden from discriminating against employees on the basis of gender. Employers are prohibited from classifying jobs as male or female and from advertising in help-wanted columns that are designated male or female unless the employer can prove that the gender of the applicant is essential to the job. Employers also cannot have separate male and female seniority lists or refuse to promote employees based on gender.

Generally, to succeed in a suit for gender discrimination, a plaintiff must demonstrate that gender was a determining factor in the employer's decision to fire or refuse to hire or promote her or him. Typically, this involves looking at all of the surrounding circumstances. **CASE EXAMPLE 25.7** In 2009, the EEOC filed a lawsuit against an Indiana plastics manufacturer, Polycon Industries, Inc., and its parent company, Crown Packaging International, Inc. The EEOC alleged that the companies reserved higher-paying production jobs for male employees and refused to promote female workers to these jobs because of their gender. The EEOC decided to pursue the case when it received complaints from women who had applied for production jobs but who were never even interviewed.[9] ●

The Pregnancy Discrimination Act of 1978,[10] which amended Title VII, expanded the definition of gender discrimination to include discrimination based on pregnancy. Women affected by pregnancy, childbirth, or related medical conditions must be treated—for all employment-related purposes, including the receipt of benefits under employee benefit programs—the same as other persons not so affected but similar in ability to work.

---

8. The EEOC has stated that employees cannot be forced to participate—or not to participate—in a religious activity as a condition of employment. For more information, see www.eeoc/gov/types/religion.html.

9. Case No. 2:09-cv-00141-RL-PRC, filed in the U.S. District Court for the Northern District of Indiana, Hammond Division; see also EEOC Press Release, May 13, 2009.

10. 42 U.S.C. Section 2000e(k).

Ethical Issue

Does the law prohibit discrimination against transgender persons? Although some states have laws that specifically ban discrimination based on gender identity, most courts have held that federal law (Title VII) does *not* protect transgender persons from discrimination. That may be changing, however, now that one federal court has extended Title VII protection against gender discrimination to transsexuals. Diane Schroer (previously David Schroer) was born male but always identified with the female gender. Schroer, who has master's degrees in history and international relations, served twenty-five years in the military and was a commander of special forces. After retiring with top-secret clearance, she applied for a terrorism specialist position at the Library of Congress. At the job interview, Schroer dressed as a man and received the highest interview score of all eighteen candidates. The selection committee unanimously voted to offer her the job.

(Jason Redmond/Reuters/Landov)

A human resources specialist from the city of West Hollywood, California, discusses job opportunities with two transgender individuals.

Schroer then met with Charlotte Preece, Schroer's future boss, and said that she had been diagnosed with gender identity disorder and was planning to have sex reassignment surgery. The next day, the Library of Congress withdrew its offer to hire Schroer. When Schroer sued alleging gender discrimination, the Library of Congress claimed that it had withdrawn its offer because Schroer was untrustworthy and would be unable to receive the needed security clearance. The court, however, found that these reasons were pretexts (excuses) and ruled in favor of Schroer. The court held that the Library of Congress had refused to hire Schroer because her appearance and background did not comport with the selection committee's stereotypes about how women and men should act and appear. The court concluded that the revocation of the job offer violated Title VII because it was discrimination "because of sex" even though Title VII does not include transsexuals as a protected class.[11] In 2009, Schroer was awarded nearly $500,000 in back pay and damages.

EQUAL PAY ACT The Equal Pay Act of 1963, which amended the Fair Labor Standards Act of 1938 (discussed in Chapter 24), prohibits employers from gender-based wage discrimination. For the act's equal pay requirements to apply, the male and female employees must work at the same establishment doing similar work (a barber and a beautician, for example). To determine whether the Equal Pay Act has been violated, a court will look to the primary duties of the two jobs. It is the job content rather than the job description that controls in all cases. If a court finds that the wage differential is due to any factor other than gender, such as a seniority or merit system, then it does not violate the Equal Pay Act.

2009 EQUAL PAY LEGISLATION Forty-five years after the Equal Pay Act was enacted, there was still a significant gap between the wages earned by male and female employees. Women in the United States typically earn about three-quarters of what men earn. This continuing disparity prompted Congress to pass the Paycheck Fairness Act of 2009, which closed some of the loopholes in the Equal Pay Act. Because the courts had interpreted the defense of "any factor other than sex" so broadly, employers had been able to justify alleged wage discrimination simply by not using the word *gender* or *sex*. The Paycheck Fairness Act clarified employers' defenses and prohibited the use of gender-based differentials in assessing an employee's education, training, or experience. The act also provided additional remedies for wage discrimination, including compensatory and punitive damages, which are available as remedies for discrimination based on race and national origin.

ON THE WEB The National Women's Law Center maintains a Web site that provides state-by-state statistics on the disparity in pay between female and male employees. Go to www.nwlc.org/fairpay/statefacts.html.

In 2009, Congress also overturned a 2007 decision by the United States Supreme Court, which had required a plaintiff alleging wage discrimination to file a complaint within 180

11. *Schroer v. Billington*, 577 F.Supp.2d 293 (D.D.C. 2008).

days of the decision that set the discriminatory pay.[12] Congress rejected this limit when it enacted the Lilly Ledbetter Fair Pay Act of 2009.[13] The act made discriminatory wages actionable under federal law regardless of when the discrimination began. Each time a person is paid discriminatory wages, benefits, or other compensation, a cause of action arises (and the plaintiff has 180 days from that date to file a complaint). In other words, if a plaintiff continues to work for the employer while receiving discriminatory wages, the time period for filing a complaint is basically unlimited.

President Barack Obama signed the Lilly Ledbetter Fair Pay Act on January 29, 2009. Who will benefit from this law?

Constructive Discharge

Constructive Discharge A termination of employment brought about by making the employee's working conditions so intolerable that the employee reasonably feels compelled to leave.

The majority of Title VII complaints involve unlawful discrimination in decisions to hire or fire employees. In some situations, however, employees who leave their jobs voluntarily can claim that they were "constructively discharged" by the employer. **Constructive discharge** occurs when the employer causes the employee's working conditions to be so intolerable that a reasonable person in the employee's position would feel compelled to quit.

PROVING CONSTRUCTIVE DISCHARGE The plaintiff must present objective proof of intolerable working conditions, which the employer knew or had reason to know about yet failed to correct within a reasonable time period. Courts generally also require the employee to show causation—that the employer's unlawful discrimination caused the working conditions to be intolerable. Put a different way, the employee's resignation must be a foreseeable result of the employer's discriminatory action.

EXAMPLE 25.8 Khalil's employer humiliates him in front of his co-workers by informing him that he is being demoted to an inferior position. Khalil's co-workers then continually insult and harass him about his national origin (he is from Iran). The employer is aware of this discriminatory treatment but does nothing to remedy the situation, despite repeated complaints from Khalil. After several months, Khalil quits his job and files a Title VII claim. In this situation, Khalil would likely have sufficient evidence to maintain an action for constructive discharge in violation of Title VII. • Although courts weigh the facts on a case-by-case basis, employee demotion is one of the most frequently cited reasons for a finding of constructive discharge, particularly when the employee was subjected to humiliation.

APPLIES TO ALL TITLE VII DISCRIMINATION Note that constructive discharge is a theory that plaintiffs can use to establish any type of discrimination claims under Title VII, including race, color, national origin, religion, gender, pregnancy, and sexual harassment. Constructive discharge has also been successfully used in situations that involve discrimination based on age or disability (both of which will be discussed later in this chapter). Constructive discharge is most commonly asserted in cases involving sexual harassment, however.

When constructive discharge is claimed, the employee can pursue damages for loss of income, including back pay. These damages ordinarily are not available to an employee who left a job voluntarily.

Sexual Harassment

Sexual Harassment In the employment context, the demanding of sexual favors in return for job promotions or other benefits, or language or conduct that is so sexually offensive that it creates a hostile working environment.

Title VII also protects employees against **sexual harassment** in the workplace. Sexual harassment can take two forms: *quid pro quo* harassment and hostile-environment harassment. *Quid pro quo* is a Latin phrase that is often translated to mean "something in exchange for something else." *Quid pro quo* harassment occurs when sexual favors

12. *Ledbetter v. Goodyear Tire Co.*, 550 U.S. 618, 127 S.Ct. 2162, 167 L.Ed.2d 982 (2007).
13. Pub. L. No. 111-2, 123 Stat. 5 (January 5, 2009), amending 42 U.S.C. Section 2000e-5[e].

(Charles Eckert/MCT/Landov)

A federal jury decided that Madison Square Garden in New York City had to pay $11.6 million in damages for sexual harassment to fired executive Anucha Browne Sanders (center).

are demanded in return for job opportunities, promotions, salary increases, and the like. According to the United States Supreme Court, hostile-environment harassment occurs when "the workplace is permeated with discriminatory intimidation, ridicule, and insult, that is sufficiently severe or pervasive to alter the conditions of the victim's employment and create an abusive working environment."[14]

The courts determine whether the sexually offensive conduct was sufficiently severe or pervasive as to create a hostile environment on a case-by-case basis. Typically, a single incident of sexually offensive conduct is not enough to create a hostile environment (although there have been exceptions when the conduct was particularly objectionable). Note also that if the employee who is alleging sexual harassment has signed an arbitration clause (see Chapter 3), she or he will most likely be required to arbitrate the claim.[15]

Preventing Legal Disputes

To avoid sexual-harassment complaints, you should be proactive in preventing sexual harassment in the workplace. Establish written policies, distribute them to employees, and review them annually. Make it clear that the policies prohibiting harassment and discrimination apply to everyone at all levels of your organization. Provide training. Assure employees that no one will be punished for making a complaint. If you receive complaints, always take them seriously and investigate–no matter how trivial they might seem. Prompt remedial action is key, but it must not include any adverse action against the complainant (such as immediate termination). Also, never discourage employees from seeking the assistance of government agencies (such as the EEOC) or threaten or punish them for doing so. It is generally best to obtain the advice of counsel when you receive a serious sexual-harassment complaint.

HARASSMENT BY SUPERVISORS For an employer to be held liable for a supervisor's sexual harassment, the supervisor normally must have taken a tangible employment action against the employee. A **tangible employment action** is a significant change in employment status or benefits, such as when an employee is fired, refused a promotion, demoted, or reassigned to a position with significantly different responsibilities. Only a supervisor, or another person acting with the authority of the employer, can cause this sort of injury. A constructive discharge also qualifies as a tangible employment action.[16]

Tangible Employment Action A significant change in employment status, such as a change brought about by firing or failing to promote an employee; reassigning the employee to a position with significantly different responsibilities; or effecting a significant change in employment benefits.

THE *ELLERTH/FARAGHER* AFFIRMATIVE DEFENSE In 1998, the United States Supreme Court issued several important rulings that have had a lasting impact on cases alleging sexual harassment by supervisors.[17] The Court held that an employer (a city) was liable for a supervisor's harassment of employees even though the employer was unaware of the behavior. Although the city had a written policy against sexual harassment, it had not distributed the policy to its employees and had not established any complaint procedures for employees who felt that they had been sexually harassed. In another case, the Court held that an employer can be liable for a supervisor's sexual harassment even though the employee does not suffer adverse job consequences.

14. *Harris v. Forklift Systems,* 510 U.S. 17, 114 S.Ct. 367, 126 L.Ed.2d 295 (1993); see also *Billings v. Town of Grafton,* 515 F.3d 39 (1st Cir. 2008).
15. See, for example, *EEOC v. Cheesecake Factory, Inc.,* 2009 WL 1259359 (D.Ariz. 2009).
16. See, for example, *Pennsylvania State Police v. Suders,* 542 U.S. 129, 124 S.Ct. 2342, 159 L.Ed.2d 204 (2004).
17. *Burlington Industries, Inc. v. Ellerth,* 524 U.S. 742, 118 S.Ct. 2257, 141 L.Ed.2d 633 (1998); and *Faragher v. City of Boca Raton,* 524 U.S. 775, 118 S.Ct. 2275, 141 L.Ed.2d 662 (1998).

The Court's decisions in these cases established what has become known as the "*Ellerth/Faragher* affirmative defense" to charges of sexual harassment. The defense has two elements:

1. That the employer has taken reasonable care to prevent and promptly correct any sexually harassing behavior (by establishing effective antiharassment policies and complaint procedures, for example).
2. That the plaintiff-employee unreasonably failed to take advantage of any preventive or corrective opportunities provided by the employer to avoid harm.

An employer that can prove both elements will not be liable for a supervisor's harassment.

ON THE WEB The New York State Governor's Office of Employee Relations maintains an interactive site on sexual harassment and how to prevent it in the workplace. Go to www.goer.state.ny.us/Train/onlinelearning/SH/intro.html.

Retaliation by Employers Employers sometimes retaliate against employees who complain about sexual harassment or other Title VII violations. Retaliation can take many forms. An employer might demote or fire the person, or otherwise change the terms, conditions, and benefits of his or her employment. Title VII prohibits retaliation, and employees can sue their employers. In a *retaliation claim,* an individual asserts that she or he has suffered a harm as a result of making a charge, testifying, or participating in a Title VII investigation or proceeding.

In 2006, the United States Supreme Court made it easier to bring retaliation claims by ruling that plaintiffs do not have to prove that the challenged action adversely affected their workplace or employment.[18] Instead, to prove retaliation, plaintiffs must show that the challenged action was one that would likely have dissuaded a reasonable worker from making or supporting a charge of discrimination.

In 2009, the Court again strengthened Title VII protections against retaliation. The Court held that the law's retaliation protection extends to an employee who speaks out about discrimination not on her or his own initiative, but in answering questions during an employer's internal investigation of another employee's complaint.[19]

"Sexual harassment at work: Is it a problem for the self-employed?"

Victoria Wood, 1953–present
(English comedian and actor)

Harassment by Co-Workers and Nonemployees When the harassment of co-workers, rather than supervisors, creates a hostile working environment, an employee may still have a cause of action against the employer. Normally, though, the employer will be held liable only if the employer knew, or should have known, about the harassment and failed to take immediate remedial action.

Occasionally, a court may also hold an employer liable for harassment by *nonemployees* if the employer knew about the harassment and failed to take corrective action. **EXAMPLE 25.9** Gordon, who owns and manages a Great Bites restaurant, knows that one of his regular customers, Dean, repeatedly harasses Sharon, a waitress. If Gordon does nothing and permits the harassment to continue, he may be liable under Title VII even though Dean is not an employee of the restaurant. ●

Same-Gender Harassment In *Oncale v. Sundowner Offshore Services, Inc.,*[20] the United States Supreme Court held that Title VII protection extends to situations in which individuals are sexually harassed by members of the same gender. **CASE EXAMPLE 25.10** James Tepperwien was a security officer for three and a half years at a nuclear power plant owned by Entergy Nuclear Operations. During that time, Tepperwien twice reported to his superiors that Vito Messina, another security officer who was allegedly gay, had sexu-

18. *Burlington Northern and Santa Fe Railroad Co. v. White,* 548 U.S. 53, 126 S.Ct. 2405, 165 L.Ed.2d 345 (2006) (see the *Case Analysis Question* on page 662).
19. *Crawford v. Metropolitan Government of Nashville and Davidson County, Tennessee,* ___ U.S. ___, 129 S.Ct. 846, 172 L.Ed.2d 650 (2009).
20. 523 U.S. 75, 118 S.Ct. 998, 140 L.Ed.2d 207 (1998).

ally harassed him. After the first incident, Entergy made all the security officers read and sign its no-tolerance antiharassment policy. After the second incident, Messina was placed on administrative leave for ten weeks. After Messina returned to work, Tepperwien was disciplined for failing to report some missing equipment. He then filed another harassment complaint and quit his job, claiming that he had been constructively discharged and that Entergy had not taken sufficient steps to prevent further harassment. The court noted that a male victim of same-gender harassment must show that he was harassed because he was male. The court found that Tepperwien had presented credible evidence that Messina was a homosexual and had made sexual advances toward other security officers. This evidence was sufficient to establish a *prima facie* case of hostile-environment sexual harassment, so the case could go forward to trial, but it was not enough to show the intolerable conditions required for a finding of constructive discharge.[21] ●

PROOF OF SAME-GENDER HARASSMENT It can be difficult to prove that the harassment in same-gender cases is "based on sex." It is easier to establish a case of same-gender harassment when the harasser is homosexual, as in Case Example 25.10 just presented above. When the victim is homosexual, some courts have found that the harasser's conduct does not qualify as sexual harassment under Title VII because it was based on the employee's sexual orientation, not on his "sex."[22]

Although federal law (Title VII) does not prohibit discrimination or harassment based on a person's sexual orientation, a growing number of states have enacted laws the prohibit sexual orientation discrimination in private employment. Also, many companies have voluntarily established nondiscrimination policies that include sexual orientation. (Workers in the United States often have more protection against sexual harassment in the workplace than workers in other countries, as this chapter's *Beyond Our Borders* feature on the following page explains.)

Online Harassment

Employees' online activities can create a hostile working environment in many ways. Racial jokes, ethnic slurs, or other comments contained in e-mail, text or instant messages, and blog posts can become the basis for a claim of hostile-environment harassment or other forms of discrimination. A worker who sees sexually explicit images on a co-worker's computer screen may find the images offensive and claim that they create a hostile working environment.[23]

Nevertheless, employers may be able to avoid liability for online harassment if they take prompt remedial action. **CASE EXAMPLE 25.11** While working at WorldCom, Inc., Angela Daniels received racially harassing e-mailed jokes from another employee. Shortly afterward, the company issued a warning to the offending employee about the proper use of the e-mail system and held two meetings to discuss company policy on the use of the system. In Daniels's suit against WorldCom for racial discrimination, a federal district court concluded that the employer was not liable for its employee's racially harassing e-mails because the employer took prompt remedial action.[24] ●

Remedies under Title VII

Employer liability under Title VII may be extensive. If the plaintiff successfully proves that unlawful discrimination occurred, he or she may be awarded reinstatement, back pay, retroactive promotions, and damages. Compensatory damages are available only in cases of

---

21. *Tepperwien v. Entergy Nuclear Operations, Inc.*, 606 F.Supp.2d 427 (S.D.N.Y. 2009).

22. See, for example, *McCown v. St. John's Health System*, 349 F.3d 540 (8th Cir. 2003); and *Rene v. MGM Grand Hotel, Inc.*, 305 F.3d 1061 (9th Cir. 2002).

23. See, for example, *Doe v. XYC Corp.*, 382 N.J.Super. 122 (App.Div. 2005).

24. *Daniels v. WorldCom, Inc.*, 1998 SL 91261 (N.D.Tex. 1998). See also *Musgrove v. Mobil Oil Corp.*, 2003 WL 21653125 (N.D.Tex. 2003).

Beyond Our Borders Sexual Harassment in Other Nations

The problem of sexual harassment in the workplace is not confined to the United States. Indeed, it is a worldwide problem for female workers. In Argentina, Brazil, Egypt, Turkey, and many other countries, there is no legal protection against any form of employment discrimination. Even in those countries that do have laws prohibiting discriminatory employment practices, including gender-based discrimination, those laws often do not specifically include sexual harassment as a discriminatory practice. Several countries have attempted to remedy this omission by passing new laws or amending others to specifically prohibit sexual harassment in the workplace. Japan, for example, has amended its Equal Employment Opportunity Law to include a provision making sexual harassment illegal. Thailand has also passed its first sexual-harassment law. The European Union has adopted a directive that specifically identifies sexual harassment as a form of discrimination. Nevertheless, women's groups throughout Europe contend that corporations in European countries tend to view sexual harassment with "quiet tolerance." They contrast this attitude with that of most U.S. corporations, which have implemented specific procedures to deal with harassment claims.

• **For Critical Analysis**
Why do you think U.S. corporations are more aggressive than European companies in taking steps to prevent sexual harassment in the workplace?

intentional discrimination. Punitive damages may be recovered against a private employer only if the employer acted with malice or reckless indifference to an individual's rights. The statute limits the total amount of compensatory and punitive damages that the plaintiff can recover from specific employers—ranging from $50,000 against employers with one hundred or fewer employees to $300,000 against employers with more than five hundred employees.

Discrimination Based on Age

Age discrimination is potentially the most widespread form of discrimination, because anyone—regardless of race, color, national origin, or gender—could be a victim at some point in life. The Age Discrimination in Employment Act (ADEA) of 1967, as amended, prohibits employment discrimination on the basis of age against individuals forty years of age or older. The act also prohibits mandatory retirement for nonmanagerial workers. For the act to apply, an employer must have twenty or more employees, and the employer's business activities must affect interstate commerce. The EEOC administers the ADEA, but the act also permits private causes of action against employers for age discrimination.

"Growing old is like being increasingly penalized for a crime you have not committed."
Anthony Powell, 1905–2000
(English novelist)

The ADEA includes a provision that extends protections against age discrimination to federal government employees.[25] In 2008, the United States Supreme Court ruled that this provision encompasses not only claims of age discrimination, but also claims of retaliation for complaining about age discrimination, which are not specifically mentioned in the statute.[26] Thus, the ADEA protects federal and private-sector employees from retaliation based on age-related complaints.

Procedures under the ADEA

REMEMBER The Fourteenth Amendment prohibits any state from denying any person "the equal protection of the laws." This prohibition applies to the *federal* government through the due process clause of the Fifth Amendment.

The burden-shifting procedure under the ADEA is similar to that under Title VII. If a plaintiff can establish that she or he (1) was a member of the protected age group, (2) was qualified for the position from which she or he was discharged, and (3) was discharged under circumstances that give rise to an inference of discrimination, the plaintiff has established a *prima facie* case of unlawful age discrimination. The burden then shifts to the employer, who must articulate a legitimate reason for the discrimination. If the plaintiff can prove

25. See 29 U.S.C. Section 632(a) (2000 ed., Supp. V).
26. *Gomez-Perez v. Potter*, ___ U.S. ___, 128 S.Ct. 1931, 170 L.Ed.2d 887 (2008).

This sixty-year-old worker has just been informed that his position is being eliminated because of company restructuring. How can he establish that his firing was based on his age rather than on the restructuring?

that the employer's reason is only a pretext (excuse) and that the plaintiff's age was a determining factor in the employer's decision, the employer will be held liable under the ADEA.[27]

Replacing Older Workers with Younger Workers

Numerous age discrimination cases have been brought against employers who, to cut costs, replaced older, higher-salaried employees with younger, lower-salaried workers. Whether a firing is discriminatory or simply part of a rational business decision to prune the company's ranks is not always clear. Companies often defend a decision to discharge a worker by asserting that the worker could no longer perform his or her duties or that the worker's skills were no longer needed.

The employee must prove that the discharge was motivated, at least in part, by age bias. Proof that qualified older employees generally are discharged before younger employees or that co-workers continually made unflattering age-related comments about the discharged worker may be enough. **CASE EXAMPLE 25.12** Meenan Oil Company fired Louis Ceccoli, a seventy-one-year-old sales representative. Ceccoli's manager had made several derogatory comments about older workers and had repeatedly asked Ceccoli about his retirement plans. The EEOC filed an ADEA lawsuit. Meenan was eventually required to pay Ceccoli $80,000 and to provide antidiscrimination training to its supervisors and managers.[28] ●

The plaintiff need not prove that he or she was replaced by a person outside the protected class (under the age of forty years) as long as the person is younger than the plaintiff. The issue in all ADEA cases is whether age discrimination has, in fact, occurred, regardless of the age of the replacement worker. Nevertheless, the bigger the age gap, the more likely the individual will succeed in showing age discrimination.

When an older worker who is laid off as part of a restructuring subsequently files a suit against the company for age discrimination, a court must decide what testimony concerning the company's attitudes toward workers' ages will be allowed as evidence at trial. This issue was at the heart of the following case.

27. See, for example, *Cash Distributing Co. v. Neely*, 947 So.2d 286 (Miss. Sup.Ct. 2007).
28. See the EEOC press release at www.eeoc.ogv/press/5-13-09.html.

Case 25.1 Sprint/United Management Co. v. Mendelsohn

Supreme Court of the United States, ___ U.S. ___, 128 S.Ct. 1140, 170 L.Ed.2d 1 (2008).

In an age discrimination case, is the testimony of other employees with similar claims admissible?

FACTS Ellen Mendelsohn worked for Sprint/United Management Company (Sprint) from 1989 to 2002, when Sprint fired her during a companywide reduction in the workforce. She sued under the ADEA, alleging disparate treatment based on her age (fifty-one). Five other former Sprint employees testified that they had also suffered discrimination based on age. Three said that they had heard managers make remarks belittling older workers and indicating that age was a factor in deciding who would be fired during the restructuring. None of the five witnesses worked in the same part of the company as Mendelsohn, however, and none could testify about her supervisors. The district court excluded their testimony as to the impact on Mendelsohn because the witnesses were not "similarly situated" in the company. The appeals court held that the testimony was not *per se* irrelevant and remanded the case with instructions to admit the challenged testimony. Sprint appealed to the United States Supreme Court.

ISSUE Was the testimony of witnesses concerning the company's general attitude toward age discrimination *per se* irrelevant and *per se* inadmissible, even though they did not work in the same department as the plaintiff?

DECISION No. The United States Supreme Court vacated the appellate court's decision and remanded the case to the district court so that the trial court could clarify its ruling.

Case 25.1—Continues next page

Case 25.1–Continued

REASON The Court reasoned that the trial court had gone too far in excluding the challenged testimony and that the appellate court had erred in telling the lower court to admit the testimony. The testimony is not necessarily *per se* admissible or *per se* inadmissible. According to federal rules, the relevance of such evidence is fact based and depends on many factors. The district (trial) court should study the evidence in more detail and determine if the witnesses were providing credible evidence of a discriminatory policy at Sprint that was played out through the reduction in the workforce. The court had to assess the value of such evidence. It could not simply reject evidence that did not directly address the attitude of Mendelsohn's immediate supervisors.

FOR CRITICAL ANALYSIS—Legal Consideration *What steps should employers take to reduce the likelihood that supervisors will make negative comments about workers' ages?*

State Employees Not Covered by the ADEA

Generally, the states are immune from lawsuits brought by private individuals in federal court—unless a state consents to the suit. This immunity stems from the United States Supreme Court's interpretation of the Eleventh Amendment (the text of this amendment is included in Appendix B). **CASE EXAMPLE 25.13** In two Florida cases, professors and librarians contended that their employers—two Florida state universities—denied them salary increases and other benefits because they were getting old and their successors could be hired at lower cost. The universities claimed that as agencies of a sovereign state, they could not be sued in federal court without the state's consent. The cases ultimately reached the United States Supreme Court, which held that the Eleventh Amendment bars private parties from suing state employers for violations of the ADEA.[29] ●

ON THE WEB The Employment Law Information Network provides access to many articles on age discrimination and other employment issues at www.elinfonet.com/fedindex/2.

State immunity under the Eleventh Amendment is not absolute, however, as the Supreme Court explained in 2004. In some situations, such as when fundamental rights are at stake, Congress has the power to abrogate (abolish) state immunity to private suits through legislation that unequivocally shows Congress's intent to subject states to private suits.[30] As a general rule, though, the Court has found that state employers are immune from private suits brought by employees under the ADEA (for age discrimination, as noted above), the Americans with Disabilities Act[31] (for disability discrimination), and the Fair Labor Standards Act[32] (which relates to wages and hours—see Chapter 24). In contrast, states are not immune from the requirements of the Family and Medical Leave Act[33] (see Chapter 24).

Discrimination Based on Disability

"Jobs are physically easier, but the worker now takes home worries instead of an aching back."
Homer Bigart, 1907–1991
(American journalist)

The Americans with Disabilities Act (ADA) of 1990 was designed to eliminate discriminatory employment practices that prevent otherwise qualified workers with disabilities from fully participating in the national labor force. The ADA prohibits disability-based discrimination in workplaces with fifteen or more workers (with the exception of state government employers, who are generally immune under the Eleventh Amendment, as was just discussed). Basically, the ADA requires that employers "reasonably accommodate" the needs of persons with disabilities unless to do so would cause the employer to suffer an "undue hardship." In 2008, Congress enacted the ADA Amendments Act,[34] which broadened the coverage of the ADA's protections, as will be discussed shortly.

29. *Kimel v. Florida Board of Regents,* 528 U.S. 62, 120 S.Ct. 631, 145 L.Ed.2d 522 (2000).
30. *Tennessee v. Lane,* 541 U.S. 509, 124 S.Ct. 1978, 158 L.Ed.2d 820 (2004).
31. *Board of Trustees of the University of Alabama v. Garrett,* 531 U.S. 356, 121 S.Ct. 955, 148 L.Ed.2d 866 (2001).
32. *Alden v. Maine,* 527 U.S. 706, 119 S.Ct. 2240, 144 L.Ed.2d 636 (1999).
33. *Nevada Department of Human Resources v. Hibbs,* 538 U.S. 721, 123 S.Ct. 1972, 155 L.Ed.2d 953 (2003).
34. 42 U.S.C. Sections 12103 and 12205a.

Procedures under the ADA

To prevail on a claim under the ADA, a plaintiff must show that he or she (1) has a disability, (2) is otherwise qualified for the employment in question, and (3) was excluded from the employment solely because of the disability. As in Title VII cases, a plaintiff must pursue her or his claim through the EEOC before filing an action in court for a violation of the ADA. The EEOC may decide to investigate and perhaps even sue the employer on behalf of the employee. If the EEOC decides not to sue, then the employee is entitled to sue in court.

Significantly, the United States Supreme Court held in 2002 that the EEOC could bring a suit against an employer for disability-based discrimination even though the employee had agreed to submit any job-related disputes to arbitration (see Chapter 3). The Court reasoned that because the EEOC was not a party to the arbitration agreement, the agreement was not binding on the EEOC.[35]

Plaintiffs in lawsuits brought under the ADA may obtain many of the same remedies available under Title VII. These include reinstatement, back pay, a limited amount of compensatory and punitive damages (for intentional discrimination), and certain other forms of relief. Repeat violators may be ordered to pay fines of up to $100,000.

(Image Source via AP Images)

Co-workers discuss business matters. What is a disability under the Americans with Disabilities Act?

What Is a Disability?

The ADA is broadly drafted to cover persons with a wide range of disabilities. Specifically, the ADA defines *disability* as "(1) a physical or mental impairment that substantially limits one or more of the major life activities of such individuals; (2) a record of such impairment; or (3) being regarded as having such an impairment." Health conditions that have been considered disabilities under the federal law include blindness, alcoholism, heart disease, cancer, muscular dystrophy, cerebral palsy, paraplegia, diabetes, acquired immune deficiency syndrome (AIDS), testing positive for the human immunodeficiency virus (HIV), and morbid obesity (defined as existing when an individual's weight is two times the normal weight for his or her height). The ADA excludes from coverage certain conditions, such as kleptomania (the obsessive desire to steal).

THE SUPREME COURT NARROWLY INTERPRETED THE ADA Although the ADA's definition of disability is broad, United States Supreme Court rulings from 1999 to 2007 interpreted that definition narrowly and made it harder for employees to establish a disability under the act. In 1999, the Court held that severe myopia, or nearsightedness, which can be corrected with lenses, does not qualify as a disability under the ADA.[36] In 2002, the Court held that repetitive-stress injuries (such as carpal tunnel syndrome) ordinarily do not constitute a disability under the ADA.[37] After that, the courts began focusing on how the person functioned when using corrective devices or taking medication, not on how the person functioned without these measures.[38]

2008 AMENDMENTS REVERSE PRIOR SUPREME COURT CASES In response to the Supreme Court's limiting decisions, Congress decided to amend the ADA in 2008. Basically, the amendments reverse the Court's restrictive interpretation of disability under the ADA and prohibit employers from considering mitigating measures or medications when

---

35. *EEOC v. Waffle House, Inc.*, 534 U.S. 279, 122 S.Ct. 754, 151 L.Ed.2d 755 (2002).

36. *Sutton v. United Airlines, Inc.*, 527 U.S. 471, 119 S.Ct. 2139, 144 L.Ed.2d 450 (1999).

37. *Toyota Motor Manufacturing, Kentucky, Inc. v. Williams*, 534 U.S. 184, 122 S.Ct. 681, 151 L.Ed.2d 615 (2002). This case was invalidated by the 2008 amendments to the ADA.

38. See, for example, *Orr v. Wal-Mart Stores, Inc.*, 297 F.3d 720 (8th Cir. 2002).

determining if an individual has a disability. In other words, disability is now determined on a case-by-case basis.

A condition may fit the definition of disability in one set of circumstances, but not in another. What makes the difference in an individual situation? The court in the following case answered that question.

Case 25.2 Rohr v. Salt River Project Agricultural Improvement and Power District

United States Court of Appeals, Ninth Circuit, 555 F.3d 850 (2009).
www.ca9.uscourts.gov[a]

HISTORICAL AND SOCIAL SETTING *Diabetes is a chronic and incurable disease associated with an increased risk of heart disease, stroke, high blood pressure, blindness, kidney disease, nervous system disease, amputations, dental disease, complications of pregnancy, and sexual dysfunction. Type 1 diabetes, or juvenile diabetes, results from the body's failure to produce insulin—a hormone that is needed to convert food into energy. Type 2 results from the body's failure to properly use insulin. If left untreated, type 2 can cause seizures and a coma. In the United States, approximately 23.6 million children and adults, or 7.8 percent of the population, have diabetes.*

Is diabetes a disability under the Americans with Disabilities Act?

FACTS Larry Rohr has type 2 diabetes. He tires quickly and suffers from high blood pressure, deteriorating vision, and loss of feeling in his hands and feet. Insulin injections, other medicine, blood tests, and a strict diet are fixtures of his daily life. If he fails to follow this regimen, his blood sugar rises to a level that aggravates his disease. At the time of his diagnosis, he was a welding metallurgy specialist for the Salt River Project Agricultural Improvement and Power District, which provides utility services to homes in Arizona. Due to the effort required to manage his diabetes, particularly his strict diet schedule, Rohr's physician forbade his assignment to tasks involving overnight, out-of-town travel. Salt River told Rohr that this would prevent him from performing the essential functions of his job, such as responding to power outages. Rohr was asked to transfer, apply for disability benefits, or take early retirement. He filed a suit in a federal district court against Salt River, alleging discrimination. The court issued a summary judgment in the employer's favor. Rohr appealed.

ISSUE Is diabetes a disability under the ADA if it significantly restricts an individual's eating?

DECISION Yes. The U.S. Court of Appeals for the Ninth Circuit vacated the lower court's judgment and remanded the case for trial.

REASON The ADA's definition of disability includes a physical impairment that substantially limits a major life activity. Diabetes is a physical impairment because it affects the digestive, hemic (blood), and endocrine systems. Major life activities include eating patterns. Thus, if the symptoms of diabetes and the efforts to manage the disease significantly restrict an individual's eating, the definition of disability is met. In many instances, failure to take insulin can result in severe health problems and even death. Determining how much insulin to take can require frequent, self-administered blood tests and adjustments in activity and food levels. Rohr must follow these steps. Because insulin alone does not stabilize his blood sugar levels, he must strictly monitor what, and when, he eats every day. Failure to do so would endanger his health. "Straying from a diet for more than one or two meals is not a cause for medical concern for most people, and skipping a meal, or eating a large one, does not expose them to the risk of fainting." But for Rohr, the effort to control his diet is substantially limiting.

FOR CRITICAL ANALYSIS—Technological Consideration *If Rohr could monitor his condition and regimen through a cell phone or other portable Internet connection, would the result in this case likely have been affected? Explain.*

a. In the left-hand column, in the "Decisions" pull-down menu, click on "Opinions." On that page, click on "Advanced Search." In the "by Case No.:" box, type "06-16527" and click on "Search." In the result, click on the case title to access the opinion.

Reasonable Accommodation

The ADA does not require that employers accommodate the needs of job applicants or employees with disabilities who are not otherwise qualified for the work. If a job applicant or an employee with a disability, with reasonable accommodation, can perform essential job functions, however, the employer must make the accommodation. Required modifications may include installing ramps for a wheelchair, establishing more flexible working hours, creating or modifying job assignments, and creating or improving training materials and procedures. Generally, employers should give primary consideration to employees' preferences in deciding what accommodations should be made.

ON THE WEB An abundance of helpful information on disability-based discrimination, including the text of the ADA, can be found online at www.jan.wvu.edu.

(Paul Tople/MCT/Landov)

This paraplegic employee has a customized van that he parks in the handicap parking area outside his workplace. In general, providing such parking for employees who have a disability is considered a reasonable accommodation that employers must make.

DON'T FORGET **Preemployment screening procedures must be applied equally in regard to all job applicants.**

UNDUE HARDSHIP Employers who do not accommodate the needs of persons with disabilities must demonstrate that the accommodations will cause "undue hardship" in terms of being significantly difficult or expensive for the employer. Usually, the courts decide whether an accommodation constitutes an undue hardship on a case-by-case basis by looking at the employer's resources in relation to the specific accommodation.

EXAMPLE 25.14 Bryan Lockhart, who uses a wheelchair, works for a cell phone company that provides parking for its employees. Lockhart informs the company supervisors that the parking spaces are so narrow that he is unable to extend the ramp on his van that allows him to get in and out of the vehicle. Lockhart therefore requests that the company reasonably accommodate his needs by paying a monthly fee for him to use a larger parking space in an adjacent lot. In this situation, a court would likely find that it would not be an undue hardship for the employer to pay for additional parking for Lockhart. •

JOB APPLICATIONS AND PREEMPLOYMENT PHYSICAL EXAMS Employers must modify their job-application process so that those with disabilities can compete for jobs with those who do not have disabilities. For instance, a job announcement might be modified to allow job applicants to respond by e-mail or letter, as well as by telephone, so that it does not discriminate against potential applicants with hearing impairments.

Employers are restricted in the kinds of questions they may ask on job-application forms and during preemployment interviews. Furthermore, they cannot require persons with disabilities to submit to preemployment physicals unless such exams are required of all other applicants. Employers can condition an offer of employment on the applicant's successfully passing a medical examination, but can disqualify the applicant only if the medical problems they discover would render the applicant unable to perform the job.

CASE EXAMPLE 25.15 When filling the position of delivery truck driver, a company cannot screen out all applicants who are unable to meet the U.S. Department of Transportation's hearing standard. The company would first have to prove that drivers who are deaf are not qualified to perform the essential job function of driving safely and pose a higher risk of accidents than drivers who are not deaf.[39] •

SUBSTANCE ABUSERS Drug addiction is a disability under the ADA because drug addiction is a substantially limiting impairment. Those who are actually using illegal drugs are not protected by the act, however. The ADA protects only persons with *former* drug addictions—those who have completed or are now in a supervised drug-rehabilitation program. Individuals who have used drugs casually in the past are not protected under the act. They are not considered addicts and therefore do not have a disability (addiction).

People suffering from alcoholism are protected by the ADA. Employers cannot legally discriminate against employees simply because they are suffering from alcoholism and must treat them in the same way they treat other employees. Of course, employers have the right to prohibit the use of alcohol in the workplace and can require that employees not be under the influence of alcohol while working. Employers can also fire or refuse to hire a person who is an alcoholic if he or she poses a substantial risk of harm either to himself or herself or to others and the risk cannot be reduced by reasonable accommodation.

HEALTH INSURANCE PLANS Workers with disabilities must be given equal access to any health insurance provided to other employees. Employers can exclude from coverage preexisting health conditions and certain types of diagnostic or surgical procedures, though. An employer can also put a limit, or cap, on health-care payments under its particular group health policy—as long as such caps are "applied equally to all insured employees" and do not "discriminate on the basis of disability." Whenever a group health-care plan

ON THE WEB **The Equal Employment Opportunity Commission posts a manual that provides guidance on reasonable accommodation and undue hardship under the ADA. Go to www.eeoc.gov/policy/docs/accommodation.html.**

39. *Bates v. United Parcel Service, Inc.*, 465 F.3d 1069 (9th Cir. 2006).

makes a disability-based distinction in its benefits, the plan violates the ADA (unless the employer can justify its actions under the *business necessity* defense, which will be discussed shortly).

Association Discrimination

The ADA contains an "association provision" that protects qualified individuals from employment discrimination based on an identified disability of a person with whom the qualified individual is known to have a relationship or an association.[40] The purpose of this provision is to prevent employers from taking adverse employment actions based on stereotypes or assumptions about individuals who associate with people who have disabilities. An employer cannot, for instance, refuse to hire the parent of a child with a disability based on the assumption that the person will miss work too often or be unreliable.

To establish a *prima facie* case of association discrimination under the ADA, the plaintiff must show that she or he (1) was qualified for the job, (2) was subjected to adverse employment action, and (3) was known by her or his employer to have a relative or an associate with a disability. In addition, the plaintiff must show that the adverse employment action occurred under circumstances raising a reasonable inference that the disability of the relative or associate was a determining factor in the employer's decision.

In the following case, a man claimed that his employer unlawfully discriminated against him based on his wife's disability. Although the case involved a state law that offers slightly more protection than the ADA, the opinion shows how courts analyze association discrimination claims.

---

40. 42 U.S.C. Section 12112(b)(4).

Case 25.3 Francin v. Mosby, Inc.

Missouri Court of Appeals, 248 S.W.3d 619 (2008).
www.courts.mo.gov[a]

Was an employee fired because of a spouse's illness?

(©Eric Von Seggern, 2009. Used under license from Shutterstock.com)

FACTS Randall Francin began working at Mosby, Inc. (doing business as Elsevier), in 1991. He worked as a production assistant until 2002, when his position was eliminated due to organizational restructuring. Francin was rehired soon after as an associate editor. In this new position, Francin updated drug information and proofread information contained in drug inserts. In 2003, Francin's wife was diagnosed with amyotrophic lateral sclerosis. He discussed his rights for leave under the Family and Medical Leave Act (discussed in Chapter 24) with a company human resources representative. Early in 2004, Francin received a "merit award increase" in salary, and his supervisor resigned. During an interview with his new boss, Francin discussed his wife's illness. On September 21, 2004, Francin was fired. Francin filed a suit under the Missouri Human Rights Act, alleging that Elsevier discriminated against him because of his association with a person with a disability. Elsevier filed a motion for summary judgment, which was granted by the trial court. On appeal, Francin claimed that the trial court erred in granting summary judgment because there was a genuine issue of material fact concerning whether his wife's disability was a contributing factor in the decision to terminate his employment.

ISSUE Did the trial court err in granting summary judgment to Elsevier because there was a genuine dispute of material fact?

DECISION Yes. The Missouri intermediate appellate court reversed the trial court's decision and remanded the case for further proceedings.

REASON Summary judgment is appropriate only when there are no genuine disputes of material fact. The appellate court found sufficient evidence that Francin's wife's illness was a contributing factor to his termination and thus was a material fact in this case. In particular, the court cited the contradictory evidence of Francin's positive job performance with the close timing of his termination after disclosing his wife's condition to his new boss.

WHAT IF THE FACTS WERE DIFFERENT? *Assume that Francin had only discussed his wife's illness with a human resources officer in the company and had never mentioned it to his new boss. Would the outcome of the appeal have been different? Explain.*

---

a. Click on "Opinions & Minutes" under the "Quick Links" menu. Select the link for opinions from the Missouri Court of Appeals, Eastern District, and using the "Search Opinions" function, enter "Randall Francin." Click on the case title to access this opinion. This is the official Web site of the Missouri courts.

Hostile-Environment Claims under the ADA

As discussed earlier in this chapter, under Title VII of the Civil Rights Act of 1964, an employee may base certain types of employment-discrimination causes of action on a hostile-environment theory. Using this theory, a worker may successfully sue her or his employer, even if the worker was not fired or otherwise discriminated against.

Although the ADA does not expressly provide for hostile-environment claims, a number of courts have allowed such actions. Only a few plaintiffs have been successful, however. For a claim to succeed, the conduct complained of must be sufficiently severe or pervasive to permeate the workplace and alter the conditions of employment such that a reasonable person would find the environment hostile or abusive. **CASE EXAMPLE 25.16** Lester Wenigar was a fifty-seven-year-old man with a low IQ and limited mental capacity who worked at a farm doing manual labor and as a night watchman. His employer frequently shouted at him and called him names, did not allow him to take breaks, and provided him with substandard living quarters (a storeroom over a garage without any heat or windows). In this situation, because the employer's conduct was severe and offensive, a court would likely find that the working conditions constituted a hostile environment under the ADA.[41] ●

Defenses to Employment Discrimination

The first line of defense for an employer charged with employment discrimination is, of course, to assert that the plaintiff has failed to meet his or her initial burden of proving that discrimination occurred. Once a plaintiff succeeds in proving that discrimination occurred, the burden shifts to the employer to justify the discriminatory practice. Often, employers attempt to justify the discrimination by claiming that it was the result of a business necessity, a bona fide occupational qualification, or a seniority system. In some cases, as noted earlier, an effective antiharassment policy and prompt remedial action when harassment occurs may shield employers from liability for sexual harassment under Title VII.

Business Necessity

Business Necessity A defense to allegations of employment discrimination in which the employer demonstrates that an employment practice that discriminates against members of a protected class is related to job performance.

An employer may defend against a claim of disparate-impact (unintentional) discrimination by asserting that a practice that has a discriminatory effect is a **business necessity.** **EXAMPLE 25.17** If requiring a high school diploma is shown to have a discriminatory effect, an employer might argue that a high school education is necessary for workers to perform the job at a required level of competence. If the employer can demonstrate to the court's satisfaction that a definite connection exists between a high school education and job performance, the employer normally will succeed in this business necessity defense. ●

Bona Fide Occupational Qualification

Bona Fide Occupational Qualification (BFOQ) Identifiable characteristics reasonably necessary to the normal operation of a particular business. These characteristics can include gender, national origin, and religion, but not race.

Another defense applies when discrimination against a protected class is essential to a job—that is, when a particular trait is a **bona fide occupational qualification (BFOQ).** Race, however, can never be a BFOQ. Generally, courts have restricted the BFOQ defense to instances in which the employee's gender is essential to the job. **EXAMPLE 25.18** A women's clothing store might legitimately hire only female sales attendants if part of an attendant's job involves assisting clients in the store's dressing rooms. Similarly, the Federal Aviation Administration can legitimately impose age limits for airline pilots—but an airline cannot impose weight limits only on female flight attendants. ●

41. *Wenigar v. Johnson*, 712 N.W.2d 190 (Minn.App. 2006). This case involved a hostile-environment claim under the Minnesota disability statute rather than the ADA, but the court relied on another court's decision under the ADA.

Seniority Systems

An employer with a history of discrimination might have no members of protected classes in upper-level positions. Even if the employer now seeks to be unbiased, it may face a lawsuit in which the plaintiff asks a court to order that minorities be promoted ahead of schedule to compensate for past discrimination. If no present intent to discriminate is shown, however, and if promotions or other job benefits are distributed according to a fair **seniority system** (in which workers with more years of service are promoted first or laid off last), the employer normally has a good defense against the suit.

Seniority System In regard to employment relationships, a system in which those who have worked longest for the employer are first in line for promotions, salary increases, and other benefits. They are also the last to be laid off if the workforce must be reduced.

According to the United States Supreme Court, this defense may also apply to alleged discrimination under the ADA. The case involved a baggage handler who had injured his back and requested an assignment to a position at U.S. Airways, Inc. The airline refused to give the employee the position because another employee had seniority. The Court sided with U.S. Airways. If an employee with a disability requests an accommodation that conflicts with an employer's seniority system, the accommodation generally will not be considered "reasonable" under the act.[42]

After-Acquired Evidence of Employee Misconduct

In some situations, employers have attempted to avoid liability for employment discrimination on the basis of "after-acquired evidence"—that is, evidence that the employer discovers after a lawsuit is filed—of an employee's misconduct. **EXAMPLE 25.19** An employer fires a worker who then sues the employer for employment discrimination. During pretrial investigation, the employer learns that the employee made material misrepresentations on his employment application—misrepresentations that, had the employer known about them, would have served as grounds to fire the individual. •

According to the United States Supreme Court, after-acquired evidence of wrongdoing cannot be used to shield an employer entirely from liability for employment discrimination. It may, however, be used to limit the amount of damages for which the employer is liable.[43]

Affirmative Action

Federal statutes and regulations providing for equal opportunity in the workplace were designed to reduce or eliminate discriminatory practices with respect to hiring, retaining, and promoting employees. **Affirmative action** programs go a step further and attempt to "make up" for past patterns of discrimination by giving members of protected classes preferential treatment in hiring or promotion. During the 1960s, all federal and state government agencies, private companies that contracted to do business with the federal government, and institutions that received federal funding were required to implement affirmative action policies.

Affirmative Action Job-hiring policies that give special consideration to members of protected classes in an effort to overcome present effects of past discrimination.

Title VII of the Civil Rights Act of 1964 neither requires nor prohibits affirmative action. Thus, most private firms have not been required to implement affirmative action policies, though many have voluntarily done so. Affirmative action programs have been controversial, however, particularly when they have resulted in reverse discrimination (which was discussed on page 641).

ON THE WEB The American Association for Affirmative Action provides a wealth of information about affirmative action at its Web site. Go to www.affirmativeaction.org/resources.html.

Constitutionality of Affirmative Action Programs

Because of their inherently discriminatory nature, affirmative action programs may violate the equal protection clause of the Fourteenth Amendment to the U.S. Constitution. The United States Supreme Court has held that any federal, state, or local affirmative action

42. *U.S. Airways, Inc. v. Barnett*, 535 U.S. 391, 122 S.Ct. 1516, 152 L.Ed.2d 589 (2002).
43. *McKennon v. Nashville Banner Publishing Co.*, 513 U.S. 352, 115 S.Ct. 879, 130 L.Ed.2d 852 (1995).

(AP Photo/Jessica Hill)

Some high schools in Seattle, Washington, make their student selections based on diversity criteria, rather than on pure past scholastic achievement. Under what circumstances is this constitutional?

program that uses racial or ethnic classifications as the basis for making decisions is subject to strict scrutiny by the courts.[44] Recall from Chapter 2 that strict scrutiny is the highest standard, which means that most programs do not survive a court's analysis under this test.

Today, an affirmative action program normally is constitutional only if it attempts to remedy past discrimination and does not make use of quotas or preferences. Furthermore, once such a program has succeeded in the goal of remedying past discrimination, it must be changed or dropped.

Affirmative Action in Schools

Most of the affirmative action cases that have reached the United States Supreme Court in the last twenty years have been in the context of university admissions programs and schools, rather than employment. Generally, the Court has found that a school admissions policy that *automatically* awards minority applicants a specified number of points needed to guarantee admission violates the equal protection clause.[45] A school can, however, "consider race or ethnicity more flexibly as a 'plus' factor in the context of individualized consideration of each and every applicant."[46] In other words, it is unconstitutional for schools to apply a mechanical formula that gives "diversity bonuses" based on race or ethnicity.

CASE EXAMPLE 25.20 In 2007, the United States Supreme Court ruled on two cases involving the use of racial classifications in assigning students to schools in Seattle, Washington, and Jefferson County, Kentucky. Both school districts had adopted student assignment plans that relied on race to determine which schools certain children would attend. The Seattle school district plan classified children as "white" or "nonwhite" and used the racial classifications as a "tiebreaker" to determine which high school the students would attend. The school district in Jefferson County classified students as "black" or "other" to assign children to elementary schools. Parent groups from the relevant public schools filed lawsuits claiming that the racial preferences violated the equal protection clause. The Court held that the school districts failed to show that the use of racial classifications in their student assignment plans was necessary to achieve their stated goal of racial diversity. Hence, the Court found that the affirmative action programs of both school districts were unconstitutional.[47] ●

State Statutes

Although the focus of this chapter has been on federal legislation, most states also have statutes that prohibit employment discrimination. Generally, the same kinds of discrimination are prohibited under federal and state legislation. In addition, state statutes often provide protection for certain individuals who are not protected under federal laws. For example, anyone over the age of eighteen is entitled to sue for age discrimination under New Jersey state law, which specifies no threshold age limit.

Furthermore, as mentioned in Chapter 24, state laws prohibiting discrimination may apply to firms with fewer employees than the threshold number required under federal statutes, thus offering protection to more workers. State laws may also allow for additional damages, such as damages for emotional distress, which are not available under federal

44. See the landmark decision in *Adarand Constructors, Inc. v. Peña,* 515 U.S. 200, 115 S.Ct. 2097, 132 L.Ed.2d 158 (1995).

45. *Gratz v. Bollinger,* 539 U.S. 244, 123 S.Ct. 2411, 156 L.Ed.2d 257 (2003).

46. *Grutter v. Bollinger,* 539 U.S. 306, 123 S.Ct. 2325, 156 L.Ed.2d 304 (2003).

47. The Court consolidated the two cases and issued one opinion for both. See *Parents Involved in Community Schools v. Seattle School District No. 1,* 551 U.S. 701, 127 S.Ct. 2738, 168 L.Ed.2d 508 (2007).

statutes.[48] Finally, some states, including California and Washington, have passed laws that end affirmative action programs in that state or modify admissions policies at state-sponsored universities.

48. For a reverse discrimination case in which a former police officer was awarded nearly $80,000 in emotional distress damages based on a violation of New Jersey's law against discrimination, see *Klawitter v. City of Trenton*, 395 N.J.Super. 302, 928 A.2d 900 (2007).

Reviewing . . . Employment Discrimination

Amaani Lyle, an African American woman, took a job as a scriptwriters' assistant at Warner Brothers Television Productions. She worked for the writers of *Friends,* a popular, adult-oriented television series. One of her essential job duties was to type detailed notes for the scriptwriters during brainstorming sessions in which they discussed jokes, dialogue, and story lines. The writers then combed through Lyle's notes after the meetings for script material. During these meetings, the three male scriptwriters told lewd and vulgar jokes and made sexually explicit comments and gestures. They often talked about their personal sexual experiences and fantasies, and some of these conversations were then used in episodes of *Friends.*

During the meetings, Lyle never complained that she found the writers' conduct offensive. After four months, she was fired because she could not type fast enough to keep up with the writers' conversations during the meetings. She filed a suit against Warner Brothers alleging sexual harassment and claiming that her termination was based on racial discrimination. Using the information presented in the chapter, answer the following questions.

1. Would Lyle's claim of racial discrimination be for intentional (disparate treatment) or unintentional (disparate impact) discrimination? Explain.
2. Can Lyle establish a *prima facie* case of racial discrimination? Why or why not?
3. Lyle was told when she was hired that typing speed was extremely important to her position. At the time, she maintained that she could type eighty words per minute, so she was not given a typing test. It later turned out that Lyle could type only fifty words per minute. What impact might typing speed have on Lyle's lawsuit?
4. Lyle's sexual-harassment claim is based on the hostile work environment created by the writers' sexually offensive conduct at meetings that she was required to attend. The writers, however, argue that their behavior was essential to the "creative process" of writing *Friends,* a show that routinely contained sexual innuendos and adult humor. Which defense discussed in the chapter might Warner Brothers assert using this argument?

Linking the Law to Management

Human Resource Management Comes to the Fore

In the good old days (at least according to company old-timers), the boss determined that the company needed additional workers. So the boss would put an ad in the newspaper, interview job applicants, and pick the ones he or she liked. If the new hires did not work out, they would simply be fired, and the process would start over again. In big companies, a personnel officer would do the hiring and firing. The point is that for much of the business history of the United States, there were no rules, regulations, or laws that placed constraints on the hiring or firing process.

As you learned in this chapter, in today's business environment an ill-conceived hiring and firing process can land a company in court facing a discrimination lawsuit. Moreover, managers today have to make sure that those who work under them do not engage in discriminatory behavior while on the job. Enter the human resource management specialist.

What Is Human Resource Management?

Human resource management (HRM) encompasses the activities required to acquire, maintain, and develop an organization's employees. HRM involves the design and application of formal systems in an organization to ensure the effective and efficient use of human talent to accomplish organizational goals.

Some of you reading this may end up in a human resources department. If so, you will need to be aware of the legal issues that you learned in this chapter (and in Chapters 23 and 24). In addition, all managers in large organizations have to be skilled in the basics of HRM. So-called flat organizations require that managers play an active role in recruiting and selecting the right personnel, as well as developing effective training programs.

The Acquisition Phase of HRM

Acquiring talented employees is the first step in an HRM system. All recruitment must be done without violating of any of the laws and regulations outlined in this chapter. Obviously, recruitment must be colorblind, as well as indifferent to gender, religion, national origin, and age. A skilled HRM professional must devise recruitment methods that do not have even the slightest hint of discriminatory basis. Recruitment methods must also give an equal chance to people with disabilities. If a candidate with a disability must be rejected, the HRM professional must make sure that the rejection is based on the applicant's lack of training or ability, not on his or her disability.

On-the-Job HRM Issues

In addition, the HRM professional must monitor the on-the-job working environment. As you learned in this chapter, if some employees harass a co-worker, the courts could decide that such actions constituted constructive discharge. Sexual harassment is another major issue to consider. An HRM professional must work closely with an employment law specialist to develop a set of antiharassment rules and make sure that all employees are familiar with them. In addition, the HRM professional must create and supervise a grievance system so that any harassment can be stopped before it becomes actionable.

HRM Issues Concerning Employee Termination

In many states, employment is at will. In principle, a company can fire any employee for cause or no cause at any time. In reality, even in employment-at-will jurisdictions, lawsuits can arise for improper termination. An informed HRM specialist will develop a system to protect her or his company from termination lawsuits. There should be well-documented procedures that outline how the company will deal with an employee's improper or incompetent behavior. The company should also have an established policy about the amount of severance pay that terminated employees will receive. Sometimes, it is better to err on the side of generosity to maintain the goodwill of terminated employees.

FOR CRITICAL ANALYSIS

What are some types of actions that an HRM professional can take to reduce the probability of harassment lawsuits against her or his company?

Key Terms

affirmative action 656
bona fide occupational qualification (BFOQ) 655
business necessity 655
constructive discharge 644
disparate-impact discrimination 640
disparate-treatment discrimination 639
employment discrimination 638
***prima facie* case** 640
protected class 638
seniority system 656
sexual harassment 644
tangible employment action 645

Chapter Summary: Employment Discrimination

Title VII of the Civil Rights Act of 1964 (See pages 639–648.)	Title VII prohibits employment discrimination based on race, color, national origin, religion, or gender. 1. *Procedures*—Employees must file a claim with the Equal Employment Opportunity Commission (EEOC). The EEOC may sue the employer on the employee's behalf; if not, the employee may sue the employer directly. 2. *Types of discrimination*—Title VII prohibits both intentional (disparate-treatment) and unintentional (disparate-impact) discrimination. Disparate-impact discrimination occurs when an employer's practice, such as hiring only persons with a certain level of education, has the effect of discriminating against a class of persons protected by Title VII. Title VII also extends to discriminatory practices, such as various forms of harassment, in the online environment. 3. *Remedies for discrimination under Title VII*—If a plaintiff proves that unlawful discrimination occurred, he or she may be awarded reinstatement, back pay, and retroactive promotions. Damages (both compensatory and punitive) may be awarded for intentional discrimination.
Discrimination Based on Age (See pages 648–650.)	The Age Discrimination in Employment Act (ADEA) of 1967 prohibits employment discrimination on the basis of age against individuals forty years of age or older. Procedures for bringing a case under the ADEA are similar to those for bringing a case under Title VII.

Continued

Chapter Summary: Employment Discrimination—Continued

Discrimination Based on Disability (See pages 650–655.)	The Americans with Disabilities Act (ADA) of 1990 prohibits employment discrimination against persons with disabilities who are otherwise qualified to perform the essential functions of the jobs for which they apply. 1. *Procedures and remedies*—To prevail on a claim under the ADA, the plaintiff must show that she or he has a disability, is otherwise qualified for the employment in question, and was excluded from the employment solely because of the disability. Procedures under the ADA are similar to those required in Title VII cases; remedies are also similar to those under Title VII. 2. *Definition of disability*—The ADA defines the term *disability* as a physical or mental impairment that substantially limits one or more major life activities, a record of such impairment, or being regarded as having such an impairment. 3. *Reasonable accommodation*—Employers are required to reasonably accommodate the needs of persons with disabilities. Reasonable accommodations may include altering job-application procedures, modifying the physical work environment, and permitting more flexible work schedules. Employers are not required to accommodate the needs of all workers with disabilities. For example, employers need not accommodate workers who pose a definite threat to health and safety in the workplace or those who are not otherwise qualified for their jobs.
Defenses to Employment Discrimination (See pages 655–656.)	If a plaintiff proves that employment discrimination occurred, employers may avoid liability by successfully asserting certain defenses. Employers may assert that the discrimination was required for reasons of business necessity, to meet a bona fide occupational qualification, or to maintain a legitimate seniority system. Evidence of prior employee misconduct acquired after the employee has been fired is not a defense to discrimination.
Affirmative Action (See pages 656–657.)	Affirmative action programs attempt to "make up" for past patterns of discrimination by giving members of protected classes preferential treatment in hiring or promotion. Such programs are subject to strict scrutiny by the courts and are often struck down for violating the Fourteenth Amendment.
State Statutes (See pages 657–658.)	Generally, state laws also prohibit the kinds of discrimination prohibited by federal statutes. State laws may provide for more extensive protection and remedies than federal laws. Also, some states, such as California and Washington, have banned state-sponsored affirmative action programs.

ExamPrep

ISSUE SPOTTERS

1 Ruth is a supervisor for Subs & Suds, a restaurant. Tim is a Subs & Suds employee. The owner announces that some employees will be discharged. Ruth tells Tim that if he has sex with her, he can keep his job. Is this sexual harassment? Why or why not?

2 Koko, a person with a disability, applies for a job at Lively Sales Corporation for which she is well qualified, but she is rejected. Lively continues to seek applicants and eventually fills the position with a person who does not have a disability. Could Koko succeed in a suit against Lively for discrimination? Explain.

BEFORE THE TEST

Check your answers to the Issue Spotters, and at the same time, take the interactive quiz for this chapter. Go to www.cengage.com/blaw/blt and click on "Chapter 25." First, click on "Answers to Issue Spotters" to check your answers. Next, click on "Interactive Quiz" to assess your mastery of the concepts in this chapter. Then click on "Flashcards" to review this chapter's Key Term definitions.

For Review

Answers for the even-numbered questions in this For Review section can be found on this text's accompanying Web site at www.cengage.com/blaw/blt. *Select "Chapter 25" and click on "For Review."*

1 Generally, what kind of conduct is prohibited by Title VII of the Civil Rights Act of 1964, as amended?
2 What is the difference between disparate-treatment discrimination and disparate-impact discrimination?
3 What remedies are available under Title VII of the 1964 Civil Rights Act, as amended?
4 What federal acts prohibit discrimination based on age and discrimination based on disability?
5 What are three defenses to claims of employment discrimination?

Hypothetical Scenarios and Case Problems

25–1 **Title VII Violations.** Discuss fully whether either of the following actions would constitute a violation of Title VII of the 1964 Civil Rights Act, as amended.

1 Tennington, Inc., is a consulting firm and has ten employees. These employees travel on consulting jobs in seven states. Tennington has an employment record of hiring only white males.

2 Novo Films, Inc., is making a film about Africa and needs to employ approximately one hundred extras for this picture. To hire these extras, Novo advertises in all major newspapers in Southern California. The ad states that only African Americans need apply.

25–2 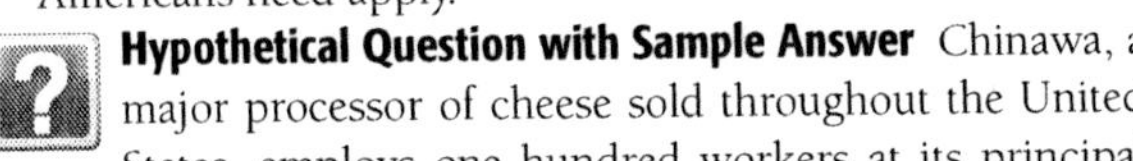 **Hypothetical Question with Sample Answer** Chinawa, a major processor of cheese sold throughout the United States, employs one hundred workers at its principal processing plant. The plant is located in Heartland Corners, which has a population that is 50 percent white and 25 percent African American, with the balance Hispanic American, Asian American, and others. Chinawa requires a high school diploma as a condition of employment for its cleaning crew. Three-fourths of the white population complete high school, compared with only one-fourth of those in the minority groups. Chinawa has an all-white cleaning crew. Has Chinawa violated Title VII of the Civil Rights Act of 1964? Explain.

—For a sample answer to Question 25–2, go to Appendix E at the end of this text.

25–3 **Religious Discrimination.** Gina Gomez, a devout Roman Catholic, worked for Sam's Department Stores, Inc., in Phoenix, Arizona. Sam's considered Gomez a productive employee because her sales exceeded $200,000 per year. At the time, the store gave its managers the discretion to grant unpaid leave to employees but prohibited vacations or leave during the holiday season—October through December. Gomez felt that she had a "calling" to go on a "pilgrimage" in October 2009 to Medjugorje, Bosnia and Herzegovina, where some persons claimed to have had visions of the Virgin Mary. The Catholic Church had not designated the site an official pilgrimage site, the visions were not expected to be stronger in October, and tours were available at other times. The store managers denied Gomez's request for leave, but she had a nonrefundable ticket and left anyway. Sam's terminated her employment, and she could not find another job. Can Gomez establish a *prima facie* case of religious discrimination? Explain.

25–4 **Case Problem with Sample Answer** For twenty years, Darlene Jespersen worked as a bartender at Harrah's Casino in Reno, Nevada. In 2000, Harrah's implemented a "Personal Best" program that included new grooming standards. Among other requirements, women were told to wear makeup "applied neatly in complimentary colors." Jespersen, who never wore makeup off the job, felt so uncomfortable wearing it on the job that it interfered with her ability to perform. Unwilling to wear makeup and not qualifying for another position at Harrah's with similar compensation, Jespersen quit the casino. She filed a suit in a federal district court against Harrah's Operating Co., the casino's owner, alleging that the makeup policy discriminated against women in violation of Title VII of the Civil Rights Act of 1964. Harrah's argued that any burdens under the new program fell equally on both genders, citing the "Personal Best" short-hair standard that applied only to men. Jespersen responded by describing her personal reaction to the makeup policy and emphasizing her exemplary record during her tenure at Harrah's. In whose favor should the court rule? Why? [*Jespersen v. Harrah's Operating Co.*, 444 F.3d 1104 (9th Cir. 2006)]

—After you have answered Problem 25–4, compare your answer with the sample answer given on the Web site that accompanies this text. Go to www.cengage.com/blaw/blt, select "Chapter 25," and click on "Case Problem with Sample Answer."

25–5 **Discrimination Based on Disability.** Cerebral palsy limits Steven Bradley's use of his legs. He uses forearm crutches for short-distance walks and a wheelchair for longer distances. Standing for more than ten or fifteen minutes is difficult. With support, however, Bradley can climb stairs and get on and off a stool. His condition also restricts the use of his fourth finger to, for example, type, but it does not limit his ability to write—he completed two years of college. His grip strength is normal, and he can lift heavy objects. In 2001, Bradley applied for a "greeter" or "cashier" position at a Wal-Mart Stores, Inc., Supercenter in Richmond, Missouri. The job descriptions stated, "No experience or qualification is required." Bradley indicated that he was available for full- or part-time work from 4:00 P.M. to 10:00 P.M. any evening. His employment history showed that he currently worked as a proofreader and that he had previously worked as an administrator. His application was rejected, according to Janet Daugherty, the personnel manager, based on his "work history" and the "direct threat" that he posed to the safety of himself and others. Bradley claimed, however, that the store refused to hire him due to his disability. What steps must Bradley follow to pursue his claim? What does he need to show to prevail? Is he likely to meet these requirements? Discuss. [*EEOC v. Wal-Mart Stores, Inc.*, 477 F.3d 561 (8th Cir. 2007)]

25–6 **Discrimination Based on Gender.** The Milwaukee County Juvenile Detention Center established a new policy that required each unit of the facility to be staffed at all times by at least one officer of the same gender as the detainees housed at a unit. The purpose of the policy, administrators said, was to reduce the likelihood of sexual abuse of juveniles by officers of the other gender. Because there were many more male units in the center than female units, the policy had the effect of reducing the number of shifts available for women officers and increasing the number of shifts for men. Two female officers sued for gender discrimination. The district court held for the county, finding that the policy of assignment was based on a bona fide occupational qualification (BFOQ) and so was not illegal gender discrimination. The officers appealed. What would be evidence that the county had a valid BFOQ? [*Henry v. Milwaukee County*, 539 F.3d 573 (7th Cir. 2008)]

25–7 **Sexual Harassment.** The Metropolitan Government of Nashville and Davidson County, Tennessee (Metro), began looking into rumors of sexual harassment by the Metro School District's employee relations director, Gene Hughes. Veronica Frazier, a Metro human resources officer, asked Vicky Crawford, a Metro employee, whether she had witnessed "inappropriate behavior" by Hughes. Crawford described several instances of sexually harassing behavior. Two other employees also reported being sexually harassed by Hughes. Metro took no action against Hughes, but soon after completing the investigation, Metro accused Crawford of embezzlement and fired her. The two other employees were also fired. Crawford filed a suit in a federal district court against Metro, claiming retaliation under Title VII. What arguments can be made that Crawford's situation does or does not qualify as a retaliation claim under Title VII? Discuss. [*Crawford v. Metropolitan Government of Nashville and Davidson County, Tennessee*, __ U.S. __, 129 S.Ct. 846, 172 L.Ed.2d 650 (2009)]

25–8 **A Question of Ethics** *Titan Distribution, Inc., employed Quintak, Inc., to run its tire mounting and distribution operation in Des Moines, Iowa. Robert Chalfant worked for Quintak as a second-shift supervisor at Titan. He suffered a heart attack in 1992 and underwent heart bypass surgery in 1997. He also had arthritis. In July 2002, Titan decided to terminate Quintak. Chalfant applied to work at Titan. On his application, he described himself as having a disability. After a physical exam, Titan's doctor concluded that Chalfant could work in his current capacity, and he was notified that he would be hired. Despite the notice, Nadis Barucic, a Titan employee, wrote "not pass px" at the top of Chalfant's application, and he was not hired. He took a job with AMPCO Systems, a parking ramp management company. This work involved walking up to five miles a day and lifting more weight than he had at Titan. In September, Titan eliminated its second shift. Chalfant filed a suit in a federal district court against Titan, in part, under the Americans with Disabilities Act (ADA). Titan argued that the reason it had not hired Chalfant was not that he did not pass the physical, but no one—including Barucic—could explain why she had written "not pass px" on his application. Later, Titan claimed that Chalfant was not hired because the entire second shift was going to be eliminated.* [Chalfant v. Titan Distribution, Inc., *475 F.3d 982 (8th Cir. 2007)*]

1 What must Chalfant establish to make his case under the ADA? Can he meet these requirements? Explain.

2 In employment-discrimination cases, punitive damages can be appropriate when an employer acts with malice or reckless indifference to an employee's protected rights. Would an award of punitive damages to Chalfant be appropriate in this case? Discuss.

Critical Thinking and Writing Assignments

25–9 **Critical Legal Thinking.** Why has the federal government limited the application of the statutes discussed in this chapter to firms with a specified number of employees, such as fifteen or twenty? Should these laws apply to all employers, regardless of size? Why or why not?

25–10 **Case Analysis Question** Go to Appendix F at the end of this text and examine Case No. 5 [*Burlington Northern and Santa Fe Railway Co. v. White*, 548 U.S. 53, 126 S.Ct. 2405, 165 L.Ed.2d 345 (2006)]. This case has been excerpted there in great detail. Review and then brief the case, making sure that your brief answers the following questions.

1 **Issue:** What was the plaintiff's complaint, the defendant's response, and the chief legal dispute between them?

2 **Rule of Law:** Which provisions of Title VII did the Court consider here, and which rule of statutory interpretation governed the Court's consideration?

3 **Applying the Rule of Law:** How did the Court interpret these provisions, and how did that interpretation apply to the circumstances in this case?

4 **Conclusion:** Based on its application of the principles in this case, what did the Court conclude?

Practical Internet Exercises

Go to this text's Web site at www.cengage.com/blaw/blt, select "Chapter 25," and click on "Practical Internet Exercises." There you will find the following Internet research exercises that you can perform to learn more about the topics covered in this chapter.

Practical Internet Exercise 25–1: LEGAL PERSPECTIVE—**Americans with Disabilities**
Practical Internet Exercise 25–2: MANAGEMENT PERSPECTIVE—**Equal Employment Opportunity**
Practical Internet Exercise 25–3: SOCIAL PERSPECTIVE—**Religious and National-Origin Discrimination**

Unit Four Cumulative Business Hypothetical

Two brothers, Ray and Paul Ashford, start a business—Ashford Brothers, Inc.—manufacturing a new type of battery system for hybrid automobiles. The batteries hit the market at the perfect time and are in great demand.

1. Loren, one of Ashford's salespersons, anxious to make a sale, intentionally quotes a price to a customer that is $500 lower than Ashford had authorized for that particular product. The customer purchases the product at the quoted price. When Ashford learns of the deal, it claims that it is not legally bound to the sales contract because it did not authorize Loren to sell the product at that price. Is Ashford bound to the contract? Discuss fully.
2. One day Gina, an Ashford employee, suffered a serious burn when she accidentally spilled some acid on her hand. The accident occurred because another employee, who was suspected of using illegal drugs, carelessly bumped into her. The hand required a series of skin-graft operations before it healed sufficiently to allow Gina to return to work. Gina wants to obtain compensation for her lost wages and medical expenses. Can she do that? If so, how?
3. After Gina's injury, Ashford decides to conduct random drug tests on all of its employees. Several employees claim that the testing violates their privacy rights. If the dispute is litigated, what factors will the court consider in deciding whether the random drug testing is legally permissible?
4. Ashford provides health insurance for its two hundred employees, including Dan. For personal medical reasons, Dan takes twelve weeks' leave. During this period, can Dan continue his coverage under Ashford's health-insurance plan? After Dan returns to work, Ashford closes Dan's division and terminates the employees, including Dan. Can Dan continue his coverage under Ashford's health-insurance plan? If so, at whose expense?
5. Aretha, another employee at Ashford, is disgusted by the sexually offensive behavior of several male employees. She has complained to her supervisor on several occasions about the offensive behavior, but the supervisor merely laughs at her concerns. Aretha decides to bring a legal action against the company for sexual harassment. Does Aretha's complaint concern *quid pro quo* harassment or hostile-environment harassment? What federal statute protects employees from sexual harassment? What remedies are available under that statute? What procedures must Aretha follow in pursuing her legal action?

Unit Four Extended Case Study: *Media General Operations, Inc. v. National Labor Relations Board*

The National Labor Relations Act (NLRA), which was discussed in Chapter 24, ensures that employees are not discriminated against for engaging in collective action in the workplace. It protects the rights of employees to organize and engage in collective bargaining and related activities. This protection prevents employers from retaliating against workers for participating in "concerted activities" and provides a process for enforcing of the rights that the NLRA guarantees.

In this Extended Case Study, we review the case of Media General Operations, Inc. v. National Labor Relations Board,[1] *which involved a worker who was fired for making a profane reference to a company executive during collective bargaining contract negotiations between the employer and the employees' union. Was the worker's derogatory remark a protected "concerted activity" under the NLRA or an unprotected "attack"?*

1. 560 F.3d 181 (4th Cir. 2009).

CASE BACKGROUND

Gregg McMillen was a journeyman pressman for *The Tampa Tribune,* a newspaper published by Media General Operations, Inc., which does business as *The Tampa Tribune.* The Graphic Communications Conference of the International Brotherhood of Teamsters, Local 180 represented McMillen and the other pressroom employees.

Negotiations between the union and the publisher over a contract to cover the employees had failed to yield results more than a year after the previous contract expired. Bill Barker, vice president of the Tribune, wrote to the pressroom workers, accusing the union of delaying the process. About two dozen employees, including McMillen, protested in a letter to Barker.

Barker responded with a letter that repeated his view. During a subsequent shift, McMillen walked into the pressroom office where Glenn Lerro, the pressroom foreman, and Joel Bridges, the assistant foreman, asked him whether he had seen the letter. He said no, referring to the company executive as "that f * * * ing idiot." He later apologized to Lerro for the remark. Three days later, he was fired for violating a workplace rule that bars the use of "threatening, abusive, or harassing language."

McMillen filed a charge with the National Labor Relations Board (NLRB), which concluded that McMillen's discharge violated the NLRA. On appeal, an administrative law judge (ALJ) found that McMillen's remark was not a protected act. The NLRB reversed this decision. The publisher appealed to the U.S. Court of Appeals for the Fourth Circuit.

MAJORITY OPINION

DUNCAN, Circuit Judge:

* * * *

* * * *Four factors * * * determine whether the Act's protection applies: (1) the place of the discussion; (2) the subject matter of the discussion; (3) the nature of the employee's outburst; and (4) whether the outburst was, in any way, provoked by an employer's unfair labor practice. If the balance is such that the conduct crosses the line from protected activity * * * to opprobrious [despicable] conduct, the worker loses the protection of the Act.* [Emphasis added.]

In the instant case, the ALJ found and the Board agreed that the first two factors weighed in favor of McMillen retaining the Act's protections. The discussion during which the derogatory remark was made took place away from the pressroom floor in an office that was used by pressroom supervisors and thus was at least semi-private. In addition, McMillen's comment occurred in the context of a discussion of Barker's letters, and those letters dealt with the ongoing contract negotiations between the Tribune and the Union. The Board also agreed with the ALJ that the fourth factor militated against extending the protection of the Act, since McMillen never claimed that he was responding to an unfair labor practice. Instead, his outburst was in response to a series of admittedly legal and truthful letters written by Barker.

Where the two adjudicators parted ways was on the significance of the third factor. The ALJ determined that the nature of the outburst was "so egregious [offensive]" that it removed McMillen's statement from the Act's protection. The Board disagreed. Analyzing the record, it found that the nature of the remark was only moderately prejudicial to McMillen's retention of the Act's protection. The Board based this determination on the fact that the remark was not made directly to Barker, that it was an isolated statement for which McMillen later apologized, and that it was neither a direct challenge to Barker's authority nor did it undermine employee discipline. Because of this different weighting of the third factor, the Board overturned the ALJ's conclusion and found that on the balance of the factors McMillen was entitled to the protection of the Act.

We disagree. The Board overreached as a matter of law in finding that the conduct in question was not so egregious as to forfeit the protection of the Act.

The lack of concurrence between Barker's lawful letter and McMillen's comment particularly disfavors protection. This was not a spontaneous outburst in response to an illegal threat but an *ad hominem* [appealing to people's emotions] attack made in the context of a discussion McMillen initiated with two supervisors. It was a response to an undisputedly legal letter issued in exercise of the company's rights. In addition, McMillen had not even read the letter in question, which further divorces his derogatory remark from the context of the ongoing labor dispute and thus makes the remark of a nature less eligible for protection. Insulting, obscene personal attacks by an employee against a supervisor need not be tolerated, even when they occur during otherwise protected activity.

It is also of particular significance * * * that McMillen made his derogatory remark in response to a series of *lawful* letters sent by his employer. Thus, the fourth factor of the * * * test weighs more than slightly against extending the Act's protection.

* * * McMillen's opprobrious *ad hominem* attack on a supervisor made at a point temporally remove[d] from and concerned only with lawful behavior by the employer falls outside the zone of protection.

* * * *

* * * We therefore reverse the judgment of the Board and reinstate the opinion of [the] ALJ.

DISSENTING OPINION

KING, Circuit Judge, dissenting.

* * * *

* * * The panel majority * * * seems to reject the Board's analysis of at least two * * * factors (factors one and three). The

Continued

majority's analysis of these factors, however, is * * * problematic and unconvincing * * * . For example, the majority suggests that factor one, i.e., the place of the discussion, should weigh against the Act's protection because McMillen's comment was made in a "setting * * * physically * * * removed from the site of the ongoing collective bargaining negotiations." * * * The majority's apparent view—that only employee conduct occurring at the physical site of labor negotiations should be accorded protection—is not only grossly unfair, but also completely at odds with precedent. That is, the typical factor one assessment focuses on whether the employee conduct, because of the place where it occurred, somehow undermined workplace discipline. Here, the majority does not—and cannot—identify anything in this record supportive of the notion that McMillen's comment undermined workplace discipline.

The panel majority further suggests that factor three—the nature of the employee's outburst—should be given more than the "moderate" weight against protection assigned to it by the Board. More specifically, the majority * * * [indicates] that insulting, obscene personal attacks by an employee against a supervisor need not be tolerated * * * . [But] care must be exercised in evaluating employee language uttered in the course of engaging in activity protected by * * * the Act, and * * * an employee's exercise of rights under the Act must not be stifled by the threat of liability for the over enthusiastic use of rhetoric. Strikingly, * * * it has been held that calling an employer's president a "son-of-a-bitch" was not so outrageous as to justify discharge. In light of this and other precedent, it was entirely rational and consistent with the Act for the Board to rule that McMillen's comment should weigh only moderately against the Act's protection.

* * * The Board's disposition of this dispute was well within the parameters of its legal authority and binding precedent, and it is instead the panel majority that has reached beyond its bounds.

QUESTIONS FOR ANALYSIS

1. **Law.** What was the majority's decision in this case? On what was this decision based?
2. **Law.** What was the dissent's position with respect to the majority's reasoning and decision? If the majority of the court had agreed with the dissent, what would have resulted?
3. **Technology.** Would the decision in this case likely have been different if the employee had made the derogatory remark online?
4. **Cultural Dimensions.** What is the possible effect on an employee who is aware of the outcome in this case?
5. **Implications for the Investor.** What does the outcome in this case suggest to an employer engaged in collective bargaining negotiations with an employees' union?

Unit Five

Business Organizations

Unit Contents

26 Sole Proprietorships and Private Franchises

27 All Forms of Partnership

28 Limited Liability Companies and Special Business Forms

29 Corporate Formation, Merger, and Termination

30 Corporate Directors, Officers, and Shareholders

31 Investor Protection,
Insider Trading, and Corporate Governance

(Othermore/Creative Commons)

Chapter 26

Sole Proprietorships and Private Franchises

"Why not go out on a limb? Isn't that where the fruit is?"

—Frank Scully, 1892–1964
(American author)

Chapter Outline

- Sole Proprietorships
- Franchises
- The Franchise Contract
- Termination of the Franchise

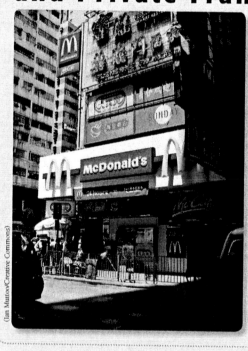

(Ian Muttoo/Creative Commons)

Learning Objectives

After reading this chapter, you should be able to answer the following questions:

1. What advantages and disadvantages are associated with the sole proprietorship?
2. What is a franchise? What are the most common types of franchises?
3. What laws govern a franchising relationship?
4. What terms and conditions are typically included in a franchise contract?
5. What is wrongful termination? In what types of situations do courts typically find that a franchisor has wrongfully terminated a franchise?

Entrepreneur One who initiates and assumes the financial risk of a new business enterprise and undertakes to provide or control its management.

Many Americans would agree with Frank Scully's comment in the chapter-opening quotation that to succeed in business one must "go out on a limb." Certainly, an entrepreneur's primary motive for undertaking a business enterprise is to make profits. An **entrepreneur** is by definition one who initiates and assumes the financial risks of a new enterprise and undertakes to provide or control its management.

One of the questions faced by anyone who wishes to start a business is what form of business organization should be chosen for the endeavor. In making this determination, the entrepreneur needs to consider a number of important factors, including (1) ease of creation, (2) the liability of the owners, (3) tax considerations, and (4) the need for capital. In studying this unit on business organizations, keep these factors in mind as you read about the various business organizational forms available to entrepreneurs.

Traditionally, entrepreneurs have used three major forms to structure their business enterprises—the sole proprietorship, the partnership, and the corporation. In this chapter, we examine sole proprietorships and discuss franchises as well. Although the franchise is not really a business organizational form, it is widely used today by entrepreneurs seeking to make profits.

Sole Proprietorships

Sole Proprietorship The simplest form of business organization, in which the owner is the business. The owner reports business income on his or her personal income tax return and is legally responsible for all debts and obligations incurred by the business.

The simplest form of business organization is a **sole proprietorship.** In this form, the owner is the business; thus, anyone who does business without creating a separate business organization has a sole proprietorship. More than two-thirds of all U.S. businesses are sole proprietorships. They are usually small enterprises—about 99 percent of the sole proprietorships in the United States have revenues of less than $1 million per year. Sole proprietors can own and manage any type of business, ranging from an informal, home-office undertaking to a large restaurant or construction firm.

Advantages of the Sole Proprietorship

(Tay Rees/Stone/Getty Images)

This woman owns a gift shop. She owns the business by herself. What are the advantages of doing business as a sole proprietorship?

A major advantage of the sole proprietorship is that the proprietor owns the entire business and has a right to receive all of the profits (because he or she assumes all of the risk). In addition, it is often easier and less costly to start a sole proprietorship than to start any other kind of business, as few legal formalities are involved.[1] No documents need to be filed with the government to start a sole proprietorship (though a state business license may be required to operate certain types of businesses).

This form of business organization also offers more flexibility than does a partnership or a corporation. The sole proprietor is free to make any decision she or he wishes concerning the business—including whom to hire, when to take a vacation, and what kind of business to pursue. In addition, the proprietor can sell or transfer all or part of the business to another party at any time and does not need approval from anyone else (as would be required from partners in a partnership or normally from shareholders in a corporation).

A sole proprietor pays only personal income taxes (including Social Security and Medicare taxes) on the business's profits, which are reported as personal income on the proprietor's personal income tax return. Sole proprietors are also allowed to establish certain retirement accounts that are tax-exempt until the funds are withdrawn.

Disadvantages of the Sole Proprietorship

The major disadvantage of the sole proprietorship is that the proprietor alone bears the burden of any losses or liabilities incurred by the business enterprise. In other words, the sole proprietor has unlimited liability, or legal responsibility, for all obligations incurred in doing business. Any lawsuit against the business or its employees can lead to unlimited personal liability for the owner of a sole proprietorship. Creditors can go after the owner's personal assets to satisfy any business debts. This unlimited liability is a major factor to be considered in choosing a business form.

EXAMPLE 26.1 Sheila Fowler operates a golf shop as a sole proprietorship. The business is located near a major golf course. A professional golfer, Dean Maheesh, is seriously injured when a display of golf clubs, which one of Fowler's employees had failed to secure, falls on him. If Maheesh sues Fowler's shop (a sole proprietorship) and wins, her personal liability could easily exceed the limits of her insurance policy. In this situation, Fowler could lose not only her business, but also her house, car, and any other personal assets that can be attached to pay the judgment. •

"*Always tell yourself: The difference between running a business and ruining a business is I.*"
Anonymous

The sole proprietorship also has the disadvantage of lacking continuity on the death of the proprietor. When the owner dies, so does the business—it is automatically dissolved. Another disadvantage is that the proprietor's opportunity to raise capital is limited to personal funds and the funds of those who are willing to make loans.

1. Although starting a sole proprietorship involves relatively few legal formalities compared with other business organizational forms, even small sole proprietorships may need to comply with certain zoning requirements, obtain appropriate licenses, and the like.

The personal liability of a sole proprietorship's owner was at issue in the following case. The case involved the federal Cable Communications Act, which prohibits a commercial establishment from broadcasting television programs to its patrons without authorization. The court had to decide whether the owner of the sole proprietorship that had installed a satellite television system was personally liable for violating this act by identifying a restaurant as a "residence" for billing purposes.

Case 26.1 Garden City Boxing Club, Inc. v. Dominguez

United States District Court, Northern District of Illinois, Eastern Division, __ F.Supp.2d __ (2006).

(AP Photo/Laura Rauch)

Who is liable for paying the fee for closed-circuit broadcast rights to a prizefight when the end-user is misidentified, causing revenue reduction?

FACTS Garden City Boxing Club, Inc. (GCB), which is based in San Jose, California, owned the exclusive right to broadcast several prizefights via closed-circuit television, including the match between Oscar De La Hoya and Fernando Vargas on September 14, 2002. GCB sold the right to receive the broadcasts to bars and other commercial venues. The fee was $20 multiplied by an establishment's maximum fire code occupancy. Antenas Enterprises in Chicago, Illinois, sells and installs satellite television systems under a contract with DISH Network. After installing a system, Antenas sends the buyer's address and other identifying information to DISH. In January 2002, Luis Garcia, an Antenas employee, identified a new customer as José Melendez at 220 Hawthorn Commons in Vernon Hills. The address was a restaurant–Mundelein Burrito–but Garcia designated the account as residential. Mundelein's patrons watched the De La Hoya–Vargas match, as well as three other fights on other dates, for which the restaurant paid only the residential rate to DISH and nothing to GCB. GCB filed a suit in a federal district court against Luis Dominguez, the sole proprietor of Antenas, to collect the fee.

ISSUE Is Dominguez personally liable for the restaurant's commercial fee to GCB?

DECISION Yes. The court issued a summary judgment in GCB's favor, holding that the plaintiff was entitled to the amount of the fee, plus damages and attorneys' fees.

REASON The court found that Mundelein Burrito was clearly a commercial establishment. "The structure of the building, an exterior identification sign, and its location in a strip mall made this obvious." Under the Cable Communications Act, "an authorized intermediary of a communication violates the Act when it divulges communication through an electronic channel to one other than the addressee." Antenas's improper designation of Mundelein Burrito as residential allowed the unauthorized broadcast of four prizefights to the restaurant. Antenas is a sole proprietorship. Furthermore, a sole proprietorship has no legal identity apart from that of the individual who owns it. A sole proprietor is personally responsible for the acts that his or her employees commit within the scope of their employment. Dominguez owns Antenas, and Garcia is Dominguez's employee. "Accordingly, Dominguez is personally liable for the damages caused by the violation of * * * the [Cable Communications] Act."

WHAT IF THE FACTS WERE DIFFERENT? *If Mundelein Burrito had identified itself as a residence when ordering the satellite system, how might the result in this case have been different?*

Franchises

Franchise Any arrangement in which the owner of a trademark, trade name, or copyright licenses another to use that trademark, trade name, or copyright in the selling of goods or services.

Franchisee One receiving a license to use another's (the franchisor's) trademark, trade name, or copyright in the sale of goods and services.

Franchisor One licensing another (the franchisee) to use the owner's trademark, trade name, or copyright in the selling of goods or services.

Instead of setting up a business form through which to market their own products or services, many entrepreneurs opt to purchase a franchise. A **franchise** is defined as any arrangement in which the owner of a trademark, a trade name, or a copyright licenses others to use the trademark, trade name, or copyright in the selling of goods or services. A **franchisee** (a purchaser of a franchise) is generally legally independent of the **franchisor** (the seller of the franchise). At the same time, the franchisee is economically dependent on the franchisor's integrated business system. In other words, a franchisee can operate as an independent businessperson but still obtain the advantages of a regional or national organization.

Today, franchising companies and their franchisees account for a significant portion of all retail sales in this country. Well-known franchises include McDonald's, 7-Eleven, and Burger King. Franchising has also become a popular way for businesses to expand their operations internationally, as will be discussed in this chapter's *Beyond Our Borders* feature on page 675.

Types of Franchises

KEEP IN MIND **Because a franchise involves the licensing of a trademark, a trade name, or a copyright, the law governing intellectual property may apply in some situations.**

Many different kinds of businesses now sell franchises, and numerous types of franchises are available. Generally, though, the majority of franchises fall into one of three classifications: distributorships, chain-style business operations, or manufacturing or processing-plant arrangements.

DISTRIBUTORSHIP In a *distributorship,* a manufacturer (the franchisor) licenses a dealer (the franchisee) to sell its product. Often, a distributorship covers an exclusive territory. An example of this type of franchise is an automobile dealership or beer distributorship.

EXAMPLE 26.2 Black Butte Beer Company distributes its brands of beer through a network of authorized wholesale distributors, each with an assigned territory. Marik signs a distributorship contract for the area from Gainesville to Ocala, Florida. If the contract states that Marik is the exclusive distributor in that area, then no other franchisee may distribute Black Butte beer in that region. •

CHAIN-STYLE BUSINESS OPERATION In a *chain-style business operation,* a franchise operates under a franchisor's trade name and is identified as a member of a select group of dealers that engage in the franchisor's business. The franchisee is generally required to follow standardized or prescribed methods of operation. Often, the franchisor requires that the franchisee maintain certain standards of operation. In addition, the franchisee may be required to obtain materials and supplies exclusively from the franchisor. McDonald's and most other fast-food chains are examples of this type of franchise. Chain-style franchises are also common in service-related businesses, including real estate brokerage firms such as Century 21 and tax-preparing services such as H&R Block, Inc.

MANUFACTURING OR PROCESSING-PLANT ARRANGEMENT In a *manufacturing or processing-plant arrangement,* the franchisor transmits to the franchisee the essential ingredients or formula to make a particular product. The franchisee then markets the product either at wholesale or at retail in accordance with the franchisor's standards. Examples of this type of franchise are Pepsi-Cola and other soft-drink bottling companies.

Laws Governing Franchising

(Baloo—Rex May)

"Hi. Would you guys be interested in a Starbux franchise?"

Because a franchise relationship is primarily a contractual relationship, it is governed by contract law. If the franchise exists primarily for the sale of products manufactured by the franchisor, the law governing sales contracts as expressed in Article 2 of the Uniform Commercial Code applies (see Chapters 15 through 17). Additionally, the federal government and most states have enacted laws governing certain aspects of franchising. Generally, these laws are designed to protect prospective franchisees from dishonest franchisors and to prohibit franchisors from terminating franchises without good cause.

FEDERAL REGULATION OF FRANCHISING The federal government regulates franchising through laws that apply to specific industries and through the Franchise Rule, created by the Federal Trade Commission (FTC).

Industry-Specific Standards. Congress has enacted laws that protect franchisees in certain industries, such as automobile dealerships and service stations. These laws protect the franchisee from unreasonable demands and bad faith terminations of the franchise by the franchisor. If an automobile manufacturer-franchisor terminates a franchise because of a dealer-franchisee's failure to comply with unreasonable demands (for example, failure to attain an unrealistically high sales quota), the manufacturer may be liable for damages.[2] Similarly, federal law prescribes the conditions under which a franchisor of service stations can terminate the franchise.[3] Federal antitrust laws (to be discussed in Chapter 32) also apply in certain circumstances to prohibit certain types of anticompetitive agreements.

The Franchise Rule. The FTC's Franchise Rule requires franchisors to disclose certain material facts that a prospective franchisee needs to make an informed decision concerning the purchase of a franchise.[4] The rule was designed to enable potential franchisees to weigh the risks and benefits of an investment. The rule requires the franchisor to make numerous written disclosures to prospective franchisees. For example, if a franchisor provides projected earnings figures, the franchisor must indicate whether the figures are based on actual data or hypothetical examples. If a franchisor makes sales or earnings projections based on actual data for a specific franchise location, the franchisor must disclose the number and percentage of its existing franchises that have achieved this result.

"Business opportunities are like buses, there's always another one coming."
Richard Branson, 1950–present
(British entrepreneur)

All representations made to a prospective franchisee must have a reasonable basis. Franchisors are also required to explain termination, cancellation, and renewal provisions of the franchise contract to potential franchisees before the agreement is signed. Those who violate the Franchise Rule are subject to substantial civil penalties, and the FTC can sue on behalf of injured parties to recover damages.

Can a franchisor satisfy the Franchise Rule by providing disclosures via the Internet? See this chapter's *Adapting the Law to the Online Environment* feature for a discussion of this topic.

Ethical Issue

Should the law require franchisors to give prospective franchisees information about potential earnings? The most common question that entrepreneurs who are thinking about starting a franchise ask is, "How much will I make?" Surprisingly, the law does not require franchisors to provide any estimate of, or actual data on, the earnings potential of a franchise. Franchisors can voluntarily choose to provide earnings data on their uniform disclosure documents but are not required to do so. If franchisors do make earnings claims, as previously mentioned, they must specify whether these figures are actual or hypothetical, follow specific rules, and have a reasonable basis for these claims. About 75 percent of franchisors choose not to provide information about earnings potential (which is Item 19 on the disclosure form).

The failure of the latest version of the FTC's Franchise Rule to require disclosure of earnings potential has led to many complaints from franchisees.[5] After all, some franchisees invest their life savings in franchises that ultimately fail because of unrealistic earnings expectations. Moreover, the franchisee may be legally responsible to continue operating and paying the franchisor even when the business is not turning a profit. For instance, Thomas Anderson asked the franchisor, Rocky Mountain Chocolate Factory, Inc. (RMCF), and five of its franchisees for earnings information before he entered into a franchise agreement, but he did not receive any data. When his chocolate franchise failed to become profitable, Anderson and his partner were ordered by a court to pay $33,109 in past due royalties and interest to RMCF (plus court costs and expenses).[6]

---

2. Automobile Dealers' Franchise Act of 1965, also known as the Automobile Dealers' Day in Court Act, 15 U.S.C. Sections 1221 *et seq.*
3. Petroleum Marketing Practices Act (PMPA) of 1979,15 U.S.C. Sections 2801 *et seq.*
4. 16 C.F.R. Part 436.
5. For example, Beth Tomei and nine other franchisees filed a class-action arbitration claim against their franchisor, Butterfly Life, a women's fitness company, for failure to disclose financial information. The arbitration was dismissed in 2009, however, because the plaintiff-franchisees reportedly failed to pay their allocated share of the arbitration fees.
6. *Rocky Mountain Chocolate Factory, Inc. v. SDMS, Inc.*, 2009 WL 579516 (D.Colo. 2009).

Adapting the Law to the Online Environment

Satisfying the FTC's Franchise Rule in the Internet Age

The Federal Trade Commission (FTC) issued its Franchise Rule in 1978, when the normal medium for transmission of information in a permanent form was on paper. When the Internet became a reality for a large number of people in the 1990s, the FTC was faced with the possibility that franchisors might use Web sites to provide downloadable information to prospective franchisees. Was such online information the equivalent of an offer that requires compliance with the FTC's Franchise Rule? The FTC said yes.

In the 1990s, the FTC issued advisory opinions allowing electronic disclosures by CD-ROM and DVD, as long as the prospective franchisee was given the option of receiving the disclosure in electronic or paper format and chose electronic. The CD-ROM or DVD had to have a label indicating that it contained the disclosures required by the FTC and the date when it was issued. In 1999, the FTC began its formal rulemaking process (see Chapter 1) to create regulations that would apply to online disclosures.[a]

Franchise.com and Others Get the Green Light

In 2001, Franchise.com, a marketer of existing franchises, became the first Web-based franchise operation to win the FTC's approval of its plan to provide electronic disclosure services for all of its franchisor advertisers. Franchise.com requires any franchisor that wishes to advertise on its Web site to provide a disclosure document containing the FTC's proposed cover-page statement regarding electronic disclosures. When a prospective franchisee comes to the Franchise.com Web site, he or she must agree to receive disclosures electronically by clicking on the appropriate button. The prospect can then obtain information on a particular franchise through the Web site. Whenever prospective franchisees access their accounts at the Web site, there are hyperlinks to written summary documents. Each time a prospective franchisee clicks on the hyperlinks, she or he is advised to download or print the disclosure document for future reference.

In 2003, McGarry Internet, Ltd., of Dublin, Ireland, received similar approval. This company sends each prospective franchisee a Uniform Franchise Offering Circular via e-mail. In 2005, the FTC approved the request of VaultraNet, which had developed an Internet-based file delivery and signature system that it uses to provide disclosure documents to prospective franchisees.

Amendments to the Franchise Rule

In 2007, amendments to the Franchise Rule allowed franchisors to provide online disclosure documents as long as they met certain requirements. In 2008, the final amended version of the rule became mandatory. Prospective franchisees must be able to download or save all electronic disclosure documents. Additional disclosures are required about lawsuits that the franchisor has filed and any past settlement agreements. A franchisor must also disclose whether the franchisor or an affiliate has the right to use other channels of distribution, such as the Internet, to make sales within the franchisee's territory. These amendments bring the federal rule into closer alignment with state franchise disclosure laws.

FOR CRITICAL ANALYSIS

Why do you think it took so long for the FTC to issue final rules about franchisors using the Internet?

a. 16 C.F.R. Part 436, 64 Fed.Reg. 57,294 (October 22, 1999).

State Regulation of Franchising State legislation varies but often is aimed at protecting franchisees from unfair practices and bad faith terminations by franchisors. Approximately fifteen states have laws similar to the federal rules requiring franchisors to provide presale disclosures to prospective franchisees.[7]

State laws may also require that a disclosure document (known as an *offering circular*) be registered or filed with a state official, or they may require that the franchisor's advertising be submitted to the state for review or approval. To protect franchisees, a state law might require the disclosure of information such as the actual costs of operation, recurring expenses, and profits earned, along with data substantiating these figures. State deceptive trade practices acts (see Chapter 33) may also apply and prohibit certain types of actions on the part of franchisors.

ON THE WEB For information about the FTC's regulations on franchising, as well as state laws regulating franchising, go to www.ftc.gov/bcp/franchise/netfran.htm.

To prevent arbitrary or bad faith terminations, state law may prohibit termination without "good cause" or require that certain procedures be followed in terminating a franchising relationship. **CASE EXAMPLE 26.3** FMS, Inc., entered into a franchise agreement with Samsung

7. These states include California, Hawaii, Illinois, Indiana, Maryland, Michigan, Minnesota, New York, North Dakota, Oregon, Rhode Island, South Dakota, Virginia, Washington, and Wisconsin.

Construction Equipment North America to become an authorized dealership for the sale of Samsung brand construction equipment. Then Samsung sold its construction-equipment business to Volvo Construction Equipment North America, Inc., which was to continue selling Samsung brand equipment. Volvo did so for a while but then started modifying and rebranding construction equipment under its own name.

When Volvo canceled FMS's franchise agreement, FMS filed a lawsuit alleging that Volvo, among other things, had violated Maine's franchise law, which prohibits termination of a franchise without "good cause." A federal appellate court, however, found that because Volvo was no longer manufacturing the Samsung brand equipment, it did have good cause to terminate FMS's franchise. If Volvo had continued making the Samsung brand equipment, the statute would have prevented it from terminating the FMS franchise, but the statute did not prohibit it from discontinuing the dealership as to the rebranded equipment.[8] ●

The Franchise Contract

The franchise relationship is defined by a contract between the franchisor and the franchisee. The franchise contract specifies the terms and conditions of the franchise and spells out the rights and duties of the franchisor and the franchisee. If either party fails to perform the contractual duties, that party may be subject to a lawsuit for breach of contract. Generally, statutes and case law governing franchising tend to emphasize the importance of good faith and fair dealing in franchise relationships.

ON THE WEB A good source for information on the purchase and sale of franchises is Franchising.org, at www.franchising.org.

Because each type of franchise relationship has its own characteristics, it is difficult to describe the broad range of details a franchising contract may include. In the remaining pages of this chapter, we will look at some of the major issues that typically are addressed in a franchise contract. The *Business Application* feature at the end of this chapter describes some steps a franchisee can take to avoid problems common in franchise agreements.

Payment for the Franchise

The franchisee ordinarily pays an initial fee or lump-sum price for the franchise license (the privilege of being granted a franchise). This fee is separate from the various products that the franchisee purchases from or through the franchisor. In some industries, the franchisor relies heavily on the initial sale of the franchise for realizing a profit. In other industries, the continued dealing between the parties brings profit to both. In most situations, the franchisor will receive a stated percentage of the annual (or monthly) sales or annual volume of business done by the franchisee. The franchise agreement may also require the franchisee to pay a percentage of advertising costs and certain administrative expenses.

Business Premises

The franchise agreement may specify whether the premises for the business must be leased or purchased outright. In some cases, a building must be constructed or remodeled to meet the terms of the agreement. The agreement usually will specify whether the franchisor supplies equipment and furnishings for the premises or whether this is the responsibility of the franchisee.

Location of the Franchise

Typically, the franchisor will determine the territory to be served. Some franchise contracts give the franchisee exclusive rights, or "territorial rights," to a certain geographic area. Other franchise contracts, though they define the territory allotted to a particular franchise,

8. *FMS, Inc. v. Volvo Construction Equipment North America, Inc.*, 557 F.3d 758 (7th Cir. 2009).

Beyond Our Borders Franchising in Foreign Nations

In the last twenty years, many U.S. companies (particularly fast-food chains and coffeehouses) have successfully expanded through franchising in nations around the globe. Franchises offer businesses a way to expand internationally without violating the legal restrictions that many nations impose on foreign ownership of businesses. Although Canada has been the most popular location for franchises in the past, during the last few years, franchisors have expanded their target locations to Asia, South America, Central America, and Mexico.

Cultural and Legal Differences Are Important

Businesspersons must exercise caution when entering international franchise relationships—perhaps even more so than when entering other types of international contracts. Differences in language, culture, laws, and business practices can seriously complicate the franchising relationship. If a U.S. franchisor has quality control standards that do not mesh with local business practices, for example, how can the franchisor maintain the quality of its product and protect its good reputation? If the law in China, for example, does not provide for the same level of intellectual property protection, how can a U.S. franchisor protect its trademark rights or prevent its "secret recipe or formula" from being copied?

The Need to Adequately Assess the Market

Because of the complexities of international franchising, successful franchisors recommend that a company seeking to franchise overseas conduct thorough research to determine whether its particular type of business will be well received in that location. It is important to know the political and cultural climate of the target country, as well as the economic trends. Marketing surveys to assess the potential success of the franchise location are crucial in international markets. Also, because complying with U.S. disclosure laws may not satisfy the legal requirements of other nations, most successful franchisors retain counsel knowledgeable in the laws of the target location. Competent counsel can draft dispute-settlement provisions (such as an arbitration clause) for international franchising contracts and advise the parties about the tax implications of operating a foreign franchise (such as import taxes and customs duties).

• For Critical Analysis *Should a U.S.-based franchisor be allowed to impose contract terms and quality control standards on franchisees in foreign nations that are different from those imposed on domestic franchisees? Why or why not?*

(AP Photo/Saurabh Das)

The RJ Corporation of India signed a franchise agreement with Disney Consumer Products. What do you think some of the elements of that agreement were?

either specifically state that the franchise is nonexclusive or are silent on the issue of territorial rights.

Many franchise cases involve disputes over territorial rights, and the implied covenant of good faith and fair dealing often comes into play in this area of franchising. If the franchise contract does not grant exclusive territorial rights to a franchisee and the franchisor allows a competing franchise to be established nearby, the franchisee may suffer a significant loss in profits. In this situation, a court may hold that the franchisor's actions breached an implied covenant of good faith and fair dealing.

Quality Control by the Franchisor

Although the day-to-day operation of the franchise business is normally left to the franchisee, the franchise agreement may provide for the amount of supervision and control agreed on by the parties. When the franchisee prepares a product, such as food, or provides a service, such as a motel, the contract often provides that the franchisor will establish certain standards for the facility. Typically, the contract will state that the franchisor is permitted to make periodic inspections to ensure that the standards are being maintained so as to protect the franchise's name and reputation.

As a general rule, the validity of a provision permitting the franchisor to establish and enforce certain quality standards is unquestioned. Because the franchisor has a legitimate interest in maintaining the quality of the product or service to protect its name and reputation, it can exercise greater control in this area than would otherwise be tolerated.

RECALL **Under the doctrine of *respondeat superior,* an employer may be liable for the torts of employees if they occur within the scope of employment, without regard to the personal fault of the employer.**

Pricing Arrangements

Franchises provide the franchisor with an outlet for the firm's goods and services. Depending on the nature of the business, the franchisor may require the franchisee to purchase certain supplies from the franchisor at an established price.[9] A franchisor cannot, however, set the prices at which the franchisee will resell the goods because such price setting may be a violation of state or federal antitrust laws, or both. A franchisor can suggest retail prices but cannot mandate them.

Termination of the Franchise

The duration of the franchise is a matter to be determined between the parties. Sometimes, a franchise will start out for a short period, such as a year, so that the franchisor can determine whether it wants to stay in business with the franchisee. Other times, the duration of the franchise contract correlates with the term of the lease for the business premises, and both are renewable at the end of that period.

Usually, the franchise agreement will specify that termination must be "for cause," such as death or disability of the franchisee, insolvency of the franchisee, breach of the franchise agreement, or failure to meet specified sales quotas. Most franchise contracts provide that notice of termination must be given. If no set time for termination is specified, then a reasonable time, with notice, will be implied. A franchisee must be given reasonable time to wind up the business—that is, to do the accounting and return the copyright or trademark or any other property of the franchisor.

A franchise agreement may grant the franchisee the opportunity to cure an ordinary, curable breach within a certain period of time after notice to forestall, or even avoid, the termination of the contract. Could a franchisee's conduct so seriously undermine the requirements of the agreement that the franchisor could cancel the contract despite a notice-and-cure provision? That was the issue in the following case.

9. Although a franchisor can require franchisees to purchase supplies from it, requiring a franchisee to purchase exclusively from the franchisor may violate federal antitrust laws (see Chapter 32).

Case 26.2 LJL Transportation, Inc. v. Pilot Air Freight Corp.

Supreme Court of Pennsylvania, 599 Pa. 546, 962 A.2d 639 (2009).
www.pacourts.us/T/SupremeCourt[a]

Does a franchisee's diversion of air transportation to a company other than the one stipulated in the franchise agreement warrant its termination?

FACTS Pilot Air Freight Corporation moves freight through a network of company-owned and company-franchised locations at airports and other sites. Franchisees included LJL Transportation Inc., which is owned by Louis Pektor and Leo Decker. The franchise agreement required LJL to assign all shipments to the Pilot network. The agreement also provided that "Pilot shall allow Franchisee an opportunity to cure a default within ninety (90) days of receipt of written notice." After eight years as a Pilot franchisee, LJL began to divert shipments to Northeast Transportation, a competing service owned by Pektor and Decker. On learning of the diversions, Pilot terminated the franchise agreement. LJL filed a suit in a Pennsylvania state court against Pilot, alleging breach of contract and asserting a right to cure. The court issued a summary judgment in Pilot's favor, and a state intermediate appellate court affirmed. LJL appealed.

ISSUE Can a franchisee's conduct justify the immediate termination of a franchise agreement even if it includes a "right-to-cure" clause?

DECISION Yes. The Pennsylvania Supreme Court affirmed the lower court's judgment. A franchise agreement may be terminated immediately "when there is a material breach of the contract so serious it goes directly to the heart and essence of the contract, rendering the breach incurable."

a. In the "Conducting Business with the Court" section, click on "Supreme Court Opinions." On that page, in the "Caption" box type "LJL"; in the "Month" pull-down menu, select "January"; in the "Year" pull-down menu, choose "2009"; and click on "Search." In the result, click on the link to access the opinion. The Unified Judicial System of Pennsylvania maintains this Web site.

Case 26.2–Continued

REASON Good faith and honesty are requirements for the performance and enforcement of a contract. Self-dealing contravenes (disregards) those requirements, violating the trust on which an agreement is based. A franchisee's breach of these duties goes to the contract's "heart." Allowing the franchisee to attempt to undo such conduct through the exercise of a right-to-cure clause would be an inadequate remedy because it could not effectively right the wrong. "Such a breach is so fundamentally destructive, it understandably and inevitably causes the trust that is the bedrock foundation and veritable lifeblood of the parties' contractual relationship to essentially evaporate." In this situation, a franchisor can terminate the franchise agreement without notice despite any right-to-cure provision.

FOR CRITICAL ANALYSIS—Ethical Consideration *From an ethical perspective, if LJL had been allowed to invoke the right-to-cure provision, could it have undone its wrongdoing so that the franchise relationship could have continued? Why or why not?*

WHY IS THIS CASE IMPORTANT? *This was a case of "first impression" for this jurisdiction–Pennsylvania. The court reviewed the decisions of courts in other jurisdictions in cases involving similar facts and applied their reasoning to reach the same conclusion in this case. These holdings emphasize that a party to a contract cannot breach it in an egregious manner and still expect to take advantage of its provisions to avoid the consequences.*

Wrongful Termination

Because a franchisor's termination of a franchise often has adverse consequences for the franchisee, much franchise litigation involves claims of wrongful termination. Generally, the termination provisions of contracts are more favorable to the franchisor. This means that the franchisee, who normally invests a substantial amount of time and funds to make the franchise operation successful, may receive little or nothing for the business on termination. The franchisor owns the trademark and hence the business.

It is in this area that statutory and case law become important. The federal and state laws discussed earlier attempt, among other things, to protect franchisees from the arbitrary or unfair termination of their franchises by the franchisors. Generally, both statutory and case law emphasize the importance of good faith and fair dealing in terminating a franchise relationship.

Preventing Legal Disputes

To avoid potential disputes regarding franchise termination, always do preliminary research on a franchisor before agreeing to enter into a franchise contract. Find out whether the franchisor has terminated franchises in the past, how many times, and for what reasons. Contact five to ten franchisees of the same franchisor and ask questions about their relationships and any problems. If the franchisor has been honest, reliable, and reasonable with its franchisees in the past, you will have a better chance of avoiding disputes over wrongful termination in the future.

The Importance of Good Faith and Fair Dealing

In determining whether a franchisor has acted in good faith when terminating a franchise agreement, the courts generally try to balance the rights of both parties. If a court perceives that a franchisor has arbitrarily or unfairly terminated a franchise, the franchisee will be provided with a remedy for wrongful termination. If a franchisor's decision to terminate a franchise was made in the normal course of the franchisor's business operations, however, and reasonable notice of termination was given to the franchisee, generally a court will not consider termination wrongful.

At issue in the following case was whether General Motors Corporation acted wrongfully in terminating its franchise with a motor vehicle dealer in Connecticut.

Case 26.3 Chic Miller's Chevrolet, Inc. v. General Motors Corp.

United States District Court, District of Connecticut, 352 F.Supp.2d 251 (2005).

(Photo by Justin Sullivan/Getty Images)

Did GM act wrongfully in terminating a Chevrolet dealership's franchise?

FACTS Chapin Miller began work as a mail clerk with General Motors Acceptance Corporation (GMAC). By 1967, Miller had succeeded sufficiently within the organization to acquire Chic Miller's Chevrolet, a General Motors Corporation (GM) dealership, in Bristol, Connecticut. As part of its operations, Chic Miller's entered into lending agreements, commonly known as floor plan financing, to enable it to buy new vehicles from GM. At first, the dealership had floor plan financing through GMAC. In 2001, however, Miller believed that GMAC was charging interest "at an inappropriately high rate" and negotiated a lower rate from Chase Manhattan Bank. In November 2002, Chase declined to provide further financing. Unable to obtain a loan from any other lender, Chic Miller's contacted GMAC, which also refused to make a deal. Under the parties' "Dealer Sales and Service Agreement," GM could terminate a dealership for "Failure of Dealer to maintain the line of credit." GM sent several notices of termination, but Chic Miller's remained open until March 2003, when it closed for seven days. GM sent a final termination notice. Chic Miller's filed a suit in a federal district court against GM, alleging, among other things, a failure to act in good faith in terminating the franchise. GM filed a motion for summary judgment.

ISSUE Did GM act wrongfully in terminating its franchise with Chic Miller's?

DECISION No. The court granted GM's motion for summary judgment. GM acted in good faith, with good cause under the applicable state statute, in terminating Chic Miller's franchise.

REASON The court stated that to terminate a franchise under the Connecticut Franchise Act, "a franchisor must: provide notice that complies with statutory requirements; have 'good cause' for the termination; and act 'in good faith.' " The court explained that there is "good cause" under the statute "if there is a failure by the dealer to comply with a provision of the franchise which is both reasonable and of material significance to the franchise relationship." In this case, the dealer failed to maintain floor plan financing, a material requirement under the franchise agreement. "[W]ithout floor plan financing, a dealership is unable to purchase motor vehicle inventory, which, in turn, severely limits a dealership's ability to earn income from vehicle sales." The dealership "will eventually lose its ability to generate revenues and become financially insolvent, and will not be able to conduct customary sales and service operations." Here, the dealer also failed to conduct sales and service operations for seven consecutive business days, another material requirement under the parties' contract.

WHAT IF THE FACTS WERE DIFFERENT? *Suppose that in March 2003, Chic Miller's had placed one newspaper ad promoting its services and had sold one car. Would the result have been different? Why or why not?*

Reviewing . . . Sole Proprietorships and Private Franchises

Carlos Del Rey decided to open a fast-food Mexican restaurant and signed a franchise contract with a national chain called La Grande Enchilada. Under the franchise agreement, Del Rey purchased the building, and La Grande Enchilada supplied the equipment. The contract required the franchisee to strictly follow the franchisor's operating manual and stated that failure to do so would be grounds for terminating the franchise contract. The manual set forth detailed operating procedures and safety standards, and provided that a La Grande Enchilada representative would inspect the restaurant monthly to ensure compliance. Nine months after Del Rey began operating his La Grande Enchilada, a spark from the grill ignited an oily towel in the kitchen. No one was injured, but by the time firefighters were able to put out the fire, the kitchen had sustained extensive damage. The cook told the fire department that the towel was "about two feet from the grill" when it caught fire, which was in compliance with the franchisor's manual that required towels to be at least one foot from the grills. Nevertheless, the next day La Grande Enchilada notified Del Rey that his franchise would terminate in thirty days for failure to follow the prescribed safety procedures. Using the information presented in the chapter, answer the following questions.

1. What type of franchise was Del Rey's La Grande Enchilada restaurant?
2. If Del Rey operates the restaurant as a sole proprietorship, then who bears the loss for the damaged kitchen? Explain.
3. Assume that Del Rey files a lawsuit against La Grande Enchilada, claiming that his franchise was wrongfully terminated. What is the main factor a court would consider in determining whether the franchise was wrongfully terminated?
4. Would a court be likely to rule that La Grande Enchilada had good cause to terminate Del Rey's franchise in this situation? Why or why not?

Business Application

What Problems Can a Franchisee Anticipate?*

A franchise arrangement appeals to many prospective businesspersons for several reasons. Entrepreneurs who purchase franchises can operate independently and without the risks associated with products that have never before been marketed. Additionally, the franchisee can usually rely on the assistance and guidance of a management network that is regional or national in scope and has been in place for some time. Franchisees do face potential problems, however. Generally, to avoid possibly significant economic and legal difficulties, it is imperative that you obtain all relevant details about the business and that you have an attorney evaluate the franchise contract for possible pitfalls.

The Franchise Fee

Almost all franchise contracts require a franchise fee payable up front or in installments. This fee often ranges between $10,000 and $50,000. For nationally known franchises, such as McDonald's, the fee may be $500,000 or more. To calculate the true cost of the franchise, however, you must also include the fees that are paid once the franchise opens for business. For example, as a franchisee, you would probably pay 2 to 8 percent of your gross sales as royalties to the franchisor (for the use of the franchisor's trademark, for example). Another 1 to 2 percent of gross sales might go to the franchisor to cover advertising costs. Although your business would benefit from the advertising, the cost of that advertising might exceed the benefits you would realize.

Electronic Encroachment and Termination Provisions

Even when the franchise contract gives the franchisee exclusive territorial rights, a problem that many franchisees do not anticipate is the adverse effects on their businesses of so-called electronic encroachment. For example, a franchise contract may give the franchisee exclusive rights to operate a franchise in a certain territory but include no provisions to prevent the franchisor from selling its products to customers located within the franchisee's territory via telemarketing, mail-order catalogues, or online services over the Internet. As a prospective franchisee, you should make sure that your franchise contract covers such contingencies and protects you against any losses you might incur from these types of competition in your area.

A major economic consequence, usually of a negative nature, will occur if the franchisor can or does terminate your franchise agreement. Before you sign a franchise contract, make sure that the contract provisions regarding termination are reasonable, are clearly specified, and provide you with adequate notice and sufficient time to wind up business.

CHECKLIST FOR THE FRANCHISEE

1. **Find out all you can about the franchisor: How long has the franchisor been in business? How profitable is the business? Is there a growing market for the product?**
2. **Obtain the most recent financial statement from the franchisor and a complete description of the business.**
3. **Obtain a clear and complete statement of all fees that you will be required to pay.**
4. **Determine whether the franchisor will help you find a suitable location, train management and employees, assist with promotion and advertising, and supply capital or credit.**
5. **Visit other franchisees in the same business. Ask them about their profitability and their experiences with the product, the market, and the franchisor.**
6. **Evaluate your training and experience in the business on which you are about to embark. Are they sufficient to ensure success as a franchisee?**
7. **Carefully examine the franchise contract provisions relating to termination of the franchise agreement. Are they specific enough to allow you to sue for breach of contract in the event the franchisor wrongfully terminates the contract? Find out how many franchises have been terminated in the past several years.**
8. **Will you have an exclusive geographic territory and, if so, for how many years? Does the franchisor have a right to engage in telemarketing, electronic marketing, and Internet or mail-order sales to customers within this territory?**
9. **Finally, the most important way to protect yourself is to have an attorney familiar with franchise law examine the contract before you sign it.**

* This *Business Application* is not meant to substitute for the services of an attorney who is licensed to practice law in your state.

Key Terms

entrepreneur 668
franchise 670
franchisee 670
franchisor 670
sole proprietorship 669

Chapter Summary: Sole Proprietorships and Private Franchises

Sole Proprietorships (See pages 669–670.)	The simplest form of business organization; used by anyone who does business without creating a separate organization. The owner is the business. The owner pays personal income taxes on all profits and is personally liable for all business debts.
Franchises (See pages 670–674.)	1. *Types of franchises*– a. Distributorship (for example, automobile dealerships). b. Chain-style operation (for example, fast-food chains). c. Manufacturing/processing-plant arrangement (for example, soft-drink bottling companies, such as Pepsi-Cola). 2. *Laws governing franchising*– a. Franchises are governed by contract law. b. Franchises are also governed by federal and state statutory laws and agency regulations.
The Franchise Contract (See pages 674–676.)	The franchise relationship is defined by a contract between the franchisor and the franchisee. The contract normally spells out the following terms: 1. *Payment for the franchise*–Ordinarily, the contract requires the franchisee (purchaser) to pay an initial fee or lump-sum price for the franchise license. 2. *Business premises*–Specifies whether the business premises will be leased or purchased by the franchisee. 3. *Location of the franchise*–Specifies the territory to be served by the franchisee. 4. *Business organization*–The franchisor may specify particular requirements for the form and capital structure of the business. 5. *Quality control*–The franchisor may require the franchisee to abide by certain standards of quality relating to the product or service offered. 6. *Pricing arrangements*–The franchisor may require the franchisee to purchase certain supplies from the franchisor at an established price but cannot set retail resale prices.
Termination of the Franchise (See pages 676–678.)	Usually, the contract provides for the date and/or conditions of termination of the franchise arrangement. Both federal and state statutes attempt to protect franchisees from franchisors who unfairly or arbitrarily terminate franchises.

ExamPrep

ISSUE SPOTTERS

1 Frank plans to open a sporting goods store and to hire Gogi and Hap. Frank will invest only his own money. He expects that he will not make a profit for at least eighteen months and will make only a small profit in the three years after that. He hopes to expand eventually. Which form of business organization would be most appropriate?

2 Thirsty Bottling Company and U.S. Beverages, Inc. (USB), enter into a franchise agreement that states the franchise may be terminated at any time "for cause." Thirsty fails to meet USB's specified sales quota. Does this constitute "cause" for termination? Why or why not?

BEFORE THE TEST

Check your answers to the Issue Spotters, and at the same time, take the interactive quiz for this chapter. Go to www.cengage.com/blaw/blt and click on "Chapter 26." First, click on "Answers to Issue Spotters" to check your answers. Next, click on "Interactive Quiz" to assess your mastery of the concepts in this chapter. Then click on "Flashcards" to review this chapter's Key Term definitions.

For Review

Answers for the even-numbered questions in this For Review *section can be found on this text's accompanying Web site at* www.cengage.com/blaw/blt. *Select "Chapter 26" and click on "For Review."*

1 What advantages and disadvantages are associated with the sole proprietorship?
2 What is a franchise? What are the most common types of franchises?
3 What laws govern a franchising relationship?
4 What terms and conditions are typically included in a franchise contract?
5 What is wrongful termination? In what types of situations do courts typically find that a franchisor has wrongfully terminated a franchise?

Hypothetical Scenarios and Case Problems

26–1 Control of a Franchise. National Foods, Inc., sells franchises to its fast-food restaurants, known as Chicky-D's. Under the franchise agreement, franchisees agree to hire and train employees strictly according to Chicky-D's standards. The regional supervisors at Chicky-D's are required to approve all job candidates before they are hired and all general policies affecting those employees. Chicky-D's reserves the right to terminate a franchise for violating the franchisor's rules. In practice, however, Chicky-D's regional supervisors routinely approve new employees and individual franchisees' policies. After several incidents of racist comments and conduct by Tim, a recently hired assistant manager at a Chicky-D's, Sharon, a counterperson at the restaurant, resigns. Sharon files a suit in a federal district court against National. National files a motion for summary judgment, arguing that it is not liable for harassment by franchise employees. Will the court grant National's motion? Why or why not?

26–2 Hypothetical Question with Sample Answer Omega Computers, Inc., is a franchisor that grants exclusive physical territories to its franchisees with retail locations, including Pete's Digital Products. Omega sells more than two hundred of the franchises before establishing an interactive Web site. On the site, a customer can order Omega's products directly from the franchisor. When Pete's sets up a Web site through which a customer can also order Omega's products, Omega and Pete's file suits against each other, alleging that each is in violation of the franchise relationship. To decide this issue, what factors should the court consider? How might these parties have avoided this conflict? Discuss.

—For a sample answer to Question 26–2, go to Appendix E at the end of this text.

26–3 Franchising. Maria, Pablo, and Vicky are recent college graduates who would like to go into business for themselves. They are considering purchasing a franchise. If they enter into a franchising arrangement, they would have the support of a large company that could answer any questions they might have. Also, a firm that has been in business for many years would be experienced in dealing with some of the problems that novice businesspersons might encounter. These and other attributes of franchises can lessen some of the risks of the marketplace. What other aspects of franchising—positive and negative—should Maria, Pablo, and Vicky consider before committing themselves to a particular franchise?

26–4 Franchise Termination. J.C., Inc., operated McDonald's restaurants in Lancaster, Ohio, under a franchise agreement with McDonald's Corp. The agreement required J.C. to make monthly payments of certain percentages of the gross sales to McDonald's. If any payment was more than thirty days late, McDonald's had the right to terminate the franchise. The agreement stated, "No waiver by [McDonald's] of any breach . . . shall constitute a waiver of any subsequent breach." McDonald's sometimes accepted J.C.'s late payments, but when J.C. defaulted on the payments in July 2010, McDonald's gave notice of thirty days to comply or surrender possession of the restaurants. J.C. missed the deadline. McDonald's demanded that J.C. vacate the restaurants. J.C. refused. McDonald's alleged that J.C. had violated the franchise agreement. J.C. claimed that McDonald's had breached the implied covenant of good faith and fair dealing. Which party should prevail and why? [*McDonald's Corp. v. C.B. Management Co.*, 13 F.Supp.2d 705 (N.D.Ill. 1998)]

26–5 Sole Proprietorship. James Ferguson operates "Jim's 11-E Auto Sales" in Jonesborough, Tennessee, as a sole proprietorship. In 1999, Consumers Insurance Co. issued a policy to "Jim Ferguson, Jim's 11E Auto Sales" covering "Owned 'Autos' Only." *Auto* was defined to include "a land motor vehicle," which was not further explained in the policy. Coverage included damage caused by the owner or driver of an underinsured motor vehicle. In 2000, Ferguson bought and titled in his own name a 1976 Harley-Davidson motorcycle, intending to repair and sell the cycle through his dealership. In October 2001, while riding the motorcycle, Ferguson was struck by an auto driven by John Jenkins. Ferguson filed a suit in a Tennessee state court against Jenkins—who was underinsured with respect to Ferguson's medical bills—and Consumers. The insurer argued, among other things, that because the motorcycle was bought and titled in Ferguson's own name, and he was riding it at the time of the accident, it was his personal vehicle and thus was not covered under the dealership's policy. What is the relationship between a sole proprietor and a sole proprietorship? How might this status affect the court's decision in this case? [*Ferguson v. Jenkins*, 204 S.W.3d 779 (Tenn.App. 2006)]

26–6 Case Problem with Sample Answer Walid Elkhatib, a Palestinian Arab, emigrated to the United States in 1971 and became a U.S. citizen. Eight years later, Elkhatib bought a Dunkin' Donuts, Inc., franchise in Bellwood, Illinois. Dunkin' Donuts began offering breakfast sandwiches with bacon, ham, or sausage through its franchises in 1984, but Elkhatib refused to sell these items at his store on the ground that his religion forbade the handling of pork. In 1995, Elkhatib opened a second franchise in Berkeley, Illinois, at which he also refused to sell pork products. The next year, at both locations, Elkhatib began selling meatless sandwiches. In 1998, Elkhatib opened a third franchise in Westchester, Illinois. When he proposed to relocate this franchise, Dunkin' Donuts refused to approve the new location and added that it would not renew any of his franchise agreements because he did not carry the full sandwich line. Elkhatib filed a suit in a federal district court against Dunkin' Donuts and others. The defendants filed a motion for summary judgment. Did Dunkin' Donuts act in good faith in its relationship with Elkhatib? Explain. [*Elkhatib v. Dunkin' Donuts, Inc.*, 493 F.3d 827 (7th Cir. 2007)]

—After you have answered Problem 26–6, compare your answer with the sample answer given on the Web site that accompanies this text. Go to www.cengage.com/blaw/blt, select "Chapter 26," and click on "Case Problem with Sample Answer."

26–7 **Sole Proprietorship.** Julie Anne Gaskill is an oral and maxillofacial surgeon in Bowling Green, Kentucky. Her medical practice is a sole proprietorship consisting of her as the sole surgeon, with office staff. She sees every patient, exercises all professional judgment and skill, and manages the business. When Gaskill and her spouse, John Robbins, initiated divorce proceedings in a Kentucky state court, her accountant estimated the value of the practice at $221,610, excluding goodwill. Robbins's accountant estimated the value at $669,075, including goodwill. Goodwill is the ability or reputation of a business to draw customers, get them to return, and contribute to future profitability. How can a sole proprietor's reputation, skill, and relationships with customers be valued? Could these qualities be divided into "enterprise" and "personal" goodwill, with some goodwill associated with the business and some solely due to the personal qualities of the proprietor? If so, what might comprise each type? Is this an effective method for valuing Gaskill's practice? Discuss. [*Gaskill v. Robbins*, 282 S.W.3d 306 (Ky. 2009)]

26–8 **A Question of Ethics** *In August 2004, Ralph Vilardo contacted Travel Center, Inc., in Cincinnati, Ohio, to buy a trip to Florida in December for his family to celebrate his fiftieth wedding anniversary. Vilardo paid $6,900 to David Sheets, the sole proprietor of Travel Center. Vilardo also paid $195 to Sheets for a separate trip to Florida in February 2005. Sheets assured Vilardo that everything was set, but in fact no arrangements were made. Later, two unauthorized charges for travel services totaling $1,182.35 appeared on Vilardo's credit-card statement. Vilardo filed a suit in an Ohio state court against Sheets and his business, alleging, among other things, fraud and violations of the state consumer protection law. Vilardo served Sheets and Travel Center with copies of the complaint, the summons, a request for admissions, and other documents filed with the court, including a motion for summary judgment. Responses to each of these filings were subject to certain time limits. Sheets responded once on his own behalf with a denial of all of Vilardo's claims. Travel Center did not respond. [*Vilardo v. Sheets, __ N.E.2d __ (12 Dist. 2006)]*

1 Almost four months after Vilardo filed his complaint, Sheets decided that he was unable to adequately represent himself and retained an attorney who asked the court for more time. Should the court grant this request? Why or why not? Ultimately, what should the court rule in this case?
2 Sheets admitted that "Travel Center" was a sole proprietorship. He also argued that liability might be imposed on his business but not on himself. How would you rule with respect to this argument? Would there be anything unethical about allowing Sheets to avoid liability on this basis? Explain.

Critical Thinking and Writing Assignments

26–9 **Critical Legal Thinking.** Suppose that a franchisor requires the franchisee to purchase a particular type of van that will be used to deliver the franchised carpet-cleaning services to the public. If the van is involved in an accident that causes injury to a person, should the franchisor be held liable for the injuries? What are the arguments for and against holding the franchisor liable under the circumstances?

26–10 **Critical Thinking and Writing Assignment for Business.** Jordan Mendelson is interested in starting a kitchen franchise business. Customers will come to the business to assemble gourmet dinners and then take the prepared meals to their homes for cooking. The franchisor requires each store to use a specific layout and provides the recipes for various dinners, but the franchisee is not required to purchase the food products from the franchisor. What general factors should Mendelson consider before entering a contract to start such a franchise? Is location important? Are there any laws that Mendelson should consider due to the fact that this franchise involves food preparation and sales? Should Mendelson operate this business as a sole proprietorship? Why or why not?

Practical Internet Exercises

Go to this text's Web site at www.cengage.com/blaw/blt, select "Chapter 26," and click on "Practical Internet Exercises." There you will find the following Internet research exercises that you can perform to learn more about the topics covered in this chapter.

Practical Internet Exercise 26–1: Legal Perspective—**Starting a Business**
Practical Internet Exercise 26–2: Management Perspective—**Franchises**

Chapter 27

All Forms of Partnership

"All men's gains . . . are the fruit of venturing."

—Herodotus, fifth century B.C.E. (Greek historian)

Chapter Outline

- Basic Partnership Concepts
- Partnership Formation
- Partnership Operation, Dissociation, and Termination
- Limited Liability Partnerships
- Limited Partnerships

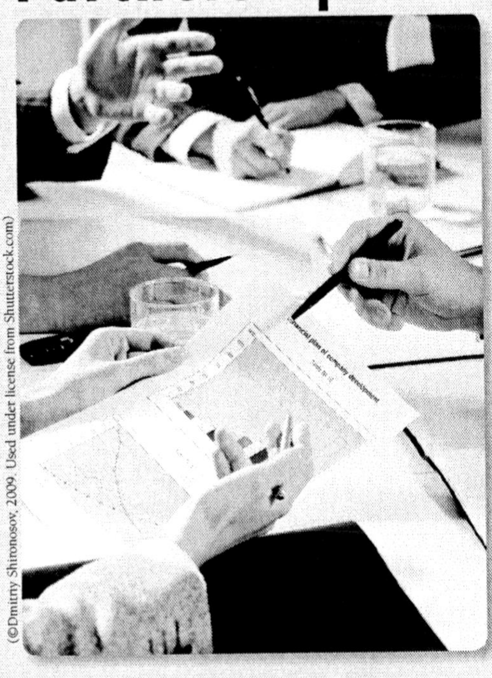

(©Dmitry Shironosov, 2009. Used under license from Shutterstock.com)

Learning Objectives

After reading this chapter, you should be able to answer the following questions:

1. What are the three essential elements of a partnership?
2. What are the rights and duties of partners in an ordinary partnership?
3. What is meant by joint and several liability? Why is this often considered to be a disadvantage of the partnership form of business?
4. What advantages do limited liability partnerships offer to businesspersons that are not offered by general partnerships?
5. What are the key differences between the rights and liabilities of general partners and those of limited partners?

Traditionally, the two most common forms of business organization selected by two or more persons entering into business together are the partnership and the corporation. A *partnership* arises from an agreement, express or implied, between two or more persons to carry on a business for profit. Partners are co-owners of a business and have joint control over its operation and the right to share in its profits. In this chapter, we focus on partnerships. (Corporations will be discussed in Chapters 28 through 30.)

We open the chapter with an examination of ordinary partnerships, or *general partnerships,* and the rights and duties of partners in this traditional business entity. We then examine some special forms of partnerships known as *limited liability partnerships* and *limited partnerships,* which receive different treatment under the law. As the chapter-opening quotation indicates, all gains are the "fruit of venturing," and partnerships—to the extent that they encourage business ventures—contribute to those gains.

Basic Partnership Concepts

Partnerships are governed both by common law concepts—in particular, those relating to agency—and by statutory law. As in so many other areas of business law, the National Conference of Commissioners on Uniform State Laws has drafted uniform laws for partnerships, and these uniform laws have been widely adopted by the states.

Agency Concepts and Partnership Law

When two or more persons agree to do business as partners, they enter into a special relationship with one another. To an extent, their relationship is similar to an agency relationship because each partner is deemed to be the agent of the other partners and of the partnership. The common law agency concepts outlined in Chapter 23 thus apply—specifically, the imputation of knowledge of, and responsibility for, acts done within the scope of the partnership relationship. In their relationships with one another, partners, like agents, are bound by fiduciary ties.

In one important way, however, partnership law is distinct from agency law. A partnership is based on a voluntary contract between two or more competent persons who agree to commit financial capital, labor, and skill to a business with the understanding that profits and losses will be shared. In a nonpartnership agency relationship, the agent usually does not have an ownership interest in the business nor is he or she obliged to bear a portion of the ordinary business losses.

The Uniform Partnership Act

ON THE WEB You can find summaries, texts, and the legislative history of numerous uniform acts, including the UPA, at the Web site of the National Conference of Commissioners on Uniform State Laws at www.nccusl.org.

The Uniform Partnership Act (UPA) governs the operation of partnerships *in the absence of express agreement* and has done much to reduce controversies in the law relating to partnerships. In other words, the partners are free to establish rules for their partnership that differ from those stated in the UPA. Except for Louisiana, every state has adopted the UPA. The majority of states have adopted the most recent version of the UPA, which was issued in 1994 and amended in 1997 to provide limited liability for partners in a limited liability partnership.[1] We therefore base our discussion of the UPA in this chapter on the 1997 version of the act and refer to older versions of the UPA in footnotes when appropriate.

Definition of Partnership

Partnership An agreement by two or more persons to carry on, as co-owners, a business for profit.

Parties sometimes find themselves in conflict over whether their business enterprise is a legal partnership, especially in the absence of a formal, written partnership agreement. The UPA defines a **partnership** as "an association of two or more persons to carry on as co-owners a business for profit" [UPA 101(6)]. Note that the UPA's definition of *person* includes corporations, so a corporation can be a partner in a partnership [UPA 101(10)]. The *intent* to associate is a key element of a partnership, and a person cannot join a partnership unless all of the other partners consent [UPA 401(i)].

When Does a Partnership Exist?

In resolving disputes over whether partnership status exists, courts will usually look for the following three essential elements, which are implicit in the UPA's definition of a general partnership:

KEEP IN MIND Two or more persons are required to form a partnership. Other forms of business can be organized by a single individual.

1. A sharing of profits and losses.
2. A joint ownership of the business.
3. An equal right to be involved in the management of the business.

Joint ownership of property does not in and of itself create a partnership. In fact, the sharing of gross revenues and even profits from such ownership is usually not enough

1. At the time this book went to press, two-thirds of the states, as well as the District of Columbia, Puerto Rico, and the U.S. Virgin Islands, had adopted the UPA with the 1997 amendments. Excerpts from the latest version of the UPA are presented on the Web site that accompanies this text.

"Oh, thank you, Lord! Do I have to tell my partner?"

to create a partnership [UPA 202(c)(1), (2)]. **EXAMPLE 27.1** Chiang and Burke jointly own a piece of rural property. They lease the land to a farmer with the understanding that—in lieu of set rental payments—they will receive a share of the profits from the farming operation conducted by the farmer. This arrangement normally would not make Chiang, Burke, and the farmer partners. •

Note, though, that while the sharing of profits from ownership of property does not prove the existence of a partnership, sharing *both profits and losses* usually does. **EXAMPLE 27.2** Two sisters, Zoe and Cienna, buy a restaurant together, open a joint bank account from which they pay for expenses and supplies, and share the net profits (or losses) that the restaurant generates. Zoe manages the restaurant and Cienna handles the bookkeeping. After eight years, Cienna stops doing the bookkeeping and does no other work for the restaurant. Zoe, who is now operating the restaurant by herself, no longer wants to share the profits with Cienna. Zoe claims that she and Cienna did not establish a partnership. In this situation, a court would find that a partnership existed because the sisters shared management responsibilities, had a joint bank account, and shared the profits and losses of the restaurant equally. •

Entity versus Aggregate Theory of Partnerships

At common law, a partnership was treated only as an aggregate of individuals and never as a separate legal entity. Thus, at common law a lawsuit could never be brought by or against the firm in its own name; each individual partner had to sue or be sued.

Today, in contrast, a majority of the states follow the UPA and treat a partnership as an entity for most purposes. For example, a partnership usually can sue or be sued, collect judgments, and have all accounting procedures in the name of the partnership entity [UPA 201, 307(a)]. As an entity, a partnership may hold the title to real or personal property in its name rather than in the names of the individual partners. Additionally, federal procedural laws permit the partnership to be treated as an entity in suits in federal courts and bankruptcy proceedings.

Pass-Through Entity A business entity that has no tax liability. The entity's income is passed through to the owners, and the owners pay taxes on the income.

Information Return A tax return submitted by a partnership that only reports the income and losses earned by the business. The partnership as an entity does not pay taxes on the income received by the partnership.

For federal income tax purposes, however, the partnership is treated as an aggregate of the individual partners rather than as a separate legal entity. The partnership is a pass-through entity and not a tax-paying entity. A **pass-through entity** is a business entity that has no tax liability; the entity's income is passed through to the owners of the entity, who pay taxes on it. Thus, the income or losses the partnership incurs are "passed through" the entity framework and attributed to the partners on their individual tax returns. The partnership itself has no tax liability and is responsible only for filing an **information return** with the Internal Revenue Service. The firm itself pays no taxes. A partner's profit from the partnership (whether distributed or not) is taxed as individual income to the individual partner.

Partnership Formation

As a general rule, agreements to form a partnership can be *oral, written,* or *implied by conduct.* Some partnership agreements, however, must be in writing (or an electronic record) to be legally enforceable under the Statute of Frauds (see Chapter 12 for details).

Articles of Partnership A written agreement that sets forth each partner's rights and obligations with respect to the partnership.

A partnership agreement, called **articles of partnership,** can include any terms that the parties wish, unless they are illegal or contrary to public policy or statute [UPA 103]. The terms commonly included in a partnership agreement are listed in Exhibit 27–1 on the following page. (Creating a partnership agreement in another country may involve additional requirements, as this chapter's *Beyond Our Borders* feature on page 687 explains.)

Exhibit 27–1 Common Terms Included in a Partnership Agreement

Basic structure	1. Name of the partnership. 2. Names of the partners. 3. Location of the business and the state law under which the partnership is organized. 4. Purpose of the partnership. 5. Duration of the partnership.
Capital contributions	1. Amount of capital that each partner is contributing. 2. The agreed-on value of any real or personal property that is contributed instead of cash. 3. How losses and gains on contributed capital will be allocated and whether contributions will earn interest.
Sharing of profits and losses	1. Percentage of the profits and losses of the business that each partner will receive. 2. When distributions of profit will be made and how net profit will be calculated.
Management and control	1. How management responsibilities will be divided among the partners. 2. Name(s) of the managing partner or partners and whether other partners have voting rights.
Accounting and partnership records	1. Name of the bank in which the partnership will maintain its business and checking accounts. 2. Statement that an accounting of partnership records will be maintained and that any partner, or her or his agent, can review these records at any time. 3. The dates of the partnership's fiscal year (if used) and when the annual audit of the books will take place.
Dissociation and dissolution	1. Events that will cause the dissociation of a partner or dissolve the partnership, such as the retirement, death, or incapacity of any partner. 2. How partnership property will be valued and apportioned on dissociation and dissolution. 3. Whether an arbitrator will determine the value of partnership property on dissociation and dissolution and whether that determination will be binding.
Arbitration	1. Whether arbitration is required for any dispute relating to the partnership agreement.

Duration of the Partnership

The partnership agreement can specify the duration of the partnership by stating that it will continue until a certain date or the completion of a particular project. A partnership that is specifically limited in duration is called a *partnership for a term*. Generally, withdrawing from a partnership for a term prematurely (before the expiration date) constitutes a breach of the agreement, and the responsible partner can be held liable for any resulting losses [UPA 602(b)(2)]. If no fixed duration is specified, the partnership is a *partnership at will*.

An attorney is having two partners sign a formal partnership agreement. What might be included in this agreement?

Partnership by Estoppel

Occasionally, persons who are not partners may nevertheless hold themselves out as partners and make representations that third parties rely on in dealing with them. In such a situation, a court may conclude that a *partnership by estoppel* exists. The law does not confer any partnership rights on these persons, but it may impose liability on them. This is also

Beyond Our Borders Doing Business with Foreign Partners

U.S. businesspersons who wish to operate a partnership in another country often discover that the country requires local participation. This means that nationals of the host country must own a specific share of the business. In other words, the partnership will have to include one or more partners who live in the host country. Sometimes, U.S. businesspersons are reluctant to establish partnerships in a country that requires local participation. They fear that if the partnership breaks up, the technology and expertise developed by the partnership business may end up in the hands of a future competitor. In that event, the U.S. parties may have little recourse under the host country's laws against their former partners' use of the intellectual property.

• **For Critical Analysis**

Do local participation rules benefit countries in the long run? Explain.

true when a partner represents, expressly or impliedly, that a nonpartner is a member of the firm. Whenever a third person has reasonably and detrimentally relied on the representation that a nonpartner was part of the partnership, a partnership by estoppel is deemed to exist. When this occurs, the nonpartner is regarded as an agent whose acts are binding on the partnership [UPA 308].

CASE EXAMPLE 27.3 Gary Chavers operated Chavers Welding and Construction (CWC). His sons Reggie and Mark worked in the business as well. CWC contracted with Epsco, Inc., to provide payroll and employee services. Initially, Epsco collected payments for its services each week, but later Epsco extended credit to CWC, which the Chaverses had represented was a partnership. Eventually, when CWC's account was more than $80,000 delinquent, Epsco filed a lawsuit to recover payment. Gary filed for bankruptcy, and his obligation to Epsco was discharged. Reggie and Mark claimed that their father owned CWC as a sole proprietor and that they were not partners in the business. The court, however, held that the sons were liable for CWC's debts based on partnership by estoppel. Because the Chaverses had represented to Epsco that CWC was a partnership and Epsco had relied on this representation when extending credit, the sons could not claim that no partnership existed.[2] •

Partnership Operation, Dissociation, and Termination

The rights and duties of partners are governed largely by the specific terms of their partnership agreement. In the absence of provisions to the contrary in the partnership agreement, the law imposes the rights and duties discussed here. The character and nature of the partnership business generally influence the application of these rights and duties.

Rights of Partners

The rights of partners in a partnership relate to the following areas: management, interest in the partnership, compensation, inspection of books, accounting, and property.

Management Rights In a general partnership, all partners have equal rights in managing the partnership [UPA 401(f)]. Unless the partners agree otherwise, each partner has one vote in management matters *regardless of the proportional size of his or her interest in the firm*. Often, in a large partnership, partners will agree to delegate daily management responsibilities to a management committee made up of one or more of the partners.

The majority rule controls decisions in ordinary matters connected with partnership business, unless otherwise specified in the agreement. Decisions that significantly affect the

2. *Chavers v. Epsco, Inc.*, 352 Ark. 65, 98 S.W.3d 421 (2003).

nature of the partnership or that are not apparently for carrying on the ordinary course of the partnership business, or business of the kind, however, require the *unanimous* consent of the partners [UPA 301(2), 401(i), (j)].

Unanimous consent is likely to be required for a decision to undertake any of the following actions:

1. To alter the essential nature of the firm's business as expressed in the partnership agreement or to alter the capital structure of the partnership.
2. To admit new partners or to enter a wholly new business.
3. To assign partnership property to a trust for the benefit of creditors.
4. To dispose of the partnership's goodwill.
5. To confess judgment against the partnership or to submit partnership claims to arbitration. (A **confession of judgment** is the act of a debtor permitting a judgment to be entered against her or him by a creditor, for an agreed sum, without the institution of legal proceedings.)
6. To undertake any act that would make further conduct of partnership business impossible.
7. To amend the partnership agreement.

Confession of Judgment The act or agreement of a debtor permitting a judgment to be entered against him or her by a creditor, for an agreed sum, without the institution of legal proceedings.

Interest in the Partnership Each partner is entitled to the proportion of business profits and losses designated in the partnership agreement. If the agreement does not apportion profits (indicate how the profits will be shared), the UPA provides that profits will be shared equally. If the agreement does not apportion losses, losses will be shared in the same ratio as profits [UPA 401(b)].

EXAMPLE 27.4 The partnership agreement for Rico and Brent provides for capital contributions of $60,000 from Rico and $40,000 from Brent, but it is silent as to how Rico and Brent will share profits or losses. In this situation, Rico and Brent will share both profits and losses equally. If their partnership agreement provided for profits to be shared in the same ratio as capital contributions, however, 60 percent of the profits would go to Rico, and 40 percent would go to Brent. If their partnership agreement was silent as to losses, losses would be shared in the same ratio as profits (60 percent and 40 percent, respectively). ●

"Forty for you, sixty for me—and equal partners we will be."

Anonymous

Compensation Devoting time, skill, and energy to partnership business is a partner's duty and generally is not a compensable service. Rather, as mentioned, a partner's income from the partnership takes the form of a distribution of profits according to the partner's share in the business. Partners can, of course, agree otherwise. For example, the managing partner of a law firm often receives a salary in addition to her or his share of profits for performing special administrative or managerial duties.

Inspection of Books Partnership books and records must be kept accessible to all partners. Each partner has the right to receive (and the corresponding duty to produce) full and complete information concerning the conduct of all aspects of partnership business [UPA 403]. Each firm keeps books for recording and preserving such information. Partners contribute the information, and a bookkeeper or an accountant typically has the duty to preserve it. The books must be kept at the firm's principal business office and cannot be removed without the consent of all of the partners. Every partner, whether active or inactive, is entitled to inspect all books and records on demand and can make copies of the materials. The personal representative of a deceased partner's estate has the same right of access to partnership books and records that the decedent would have had [UPA 403].

Accounting of Partnership Assets or Profits An accounting of partnership assets or profits is required to determine the value of each partner's share in the partnership. An accounting can be performed voluntarily, or it can be compelled by court order. Under UPA 405(b), a partner has the right to bring an action for an accounting during the term of the partnership, as well as on the firm's *dissolution* and *winding up* (see pages 694 and 695).

PROPERTY RIGHTS Property acquired *by* a partnership is the property of the partnership and not of the partners individually [UPA 203]. Partnership property includes all property that was originally contributed to the partnership and anything later purchased by the partnership or in the partnership's name (except in rare circumstances) [UPA 204]. A partner may use or possess partnership property only on behalf of the partnership [UPA 401(g)]. A partner is *not* a co-owner of partnership property and has no right to sell, mortgage, or transfer partnership property to another.[3]

In other words, partnership property is owned by the partnership as an entity and not by the individual partners. Thus, a creditor of an individual partner cannot seek to use partnership property to satisfy the partner's debt. Such a creditor can, however, petition a court for a **charging order** to attach the individual partner's interest in the partnership (her or his proportionate share of the profits and losses and right to receive distributions) to satisfy the partner's obligation. (A partner can also assign her or his right to a share of the partnership profits to another to satisfy a debt.)

Charging Order In partnership law, an order granted by a court to a judgment creditor that entitles the creditor to attach profits or assets of a partner on the dissolution of the partnership.

Duties and Liabilities of Partners

The duties and liabilities of partners are basically derived from agency law. Each partner is an agent of every other partner and acts as both a principal and an agent in any business transaction within the scope of the partnership agreement. Each partner is also a general agent of the partnership in carrying out the usual business of the firm "or business of the kind carried on by the partnership" [UPA 301(1)]. Thus, every act of a partner concerning partnership business, or "business of the kind," and every contract signed in the partnership's name bind the firm.

FIDUCIARY DUTIES The fiduciary duties a partner owes to the partnership and the other partners are the *duty of loyalty* and the *duty of care* [UPA 404(a)]. The duty of loyalty requires a partner to account to the partnership for "any property, profit, or benefit" derived by the partner from the partnership's business or the use of its property [UPA 404(b)]. A partner must also refrain from competing with the partnership in business or dealing with the firm as an adverse party.

A partner's duty of care involves refraining from "grossly negligent or reckless conduct, intentional misconduct, or a knowing violation of law" [UPA 404(c)].[4] A partner is not liable to the partnership for simple negligence or honest errors in judgment in conducting partnership business, though.

"Surround yourself with partners who are better than you are."
David Ogilvy, 1911–1999
(Scottish advertising executive)

These duties may not be waived or eliminated in the partnership agreement, and in fulfilling them each partner must act consistently with the obligation of good faith and fair dealing, which applies to all contracts, including partnership agreements [UPA 103(b), 404(d)]. The agreement can specify acts that the partners agree will violate a fiduciary duty.

Note that a partner may pursue his or her own interests without automatically violating these duties [UPA 404(e)]. The key is whether the partner has disclosed the interest to the other partners. **EXAMPLE 27.5** Jayne Trell, a partner at Jacoby & Meyers, owns a shopping mall. Trell may vote against a partnership proposal to open a competing mall, provided that

3. Under the previous version of the UPA, partners were *tenants in partnership*, and every partner was a co-owner with all other partners of the partnership property. The current UPA does not recognize this concept.

4. The previous version of the UPA touched only briefly on the duty of loyalty and left the details of the partners' fiduciary duties to be developed under the law of agency.

she has fully disclosed her interest in the shopping mall to the other partners at the firm. ● A partner cannot make secret profits or put self-interest before his or her duty to the interest of the partnership, however.

AUTHORITY OF PARTNERS The UPA affirms general principles of agency law that pertain to the authority of a partner to bind a partnership in contract. A partner may also subject the partnership to tort liability under agency principles. When a partner is carrying on partnership business or business of the kind with third parties in the usual way, both the partner and the firm share liability.

The partnership will not be liable, however, if the third parties know that the partner has no such authority. **EXAMPLE 27.6** Patricia, a partner in Heise, Green, and Stevens, applies for a loan on behalf of the partnership without authorization from the other partners. The bank manager knows that Patricia has no authority. If the bank manager grants the loan, Patricia will be personally bound, but the firm will not be liable. ●

A partnership may file in a designated state office a "statement of partnership authority" to limit the capacity of a partner to act as the firm's agent or transfer property on its behalf [UPA 105, 303]. Any limit on a partner's authority, however, normally does not affect a third party who does not know about the statement (except in real estate transactions when the statement has been recorded with the appropriate state office).

Agency concepts relating to actual (express and implied) authority, apparent authority, and ratification are also applicable to partnerships. The extent of *implied authority* is generally broader for partners than for ordinary agents, though.

The Scope of Implied Powers. The character and scope of the partnership business and the customary nature of the particular business operation determine the implied powers of the partners. For example, a *trading partnership* is a business that has goods in inventory and makes profits buying and selling those goods. A partner in a trading partnership has a wide range of implied powers, such as to advertise products, hire employees, and extend the firm's credit by issuing or signing checks (see Chapters 18 and 19).

In an ordinary partnership, the partners can exercise all implied powers reasonably necessary and customary to carry on that particular business. Some customarily implied powers include the authority to make warranties on goods in the retail sales business and the power to enter into contracts consistent with the firm's regular course of business. Most partners also have the implied authority to make representations to others concerning partnership affairs, and these statements may be admissible as evidence against the partnership. A partner might also have the implied power to convey real property in the firm's name when such conveyances are part of the ordinary course of partnership business.

Authorized versus Unauthorized Actions. If a partner acts within the scope of authority, the partnership is legally bound to honor the partner's commitments to third parties. For instance, a partner's authority to sell partnership products carries with it the implied authority to transfer title and to make the usual warranties. **EXAMPLE 27.7** Jamie Schwab is a partner in a firm that operates a retail tire store. When Schwab negotiates a contract with a customer for the sale of a set of tires, he promises that "each tire will be warranted for normal wear for 40,000 miles." Because Schwab has authority to make warranties, the partnership is bound to honor the warranty. Schwab would not, however, have the authority to sell the partnership's office equipment, fixtures, or other property without the consent of all of the other partners. ●

In addition, because partnerships are formed to generate profits, a partner generally does not have the authority to make charitable contributions without the consent of the other partners. Such actions are not binding on the partnership unless they are ratified by all of the other partners.

LIABILITY OF PARTNERS One significant disadvantage associated with a traditional partnership is that partners are *personally* liable for the debts of the partnership. Moreover, in most states the liability is essentially unlimited because the acts of one partner in the ordinary course of business subject the other partners to personal liability [UPA 305]. The following subsections explain the rules on a partner's liability. The *Business Application* feature at the end of this chapter discusses the effect that liability rules are having on the rate of partnership formation.

Joint Liability Shared liability. In partnership law, partners incur joint liability for partnership obligations and debts. For example, if a third party sues a partner on a partnership debt, the partner has the right to insist that the other partners be sued with him or her.

Joint Liability. At one time, each partner in a partnership generally was jointly liable for the partnership's obligations. **Joint liability** means that a third party must sue all of the partners as a group, but each partner can be held liable for the full amount.[5] If a third party sued the partnership on a contractual debt, the lawsuit had to name all of the partners as defendants to seek partnership assets to pay any judgment. With joint liability, the partnership's assets must be exhausted before creditors can reach the partners' individual assets.[6]

Joint and Several Liability In partnership law, a doctrine under which a plaintiff may sue, and collect a judgment from, all of the partners together (jointly) or one or more of the partners separately (severally, or individually). This is true even if one of the partners sued did not participate in, ratify, or know about whatever it was that gave rise to the cause of action.

Joint and Several Liability. In the majority of states, under UPA 306(a), partners are jointly and severally (separately or individually) liable for all partnership obligations, including contracts, torts, and breaches of trust. **Joint and several liability** means that a third party may sue all of the partners together (jointly) or one or more of the partners separately (severally) at his or her option. This is true even if the partner did not participate in, ratify, or know about whatever it was that gave rise to the cause of action. Normally, though, the partnership's assets must be exhausted before a creditor can enforce a judgment against a partner's separate assets [UPA 307(d)].

A judgment against one partner severally (separately) does not extinguish the others' liability. (Similarly, a release of one partner does not discharge the partners' several liability.) Those partners not sued in the first action may be sued subsequently, unless the first action was conclusive on the question of the partnership's liability. In other words, if an action is brought against one partner and the court holds that the partnership was in no way liable, the third party cannot bring an action against another partner and succeed on the issue of the partnership's liability.

Liability of an Incoming Partner. A partner newly admitted to an existing partnership is not personally liable for any partnership obligations incurred before the person became a partner [UPA 306(b)]. The new partner's liability to existing creditors of the partnership is limited to her or his capital contribution to the firm. **EXAMPLE 27.8** Smartclub, an existing partnership with four members, admits a new partner, Alex Jaff. He contributes $100,000 to the partnership. Smartclub has debts amounting to $600,000 at the time Jaff joins the firm. Although Jaff's capital contribution of $100,000 can be used to satisfy Smartclub's prior obligations, Jaff is not personally liable for partnership debts that were incurred before he became a partner. Thus, his personal assets cannot be used to satisfy the partnership's preexisting debt. If, however, the managing partner at Smartclub borrows funds for the partnership after Jaff becomes a partner, Jaff will be personally liable for those amounts. ●

5. Under the previous version of the UPA, which is still in effect in a few states, partners were subject to *joint liability* on partnership debts arising from contracts, but not on partnership debts arising from torts. States that still follow the previous version of the UPA include Connecticut, West Virginia, and Wyoming.

6. For a case applying joint liability to a partnership, see *Shar's Cars, LLC v. Elder*, 97 P.3d 724 (Utah App. 2004).

Partner's Dissociation

Dissociation The severance of the relationship between a partner and a partnership when the partner ceases to be associated with the carrying on of the partnership business.

Dissociation occurs when a partner ceases to be associated in the carrying on of the partnership business. Although a partner always has the *power* to dissociate from the firm, he or she may not have the *right* to dissociate. Dissociation normally entitles the partner to have his or her interest purchased by the partnership and terminates his or her actual authority to act for the partnership and to participate with the partners in running the business. Otherwise, the partnership continues to do business without the dissociating partner.[7]

EVENTS CAUSING DISSOCIATION Under UPA 601, a partner can be dissociated from a partnership in any of the following ways:

1. By the partner's voluntarily giving notice of and "express will to withdraw."
2. By the occurrence of an event agreed to in the partnership agreement.
3. By a unanimous vote of the other partners under certain circumstances, such as when a partner transfers substantially all of her or his interest in the partnership, or when it becomes unlawful to carry on partnership business with that partner.
4. By order of a court or arbitrator if the partner has engaged in wrongful conduct that affects the partnership business, breached the partnership agreement or violated a duty owed to the partnership or the other partners, or engaged in conduct that makes it "not reasonably practicable to carry on the business in partnership with the partner" [UPA 601(5)].
5. By the partner's declaring bankruptcy, assigning his or her interest in the partnership for the benefit of creditors, or becoming physically or mentally incapacitated, or by the partner's death. Note that although the bankruptcy or death of a partner represents that partner's "dissociation" from the partnership, it is not an *automatic* ground for the partnership's dissolution (*dissolution* will be discussed on page 694).

WRONGFUL DISSOCIATION As mentioned, a partner has the power to dissociate from a partnership at any time, but if she or he lacks the right to dissociate, then the dissociation is considered wrongful under the law [UPA 602]. When a partner's dissociation is in breach of the partnership agreement, for instance, it is wrongful. **EXAMPLE 27.9** Jensen & Whalen's partnership agreement states that it is a breach of the agreement for any partner to assign partnership property to a creditor without the consent of the other partners. If Janis, a partner, makes such an assignment, she not only has breached the agreement but has also wrongfully dissociated from the partnership. ● Similarly, if a partner refuses to perform duties required by the partnership agreement—such as accounting for profits earned from the use of partnership property—this breach can be treated as a wrongful dissociation. A partner who wrongfully dissociates is liable to the partnership and to the other partners for damages caused by the dissociation.

EFFECTS OF DISSOCIATION Dissociation (rightful or wrongful) terminates some of the rights of the dissociated partner, requires that the partnership purchase his or her interest, and alters the liability of the parties to third parties. On a partner's dissociation, his or her right to participate in the management and conduct of the partnership business terminates [UPA 603]. The partner's duty of loyalty also ends.

A partner's duty of care continues only with respect to events that occurred before dissociation, unless the partner participates in *winding up* the partnership's business (to be

7. Under the previous version of the UPA, when a partner withdrew from a partnership, the partnership was considered dissolved, its business had to be wound up, and the proceeds had to be distributed to creditors and among the partners. The new UPA dramatically changed the law governing partnership breakups and does not require that a partnership be dissolved just because one partner has left the firm.

discussed shortly). **EXAMPLE 27.10** Debbie Pearson, a partner who leaves an accounting firm, Bubb & Pearson, can immediately compete with that firm for new clients. She must exercise care in completing ongoing client transactions, however, and must account to Bubb & Pearson for any fees received from the former clients based on those transactions. ●

Buyout Price The amount payable to a partner on his or her dissociation from a partnership, based on the amount distributable to that partner if the firm were wound up on that date, and offset by any damages for wrongful dissociation.

After a partner's dissociation, his or her interest in the partnership must be purchased according to the rules in UPA 701. The **buyout price** is based on the amount that would have been distributed to the partner if the partnership were wound up on the date of dissociation. Offset against the price are amounts owed by the partner to the partnership, including any damages for the partner's wrongful dissociation. In the following case, the court had to decide how the buyout price of a partner's interest should be determined on his dissociation from his family's ranch business.

Case 27.1 Warnick v. Warnick

Supreme Court of Wyoming, 2006 WY 58, 133 P.3d 997 (2006).

(Rob Lee/Creative Commons)

Does the buyout price of a partner in a ranch include the expenses of a hypothetical sale?

FACTS In 1978, Wilbur and Dee Warnick and their son Randall bought a ranch in Sheridan County, Wyoming, for $335,000. To operate the ranch, they formed a partnership—Warnick Ranches. The partners' initial capital contributions totaled $60,000, of which Wilbur paid 36 percent, Dee paid 30 percent, and Randall paid 34 percent. Wilbur and Dee moved onto the ranch in 1981. Randall lived and worked on the ranch during the 1981 and 1982 summer haying seasons and again from 1991 to 1998. The partners each contributed funds to the operation and received cash distributions from the partnership. In 1999, Randall dissociated from the partnership. When the parties could not agree on a buyout price, Randall filed a suit in a Wyoming state court against the other partners and the partnership to recover what he believed to be a fair buyout price. The court awarded Randall $115,783.13—the amount of his cash contributions, plus 34 percent of the increase in the value of the partnership's assets above all partners' cash contributions, with interest from the date of his dissociation. The defendants appealed to the Wyoming Supreme Court, arguing that, in the calculation, $50,000 should be deducted from the appraised value of the ranch, its livestock, and its equipment for the estimated expenses of selling these assets.

ISSUE In determining the buyout price of a dissociated partner, do the costs of liquidating partnership assets include the expenses of a hypothetical sale?

DECISION No. The court affirmed the judgment of the lower court, holding that "purely hypothetical costs of sale are not a required deduction in valuing partnership assets."

REASON The state supreme court explained that under Wyoming Statutes Section 17-21-701 (Wyoming's version of UPA 701), the buyout price is "the amount that would have been paid to the dissociating partner following a settlement of partnership accounts upon the winding up of the partnership, if, on the date of dissociation, the assets of the partnership were sold at a price equal to the greater of the liquidation value or the value based on a sale of the business as a going concern without the dissociating partner." The first step in the calculation is to value the partnership's assets according to the two methods. In making the determination in this case, the defendants "assume that the liquidation value of the ranch is the amount of cash that would remain following a sale." But liquidation value refers to the prices of assets if they are sold separately, as opposed to the value of the business as a whole. For this purpose, an asset's price is the amount that "a willing and informed buyer would pay a willing and informed seller, with neither being under any compulsion to deal." Such a seller would factor the cost of a sale into the price, as the appraiser and the lower court likely did here. Besides "the assets of this partnership were not, in fact, liquidated. Instead, * * * the assets were retained by Warnick Ranches."

FOR CRITICAL ANALYSIS—Economic Consideration *How and why might the value of a partnership interest in a going concern differ from the value of the same interest as a result of a liquidation?*

Liability to Third Parties For two years after a partner dissociates from a continuing partnership, the partnership may be bound by the acts of the dissociated partner based on apparent authority [UPA 702]. In other words, the partnership may be liable to a third party with whom a dissociated partner enters into a transaction if the third party reasonably believed that the dissociated partner was still a partner. Similarly, a dissociated partner may be liable for partnership obligations entered into during a two-year period following dissociation [UPA 703]. To avoid this possible liability, a partnership should notify its creditors, customers, and clients of a partner's dissociation. Also, either the partnership or the dissociated partner can file a statement of dissociation in the appropriate state office to limit the dissociated partner's authority to ninety days after the filing [UPA 704].

Partnership Termination

The same events that cause dissociation can result in the end of the partnership if the remaining partners no longer wish to (or are unable to) continue the partnership business. The termination of a partnership is referred to as **dissolution**, which essentially means the commencement of the winding up process. **Winding up** is the actual process of collecting, liquidating, and distributing the partnership assets.[8]

Dissolution The formal disbanding of a partnership or a corporation. It can take place by (1) acts of the partners or, in a corporation, acts of the shareholders and board of directors; (2) the subsequent illegality of the firm's business; (3) the expiration of a time period stated in a partnership agreement or a certificate of incorporation; or (4) judicial decree.

Winding Up The second of two stages in the termination of a partnership or corporation. Once the firm is dissolved, it continues to exist legally until the process of winding up all business affairs (collecting and distributing the firm's assets) is complete.

DISSOLUTION Dissolution of a partnership generally can be brought about by acts of the partners, by operation of law, or by judicial decree [UPA 801]. Any partnership (including one for a fixed term) can be dissolved by the partners' agreement. Similarly, if the partnership agreement states that it will dissolve on a certain event, such as a partner's death or bankruptcy, then the occurrence of that event will dissolve the partnership. A partnership for a fixed term or a particular undertaking is dissolved by operation of law at the expiration of the term or on the completion of the undertaking. Under the UPA, a court may order dissolution when it becomes obviously impractical for the firm to continue—for example, if the business can only be operated at a loss [UPA 801(5)].

Even when one partner has brought a court action seeking to dissolve a partnership, the partnership continues to exist until it is legally dissolved by the court or by the parties' agreement. **CASE EXAMPLE 27.11** Ellin Curley and Lawrence Kaiser were a married couple when they formed a general partnership, K&K Associates. Later, Curley and Kaiser divorced and entered into an amended partnership agreement that stated that Curley owned 80 percent of the firm and Kaiser owned 20 percent. K&K invested capital in Alpine Focus Fund, LP, but the investment suffered losses. Curley attempted to collect from Kaiser his share of the amount lost, but Kaiser refused to pay. Curley then filed a suit for breach of contract and requested judicial dissolution of K&K.

While the lawsuit was pending, Kaiser died, and his new wife was substituted as the defendant. A provision in the amended agreement stated that if Kaiser died while still a partner, K&K would terminate and the value of Kaiser's ownership interest in the closing capital account would be zero. The defense argued that the court should not enforce this provision because the partnership no longer existed. The court ruled that although the court proceeding had started the dissolution process, the partnership still existed at the time of Kaiser's death. Therefore, the provision in the amended agreement effectively terminated the partnership and reduced Kaiser's interest in the closing capital account to zero.[9] ●

Do former partners remain jointly and severally liable for a partnership's obligations even after the partnership has been dissolved? Generally, dissolution has no effect on a partnership's liabilities to third parties. Partners remain liable for partnership debts even after the partnership has ceased to exist. For example, in one case the plaintiff alleged that when he was about twelve years old, Nelson Faerber, Jr., a school board member and prominent attorney, began sexually molesting him. For almost six years, Faerber, who was a partner at a Florida law firm, purportedly molested the boy on numerous occasions and at various locations, including the law firm's offices and the plaintiff's

8. Although "winding down" would seem to more accurately describe the process of settling accounts and liquidating the assets of a partnership, "winding up" has been traditionally used in English and U.S. statutory and case law to denote this final stage of a partnership's existence.

9. *Curley v. Kaiser*, 112 Conn.App. 213, 962 A.2d 167 (2009).

middle school. Faerber had died before the plaintiff filed the lawsuit, so the suit named several other defendants, including Faerber's wife, the school, and members of Faerber's former law firm. The law firm argued that the court should dismiss the case against it because the firm no longer existed. The court disagreed, however, holding that "under Florida law, partners remain jointly and severally liable for partnership liability, notwithstanding dissolution and division of property."[10] Although the holding in this case might seem unfair, it illustrates how unlimited liability in general partnerships can extend even beyond the partnership's termination.

WINDING UP After dissolution, the partnership continues for the limited purpose of the winding up process. The partners cannot create new obligations on behalf of the partnership. They have authority only to complete transactions begun but not finished at the time of dissolution and to wind up the business of the partnership [UPA 803, 804(1)]. Winding up includes collecting and preserving partnership assets, discharging liabilities (paying debts), and accounting to each partner for the value of her or his interest in the partnership. Partners continue to have fiduciary duties to one another and to the firm during this process. UPA 401(h) provides that a partner is entitled to compensation for services in winding up partnership affairs (and reimbursement for expenses incurred in the process) above and apart from his or her share in the partnership profits.

DON'T FORGET Secured creditors have priority over unsecured creditors to any assets that serve as collateral for a partnership's debts.

Both creditors of the partnership and creditors of the individual partners can make claims on the partnership's assets. In general, partnership creditors share proportionately with the partners' individual creditors in the assets of the partners' estates, which include their interests in the partnership. A partnership's assets are distributed according to the following priorities [UPA 807]:

1. Payment of debts, including those owed to partner and nonpartner creditors.
2. Return of capital contributions and distribution of profits to partners.[11]

If the partnership's liabilities are greater than its assets, the partners bear the losses—in the absence of a contrary agreement—in the same proportion in which they shared the profits (rather than, for example, in proportion to their contributions to the partnership's capital).

Preventing Legal Disputes 

Before entering a partnership, agree on how the assets will be valued and divided in the event the partnership dissolves. Make express arrangements that will provide for a smooth dissolution. You and your partners can enter a buy-sell, or buyout, agreement, which provides that one or more partners will buy out the other or others, should the relationship deteriorate. Agreeing beforehand on who buys what, under what circumstances, and, if possible, at what price may eliminate costly negotiations or litigation later. Alternatively, your agreement can specify that one or more partners will determine the value of the interest being sold and that the other or others will decide whether to buy or sell.

Limited Liability Partnerships

Limited Liability Partnership (LLP) A hybrid form of business organization that is used mainly by professionals who normally do business in a partnership. An LLP is a pass-through entity for tax purposes, but the personal liability of the partners is limited.

The **limited liability partnership (LLP)** is a hybrid form of business designed mostly for professionals who normally do business as partners in a partnership. The first state to enact an LLP statute was Texas, in 1991. Other states quickly followed suit, and by 1997, almost all of the states had enacted LLP statutes.

10. *Doe v. Faerber,* 446 F.Supp.2d 1311 (M.D.Fla. 2006). See also *Red River Wings, Inc. v. Hoot, Inc.,* 751 N.W.2d 206 (N.D. 2008).
11. Under the previous version of the UPA, creditors of the partnership had priority over creditors of the individual partners. Also, in distributing partnership assets, third party creditors were paid before partner creditors, and capital contributions were returned before profits.

The major advantage of the LLP is that it allows a partnership to continue as a pass-through entity for tax purposes but limits the personal liability of the partners. The LLP is especially attractive for two categories of businesses: professional service firms and family businesses. In fact, all of the "Big Four" accounting firms—the four largest international accountancy and professional services firms—are organized as LLPs, including Ernst & Young, LLP, and PricewaterhouseCoopers, LLP.

Formation of an LLP

LLPs must be formed and operated in compliance with state statutes, which may include provisions of the UPA. The appropriate form must be filed with a central state agency, usually the secretary of state's office, and the business's name must include either "Limited Liability Partnership" or "LLP" [UPA 1001, 1002]. In addition, an LLP must file an annual report with the state to remain qualified as an LLP in that state [UPA 1003].

In most states, it is relatively easy to convert a traditional partnership into an LLP because the firm's basic organizational structure remains the same. Additionally, all of the statutory and common law rules governing partnerships still apply (apart from those modified by the LLP statute). Normally, LLP statutes are simply amendments to a state's already existing partnership law.

Liability in an LLP

An LLP allows professionals, such as attorneys and accountants, to avoid personal liability for the malpractice of other partners. A partner in an LLP is still liable for her or his own wrongful acts, such as negligence, however. Also liable is the partner who supervised the individual who committed a wrongful act. This generally is true for all types of partners and partnerships, not just LLPs.

EXAMPLE 27.12 A group of five lawyers is operating as a partnership. One of the attorneys, Dan Kolcher, is sued for malpractice and loses. If the firm was organized as a general partnership and the firm did not have sufficient malpractice insurance to pay the judgment, the personal assets of the other attorneys could be used to satisfy the obligation. Because the firm is organized as an LLP, however, no other partner at the law firm can be held *personally* liable for Kolcher's malpractice, unless she or he acted as Kolcher's supervisor. In the absence of a supervisor, only Kolcher's personal assets can be used to satisfy the judgment (to the extent that it exceeds the liability insurance coverage). ●

Although LLP statutes vary from state to state, generally each state statute limits the liability of partners in some way. For example, Delaware law protects each innocent partner from the "debts and obligations of the partnership arising from negligence, wrongful acts, or misconduct." The UPA more broadly exempts partners from personal liability for any partnership obligation, "whether arising in contract, tort, or otherwise" [UPA 306(c)]. Although the language of some of these statutes may seem to apply specifically to attorneys, any group of professionals can organize as an LLP.

ON THE WEB For an example of a state law (that of Iowa) governing limited liability partnerships, go to www.sos.state.ia.us/business/limliabpart.html.

LIABILITY OUTSIDE THE STATE OF FORMATION When an LLP formed in one state wants to do business in another state, it may be required to register in the second state—for example, by filing a statement of foreign qualification [UPA 1102]. Because state LLP statutes are not uniform, a question arises in this situation. If the LLP statutes in the two states provide different liability protection, which law applies? Most states apply the law of the state in which the LLP was formed, even when the firm does business in another state, which is also the rule under UPA 1101.

SHARING LIABILITY AMONG PARTNERS When more than one partner in an LLP is negligent, there is a question as to how liability is to be shared. Is each partner jointly and severally liable for the entire result, as a general partner would be in most states? Some states provide for proportionate liability—that is, for separate determinations of the negligence of the partners. **EXAMPLE 27.13** Accountants Don and Jane are partners in an LLP, with Don supervising Jane. Jane negligently fails to file tax returns for their client, Centaur Tools. Centaur files a suit against Don and Jane. In a state that does not allow for proportionate liability, Don can be held liable for the entire loss. Under a proportionate liability statute, Don will be liable for no more than his portion of the responsibility for the missed tax deadline. (Even if Jane settles the case quickly, Don will still be liable for his portion.) ●

Family Limited Liability Partnerships

Family Limited Liability Partnership (FLLP) A type of limited liability partnership owned by family members or fiduciaries of family members.

A **family limited liability partnership (FLLP)** is a limited liability partnership in which the partners are persons related to each other, essentially as spouses, parents, grandparents, siblings, cousins, nephews, or nieces. A person acting in a fiduciary capacity for persons so related can also be a partner. All of the partners must be natural persons or persons acting in a fiduciary capacity for the benefit of natural persons.

Probably the most significant use of the FLLP form of business organization is in agriculture.[12] Family-owned farms sometimes find this form to their benefit. The FLLP offers the same advantages as other LLPs with some additional advantages, such as, in Iowa, an exemption from real estate transfer taxes when partnership real estate is transferred among partners.[13]

Limited Partnerships

Limited Partnership A partnership consisting of one or more general partners (who manage the business and are liable to the full extent of their personal assets for debts of the partnership) and one or more limited partners (who contribute only assets and are liable only up to the extent of their contributions).

General Partner In a limited partnership, a partner who assumes responsibility for the management of the partnership and liability for all partnership debts.

Limited Partner In a limited partnership, a partner who contributes capital to the partnership but has no right to participate in the management and operation of the business. The limited partner assumes no liability for partnership debts beyond the capital contributed.

We now look at a business organizational form that limits the liability of *some* of its owners—the **limited partnership.** Limited partnerships originated in medieval Europe and have been in existence in the United States since the early 1800s. In many ways, limited partnerships are like the general partnerships discussed at the outset of this chapter, but they differ from general partnerships in several ways. Because of this, they are sometimes referred to as *special partnerships*.

A limited partnership consists of at least one **general partner** and one or more **limited partners.** A general partner assumes management responsibility for the partnership and so has full responsibility for the partnership and for all debts of the partnership. A limited partner contributes cash or other property and owns an interest in the firm but does not undertake any management responsibilities and is not personally liable for partnership debts beyond the amount of his or her investment. A limited partner can forfeit limited liability by taking part in the management of the business. Exhibit 27–2 on the following page compares characteristics of general and limited partnerships.[14]

Until 1976, the law governing limited partnerships in all states except Louisiana was the Uniform Limited Partnership Act (ULPA). Since 1976, most states and the District of Columbia have adopted the revised version of the ULPA, known as the Revised Uniform Limited Partnership Act (RULPA). Because the RULPA is the dominant law governing limited partnerships in the United States, we will refer to the RULPA in the following discussion of limited partnerships. Note, however, that amendments to make the RULPA more flexible were proposed to the states in 2001 and fifteen states have adopted the 2001 version of this uniform law.

---

12. For a case example, see *Cannon v. Bertrand*, 2 So.3d 393 (La. 2009).
13. Iowa Statutes Section 428A.2.
14. Under the UPA, a general partnership can be converted into a limited partnership and vice versa [UPA 902, 903]. The UPA also provides for the merger of a general partnership with one or more general or limited partnerships under rules that are similar to those governing corporate mergers [UPA 905].

Exhibit 27–2 A Comparison of General Partnerships and Limited Partnerships

CHARACTERISTIC	GENERAL PARTNERSHIP (UPA)	LIMITED PARTNERSHIP (RULPA)
Creation	By agreement of two or more persons to carry on a business as co-owners for profit.	By agreement of two or more persons to carry on a business as co-owners for profit. Must include one or more general partners and one or more limited partners. Filing of a certificate with the secretary of state is required.
Sharing of profits and losses	By agreement; or, in the absence of agreement, profits are shared equally by the partners, and losses are shared in the same ratio as profits.	Profits are shared as required in the certificate agreement, and losses are shared likewise, up to the amount of the limited partners' capital contributions. In the absence of a provision in the certificate agreement, profits and losses are shared on the basis of percentages of capital contributions.
Liability	Unlimited personal liability of all partners.	Unlimited personal liability of all general partners; limited partners liable only to the extent of their capital contributions.
Capital contribution	No minimum or mandatory amount; set by agreement.	Set by agreement.
Management	By agreement, or in the absence of agreement, all partners have an equal voice.	General partner or partners only. Limited partners have no voice or else are subject to liability as general partners (but only if a third party has reason to believe that the limited partner is a general partner). A limited partner may act as an agent or employee of the partnership and vote on amending the certificate or on the sale or dissolution of the partnership.
Duration	Terminated by agreement of the partners, but can continue to do business even when a partner dissociates from the partnership.	Terminated by agreement in the certificate or by retirement, death, or mental incompetence of a general partner in the absence of the right of the other general partners to continue the partnership. Death of a limited partner, unless he or she is the only remaining limited partner, does not terminate the partnership.
Distribution of assets on liquidation—Order of priorities	1. Payment of debts, including those owed to partner and nonpartner creditors. 2. Return of capital contributions and distribution of profit to partners.	1. Outside creditors and partner creditors. 2. Partners and former partners entitled to distributions or partnership assets. 3. Unless otherwise agreed, return of capital contributions and distribution of profit to partners.

Formation of a Limited Partnership

Certificate of Limited Partnership The basic document filed with a designated state official by which a limited partnership is formed.

In contrast to the informal, private, and voluntary agreement that usually suffices for a general partnership, the formation of a limited partnership is a public and formal proceeding that must follow statutory requirements. A limited partnership must have at least one general partner and one limited partner, as mentioned previously. Additionally, the partners must sign a **certificate of limited partnership**, which requires information similar to that found in a corporate charter (see Chapter 28). The certificate must be filed with the designated state official—under the RULPA, the secretary of state. The certificate is usually open to public inspection.

Liabilities of Partners in a Limited Partnership

General partners, unlike limited partners, are personally liable to the partnership's creditors; thus, at least one general partner is necessary in a limited partnership so that someone has personal liability. This policy can be circumvented in states that allow a corporation to be the general partner in a partnership. Because the corporation has limited liability by virtue of corporate laws, if a corporation is the general partner, no one in the limited partnership has personal liability.

In contrast to the personal liability of general partners, the liability of a limited partner is limited to the capital that she or he contributes or agrees to contribute to the partnership [RULPA 502]. Limited partners enjoy this limited liability only so long as they do not participate in management [RULPA 303]. A limited partner who participates in management will be just as liable as a general partner to any creditor who transacts business with the limited partnership and believes, based on the limited partner's conduct, that the limited partner is a general partner [RULPA 303]. The extent of review and advisement a limited partner can engage in before being exposed to liability remains rather vague, though.

NOTE A limited partner is liable only to the extent of any contribution that she or he made to the partnership, but can lose this limited liability by participating in management.

Rights and Duties in a Limited Partnership

With the exception of the right to participate in management, limited partners have essentially the same rights as general partners. Limited partners have a right of access to the partnership's books and to information regarding partnership business.

General and limited partners also owe each other a fiduciary duty to exercise good faith in transactions related to the partnership. Can this duty be waived through a provision in the partnership agreement? That was the issue in the following case.

Case 27.2 1515 North Wells, LP v. 1513 North Wells, LLC

Appellate Court of Illinois, First District, 392 Ill.App.3d 863 (Ill.App. 1 Dist 2009).
www.state.il.us/court/default.asp[a]

A limited partnership agreement to build condominiums allowed partners to engage in "whatever activities" they chose. Can that excuse the breach of fiduciary duties of the partners?

FACTS Thomas Bracken (owner of 1513 North Wells, LLC), Mark Sutherland, and Alex Pearsall were limited partners in 1515 North Wells, LP. Sutherland and Pearsall's company, SP Development Corporation, was 1515's general partner. The partnership was formed to build a condominium with residential and commercial space. SP chose another Sutherland and Pearsall company, Sutherland and Pearsall Development, to be the general contractor for the 1515 project. Meanwhile, Bracken borrowed $250,000 from 1515. When he did not repay the loan, 1515 filed a suit in an Illinois state court to collect. In response, Bracken filed a claim that included SP Development Corporation, alleging breach of fiduciary duty. The court ordered Bracken to repay the loan and SP to pay Bracken $900,000. SP appealed, arguing that a provision in 1515's partnership agreement, which allowed all partners to engage in "whatever activities they choose," effectively "relaxed" SP's fiduciary duty.

ISSUE Can a general partner breach a fiduciary duty to a limited partner even if their agreement allows partners to engage in "whatever activities they choose"?

DECISION Yes. The state intermediate appellate court affirmed the lower court's judgment. A partnership agreement cannot "contract away" the fiduciary duty that a general partner owes to limited partners.

REASON Under UPA 103(b)(3), a partnership agreement cannot "eliminate or reduce a partner's fiduciary duties." An agreement can permit the partners to engage in activities within or outside the areas of partnership business. But this does not allow them to conduct deals at the expense of the other partners. The provision in 1515's partnership agreement that allowed the partners to engage in "whatever activities" thus could not excuse their liability for a breach of fiduciary duty. To establish a successful claim on this basis, a partner must prove a fiduciary duty, a breach of the duty, and damages caused by the breach. In this case, "there was ample evidence to support the court's finding of a breach of fiduciary duty." The court cited the contract that SP awarded to Sutherland and Pearsall Development. SP had chosen this company even though it had submitted the only bid, which consisted of a "cost plus fee" contract (it did not state a maximum price). SP had also granted the contractor—not 1515—the right to keep any revenue generated by the sales of condominium upgrades.

FOR CRITICAL ANALYSIS—Ethical Consideration *Did any of the parties involved in this case commit an ethical violation? Discuss.*

a. In the "Documents" pull-down menu, click on "Court Opinions." On that page, click on "Supreme and Appellate Court Opinion Archive." In the result, in the "Select a Court" column, select "1st District Appellate"; in the "Select an Archive Year" column, choose "2009"; and click on "Get Opinions." In that result, scroll to the name of the case and click on it to access the opinion. The Administrative Office of the Illinois Courts maintains this Web site.

Dissociation and Dissolution

"A friendship founded on business is a good deal better than a business founded on friendship."

John D. Rockefeller, 1839–1937
(American industrialist)

A general partner has the power to voluntarily dissociate, or withdraw, from a limited partnership unless the partnership agreement specifies otherwise. A limited partner theoretically can withdraw from the partnership by giving six months' notice unless the partnership agreement specifies a term, which most do. Also, some states have passed laws prohibiting the withdrawal of limited partners.

In a limited partnership, a general partner's voluntary dissociation from the firm normally will lead to dissolution *unless* all partners agree to continue the business. Similarly, the bankruptcy, retirement, death, or mental incompetence of a general partner will cause the dissociation of that partner and the dissolution of the limited partnership unless the other members agree to continue the firm [RULPA 801]. Bankruptcy of a limited partner, however, does not dissolve the partnership unless it causes the bankruptcy of the firm. Death or an assignment of the interest of a limited partner does not dissolve a limited partnership [RULPA 702, 704, 705]. A limited partnership can be dissolved by court decree [RULPA 802].

On dissolution, creditors' claims, including those of partners who are creditors, take first priority. After that, partners and former partners receive unpaid distributions of partnership assets and, except as otherwise agreed, amounts representing returns on their contributions and amounts proportionate to their shares of the distributions [RULPA 804].

In the following case, two limited partners wanted the business of the partnership to be sold on its dissolution, while another limited partner (actor Kevin Costner) and the general partner wanted it to continue.

Case 27.3 In re Dissolution of Midnight Star Enterprises, LP

Supreme Court of South Dakota, 2006 SD 98, 724 N.W.2d 334 (2006).

(Davide Lanzilao/Contrasto/Redux)

Actor Kevin Costner wanted a partnership to continue doing business. Can another partner force the sale of the business?

FACTS Midnight Star Enterprises, LP, consists of a casino, bar, and restaurant in Deadwood, South Dakota. The owners are Midnight Star Enterprises, Limited (MSEL), the general partner, which owns 22 partnership units; actor Kevin Costner, a limited partner, who owns 71.50 partnership units; and Carla and Francis Caneva, limited partners, who own 3.25 partnership units each. Costner also owns MSEL and thus controls 93.5 partnership units. The Canevas were the business's managers, for which they received salaries and bonuses. When MSEL voiced concerns about the management, communication among the partners broke down. MSEL filed a petition in a South Dakota state court to dissolve the partnership. MSEL hired Paul Thorstenson, an accountant, to determine the firm's fair market value, which he calculated to be $3.1 million. The Canevas solicited a competitor's offer to buy the business for $6.2 million, which the court ruled was the appropriate amount. At the Canevas' request, the court ordered MSEL and Costner to buy the business for that price within ten days or sell it on the open market to the highest bidder. MSEL appealed to the South Dakota Supreme Court.

ISSUE Can a partner force the sale of a limited partnership when the other partners want to continue the business?

DECISION No. The South Dakota Supreme Court reversed the judgment of the lower court and remanded the case to allow MSEL and Costner to pay the Canevas the value of their 6.5 partnership units after a revaluation of the partnership.

REASON The state supreme court concluded that the partnership agreement did not require the business to be sold on the open market on the partnership's dissolution. Under the agreement, during liquidation, the firm's property could be distributed in kind among the partners if it was first offered for sale to a third party. In other words, only a decision to make an in-kind distribution of assets required that the business be offered for sale on the open market. The court also concluded that the correct value of the business was the accountant's figure, which was based on a fair market value analysis using a hypothetical buyer. This analysis provided a reasonable basis for determining value "by removing the irrationalities, strategies, and emotions" that exist in an actual offer. Besides, the partnership agreement required a "fair market value" of the assets. Finally, "[s]ince it was error for the [lower] court to value Midnight Star at $6.2 million, it was also error to force the general partners to buy the business for $6.2 million or

Case 27.3–Continued

sell the business." The state supreme court reasoned that "forced sales typically end up in economic waste." A buyout is an acceptable alternative, as long as the partners receive the fair value of their property interest. "Instead of ordering the majority partners to purchase the whole partnership for the appraised value, the majority partners should only be required to pay any interests the withdrawing partner is due."

FOR CRITICAL ANALYSIS—Ethical Consideration *Under what circumstances on the dissolution of a limited partnership might a forced sale of its property be appropriate?*

Limited Liability Limited Partnerships

Limited Liability Limited Partnership (LLLP) A type of limited partnership in which the liability of all of the partners, including general partners, is limited to the amount of their investments.

A **limited liability limited partnership (LLLP)** is a type of limited partnership. An LLLP differs from a limited partnership in that a general partner in an LLLP has the same liability as a limited partner in a limited partnership. In other words, the liability of *all* partners is limited to the amount of their investments in the firm.

A few states provide expressly for LLLPs.[15] In states that do not provide for LLLPs but do allow for limited partnerships and limited liability partnerships, a limited partnership should probably still be able to register with the state as an LLLP.

15. See, for example, Colorado Revised Statutes Annotated Section 7-62-109. Other states that provide expressly for limited liability limited partnerships include Delaware, Florida, Missouri, Pennsylvania, Texas, and Virginia.

Reviewing . . . All Forms of Partnership

Grace Tarnavsky and her sons, Manny and Jason, bought a ranch known as the Cowboy Palace in March 2006, and the three orally agreed to share the business for five years. Grace contributed 50 percent of the investment, and each son contributed 25 percent. Manny agreed to handle the livestock, and Jason agreed to do the bookkeeping. The Tarnavskys took out joint loans and opened a joint bank account into which they deposited the ranch's proceeds and from which they made payments toward property, cattle, equipment, and supplies. In September 2010, Manny severely injured his back while baling hay and became permanently unable to handle livestock. Manny therefore hired additional laborers to tend the livestock, causing the Cowboy Palace to incur significant debt. In September 2011, Al's Feed Barn filed a lawsuit against Jason to collect $12,400 in unpaid debts. Using the information presented in the chapter, answer the following questions.

1. Was this relationship a partnership for a term or a partnership at will?
2. Did Manny have the authority to hire additional laborers to work at the ranch after his injury? Why or why not?
3. Under the UPA, can Al's Feed Barn bring an action against Jason individually for Cowboy Palace's debt? Why or why not?
4. Suppose that after his back injury in 2010, Manny sent his mother and brother a notice indicating his intent to withdraw from the partnership. Can he still be held liable for the debt to Al's Feed Barn? Why or why not?

Business Application

Why Are General Partnerships Declining in Popularity?*

Forty years ago, there were three basic forms of business organization–the sole proprietorship, the general partnership, and the corporation. When several people wanted to join together to create a business, they formed a general partnership. General partnerships are easy to form through a simple agreement and allow two or more persons to pool their capital and individual expertise for the benefit of all. The partners in a general

*This *Business Application* is not meant to substitute for the services of an attorney who is licensed to practice law in your state.

Continued

partnership do not need to file documents with the state to form their business or obtain any certificate (except perhaps a business license).

Traditional partnerships are also flexible. They can be limited to a specified purpose or stated time period, or they can continue until one or more of the partners decide to terminate the business. The partners themselves can decide how to split the profits and losses of the business, and partnerships can obtain credit from lenders more easily than sole proprietorships can.

Another advantage is that the partnership entity itself has no income tax liability. Instead, the individual partners pay taxes on the profits derived from the partnership. Thus, partnerships avoid double taxation, which occurs with corporations, as you will learn in Chapter 29.

A Distinct Disadvantage—Unlimited Personal Liability

Despite their many advantages, general partnerships have one very important disadvantage—the unlimited personal liability of the individual partners. Partners in a general partnership are personally liable not only for the firm's debts, but also for the acts of other partners committed within the scope of the partnership business. Because partners have joint and several liability, a partner's personal assets can be in jeopardy even though he or she was not involved in the act that gave rise to the liability. Reportedly, Mark Twain (1835–1910), the author of *The Adventures of Huckleberry Finn,* lost more than one small fortune due to his participation in unsuccessful partnerships. In today's business world, liability for a partner's misconduct—including the Twitters and Tweets of another partner that lead to a defamation lawsuit and a substantial damages award—can be particularly devastating.

General partnerships have some other disadvantages as well. They cannot receive a Chapter 7 discharge in bankruptcy, for example, and one partner's death can sometimes result in the firm's dissolution. Nevertheless, these problems are minor compared to the unlimited personal liability.

A Possible Solution—Limited Liability Entities

Not surprisingly, the disadvantageous liability of general partnerships has created a demand for business organizational forms that offer the benefits of partnerships while providing limited liability as well. These forms include the limited partnership, the limited liability partnership, the limited liability limited partnership (discussed in this chapter); the limited liability company (see Chapter 28); and the S corporation (see Chapter 29). These limited liability entities have increased dramatically in popularity in recent years at the expense of general partnerships.

CHECKLIST FOR FORMING A GENERAL PARTNERSHIP

1. **Decide how important ease and informality are to the creation of your business organization. For example, to accomplish a single project within a limited time, a general partnership may be the ideal business form.**
2. **Choose your partners carefully. Remember that you can be personally liable for their actions.**
3. **The partnership should carry sufficient insurance to protect against third parties reaching each partner's individual assets and to allow the partnership to continue on after a partner's death.**
4. **Before you form a partnership, decide how profits and losses are to be shared and the amount of each partner's capital contribution. Express these decisions in a written partnership agreement.**

Key Terms

articles of partnership 685
buyout price 693
certificate of limited partnership 698
charging order 689
confession of judgment 688
dissociation 692
dissolution 694
family limited liability partnership (FLLP) 697
general partner 697
information return 685
joint and several liability 691
joint liability 691
limited liability limited partnership (LLLP) 701
limited liability partnership (LLP) 695
limited partner 697
limited partnership 697
partnership 684
pass-through entity 685
winding up 694

Chapter Summary: All Forms of Partnership

Partnerships **(See pages 683–695.)**	1. A partnership is created by agreement of the parties. 2. A partnership is treated as an entity except for limited purposes. 3. Each partner pays a proportionate share of income taxes on the net profits of the partnership, whether or not they are distributed; the partnership files only an information return with the Internal Revenue Service. 4. Each partner has an equal voice in management unless the partnership agreement provides otherwise. 5. In the absence of an agreement, partners share profits equally and share losses in the same ratio as they share profits.

Chapter Summary: All Forms of Partnership—Continued

Partnerships—Continued	6. The capital contribution of each partner is determined by agreement. 7. Partners have unlimited liability for partnership debts. 8. A partnership can be terminated by agreement or can be dissolved by action of the partners (dissociation from a partnership at will), operation of law (subsequent illegality), or court decree.
Limited Liability Partnerships (LLPs) (See pages 695–697.)	1. *Formation*—The appropriate form must be filed with a state agency, usually the secretary of state's office. Typically, an LLP is formed by professionals who work together as partners in a partnership. Under most state LLP statutes, it is relatively easy to convert a traditional partnership into an LLP. 2. *Liability of partners*—LLP statutes vary, but under the UPA, professionals generally can avoid personal liability for acts committed by other partners. The extent to which partners' limited liability will be recognized when the partnership does business in another state depends on the other state's laws. Partners in an LLP continue to be liable for their own wrongful acts and for the wrongful acts of those whom they supervise. 3. *Family limited liability partnership (FLLP)*—A form of LLP in which all of the partners are family members or fiduciaries of family members; the most significant use of the FLLP is by families engaged in agricultural enterprises.
Limited Partnerships (See pages 697–701.)	1. *Formation*—A certificate of limited partnership must be filed with the secretary of state's office or other designated state official. The certificate must include information about the business, similar to the information included in a corporate charter. The partnership consists of one or more general partners and one or more limited partners. 2. *Rights and liabilities of partners*—With some exceptions, the rights of partners are the same as the rights of partners in a general partnership. General partners have unlimited liability for partnership obligations; limited partners are liable only to the extent of their contributions. 3. *Limited partners and management*—Only general partners can participate in management. Limited partners have no voice in management; if they do participate in management activities, they risk having general-partner liability. 4. *Dissolution*—Generally, a limited partnership can be dissolved in much the same way as an ordinary partnership. The death or assignment of the interest of a limited partner does not dissolve the partnership; bankruptcy of a limited partner also will not dissolve the partnership unless it causes the bankruptcy of the firm. 5. *Limited liability limited partnerships (LLLPs)*—A special type of limited partnership in which the liability of all partners, including general partners, is limited to the amount of their investments.

ExamPrep

ISSUE SPOTTERS

1 Darnell and Eliana are partners in D&E Designs, an architectural firm. When Darnell dies, his widow claims that as Darnell's heir, she is entitled to take his place as Eliana's partner or to receive a share of the firm's assets. Is she right? Why or why not?

2 Finian and Gloria are partners in F&G Delivery Service. When business is slow, without Gloria's knowledge, Finian leases the delivery vehicles as moving vans. Because the vehicles would otherwise be sitting idle in a parking lot, can Finian keep the income resulting from the leasing of the delivery vehicles? Explain your answer.

BEFORE THE TEST

Check your answers to the Issue Spotters, and at the same time, take the interactive quiz for this chapter. Go to www.cengage.com/blaw/blt and click on "Chapter 27." First, click on "Answers to Issue Spotters" to check your answers. Next, click on "Interactive Quiz" to assess your mastery of the concepts in this chapter. Then click on "Flashcards" to review this chapter's Key Term definitions.

For Review

Answers for the even-numbered questions in this For Review section can be found on this text's accompanying Web site at www.cengage.com/blaw/blt. Select "Chapter 27" and click on "For Review."

1 What are the three essential elements of a partnership?
2 What are the rights and duties of partners in an ordinary partnership?
3 What is meant by joint and several liability? Why is this often considered to be a disadvantage of the partnership form of business?
4 What advantages do limited liability partnerships offer to businesspersons that are not offered by general partnerships?
5 What are the key differences between the rights and liabilities of general partners and those of limited partners?

Hypothetical Scenarios and Case Problems

27–1 Partnership Formation. Daniel is the owner of a chain of shoe stores. He hires Rubya to be the manager of a new store, which is to open in Grand Rapids, Michigan. Daniel, by written contract, agrees to pay Rubya a monthly salary and 20 percent of the profits. Without Daniel's knowledge, Rubya represents himself to Classen as Daniel's partner, showing Classen the agreement to share profits. Classen extends credit to Rubya. Rubya defaults. Discuss whether Classen can hold Daniel liable as a partner.

27–2 Hypothetical Question with Sample Answer Dorinda, Luis, and Elizabeth form a limited partnership. Dorinda is a general partner, and Luis and Elizabeth are limited partners. Discuss fully whether each of the separate events below constitutes a dissolution of the limited partnership.

1 Luis assigns his partnership interest to Ashley.
2 Elizabeth is petitioned into involuntary bankruptcy.
3 Dorinda dies.

—For a sample answer to Question 27–2, go to Appendix E at the end of this text.

27–3 Distribution of Partnership Assets. Shawna and David formed a partnership. At the time of the partnership's formation, Shawna's capital contribution was $10,000, and David's was $15,000. Later, Shawna made a $10,000 loan to the partnership when it needed working capital. The partnership agreement provided that profits were to be shared with 40 percent for Shawna and 60 percent for David. The partnership was dissolved after David's death. At the end of the dissolution and the winding up of the partnership, the partnership's assets were $50,000, and the partnership's debts were $8,000. Discuss fully how the assets should be distributed.

27–4 Indications of Partnership. At least six months before the 1996 Summer Olympic Games in Atlanta, Georgia, Stafford Fontenot, Steve Turner, Mike Montelaro, Joe Sokol, and Doug Brinsmade agreed to sell Cajun food at the games and began making preparations. Calling themselves "Prairie Cajun Seafood Catering of Louisiana," on May 19 the group applied for a license with the Fulton County, Georgia, Department of Public Health–Environmental Health Services. Later, Ted Norris sold a mobile kitchen for an $8,000 check drawn on the "Prairie Cajun Seafood Catering of Louisiana" account and two promissory notes, one for $12,000 and the other for $20,000. The notes, which were dated June 12, listed only Fontenot "d/b/a Prairie Cajun Seafood" as the maker (*d/b/a* is an abbreviation for "doing business as"). On July 31, Fontenot and his friends signed a partnership agreement, which listed specific percentages of profits and losses. They drove the mobile kitchen to Atlanta, but business was "disastrous." When the notes were not paid, Norris filed a suit in a Louisiana state court against Fontenot, seeking payment. What are the elements of a partnership? Was there a partnership among Fontenot and the others? Who is liable on the notes? Explain. [*Norris v. Fontenot,* 867 So.2d 179 (La.App. 3 Cir. 2004)]

27–5 Case Problem with Sample Answer In August 2003, Tammy Duncan began working as a waitress at Bynum's Diner, which was owned by her mother, Hazel Bynum, and her stepfather, Eddie Bynum, in Valdosta, Georgia. Less than a month later, the three signed an agreement under which Eddie was to relinquish his management responsibilities, allowing Tammy to be co-manager. At the end of this six-month period, Eddie would revisit this agreement and could then extend it for another six-month period. The diner's bank account was to remain in Eddie's name. There was no provision with regard to the diner's profit, if any, and the parties did not change the business's tax information. Tammy began doing the bookkeeping, as well as waiting tables and performing other duties. On October 30, she slipped off a ladder and injured her knees. At the end of the six-month term, Tammy quit working at the diner. The Georgia State Board of Workers' Compensation determined that she had been the diner's employee and awarded her benefits under the diner's workers' compensation policy with Cypress Insurance Co. Cypress filed a suit in a Georgia state court against Tammy, arguing that she was not an employee, but a co-owner. What are the essential elements of a partnership? Was Tammy a partner in the business of the diner? Explain. [*Cypress Insurance Co. v. Duncan,* 281 Ga.App. 469, 636 S.E.2d 159 (2006)]

—After you have answered Problem 27–5, compare your answer with the sample answer given on the Web site that accompanies this text. Go to www.cengage.com/blaw/blt, select "Chapter 27," and click on "Case Problem with Sample Answer."

27–6 Partnership Dissolution. Nine minority partners each owned one-half of 1 percent of J&J Celcom, a partnership with AT&T, which owned the rest. AT&T, using its majority power, voted to buy out the minority partners. It offered each partner a price that was slightly higher than the price provided by a third party's appraisal. Some of the partners accepted the offer, but others did not. AT&T then voted to dissolve the partnership, forcing the remaining minority partners to accept the appraisal price. Those partners sued. The trial court held for AT&T, and the minority partners appealed. The appeals court held that the price offered was the fair market price, but certified the following question to Washington State's highest court: "Does a controlling partner violate the duty of loyalty to the partnership or to dissenting minority partners where the controlling partner causes the partnership to sell all its assets" to another party? Why or why not? [*J&J Celcom v. AT&T Wireless Services, Inc.*, 162 Wash.2d 102, 169 P.3d 823 (Sup.Ct. 2007)]

27–7 Limited Partnership. James Carpenter contracted with Austin Estates, LP, to buy property in Texas. Carpenter asked Sandra McBeth to invest in the deal. He admitted that a dispute had arisen with the city of Austin over water for the property, but he assured her that it would not be a significant obstacle. McBeth agreed to invest $800,000 to hold open the option to buy the property. She became a limited partner in StoneLake Ranch, LP. Carpenter acted as the firm's general partner. Despite his statements to McBeth, the purchase was delayed due to the water dispute. Unable to complete the purchase timely, Carpenter paid the $800,000 to Austin Estates without notifying McBeth. Later, Carpenter and others—*excluding* McBeth—bought the property and sold it at a profit. McBeth filed a suit in a Texas state court against Carpenter. What is the nature of the fiduciary duty that a general partner owes a limited partner? Did Carpenter breach that duty in this case? Explain. [*McBeth v. Carpenter*, 565 F.3d 171 (5th Cir. 2009)]

27–8 A Question of Ethics *In 1991, Hassan Mardanlou and Ali Ghaffarian signed a lease for 3960 South State Street in Salt Lake City, Utah. Ghaffarian paid $6,000 for the first and last months' rent, and said to Mardanlou, "We are in this together, partner." Mardanlou bought business cards for "Access Auto" with his and Ghaffarian's names on the cards. Both men were listed on Access Auto's insurance policy. Mardanlou bought the firm's furniture. Ghaffarian did the bookkeeping and bought the inventory. Mardanlou did not have access to the books but wrote checks on the firm's account, sold its inventory, and managed the sales staff. In March 1993, Ghaffarian gave Mardanlou a check for $10,000. Otherwise, Mardanlou was paid a fixed amount each month. Later that year, without telling Mardanlou, Ghaffarian bought the leased property with the firm's funds but titled it in his name. In 1995, Mardanlou learned of this deal and confronted Ghaffarian, who said, "Don't worry, we're partners." Ghaffarian filed the firm's tax returns in his name only, despite Mardanlou's repeated objections. Finally, in 1997, Mardanlou quit the firm and filed a suit in a Utah state court against Ghaffarian to dissolve the partnership and obtain a share of the profits. [*Mardanlou v. Ghaffarian*, *2006 UT App 165, 135 P.3d 904 (2006)]*

1 What factors indicate that Mardanlou and Ghaffarian were partners? What factors indicate that they were not partners? If you were the judge, how would you resolve this dispute?
2 Is Mardanlou entitled to a share of the value of the real property that Ghaffarian bought in his own name? If so, how much? From an ethical point of view, what solution appears to be the fairest? Discuss.
3 Is Mardanlou entitled to a share of Access Auto's profits? Why or why not?

Critical Thinking and Writing Assignments

27–9 Critical Thinking and Writing Assignment for Business. Sandra Lerner and Patricia Holmes were friends. One evening, while applying nail polish to Lerner, Holmes layered a raspberry color over black to produce a new color, which Lerner liked. Later, the two created other colors with names like "Bruise," "Smog," and "Oil Slick," and titled their concept "Urban Decay." Lerner and Holmes started a firm to produce and market the polishes but never discussed the sharing of profits and losses. They agreed to build the business and then sell it. Together, they did market research, worked on a logo and advertising, obtained capital, and hired employees. Then Lerner began working to edge Holmes out of the firm.

1 Lerner claimed that there was no partnership agreement because there was no provision on how to divide profits. Was she right? Why or why not?
2 Suppose that Lerner, but not Holmes, had contributed a significant amount of personal funds into developing and marketing the new nail polish. Would this entitle Lerner to receive more of the profit? Explain.
3 Did Lerner violate her fiduciary duty? Why or why not?

Practical Internet Exercises

Go to this text's Web site at www.cengage.com/blaw/blt, select "Chapter 27," and click on "Practical Internet Exercises." There you will find the following Internet research exercises that you can perform to learn more about the topics covered in this chapter.

Practical Internet Exercise 27–1: LEGAL PERSPECTIVE—**Liability of Dissociated Partners**
Practical Internet Exercise 27–2: ECONOMIC PERSPECTIVE—**Taxation of Partnerships**
Practical Internet Exercise 27–3: MANAGEMENT PERSPECTIVE—**Limited Partnerships and Limited Liability Partnerships**

Chapter 28

Limited Liability Companies and Special Business Forms

"To play it safe is not to play."

—Robert Altman, 1925–2006
(American film director)

Chapter Outline

- Limited Liability Companies
- LLC Operation and Management
- Dissociation and Dissolution of an LLC
- Special Business Forms

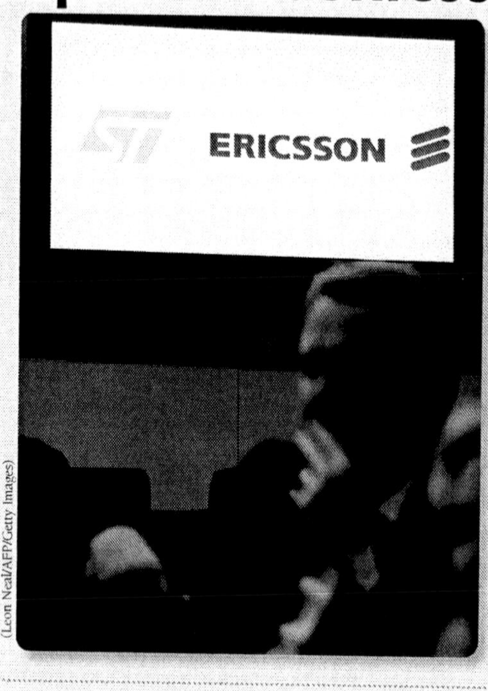

(Leon Neal/AFP/Getty Images)

Learning Objectives

After reading this chapter, you should be able to answer the following questions:

1. What advantages do limited liability companies offer to businesspersons that are not offered by sole proprietorships or partnerships?
2. How are limited liability companies formed, and who decides how they will be managed and operated?
3. What are the two options for managing limited liability companies?
4. What is a joint venture? How is it similar to a partnership? How is it different?
5. What are the essential characteristics of joint stock companies, syndicates, business trusts, and cooperatives, respectively?

In the United States, public policy encourages trade and commerce. To promote commerce and profit-making activities, our government allows entrepreneurs to choose from a variety of business organizational forms when undertaking their business ventures. Many businesspersons would agree with the chapter-opening quotation that in business "to play it safe is not to play." Because risk is associated with the potential for higher profits, businesspersons are motivated to choose organizational forms that limit their liability while allowing them to take risks that may maximize their profit.

Limited Liability Company (LLC) A hybrid form of business enterprise that offers the limited liability of a corporation and the tax advantages of a partnership.

In the preceding chapters, we examined sole proprietorships and various partnership forms. Here, we examine a relatively new form of business organization, the **limited liability company (LLC).** The LLC is a hybrid that combines the limited liability aspects of a corporation and the tax advantages of a partnership. We examine the origins and evolution of the LLC in the *Landmark in the Law* feature. Then we look at important characteristics of the LLC, including formation, jurisdictional requirements, and the advantages and disadvantages of choosing to do business as an LLC. Next, we examine the operation and management options in an LLC. The chapter concludes with a discussion of various other special business forms, including joint ventures, syndicates, joint stock companies, business trusts, and cooperatives.

Landmark in the Law Limited Liability Company (LLC) Statutes

In 1977, Wyoming became the first state to pass legislation authorizing the creation of a limited liability company (LLC). Although LLCs emerged in the United States in the late 1970s, they have been used for more than a century in other foreign jurisdictions, including several European and South American nations.

Taxation of LLCs Despite Wyoming's adoption of an LLC statute, the tax status of LLCs in the United States was not clear until 1988, when the Internal Revenue Service (IRS) ruled that Wyoming LLCs would be taxed as partnerships instead of as corporations, providing that certain requirements were met. Before this ruling, only one additional state—Florida, in 1982—had authorized LLCs. The 1988 IRS ruling encouraged other states to enact LLC statutes, and in less than a decade, all states had done so.

IRS rules that went into effect in 1997 also encouraged more widespread use of LLCs in the business world. Under these rules, any unincorporated business is automatically taxed as a partnership unless it indicates otherwise on the tax form. The exceptions involve publicly traded companies, companies formed under a state incorporation statute, and certain foreign-owned companies. If a business chooses to be taxed as a corporation, it can indicate this preference by checking a box on the IRS form.

Foreign Entities May Be LLC Members Part of the impetus behind the creation of LLCs in this country is that foreign investors are allowed to become LLC members. Generally, in an era increasingly characterized by global business efforts and investments, the LLC offers U.S. firms and potential investors from other countries greater flexibility and opportunities than are available through partnerships or corporations.

- **Application to Today's World** *Once it became clear that LLCs could be taxed as partnerships, the LLC form of business organization was widely adopted. Members could avoid the personal liability associated with the partnership form of business as well as the double taxation of the corporate form of business (see Chapter 29). Today, LLCs are a common form of business organization.*

- **Relevant Web Sites** To locate information on the Web concerning limited liability company statutes, go to this text's Web site at www.cengage.com/blaw/blt, select "Chapter 28," and click on "URLs for Landmarks."

Limited Liability Companies

Limited liability companies are governed by state LLC statutes. These laws vary, of course, from state to state. In an attempt to create more uniformity among the states in this respect, in 1995 the National Conference of Commissioners on Uniform State Laws (NCCUSL) issued the Uniform Limited Liability Company Act (ULLCA), but less than one-fifth of the states adopted it.[1] In 2006, the NCCUSL issued a revised version of this uniform law (the Re-ULLCA), which has been adopted in a few states. Thus, the law governing LLCs remains far from uniform. Some provisions are common to most state statutes, however, and we base our discussion of LLCs in this section on these common elements.

Member A person who has an ownership interest in a limited liability company.

Flight Options, LLC, offers charter jet services. Why did the company choose to organize as an LLC?

(Michael Brands/*The New York Times*/Redux)

The Nature of the LLC

Limited liability companies share many characteristics with corporations. Like corporations, LLCs are creatures of the state. In other words, they must be formed and operated in compliance with state law. Like shareholders in a corporation, owners of an LLC, who are called **members,** enjoy limited liability [ULLCA 303]. Also like corporations, LLCs are legal entities apart from their members. As a legal person, the LLC can sue or be sued, enter into contracts, and hold title to property [ULLCA 201]. The terminology used to describe LLCs formed in other states or nations is

1. Excerpts from the Uniform Limited Liability Company Act (ULLCA) are presented on the Web site that accompanies this text.

also similar to the terminology used in corporate law. For example, an LLC formed in one state but doing business in another state is referred to in the second state as a *foreign LLC.*

If an LLC is sued for wrongful discharge, can its members, managers, and agents be held liable, based on their status in the LLC, even though they did not participate in the dismissal that led to the lawsuit? That was the question in the following case.

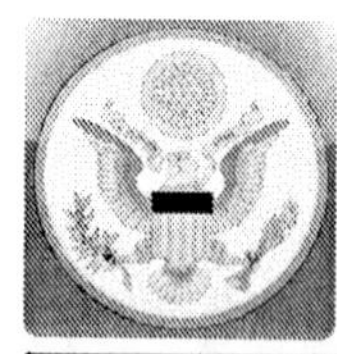

Case 28.1 McFarland v. Virginia Retirement Services of Chesterfield, LLC

United States District Court, Eastern District of Virginia, 477 F.Supp.2d 727 (2007).

Staff members at a retirement community LLC have elderly residents walk in ninety-five-degree heat. What factors determine accountability and liability?

FACTS Virginia Retirement Services of Chesterfield, LLC, does business as Magnolias of Chesterfield (Magnolia), a retirement community. In 2005, Penny McFarland became Magnolia's activities director. McFarland was responsible for coordinating and conducting resident activities. In 2006, Effie Stovall, McFarland's supervisor, told the staff to take the residents outside for a walk. The temperature was ninety-five degrees. Out of concern for the residents, someone complained to the state licensing board. An inspector contacted McFarland, who immediately told Stovall. When Mary Dunmoyer, Magnolia's executive director, learned of the contact, she had Stovall discharge McFarland for trying to "sabotage" the community. McFarland filed a suit in a federal district court against Magnolia, Dunmoyer, and other individual defendants, alleging, among other things, wrongful discharge–that she was terminated because she had provided information regarding the health and safety of Magnolia's residents in response to the inspector's inquiry. The individual defendants, who were members, managers, or agents of Magnolia, filed a motion to be dismissed from the suit.

ISSUE Can a member, manager, or agent of an LLC be held responsible for its contractual obligations or tort liability based *solely* on the individual's position in the LLC?

DECISION No. The district court dismissed the individual defendants, except for Dunmoyer, from McFarland's suit.

REASON Under Virginia state law, members, managers, and agents of an LLC are not responsible for its liabilities "solely" by virtue of their status. The district court pointed out that only "officers or agents who have played a key role in contributing to the company's tortious conduct" can be part of a wrongful discharge claim. With the exception of Dunmoyer, none of the other individual defendants were alleged to have personally participated in McFarland's discharge. Thus, the court found that they should be dropped from the suit.

FOR CRITICAL ANALYSIS—Legal Consideration *Why is the liability of the members of an LLC limited with respect to the firm's debts and other obligations?*

LLC Formation

Articles of Organization The document filed with a designated state official by which a limited liability company is formed.

To form an LLC, **articles of organization** must be filed with a central state agency—usually the secretary of state's office [ULLCA 202].[2] Typically, the articles are required to include such information as the name of the business, its principal address, the name and address of a registered agent, the names of the members, and information on how the LLC will be managed [ULLCA 203]. The business's name must include the words *Limited Liability Company* or the initials *LLC* [ULLCA 105(a)]. Although a majority of the states permit one-member LLCs, some states require at least two members.

Businesspersons sometimes enter into contracts on behalf of a business organization that is not yet formed. As you will read in Chapter 29, persons who are forming a corporation may enter into contracts during the process of incorporation but before the corporation becomes a legal entity. These contracts are referred to as preincorporation contracts. Once the corporation is formed and adopts the preincorporation contract (by means of a *novation,* discussed in Chapter 13), it can enforce the contract terms.

Where must an LLC's articles of organization be filed?

2. In addition to requiring the filing of articles of organization, a few states require that a notice of the intention to form an LLC be published in a local newspaper.

ON THE WEB You can find information on how to form an LLC, including the fees charged in each state for filing LLC articles of organization, at the Web site of Bizcorp, Inc. Go to www.bizcorp.com.

In the following case, the question was whether the same principle extends to LLCs. A person in the process of forming an LLC entered into a preorganization contract under which it would be obligated to purchase the Park Plaza Hotel in Hollywood, California. Once the LLC legally existed, the owners of the hotel refused to sell the property to the LLC, claiming that the contract was unenforceable.

Case 28.2 02 Development, LLC v. 607 South Park, LLC

Court of Appeal of California, Second District, 159 Cal.App.4th 609, 71 Cal.Rptr.3d 608 (2008).

(Creative Commons)

Can a purchase agreement for a hotel be assigned to an LLC before its organization?

FACTS In March 2004, 607 South Park, LLC, entered into a written agreement to sell Park Plaza Hotel to 607 Park View Associates, Ltd., for $8.7 million. The general partner of 607 Park View Associates was Creative Environments of Hollywood, Inc. In February 2005, Creative Environments assigned the rights to the hotel purchase to another company, 02 Development, LLC. At the time, 02 Development did not yet exist; it was legally created several months later. When 607 South Park refused to sell the hotel, 02 Development sued for breach of the hotel purchase agreement. 607 South Park moved for summary judgment, arguing that no enforceable contract existed because at the time of the assignment, 02 Development did not yet legally exist. Furthermore, 607 South Park argued, 02 Development suffered no damages because it was "not ready, willing, and able to fund the purchase of the hotel." The trial court granted the motion and entered judgment in favor of 607 South Park. 02 Development appealed.

ISSUE Can an LLC enforce a contract that had been assigned to it prior to the date of its legal formation?

DECISION Yes. A state intermediate appellate court reversed the judgment and directed the trial court to enter an order denying 607 South Park's motion for summary judgment. According to the appellate court, LLCs should be treated the same as corporations with respect to preorganization contracts.

REASON South Park's primary argument was that 02 Development did not exist at the time of the contract and was not a party to the contract. The court, however, reasoned that it is established law that corporations are liable on preincorporation contracts and that the same principle should extend to LLCs. "When the assignment agreement was executed, 02 Development did not exist so it was not then a party to the agreement. But once 02 Development came into existence, it could enforce any preorganization contract made on its behalf, such as the assignment agreement, if it adopted or ratified it." 607 South Park had not argued that LLCs should be treated differently than corporations. Instead, 607 South Park had argued that 02 Development was required to present admissible evidence that it would have been financially able to close the transaction, but the court rejected this notion. "607 South Park presented no evidence that 02 Development would have been unable to arrange for the necessary funding to close the transaction on time if 607 South Park had given it the opportunity instead of repudiating a contract in advance." Consequently, the trial court erred when it granted 607 South Park's motion for summary judgment.

FOR CRITICAL ANALYSIS—Social Consideration *Why was it unimportant to the appellate court that the trial court did not require 02 Development to prove that it had funding commitments for $8.7 million?*

Jurisdictional Requirements

One of the significant differences between LLCs and corporations involves federal jurisdictional requirements. The federal jurisdiction statute provides that a corporation is deemed to be a citizen of the state where it is incorporated and maintains its principal place of business. The statute does not mention the citizenship of partnerships, LLCs, and other unincorporated associations, but the courts have tended to regard these entities as citizens of every state in which their members are citizens.

The state citizenship of LLCs may come into play when a party sues an LLC based on diversity of citizenship. Remember from Chapter 3 that in some circumstances, such as when parties to a lawsuit are from different states, a federal court can exercise diversity jurisdiction in cases in which the amount in controversy exceeds $75,000. *Total* diversity of citizenship must exist, however. **EXAMPLE 28.1** Fong, a citizen of New York, wishes to bring a lawsuit against Skycel, an LLC formed under the laws of Connecticut. One of Skycel's members also lives in New York. Fong will not be able to bring the action against Skycel in federal court—on the basis of diversity jurisdiction—because the defendant LLC is also impliedly a citizen of New York. The same would be true if Fong was filing a suit against multiple defendants and one of the defendants lived in New York. ●

Advantages of the LLC

The LLC offers many advantages to businesspersons, which is why this form of business organization has become increasingly popular. See the *Business Application* feature at the end of this chapter for a discussion of the factors that entrepreneurs need to consider when choosing between LLCs and limited liability partnerships (LLPs).

Limited Liability A key advantage of the LLC is that the liability of members is limited to the amount of their investments. Although the LLC as an entity can be held liable for any loss or injury caused by the wrongful acts or omissions of its members, the members themselves generally are not personally liable.

The focus in the following case was on a member's personal liability for the alleged "acts" of his firm.

Case 28.3 Allen v. Dackman

Court of Special Appeals of Maryland, 184 Md.App. 1, 964 A.2d 210 (2009).
www.courts.state.md.us/index.html[a]

HISTORICAL AND ENVIRONMENTAL SETTING *Lead is a toxic metal that was used for centuries in water pipes and other products. Lead can be emitted into the air from motor vehicles and industrial sources, and it can leach into drinking water from plumbing. One of the most common sources of lead is deteriorating lead-based paint. This paint can be found in many houses and apartments built before 1978, the year that the federal government banned lead-based paint in housing. If ingested, lead can cause various harmful health effects, ranging from behavioral problems and learning disabilities to seizures and death. Children six years old and under are especially at risk.*

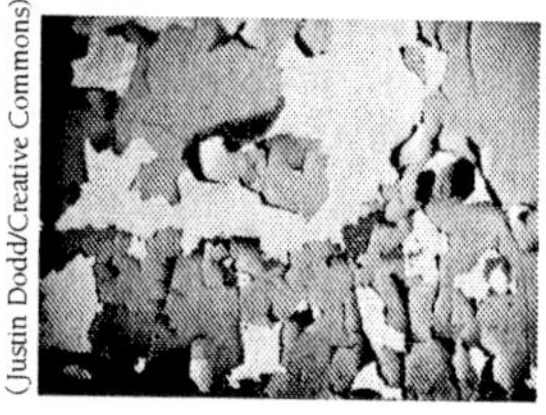
(Justin Dodd/Creative Commons)

Can a member of an LLC be held personally liable for illness sustained from lead paint in a rental property?

FACTS When Monica Allen and Shantese Thomas were three years old and one year old, respectively, they came to live with their grandmother, Tracy Allen, at 3143 Elmora Avenue in Baltimore, Maryland. Allen leased the dwelling from Mildred Thompkins. Less than a year later, after Thompkins failed to pay the taxes on the property, Hard Assets, LLC, acquired it. For fifteen years, the firm had bought and sold tax-delinquent properties. Jay Dackman, a member of the LLC, ran the business. Hard Assets intended to sell the property, rather than keep it as a rental, so Allen and her grandchildren were asked to vacate the premises. Within a few months, the property was sold. While living there, Monica and Shantese were allegedly injured from exposure to lead-based paint. To recover, their mother, Monica Allen, filed a suit in a Maryland state court against Dackman, alleging violations of the city's housing code and negligence. The court issued a judgment in Dackman's favor. Allen appealed.

ISSUE Can a member of an LLC avoid personal liability for the alleged injuries of residents who live on property owned by the LLC?

DECISION Yes. A state intermediate appellate court affirmed the lower court's judgment. Dackman, as a member of Hard Assets, could not be held personally liable for the LLC's asserted obligations or liabilities.

REASON Under the city's housing code, an "owner" is a person who "controls" the title to property, and an "operator" is a person who has control of a building in which "dwelling units * * * are let." Dackman was not an "owner" within this definition because he did not personally "control" the property. He ran Hard Assets' business, but he lacked the right, as an individual, to transfer the title to the property. He was not an "operator" because Hard Assets did not offer the property for lease and did not receive rent, or attempt to collect rent, from the Allens. Dackman could not be liable on the negligence claim because, under Maryland's Limited Liability Company Act, "no member shall be personally liable for the obligations of the limited liability company, whether arising in contract, tort or otherwise, solely by reason of being a member of the limited liability company."

FOR CRITICAL ANALYSIS—Social Consideration *Is Hard Assets liable for the alleged injuries to Monica and Shantese? Explain.*

a. In the "Appellate Courts" section, click on "reported opinions." On that page, in the "Court" box choose "Court of Special Appeals"; in the "Filing Year" box, select "2009"; in the "Sorting Order" box, choose "by appellant's (or first party's) name"; and click on "Submit." In the result, click on the link to access the opinion. The Maryland Judiciary maintains this Web site.

(Photo Courtesy of ECD Ovonics)

Stan Ovshinsky, founder of Ovonic Hydrogen Systems, LLC, a developer of alternative energy technologies. What are some of the advantages of doing business as an LLC instead of a corporation? Are there any disadvantages?

TAXATION Another advantage is the flexibility of the LLC in regard to taxation. An LLC that has *two or more members* can choose to be taxed either as a partnership or as a corporation. As you will read in Chapter 29, a corporate entity must pay income taxes on its profits, and the shareholders pay personal income taxes on profits distributed as dividends. An LLC that wants to distribute profits to its members may prefer to be taxed as a partnership to avoid the "double taxation" that is characteristic of the corporate entity.

Unless an LLC indicates that it wishes to be taxed as a corporation, the IRS automatically taxes it as a partnership. This means that the LLC as an entity pays no taxes; rather, as in a partnership, profits are "passed through" the LLC to the members who then personally pay taxes on the profits. If an LLC's members want to reinvest the profits in the business, however, rather than distribute the profits to members, they may prefer that the LLC be taxed as a corporation. Corporate income tax rates may be lower than personal tax rates. Part of the attractiveness of the LLC is this flexibility with respect to taxation.

For federal income tax purposes, one-member LLCs are automatically taxed as sole proprietorships unless they indicate that they wish to be taxed as corporations. With respect to state taxes, most states follow the IRS rules.

MANAGEMENT AND FOREIGN INVESTORS Still another advantage of the LLC for businesspersons is the flexibility it offers in terms of business operations and management—as will be discussed shortly. Finally, because foreign investors can participate in an LLC, the LLC form of business is attractive as a way to encourage investment. For a discussion of business organizations in other nations that are similar to the LLC, see this chapter's *Beyond Our Borders* feature on the following page.

Disadvantages of the LLC

REMEMBER A uniform law is a "model" law. It does not become the law of any state until the state legislature adopts it, either in part or in its entirety.

The main disadvantage of the LLC is that state LLC statutes are not uniform. Therefore, businesses that operate in more than one state may not receive consistent treatment in these states. Generally, though, most states apply to a foreign LLC (an LLC formed in another state) the law of the state where the LLC was formed. Difficulties can arise, nonetheless, when one state's court must interpret and apply another state's laws.

LLC Operation and Management

As mentioned, an advantage of the LLC form of business is the flexibility it offers in terms of operation and management. We discuss the operating agreement, management options, and general operating procedures of LLCs next.

The LLC Operating Agreement

Operating Agreement In a limited liability company, an agreement in which the members set forth the details of how the business will be managed and operated. State statutes typically give the members wide latitude in deciding for themselves the rules that will govern their organization.

The members of an LLC can decide how to operate the various aspects of the business by forming an **operating agreement** [ULLCA 103(a)]. Operating agreements typically contain provisions relating to management, how profits will be divided, the transfer of membership interests, whether the LLC will be dissolved on the death or departure of a member, and other important issues.

A WRITING IS PREFERRED In many states, an operating agreement is not required for an LLC to exist, and if there is one, it need not be in writing. Generally, though, LLC members should protect their interests by creating a written operating agreement. As in any business, disputes may arise over any number of issues. If there is no agreement covering the topic under dispute, such as how profits will be divided, the state LLC statute will govern the outcome. For example, most LLC statutes provide that if the members have not specified how profits will be divided, they will be divided equally among the members.

Beyond Our Borders — Limited Liability Companies in Other Nations

Limited liability companies are not unique to the United States. Many nations have business forms that provide limited liability, although these organizations may differ significantly from domestic LLCs. In Germany, for example, the *GmbH*, or *Gesellschaft mit beschränkter Haftung* (which means "company with limited liability"), is a type of business entity that has been available since 1892. The GmbH is now the most widely used business form in Germany. A GmbH, however, is owned by shareholders and thus resembles a U.S. corporation in certain respects. German laws also impose numerous restrictions on the operations and business transactions of GmbHs, whereas LLCs in the United States are not even required to have an operating agreement.

Business forms that limit the liability of owners can also be found in various other countries. Limited liability companies known as *limitadas* are common in many Latin American nations. In France, a *société à responsabilité limitée* (meaning "society with limited liability") is an entity that provides business owners with limited liability. Although laws in the United Kingdom and Ireland use the term *limited liability partnership,* the entities are similar to our domestic LLCs. In 2006, Japan enacted legislation that created a new type of business organization, called the *godo kaisha (GK),* which is also quite similar to a U.S. LLC. In most nations, some type of document that is similar to the LLC's articles of organization must be filed with the government to form the business. Many countries limit the number of owners that such businesses may have, and some also require the member-owners to choose one or more persons who will manage the business affairs.

• For Critical Analysis

Clearly, limited liability is an important aspect of doing business globally. Why might a nation limit the number of member-owners in a limited liability entity?

PARTNERSHIP LAW MAY APPLY When an issue, such as the authority of individual members, is not covered by an operating agreement or by an LLC statute, the courts often apply principles of partnership law. These principles can give the members of an LLC broad authority to bind the LLC unless an operating agreement provides otherwise. **CASE EXAMPLE 28.2** Clifford Kuhn, Jr., and Joseph Tumminelli formed Touch of Class Limousine Service as an LLC. They did not create a written operating agreement but orally agreed that Kuhn would provide the financial backing and procure customers, and that Tumminelli would manage the company's day-to-day operations. Tumminelli embezzled $283,000 from the company after cashing customers' checks at Quick Cash, Inc., a local check-cashing service. Kuhn filed a lawsuit against Tumminelli, the banks, and others in a New Jersey state court to recover the embezzled funds. He argued that Quick Cash and the banks were liable because Tumminelli did not have the authority to cash the company's checks and convert the funds. The court, however, held that in the absence of a written operating agreement to the contrary, a member of an LLC, like a partner in a partnership, does have the authority to cash the firm's checks.[3] ●

Management of an LLC

"Business is the salt of life."
Voltaire, 1694–1778
(French author and philosopher)

Basically, the members of an LLC have two options for managing the firm. It can be either a "member-managed" LLC or a "manager-managed" LLC. Most LLC statutes and the ULLCA provide that unless the articles of organization specify otherwise, an LLC is assumed to be member managed [ULLCA 203(a)(6)].

In a *member-managed* LLC, all of the members participate in management, and decisions are made by majority vote [ULLCA 404(a)]. In a *manager-managed* LLC, the members designate a group of persons to manage the firm. The management group may consist of only members, both members and nonmembers, or only nonmembers.

Under the ULLCA, managers in a manager-managed LLC owe fiduciary duties (the duty of loyalty and the duty of care) to the LLC and its members, just as corporate directors and officers owe fiduciary duties to the corporation and its shareholders [ULLCA 409(a), (h)].

3. *Kuhn v. Tumminelli,* 366 N.J.Super. 431, 841 A.2d 496 (2004).

But because not all states have adopted the ULLCA, some state statutes provide that managers owe fiduciary duties only to the LLC and not to the other members. Although to whom the duty is owed may seem insignificant at first glance, it actually can have a dramatic effect on the outcome of litigation.

Ethical Issue

Do managers in a manager-managed LLC owe fiduciary duties to other members? **Fiduciary duties, such as the duty of loyalty and the duty of care, have an ethical component because they require a person to act honestly and faithfully toward another. In states that have adopted the ULLCA, the managers of a manager-managed LLC owe fiduciary duties to the members and thus basically are required to behave ethically toward them. In other states, however, the LLC statutes may not include such a requirement. Consequently, even when a manager-member has acted unfairly and unethically toward other members, the members may not be able to sue the manager for a breach of fiduciary duties.**

In North Carolina and Virginia, for example, the LLC statutes do not explicitly create fiduciary duties for managers to members. Instead, the statutes require that a manager exercise good business judgment in the best interests of the company. Because the statutes are silent on the manager's duty to members, in 2009 courts in those two states held that a manager-member owed fiduciary duties only to the LLC and not to the members.[4] In contrast, in two other 2009 cases, courts in Idaho and Kentucky held that a manager-member owes fiduciary duties to the LLC's members and that the members can sue the manager for breaching fiduciary duties.[5]

Operating Procedures

The members of an LLC can also set forth in their operating agreement provisions governing decision-making procedures. For instance, the agreement can include procedures for choosing or removing managers. Although most LLC statutes are silent on this issue, the ULLCA provides that members may choose and remove managers by majority vote [ULLCA 404(b)(3)].

The members are also free to include in the agreement provisions designating when and for what purposes they will hold formal members' meetings. In contrast to the state laws governing corporations, which generally provide for shareholders' meetings (see Chapter 29), most state LLC statutes have no provisions regarding members' meetings.

(PhotoDisc)

Members of a manager-managed LLC hold a formal members' meeting. What is the difference between a member-managed LLC and a manager-managed LLC? How are managers typically chosen?

Members may also specify in their agreement how voting rights will be apportioned. If they do not, LLC statutes in most states provide that voting rights are apportioned according to each member's capital contributions. Some states provide that, in the absence of an agreement to the contrary, each member has one vote.

Dissociation and Dissolution of an LLC

Recall from Chapter 27 that in the context of partnerships, *dissociation* occurs when a partner ceases to be associated in the carrying on of the business. The same concept applies to LLCs. A member of an LLC has the *power* to dissociate from the LLC at any time, but she or he may not have the *right* to dissociate. Under the ULLCA, the events that trigger a member's dissociation from an LLC are similar to the events causing a partner to be dissociated

4. *Remora Investments, LLC v. Orr,* 277 Va. 316, 673 S.E.2d 845 (2009); Virginia Code Sections 13.1–1024.1; and *Kaplan v. O.K. Technologies, LLC,* 675 S.E.2d 133 (N.C.App. 2009); North Carolina General Statutes Section 57C-3-22(b).

5. *Bushi v. Sage Health Care, LLC,* 146 Idaho 764, 203 P.3d 694 (2009); Idaho Code Sections 30-6-101 *et seq.*; and *Patmon v. Hobbs,* 280 S.W.3d 589 (Ky.App. 2009); Kentucky Revised Statutes Section 275.170.

under the Uniform Partnership Act (UPA). These include voluntary withdrawal, expulsion by other members or by court order, bankruptcy, incompetence, and death. Generally, even if a member dies or otherwise dissociates from an LLC, the other members may continue to carry on the LLC's business, unless the operating agreement provides otherwise.

The Effect of Dissociation

When a member dissociates from an LLC, he or she loses the right to participate in management and the right to act as an agent for the LLC. The member's duty of loyalty to the LLC also terminates, and the duty of care continues only with respect to events that occurred before dissociation. Generally, the dissociated member also has a right to have his or her interest in the LLC bought out by the other members. The LLC's operating agreement may contain provisions establishing a buyout price, but if it does not, the member's interest is usually purchased at a fair value. In states that have adopted the ULLCA, the LLC must purchase the interest at "fair" value within 120 days after the dissociation.

If the member's dissociation violates the LLC's operating agreement, it is considered legally wrongful, and the dissociated member can be held liable for damages caused by the dissociation. **EXAMPLE 28.3** Chadwick and Barrel are members in an LLC. Chadwick manages the accounts, and Barrel, who has many connections in the community and is a skilled investor, brings in the business. If Barrel wrongfully dissociates from the LLC, the LLC's business will suffer, and Chadwick can hold Barrel liable for the loss of business resulting from her withdrawal. ●

Dissolution

Regardless of whether a member's dissociation was wrongful or rightful, normally the dissociated member has no right to force the LLC to dissolve. The remaining members can opt to either continue or dissolve the business. Members can also stipulate in their operating agreement that certain events will cause dissolution, or they can agree that they have the power to dissolve the LLC by vote. As with partnerships, a court can order an LLC to be dissolved in certain circumstances, such as when the members have engaged in illegal or oppressive conduct, or when it is no longer feasible to carry on the business.

When an LLC is dissolved, any members who did not wrongfully dissociate may participate in the winding up process. To wind up the business, members must collect, liquidate, and distribute the LLC's assets. Members may preserve the assets for a reasonable time to optimize their return, and they continue to have the authority to perform reasonable acts in conjunction with winding up. In other words, the LLC will be bound by the reasonable acts of its members during the winding up process. Once all the LLC's assets have been sold, the proceeds are distributed to pay off debts to creditors first (including debts owed to members who are creditors of the LLC). The member's capital contributions are returned next, and any remaining amounts are then distributed to members in equal shares or according to their operating agreement.

Preventing Legal Disputes

When forming an LLC, carefully draft the operating agreement. Stipulate the events that will cause dissociation and how the fair-value buyout price will be calculated. Set a time limit within which the LLC must pay the dissociated member (or her or his estate) in the event of withdrawal, disability, or death. Include provisions that clearly limit the authority of dissociated members to act on behalf of the LLC and provide a right to seek damages from members who exceed the agreed-on parameters. Also, notify third parties if any member dissociates and file a notice of dissociation with the state to limit the extent of the former member's apparent authority to act on behalf of the LLC. The operating agreement should specify any events that will automatically cause a dissolution, as well as which members will have a right to participate in—or make decisions about—the winding up.

Special Business Forms

Besides the traditional business forms and limited liability companies discussed in this unit, several other forms can be used to organize a business. For the most part, these special business forms are hybrid organizations—that is, they have characteristics similar to those of partnerships or corporations or combine features of both. These forms include joint ventures, syndicates, joint stock companies, business trusts, and cooperatives.

Joint Ventures

Joint Venture A joint undertaking of a specific commercial enterprise by an association of persons. A joint venture normally is not a legal entity and is treated like a partnership for federal income tax purposes.

A **joint venture,** sometimes referred to as a *joint adventure,* is a relationship in which two or more persons or business entities combine their efforts or their property for a single transaction or project or a related series of transactions or projects. Unless otherwise agreed, joint venturers share profits and losses equally. For instance, when several contractors combine their resources to build and sell houses in a single development, their relationship is a joint venture.

Joint ventures range in size from very small activities to huge, multimillion-dollar joint actions carried out by some of the world's largest corporations. Large organizations often investigate new markets or new ideas by forming joint ventures with other enterprises. For instance, Intel Corporation and Micron Technology, Inc., formed a joint venture to manufacture NAND flash memory, a data-storage chip widely used in digital cameras, cell phones, and portable music players, including some iPods made by Apple, Inc. Similarly, Mitsubishi Chemical Corporation formed a joint venture with Exxon Chemical Corporation to start Mytex Polymers, a company that produces certain plastic compounds used by automakers in the United States and Japan.

SIMILARITIES TO PARTNERSHIPS The joint venture resembles a partnership and is taxed like a partnership. For this reason, most courts apply the same principles to joint ventures as they apply to partnerships. Joint venturers owe to each other the same fiduciary duties, including the duty of loyalty, that partners owe each other. If one of the venturers secretly buys land that was to be acquired by the joint venture, the other joint venturers may be awarded damages for the breach of loyalty. A joint venturer can also be held personally liable for the venture's debts (because joint venturers share profits and *losses*). Like partners, joint venturers have equal rights to manage the activities of the enterprise, but they can agree to give control of the operation to one of the members.

Joint venturers also have authority as agents to enter into contracts for the business that will bind the joint venture. **CASE EXAMPLE 28.4** Murdo Cameron developed components to make replicas of vintage P-51 Mustang planes. Cameron agreed in writing with Douglas Anderson to collaborate on the design and manufacture of one P-51 for each of them. They agreed that Anderson would build the first plane and that Cameron would provide an engine, which Anderson would pay for after the plane's first flight. Without Cameron's knowledge, Anderson borrowed funds from SPW Associates, LLP, to finance the construction, using the first plane as security for the loan. After Anderson built one plane, he defaulted on the loan. SPW filed a lawsuit asking a state court to declare that SPW was entitled to the aircraft. The court ruled that Anderson and Cameron had entered into a joint venture and that the plane was the venture's property. Under partnership law, partners have the power as agents to bind the partnership. Because this principle applies to joint ventures, Anderson had the authority to grant SPW a security interest in the plane, and SPW was entitled to its possession.[6] ●

"Business without profit is not business any more than a pickle is candy."

Charles Abbott, 1762–1832
(British jurist)

6. *SPW Associates, LLP v. Anderson,* 2006 ND 159, 718 N.W.2d 580 (N.D.Sup.Ct. 2006).

DIFFERENCES FROM PARTNERSHIPS Joint ventures differ from partnerships in several important ways. The members of a joint venture have less implied and apparent authority than the partners in a partnership. As discussed in Chapter 27, each partner is treated as an agent of the other partners. Because the activities of a joint venture are more limited than the business of a partnership, the members of a joint venture are presumed to have less power to bind their co-venturers. In Case Example 28.4 on the previous page, for instance, if Anderson's contract had not been directly related to the business of building vintage planes, the court might have concluded that Anderson lacked the authority to bind the joint venture. Also, unlike most partnerships, a joint venture normally terminates when the project or the transaction for which it was formed has been completed, though the members can specify how long the relationship will last.

CONTRAST A partnership involves a continuing relationship of the partners. A joint venture is often a one-time association.

Syndicates

A group of individuals or firms that get together to finance a particular project, such as the building of a shopping center or the purchase of a professional basketball franchise, is called a **syndicate** or an *investment group*. The form of such groups varies considerably. A syndicate may exist as a corporation or as a general or limited partnership. In some instances, the members do not have a legally recognized business arrangement but merely purchase and own property jointly.

Syndicate A group of individuals or firms brought together for the purpose of financing a project that they would not or could not undertake independently; also called an *investment group*.

Joint Stock Companies

A **joint stock company** is a true hybrid of a partnership and a corporation. It has many characteristics of a corporation in that (1) its ownership is represented by transferable shares of stock, (2) it is usually managed by directors and officers of the company or association, and (3) it can have a perpetual existence. Most of its other features, however, are more characteristic of a partnership, and it is usually treated like a partnership. As with a partnership, a joint stock company is formed by agreement (not statute), property is usually held in the names of the members, shareholders have personal liability, and the company generally is not treated as a legal entity for purposes of a lawsuit. In a joint stock company, however, shareholders are not considered to be agents of one another, as would be the case if the company were a true partnership (see Chapter 27).

Joint Stock Company A hybrid form of business organization that combines characteristics of a corporation and a partnership. Usually, a joint stock company is regarded as a partnership for tax and other legal purposes.

Business Trusts

A **business trust** is created by a written trust agreement that sets forth the interests of the beneficiaries and the obligations and powers of the trustees. With a business trust, legal ownership and management of the property of the business stay with one or more of the trustees, and the profits are distributed to the beneficiaries.

The business trust was started in Massachusetts in an attempt to obtain the limited liability advantage of corporate status while avoiding certain restrictions on a corporation's ownership of, and ability to develop, real property. A business trust resembles a corporation in many respects. Beneficiaries of the trust, for example, are not personally responsible for the debts or obligations of the business trust. In fact, in a number of states, business trusts must pay corporate taxes.

Business Trust A form of business organization in which investors (trust beneficiaries) transfer cash or property to trustees in exchange for trust certificates that represent their investment shares. The certificate holders share in the trust's profits but have limited liability.

Cooperatives

A **cooperative** is an association that is organized to provide an economic service to its members (or shareholders); it may or may not be incorporated. Most cooperatives are organized under state statutes for cooperatives, general business corporations, or LLCs. Generally, an incorporated cooperative will distribute dividends, or profits, to its own-

Cooperative An association, which may or may not be incorporated, that is organized to provide an economic service to its members. Unincorporated cooperatives are often treated like partnerships for tax and other legal purposes. Examples of cooperatives include consumer purchasing cooperatives, credit cooperatives, and farmers' cooperatives.

ers on the basis of their transactions with the cooperative rather than on the basis of the amount of capital they contributed. Members of incorporated cooperatives have limited liability, as do shareholders of corporations and members of LLCs. Cooperatives that are unincorporated are often treated like partnerships. The members have joint liability for the cooperative's acts.

This form of business generally is adopted by groups of individuals who wish to pool their resources to gain some advantage in the marketplace. Consumer purchasing co-ops are formed to obtain lower prices through quantity discounts. Seller marketing co-ops are formed to control the market and thereby enable members to sell their goods at higher prices. Co-ops range in size from small, local, consumer cooperatives to national businesses such as Ace Hardware and Land O' Lakes, a well-known producer of dairy products.

Reviewing . . . Limited Liability Companies and Special Business Forms

The city of Papagos, Arizona, had a deteriorating bridge in need of repair on a prominent public roadway. The city posted notices seeking proposals for an artistic bridge design and reconstruction. Davidson Masonry, LLC—owned and managed by Carl Davidson and his wife, Marilyn Rowe—decided to submit a bid for a decorative concrete project that incorporated artistic metalwork. They contacted Shana Lafayette, a local sculptor who specialized in large-scale metal creations, to help them design the bridge. The city selected their bridge design and awarded them the contract for a commission of $184,000. Davidson Masonry and Lafayette then entered into an agreement to work together on the bridge project. Davidson Masonry agreed to install and pay for concrete and structural work, and Lafayette agreed to install the metalwork at her expense. They agreed that overall profits would be split, with 25 percent going to Lafayette and 75 percent going to Davidson Masonry. Lafayette designed numerous metal salmon sculptures that were incorporated into colorful decorative concrete forms designed by Rowe, while Davidson performed the structural engineering. The group worked together successfully until the completion of the project. Using the information presented in the chapter, answer the following questions.

1. Would Davidson Masonry automatically be taxed as a partnership or a corporation? Why or why not?
2. Is Davidson Masonry member managed or manager managed?
3. When Davidson Masonry and Lafayette entered into an agreement to work together, what kind of special business form was created? Explain.
4. Suppose that during construction, Lafayette had entered into an agreement to rent space in a warehouse that was close to the bridge so that she could work on her sculptures near the location at which they would eventually be installed. She entered into the contract without the knowledge or consent of Davidson Masonry. In this situation, would a court be likely to hold that Davidson Masonry was bound by the contract that Lafayette entered? Why or why not?

Business Application

How Do You Choose between LLCs and LLPs?*

One of the most important decisions that an entrepreneur makes is the selection of the form in which to do business. To make the best decision, a businessperson needs to understand all aspects of the various forms, including legal, tax, licensing, and business considerations. In addition, all of the participants in the business should understand their actual relationship, regardless of the organizational structure.

Number of Participants

During the last fifteen years, new forms of business organizations, including limited liability partnerships (LLPs—discussed in Chapter 27) and limited liability companies (LLCs), have been added to the options for business entities. An initial consideration in choosing between these forms

*This *Business Application* is not meant to substitute for the services of an attorney who is licensed to practice law in your state.

Continued

is the number of participants. An LLP must have two or more partners, but in many states, an LLC can have a single member (owner).

Liability Considerations

The members of an LLC are not liable for the obligations of the organization. Members' liability is limited to the amount of their property (investment) interest. The liability of the partners in an LLP varies from state to state. About half of the states exempt the partners from liability for any obligation of the firm. In some states, the partners are individually liable for the contractual obligations of the firm but are not liable for obligations arising from the torts of others. In either situation, each partner may be on his or her own with respect to liability unless the other partners agree to help.

Distributions from the Firm

Members and partners generally are paid by allowing them to withdraw funds from the firm against their share of the profits. In many states, a member of an LLC must repay so-called wrongful distributions even if she or he did not know that the distributions were wrongful (wrongful distributions include those made when the LLC is insolvent). Under most LLP statutes, by contrast, the partners must repay only distributions that were fraudulent.

Management Structure

Both LLPs and LLCs can set up whatever management structure the participants desire. Also, all unincorporated business organizations, including LLPs and LLCs with two or more members, are treated as partnerships for federal income tax purposes (unless an LLC elects to be treated as a corporation[a]). This means that the firms are not taxed at the entity level. Their income is passed through to the partners or members, who report it on their individual income tax returns. Some states impose additional taxes on LLCs.

a. The chief benefits of electing corporate status for tax purposes are that the members generally are not subject to self-employment taxes and that fringe benefits may be provided to employee-members on a tax-reduced basis. The tax laws are complicated, however, and a professional should be consulted about the details.

The Nature of the Business

The business in which a firm engages is another factor to consider in choosing a business form. For example, with a few exceptions, professionals, such as accountants, attorneys, and physicians, may organize as either an LLP or an LLC in any state. In many states, however, the organizational form of an entity that engages in a certain profession and the liability of the owners are prescribed by state law.

Financial and Personal Relationships

Although the legal consequences of choosing a business form are certainly important, they are often secondary to the financial and personal relationships among the participants. Work effort, motivation, ability, and other personal attributes can be significant factors, as may fundamental business concerns such as the expenses and debts of the firm—and the extent of personal liability for these obligations. Another practical factor to consider is the willingness of others to do business with an LLP or an LLC. A supplier, for example, may not be willing to extend credit to a firm whose partners or members will not accept personal liability for the debt.

CHECKLIST FOR CHOOSING A LIMITED LIABILITY BUSINESS FORM

1. **Determine the number of participants, the forms a state allows, and the limits on liability the state provides for the participants.**
2. **Evaluate the tax considerations.**
3. **Consider the business in which the firm engages, or will engage, and any restrictions imposed on that type of business.**
4. **Weigh such practical concerns as the financial and personal relationships among the participants and the willingness of others to do business with a particular organizational form.**

Key Terms

articles of organization 708
business trust 716
cooperative 716
joint stock company 716
joint venture 715
limited liability company (LLC) 706
member 707
operating agreement 711
syndicate 716

Chapter Summary: Limited Liability Companies and Special Business Forms

Limited Liability Companies (LLCs) (See pages 707–711.)	1. *Formation*—Articles of organization must be filed with the appropriate state office—usually the office of the secretary of state—setting forth the name of the business, its principal address, the names of the owners (called *members*), and other relevant information.

Chapter Summary: Limited Liability Companies and Special Business Forms—Continued

Limited Liability Companies (LLCs)—Continued	2. *Advantages and disadvantages of the LLC*—Advantages of the LLC include limited liability, the option to be taxed as a partnership or as a corporation, and flexibility in deciding how the business will be managed and operated. The main disadvantage is the absence of uniformity in state LLC statutes.
LLC Operation and Management (See pages 711–713.)	1. *Operating agreement*—When an LLC is formed, the members decide, in an operating agreement, how the business will be managed and what rules will apply to the organization. 2. *Management*—An LLC may be managed by members only, by some members and some nonmembers, or by nonmembers only.
Dissociation and Dissolution of an LLC (See pages 713–714.)	Members of an LLC have the power to dissociate from the LLC at any time, but they may not have the right to dissociate. Dissociation does not always result in the dissolution of an LLC; the remaining members can choose to continue the business. Dissociated members have a right to have their interest purchased by the other members. If the LLC is dissolved, the business must be wound up and the assets sold. Creditors are paid first; then members' capital investments are returned. Any remaining proceeds are distributed to members.
Special Business Forms (See pages 715–717.)	1. *Joint venture*—An organization created by two or more persons in contemplation of a limited activity or a single transaction; similar to a partnership in many respects. 2. *Syndicate*—An investment group that undertakes to finance a particular project; may exist as a corporation or as a general or limited partnership. 3. *Joint stock company*—A business form similar to a corporation in some respects (transferable shares of stock, management by directors and officers, perpetual existence) but otherwise resembling a partnership. 4. *Business trust*—A business form created by a written trust agreement that sets forth the interests of the beneficiaries and the obligations and powers of the trustee(s); similar to a corporation in many respects. Beneficiaries are not personally liable for the debts or obligations of the business trust. 5. *Cooperative*—An association organized to provide an economic service, without profit, to its members; may take the form of a corporation or a partnership.

ExamPrep

ISSUE SPOTTERS

1 Gomer, Harry, and Ida are members of Jeweled Watches, LLC. What are their options with respect to the management of their firm?

2 Greener Delivery Company and Hiway Trucking, Inc., form a business trust. Insta Equipment Company and Jiffy Supply Corporation form a joint stock company. Kwik Mart, Inc., and Luscious Produce, Inc., form an incorporated cooperative. What do these forms of business organization have in common?

BEFORE THE TEST

Check your answers to the Issue Spotters, and at the same time, take the interactive quiz for this chapter. Go to www.cengage.com/blaw/blt and click on "Chapter 28." First, click on "Answers to Issue Spotters" to check your answers. Next, click on "Interactive Quiz" to assess your mastery of the concepts in this chapter. Then click on "Flashcards" to review this chapter's Key Term definitions.

For Review

Answers for the even-numbered questions in this For Review section can be found on this text's accompanying Web site at www.cengage.com/blaw/blt. *Select "Chapter 28" and click on "For Review."*

1 What advantages do limited liability companies offer to businesspersons that are not offered by sole proprietorships or partnerships?

2 How are limited liability companies formed, and who decides how they will be managed and operated?

3 What are the two options for managing limited liability companies?
4 What is a joint venture? How is it similar to a partnership? How is it different?
5 What are the essential characteristics of joint stock companies, syndicates, business trusts, and cooperatives, respectively?

Hypothetical Scenarios and Case Problems

28–1 Limited Liability Companies. John, Lesa, and Trevor form a limited liability company. John contributes 60 percent of the capital, and Lesa and Trevor each contribute 20 percent. Nothing is decided about how profits will be divided. John assumes that he will be entitled to 60 percent of the profits, in accordance with his contribution. Lesa and Trevor, however, assume that the profits will be divided equally. A dispute over the profits arises, and ultimately a court has to decide the issue. What law will the court apply? In most states, what will result? How could this dispute have been avoided in the first place? Discuss fully.

28–2 Hypothetical Question with Sample Answer Faraway Corp. is considering entering into two contracts, one with a joint stock company that distributes home products east of the Mississippi River and the other with a business trust formed by a number of sole proprietors who are sellers of home products on the West Coast. Both contracts involve large capital outlays for Faraway, which will supply each business with soft-drink dispensers. In both business organizations, at least two shareholders or beneficiaries are personally wealthy, but each organization has limited financial resources. The owner-managers of Faraway are not familiar with either form of business organization. Because each form resembles a corporation, they are concerned about whether they will be able to collect payments from the wealthy members of the business organizations in the event that either organization breaches the contract by failing to make the payments. Discuss fully Faraway's concern.

—For a sample answer to Question 28–2, go to Appendix E at the end of this text.

28–3 Limited Liability Companies. Joe, a resident of New Jersey, wants to open a restaurant. He asks his friend Kay, who is an experienced attorney and a New Yorker, for her business and legal advice in exchange for a 20 percent ownership interest in the restaurant. Kay helps Joe negotiate a lease for the restaurant premises and advises Joe to organize the business as a limited liability company (LLC). Joe forms Café Olé, LLC, and, with Kay's help, obtains financing. Then, the night before the restaurant opens, Joe tells Kay that he is "cutting her out of the deal." The restaurant proves to be a success. Kay wants to file a suit in a federal district court against Joe and the LLC. Can a federal court exercise jurisdiction over the parties based on diversity of citizenship? Explain.

28–4 Foreign Limited Liability Companies. Whalen Murdock and Cary Hansen organized Capital Care, LLC, in Nebraska. Capital Care operated, and Murdock and Hansen managed, Heartland Care Center in Abilene, Kansas. Burk Properties, Inc., held a mortgage on the Heartland facilities. When Heartland failed as a business, its residents were transferred to other facilities. Heartland employees who provided care to the residents for five days during the transfers were not paid wages. The employees filed claims with the Kansas Department of Human Resources for the unpaid wages. Kansas state law provides that a *corporate* officer or manager may be liable for a firm's unpaid wages, but protects LLC members from personal liability generally and states that an LLC cannot be construed as a corporation. Under Nebraska state law, the members of an LLC can be personally liable for wages due the LLC's employees. Should Murdock and Hansen be held personally liable for the unpaid wages? Explain.

28–5 Case Problem with Sample Answer Westbury Properties, Inc., and others (collectively the Westbury group) owned, managed, and developed real property. Jerry Stoker and the Stoker Group, Inc. (the Stokers), also developed real property. The Westbury group entered into agreements with the Stokers concerning a large tract of property in Houston County, Georgia. The parties formed limited liability companies (LLCs), including Bellemeade, LLC (the LLC group), to develop various parcels of the tract for residential purposes. The operating agreements provided that "no Member shall be accountable to the [LLC] or to any other Member with respect to [any other] business or activity even if the business or activity competes with the [LLC's] business." The Westbury group entered into agreements with other parties to develop additional parcels within the tract in competition with the LLC group. The Stokers filed a suit in a Georgia state court against the Westbury group, alleging, among other things, breach of fiduciary duty. What duties do the members of an LLC owe to each other? Under what principle might the terms of an operating agreement alter these duties? In whose favor should the court rule? Discuss. [*Stoker v. Bellemeade, LLC*, 272 Ga.App. 817, 615 S.E.2d 1 (2005)]

—After you have answered Problem 28–5, compare your answer with the sample answer given on the Web site that accompanies this text. Go to www.cengage.com/blaw/blt, select "Chapter 28," and click on "Case Problem with Sample Answer."

28–6 Limited Liability Companies. A limited liability company (LLC) owned a Manhattan apartment building that was sold. The owners of 25 percent of the membership interests in the LLC filed a lawsuit on behalf of the company (the LLC)—called a derivative suit—claiming that those in majority control of the LLC sold the building for less than its market value and personally profited from the deal. The trial court dismissed the suit, holding that the plaintiffs individually could not bring a derivative suit "to redress wrongs suffered by the corporation" because such actions were permitted only for corporations and could not be brought for a LLC. The appellate court reversed, holding that derivative suits on behalf of LLCs are permitted. That decision was appealed. A key problem was that the state law governing LLCs did not address the issue. How should such matters logically be resolved? Are the minority owners in an LLC at the mercy of the decisions of the majority owners? [*Tzolis v. Wolff*, 10 N.Y.3d 100, 884 N.E.2d 1005 (2008)]

28-7 **Joint Venture.** Holiday Isle Resort & Marina, Inc., operated four restaurants, five bars, and various food kiosks at its resort in Islamorada, Florida. Holiday entered into a "joint venture agreement" with Rip Tosun to operate a fifth restaurant called Rip's—A Place For Ribs. The agreement gave Tosun authority over the employees and "full authority as to the conduct of the business." It also prohibited Tosun from competing with Rip's without Holiday's approval but did not prevent Holiday from competing. Later, Tosun sold half of his interest in Rip's to Thomas Hallock. Soon, Tosun and Holiday opened the Olde Florida Steakhouse next to Rip's. Holiday stopped serving breakfast at Rip's and diverted employees and equipment from Rip's to the Steakhouse, which then started offering breakfast. Hallock filed a suit in a Florida state court against Holiday. Did Holiday breach the joint venture agreement? Did it breach the duties that joint venturers owe each other? Explain. [*Hallock v. Holiday Isle Resort & Marina, Inc.*, 4 So.3d 17 (Fla.App. 3 Dist. 2009)]

28-8  **A Question of Ethics** *Blushing Brides, LLC, a publisher of wedding planning magazines in Columbus, Ohio, opened an account with Gray Printing Co. in July 2000. On behalf of Blushing Brides, Louis Zacks, the firm's member-manager, signed a credit agreement that identified the firm as the "purchaser" and required payment within thirty days. Despite the agreement, Blushing Brides typically took up to six months to pay the full amount for its orders. Gray printed and shipped 10,000 copies of a fall/winter 2001 issue for Blushing Brides but had not been paid when the firm ordered 15,000 copies of a spring/summer 2002 issue. Gray refused to print the new order without an assurance of payment. Zacks signed a promissory note for $14,778, plus interest at 6 percent per year, payable to Gray on June 22. Gray printed the new order but by October had been paid only $7,500. Gray filed a suit in an Ohio state court against Blushing Brides and Zacks to collect the balance.* [Gray Printing Co. v. Blushing Brides, LLC, __ N.E.2d __ (10 Dist. 2006)]

1 Under what circumstances is a member of an LLC liable for the firm's debts? In this case, is Zacks personally liable under the credit agreement for the unpaid amount on Blushing Brides' account? Did Zacks's promissory note affect the parties' liability on the account? Explain.
2 Should a member of an LLC assume an ethical responsibility to meet the obligations of the firm? Discuss.
3 Gray shipped only 10,000 copies of the spring/summer 2002 issue of Blushing Brides' magazine, waiting for the publisher to identify a destination for the other 5,000 copies. The magazine had a retail price of $4.50 per copy. Did Gray have a legal or ethical duty to "mitigate the damages" by attempting to sell or otherwise distribute these copies itself? Why or why not?

Critical Thinking and Writing Assignments

28-9 **Critical Legal Thinking.** Although a limited liability entity may be the best organizational form for most businesses, a significant number of firms may be better off as a corporation or some other form of organization. How does the fact that most of the limited liability entities are new forms for doing business affect the reasons for choosing another form of organization in which to do business? Explain.

Practical Internet Exercises

Go to this text's Web site at www.cengage.com/blaw/blt, select "Chapter 28," and click on "Practical Internet Exercises." There you will find the following Internet research exercises that you can perform to learn more about the topics covered in this chapter.

Practical Internet Exercise 28-1: LEGAL PERSPECTIVE—**Limited Liability Companies**
Practical Internet Exercise 28-2: MANAGEMENT PERSPECTIVE—**Joint Ventures**

Chapter 29

Corporate Formation, Merger, and Termination

(AP Photo/Don Ryan)

"A corporation is an artificial being, invisible, intangible, and existing only in contemplation of law."

—John Marshall, 1755–1835 (Chief justice of the United States Supreme Court, 1801–1835)

Chapter Outline

- Corporate Nature and Classification
- Corporate Formation and Powers
- Defects in Formation and Corporate Status
- Corporate Financing
- Mergers and Acquisitions
- Termination

Learning Objectives

After reading this chapter, you should be able to answer the following questions:

1. What steps are involved in bringing a corporation into existence?
2. What is the difference between a *de jure* corporation and a *de facto* corporation?
3. In what circumstances might a court disregard the corporate entity ("pierce the corporate veil") and hold the shareholders personally liable?
4. What are the basic differences between a merger, a consolidation, and a share exchange?
5. What are the two ways in which a corporation can be voluntarily dissolved?

The corporation is a creature of statute. As John Marshall indicated in the chapter-opening quotation, a corporation is an artificial being, existing only in law and neither tangible nor visible. Its existence generally depends on state law, although some corporations, especially public organizations, can be created under state or federal law.

Each state has its own body of corporate law, and these laws are not entirely uniform. The Model Business Corporation Act (MBCA) is a codification of modern corporation law that has been influential in the drafting and revision of state corporation statutes. Today, the majority of state statutes are guided by the revised version of the MBCA, which is often referred to as the Revised Model Business Corporation Act (RMBCA).[1] You should keep in mind, however, that there is considerable variation among the statutes of the states that have used the MBCA or the RMBCA as a basis for their statutes, and several states do not follow either act. Consequently, individual state corporation laws should be relied on rather than the MBCA or the RMBCA.

In this chapter, we examine the nature of the corporate form of business enterprise, the various classifications of corporations, and the formation and financing of today's corporations. We also discuss how a corporation can expand its operations by combining with

1. Excerpts from the Revised Model Business Corporation Act (RMBCA) are presented on the Web site that accompanies this text.

another corporation through a merger, a consolidation, a purchase of assets, or a purchase of a controlling interest in the other corporation. The last part of this chapter will discuss the typical reasons for—and methods used in—terminating a corporation's existence.

Corporate Nature and Classification

Corporation A legal entity formed in compliance with statutory requirements that is distinct from its shareholder-owners.

A **corporation** is a legal entity created and recognized by state law. It can consist of one or more *natural persons* (as opposed to the artificial *legal person* of the corporation) identified under a common name. A corporation can be owned by a single person, or it can have hundreds, thousands, or even millions of owners (shareholders). The corporation substitutes itself for its shareholders in conducting corporate business and in incurring liability, yet its authority to act and the liability for its actions are separate and apart from the individuals who own it.

(AP Photo/Paul Sakuma)

Yahoo! has a shareholders' meeting once a year. To what extent do those attending have any say over what direction the company takes?

The shareholder form of business organization emerged in Europe at the end of the seventeenth century. These organizations, called joint stock companies (see Chapter 28), frequently collapsed because their organizers absconded with the funds or proved to be incompetent. Because of this history of fraud and collapse, organizations resembling corporations were regarded with suspicion in the United States during its early years. Although several business corporations were formed after the Revolutionary War, the corporation did not come into common use for private business until the nineteenth century.

Corporate Personnel

In a corporation, the responsibility for the overall management of the firm is entrusted to a *board of directors*, whose members are elected by the shareholders. The board of directors hires *corporate officers* and other employees to run the daily business operations of the corporation.

CONTRAST The death of a sole proprietor results in the dissolution of a business. The death of a corporate shareholder, however, rarely causes the dissolution of a corporation.

When an individual purchases a share of stock in a corporation, that person becomes a shareholder and thus an owner of the corporation. Unlike the members of a partnership, the body of shareholders can change constantly without affecting the continued existence of the corporation. A shareholder can sue the corporation, and the corporation can sue a shareholder. Also, under certain circumstances, a shareholder can sue on behalf of a corporation. The rights and duties of corporate personnel will be examined in detail in Chapter 30.

Very large corporations have numerous directors. What does a board of directors do?

(©bonsai, 2009. Used under license from Shutterstock.com)

The Constitutional Rights of Corporations

A corporation is recognized as a "person," and it has many of the same rights and privileges under state and federal law that U.S. citizens enjoy. The Bill of Rights guarantees persons certain protections, and corporations are considered persons in most instances. Under the First Amendment, corporations are entitled to freedom of speech, although commercial speech (such as advertising) and political speech (such as contributions to political causes or candidates) receive significantly less protection than noncommercial speech. A corporation has the same right of access to the courts as a natural person and can sue or be sued. It also has a right to due process (see Chapter 2), as well as freedom from unreasonable searches and seizures (see Chapter 6) and from double jeopardy.

Generally, though, a corporation is not entitled to claim the Fifth Amendment privilege against self-incrimination. Agents or officers of the corporation therefore cannot refuse to produce corporate records on the ground that doing so might incriminate them. Additionally, the privileges and immunities clause of the U.S. Constitution, which requires each state to treat citizens of other states equally with respect to certain rights, such as travel, does not apply to corporations.

The Limited Liability of Shareholders

ON THE WEB Corporate statutes for all but a few states are now online at topics.law.cornell.edu/wex/table_corporations.

One of the key advantages of the corporate form is the limited liability of its owners (shareholders). Corporate shareholders normally are not personally liable for the obligations of the corporation beyond the extent of their investments. In certain limited situations, however, a court can pierce the "corporate veil" and impose liability on shareholders for the corporation's obligations—a concept that will be explained later in this chapter. Additionally, to enable the firm to obtain credit, shareholders in small companies sometimes voluntarily assume personal liability, as guarantors, for corporate obligations.

Corporate Earnings and Taxation

Dividend A distribution to corporate shareholders of corporate profits or income, disbursed in proportion to the number of shares held.

Retained Earnings The portion of a corporation's profits that has not been paid out as dividends to shareholders.

When a corporation earns profits, it can either pass them on to shareholders in the form of **dividends** or retain them as profits. These **retained earnings**, if invested properly, will yield higher corporate profits in the future and thus cause the price of the company's stock to rise. Individual shareholders can then reap the benefits of these retained earnings in the capital gains that they receive when they sell their stock.

CORPORATE TAXATION Whether a corporation retains its profits or passes them on to the shareholders as dividends, those profits are subject to income tax by various levels of government. As you will read later in this chapter, failure to pay taxes can lead to severe consequences. The state can suspend the entity's corporate status until the taxes are paid or even dissolve the corporation for failing to pay taxes.

Another important aspect of corporate taxation is that corporate profits can be subject to double taxation. The company pays tax on its profits, and then if the profits are passed on to the shareholders as dividends, the shareholders must also pay income tax on them. The corporation normally does not receive a tax deduction for dividends it distributes to shareholders. This double-taxation feature is one of the major disadvantages of the corporate business form.

A taxation issue of increasing importance to corporations is whether they are required to collect state sales taxes on goods or services sold to consumers via the Internet. See this chapter's *Adapting the Law to the Online Environment* feature for a discussion of this issue.

Holding Company A company whose business activity is holding shares in another company.

HOLDING COMPANIES Some U.S. corporations use holding companies to reduce—or at least defer—their U.S. income taxes. At its simplest, a **holding company** (sometimes referred to as a *parent company*) is a company whose business activity consists of holding shares in another company. Typically, the holding company is established in a low-tax or no-tax offshore jurisdiction, such as those shown in Exhibit 29–1 on page 726. Among the best known are the Cayman Islands, Dubai, Hong Kong, Luxembourg, Monaco, and Panama.

Sometimes, a U.S. corporation sets up a holding company in a low-tax offshore environment and then transfers its cash, bonds, stocks, and other investments to the holding company. In general, any profits received by the holding company on these investments are taxed at the rate of the offshore jurisdiction where the company is registered, not the rates applicable to the parent company or its shareholders in their country of residence. Thus, deposits of cash, for example, may earn interest that is taxed at only a minimal rate. Once the profits are brought "onshore," though, they are taxed at the federal corporate income tax rate, and any payments received by the shareholders are also taxable at the full U.S. rates.

Adapting the Law to the Online Environment

Economic Recession Fuels the Internet Taxation Debate

As discussed in the *Adapting the Law to the Online Environment* feature in Chapter 15 on page 363, governments at the state and federal levels have long debated whether states should be able to collect sales taxes on online sales to in-state customers. State governments claim that their inability to tax online sales has caused them to lose billions of dollars in sales tax revenue. The issue has taken on new urgency as the states search desperately for revenue in the wake of the economic recession that began in December 2007.

Supreme Court Precedent Requires Physical Presence

In 1992, the United States Supreme Court ruled that no individual state can compel an out-of-state business that lacks a substantial physical presence (such as a warehouse, office, or retail store) within that state to collect and remit state taxes.[a] The Court recognized that Congress has the power to pass legislation requiring out-of-state corporations to collect and remit state sales taxes, but Congress so far has chosen not to tax Internet transactions. In fact, Congress temporarily prohibited the states from taxing Internet sales, and that ban was extended until 2014.[b] Thus, only online retailers that also have a physical presence within a state must collect state taxes on any Web sales made to residents of that state. (Otherwise, state residents are required to self-report their purchases and pay use taxes to the state, which rarely happens.)

New York Changed Its Definition of Physical Presence

In an effort to collect taxes on Internet sales made by out-of-state corporations, New York changed its tax laws in 2008 to redefine *physical presence.* Under the new law, if an online retailer pays any party within the state to solicit business for its products, that retailer has a physical presence in the state and must collect state taxes.[c] For example, Amazon.com, America's largest online retailer, pays thousands of associates in New York to post ads that link to Amazon's Web site. Consequently, the law requires Amazon to collect tax on any sales to New York residents.

Both Amazon and Overstock.com, a Utah corporation, filed lawsuits in 2009 claiming that the new law was unconstitutional. A New York court dismissed Amazon's case, finding that the law provided a sufficient basis for requiring collection of New York taxes. As long as the seller has a substantial connection with the state, the taxes need not derive from in-state activity. The court also observed that "out-of-state sellers can shield themselves from a tax-collection obligation by altogether prohibiting in-state solicitation activities . . . on their behalf."[d] As a result, Amazon now collects and pays state sales taxes on shipments to New York.

Overstock also lost its lawsuit, but it is appealing the decision.[e] In the meantime, to avoid having to collect the sales tax, Overstock canceled agreements with its New York affiliates that were being paid to direct traffic to its Web site. In 2009, Amazon ended its arrangements with affiliates in Rhode Island and North Carolina for the same reason.

FOR CRITICAL ANALYSIS

Should the fact that an out-of-state corporation pays affiliates in a state to direct consumers to its Web site be sufficient to require the corporation to collect taxes on Web sales to state residents? Why or why not?

a. See *Quill Corp. v. North Dakota,* 504 U.S. 298, 112 S.Ct. 1904, 119 L.Ed.2d 91 (1992).

b. Internet Tax Freedom Act, Pub. L. No. 105-277; 47 U.S.C. Section 151 note (1998); extended to 2014 by Pub. L. No. 110-108.

c. New York Tax Law Section 1101(b)(8)(vi).

d. *Amazon.com, LLC v. New York State Department of Taxation and Finance,* 23 Misc.3d 418, 877 N.Y.S.2d 842 (2009).

e. *Overstock.com, Inc. v. New York State Department of Taxation and Finance,* 2009 WL 1259061 (2009).

Ethical Issue

Is it ethical for a corporation to establish an offshore holding company to reduce U.S. taxes? The use of offshore holding companies and other methods of reducing tax liability has come under criticism in recent years. In 2008, a study by the Government Accountability Office found that nearly two-thirds of U.S. corporations paid no federal income taxes between 1998 and 2005. Moreover, some of the corporations that received substantial amounts of federal bailout funds during the credit crisis had numerous subsidiaries in offshore tax havens—for example, Citigroup had 427 and Bank of America had 115.[2]

Although the use of offshore holding companies to defer or reduce tax liability is often decried as both unethical and unpatriotic, some observers are not so sure. They point out that those who run corporations have a duty to minimize (legally, of course) taxes owed by the corporation and by its shareholders. Nevertheless, given the nation's weak economic forecast, some politicians are seeking

2. Lynnley Browning, "Many U.S. Firms Operate in Tax Havens Abroad, Study Says," *The New York Times, Business Edition,* January 17, 2009.

Exhibit 29–1 Offshore Low-Tax Jurisdictions

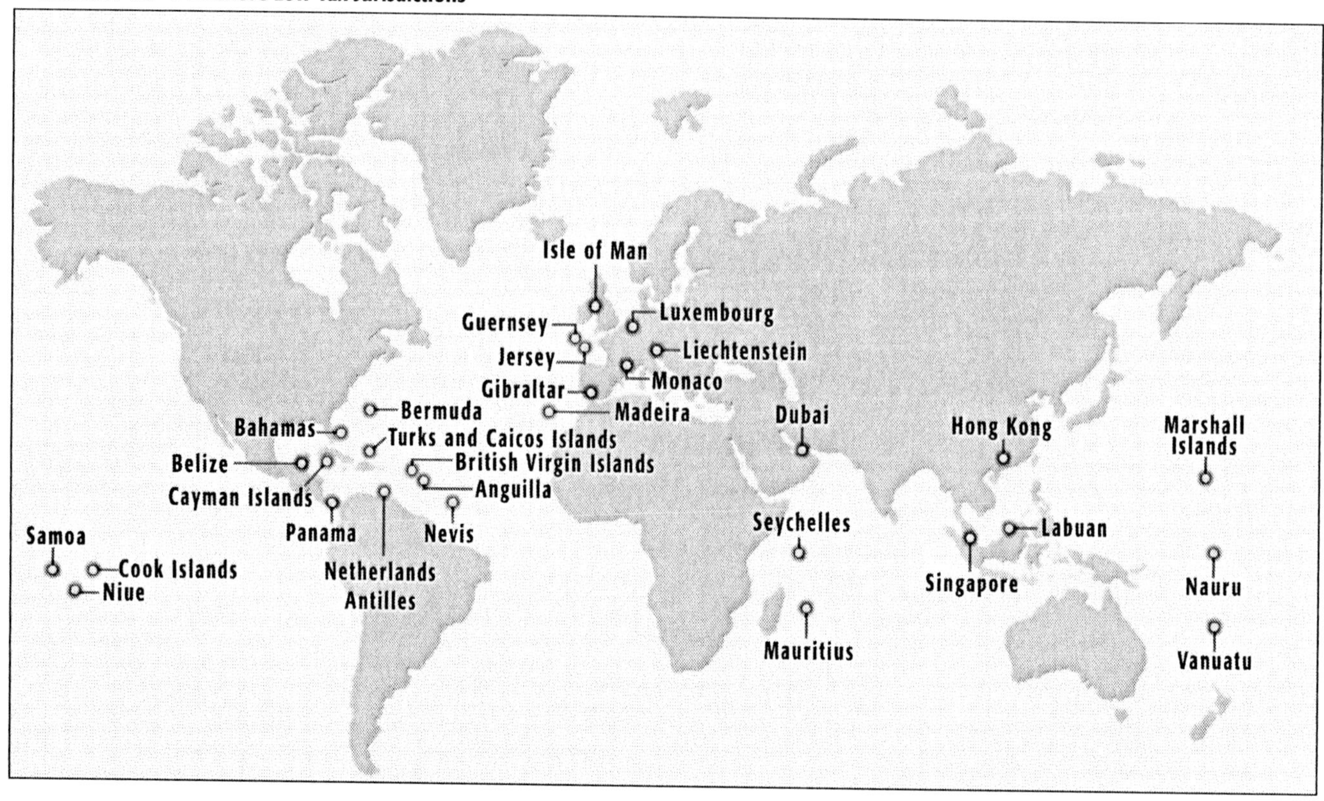

to crack down on these offshore tax havens and force corporations to pay larger amounts of taxes. In 2009, President Barack Obama proposed measures to restrict multinational companies from deferring the payment of taxes on profits earned overseas. The plan would also prevent corporations from inflating the amount of foreign taxes they paid in order to cut their U.S. tax bill and would prohibit wealthy Americans from establishing offshore bank accounts to evade U.S. taxes.

Torts and Criminal Acts

A corporation is liable for the torts committed by its agents or officers within the course and scope of their employment. This principle applies to a corporation exactly as it applies to the ordinary agency relationships discussed in Chapter 23. It follows the doctrine of *respondeat superior.*

Recall from Chapter 6 that under modern criminal law, a corporation may be held liable for the criminal acts of its agents and employees, provided the punishment is one that can be applied to the corporation. Although corporations cannot be imprisoned, they can be fined. (Of course, corporate directors and officers can be imprisoned, and many have been in recent years.) In addition, under sentencing guidelines for crimes committed by corporate employees (white-collar crimes), corporate lawbreakers can face fines amounting to hundreds of millions of dollars.[3]

3. Note that the Sarbanes-Oxley Act of 2002, discussed in Chapter 8, stiffened the penalties for certain types of corporate crime and ordered the U.S. Sentencing Commission to revise the sentencing guidelines accordingly.

CASE EXAMPLE 29.1 Brian Gauthier was a truck driver who worked for Angelo Todesca Corporation. Gauthier drove the AT-56, a ten-wheel dump truck. Although Angelo's safety manual required its trucks to be equipped with back-up alarms that automatically sounded when the trucks were put into reverse, the AT-56's alarm was missing. Angelo ordered a new alarm but allowed Gauthier to continue driving the AT-56. At a worksite, when Gauthier backed up the AT-56 to dump its load, he struck and killed a police officer who was directing traffic through the site and facing away from the truck. The state charged Angelo and Gauthier with the crime of vehicular homicide. Angelo argued that a "corporation" could not be guilty of vehicular homicide because it cannot "operate" a vehicle. The court ruled that if an employee commits a crime "while engaged in corporate business that the employee has been authorized to conduct," a corporation can be held liable for the crime. Hence, the court held that Angelo was liable for Gauthier's negligent operation of its truck, which resulted in a person's death.[4] ●

Classification of Corporations

Corporations can be classified in several ways. The classification of a corporation normally depends on its location, purpose, and ownership characteristics, as described in the following subsections.

Domestic Corporation In a given state, a corporation that does business in, and is organized under the law of, that state.

Foreign Corporation In a given state, a corporation that does business in the state without being incorporated therein.

Alien Corporation A designation in the United States for a corporation formed in another country but doing business in the United States.

DOMESTIC, FOREIGN, AND ALIEN CORPORATIONS A corporation is referred to as a **domestic corporation** by its home state (the state in which it incorporates). A corporation formed in one state but doing business in another is referred to in the second state as a **foreign corporation.** A corporation formed in another country (say, Mexico) but doing business in the United States is referred to in the United States as an **alien corporation.**

A corporation does not have an automatic right to do business in a state other than its state of incorporation. In some instances, it must obtain a *certificate of authority* in any state in which it plans to do business. Once the certificate has been issued, the corporation generally can exercise in that state all of the powers conferred on it by its home state. If a foreign corporation does business in a state without obtaining a certificate of authority, the state can impose substantial fines and sanctions on the corporation, and sometimes even on its officers, directors, or agents. Note that most state statutes specify certain activities, such as soliciting orders via the Internet, that are not considered doing business within the state. Thus, a foreign corporation normally does not need a certificate of authority to sell goods or services via the Internet or by mail.

AMTRAK is a public corporation. How does a public corporation differ from a private corporation?

(Paul Sullivan/Creative Commons)

PUBLIC AND PRIVATE CORPORATIONS A public corporation is one formed by the government to meet some political or governmental purpose. Cities and towns that incorporate are common examples. In addition, many federal government organizations, such as the U.S. Postal Service, the Tennessee Valley Authority, and AMTRAK, are public corporations. Note that a public corporation is not the same as a *publicly held* corporation (often called a *public company*). A publicly held corporation is any corporation whose shares are publicly traded in securities markets, such as the New York Stock Exchange or the over-the-counter market.

In contrast to public corporations (*not* public companies), private corporations are created either wholly or in part for private benefit. Most corporations are private. Although they may serve a public

4. *Commonwealth v. Angelo Todesca Corp.*, 446 Mass. 128, 842 N.E.2d 930 (2006).

NOTE A private corporation is a voluntary association, but a public corporation is not.

purpose, as a public electric or gas utility does, they are owned by private persons rather than by the government.[5]

Nonprofit Corporations Corporations formed for purposes other than making a profit are called *nonprofit* or *not-for-profit* corporations. Private hospitals, educational institutions, charities, and religious organizations, for example, are frequently organized as nonprofit corporations. The nonprofit corporation is a convenient form of organization that allows various groups to own property and to form contracts without exposing the individual members to personal liability.

Close Corporation A corporation whose shareholders are limited to a small group of persons, often only family members. In a close corporation, the shareholders' rights to transfer shares to others are usually restricted.

Close Corporations Most corporate enterprises in the United States fall into the category of close corporations. A **close corporation** is one whose shares are held by members of a family or by relatively few persons. Close corporations are also referred to as *closely held, family,* or *privately held* corporations. Usually, the members of the small group constituting a close corporation are personally known to one another. Because the number of shareholders is so small, there is no trading market for the shares.

In practice, a close corporation is often operated like a partnership. Some states have enacted special statutory provisions that apply to close corporations. These provisions expressly permit close corporations to depart significantly from certain formalities required by traditional corporation law.[6]

Additionally, a provision added to the RMBCA in 1991 gives close corporations a substantial amount of flexibility in determining the rules by which they will operate [RMBCA 7.32]. If all of a corporation's shareholders agree in writing, the corporation can operate without directors, bylaws, annual or special shareholders' or directors' meetings, stock certificates, or formal records of shareholders' or directors' decisions.[7]

Management of Close Corporations. A close corporation has a single shareholder or a closely knit group of shareholders, who usually hold the positions of directors and officers. Management of a close corporation resembles that of a sole proprietorship or a partnership. As a corporation, however, the firm must meet all specific legal requirements set forth in state statutes.

To prevent a majority shareholder from dominating a close corporation, the corporation may require that more than a simple majority of the directors approve any action taken by the board. Typically, this would apply only to extraordinary actions, such as changing the amount of dividends or dismissing an employee-shareholder, and not to ordinary business decisions.

Transfer of Shares in Close Corporations. By definition, a close corporation has a small number of shareholders. Thus, the transfer of one shareholder's shares to someone else can cause serious management problems. The other shareholders may find themselves required to share control with someone they do not know or like.

EXAMPLE 29.2 Three brothers—Terry, Damon, and Henry Johnson—are the only shareholders of Johnson's Car Wash, Inc. Terry and Damon do not want Henry to sell

5. The United States Supreme Court first recognized the property rights of private corporations and clarified the distinction between public and private corporations in the landmark case *Trustees of Dartmouth College v. Woodward,* 17 U.S. (4 Wheaton) 518, 4 L.Ed. 629 (1819).

6. For example, in some states (such as Maryland), a close corporation need not have a board of directors.

7. Shareholders cannot agree, however, to eliminate certain rights of shareholders, such as the right to inspect corporate books and records or the right to bring *derivative actions* (lawsuits on behalf of the corporation—see Chapter 30).

his shares to an unknown third person. To avoid this situation, the corporation could restrict the transferability of shares to outside persons. Shareholders could be required to offer their shares to the corporation or the other shareholders before selling them to an outside purchaser. In fact, a few states have statutes that prohibit the transfer of close corporation shares unless certain persons—including shareholders, family members, and the corporation—are first given the opportunity to purchase the shares for the same price. •

Control of a close corporation can also be stabilized through the use of a *shareholder agreement*. A shareholder agreement can provide that when one of the original shareholders dies, her or his shares of stock in the corporation will be divided in such a way that the proportionate holdings of the survivors, and thus their proportionate control, will be maintained. Courts are generally reluctant to interfere with private agreements, including shareholder agreements.

Misappropriation of Close Corporation Funds. Sometimes, a majority shareholder in a close corporation takes advantage of his or her position and misappropriates company funds. In such situations, the normal remedy for the injured minority shareholders is to have their shares appraised and to be paid the fair market value for them. In the following case, two wronged minority shareholders pursued an additional remedy.

Case 29.1 Williams v. Stanford

District Court of Appeal of Florida, First District, 977 So.2d 722 (2008).

(Bill Jacobus/Creative Commons)

A majority shareholder in a construction close corporation mismanaged funds. What rights do minority sharholders have when adverse events occur?

FACTS Two brothers, Paul and James Williams, together held 30 percent of the stock in Brown and Standard (B&S), Inc., a construction company. John Stanford owned the other 70 percent of the close corporation shares. The Williams brothers worked for B&S for five years when they became suspicious of Stanford's financial management. Stanford reported net losses for the company. When the brothers asked to see the B&S books, they were fired. Later, it was shown that Stanford had misappropriated at least $250,000 in B&S funds for his personal use. The Williams brothers brought a *shareholder's derivative suit* (see Chapter 30) on behalf of B&S, naming Stanford as the defendant and accusing him of a breach of fiduciary duty. Before trial, Stanford resigned from B&S and closed the company. He gave the assets and liabilities of B&S to a new company he formed and owned, J. C. Stanford & Sons. He offered the Williams brothers $25,000 each for their stock in B&S. They responded with a request for $125,000 each. The trial court held that by law the Williams brothers, by making a counteroffer, gave up their rights to bring a suit against the company. Hence, the court granted summary judgment for Stanford. The Williams brothers appealed.

ISSUE If the majority shareholder in a close corporation was misappropriating and mismanaging corporate funds, can the minority shareholders seek to rescind the transfer of corporate assets in addition to appraisal rights?

DECISION Yes. The appeals court reversed the trial court's ruling and held that the Williams brothers were entitled to a trial to determine if they could prove abuse of the company by Stanford. Although this did not follow the usual procedure for appraisal of minority shares, given the strong suspicion of fraud in this instance, the court was willing to allow for greater review.

REASON The minority shareholders claimed that their shares were worth more than the $25,000 Stanford offered. When dissenting shareholders seek more than an appraisal of their shares in the wake of dubious transactions, the courts must balance the principle that an adequate remedy should exist for the shareholders against the consideration that courts should not become bogged down in a wide range of disputes about the fairness of cash-out prices offered to minority shareholders. When shareholders point to specific acts of self-dealing or misrepresentation, they are entitled to equitable remedies beyond the normal appraisal option that dissenting shareholders must accept.

FOR CRITICAL ANALYSIS—Ethical Consideration *Was it ethical for the Williams brothers to demand $125,000 each for their shares? Why or why not?*

S Corporation A close business corporation that has met certain requirements set out in the Internal Revenue Code and thus qualifies for special income tax treatment. Essentially, an S corporation is taxed the same as a partnership, but its owners enjoy the privilege of limited liability.

S CORPORATIONS A close corporation that meets the qualifying requirements specified in Subchapter S of the Internal Revenue Code can operate as an **S corporation.** If a corporation has S corporation status, it can avoid the imposition of income taxes at the corporate level while retaining many of the advantages of a corporation, particularly limited liability. Among the numerous requirements for S corporation status, the following are the most important:

1. The corporation must be a domestic corporation.
2. The corporation must not be a member of an affiliated group of corporations.
3. The shareholders of the corporation must be individuals, estates, or certain trusts. Partnerships and nonqualifying trusts cannot be shareholders. Corporations can be shareholders under certain circumstances.
4. The corporation must have no more than one hundred shareholders.
5. The corporation must have only one class of stock, although all shareholders do not have to have the same voting rights.
6. No shareholder of the corporation may be a nonresident alien.

An S corporation is treated differently from a regular corporation for tax purposes. An S corporation is taxed like a partnership, so the corporate income passes through to the shareholders, who pay personal income tax on it. This treatment enables the S corporation to avoid the double taxation that is imposed on regular corporations. In addition, the shareholders' tax brackets may be lower than the tax bracket that the corporation would have been in if the tax had been imposed at the corporate level. This tax saving is particularly attractive when the corporation wants to accumulate earnings for some future business purpose. If the corporation has losses, the S election allows the shareholders to use the losses to offset other taxable income. Nevertheless, because the limited liability company (see Chapter 28) and the limited liability partnership (see Chapter 27) offer similar tax advantages and greater flexibility, the S corporation has lost some of its significance.

CONTRAST Unlike the shareholders of most other corporations, the shareholders of professional corporations generally must be licensed professionals.

PROFESSIONAL CORPORATIONS Professionals such as physicians, lawyers, dentists, and accountants can incorporate. Professional corporations typically are identified by the letters *S.C.* (service corporation), *P.C.* (professional corporation), or *P.A.* (professional association).

In general, the laws governing the formation and operation of professional corporations are similar to those governing ordinary business corporations. There are some differences in terms of liability, however, because the shareholder-owners are professionals who are held to a higher standard of conduct. For liability purposes, some courts treat a professional corporation somewhat like a partnership and hold each professional liable for any malpractice committed within the scope of the business by the others in the firm. With the exception of malpractice or a breach of duty to clients or patients, a shareholder in a professional corporation generally cannot be held liable for the torts committed by other professionals at the firm.

Corporate Formation and Powers

Up to this point, we have discussed some of the general characteristics of corporations. We now examine the process by which corporations come into existence. Incorporating a business is much simpler today than it was twenty years ago, and many states allow businesses to incorporate via the Internet. If the owners of a partnership or sole proprietorship wish to expand the business, they may decide to incorporate because a corporation can obtain more capital by issuing shares of stock.

Promotional Activities

"A man to carry on a successful business must have imagination. He must see things as in a vision, a dream of the whole thing."

Charles M. Schwab, 1862–1939
(American industrialist)

In the past, preliminary steps were taken to organize and promote the business prior to incorporating. Contracts were made with investors and others on behalf of the future corporation. Today, due to the relative ease of forming a corporation in most states, persons incorporating their business rarely, if ever, engage in preliminary promotional activities. Nevertheless, it is important for businesspersons to understand that they are personally liable for all preincorporation contracts made with investors, accountants, or others on behalf of the future corporation. This personal liability continues until the corporation assumes the preincorporation contracts by *novation* (discussed in Chapter 13).

EXAMPLE 29.3 Jade Sorrel contracts with an accountant, Ray Cooper, to provide tax advice for a proposed corporation, Blackstone, Inc. Cooper provides the services to Sorrel, knowing that the corporation has not yet been formed. Once Blackstone, Inc., is formed, Cooper sends an invoice to the corporation and to Sorrel personally, but the bill is not paid. Because Sorrel is personally liable for the preincorporation contract, Cooper can file a lawsuit against Sorrel for breaching the contract for accounting services. Cooper cannot seek to hold Blackstone, Inc., liable unless he has entered into a novation contract with the corporation. •

Incorporation Procedures

ON THE WEB For answers to "frequently asked questions" on the topic of incorporation, go to www.bizfilings.com/products/ccorp_FAQ.asp.

Exact procedures for incorporation differ among states, but the basic steps are as follows: (1) select a state of incorporation, (2) secure the corporate name by confirming its availability, (3) prepare the articles of incorporation, and (4) file the articles of incorporation with the secretary of state accompanied by payment of the specified fees. These steps are discussed in more detail in the following subsections.

Selecting the State of Incorporation The first step in the incorporation process is to select a state in which to incorporate. Because state corporation laws differ, individuals may look for the states that offer the most advantageous tax or other provisions. Another consideration is the fee that a particular state charges to incorporate, as well as the annual fees and the fees for specific transactions (such as stock transfers).

Delaware has historically had the least restrictive laws and provisions that favor corporate management. Consequently, many corporations, including a number of the largest, have incorporated there. Delaware's statutes permit firms to incorporate in that state and conduct business and locate their operating headquarters elsewhere. Most other states now permit this as well. Note, though, that closely held corporations, particularly those of a professional nature, generally incorporate in the state where their principal shareholders live and work. For reasons of convenience and cost, businesses often choose to incorporate in the state in which the corporation's business will primarily be conducted.

Each corporation must select a name that is not already in use and that could not be confused with an existing corporate name. What level of government usually approves corporate names?

(AP Photo/Al Behrman)

Securing the Corporate Name The choice of a corporate name is subject to state approval to ensure against duplication or deception. State statutes usually require that the secretary of state run a check on the proposed name in the state of incorporation. Some states require that the persons incorporating a firm, at their own expense, run a check on the proposed name, which can often be accomplished via Internet-based services. Once cleared, a name can be reserved for a short time, for a fee, pending the completion of the articles of incorporation. All corporate statutes require the corporation name to include the word *Corporation, Incorporated, Company,* or *Limited,* or abbreviations of these terms.

A new corporation's name cannot be the same as (or deceptively similar to) the name of an existing corporation doing business within the state. The name should also be one that can be used as the business's Internet domain name. **EXAMPLE 29.4** If an existing corporation is named Digital Synergy, Inc., you cannot choose the name Digital Synergy Company because that name is deceptively similar to the first. The state will be unlikely to allow the corporate name because it could impliedly transfer a part of the goodwill established by the first corporate user to the second corporation. In addition, you would not want to choose the name Digital Synergy Company because you would be unable to acquire an Internet domain name using even part of the name of the business. ●

If those incorporating a firm contemplate doing business in other states—or over the Internet—they also need to check on existing corporate names in those states as well. Otherwise, if the firm does business under a name that is the same as or deceptively similar to an existing company's name, it may be liable for trade name infringement.

Preventing Legal Disputes

Be cautious when choosing a corporate name. Recognize that even if a particular state does not require the incorporator to run a name check, doing so can help prevent future disputes. Many states provide online search capabilities, but these searches usually are limited and will only compare the proposed name to the names of active corporations within that state. Trade name disputes may also arise, however, if you use a business name that is deceptively similar to the name of a partnership or limited liability company. Disputes are even more likely to arise among online firms. Always check on the availability of a particular domain name before selecting a corporate name. It pays to be overly cautious and incur some additional cost to hire a professional to conduct a name search.

Articles of Incorporation The document filed with the appropriate governmental agency, usually the secretary of state, when a business is incorporated. State statutes usually prescribe what kind of information must be contained in the articles of incorporation.

PREPARING THE ARTICLES OF INCORPORATION The primary document needed to incorporate a business is the **articles of incorporation.** The articles include basic information about the corporation and serve as a primary source of authority for its future organization and business functions. The person or persons who execute (sign) the articles are called *incorporators*. Generally, the articles of incorporation *must* include the following information [RMBCA 2.02]:

1. The name of the corporation.
2. The number of shares the corporation is authorized to issue.
3. The name and address of the corporation's initial registered agent.
4. The name and address of each incorporator.

ON THE WEB For sample articles of incorporation, go to www.samplearticleofincorporation.com.

In addition, the articles *may* set forth other information, such as the names and addresses of the initial board of directors, the duration and purpose of the corporation, a par value of shares of the corporation, and any other information pertinent to the rights and duties of the corporation's shareholders and directors. Articles of incorporation vary widely depending on the size and type of corporation and the jurisdiction. Frequently, the articles do not provide much detail about the firm's operations, which are spelled out in the company's **bylaws** (internal rules of management adopted by the corporation at its first organizational meeting).

Bylaws A set of governing rules adopted by a corporation or other association.

Shares of the Corporation. The articles must specify the number of shares of stock authorized for issuance. For instance, a company might state that the aggregate number of shares that the corporation has the authority to issue is five thousand. Large corporations often state a par value of each share, such as twenty cents per share, and specify the various types or classes of stock authorized for issuance (see the discussion of *common* and *preferred stock* later in this chapter). Sometimes, the articles set forth the capital structure of the corporation and other relevant information concerning equity, shares, and credit.

Registered Office and Agent. The corporation must indicate the location and address of its registered office within the state. Usually, the registered office is also the principal office of the corporation. The corporation must also give the name and address of a specific person who has been designated as an *agent* and can receive legal documents (such as orders to appear in court) on behalf of the corporation.

Incorporators. Each incorporator must be listed by name and address. The incorporators need not have any interest at all in the corporation, and sometimes signing the articles is their only duty. Many states do not have residency or age requirements for incorporators. States vary on the required number of incorporators; it can be as few as one or as many as three. Incorporators frequently participate in the first organizational meeting of the corporation.

Duration and Purpose. A corporation has perpetual existence unless the articles state otherwise. The RMBCA does not require a specific statement of purpose to be included in the articles. A corporation can be formed for any lawful purpose. Some incorporators choose to include a general statement of purpose "to engage in any lawful act or activity," while others opt to specify the intended business activities ("to engage in the production and sale of agricultural products," for example). It is increasingly common for the articles to state that the corporation is organized for "any legal business," with no mention of specifics, to avoid the need for future amendments to the corporate articles.

KEEP IN MIND Unlike the articles of incorporation, bylaws do not need to be filed with a state official.

Internal Organization. The articles can describe the internal management structure of the corporation, although this is usually included in the bylaws adopted after the corporation is formed. The articles of incorporation commence the corporation; the bylaws are formed after commencement by the board of directors. Bylaws cannot conflict with the corporation statute or the articles of incorporation [RMBCA 2.06].

Under the RMBCA, shareholders may amend or repeal the bylaws. The board of directors may also amend or repeal the bylaws unless the articles of incorporation or provisions of the corporation statute reserve this power to the shareholders exclusively [RMBCA 10.20]. Typical bylaw provisions describe such matters as voting requirements for shareholders, the election of the board of directors, the methods of replacing directors, and the manner and time of holding shareholders' and board meetings (these corporate activities will be discussed in Chapter 30).

FILING THE ARTICLES WITH THE STATE Once the articles of incorporation have been prepared, signed, and authenticated by the incorporators, they are sent to the appropriate state official, usually the secretary of state, along with the required filing fee. In most states, the secretary of state then stamps the articles as "Filed" and returns a copy of the articles to the incorporators. Once this occurs, the corporation officially exists. (Note that some states issue a *certificate of incorporation,* which is similar to articles of incorporation, representing the state's authorization for the corporation to conduct business. This procedure was typical under the unrevised MBCA.)

First Organizational Meeting to Adopt Bylaws

After incorporation, the first organizational meeting must be held. Usually, the most important function of this meeting is the adoption of bylaws—the internal rules of management for the corporation. If the articles of incorporation named the initial board of directors, then the directors, by majority vote, call the meeting to adopt the bylaws and complete the company's organization. If the articles did not name the directors (as is typical), then the incorporators hold the meeting to elect the directors, adopt bylaws, and complete the routine business of incorporation (authorizing the issuance of shares and hiring employees, for example). The business transacted depends on the requirements of the state's corporation statute, the nature of the corporation, the provisions made in the articles, and the desires of the incorporators.

Corporate Powers

When a corporation is created, the express and implied powers necessary to achieve its purpose also come into existence. The express powers of a corporation are found in its articles of incorporation, in the law of the state of incorporation, and in the state and federal constitutions.

ON THE WEB For an example of one state's (Minnesota's) statute governing corporations, go to www.revisor.leg.state.mn.us/statutes/?id=302A.

Corporate bylaws also establish the express powers of the corporation. Because state corporation statutes frequently provide default rules that apply if the company's bylaws are silent on an issue, it is important that the bylaws set forth the specific operating rules of the corporation. In addition, after the bylaws are adopted, the corporation's board of directors will pass resolutions that also grant or restrict corporate powers.

The following order of priority is used when conflicts arise among documents involving corporations:

1. The U.S. Constitution
2. State constitutions
3. State statutes
4. The articles of incorporation
5. Bylaws
6. Resolutions of the board of directors

IMPLIED POWERS When a corporation is created, it acquires certain implied powers. Barring express constitutional, statutory, or other prohibitions, the corporation has the implied power to perform all acts reasonably appropriate and necessary to accomplish its corporate purposes. For this reason, a corporation has the implied power to borrow funds within certain limits, to lend funds, and to extend credit to those with whom it has a legal or contractual relationship.

To borrow funds, the corporation acts through its board of directors to authorize the loan. Most often, the president or chief executive officer of the corporation will execute the necessary papers on behalf of the corporation. In so doing, corporate officers have the implied power to bind the corporation in matters directly connected with the *ordinary* business affairs of the enterprise. There is a limit to what a corporate officer can do, though. A corporate officer does not have the authority to bind the corporation to an action that will greatly affect the corporate purpose or undertaking, such as the sale of substantial corporate assets.

Ultra Vires A Latin term meaning "beyond the powers"; in corporate law, acts of a corporation that are beyond its express and implied powers to undertake.

ULTRA VIRES DOCTRINE The term ***ultra vires*** means "beyond the powers." In corporate law, acts of a corporation that are beyond its express and implied powers are *ultra vires* acts. Most cases dealing with *ultra vires* acts have involved contracts made for unauthorized purposes. **EXAMPLE 29.5** Suarez is the chief executive officer of SOS Plumbing, Inc. The stated purpose of SOS is to install and repair plumbing. If Suarez enters into a contract with Carlini for SOS to purchase ten cases of brandy, this contract would likely be *ultra vires* because it is not reasonably related to the corporation's purpose. ●

Under Section 3.04 of the RMBCA, the shareholders can seek an injunction from a court to prevent (or stop) the corporation from engaging in *ultra vires* acts. The attorney general in the state of incorporation can also bring an action to obtain an injunction against the *ultra vires* transactions or to institute dissolution proceedings against the corporation on the basis of *ultra vires* acts. The corporation or its shareholders (on behalf of the corporation) can seek damages from the officers and directors who were responsible for the *ultra vires* acts. As mentioned previously, most corporations today are organized for "any legal business" and do not state a specific purpose; thus, the importance of the *ultra vires* doctrine has declined in recent years.

 Defects in Formation and Corporate Status

The procedures for incorporation are very specific. If they are not followed precisely, others may be able to challenge the existence of the corporation. Errors in the incorporation procedures can become important when, for example, a third party who is attempting to enforce a contract or bring a suit for a tort injury learns of them. On the basis of improper incorporation, the plaintiff could attempt to hold the would-be shareholders personally liable. Additionally, when the corporation seeks to enforce a contract against a defaulting party, that party may be able to avoid liability on the ground of a defect in the incorporation procedure.

To prevent injustice, courts will sometimes attribute corporate status to an improperly formed corporation by holding it to be a *de jure* corporation or a *de facto* corporation. Occasionally, a corporation may be held to exist by estoppel. Additionally, in certain circumstances involving abuse of the corporate form, a court may disregard the corporate entity and hold the shareholders personally liable.

De Jure and *De Facto* Corporations

If a corporation has substantially complied with all conditions precedent to incorporation, the corporation is said to have *de jure* (rightful and lawful) existence. In most states and under the RMBCA, the secretary of state's filing of the articles of incorporation is conclusive proof that all mandatory statutory provisions have been met [RMBCA 2.03(b)]. Because a *de jure* corporation is one that is properly formed, neither the state nor a third party can attack its existence.[8]

Sometimes, there is a defect in complying with statutory mandates—for example, the corporation failed to hold an organizational meeting. Under these circumstances, the corporation may have *de facto* (actual) status, meaning that it will be treated as a legal corporation despite the defect in its formation. A corporation with *de facto* status cannot be challenged by third persons (only by the state). In other words, the shareholders of a *de facto* corporation are still protected by limited liability (provided they are unaware of the defect). The following elements are required for *de facto* status:

1. There must be a state statute under which the corporation can be validly incorporated.
2. The parties must have made a good faith attempt to comply with the statute.
3. The enterprise must already have undertaken to do business as a corporation.

Corporation by Estoppel

If a business association holds itself out to others as being a corporation but has made no attempt to incorporate, the firm normally will be estopped (prevented) from denying corporate status in a lawsuit by a third party. This usually occurs when a third party contracts with an entity that claims to be a corporation but has not filed articles of incorporation—or contracts with a person claiming to be an agent of a corporation that does not in fact exist. When justice requires, the courts treat an alleged corporation as if it were an actual corporation for the purpose of determining the rights and liabilities of its officers and directors involved in a particular situation. A corporation by estoppel is thus determined by the situation. Recognition of its corporate status does not extend beyond the resolution of the problem at hand.

In the following case, a party sought to avoid liability on a contract with a firm that had not yet filed its articles of incorporation. Could the party escape liability on the ground that the corporation did not exist at the time of the contract?

8. There is an exception: a few states allow state authorities, in a *quo warranto* proceeding, to bring an action against the corporation for noncompliance with a necessary condition *subsequent* to incorporation. This might occur if the corporation fails to file annual reports, for example.

Case 29.2 Brown v. W.P. Media, Inc.

Supreme Court of Alabama, __ So.2d __ (2009).

HISTORICAL AND TECHNOLOGICAL SETTING *The term* wireless network *commonly refers to a telecommunications network whose interconnection is accomplished without wires. As early as World War II, wireless networks using radio waves transmitted information long distances, overseas, or behind enemy lines. Today's wireless networks are computer networks. Cell phones communicate through wide-ranging wireless networks. Businesses use wireless networks to exchange data quickly. Wireless networks can also be a relatively inexpensive and fast method to connect to the Internet.*

When a joint venture to build a wireless network fails, does liability exist when the articles of incorporation were filed after the original obligations were made?

FACTS In 2001, W.P. Media, Inc., and Alabama MBA, Inc., agreed to a joint venture—to be called Alabaster Wireless MBA, LLC—to provide wireless Internet services to consumers. W.P. Media was to create a wireless network and provide ongoing technical support. Alabama MBA was to contribute capital of $79,300, and W.P. Media was to contribute "proprietary technology" in the same amount. Hugh Brown signed the parties' contract on Alabama MBA's behalf as the chairman of its board. At the time, however, Alabama MBA's articles of incorporation had not yet been filed. Brown filed the articles of incorporation in 2002. Later, Brown and Alabama MBA filed a suit in an Alabama state court, alleging that W.P. Media had breached their contract by not building the wireless network. The court issued a summary judgment in the defendant's favor. The plaintiffs appealed.

ISSUE Can a party be liable on an obligation to a firm that had not filed its articles of incorporation when the obligation arose?

DECISION Yes. The Alabama Supreme Court reversed the lower court's judgment and remanded the case. Under the principle of estoppel, W.P. Media could not deny Alabama MBA's corporate existence.

REASON A firm that represents itself as a corporation in contracting with a third party may be estopped (prevented) from denying corporate status to avoid liability even if the firm was not incorporated at the time of the contract. Likewise, a third party that recognizes an organization as a corporation may be estopped from denying its corporate status. Here, Alabama MBA was represented as "a viable, legal corporation." The parties' contract identified Alabama MBA as a corporation, and Brown signed the contract as Alabama MBA's "chairman of the board." W.P. Media did not act as though it doubted that representation. It agreed to operate Alabaster and participated in the venture before and after Alabama MBA filed its articles of incorporation. W.P. Media did not challenge the validity of the contract until after it was sued for breaching it. Because W.P. Media treated Alabama MBA as a corporation, W.P. Media is estopped from denying Alabama MBA's corporate existence.

WHAT IF THE FACTS WERE DIFFERENT? *Would the result in this case have been different if the parties' contract to build and operate a wireless network had been negotiated and agreed to entirely online? Discuss.*

Piercing the Corporate Veil

Piercing the Corporate Veil An action in which a court disregards the corporate entity and holds the shareholders personally liable for corporate debts and obligations.

Occasionally, the owners use a corporate entity to perpetrate a fraud, circumvent the law, or in some other way accomplish an illegitimate objective. In these situations, the court will ignore the corporate structure by **piercing the corporate veil** and exposing the shareholders to personal liability. Generally, when the corporate privilege is abused for personal benefit or when the corporate business is treated so carelessly that the corporation and the controlling shareholder are no longer separate entities, the court will require the owner to assume personal liability to creditors for the corporation's debts. In short, when the facts show that great injustice would result from the use of a corporation to avoid individual responsibility, a court will look behind the corporate structure to the individual shareholder.

Factors That Lead Courts to Pierce the Corporate Veil The following are some of the factors that frequently cause the courts to pierce the corporate veil:

1. A party is tricked or misled into dealing with the corporation rather than the individual.
2. The corporation is set up never to make a profit or always to be insolvent, or it is too "thinly" capitalized—that is, it has insufficient capital at the time of formation to meet its prospective debts or other potential liabilities.

3. Statutory corporate formalities, such as holding required corporation meetings, are not followed.
4. Personal and corporate interests are **commingled** (mixed together) to such an extent that the corporation has no separate identity.

Commingle To put funds or goods together into one mass so that they are mixed to such a degree that they no longer have separate identities. In corporate law, if personal and corporate interests are commingled to the extent that the corporation has no separate identity, a court may "pierce the corporate veil" and expose the shareholders to personal liability.

A Potential Problem for Close Corporations The potential for corporate assets to be used for personal benefit is especially great in a close corporation, in which the shares are held by a single person or by only a few individuals, usually family members. In such a situation, the separate status of the corporate entity and the sole shareholder (or family-member shareholders) must be carefully preserved. Certain practices invite trouble for the one-person or family-owned corporation: the commingling of corporate and personal funds, the failure to hold board of directors' meetings and record the minutes, or the shareholders' continuous personal use of corporate property (for example, vehicles).

In the following case, when a close corporation's creditors sought payment of its debts, the owners took the small value in the business for themselves, filed a bankruptcy petition for the firm, and incorporated under a new name to continue the business. Could the court recover the business assets from the new corporation for distribution to the original firm's creditors?

Case 29.3 In re Aqua Clear Technologies, Inc.

United States Bankruptcy Court, Southern District of Florida, 361 Bankr. 567 (2007).

(©Andre Blais, 2009. Used under license from Shutterstock.com)

Can a water-softener company that has already filed for bankruptcy simply create a new company with the assets from the first corporation without paying its debts?

FACTS Harvey and Barbara Jacobson owned Aqua Clear Technologies, Inc., a small Florida business that installed and serviced home water-softening systems. Barbara was Aqua's president, and Sharon, the Jacobsons' daughter, was an officer, but neither participated in the business. Although Harvey controlled the day-to-day operations, he was not an Aqua officer, director, or employee, but an independent contractor in service to the company. Aqua had no compensation agreement with the Jacobsons. Instead, whenever Harvey decided that there were sufficient funds, they took funds out of the business for their personal expenses, including the maintenance of their home and payments for their cars, health-insurance premiums, and charges on their credit cards. In December 2004, Aqua filed a bankruptcy petition in a federal bankruptcy court. Three weeks later, Harvey incorporated Discount Water Services, Inc., and continued to service water-softening systems for Aqua's customers. Discount appropriated Aqua's equipment and inventory without a formal transfer and advertised Aqua's phone number as Discount's. Kenneth Welt, Aqua's trustee, initiated a proceeding against Discount, seeking, among other things, to recover Aqua's assets. The trustee contended that Discount was Aqua's "alter ego." (An *alter ego* is the double of something—in this case, the original company.)

ISSUE Can a firm's owners file for corporate bankruptcy and then open another corporation that engages in substantially the same business with the same equipment without paying the first corporation's debts?

DECISION No. The court issued a judgment against Discount, and in the trustee's favor, for $108,732.64, which represented the amount of the claims listed in Aqua Clear's bankruptcy schedules. The court also agreed to add the administrative expenses and all other claims allowed against Aqua Clear once those amounts were determined.

REASON The bankruptcy court pointed out that Aqua Clear—the debtor—and Discount Water "were in substantially the same business. They used the same telephone number. They operated from the same business location. They serviced the same geographic area and many of the same customers." Furthermore, the debtor and Discount Water had identical officers and directors. Consequently, "the Court may presume fraud when a transfer occurs between two corporations controlled by the same officers and directors." The court then pointed out that Aqua Clear had sent a letter to its health-insurance carrier stating that it was simply changing its name to Discount Water Services, Inc. Most of the Jacobsons' actions were designed to interfere with the collection efforts of judgment creditors. "The bottom line question is whether each entity has run its own race, or whether there has been a relay-style passing of the baton from one to the other."

FOR CRITICAL ANALYSIS—Global Consideration *If the Jacobsons' business had been global in scope, should the court have issued a different judgment? Explain.*

 Corporate Financing

Part of the process of corporate formation involves corporate financing. (See the *Linking the Law to Finance* feature on pages 746 and 747 for details on how a start-up company can obtain financing for expanding the business through incorporation.) Corporations are financed by the issuance and sale of corporate securities. **Securities** (stocks and bonds) evidence the right to participate in earnings and the distribution of corporate property or the obligation to pay funds.

Securities Generally, stocks, bonds, notes, debentures, warrants, or other items that evidence an ownership interest in a corporation or a promise of repayment by a corporation.

Stock An equity (ownership) interest in a corporation, measured in units of shares.

Bond A security that evidences a corporate (or government) debt. It does not represent an ownership interest in the issuing entity.

Stocks, or *equity securities,* represent the purchase of ownership in the business firm. **Bonds** (debentures), or *debt securities,* represent the borrowing of funds by firms (and governments). Of course, not all debt is in the form of debt securities. For example, some debt is in the form of accounts payable and notes payable, which typically are short-term debts. Bonds are simply a way for the corporation to split up its long-term debt so that it can be more easily marketed.

"Gentlemen prefer bonds."

Andrew Mellon, 1855–1937
(American banker)

Bonds

Bonds are issued by business firms and by governments at all levels as evidence of the funds they are borrowing from investors. Bonds normally have a designated *maturity date*—the date when the principal, or face, amount of the bond is returned to the investor. They are sometimes referred to as *fixed-income securities* because their owners (that is, the creditors) receive fixed-dollar interest payments, usually semiannually, during the period of time prior to maturity.

Because debt financing represents a legal obligation on the part of the corporation, various features and terms of a particular bond issue are specified in a lending agreement called a **bond indenture.** A corporate trustee, often a commercial bank trust department, represents the collective well-being of all bondholders in ensuring that the corporation meets the terms of the bond issue. The bond indenture specifies the maturity date of the bond and the pattern of interest payments until maturity. The different types of corporate bonds are described in Exhibit 29–2.

***Exhibit* 29–2 Types of Corporate Bonds**

Debenture bonds	Bonds for which no specific assets of the corporation are pledged as backing. Rather, they are backed by the general credit rating of the corporation, plus any assets that can be seized if the corporation allows the debentures to go into default.
Mortgage bonds	Bonds that pledge specific property. If the corporation defaults on the bonds, the bondholders can take the property.
Convertible bonds	Bonds that can be exchanged for a specified number of shares of common stock under certain conditions.
Callable bonds	Bonds that may be called in and the principal repaid at specified times or under conditions specified in the bonds when they are issued.

Stocks

Bond Indenture A contract between the issuer of a bond and the bondholder.

Issuing stocks is another way that corporations can obtain financing. The ways in which stocks differ from bonds are summarized in Exhibit 29–3. Basically, as mentioned, stocks represent ownership in a business firm, whereas bonds represent borrowing by the firm.

Exhibit 29–4 on page 740 summarizes the types of stocks issued by corporations. We look now at the two major types of stock—*common stock* and *preferred stock.*

Common Stock Shares of ownership in a corporation that give the owner of the stock a proportionate interest in the corporation with regard to control, earnings, and net assets. Shares of common stock are lowest in priority with respect to payment of dividends and distribution of the corporation's assets on dissolution.

COMMON STOCK The true ownership of a corporation is represented by **common stock.** Common stock provides a proportionate interest in the corporation with regard to (1) control, (2) earnings, and (3) net assets. A shareholder's interest is generally in proportion to the number of shares he or she owns out of the total number of shares issued.

Voting rights in a corporation apply to the election of the firm's board of directors and to any proposed changes in the ownership structure of the firm. For example, a holder of common stock generally has the right to vote in a decision on a proposed merger, as mergers

Exhibit 29–3 **How Do Stocks and Bonds Differ?**

STOCKS	BONDS
1. Stocks represent ownership.	1. Bonds represent debt.
2. Stocks (common) do not have a fixed dividend rate.	2. Interest on bonds must always be paid, whether or not any profit is earned.
3. Stockholders can elect the board of directors, which controls the corporation.	3. Bondholders usually have no voice in, or control over, management of the corporation.
4. Stocks do not have a maturity date; the corporation usually does not repay the stockholder.	4. Bonds have a maturity date, when the corporation is to repay the bondholder the face value of the bond.
5. All corporations issue or offer to sell stocks. This is the usual definition of a corporation.	5. Corporations do not necessarily issue bonds.
6. Stockholders have a claim against the property and income of a corporation after all creditors' claims have been met.	6. Bondholders have a claim against the property and income of a corporation that must be met *before* the claims of stockholders.

can change the proportion of ownership. State corporation law specifies the types of actions for which shareholder approval must be obtained.

Firms are not obligated to return a principal amount per share to each holder of common stock because no firm can ensure that the market price per share of its common stock will not decline over time. The issuing firm also does not have to guarantee a dividend; indeed, some corporations never pay dividends.

Holders of common stock are investors who assume a *residual* position in the overall financial structure of a business. In terms of receiving payment for their investments, they are last in line. They are entitled to the earnings that are left after preferred stockholders, bondholders, suppliers, employees, and other groups have been paid. Once those groups are paid, however, the owners of common stock may be entitled to *all* the remaining earnings as dividends. (The board of directors normally is not under any duty to declare the remaining earnings as dividends, however.)

Preferred Stock Classes of stock that have priority over common stock as to both payment of dividends and distribution of assets on the corporation's dissolution.

PREFERRED STOCK **Preferred stock** is stock with *preferences*. Usually, this means that holders of preferred stock have priority over holders of common stock as to dividends and as to payment on dissolution of the corporation. Holders of preferred stock may or may not have the right to vote.

Preferred stock is not included among the liabilities of a business because it is equity. Like other equity securities, preferred shares have no fixed maturity date on which the firm must pay them off. Although firms occasionally buy back preferred stock, they are not legally obligated to do so. Holders of preferred stock are investors who have assumed a rather cautious position in their relationship to the corporation. They have a stronger position than common shareholders with respect to dividends and claims on assets, but they will not share in the full prosperity of the firm if it grows successfully over time. This is because the value of preferred shares will not rise as rapidly as that of common shares during a period of financial success. Preferred stockholders do receive fixed dividends periodically, however, and they may benefit to some extent from changes in the market price of the shares.

The return and the risk for preferred stock lie somewhere between those for bonds and those for common stock. Preferred stock is more similar to bonds than to common stock, even though preferred stock appears in the ownership section of the firm's balance sheet. As a result, preferred stock is often categorized with corporate bonds as a fixed-income security, even though the legal status is not the same.

Venture Capital and Private Equity Capital

As discussed, corporations traditionally obtain financing through issuing and selling securities (stocks and bonds) in the capital market. In reality, however, many investors do not want to purchase stock in a business that lacks a track record, and banks are generally reluctant to extend loans to high-risk enterprises. Numerous corporations fail because they are

Exhibit 29–4 Types of Stocks

Common stock	Voting shares that represent ownership interest in a corporation. Common stock has the lowest priority with respect to payment of dividends and distribution of assets on the corporation's dissolution.
Preferred stock	Shares of stock that have priority over common-stock shares as to payment of dividends and distribution of assets on dissolution. Dividend payments are usually a fixed percentage of the face value of the share.
Cumulative preferred stock	Preferred shares on which required dividends not paid in a given year must be paid in a subsequent year before any common-stock dividends are paid.
Participating preferred stock	Preferred shares entitling the owner to receive the preferred-stock dividend and additional dividends if the corporation has paid dividends on common stock.
Convertible preferred stock	Preferred shares that, under certain conditions, can be converted into a specified number of common shares either in the issuing corporation or, sometimes, in another corporation.
Redeemable, or callable, preferred stock	Preferred shares issued with the express condition that the issuing corporation has the right to repurchase the shares as specified.

undercapitalized. Therefore, to obtain sufficient financing, many entrepreneurs seek alternative financing.

VENTURE CAPITAL Start-up businesses and high-risk enterprises often obtain venture capital financing. **Venture capital** is capital provided by professional, outside investors (*venture capitalists,* usually groups of wealthy investors and securities firms) to new business ventures. Venture capital investments are high risk—the investors must be willing to lose all of their invested funds—but offer the potential for well-above-average returns at some point in the future.

To obtain venture capital financing, the start-up business typically gives up a share of its ownership to the venture capitalists. In addition to funding, venture capitalists may provide managerial and technical expertise, and they nearly always are given some control over the new company's decisions. Many Internet-based companies, such as Google, were initially financed by venture capital.

PRIVATE EQUITY CAPITAL Private equity firms obtain their capital from wealthy investors in private markets. The firms use their **private equity capital** to invest in existing—often, publicly traded—corporations. Usually, they buy an entire corporation and then reorganize it. Sometimes, divisions of the purchased company are sold off to pay down debt. Ultimately, the private equity firm may sell shares in the reorganized (and perhaps more profitable) company to the public in an *initial public offering* (usually called an IPO—see Chapter 31). In this way, the private equity firm can make profits by selling its shares in the company to the public.

Venture Capital Capital (funds and other assets) provided by professional, outside investors (*venture capitalists,* usually groups of wealthy investors and securities firms) to start new business ventures.

Private Equity Capital Private equity capital is a financing method by which a company sells equity in an existing business to a private or institutional investor.

Mergers and Acquisitions

A corporation typically extends its operations by combining with another corporation through a merger, a consolidation, a share exchange, a purchase of assets, or a purchase of a controlling interest in the other corporation. The terms *merger* and *consolidation* traditionally referred to two legally distinct proceedings. Today, however, the term *consolidation* generally is used as a generic term to refer to all types of combinations, including mergers and acquisitions. Whether a combination is a merger, a consolidation, or a share exchange, the rights and liabilities of shareholders, the corporation, and the corporation's creditors are the same.

Merger

Merger A contractual and statutory process in which one corporation (the surviving corporation) acquires all of the assets and liabilities of another corporation (the merged corporation).

A **merger** involves the legal combination of two or more corporations in such a way that only one of the corporations continues to exist. **EXAMPLE 29.6** Corporation A and Corporation B decide to merge. They agree that A will absorb B. Therefore, on merging, B ceases to exist as a separate entity, and A continues as the *surviving corporation.* Exhibit 29–5 graphically illustrates this process.

After the merger, Corporation A is recognized as a single corporation, possessing all the rights, privileges, and powers of itself and Corporation B. It automatically acquires all of

● *Exhibit* 29–5 **Merger** Corporation A and Corporation B decide to merge. They agree that A will absorb B, so after the merger, B no longer exists as a separate entity, and A continues as the surviving corporation.

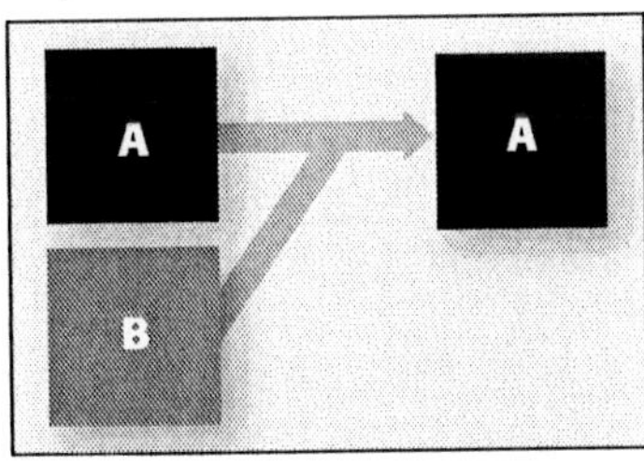

Consolidation A contractual and statutory process in which two or more corporations join to become a completely new corporation. The original corporations cease to exist, and the new corporation acquires all their assets and liabilities.

● *Exhibit* 29–6 **Consolidation** Corporation A and Corporation B consolidate to form an entirely new organization, Corporation C. In the process, A and B terminate.

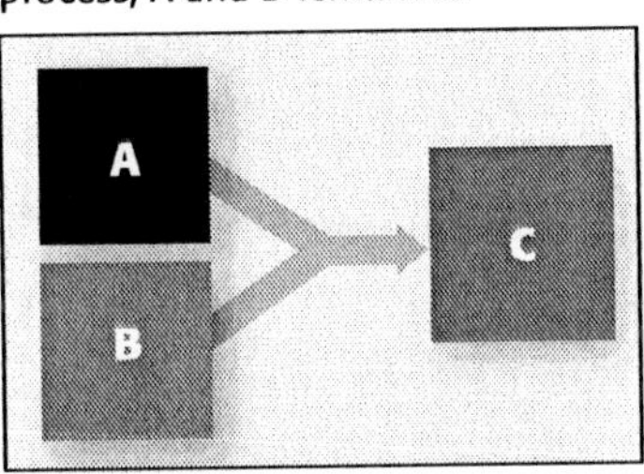

Share Exchange In a share exchange, some or all of the shares of one corporation are exchanged for some or all of the shares of another corporation, but both corporations continue to exist. Share exchanges are often used to create *holding companies* (companies that own part or all of other companies' stock).

B's property and assets without the necessity of a formal transfer. Additionally, A becomes liable for all of B's debts and obligations.[9] Finally, A's articles of incorporation are deemed amended to include any changes that are stated in the *articles of merger* (a document setting forth the terms and conditions of the merger that is filed with the secretary of state).

In a merger, the surviving corporation inherits the disappearing corporation's preexisting legal rights and obligations. If the disappearing corporation had a right of action against a third party under tort or property law, for example, the surviving corporation can bring a suit after the merger to recover the disappearing corporation's damages.

Consolidation

In a **consolidation,** two or more corporations combine in such a way that each corporation ceases to exist and a new one emerges. **EXAMPLE 29.7** Corporation A and Corporation B consolidate to form an entirely new organization, Corporation C. In the process, A and B both terminate, and C comes into existence as an entirely new entity. ● Exhibit 29–6 graphically illustrates this process.

The results of a consolidation are essentially the same as the results of a merger. C is recognized as a new corporation and a single entity; A and B cease to exist. C inherits all of the rights, privileges, and powers previously held by A and B. Title to any property and assets owned by A and B passes to C without a formal transfer. C assumes liability for all of the debts and obligations owed by A and B. The *articles of consolidation,* which state the terms of the consolidation, take the place of A's and B's original corporate articles and are thereafter regarded as C's corporate articles.

When a merger or consolidation takes place, the surviving corporation or newly formed corporation will issue shares or pay some fair consideration to the shareholders of the corporation or corporations that cease to exist. True consolidations have become less common among for-profit corporations because it is often advantageous for one of the firms to survive. In contrast, nonprofit corporations and associations may prefer consolidation because it suggests a new beginning in which neither of the two initial entities is dominant.

Share Exchange

In a **share exchange,** some or all of the shares of one corporation are exchanged for some or all of the shares of another corporation, but neither of the two corporations ceases to exist. Share exchanges are often used to create holding companies (discussed earlier in this chapter). For example, UAL Corporation is a large holding company that owns United Airlines. If one corporation owns *all* of the shares of another corporation, it is referred to as the *parent corporation,* and the wholly owned company is the *subsidiary corporation.*

Merger, Consolidation, or Share Exchange Procedures

All states have statutes authorizing mergers, consolidations, and share exchanges for domestic (in-state) and foreign (out-of-state) corporations. The procedures vary somewhat among jurisdictions. In some states, a consolidation resulting in an entirely new corporation simply follows the initial incorporation procedures discussed earlier in this chapter, whereas other business combinations must follow the procedures outlined below.

The RMBCA sets forth the following basic requirements [RMBCA 11.01–11.07]:

1. The board of directors of *each* corporation involved must approve the merger or consolidation plan.
2. The plan must specify any terms and conditions of the merger. It also must state how the value of the shares of each merging corporation will be determined and how they

9. See, for example, *Rodriguez v. Tech Credit Union Corp.,* 824 N.E.2d 442 (Ind.App. 2005).

(©HO/Reuters/Corbis)

The chairman of Chrysler discusses that company's merger with Fiat in 2009.

will be converted into shares or other securities, cash, property, or other interests in another corporation.

3. The majority of the shareholders of *each* corporation must vote to approve the plan at a shareholders' meeting. If any class of stock is entitled to vote as a separate group, the majority of each separate voting group must approve the plan. Although RMBCA 11.04(e) requires only a simple majority of the shareholders entitled to vote once a quorum is present, frequently a corporation's articles of incorporation or bylaws require greater than a majority approval (Chapter 30 will discuss *quorums* and other voting requirements). In addition, some state statutes require the approval of two-thirds of the outstanding shares of voting stock, and others require a four-fifths vote.
4. Once approved by the directors and the shareholders of both corporations, the surviving corporation files the plan (articles of merger, consolidation, or share exchange) with the appropriate official, usually the secretary of state.
5. When state formalities are satisfied, the state issues a certificate of merger to the surviving corporation or a certificate of consolidation to the newly consolidated corporation.

Short-Form Mergers

Short-Form (Parent-Subsidiary) Merger A merger of companies in which one company (the parent corporation) owns at least 90 percent of the outstanding shares of each class of stock of the other corporation (the subsidiary corporation). The merger can be accomplished without the approval of the shareholders of either corporation.

RMBCA 11.04 provides a simplified procedure for the merger of a substantially owned subsidiary corporation into its parent corporation. Under these provisions, a **short-form merger**—also referred to as a *parent-subsidiary merger*—can be accomplished *without* the approval of the shareholders of either corporation. The short-form merger can be used only when the parent corporation owns at least 90 percent of the outstanding shares of each class of stock of the subsidiary corporation. Once the board of directors of the parent corporation approves the plan, it is filed with the state, and copies are sent to each shareholder of record in the subsidiary corporation.

Shareholder Approval

As mentioned, except in a short-form merger, the shareholders of both corporations must approve a merger or consolidation plan. Shareholders invest in a corporation with the expectation that the board of directors will manage the enterprise and make decisions on ordinary business matters. For *extraordinary* matters, normally both the board of directors and the shareholders must approve of the transaction.

REMEMBER State statutes, articles of incorporation, and corporate bylaws can require the approval of more than a majority of shares for some extraordinary matters.

Mergers and other combinations are extraordinary business matters, meaning that the board of directors must normally obtain the shareholders' approval and provide appraisal rights (discussed next). Amendments to the articles of incorporation and the dissolution of the corporation also generally require shareholder approval. Sometimes, a transaction can be structured in such a way that shareholder approval is not required, but if the shareholders challenge the transaction, a court might use its equity powers to require shareholder approval. For this reason, the board of directors may request shareholder approval even when it might not be legally required.

Appraisal Rights

Appraisal Right The right of a dissenting shareholder, who objects to an extraordinary transaction of the corporation (such as a merger or a consolidation), to have his or her shares appraised and to be paid the fair value of those shares by the corporation.

What if a shareholder disapproves of a merger or a consolidation but is outvoted by the other shareholders? The law recognizes that a dissenting shareholder should not be forced to become an unwilling shareholder in a corporation that is new or different from the one in which the shareholder originally invested. Dissenting shareholders therefore are given a statutory right to be paid the fair value of the shares they held on the date of the merger or consolidation. This right is referred to as the shareholder's **appraisal right.** So long as the transaction does not involve fraud or other illegal conduct, appraisal rights are the exclusive remedy for a shareholder who is dissatisfied with the price received for the stock.

"There are two times in a man's life when he should not speculate: when he can't afford it and when he can."
Samuel Clemens (Mark Twain), 1835–1919
(American author and humorist)

Appraisal rights normally extend to regular mergers, consolidations, share exchanges, short-form mergers, and sales of substantially all of the corporate assets not in the ordinary course of business. Such rights can be particularly important in a short-form merger because the minority stockholders do not receive advance notice of the merger, the directors do not consider or approve it, and there is no vote. Appraisal rights are often the only recourse available to shareholders who object to parent-subsidiary mergers.

Each state establishes the procedures for asserting appraisal rights in that jurisdiction. Shareholders may lose their appraisal rights if they do not adhere precisely to the procedures prescribed by statute. When they lose the right to an appraisal, dissenting shareholders must go along with the transaction despite their objections.

Purchase of Assets

When a corporation acquires all or substantially all of the assets of another corporation by direct purchase, the purchasing, or *acquiring*, corporation simply extends its ownership and control over more physical assets. Because no change in the legal entity occurs, the acquiring corporation is not required to obtain shareholder approval for the purchase.[10] The U.S. Department of Justice and the Federal Trade Commission, however, have issued guidelines that significantly constrain and often prohibit mergers that could result from a purchase of assets, including takeover bids. (These guidelines are part of the federal antitrust laws that will be discussed in Chapter 32.)

Note that the corporation that is *selling* all of its assets is substantially changing its business position and perhaps its ability to carry out its corporate purposes. For that reason, the corporation whose assets are being sold must obtain the approval of both the board of directors and the shareholders. In most states and under RMBCA 13.02, a dissenting shareholder of the selling corporation can demand appraisal rights.

Potential Liability in Purchases of Assets

RECALL In a merger or consolidation, the surviving corporation inherits the disappearing corporation's rights *and* obligations.

Generally, a corporation that purchases the assets of another corporation is not responsible for the liabilities of the selling corporation. Exceptions to this rule are made in certain circumstances, however. In any of the following situations, the acquiring corporation will be held to have assumed *both* the assets and the liabilities of the selling corporation.

1. When the purchasing corporation impliedly or expressly assumes the seller's liabilities.
2. When the sale transaction is actually a merger or consolidation of the two companies.
3. When the purchaser continues the seller's business and retains the same personnel (same shareholders, directors, and officers).
4. When the sale is fraudulently executed to escape liability.

Purchase of Stock and Tender Offers

Target Corporation The corporation to be acquired in a corporate takeover; a corporation whose shareholders receive a tender offer.

Takeover The acquisition of control over a corporation through the purchase of a substantial number of the voting shares of the corporation.

An alternative to the purchase of another corporation's assets is the purchase of a substantial number of the voting shares of its stock. This enables the acquiring corporation to control the **target corporation** (the corporation being acquired). The process of acquiring control over a corporation in this way is commonly referred to as a corporate **takeover.**

10. Shareholder approval may be required in a few situations. If the acquiring corporation plans to pay for the assets with its own corporate stock and not enough authorized unissued shares are available, the shareholders must vote to approve the issuance of additional shares by amendment of the corporate articles. Also, if the acquiring corporation is a company whose stock is traded on a national stock exchange and it will be issuing a significant number (at least 20 percent) of its outstanding shares, shareholder approval can be required.

Tender Offer An offer made by one company directly to the shareholders of another (target) company to purchase their shares of stock; sometimes referred to as a *takeover bid.*

The acquiring corporation deals directly with the target company's shareholders in seeking to purchase the shares they hold. It does this by making a **tender offer** to all of the shareholders of the target corporation. The tender offer can be conditioned on receiving a specified number of shares by a certain date. The price offered is generally higher than the market price of the target corporation's stock prior to the announcement of the tender offer as a means of inducing shareholders to accept the offer. **EXAMPLE 29.8** In the 2009 merger of two Fortune 500 pharmaceutical companies, Pfizer, Inc., paid $68 billion to acquire its rival Wyeth. Wyeth shareholders reportedly received approximately $50.19 per share (part in cash and part in Pfizer stock), which amounted to a 15 percent premium over the market price of the stock. ● Federal securities laws strictly control the terms, duration, and circumstances under which most tender offers are made. In addition, many states have passed antitakeover statutes.

"In the takeover business, if you want a friend, you buy a dog."

Carl Icahn, 1936–present
(American financier)

Responses to Tender Offers

A firm may respond to a tender offer in numerous ways. Sometimes, a target firm's board of directors will see a tender offer as favorable and will recommend to the shareholders that they accept it. To resist a takeover, a target company can make a *self-tender,* which is an offer to acquire stock from its own shareholders and thereby retain corporate control.

Alternatively, a target corporation might resort to one of several other defensive tactics to resist a takeover (see Exhibit 29–7). In one commonly used tactic, known as a "poison pill," a target company gives its shareholders rights to purchase additional shares at low prices when there is a takeover attempt. The use of poison pills is an attempt to prevent takeovers by making a takeover prohibitively expensive.

Dissolution The formal disbanding of a partnership or a corporation. Dissolution of a corporation can take place by (1) an act of the state, (2) agreement of the shareholders and the board of directors, (3) the expiration of a time period stated in the certificate of incorporation, or (4) court order.

Termination

The termination of a corporation's existence has two phases—dissolution and winding up. **Dissolution** is the legal death of the artificial "person" of the corporation. *Winding up* is the process by which corporate assets are liquidated, or converted into cash and distributed among creditors and shareholders.[11]

11. Some prefer to call this phase *liquidation,* but we use the term *winding up* to mean all acts needed to bring the legal and financial affairs of the business to an end, including liquidating the assets and distributing them among creditors and shareholders. See RMBCA 14.05.

● *Exhibit* **29–7 The Terminology of Takeover Defenses**

TERM	DEFINITION
Crown jewel	When threatened with a takeover, management makes the company less attractive to the raider by selling the company's most valuable asset (the "crown jewel") to a third party.
Golden parachute	When a takeover is successful, top management usually is changed. With this in mind, a company may establish special termination or retirement benefits that must be paid to top managers if they are "retired." In other words, a departing high-level manager's parachute will be "golden" when he or she is forced to "bail out" of the company.
Greenmail	To regain control, a target company may pay a higher-than-market price to repurchase the stock that the acquiring corporation bought. When a takeover is attempted through a gradual accumulation of target stock rather than a tender offer, the intent may be to get the target company to buy back the shares at a premium price—a concept similar to blackmail.
Pac-Man	Named after the Atari video game, this is an aggressive defense in which the target corporation attempts its own takeover of the acquiring corporation.
Poison pill	The target corporation issues to its stockholders rights to purchase additional shares at low prices when there is a takeover attempt. This makes the takeover undesirably or even prohibitively expensive for the acquiring corporation.
White knight	The target corporation solicits a merger with a third party, which then makes a better (often simply a higher) tender offer to the target's shareholders. The third party that "rescues" the target is the "white knight."

Voluntary Dissolution

Dissolution can be brought about voluntarily by the directors and the shareholders. State corporation statutes establish the procedures required to voluntarily dissolve a corporation. Basically, there are two possible methods: (1) by the shareholders' unanimous vote to initiate dissolution proceedings[12] or (2) by a proposal of the board of directors that is submitted to the shareholders at a shareholders' meeting.

When a corporation is dissolved voluntarily, the corporation must file *articles of dissolution* with the state and notify its creditors of the dissolution. The corporation must also establish a date (at least 120 days after the date of dissolution) by which all claims against the corporation must be received [RMBCA 14.06].

If a corporation is dissolved and its assets are liquidated without notice to a party who has a claim against the firm, shareholders of the former corporation can be held personally liable for the debt. **CASE EXAMPLE 29.9** Christine Parent leased an automobile from Amity Autoworld, Ltd. Soon after that, Amity sold all of its automobile-franchising assets to another company named Atlantic. Parent made a written claim for monetary damages to Amity one month after the sale of its assets. Parent then filed a small claims action against Amity and obtained a $2,643 judgment, but she was unable to collect the amount because Amity had been sold to Atlantic. Parent knew that Amity's principal shareholder and chief executive officer, John Staluppi, Jr., was the son of Atlantic's principal shareholder, John Staluppi, Sr., so she filed a claim against Staluppi, Jr., personally. A state court ruled that because Amity was liquidated and dissolved without any notice to creditors, those creditors (including Parent) could hold Amity's principal shareholder, Staluppi, Jr., liable.[13] ●

Involuntary Dissolution

Because corporations are creatures of statute, the state can also dissolve a corporation in certain circumstances. The secretary of state or the state attorney general can bring an action to dissolve a corporation that has failed to pay its annual taxes or to submit required annual reports, for example. A state court can also dissolve a corporation that has engaged in *ultra vires* acts or committed fraud or misrepresentation to the state during incorporation.

Sometimes, a shareholder or a group of shareholders petitions a court for corporate dissolution. A court may dissolve a corporation if the controlling shareholders or directors have engaged in fraudulent, illegal, or oppressive conduct. **CASE EXAMPLE 29.10** Mt. Princeton Trout Club, Inc. (MPTC), was formed to own land in Colorado and provide fishing and other recreational benefits to its shareholders. The articles of incorporation prohibited MPTC from selling or leasing any of the property and assets of the corporation without the approval of a majority of the directors. Despite this provision, MPTC officers entered into leases and contracts to sell corporate property without even notifying the directors. When a shareholder, Sam Colt, petitioned for dissolution, the court dissolved MPTC based on a finding that its officers had engaged in illegal, oppressive, and fraudulent conduct.[14] ● Shareholders may also petition a court for dissolution when the board of directors is deadlocked and the affairs of the corporation can no longer be conducted because of the deadlock.[15]

---

12. Only some states allow shareholders to initiate corporate dissolution. See, for example, Delaware Code Section 275(c).
13. *Parent v. Amity Autoworld, Ltd.*, 15 Misc.3d 633, 832 N.Y.S.2d 775 (2007).
14. *Colt v. Mt. Princeton Trout Club, Inc.*, 78 P.3d 1115 (Colo.App. 2003).
15. See, for example, *Sartori v. S&S Trucking, Inc.*, 2006 MT 164, 322 Mont. 503, 139 P.3d 806 (2006).

Winding Up

When dissolution takes place by voluntary action, the members of the board of directors act as trustees of the corporate assets. As trustees, they are responsible for winding up the affairs of the corporation for the benefit of corporate creditors and shareholders. This makes the board members personally liable for any breach of their fiduciary trustee duties.

Receiver In a corporate dissolution, a court-appointed person who winds up corporate affairs and liquidates corporate assets.

When the dissolution is involuntary—or if board members do not wish to act as trustees of the assets—the court will appoint a **receiver** to wind up the corporate affairs and liquidate corporate assets. Courts may also appoint a receiver when shareholders or creditors can show that the board of directors should not be permitted to act as trustees of the corporate assets.

Reviewing . . . Corporate Formation, Merger, and Termination

Mario Bonsetti and Rico Sanchez incorporated Gnarly Vulcan Gear, Inc. (GVG), to manufacture windsurfing equipment. Bonsetti owned 60 percent of the corporation's stock, and Sanchez owned 40 percent; both men served on the board of directors. Hula Boards, Inc., owned solely by Mai Jin Li, made a public offer to Bonsetti and Sanchez to buy GVG stock. Hula offered 30 percent more than the market price per share for the GVG stock, and Bonsetti and Sanchez each sold 20 percent of their stock to Hula. Jin Li became the third member of the GVG board of directors. An irreconcilable dispute soon arose between Bonsetti and Sanchez over design modifications of their popular Baked Chameleon board. Despite Bonsetti's dissent, Sanchez and Jin Li voted to merge GVG with Hula Boards under the latter name, Gnarly Vulcan Gear was dissolved, and production of the Baked Chameleon ceased. Using the information presented in the chapter, answer the following questions.

1. What rights does Bonsetti have (in most states) as a minority shareholder dissenting to the merger of GVG and Hula Boards?
2. Could the parties have used a short-form merger procedure in this situation? Why or why not?
3. What is the term used for Hula's offer to purchase GVG stock?
4. Suppose that after the merger, a person who was injured on the Baked Chameleon board sued Hula (the surviving corporation). Can Hula be held liable for the injury? Why or why not?

Linking the Law to Finance
Sources of Funds

This chapter explained corporate formation and corporate financing. When you complete your education, you may work in corporate finance directly, or you may become involved in starting a sole proprietorship. When the start-up is up and running and sales revenues are sufficient to pay for operating expenses, you may consider incorporating the business and then seeking financing for expansion. As you learned in your finance courses, a finance manager helps directors and upper management decide on the sources of additional funding for ongoing expenses or for growth.

Difficulties Facing Finance Managers in Times of Crisis

During the recent economic crisis, many businesses experienced severe financial pressures because their traditional sources of financing dried up. In particular, commercial banks abruptly cut off lines of credit even for corporations that had solid balance sheets and stable profits. A number of corporations that were preparing to sell shares in an initial public offering (IPO) were told that there was no market for new shares, and the IPOs were canceled. Some large corporations that were considering secondary issues of additional stock found that there were no buyers for those shares either.

During the economic crisis, some finance managers had to deal with the bankruptcy of their companies. Other finance managers of troubled firms sought mergers with stronger competitors, even though those mergers meant that the value of the shares held by the current owners would be severely reduced. Some finance managers turned to the remaining players in the private equity market. The managers offered large stakes in their companies at attractive prices–anything to obtain the financing needed to avoid going under.

Sources of Funds in More Normal Times

Fortunately, during normal business periods, finance managers have a variety of options for financing. These include obtaining financing from a bank and issuing bonds or stock. When there is no financial crisis, commercial banks are ready to lend to businesses. Successful corporations typically obtain lines of credit that can be drawn down at any time and then repaid when their cash flows warrant.

In most situations, though, issuing bonds will be a less expensive option than depending on a line of credit at a commercial bank. Corporate finance managers will then have to consider the trade-off between issuing more debt or selling more common shares (equity). Although the sale of common stock does not obligate the corporation to make fixed interest payments every year, as bonds do, increasing the amount of common stock dilutes the current shareholders.

Another possibility is to sell preferred stock, which, as you learned in this chapter, has preferences. Holders of preferred stock have priority over holders of common stock with respect to dividends and to payment on the dissolution of the corporation.

Self-Financing

Sometimes, finance managers decide that the best type of financing is self-financing. That is to say, the corporation retains earnings and invests them in order to grow. Do not get the impression, though, that the use of retained earnings is costless. There is an *oppportunity cost,* which, as you learned in your economics classes, is what the company could have earned if it had invested those retained earnings in, say, U.S. Treasury bonds. Alternatively, the retained earnings could be distributed to the shareholders as dividends.

FOR CRITICAL ANALYSIS

What is the benefit of paying dividends to shareholders rather than using retained earnings to expand?

Key Terms

alien corporation 727
appraisal right 742
articles of incorporation 732
bond 738
bond indenture 738
bylaws 732
close corporation 728
commingle 737
common stock 738
consolidation 741
corporation 723
dissolution 744
dividend 724
domestic corporation 727
foreign corporation 727
holding company 724
merger 740
piercing the corporate veil 736
preferred stock 739
private equity capital 740
receiver 746
retained earnings 724
S corporation 730
securities 738
share exchange 741
short-form (parent-subsidiary) merger 742
stock 738
takeover 743
target corporation 743
tender offer 744
***ultra vires* 734**
venture capital 740

Chapter Summary: Corporate Formation, Merger, and Termination

Corporate Nature and Classification (See pages 723–730.)	A corporation is a legal entity distinct from its owners. Formal statutory requirements, which vary somewhat from state to state, must be followed in forming a corporation. 1. *Corporate parties*—The shareholders own the corporation. They elect a board of directors to govern the corporation. The board of directors hires corporate officers and other employees to run the daily business of the firm. 2. *Corporate taxation*—The corporation pays income tax on net profits; shareholders pay income tax on the disbursed dividends that they receive from the corporation (double-taxation feature). 3. *Torts and criminal acts*—The corporation is liable for the torts committed by its agents or officers within the course and scope of their employment (under the doctrine of *respondeat superior*). In some circumstances, a corporation can be held liable (and be fined) for the criminal acts of its agents and employees. In certain situations, corporate officers may be held personally liable for corporate crimes.

Continued

Chapter Summary: Corporate Formation, Merger, and Termination—Continued

Corporate Nature and Classification—Continued	4. *Domestic, foreign, and alien corporations*—A corporation is referred to as a *domestic corporation* within its home state (the state in which it incorporates). A corporation is referred to as a *foreign corporation* by any state that is not its home state. A corporation is referred to as an *alien corporation* if it originates in another country but does business in the United States. 5. *Public and private corporations*—A public corporation is one formed by a government (for example, cities, towns, and public projects). A private corporation is one formed wholly or in part for private benefit. Most corporations are private corporations. 6. *Nonprofit corporations*—Corporations formed without a profit-making purpose (for example, charitable, educational, and religious organizations and hospitals). 7. *Close corporations*—Corporations owned by a family or a relatively small number of individuals. Transfer of shares is usually restricted, and the corporation cannot make a public offering of its securities. 8. *S corporations*—Small domestic corporations (with no more than one hundred shareholders) that, under Subchapter S of the Internal Revenue Code, are given special tax treatment. These corporations allow shareholders to enjoy the limited legal liability of the corporate form but avoid its double-taxation feature. 9. *Professional corporations*—Corporations formed by professionals (for example, physicians and lawyers) to obtain the benefits of incorporation (such as limited liability). In most situations, the professional corporation is treated like other corporations, but sometimes the courts will disregard the corporate form and treat the shareholders as partners.
Corporate Formation and Powers **(See pages 730–734.)**	1. *Promotional activities*—Preliminary promotional activities are rarely if ever taken today. A person who enters contracts with investors and others on behalf of the future corporation is personally liable on all preincorporation contracts. Liability remains until the corporation is formed and assumes the contract by novation. 2. *Incorporation procedures*—Exact procedures for incorporation differ among states, but the basic steps are as follows: (a) select a state of incorporation, (b) secure the corporate name by confirming its availability, (c) prepare the articles of incorporation, and (d) file the articles of incorporation with the secretary of state accompanied by payment of the specified fees. 3. *Articles of incorporation*—The articles of incorporation must include the corporate name, the number of shares of stock the corporation is authorized to issue, the registered office and agent, and the names and addresses of the incorporators. The articles may (but are not required to) include additional information about the corporation's nature and purpose, duration, and internal organization. The state's filing of the articles of incorporation authorizes the corporation to conduct business. 4. *The first organizational meeting*—A meeting is held after incorporation. The usual purpose of this meeting is to adopt the bylaws, or internal rules of the corporation, but other business, such as election of the board of directors may also take place. 5. *Express powers*—The express powers of a corporation are granted by the following laws and documents (listed according to their priority): federal constitution, state constitutions, state statutes, articles of incorporation, bylaws, and resolutions of the board of directors. 6. *Implied powers*—Barring express constitutional, statutory, or other prohibitions, the corporation has the implied power to do all acts reasonably appropriate and necessary to accomplish its corporate purposes. 7. *Ultra vires doctrine*—Any act of a corporation that is beyond its express or implied powers to undertake is an *ultra vires* act and may lead to a lawsuit by the shareholders, corporation, or state attorney general to enjoin or recover damages for the *ultra vires* acts.
Defects in Formation and Corporate Status **(See pages 735–737.)**	1. *De jure or de facto corporation*—If a corporation has been improperly incorporated, the courts will sometimes impute corporate status to the firm by holding that it is a *de jure* corporation (cannot be challenged by the state or third persons) or a *de facto* corporation (can be challenged by the state but not by third persons). 2. *Corporation by estoppel*—If a firm is neither a *de jure* nor a *de facto* corporation but represents itself to be a corporation and is sued as such by a third party, it may be held to be a corporation by estoppel. 3. *Piercing the corporate veil*—To avoid injustice, courts may "pierce the corporate veil" and hold a shareholder or shareholders personally liable for a judgment against the corporation. This usually occurs only when the corporation was established to circumvent the law, when the corporate form is used for an illegitimate or fraudulent purpose, or when the controlling shareholder commingles his or her own interests with those of the corporation to such an extent that the corporation no longer has a separate identity.

Chapter Summary: Corporate Formation, Merger, and Termination—Continued

Corporate Financing (See pages 738–740.)	1. *Bonds*—Corporate bonds are securities representing *corporate debt*—funds borrowed by a corporation. See Exhibit 29–2 on page 738 for a description of the various types of corporate bonds. 2. *Stocks*—Stocks are equity securities issued by a corporation that represent the purchase of ownership in the business firm. Exhibit 29–3 on page 739 describes how stocks differ from bonds, and Exhibit 29–4 on page 740 describes the various types of stocks issued by corporations, including the two main types—common stock and preferred stock.
Mergers and Acquisitions (See pages 740–744.)	1. *Merger*—The legal combination of two or more corporations, with the result that the surviving corporation acquires all the assets and obligations of the other corporation, which then ceases to exist. 2. *Consolidation*—The legal combination of two or more corporations, with the result that each corporation ceases to exist and a new one emerges. The new corporation assumes all the assets and obligations of the former corporations. 3. *Share exchange*—Some or all of the shares of one corporation are exchanged for some or all of the shares of another corporation, but both corporations continue to exist. 4. *Procedure*—Determined by state statutes. The basic requirements are listed on pages 741 and 742. 5. *Short-form (parent-subsidiary) merger*—Possible when the parent corporation owns at least 90 percent of the outstanding shares of each class of stock of the subsidiary corporation. Shareholder approval is not required. The merger need be approved only by the board of directors of the parent corporation. 6. *Appraisal rights*—Rights of dissenting shareholders (given by state statute) to receive the *fair value* for their shares when a merger or consolidation takes place. 7. *Purchase of assets*—A purchase of assets occurs when one corporation acquires all or substantially all of the assets of another corporation. a. The acquiring (purchasing) corporation is not required to obtain shareholder approval; the corporation is merely increasing its assets, and no fundamental business change occurs. b. The acquired (purchased) corporation is required to obtain the approval of both its directors and its shareholders for the sale of its assets, because the sale will substantially change the corporation's business position. 8. *Purchase of stock*— A purchase of stock occurs when one corporation acquires a substantial number of the voting shares of the stock of another (target) corporation. 9. *Tender offer*—A public offer to all shareholders of the target corporation to purchase its stock at a price that generally is higher than the market price of the target stock prior to the announcement of the tender offer. Federal and state securities laws strictly control the terms, duration, and circumstances under which most tender offers are made. 10. *Target responses*—Target corporations may respond to takeover bids in various ways, including self-tender (the target firm's offer to acquire its own shareholders' stock) and the strategies listed in Exhibit 29–7 on page 744.
Termination (See pages 744–746.)	The termination of a corporation involves the following two phases: 1. *Dissolution*—The legal death of the artificial "person" of the corporation. Dissolution can be brought about voluntarily by the directors and shareholders or involuntarily by the state or through a court order. 2. *Winding up (liquidation)*—The process by which corporate assets are converted into cash and distributed to creditors and shareholders according to specified rules of preference. May be supervised by members of the board of directors (when dissolution is voluntary) or by a receiver appointed by the court to wind up corporate affairs.

ExamPrep

ISSUE SPOTTERS

1 Name Brand, Inc., is a small business. Twelve members of a single family own all of its stock. Ordinarily, corporate income is taxed at the corporate and shareholder levels. How can Name Brand avoid this double taxation of income?

2 ABC Corporation combines with DEF, Inc. ABC ceases to exist. DEF is the surviving firm. Global Corporation and Hometown Company combine. Afterwards, Global and Hometown cease to exist. GH, Inc., a new firm, functions in their place. Which of these combinations is a merger and which is a consolidation?

BEFORE THE TEST

Check your answers to the Issue Spotters, and at the same time, take the interactive quiz for this chapter. Go to www.cengage.com/blaw/blt and click on "Chapter 29." First, click on "Answers to Issue Spotters" to check your answers. Next, click on "Interactive Quiz" to assess your mastery of the concepts in this chapter. Then click on "Flashcards" to review this chapter's Key Term definitions.

For Review

Answers for the even-numbered questions in this For Review *section can be found on this text's accompanying Web site at* www.cengage.com/blaw/blt. *Select "Chapter 29" and click on "For Review."*

1 What steps are involved in bringing a corporation into existence?
2 What is the difference between a *de jure* corporation and a *de facto* corporation?
3 In what circumstances might a court disregard the corporate entity ("pierce the corporate veil") and hold the shareholders personally liable?
4 What are the basic differences between a merger, a consolidation, and a share exchange?
5 What are the two ways in which a corporation can be voluntarily dissolved?

Hypothetical Scenarios and Case Problems

29–1 **Corporate Status.** Three brothers inherited a small paper-supply business from their father, who had operated the business as a sole proprietorship. The brothers decided to incorporate under the name Gomez Corp. and retained an attorney to draw up the necessary documents. The attorney drew up the papers and had the brothers sign them, but she neglected to file the articles of incorporation with the secretary of state's office. The brothers assumed that all necessary legal work had been completed, so they proceeded to do business as Gomez Corp. One day, a Gomez Corp. employee, while making a delivery to a customer, negligently ran a red light and caused an accident. Baxter, the driver of the other vehicle, was injured and sued Gomez Corp. for damages. Baxter then learned that no state authorization had ever been issued to Gomez Corp., so he sued each of the brothers personally for damages. Can the brothers avoid personal liability for the tort of their employee? Explain.

29–2 **Hypothetical Question with Sample Answer** Jolson is the chair of the board of directors of Artel, Inc., and Douglas is the chair of the board of directors of Fox Express, Inc. Artel is a manufacturing corporation, and Fox Express is a transportation corporation. Jolson and Douglas meet to consider the possibility of combining their corporations and activities into a single corporate entity. They consider two alternative courses of action: Artel could acquire all of the stock and assets of Fox Express, or the corporations could combine to form a new corporation, called A&F Enterprises, Inc. Both Jolson and Douglas are concerned about the necessity of a formal transfer of property, liability for existing debts, and the need to amend the articles of incorporation. Discuss what the two proposed combinations are called and the legal effect each has on the transfer of property, the liabilities of the combined corporations, and the need to amend the articles of incorporation.

—For a sample answer to Question 29–2, go to Appendix E at the end of this text.

29–3 **Corporate Powers.** Kora Nayenga and two business associates formed a corporation called Nayenga Corp. for the purpose of selling computer services. Kora, who owned 50 percent of the corporate shares, served as the corporation's president. Kora wished to obtain a personal loan from his bank for $250,000, but the bank required the note to be cosigned by a third party. Kora cosigned the note in the name of the corporation. Later, Kora defaulted on the note, and the bank sued the corporation for payment. The corporation asserted, as a defense, that Kora had exceeded his authority when he cosigned the note. Had he? Explain.

29–4 **Case Problem with Sample Answer** Thomas Persson and Jon Nokes founded Smart Inventions, Inc., in 1991 to market household consumer products. The success of their first product, the Smart Mop, continued with later products, which were sold through infomercials and other means. Persson and Nokes were the firm's officers and equal shareholders, with Persson responsible for product development and Nokes operating the day-to-day activities. By 1998, they had become dissatisfied with each other's efforts. Nokes represented the firm as financially "dying," "in a grim state, . . . worse than ever," and offered to buy all of Persson's shares for $1.6 million. Persson accepted. On the day that they signed the agreement to transfer the shares, Smart Inventions began marketing a new product—the Tap Light. It was an instant success, generating millions of dollars in revenues. In negotiating with Persson, Nokes had intentionally kept the Tap Light a secret. Persson filed a suit in a California state court against

Smart Inventions and others, asserting fraud and other claims. Under what principle might Smart Inventions be liable for Nokes's fraud? Is Smart Inventions liable in this case? Explain. [*Persson v. Smart Inventions, Inc.*, 125 Cal.App.4th 1141, 23 Cal.Rptr.3d 335 (2 Dist. 2005)]

—After you have answered Problem 29–4, compare your answer with the sample answer given on the Web site that accompanies this text. Go to www.cengage.com/blaw/blt, select "Chapter 29," and click on "Case Problem with Sample Answer."

29–5 **Dissolution.** Clara Mahaffey operated Mahaffey's Auto Salvage, Inc., in Dayton, Ohio, as a sole proprietorship. In 1993, Kenneth Stumpff and Mahaffey's son, Richard Harris, joined the firm. Stumpff ran the wrecker and bought the vehicles for salvage. Harris handled the day-to-day operations and the bookkeeping. They became the company's equal 50 percent shareholders on Mahaffey's death in 2002. Harris, who inherited the land on which the firm was located, increased the rent to $1,500 per month. Within two years of Mahaffey's death, and without consulting Stumpff, Harris raised the rent to $2,500. Stumpff's wife died, and he took a leave of absence, during which the company paid him $2,500 a month and provided health insurance. After two years, Harris stopped the payments, discontinued the health benefits, and fired Stumpff, threatening to call the police if he came on the premises. Stumpff withdrew $16,000 from the firm's account, leaving a balance of $113. Harris offered to buy Stumpff's interest in the business, but Stumpff refused and filed a suit in an Ohio state court against Harris. A state statute permits the dissolution of a corporation if the owners are deadlocked in its management. Should the court order the dissolution of Mahaffey's? Why or why not? [*Stumpff v. Harris*, __ N.E.2d __ (Ohio App.2 Dist. 2006)]

29–6 **Improper Incorporation.** Denise Rubenstein and Christopher Mayor agreed to form Bayshore Sunrise Corp. (BSC) in New York to rent certain premises and operate a laundromat. BSC entered into a twenty-year commercial lease with Bay Shore Property Trust on April 15, 1999. Mayor signed the lease as the president of BSC. The next day—April 16—BSC's certificate of incorporation was filed with New York's secretary of state. Three years later, BSC defaulted on the lease, which resulted in its termination. Rubenstein and BSC filed a suit in a New York state court against Mayor, his brother-in-law Thomas Castellano, and Planet Laundry, Inc., claiming wrongful interference with a contractual relationship. The plaintiffs alleged that Mayor and Castellano conspired to squeeze Rubenstein out of BSC and arranged the default on the lease so that Mayor and Castellano could form and operate their own business, Planet Laundry, at the same address. The defendants argued that they could not be liable on the plaintiffs' claim because there had never been an enforceable lease—BSC lacked the capacity to enter into contracts on April 15. What theory might Rubenstein and BSC assert to refute this argument? Discuss. [*Rubenstein v. Mayor*, 41 A.D.3d 826, 839 N.Y.S.2d 170 (2 Dept. 2007)]

29–7 **Involuntary Dissolution.** Charles Brooks began working as an independent supplier for Georgia-Pacific, LLC, when the paper products manufacturer acquired a mill in Crossett, Arkansas. Brooks soon organized Charles Brooks Co. in corporate form. Each of the parties' contracts provided, "there is absolutely no guarantee as to the amount of work to be performed." Charles Brooks Co. borrowed funds to buy new equipment. When Georgia-Pacific reduced the quantity of timber that it bought from the supplier, the firm was unable to pay its loans. In 2002, some of the new equipment was returned to the seller. The rest was sold, but the proceeds were not enough to eliminate the debt. The same year, the Arkansas secretary of state revoked Charles Brooks Co.'s corporate status for nonpayment of franchise taxes. In 2006, Charles Brooks Co. filed a suit in a federal district court against Georgia-Pacific, alleging breach of contract. Can the plaintiff maintain this suit? Explain. [*Charles Brooks Co. v. Georgia-Pacific, LLC*, 552 F.3d 718 (8th Cir. 2009)]

29–8 **A Question of Ethics** *Mike Lyons incorporated Lyons Concrete, Inc., in Montana, but did not file its first annual report, so the state involuntarily dissolved the firm in 1996. Unaware of the dissolution, Lyons continued to do business as Lyons Concrete. In 2003, he signed a written contract with William Weimar to form and pour a certain amount of concrete on Weimar's property in Lake County for $19,810. Weimar was in a rush to complete the entire project, and he and Lyons orally agreed to additional work on a time-and-materials basis. When scheduling conflicts arose, Weimar had his own employees set some of the forms, which proved deficient. Weimar also directed Lyons to pour concrete in the rain, which undercut its quality. Mid-project, Lyons submitted an invoice for $14,389, which Weimar paid. After the work was complete, Lyons invoiced Weimar for $25,731, but he refused to pay, claiming that the $14,389 covered everything. To recover the unpaid amount, Lyons filed a mechanic's lien as "Mike Lyons d/b/a Lyons Concrete, Inc." against Weimar's property. Weimar filed a suit in a Montana state court to strike the lien, which Lyons filed a counterclaim to reassert. [*Weimar v. Lyons*, *338 Mont. 242, 164 P.3d 922 (2007)]*

1. Before the trial, Weimar asked for a change of venue on the ground that a sign on the courthouse lawn advertised "Lyons Concrete." How might the sign affect a trial on the parties' dispute? Should the court grant this request?
2. Weimar asked the court to dismiss the counterclaim on the ground that the state had dissolved Lyons Concrete in 1996. Lyons immediately filed new articles of incorporation for "Lyons Concrete, Inc." Under what doctrine might the court rule that Weimar could not deny the existence of Lyons Concrete? What ethical values underlie this doctrine? Should the court make this ruling?
3. At the trial, Weimar argued in part that there was no "fixed price" contract between the parties and that even if there was, the poor quality of the work, which required repairs, amounted to a breach, excusing Weimar's further performance. Should the court rule in Weimar's favor on this basis?

Critical Thinking and Writing Assignments

29–9 **Critical Legal Thinking.** If you had started a business, under what circumstances would you be willing to give up a substantial percentage of its ownership to obtain venture capital financing?

29–10 **Video Question** Go to this text's Web site at www.cengage.com/blaw/blt and select "Chapter 29." Click on "Video Questions" and view the video titled *Corporation or LLC: Which Is Better?* Then answer the following questions.

1 Compare the liability that Anna and Caleb would be exposed to as shareholders/owners of a corporation versus as members of a limited liability company (LLC).

2 How does the taxation of corporations different from that of LLCs?

3 Given that Anna and Caleb conduct their business (Wizard Internet) over the Internet, can you think of any drawbacks to forming an LLC?

4 If you were in the position of Anna and Caleb, would you choose to create a corporation or an LLC? Why?

Practical Internet Exercises

Go to this text's Web site at www.cengage.com/blaw/blt, select "Chapter 29," and click on "Practical Internet Exercises." There you will find the following Internet research exercises that you can perform to learn more about the topics covered in this chapter.

Practical Internet Exercise 29–1: LEGAL PERSPECTIVE—**Mergers**

Practical Internet Exercise 29–2: MANAGEMENT PERSPECTIVE—**Online Incorporation**

Chapter 30

Corporate Directors, Officers, and Shareholders

"They [corporations] cannot commit treason, nor be outlawed nor excommunicated, because they have no soul."

—Sir Edward Coke, 1552–1634
(English jurist and legal scholar)

Chapter Outline

- Roles of Directors and Officers
- Duties and Liabilities of Directors and Officers
- Role of Shareholders
- Rights of Shareholders
- Duties and Liabilities of Shareholders
- Major Business Forms Compared

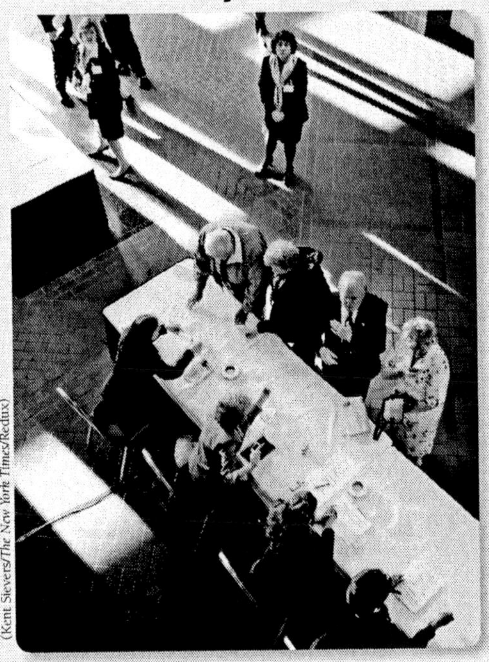
(Kent Sievers/The New York Times/Redux)

Learning Objectives

After reading this chapter, you should be able to answer the following questions:

1. What are the duties of corporate directors and officers?
2. Directors are expected to use their best judgment in managing the corporation. What must directors do to avoid liability for honest mistakes of judgment and poor business decisions?
3. What is a voting proxy? What is cumulative voting?
4. If a group of shareholders perceives that the corporation has suffered a wrong and the directors refuse to take action, can the shareholders compel the directors to act? If so, how?
5. From what sources may dividends be paid legally? In what circumstances is a dividend illegal? What happens if a dividend is illegally paid?

When Sir Edward Coke observed, in the chapter-opening quotation, that a corporation has no "soul," he was referring to the fact that a corporation is not a "natural" person but a legal fiction. No one individual shareholder or director bears sole responsibility for the corporation and its actions. Rather, a corporation joins the efforts and resources of a large number of individuals for the purpose of producing greater returns than those persons could have obtained individually.

Sometimes, actions that benefit the corporation as a whole do not coincide with the separate interests of the individuals making up the corporation. In such situations, it is important to know the rights and duties of all participants in the corporate enterprise. This chapter focuses on the rights and duties of directors, officers, and shareholders and the ways in which conflicts among them are resolved.

Roles of Directors and Officers

The board of directors is the ultimate authority in every corporation. Directors have responsibility for all policymaking decisions necessary to the management of all corporate affairs. The board selects and removes the corporate officers, determines the capital structure of the corporation, and declares dividends. Each director has one vote, and customarily the majority rules. The general areas of responsibility of the board of directors are shown in Exhibit 30–1 on the following page.

Exhibit 30–1 Directors' Management Responsibilities

AUTHORIZE MAJOR CORPORATE POLICY DECISIONS	SELECT AND REMOVE CORPORATE OFFICERS AND OTHER MANAGERIAL EMPLOYEES, AND DETERMINE THEIR COMPENSATION	MAKE CORPORATE FINANCIAL DECISIONS
Examples: • Oversee major contract negotiations and management-labor negotiations. • Initiate negotiations on the sale or lease of corporate assets outside the regular course of business. • Decide whether to pursue new product lines or business opportunities.	*Examples:* • Search for and hire corporate executives and determine the elements of their compensation packages, including stock options. • Supervise managerial employees and make decisions regarding their termination.	*Examples:* • Make decisions regarding the issuance of authorized shares and bonds. • Decide when to declare dividends that are to be paid to shareholders.

Directors are sometimes inappropriately characterized as *agents* because they act on behalf of the corporation. No *individual* director, however, can act as an agent to bind the corporation; and as a group, directors collectively control the corporation in a way that no agent is able to control a principal. In addition, although directors occupy positions of trust and control over the corporation, they are not *trustees* because they do not hold title to property for the use and benefit of others.

There are few legal requirements concerning directors' qualifications. Only a handful of states impose minimum age and residency requirements. A director may be a shareholder, but this is not necessary (unless the articles of incorporation or bylaws require ownership).

Election of Directors

Subject to statutory limitations, the number of directors is set forth in the corporation's articles or bylaws. Historically, the minimum number of directors has been three, but today many states permit fewer. Normally, the incorporators appoint the first board of directors at the time the corporation is created. The initial board serves until the first annual shareholders' meeting. Subsequent directors are elected by a majority vote of the shareholders.

ON THE WEB One of the best sources on the Web for information on publicly traded corporations, including their directors, is the EDGAR database of the Securities and Exchange Commission at www.sec.gov/edgar.shtml.

A director usually serves for a term of one year—from annual meeting to annual meeting. Most state statutes permit longer and staggered terms. A common practice is to elect one-third of the board members each year for a three-year term. In this way, there is greater management continuity.

BE AWARE The articles of incorporation may provide that a director can be removed only for cause.

Removal of Directors A director can be removed *for cause*—that is, for failing to perform a required duty—either as specified in the articles or bylaws or by shareholder action. The board of directors may also have the power to remove a director for cause, subject to shareholder review. In most states, a director cannot be removed without cause unless the shareholders have reserved the right to do so at the time of his or her election.

Vacancies on the Board of Directors If a director dies or resigns or if a new position is created through amendment of the articles or bylaws, either the shareholders or the board itself can fill the vacant position, depending on state law or the provisions of the bylaws. Note, however, that even when an election appears to be authorized by the bylaws, a court can invalidate it if the directors were attempting to manipulate the election in order to reduce the shareholders' influence.

CASE EXAMPLE 30.1 The bylaws of Liquid Audio, a Delaware corporation, authorized a board of five directors. Two directors on the board were elected each year. Another company offered to buy all of Liquid Audio's stock, but the board of directors rejected this offer. An election was coming up, and the directors feared that the shareholders would elect new directors who would allow the sale. The directors, therefore, amended the bylaws to increase the number of directors to seven, thereby diminishing the shareholders' influence in the vote. The shareholders filed an action challenging the election. The Delaware Supreme Court ruled that the directors' action was illegal because they had attempted to diminish the shareholders' right to vote effectively in an election of directors.[1] ●

Compensation of Directors

In the past, corporate directors rarely were compensated, but today they are often paid at least nominal sums and may receive more substantial compensation in large corporations because of the time, work, effort, and especially risk involved. Most states permit the corporate articles or bylaws to authorize compensation for directors. In fact, the Revised Model Business Corporation Act (RMBCA) states that unless the articles or bylaws provide otherwise, the directors may set their own compensation [RMBCA 8.11]. Directors also gain through indirect benefits, such as business contacts and prestige, and other rewards, such as stock options.

In many corporations, directors are also chief corporate officers (president or chief executive officer, for example) and receive compensation in their managerial positions. A director who is also an officer of the corporation is referred to as an **inside director**, whereas a director who does not hold a management position is an **outside director**. Typically, a corporation's board of directors includes both inside and outside directors.

Inside Director A person on the board of directors who is also an officer of the corporation.

Outside Director A person on the board of directors who does not hold a management position at the corporation.

Board of Directors' Meetings

The board of directors conducts business by holding formal meetings with recorded minutes. The dates of regular meetings are usually established in the articles or bylaws or by board resolution, and ordinarily no further notice is required. Special meetings can be called, with notice sent to all directors. Today, most states allow directors to participate in board of directors' meetings from remote locations via telephone or Web conferencing, provided that all the directors can simultaneously hear each other during the meeting [RMBCA 8.20].

ON THE WEB You can find definitions for terms used in corporate law, as well as court decisions and articles on corporate law topics, at www.law.com.

Unless the articles of incorporation or bylaws specify a greater number, a majority of the board of directors normally constitutes a quorum [RMBCA 8.24]. (A **quorum** is the minimum number of members of a body of officials or other group that must be present in order for business to be validly transacted.) Some state statutes specifically allow corporations to set a quorum as less than a majority but not less than one-third of the directors.[2]

Quorum The number of members of a decision-making body that must be present before business may be transacted.

Once a quorum is present, the directors transact business and vote on issues affecting the corporation. Each director present at the meeting has one vote.[3] Ordinary matters generally require a simple majority vote; certain extraordinary issues may require a greater-than-majority vote.

Rights of Directors

A corporate director must have certain rights to function properly in that position and make informed policy decisions for the company. The *right to participation* means that directors are entitled to participate in all board of directors' meetings and have a right to be notified of these meetings. Because the dates of regular board meetings are usually specified in the bylaws, as noted earlier, no notice of these meetings is required. If special meetings are called, however, notice is required unless waived by the director.

1. *MM Companies v. Liquid Audio, Inc.*, 813 A.2d 1118 (Del.Sup. 2003).
2. See, for example, Delaware Code Annotated Title 8, Section 141(b); and New York Business Corporation Law Section 707.
3. Except in Louisiana, which allows a director to authorize another person to cast a vote in his or her place under certain circumstances.

A director also has the *right of inspection,* which means that each director can access the corporation's books and records, facilities, and premises. Inspection rights are essential for directors to make informed decisions and to exercise the necessary supervision over corporate officers and employees. This right of inspection is almost absolute and cannot be restricted (by the articles, bylaws, or any act of the board).

When a director becomes involved in litigation by virtue of her or his position or actions, the director may also have a right to indemnification (reimbursement) for legal costs, fees, and damages incurred. Most states allow corporations to indemnify and purchase liability insurance for corporate directors [RMBCA 8.51].

Preventing Legal Disputes

If you serve as a corporate director or officer, be aware that you may at some point become involved in litigation as a result. To protect against personal liability, make sure that the corporate bylaws explicitly give directors and officers a right to indemnification (reimbursement) for any costs incurred, as well as for any judgments or settlements. Also, have the corporation purchase directors' and officers' liability insurance (D&O insurance). Having D&O insurance policies enables the corporation to avoid paying the substantial costs involved in defending a particular director or officer. Because most D&O policies have maximum coverage limits, make sure that the corporation is required to indemnify you in the event that the costs exceed the policy limits.

Committees of the Board of Directors

"I often feel like the director of a cemetery. I have a lot of people under me, but nobody listens!"

General James Gavin, 1907–1990
(U.S. Army lieutenant general)

When a board of directors has a large number of members and must deal with myriad complex business issues, meetings can become unwieldy. Therefore, the boards of large, publicly held corporations typically create committees, appoint directors to serve on individual committees, and delegate certain tasks to these committees. Committees focus on individual subjects and increase the efficiency of the board. The most common types of committees include the following:

1. *Executive committee.* The board members often elect an executive committee to handle interim management decisions between board meetings. The committee is limited to making decisions about ordinary business matters and conducting preliminary investigations into proposals. It cannot declare dividends, authorize the issuance of shares, amend the bylaws, or initiate any actions that require shareholder approval.
2. *Audit committee.* The audit committee is responsible for the selection, compensation, and oversight of the independent public accountants that audit the corporation's financial records. The Sarbanes-Oxley Act of 2002 requires all publicly held corporations to have an audit committee (as will be discussed in Chapters 31 and 34).
3. *Nominating committee.* This committee chooses the candidates for the board of directors that management wishes to submit to the shareholders in the next election. The committee can nominate but cannot select directors to fill vacancies on the board [RMBCA 8.25].
4. *Compensation committee.* The compensation committee reviews and decides the salaries, bonuses, stock options, and other benefits that are given to the corporation's top executives. The committee may also determine the compensation of directors.
5. *Litigation committee.* This committee decides whether the corporation should pursue requests by shareholders to file a lawsuit against some party that has allegedly harmed the corporation. The committee members investigate the allegations and weigh the costs and benefits of litigation.

In addition to appointing committees, the board of directors can also delegate some of its functions to corporate officers. In doing so, the board is not relieved of its overall responsibility for directing the affairs of the corporation. Instead, corporate officers and

Who hires corporate officers?

managerial personnel are empowered to make decisions relating to ordinary, daily corporate activities within well-defined guidelines.

Corporate Officers and Executives

Corporate officers and other executive employees are hired by the board of directors. At a minimum, most corporations have a president, one or more vice presidents, a secretary, and a treasurer. In most states, an individual can hold more than one office, such as president and secretary, and can be both an officer and a director of the corporation. In addition to carrying out the duties articulated in the bylaws, corporate and managerial officers act as agents of the corporation, and the ordinary rules of agency (discussed in Chapter 23) normally apply to their employment.

Corporate officers and other high-level managers are employees of the company, so their rights are defined by employment contracts. The board of directors, though, normally can remove corporate officers at any time with or without cause and regardless of the terms of the employment contracts—although in so doing, the corporation may be liable for breach of contract.

The duties of corporate officers are the same as those of directors because both groups are involved in decision making and are in similar positions of control. Hence, officers are viewed as having the same fiduciary duties of care and loyalty in their conduct of corporate affairs as directors.

Duties and Liabilities of Directors and Officers

Directors and officers are deemed fiduciaries of the corporation because their relationship with the corporation and its shareholders is one of trust and confidence. As fiduciaries, directors and officers owe ethical—and legal—duties to the corporation and to the shareholders as a whole. These fiduciary duties include the duty of care and the duty of loyalty. (Directors and officers also have a duty not to destroy evidence in the event of a lawsuit involving the corporation. The *Business Application* feature at the end of this chapter discusses how due care can be exercised to preserve electronic evidence by creating a retention policy for e-documents.)

Duty of Care

CONTRAST Shareholders own the corporation and directors make policy decisions, but the officers who run the corporation's daily business often have significant decision-making power.

Directors and officers must exercise due care in performing their duties. The standard of *due care* has been variously described in judicial decisions and codified in many state corporation codes. Generally, a director or officer is expected to act in good faith, to exercise the care that an ordinarily prudent person would exercise in similar circumstances, and to act in what he or she considers to be the best interests of the corporation [RMBCA 8.30]. Directors and officers whose failure to exercise due care results in harm to the corporation or its shareholders can be held liable for negligence (unless the *business judgment rule* applies, as will be discussed shortly).

DUTY TO MAKE INFORMED AND REASONABLE DECISIONS Directors and officers are expected to be informed on corporate matters and to conduct a reasonable investigation of the situation before making a decision. This means that they must do what is necessary to keep adequately informed: attend meetings and presentations, ask for information from those who have it, read reports, and review other written materials. In other words, directors and officers must investigate, study, and discuss matters and evaluate alternatives before making a decision. They cannot decide on the spur of the moment without adequate research.

Although directors and officers are expected to act in accordance with their own knowledge and training, they are also normally entitled to rely on information given to them by certain other persons. Most states and Section 8.30(b) of the RMBCA allow a director to make decisions in reliance on information furnished by competent officers or employees, professionals such as attorneys and accountants, and committees of the board of directors (on which the director does not serve). The reliance must be in good faith, of course, to insulate a director from liability if the information later proves to be inaccurate or unreliable.

"Executive ability is deciding quickly and getting somebody else to do the work."

J. C. Pollard, 1946–present
(British businessman)

Duty to Exercise Reasonable Supervision Directors are also expected to exercise a reasonable amount of supervision when they delegate work to corporate officers and employees. **EXAMPLE 30.2** Dale, a corporate bank director, fails to attend any board of directors' meetings for five years. In addition, Dale never inspects any of the corporate books or records and generally fails to supervise the efforts of the bank president and the loan committee. Meanwhile, Brennan, the bank president, who is a corporate officer, makes various improper loans and permits large overdrafts. In this situation, Dale (the corporate director) can be held liable to the corporation for losses resulting from the unsupervised actions of the bank president and the loan committee. ●

Dissenting Directors Directors are expected to attend board of directors' meetings, and their votes should be entered into the minutes of the meetings. Sometimes, an individual director disagrees with the majority's vote (which becomes an act of the board of directors). Unless a dissent is entered, the director is presumed to have assented. If a decision later leads to the directors being held liable for mismanagement, dissenting directors are rarely held individually liable to the corporation. For this reason, a director who is absent from a given meeting sometimes registers a dissent to actions taken at the meeting with the secretary of the board.

The Business Judgment Rule

Business Judgment Rule A rule that immunizes corporate management from liability for actions that result in corporate losses or damages if the actions are undertaken in good faith and are within both the power of the corporation and the authority of management to make.

Directors and officers are expected to exercise due care and to use their best judgment in guiding corporate management, but they are not insurers of business success. Under the **business judgment rule,** a corporate director or officer will not be liable to the corporation or to its shareholders for honest mistakes of judgment and bad business decisions.

Courts give significant deference to the decisions of corporate directors and officers, and consider the reasonableness of a decision at the time it was made, without the benefit of hindsight. Thus, corporate decision makers are not subjected to second-guessing by shareholders or others in the corporation. The business judgment rule will apply as long as the director or officer:

1. Took reasonable steps to become informed about the matter.
2. Had a rational basis for his or her decision.
3. Did not have a conflict of interest between his or her personal interest and that of the corporation.

In fact, unless there is evidence of bad faith, fraud, or a clear breach of fiduciary duties, most courts will apply the rule and protect directors and officers who make bad business decisions from liability for those choices. Consequently, if there is a reasonable basis for a business decision, a court is unlikely to interfere with that decision, even if the corporation suffers as a result.

Ethical Issue

Does the business judgment rule go too far in protecting directors and officers from liability? The business judgment rule generally insulates corporate decision makers from liability for bad decisions even though this may seem to contradict the goal of greater corporate accountability. Is the rule fair to shareholders? In 2009, a Delaware court ruled against shareholders of Citigroup, Inc., who claimed that the bank's directors had breached their fiduciary duties. The shareholders alleged that the directors caused Citigroup to engage in subprime lending (discussed in Chapter 21) even in the face of "red flags" that should have warned the bank to change its practices. Those red flags included the steady decline of the housing market, the dramatic increase in foreclosures, and the collapse of other subprime lenders. The shareholders claimed that the directors' failure to adequately protect the corporation's exposure to risk given those warning signs was a breach of their duties and resulted in significant losses to Citigroup. The court, however, found "the warning signs alleged by plaintiffs are not evidence that the directors consciously disregarded their duties or otherwise acted in bad faith; at most they evidence that the directors made bad business decisions." Thus, under the business judgment rule, the court dismissed the shareholders' claims of breach of fiduciary duty.[4]

Another 2009 case also involved the business judgment rule. Early in 2007, a foreign firm had announced its intention to acquire Lyondell Chemical Company. Over the next several months, Lyondell's directors did nothing to prepare for a possible merger. They failed to research Lyondell's market value and made no attempt to seek out other potential buyers. The $13 billion cash merger was negotiated and finalized in less than one week in July 2007, during which time the directors met for a total of only seven hours to discuss it. Shortly afterward, shareholders filed a lawsuit alleging that the directors had breached their fiduciary duties by failing to maximize the sale price of the corporation. The Delaware Supreme Court ruled that the directors were protected by the business judgment rule.[5]

Duty of Loyalty

Loyalty can be defined as faithfulness to one's obligations and duties. In the corporate context, the duty of loyalty requires directors and officers to subordinate their personal interests to the welfare of the corporation. Directors cannot use corporate funds or confidential corporate information for personal advantage and must refrain from self-dealing. For instance, a director should not oppose a tender offer (see Chapter 29) that is in the corporation's best interest simply because its acceptance may cost the director her or his position. Cases dealing with the duty of loyalty typically involve one or more of the following:

1. Competing with the corporation.
2. Usurping (taking advantage of) a corporate opportunity.
3. Having an interest that conflicts with the interest of the corporation.
4. Engaging in insider trading (using information that is not public to make a profit trading securities, as will be discussed in Chapter 31).
5. Authorizing a corporate transaction that is detrimental to minority shareholders.
6. Selling control over the corporation.

The following classic case illustrates the conflict that can arise between a corporate official's personal interest and his or her duty of loyalty.

4. *In re Citigroup, Inc., Shareholder Derivative Litigation*, 964 A.2d 106 (Del.Ch. 2009). The court did allow the shareholders to maintain a claim for waste based on the directors' approval of a chief executive officer compensation package, however.

5. *Lyondell Chemical Co. v. Ryan*, 970 A.2d 235 (Del.Sup. 2009).

Classic Case 30.1 Guth v. Loft, Inc.

Supreme Court of Delaware, 23 Del.Ch. 255, 5 A.2d 503 (1939).

HISTORICAL SETTING *In the 1920s, Loft Candy Company (Loft, Inc.), based in Long Island City, New York, was a publicly held company with a $13 million candy-and-restaurant chain. The company manufactured its own candies, syrups, and beverages and sold its products in its more than one hundred retail locations throughout the Northeast. The retail stores featured old-fashioned soda fountains and were very popular. In 1930, Charles Guth became Loft's president after a contentious stockholders' meeting. His position there set the stage for the rise of the soft drink Pepsi-Cola.*

(Dalton Rowe/ Creative Commons)

Pepsi-Cola got its start when the head of Loft Candy Company usurped a corporate opportunity.

FACTS At the time Charles Guth became Loft's president, Guth and his family owned Grace Company, which made syrups for soft drinks in a plant in Baltimore, Maryland. Coca-Cola Company supplied Loft with cola syrup. Unhappy with what he felt was Coca-Cola's high price, Guth entered into an agreement with Roy Megargel to acquire the trademark and formula for Pepsi-Cola and form Pepsi-Cola Corporation. Neither Guth nor Megargel could finance the new venture, however, and Grace Company was insolvent. Without the knowledge of Loft's board of directors, Guth used Loft's capital, credit, facilities, and employees to further the Pepsi enterprise. At Guth's direction, a Loft employee made the concentrate for the syrup, which was sent to Grace Company to add sugar and water. Loft charged Grace Company for the concentrate but allowed forty months' credit. Grace charged Pepsi for the syrup but also granted substantial credit. Grace sold the syrup to Pepsi's customers, including Loft, which paid on delivery or within thirty days. Loft also paid for Pepsi's advertising. Finally, losing profits at its stores as a result of switching from Coca-Cola, Loft filed a suit in a Delaware state court against Guth, Grace, and Pepsi, seeking their Pepsi stock and an accounting. The court entered a judgment in the plaintiff's favor. The defendants appealed to the Delaware Supreme Court.

ISSUE Did Guth violate his duty of loyalty to Loft, Inc., by acquiring the Pepsi-Cola trademark and formula for himself without the knowledge of Loft's board of directors?

DECISION Yes. The Delaware Supreme Court upheld the judgment of the lower court. The state supreme court was "convinced that the opportunity to acquire the Pepsi-Cola trademark and formula, goodwill and business belonged to [Loft], and that Guth, as its president, had no right to appropriate the opportunity to himself."

REASON The court pointed out that the officers and directors of a corporation stand in a fiduciary relationship to that corporation and to its shareholders. Corporate officers and directors must protect the corporation's interest at all times. They must also "refrain from doing anything that works injury to the corporation." In other words, corporate officers and directors must provide undivided and unselfish loyalty to the corporation, and "there should be no conflict between duty and self-interest." Whenever an opportunity is presented to the corporation, officers and directors with knowledge of that opportunity cannot seize it for themselves. "The corporation may elect to claim all of the benefits of the transaction for itself, and the law will impress a trust in favor of the corporation upon the property, interest, and profits required." Guth clearly created a conflict between his self-interest and his duty to Loft—the corporation for which he was president and director. Guth illegally appropriated the Pepsi-Cola opportunity for himself and thereby placed himself in a competitive position with the company for which he worked.

WHAT IF THE FACTS WERE DIFFERENT? *Suppose that Loft's board of directors had approved Pepsi-Cola's use of its personnel and equipment. Would the court's decision have been different? Discuss.*

IMPACT OF THIS CASE ON TODAY'S LAW *This early Delaware decision was one of the first to set forth a test for determining when a corporate officer or director has breached the duty of loyalty. The test has two basic parts—whether the opportunity was reasonably related to the corporation's line of business, and whether the corporation was financially able to undertake the opportunity. The court also considered whether the corporation had an interest or expectancy in the opportunity and recognized that when the corporation had "no interest or expectancy, the officer or director is entitled to treat the opportunity as his own."*

RELEVANT WEB SITES *To locate information on the Web concerning the* Guth v. Loft *decision, go to this text's Web site at* www.cengage.com/blaw/blt. *Select "Chapter 30" and click on "Classic Cases."*

Conflicts of Interest

Corporate directors often have many business affiliations, and a director may sit on the board of more than one corporation. Of course, directors are precluded from entering into or supporting businesses that operate in direct competition with corporations on whose boards they serve. Their fiduciary duty requires them to make a full disclosure of any potential conflicts of interest that might arise in any corporate transaction [RMBCA 8.60].

Sometimes, a corporation enters into a contract or engages in a transaction in which an officer or director has a personal interest. The director or officer must make a *full disclosure* of that interest and must abstain from voting on the proposed transaction.

"If it is not in the interest of the public, it is not in the interest of the business."
Joseph H. Defrees, 1812–1885
(U.S. congressman)

EXAMPLE 30.3 Southwood Corporation needs office space. Lambert Alden, one of its five directors, owns the building adjoining the corporation's main office building. He negotiates a lease with Southwood for the space, making a full disclosure to Southwood and the other four board directors. The lease arrangement is fair and reasonable, and it is unanimously approved by the other four directors. In this situation, Alden has not breached his duty of loyalty to the corporation, and thus the contract is valid. If it were otherwise, directors would be prevented from ever transacting business with the corporations they serve. •

Liability of Directors and Officers

Directors and officers are exposed to liability on many fronts. Corporate directors and officers may be held liable for the crimes and torts committed by themselves or by corporate employees under their supervision, as discussed in Chapter 6 and Chapter 23, respectively. Additionally, if shareholders perceive that the corporate directors are not acting in the best interests of the corporation, they may sue the directors, in what is called a *shareholder's derivative suit,* on behalf of the corporation. (This type of action will be discussed later in this chapter, in the context of shareholders' rights.) Directors and officers also can be held personally liable under a number of statutes, such as statutes enacted to protect consumers or the environment (see Chapter 33).

Role of Shareholders

BE AWARE **Shareholders normally are not agents of the corporation.**

The acquisition of a share of stock makes a person an owner and shareholder in a corporation. Shareholders thus own the corporation. Although they have no legal title to corporate property, such as buildings and equipment, they do have an equitable (ownership) interest in the firm.

As a general rule, shareholders have no responsibility for the daily management of the corporation, even if they are ultimately responsible for choosing the board of directors, which does have such control. Ordinarily, corporate officers and directors owe no duty to individual shareholders unless some contract or special relationship exists between them in addition to the corporate relationship. Their duty is to act in the best interests of the corporation and its shareholder-owners as a whole. In turn, as you will read later in this chapter, controlling shareholders owe a fiduciary duty to minority shareholders. Normally, there is no legal relationship between shareholders and creditors of the corporation. Shareholders can be creditors of the corporation, though, and they have the same rights of recovery against the corporation as any other creditor.

Starbucks chairman and chief executive officer Howard Schultz speaks to shareholders at the company's annual shareholders' meeting in Seattle, Washington. Do shareholders have any power over the actions of a corporation's board of directors?

(Robert Sorbo/Reuters/Landov)

In this section, we look at the powers and voting rights of shareholders, which are generally established in the articles of incorporation and by the state's general corporation law.

Shareholders' Powers

Shareholders must approve fundamental changes affecting the corporation before the changes can be implemented. Hence, shareholders are empowered to amend the articles of incorporation (charter) and bylaws, approve a merger or the dissolution of the corporation, and approve the sale of all or substantially all of the corporation's assets. Some of these powers are subject to prior board approval.

Members of the board of directors are elected and removed by a vote of the shareholders. The first board of directors is either named in the articles of incorporation or chosen by the incorporators to serve until the first shareholders' meeting. From that time on, the selection and retention of directors are exclusively shareholder functions.

Directors usually serve their full terms; if the shareholders judge them unsatisfactory, they are simply not reelected. Shareholders have the inherent power, however, to remove a director from office for cause (such as for breach of duty or misconduct) by a majority vote.[6] As mentioned earlier, some state statutes (and some corporate articles) permit removal of directors without cause by the vote of a majority of the holders of outstanding shares entitled to vote.

Shareholders' Meetings

Shareholders' meetings must occur at least annually. In addition, special meetings can be called to deal with urgent matters.

Notice of Meetings A corporation must notify its shareholders of the date, time, and place of an annual or special shareholders' meeting at least ten days, but not more than sixty days, before the meeting date [RMBCA 7.05].[7] Notice of a special meeting must include a statement of the purpose of the meeting, and business transacted at the meeting is limited to that purpose.

Proxies It is usually not practical for owners of only a few shares of stock of publicly traded corporations to attend shareholders' meetings. Therefore, the law allows stockholders to either vote in person or appoint another person as their agent to vote their shares at the meeting. The signed appointment form or electronic transmission authorizing an agent to vote the shares is called a **proxy** (from the Latin *procurare,* meaning "to manage, take care of").

Proxy In corporate law, a written agreement between a stockholder and another party in which the stockholder authorizes the other party to vote the stockholder's shares in a certain manner.

Management often solicits proxies, but any person can solicit proxies to concentrate voting power. Proxies have been used by a group of shareholders as a device for taking over a corporation (corporate takeovers were discussed in Chapter 29). Proxies normally are revocable (that is, they can be withdrawn), unless they are specifically designated as irrevocable. Under RMBCA 7.22(c), proxies last for eleven months, unless the proxy agreement provides for a longer period.

Proxy Materials and Shareholder Proposals When shareholders want to change a company policy, they can put their idea up for a shareholder vote. They can do this by submitting a shareholder proposal to the board of directors and asking the board to include the proposal in the proxy materials that are sent to all shareholders before meetings.

The Securities and Exchange Commission (SEC), which regulates the purchase and sale of securities (see Chapter 31), has special provisions relating to proxies and shareholder proposals. SEC Rule 14a-8 provides that all shareholders who own stock worth at least $1,000 are eligible to submit proposals for inclusion in corporate proxy materials. The corporation is required to include information on whatever proposals will be considered at the shareholders' meeting along with proxy materials. Only those proposals that relate to significant policy considerations rather than ordinary business operations must be included. For a discussion of how the SEC is adapting its rules regarding proxies to take advantage of today's communications technology, see this chapter's *Adapting the Law to the Online Environment* feature.

ON THE WEB To read an article on the SEC's new e-proxy rules, go to blogs.law.harvard.edu/corpgov/2009/01/03/e-proxy-rules-take-effect-for-all-public-companies.

6. A director can often demand court review of removal for cause.

7. A shareholder can waive the requirement of written notice by signing a waiver form. In some states, a shareholder who does not receive written notice, but who learns of the meeting and attends without protesting the lack of notice, is said to have waived notice by such conduct. State statutes and corporate bylaws typically set forth the time within which notice must be sent, what methods can be used, and what the notice must contain.

Adapting the Law to the Online Environment

Moving Company Information to the Internet

Anyone who has ever owned shares in a public company knows that such companies often are required to distribute voluminous documents relating to proxies to all shareholders. Traditionally, large packets of paper documents were sent to shareholders, but in 2007 the Securities and Exchange Commission (SEC) permitted publicly held companies to voluntarily distribute electronic proxy (e-proxy) materials. In 2009, the SEC's e-proxy rules became mandatory. Now, all public companies must post their proxy materials on the Internet, although they may still choose among several options—including paper documents sent by mail—for actually delivering the materials to shareholders.[a]

Notice and Access: E-Proxy Rules

Companies that want to distribute proxy materials only via the Internet can choose the notice and access delivery option. Under this model, the corporation posts the proxy materials on a Web site and notifies the shareholders that the proxy materials are available online.

The notice and access model involves the following steps:

1. The company posts the proxy materials on its publicly accessible Web site.
2. Subsequently, the company sends a (paper) notice to each shareholder at least forty calendar days before the date of the shareholders' meeting for which the proxy is being solicited.
3. No other materials can be sent along with the initial notice (unless the proxy is being combined with the meeting notice required by state law).
4. The notice must be written in plain English, and it must include a prominent statement of the following: the date, time, and location of the shareholders' meeting; the specific Web site at which shareholders can access the proxy materials; an explanation of how they can obtain paper copies of the proxy materials at no cost; and a clear and impartial description of each matter to be considered at the shareholders' meeting.
5. Next, the company must wait at least ten days before sending a "paper" proxy card to the shareholders. This ten-day waiting period provides shareholders with sufficient time to access the proxy materials online or to request paper copies.
6. If a shareholder requests paper proxy materials, the company must send them within three business days.
7. After receiving the initial paper notice, a shareholder can permanently elect to receive all future proxy materials on paper or by e-mail.

Other Delivery Options

Rather than using notice and access delivery, public companies can choose to deliver the full set of proxy materials to the shareholders in paper or electronic form, such as on a CD or DVD. They can also use a blend of these two options, as long as they also post the materials on a Web site. Many corporations choose one option for certain shareholders and another option for other shareholders, depending on the number of shares owned or whether the shareholders are domestic or foreign. The shareholder can always choose to receive paper documents rather than accessing materials online.

Some corporate executives want the SEC to go even further and allow corporations to disseminate important information to the public via CEO blogs. Thus far, however, the SEC has not allowed companies to distribute proxy materials (or disclose material information to the public as required before issuing shares—see Chapter 31) via blogs.

FOR CRITICAL ANALYSIS

Why might a company or other party choose to solicit proxies the old-fashioned way—by providing paper documents instead of Internet access—despite the added costs?

a. 17 C.F.R. Parts 240, 249, and 274.

Shareholder Voting

Shareholders exercise ownership control through the power of their votes. Corporate business matters are presented in the form of *resolutions*, which shareholders vote to approve or disapprove. Each common shareholder is entitled to one vote per share, although the voting techniques to be discussed shortly all enhance the power of the shareholder's vote. The articles of incorporation can exclude or limit voting rights, particularly for certain classes of shares. For example, owners of preferred shares are usually denied the right to vote [RMBCA 7.21]. If a state statute requires specific voting procedures, the corporation's articles or bylaws must be consistent with the statute.

BE CAREFUL Once a quorum is present, a vote can be taken even if some shareholders leave without casting their votes.

Quorum Requirements For shareholders to conduct business at a meeting, a quorum must be present. Generally, a quorum exists when shareholders holding more than

(AP Photo/The Charlotte Observer/John D. Simmons)

Shareholders in Wachovia Corporation leave a shareholders' meeting during which they voted on that company's takeover (see Chapter 29) by Wells Fargo. Do shareholders who oppose takeovers have any rights?

50 percent of the outstanding shares are present. In some states, obtaining the unanimous written consent of shareholders is a permissible alternative to holding a shareholders' meeting [RMBCA 7.25].

Once a quorum is present, voting can proceed. A majority vote of the shares represented at the meeting usually is required to pass resolutions. **EXAMPLE 30.4** Novo Pictures, Inc., has 10,000 outstanding shares of voting stock. Its articles of incorporation set the quorum at 50 percent of outstanding shares and provide that a majority vote of the shares present is necessary to pass resolutions concerning ordinary matters. Therefore, for this firm, a quorum of shareholders representing 5,000 outstanding shares must be present at a shareholders' meeting to conduct business. If exactly 5,000 shares are represented at the meeting, a vote of at least 2,501 of those shares is needed to pass a resolution. If 6,000 shares are represented, a vote of 3,001 will be required. ●

At times, more than a simple majority vote will be required either by a state statute or by the corporate articles. Extraordinary corporate matters, such as a merger, consolidation, or dissolution of the corporation (as discussed in Chapter 29), require a higher percentage of all corporate shares entitled to vote [RMBCA 7.27].

VOTING LISTS The corporation prepares voting lists prior to each meeting of the shareholders. Ordinarily, only persons whose names appear on the corporation's shareholder records as owners are entitled to vote.[8] The voting list contains the name and address of each shareholder as shown on the corporate records on a given cutoff, or record, date. (Under RMBCA 7.07, the record date may be as much as seventy days before the meeting.) The voting list also includes the number of voting shares held by each owner. The list is usually kept at the corporate headquarters and is available for shareholder inspection [RMBCA 7.20].

CUMULATIVE VOTING Most states permit, and some require, shareholders to elect directors by *cumulative voting,* which is a voting method designed to allow minority shareholders to be represented on the board of directors.[9] With cumulative voting, each shareholder is entitled to a total number of votes equal to the number of board members to be elected multiplied by the number of voting shares a shareholder owns. The shareholder can cast all of these votes for one candidate or split them among several nominees for director. All nominees stand for election at the same time. When cumulative voting is not required either by statute or under the articles, the entire board can be elected by a simple majority of shares at a shareholders' meeting.

Cumulative voting can best be understood by an example. **EXAMPLE 30.5** A corporation has 10,000 shares issued and outstanding. The minority shareholders hold 3,000 shares, and the majority shareholders hold the other 7,000 shares. Three members of the board are to be elected. The majority shareholders' nominees are Acevedo, Barkley, and Craycik. The minority shareholders' nominee is Drake. Can Drake be elected by the minority shareholders?

If cumulative voting is allowed, the answer is yes. Together, the minority shareholders have 9,000 votes (the number of directors to be elected times the number of shares held by the minority shareholders equals 3 times 3,000, which equals 9,000 votes). All of these

8. When the legal owner is bankrupt, incompetent, deceased, or in some other way under a legal disability, his or her vote can be cast by a person designated by law to control and manage the owner's property.

9. See, for example, California Corporations Code Section 708. Under RMBCA 7.28, however, no cumulative voting rights exist unless the articles of incorporation so provide.

Exhibit 30–2 Results of Cumulative Voting

BALLOT	MAJORITY SHAREHOLDERS' VOTES			MINORITY SHAREHOLDERS' VOTES	DIRECTORS ELECTED
	Acevedo	Barkley	Craycik	Drake	
1	10,000	10,000	1,000	9,000	Acevedo/Barkley/Drake
2	9,001	9,000	2,999	9,000	Acevedo/Barkley/Drake
3	6,000	7,000	8,000	9,000	Barkley/Craycik/Drake

votes can be cast to elect Drake. The majority shareholders have 21,000 votes (3 times 7,000 equals 21,000 votes), but these votes have to be distributed among their three nominees. The principle of cumulative voting is that no matter how the majority shareholders cast their 21,000 votes, they will not be able to elect all three directors if the minority shareholders cast all of their 9,000 votes for Drake, as illustrated in Exhibit 30–2. •

OTHER VOTING TECHNIQUES Before a shareholders' meeting, a group of shareholders can agree in writing to vote their shares together in a specified manner. Such agreements, called *shareholder voting agreements,* usually are held to be valid and enforceable. A shareholder can also appoint a voting agent and vote by proxy.

In the following case, corporate management was concerned about losing a proxy contest. The corporation's chief executive officer then entered into an agreement with a shareholder who would support management's candidates in return for a seat on the board of directors. A shareholder who opposed the deal filed a lawsuit claiming that this agreement was illegal and a breach of the officer's fiduciary duty.

Case 30.2 Portnoy v. Cryo-Cell International, Inc.

Court of Chancery of Delaware, 940 A.2d 43 (2008).

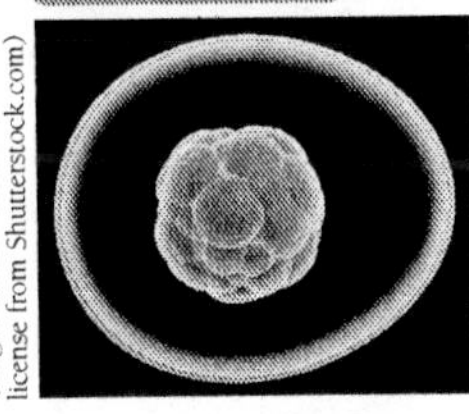

To avoid the possibility of a shareholders' vote replacing the board of directors, did the chief executive officer of a stem-cell services company breach her fiduciary duties?

FACTS Cryo-Cell International, Inc., a small public company, was struggling to survive. Several of its shareholders, including David Portnoy, mounted a proxy contest in an effort to replace the board of directors at the annual shareholders' meeting. Another shareholder, Andrew Filipowski, used management's fear of being replaced if the dissident shareholders won to create a deal for himself—he would support management in exchange for being included in management's slate of directors. The company's chief executive officer, Mercedes Walton, devised a plan that would allow management and Filipowski to win the proxy contest. Under this plan, Walton would act as a "matchmaker" and find shareholders willing to sell their shares to Filipowski. Walton promised Filipowski that if management's slate won, Cryo-Cell's board of directors would add another board seat that a Filipowski designee would fill. Walton's side deal was not made known to the shareholders when they voted. After management won the election, Walton prepared to add Filipowski's designee to the board. Portnoy then filed a lawsuit, claiming that the election results should be overturned. Portnoy argued that all of the dealings between Cryo-Cell and Filipowski were tainted by fiduciary misconduct and that the agreement to add Filipowski to the management slate in exchange for his support was not created in the company's best interests and constituted an "illegal vote-buying arrangement."

ISSUE Did the chief executive officer's promise to change the corporate bylaws and expand the number of directors after a vote constitute a breach of fiduciary duties and taint the election?

DECISION Yes. The court ruled that the incumbent board's actions and the side agreement with the company's chief executive officer (Walton) constituted serious breaches of fiduciary duty that tainted the election. The court, therefore, ordered a special shareholders' meeting at which a new election would be held. The court did not, however, find that the agreement to add Filipowski to management's slate of directors was improper.

REASON The court reasoned that a mere offer of a position on a management slate should not be considered a vote-buying agreement. "When stockholders can decide for themselves whether to see the candidate who obtained a place on a management slate by way of [bargaining

Case 30.2—Continues next page ➡

Case 30.2–Continued

with management], it seems unwise to formulate a standard that involves the potential for excessive and imprecise judicial involvement." Such an arrangement is not vote buying. In contrast, the side agreement that guaranteed Filipowski's designee an additional seat on the board was a breach of fiduciary duty. Walton had promised "she and her incumbent colleagues would use their powers as directors of Cryo-Cell to increase the size of the board and to seat [Filipowski's designee]. This was therefore a promise that would not be, for the duration of the term, subject to prior approval by the electorate." Thus, it was improper.

FOR CRITICAL ANALYSIS—Ethical Consideration *If Filipowski had promised to bring additional funding to keep Cryo-Cell from failing due to lack of capital, would the actions described in this case have been considered ethical? Explain your answer.*

Rights of Shareholders

Shareholders possess numerous rights. A significant right—the right to vote their shares—has already been discussed. We now look at some additional rights of shareholders.

(PhotoDisc)

Stock certificates are displayed. To be a shareholder, is it necessary to have physical possession of a certificate? Why or why not?

Stock Certificates

A **stock certificate** is a certificate issued by a corporation that evidences ownership of a specified number of shares in the corporation. In jurisdictions that require the issuance of stock certificates, shareholders have the right to demand that the corporation issue certificates. In most states and under RMBCA 6.26, boards of directors may provide that shares of stock will be uncertificated—that is, no actual, physical stock certificates will be issued. When shares are uncertificated, the corporation may be required to send each shareholder a letter or some other form of notice that contains the same information that would normally appear on the face of stock certificates.

Stock is intangible personal property, and the ownership right exists independently of the certificate itself. If a stock certificate is lost or destroyed, ownership is not destroyed with it. A new certificate can be issued to replace one that has been lost or destroyed. Notice of shareholders' meetings, dividends, and operational and financial reports are all distributed according to the recorded ownership listed in the corporation's books, not on the basis of possession of the certificate.

Stock Certificate A certificate issued by a corporation evidencing the ownership of a specified number of shares in the corporation.

Preemptive Rights

Sometimes, the articles of incorporation grant preemptive rights to shareholders [RMBCA 6.30]. With **preemptive rights,** a shareholder receives a preference over all other purchasers to subscribe to or purchase a prorated share of a new issue of stock. In other words, a shareholder who is given preemptive rights can purchase the same percentage of the new shares being issued as she or he already holds in the company. This allows each shareholder to maintain her or his proportionate control, voting power, or financial interest in the corporation. Generally, preemptive rights apply only to additional, newly issued stock sold for cash, and the preemptive rights must be exercised within a specified time period, which is usually thirty days.

Preemptive Rights Rights held by shareholders that entitle them to purchase newly issued shares of a corporation's stock, equal in percentage to shares already held, before the stock is offered to any outside buyers. Preemptive rights enable shareholders to maintain their proportionate ownership and voice in the corporation.

EXAMPLE 30.6 Tran Corporation authorizes and issues 1,000 shares of stock. Lebow purchases 100 shares, making her the owner of 10 percent of the company's stock. Subsequently, Tran, by vote of its shareholders, authorizes the issuance of another 1,000 shares (by amending the articles of incorporation). This increases its capital stock to a total of

2,000 shares. If preemptive rights have been provided, Lebow can purchase one additional share of the new stock being issued for each share she already owns—or 100 additional shares. Thus, she can own 200 of the 2,000 shares outstanding, and she will maintain her relative position as a shareholder. If preemptive rights are not allowed, her proportionate control and voting power may be diluted from that of a 10 percent shareholder to that of a 5 percent shareholder because of the issuance of the additional 1,000 shares. ●

Preemptive rights are most important in close corporations because each shareholder owns a relatively small number of shares but controls a substantial interest in the corporation. Without preemptive rights, it would be possible for a shareholder to lose his or her proportionate control over the firm.

Stock Warrants

Stock Warrant A certificate that grants the owner the option to buy a given number of shares of stock, usually within a set time period.

Stock warrants are rights to buy stock at a stated price by a specified date that are created by the company. Usually, when preemptive rights exist and a corporation is issuing additional shares, it issues its shareholders stock warrants. Warrants are often publicly traded on securities exchanges.

Dividends

As mentioned in Chapter 29, a *dividend* is a distribution of corporate profits or income *ordered by the directors* and paid to the shareholders in proportion to their respective shares in the corporation. Dividends can be paid in cash, property, stock of the corporation that is paying the dividends, or stock of other corporations.[10]

State laws vary, but each state determines the general circumstances and legal requirements under which dividends are paid. State laws also control the sources of revenue to be used; only certain funds are legally available for paying dividends. Depending on state law, dividends may be paid from the following sources:

1. *Retained earnings.* All states allow dividends to be paid from the undistributed net profits earned by the corporation, including capital gains from the sale of fixed assets. As mentioned in Chapter 29, the undistributed net profits are called *retained earnings.*
2. *Net profits.* A few states allow dividends to be issued from current net profits without regard to deficits in prior years.
3. *Surplus.* A number of states allow dividends to be paid out of any kind of surplus.

Illegal Dividends Sometimes, dividends are improperly paid from an unauthorized account, or their payment causes the corporation to become insolvent. Generally, shareholders must return illegal dividends only if they knew that the dividends were illegal when the payment was received (or if the dividends were paid when the corporation was insolvent). Whenever dividends are illegal or improper, the board of directors can be held personally liable for the amount of the payment.

Directors' Failure to Declare a Dividend When directors fail to declare a dividend, shareholders can ask a court to compel the directors to meet and to declare a dividend. To succeed, the shareholders must show that the directors have acted so unreasonably in withholding the dividend that their conduct is an abuse of their discretion.

Often, a corporation accumulates large cash reserves for a legitimate corporate purpose, such as expansion or research. The mere fact that the firm has sufficient earnings or surplus available to pay a dividend is not enough to compel directors to distribute funds that, in the

10. Technically, dividends paid in stock are not dividends. They maintain each shareholder's proportionate interest in the corporation. On one occasion, a distillery declared and paid a "dividend" in bonded whiskey.

(AP Photo/Chris Gardner)

A General Motors shareholder asks a question at the company's annual stockholders' meeting. Shareholders also have a limited right to inspect and copy corporate books and records, provided the request is made in advance and is not impromptu in an open forum like a shareholders' meeting. What other limitations are placed on shareholders' inspection rights?

board's opinion, should not be distributed. The courts are reluctant to interfere with corporate operations and will not compel directors to declare dividends unless abuse of discretion is clearly shown.

Inspection Rights

Shareholders in a corporation enjoy both common law and statutory inspection rights. The RMBCA provides that every shareholder is entitled to examine specified corporate records. The shareholder's right of inspection is limited, however, to the inspection and copying of corporate books and records for a *proper purpose*, provided the request is made in advance. The shareholder can inspect in person, or an attorney, accountant, or other authorized assistant can do so as the shareholder's agent.

The power of inspection is fraught with potential abuses, and the corporation is allowed to protect itself from them. For instance, a shareholder can properly be denied access to corporate records to prevent harassment or to protect trade secrets or other confidential corporate information. Some states require that a shareholder must have held his or her shares for a minimum period of time immediately preceding the demand to inspect or must hold a minimum number of outstanding shares. A shareholder who is denied the right of inspection can seek a court order to compel the inspection.

Transfer of Shares

(©Galushko Sergey, 2009. Used under license from Shutterstock.com)

Do shareholders have to sign stock certificates in order to transfer their shares to someone else?

Corporate stock represents an ownership right in intangible personal property. The law generally recognizes the right to transfer stock to another person unless there are valid restrictions on its transferability. Although stock certificates are negotiable and freely transferable by indorsement and delivery, transfer of stock in closely held corporations usually is restricted. These restrictions must be reasonable and may be set out in the bylaws or in a shareholder agreement. The existence of any restrictions on transferability must always be indicated on the face of the stock certificate.

When shares are transferred, a new entry is made in the corporate stock book to indicate the new owner. Until the corporation is notified and the entry is complete, all rights—including voting rights, the right to notice of shareholders' meetings, and the right to dividend distributions—remain with the current record owner.

Rights on Dissolution

When a corporation is dissolved and its outstanding debts and the claims of its creditors have been satisfied, the remaining assets are distributed to the shareholders in proportion to the percentage of shares owned by each shareholder. Certain classes of preferred stock can be given priority. If no class of stock has been given preferences in the distribution of assets on liquidation, then all of the stockholders share the remaining assets.

As noted in Chapter 29, in some situations, shareholders can petition a court to have the corporation dissolved. The RMBCA permits any shareholder to initiate a dissolution proceeding in any of the following circumstances [RMBCA 14.30]:

1. The directors are deadlocked in the management of corporate affairs. The shareholders are unable to break that deadlock, and irreparable injury to the corporation is being suffered or threatened.
2. The acts of the directors or those in control of the corporation are illegal, oppressive, or fraudulent.
3. Corporate assets are being misapplied or wasted.

4. The shareholders are deadlocked in voting power and have failed, for a specified period (usually two annual meetings), to elect successors to directors whose terms have expired or would have expired with the election of successors.

The Shareholder's Derivative Suit

Shareholder's Derivative Suit A suit brought by a shareholder to enforce a corporate cause of action against a third person.

When the corporation is harmed by the actions of a third party, the directors can bring a lawsuit in the name of the corporation against that party. If the corporate directors fail to bring a lawsuit, shareholders can do so "derivatively" in what is known as a **shareholder's derivative suit.** A shareholder cannot bring a derivative suit until ninety days after making a written demand on the corporation (the board of directors) to take suitable action [RMBCA 7.40]. Only if the directors refuse to take appropriate action can the derivative suit go forward.

The right of shareholders to bring a derivative action is especially important when the wrong suffered by the corporation results from the actions of corporate directors or officers. This is because the directors and officers would probably be unwilling to take any action against themselves. Nevertheless, a court will dismiss a derivative suit if the majority of directors or an independent panel determines in good faith that the lawsuit is not in the best interests of the corporation [RMBCA 7.44].

When shareholders bring a derivative suit, they are not pursuing rights or benefits for themselves personally but are acting as guardians of the corporate entity. Therefore, if the suit is successful, any damages recovered normally go into the corporation's treasury, not to the shareholders personally.[11] **EXAMPLE 30.7** Zeon Corporation is owned by two shareholders, each holding 50 percent of the corporate shares. One of the shareholders wants to sue the other for misusing corporate assets or usurping corporate opportunities. In this situation, the plaintiff-shareholder will have to bring a shareholder's derivative suit (not a suit in his or her own name) because the alleged harm was suffered by Zeon, not by the plaintiff personally. Any damages awarded will go to the corporation, not to the plaintiff-shareholder. ● (Derivative actions are less common in other countries than in the United States, as this chapter's *Beyond Our Borders* feature explains.)

Duties and Liabilities of Shareholders

One of the hallmarks of the corporate form of business organization is that shareholders are not personally liable for the debts of the corporation. If the corporation fails, shareholders can lose their investments, but generally that is the limit of their liability. As discussed in Chapter 29, in certain instances of fraud, undercapitalization, or careless observance of corporate formalities, a court will pierce the corporate veil (disregard the corporate entity)

11. The shareholders may be entitled to reimbursement for reasonable expenses involved in the derivative suit, however, including attorneys' fees.

Beyond Our Borders — Derivative Actions in Other Nations

Today, most of the claims brought against directors and officers in the United States are those alleged in shareholders' derivative suits. Other nations, however, put more restrictions on the use of such suits. German law, for example, does not provide for derivative litigation, and a corporation's duty to its employees is just as significant as its duty to its shareholder-owners. The United Kingdom has no statute authorizing derivative actions, which are permitted only to challenge directors' actions that the shareholders could not legally ratify. Japan authorizes derivative actions but also permits a company to sue the plaintiff-shareholder for damages if the action is unsuccessful.

For Critical Analysis

Do corporations benefit from shareholders' derivative suits? If so, how?

and hold the shareholders individually liable. These situations are the exception, however, not the rule. A shareholder can also be personally liable in certain other rare instances. One relates to illegal dividends, which were discussed previously. Another relates to *watered stock*. Finally, in certain instances, a majority shareholder who engages in oppressive conduct or attempts to exclude minority shareholders from receiving certain benefits can be held personally liable.

Watered Stock

Watered Stock Shares of stock issued by a corporation for which the corporation receives, as payment, less than the stated value of the shares.

When a corporation issues shares for less than their fair market value, the shares are referred to as **watered stock.**[12] Usually, the shareholder who receives watered stock must pay the difference to the corporation (the shareholder is personally liable). In some states, the shareholder who receives watered stock may be liable to creditors of the corporation for unpaid corporate debts.

EXAMPLE 30.8 During the formation of a corporation, Gomez, one of the incorporators, transfers his property, Sunset Beach, to the corporation for 10,000 shares of stock. The stock has a specific face value *(par value)* of $100 per share, and thus the total price of the 10,000 shares is $1 million. After the property is transferred and the shares are issued, Sunset Beach is carried on the corporate books at a value of $1 million. On appraisal, it is discovered that the market value of the property at the time of transfer was only $500,000. The shares issued to Gomez are therefore watered stock, and he is liable to the corporation for the difference between the value of the shares and the value of the property. •

Duties of Majority Shareholders

In some instances, a majority shareholder is regarded as having a fiduciary duty to the corporation and to the minority shareholders. This occurs when a single shareholder (or a few shareholders acting in concert) owns a sufficient number of shares to exercise *de facto* (actual) control over the corporation. In these situations, majority shareholders owe a fiduciary duty to the minority shareholders. When a majority shareholder breaches her or his fiduciary duty to a minority shareholder, the minority shareholder can sue for damages. How egregious should majority shareholders' misbehavior be to warrant—in addition to compensatory damages—an award of punitive damages? The court in the following case set out the factors to consider and then weighed the majority shareholders' acts against these standards.

12. The phrase *watered stock* was originally used to describe cattle that were kept thirsty during a long drive and then were allowed to drink large quantities of water just prior to their sale. The increased weight of the "watered stock" allowed the seller to reap a higher profit.

Case 30.3 Mazloom v. Mazloom

Court of Appeals of South Carolina, 382 S.C. 307, 675 S.E.2d 746 (2009).

(The TruthAbout/Creative Commons)

A Mini Mart was part of assets sold without payment to a legitimate owner. What duty was breached?

FACTS Four brothers—Iraj, Ahmad, Manooch, and Aboli Mazloom—incorporated a business known as AMBI, Inc. AMBI owned real estate in South Carolina on which the brothers operated a Mini Mart, a liquor store, and a one-bedroom apartment. Each brother had a 25 percent interest in AMBI. After seventeen years, Ahmad, Manooch, and Aboli dissolved AMBI, filed articles of organization for a new firm—AMA, LLC—and transferred AMBI's assets to AMA for five dollars. When Iraj learned of the changes, he had Manooch and Aboli file an amendment to AMA's articles stating that "Iraj Mazloom owns 25% (or 1/4) shares of stock in AMA." Less than five months later, Ahmad sold his interest in AMA to Manooch and Aboli, who then sold AMA's assets to Ganesh Mini Mart, LLC, for $345,000. They paid Iraj nothing. He filed a suit in a South Carolina state court against Manooch and Aboli, claiming breach of fiduciary duty. The brothers asserted that Iraj did not own shares in AMBI or AMA. The court awarded Iraj 25 percent of the proceeds from the sale of AMA's assets and other amounts, including punitive damages of $50,000. Manooch and Aboli appealed.

ISSUE Can a majority shareholders' breach of fiduciary duty to a minority shareholder support an award of punitive damages?

Case 30.3–Continued

DECISION Yes. The state intermediate appellate court affirmed the award of punitive damages to Iraj for Manooch and Aboli's breach of their duty.

REASON Factors considered in reviewing an award of punitive damages include the misconduct on which the award was based, the knowledge and culpability of the parties against whom the award was assessed, the relationship of the harm to the award, the effect that the award might have in deterring the wrongdoers and others from similar misconduct, and the wrongdoers' ability to pay. In this case, the misconduct included the brothers' failure to notify Iraj before the sale of AMBI's assets, AMBI's dissolution, and the sale of AMA's assets to a third party; the brothers' denial of Iraj's 25 percent interest in the business; and their failure to tender his share of the proceeds from the sale of the assets. The brothers were aware of their misconduct and were entirely culpable. The award was likely to deter them from similar misconduct. Furthermore, they had sufficient personal assets, including their proceeds from the AMA sale, to pay the award.

FOR CRITICAL ANALYSIS—Social Consideration *An award of punitive damages is almost completely at the discretion of a jury and trial judge. Why is that?*

WHY IS THIS CASE IMPORTANT? *Why did the three brothers attempt to cheat their sibling out of his share of the family's jointly owned business? The brothers did not plead their motive in defense. The court did not ask for it. It did not affect the consideration of their legal dispute. This case makes it clear that, regardless of the personal motivation underlying a party's actions, he or she will be held to the legal obligations arising out of a business relationship and liability will be assessed for any breach.*

Major Business Forms Compared

As mentioned in Chapter 26, when deciding which form of business organization would be most appropriate, businesspersons normally take into account several factors, including ease of creation, the liability of the owners, tax considerations, and the need for capital. Each major form of business organization offers distinct advantages and disadvantages with respect to these and other factors. Exhibit 30–3 summarizes the essential advantages and disadvantages of each of the forms of business organization discussed in Chapters 26 through 30.

Exhibit 30–3 **Major Forms of Business Compared**

CHARACTERISTIC	SOLE PROPRIETORSHIP	PARTNERSHIP	CORPORATION
Method of creation	Created at will by owner.	Created by agreement of the parties.	Authorized by the state under the state's corporation law.
Legal position	Not a separate entity; owner is the business.	Is a separate legal entity in most states.	Always a legal entity separate and distinct from its owners—a legal fiction for the purposes of owning property and being a party to litigation.
Liability	Unlimited liability.	Unlimited liability.	Limited liability of shareholders—shareholders are not liable for the debts of the corporation.
Duration	Determined by owner; automatically dissolved on owner's death.	Terminated by agreement of the partners, but can continue to do business even when a partner dissociates from the partnership.	Can have perpetual existence.
Transferability of interest	Interest can be transferred, but individual's proprietorship then ends.	Although partnership interest can be assigned, assignee does not have full rights of a partner.	Shares of stock can be transferred.
Management	Completely at owner's discretion.	Each general partner has a direct and equal voice in management unless expressly agreed otherwise in the partnership agreement.	Shareholders elect directors, who set policy and appoint officers.

Continued

Exhibit 30–3 Major Forms of Business Compared—Continued

CHARACTERISTIC	SOLE PROPRIETORSHIP	PARTNERSHIP	CORPORATION
Taxation	Owner pays personal taxes on business income.	Each partner pays pro rata share of income taxes on net profits, whether or not they are distributed.	Double taxation—corporation pays income tax on net profits, with no deduction for dividends, and shareholders pay income tax on disbursed dividends they receive.
Organizational fees, annual license fees, and annual reports	None or minimal.	None or minimal.	All required.
Transaction of business in other states	Generally no limitation.	Generally no limitation.[a]	Normally must qualify to do business and obtain certificate of authority.

CHARACTERISTIC	LIMITED PARTNERSHIP	LIMITED LIABILITY COMPANY	LIMITED LIABILITY PARTNERSHIP
Method of creation	Created by agreement to carry on a business for a profit. At least one party must be a general partner and the other(s) limited partner(s). Certificate of limited partnership is filed. Charter must be issued by the state.	Created by an agreement of the member-owners of the company. Articles of organization are filed. Charter must be issued by the state.	Created by agreement of the partners. A statement of qualification for the limited liability partnership is filed.
Legal position	Treated as a legal entity.	Treated as a legal entity.	Generally, treated same as a general partnership.
Liability	Unlimited liability of all general partners; limited partners are liable only to the extent of capital contributions.	Member-owners' liability is limited to the amount of capital contributions or investments.	Varies, but under the Uniform Partnership Act, liability of a partner for acts committed by other partners is limited.
Duration	By agreement in certificate, or by termination of the last general partner (retirement, death, and the like) or last limited partner.	Unless a single-member LLC, can have perpetual existence (same as a corporation).	Remains in existence until cancellation or revocation.
Transferability of interest	Interest can be assigned (same as general partnership), but if assignee becomes a member with consent of other partners, certificate must be amended.	Member interests are freely transferable.	Interest can be assigned same as in a traditional partnership.
Management	General partners have equal voice or by agreement. Limited partners may not retain limited liability if they actively participate in management.	Member-owners can fully participate in management or can designate a group of persons to manage on behalf of the members.	Same as a traditional partnership.
Taxation	Generally taxed as a partnership.	LLC is not taxed, and members are taxed personally on profits "passed through" the LLC.	Same as a traditional partnership.
Organizational fees, annual license fees, and annual reports	Organizational fee required; usually not others.	Organizational fee required; others vary with states.	Fees are set by each state for filing statements of qualification, foreign qualification, and annual reports.
Transaction of business in other states	Generally no limitations.	Generally no limitation, but may vary depending on state.	Must file a statement of foreign qualification before doing business in another state.

a. A few states have enacted statutes requiring that foreign partnerships qualify to do business there.

Reviewing . . . Corporate Directors, Officers, and Shareholders

David Brock is on the board of directors of Firm Body Fitness, Inc., which owns a string of fitness clubs in New Mexico. Brock owns 15 percent of the Firm Body stock, and he is also employed as a tanning technician at one of the fitness clubs. After the January financial report showed that Firm Body's tanning division was operating at a substantial net loss, the board of directors, led by Marty Levinson, discussed terminating the tanning operations. Brock successfully convinced a majority of the board that the tanning division was necessary to market the club's overall fitness package. By April, the tanning division's financial losses had risen. The board hired a business analyst who conducted surveys and determined that the tanning operations did not significantly increase membership. A shareholder, Diego Peñada, discovered that Brock owned stock in Sunglow, Inc., the company from which Firm Body purchased its tanning equipment. Peñada notified Levinson, who privately reprimanded Brock. Shortly afterwards, Brock and Mandy Vail, who owned 37 percent of the Firm Body stock and also held shares of Sunglow, voted to replace Levinson on the board of directors. Using the information presented in the chapter, answer the following questions.

1. What duties did Brock, as a director, owe to Firm Body?
2. Does the fact that Brock owned shares in Sunglow establish a conflict of interest? Why or why not?
3. Suppose that Firm Body brought an action against Brock claiming that he had breached the duty of loyalty by not disclosing his interest in Sunglow to the other directors. What theory might Brock use in his defense?
4. Now suppose that Firm Body did not bring an action against Brock. What type of lawsuit might Peñada be able to bring based on these facts?

Business Application

Creating an E-Document-Retention Policy*

If a corporation becomes the target of a civil lawsuit or criminal investigation, the company may be required to turn over any documents in its files relating to the matter during the discovery stage of litigation. These documents may include legal documents, contracts, e-mail, faxes, letters, interoffice memorandums, notebooks, diaries, and other materials, even if they are kept in personal files in the homes of directors or officers. Under the current Federal Rules of Civil Procedure, which govern civil litigation procedures (see Chapter 3), a defendant in a lawsuit must disclose all relevant electronic data compilations and documents, as well as all relevant paper documents.

Although certain documents or data might free a company of any liability arising from a claim, others might serve to substantiate a civil claim or criminal charge. It is also possible that information contained in a document—an interoffice e-mail memo, for example (or even a memo referring to that memo)—could be used to convince a jury that the company or its directors or officers had condoned a certain action that they later denied condoning.

Which E-Documents Should Be Retained?

How does a company decide which e-documents should be retained and which should be destroyed? By law, corporations are required to keep certain types of documents, such as those specified in the *Code of Federal Regulations* and in regulations issued by government agencies, such as the Occupational Safety and Health Administration. Most businesses today have a document-retention policy. Generally, any records that the company is not legally required to keep or that the company is sure it will have no legal need for should be removed from the files and destroyed. A partnership agreement, for example, should be kept. A memo about last year's company picnic should not.

Modifications May Be Necessary During an Investigation

Companies that are under investigation usually must modify their document-retention policy until the investigation has been completed. After receiving a subpoena to produce specific types of documents, company officers should instruct the appropriate employees not to destroy relevant papers or e-documents that would otherwise be disposed of as part of the company's normal document-retention program.

To avoid being charged with obstruction of justice, company officials must always exercise good faith in deciding which documents should or should not be destroyed when attempting to comply with a subpoena. The specter of criminal prosecution would appear to encourage the retention of even those documents that are only remotely related to the dispute—at least until it has been resolved.

CHECKLIST FOR AN E-DOCUMENT-RETENTION POLICY

1. **Develop guidelines that let employees know not only which e-documents should be retained and deleted but also which types of documents should not be created in the first place.**

*This *Business Application* is not meant to substitute for the services of an attorney who is licensed to practice law in your state.

Continued

2. **Find out which documents must be retained under the *Code of Federal Regulations* and other government agency regulations to which your corporation is subject.**
3. **Retain other e-documents only if their retention is in the corporation's interest.**
4. **If certain corporate documents are subpoenaed, modify your document-retention policy to keep any documents that are even remotely related to the dispute until it has been resolved.**

Key Terms

business judgment rule 758
inside director 755
outside director 755
preemptive right 766
proxy 762
quorum 755
shareholder's derivative suit 769
stock certificate 766
stock warrant 767
watered stock 770

Chapter Summary: Corporate Directors, Officers, and Shareholders

Roles of Directors and Officers (See pages 753–757.)	1. *Directors' qualifications*—Few qualifications are required; a director may be a shareholder but is not required to be. Directors are responsible for all policymaking decisions necessary to the management of all corporate affairs (see Exhibit 30–1 on page 754). 2. *Election of directors*—The first board of directors is usually appointed by the incorporators; thereafter, directors are elected by the shareholders. Directors usually serve a one-year term, although their terms can be longer or staggered. Compensation is usually specified in the corporate articles or bylaws. 3. *Board of directors' meetings*—The board of directors conducts business by holding formal meetings with recorded minutes. The date of regular meetings is usually established in the corporate articles or bylaws; special meetings can be called, with notice sent to all directors. Quorum requirements vary from state to state; usually, a quorum is a majority of the directors. Voting usually must be done in person, and in ordinary matters only a majority vote is required. 4. *Rights of directors*—Directors' rights include the rights of participation, inspection, compensation, and indemnification. 5. *Directors' committees*—A board of directors may create committees of directors and delegate various responsibilities to them. Common types of committees are listed and described on page 756. 6. *Corporate officers and executives*—Corporate officers and other executive employees are normally hired by the board of directors and have the rights defined by their employment contracts. The duties of corporate officers are the same as those of directors.
Duties and Liabilities of Directors and Officers (See pages 757–761.)	1. *Duty of care*—Directors and officers are obligated to act in good faith, to use prudent business judgment in the conduct of corporate affairs, and to act in the corporation's best interests. If a director fails to exercise this duty of care, she or he can be answerable to the corporation and to the shareholders for breaching the duty. 2. *The business judgment rule*—This rule immunizes directors and officers from liability when they acted in good faith, acted in the best interests of the corporation, and exercised due care. For the rule to apply, the directors and officers must have made an informed, reasonable, and loyal decision. 3. *Duty of loyalty*—Directors and officers have a fiduciary duty to subordinate their own interests to those of the corporation in matters relating to the corporation. 4. *Conflicts of interest*—To fulfill their duty of loyalty, directors and officers must make a full disclosure of any potential conflicts between their personal interests and those of the corporation. 5. *Liability of directors and officers*—Corporate directors and officers are personally liable for their own torts and crimes. Additionally, they may be held personally liable for the torts and crimes committed by corporate personnel under their supervision (see Chapters 6 and 23).

Chapter Summary: Corporate Directors, Officers, and Shareholders

Role of Shareholders (See pages 761–766.)	1. *Shareholders' powers*–Shareholders' powers include the approval of all fundamental changes affecting the corporation and the election of the board of directors. 2. *Shareholders' meetings*–Shareholders' meetings must occur at least annually; special meetings can be called when necessary. Notice of the date, time, and place of the meeting (and its purpose, if it is specially called) must be sent to shareholders. Shareholders may vote by proxy (authorizing someone else to vote their shares) and may submit proposals to be included in the company's proxy materials sent to shareholders before meetings. 3. *Shareholder voting*–Shareholder voting requirements and procedures are as follows: a. A minimum number of shareholders (a quorum–generally, more than 50 percent of shares held) must be present at a meeting for business to be conducted; resolutions are passed (usually) by simple majority vote. b. The corporation must prepare voting lists of shareholders of record prior to each shareholders' meeting. c. Cumulative voting may or may not be required or permitted. Cumulative voting gives minority shareholders a better chance to be represented on the board of directors. d. A shareholder voting agreement (an agreement of shareholders to vote their shares together) is usually held to be valid and enforceable.
Rights of Shareholders (See pages 766–769.)	Shareholders have numerous rights, which may include the following: 1. The right to a stock certificate, preemptive rights, and the right to stock warrants (depending on the articles of incorporation). 2. The right to obtain a dividend (at the discretion of the directors). 3. Voting rights. 4. The right to inspect the corporate records. 5. The right to transfer shares (this right may be restricted in close corporations). 6. The right to a share of corporate assets when the corporation is dissolved. 7. The right to sue on behalf of the corporation (bring a shareholder's derivative suit) when the directors fail to do so.
Duties and Liabilities of Shareholders (See pages 769–771.)	1. Shareholders may be liable for the retention of illegal dividends and for the value of watered stock. 2. In certain situations, majority shareholders may be regarded as having a fiduciary duty to minority shareholders and will be liable if that duty is breached.

ExamPrep

ISSUE SPOTTERS

1 Wonder Corporation has an opportunity to buy stock in XL, Inc. The directors decide that instead of Wonder buying the stock, the directors will buy it. Yvon, a Wonder shareholder, learns of the purchase and wants to sue the directors on Wonder's behalf. Can she do it? Explain.

2 Nico is Omega Corporation's majority shareholder. He owns enough stock in Omega that if he were to sell it, the sale would be a transfer of control of the firm. Discuss whether Nico owes a duty to Omega or the minority shareholders in selling his shares.

BEFORE THE TEST

Check your answers to the Issue Spotters, and at the same time, take the interactive quiz for this chapter. Go to www.cengage.com/blaw/blt and click on "Chapter 30." First, click on "Answers to Issue Spotters" to check your answers. Next, click on "Interactive Quiz" to assess your mastery of the concepts in this chapter. Then click on "Flashcards" to review this chapter's Key Term definitions.

For Review

Answers for the even-numbered questions in this For Review section can be found on this text's accompanying Web site at www.cengage.com/blaw/blt. Select "Chapter 30" and click on "For Review."

1 What are the duties of corporate directors and officers?

2 Directors are expected to use their best judgment in managing the corporation. What must directors do to avoid liability for honest mistakes of judgment and poor business decisions?

3 What is a voting proxy? What is cumulative voting?

4 If a group of shareholders perceives that the corporation has suffered a wrong and the directors refuse to take action, can the shareholders compel the directors to act? If so, how?

5 From what sources may dividends be paid legally? In what circumstances is a dividend illegal? What happens if a dividend is illegally paid?

Hypothetical Scenarios and Case Problems

30–1 **Voting Techniques.** Algonquin Corp. has issued and has outstanding 100,000 shares of common stock. Four stockholders own 60,000 of these shares, and for the past six years they have nominated a slate of candidates for membership on the board, all of whom have been elected. Sergio and twenty other shareholders, owning 20,000 shares, are dissatisfied with corporate management and want a representative on the board who shares their views. Explain under what circumstances Sergio and the twenty other shareholders can elect their representative to the board.

30–2 **Hypothetical Question with Sample Answer** Starboard, Inc., has a board of directors consisting of three members (Ellsworth, Green, and Morino) and approximately five hundred shareholders. At a regular meeting of the board, the board selects Tyson as president of the corporation by a two-to-one vote, with Ellsworth dissenting. The minutes of the meeting do not register Ellsworth's dissenting vote. Later, during an audit, it is discovered that Tyson is a former convict and has openly embezzled $500,000 from Starboard. This loss is not covered by insurance. The corporation wants to hold directors Ellsworth, Green, and Morino liable. Ellsworth claims no liability. Discuss the personal liability of the directors to the corporation.

—For a sample answer to Question 30–2, go to Appendix E at the end of this text.

30–3 **Rights of Shareholders.** Lucia has acquired one share of common stock of a multimillion-dollar corporation with more than 500,000 shareholders. Lucia's ownership is so small that she is wondering what her rights are as a shareholder. For example, she wants to know whether owning this one share entitles her to (1) attend and vote at shareholders' meetings, (2) inspect the corporate books, and (3) receive yearly dividends. Discuss Lucia's rights in these three matters.

30–4 **Duties of Directors and Officers.** In 1978, David Brandt and Dean Somerville incorporated Posilock Puller, Inc. (PPI), to make and market bearing pullers. Each received half of the stock. Initially operating out of McHenry, North Dakota, PPI moved to Cooperstown, North Dakota, in 1984 into a building owned by Somerville. After the move, Brandt's participation in PPI diminished, and Somerville's increased. In 1998, Somerville formed PL MFG as his own business to make components for the bearing pullers and sell the parts to PPI. The start-up costs included a $450,000 loan from Sheyenne Valley Electric Cooperative. PPI executed the loan documents and indorsed the check. The proceeds were deposited into an account for PL MFG, which did not sign a promissory note payable to PPI until 2000. When Brandt learned of PL MFG and the loan, he filed a suit in a North Dakota state court against Somerville, alleging, in part, a breach of fiduciary duty. What fiduciary duty does a director owe to his or her corporation? What does this duty require? Should the court hold Somerville liable? Why or why not? [*Brandt v. Somerville*, 2005 ND 35, 692 N.W.2d 144 (2005)]

30–5 **Duties of Majority Shareholders.** Steve and Marie Venturini were involved in the operation of Steve's Sizzling Steakhouse in Carlstadt, New Jersey, from the day their parents opened it in the 1930s. By the 1980s, Steve, Marie, and her husband, Joe, were running it. The business was a corporation with Steve and Marie each owning half of the stock. Steve died in 2001, leaving his stock in equal shares to his sons Steve and Gregg. Son Steve had never worked there. Gregg did occasional maintenance work until his father's death. Despite their lack of participation, the sons were paid more than $750 per week each. In 2002, Marie's son Blaise, who had obtained a college degree in restaurant management while working part-time at the steakhouse, took over its management. When his cousins became threatening, he denied them access to the business and its books. Marie refused Gregg and Steve's offer of about $1.4 million for her stock in the restaurant, and they refused her offer of about $800,000 for theirs. They filed a suit in a New Jersey state court against her, claiming, among other things, a breach of fiduciary duty. Should the court order the aunt to buy out the nephews or the nephews to buy out the aunt, or neither? Why? [*Venturini v. Steve's Steakhouse, Inc.*, __ N.J.Super. __, __ A.2d __ (Ch.Div. 2006)]

30–6 **Case Problem with Sample Answer** Harry Hoaas and Larry Griffiths were shareholders in Grand Casino, Inc., which owned and operated a casino in Watertown, South Dakota. Griffiths owned 51 percent of the stock and Hoaas 49 percent. Hoaas managed the casino, which Griffiths typically visited once a week. At the end of 1997, an accounting showed that the cash on hand was less than the amount posted in the casino's books. Later, more shortfalls were discovered. In October 1999, Griffiths did a complete audit. Hoaas was unable to account for $135,500 in missing cash. Griffiths then kept all of the casino's most recent profits, including Hoaas's $9,447.20 share, and, without telling Hoaas, sold the casino for $100,000 and kept all of the proceeds. Hoaas filed a suit in a South Dakota state court against Griffiths, asserting, among other things, a breach of fiduciary duty. Griffiths countered with evidence of Hoaas's misappropriation of corporate cash. What duties did these parties owe each other? Did either Griffiths or Hoaas, or both of them, breach those duties? How should their dispute be resolved? How should their finances be reconciled? Explain. [*Hoaas v. Griffiths,* 2006 SD 27, 714 N.W.2d 61 (2006)]

—After you have answered Problem 30–6, compare your answer with the sample answer given on the Web site that accompanies this text. Go to www.cengage.com/blaw/blt, select "Chapter 30," and click on "Case Problem with Sample Answer."

30–7 **Role of Directors.** The board of directors of a property management corporation in Oregon meets on a regular basis. The company paid the directors $6,000 each in the third quarter of 2003. It did not report the payments as part of its payroll and did not pay unemployment tax on the payments. The Oregon Employment Department contended that the company owed $700 in unemployment taxes on the payments to the directors. The company protested. The administrative law judge (ALJ) for the Employment Department held that the company owed the taxes because directors' fees are the same as wages for employment. The company appealed. The court of appeals affirmed the ALJ's ruling. The company appealed again. Are payments to directors the same as wages for tax purposes? Explain. [*Necanicum Investment Co. v. Employment Department,* 345 Or. 138, 190 P.3d 368 (2008)]

30–8 **Duties of Directors and Officers.** First Niles Financial, Inc., is a company whose sole business is to own and operate a bank, Home Federal Savings and Loan Association of Niles, Ohio. First Niles's directors include bank officers William Stephens, Daniel Csontos, and Lawrence Safarek; James Kramer, president of an air-conditioning company that services the bank; and Ralph Zuzolo, whose law firm serves the bank and whose title company participates in most of its real estate deals. First Niles's board put the bank up for sale. There were three bids. Farmers National Bank Corp. stated that it would not retain the board. Cortland Bancorp indicated that it would terminate the directors but consider them for future service. First Financial Corp. said nothing about the directors. The board did not pursue Farmers' offer, failed to respond timely to Cortland's request, and rejected First Financial's bid. Leonard Gantler and other First Niles shareholders filed a suit in a Delaware state court against Stephens and the others. What duties do directors and officers owe to a corporation and its shareholders? How might those duties have been breached here? Discuss. [*Gantler v. Stephens,* 965 A.2d 695 (Del.Sup. 2009)]

30–9 **A Question of Ethics** *New Orleans Paddlewheels, Inc. (NOP), is a Louisiana corporation formed in 1982, when James Smith, Sr., and Warren Reuther were its only shareholders, with each holding 50 percent of the stock. NOP is part of a sprawling enterprise of tourism and hospitality companies in New Orleans. The positions on the board of each company were split equally between the Smith and Reuther families. At Smith's request, his son James Smith, Jr. (JES), became involved in the businesses. In 1999, NOP's board elected JES as president, in charge of day-to-day operations, and Reuther as chief executive officer (CEO), in charge of marketing and development. Over the next few years, animosity developed between Reuther and JES. In October 2001, JES terminated Reuther as CEO and denied him access to the offices and books of NOP and the other companies, literally changing the locks on the doors. At the next meetings of the boards of NOP and the overall enterprise, deadlock ensued, with the directors voting along family lines on every issue. Complaining that the meetings were a "waste of time," JES began to run the entire enterprise by taking advantage of an unequal balance of power on the companies' executive committees. In NOP's subsequent bankruptcy proceeding, Reuther filed a motion for the appointment of a trustee to formulate a plan for the firm's reorganization, alleging, among other things, misconduct by NOP's management. [*In re* New Orleans Paddlewheels, Inc., *350 Bankr. 667 (E.D.La. 2006)]*

1 Was Reuther legally entitled to have access to the books and records of NOP and the other companies? JES maintained, among other things, that NOP's books were "a mess." Was JES's denial of that access unethical? Explain.

2 How would you describe JES's attempt to gain control of NOP and the other companies? Were his actions deceptive and self-serving in the pursuit of personal gain or legitimate and reasonable in the pursuit of a business goal? Discuss.

Critical Thinking and Writing Assignments

30–10 **Critical Legal Thinking.** In general, courts are reluctant to grant shareholders' petitions for corporate dissolution except in extreme circumstances, such as when corporate directors or shareholders are deadlocked and the corporation suffers as a result. Instead, a court will attempt to "save" the corporate entity whenever possible. Why is this?

Practical Internet Exercises

Go to this text's Web site at www.cengage.com/blaw/blt, select "Chapter 30," and click on "Practical Internet Exercises." There you will find the following Internet research exercises that you can perform to learn more about the topics covered in this chapter.

Practical Internet Exercise 30–1: LEGAL PERSPECTIVE—**Liability of Directors and Officers**

Practical Internet Exercise 30–2: MANAGEMENT PERSPECTIVE—**D&O Insurance**

Chapter 31

Investor Protection, Insider Trading, and Corporate Governance

"You are remembered for the rules you break."

—Douglas MacArthur, 1880–1964
(U.S. Army general)

Chapter Outline

- Securities Act of 1933
- Securities Exchange Act of 1934
- State Securities Laws
- Corporate Governance
- Online Securities Fraud

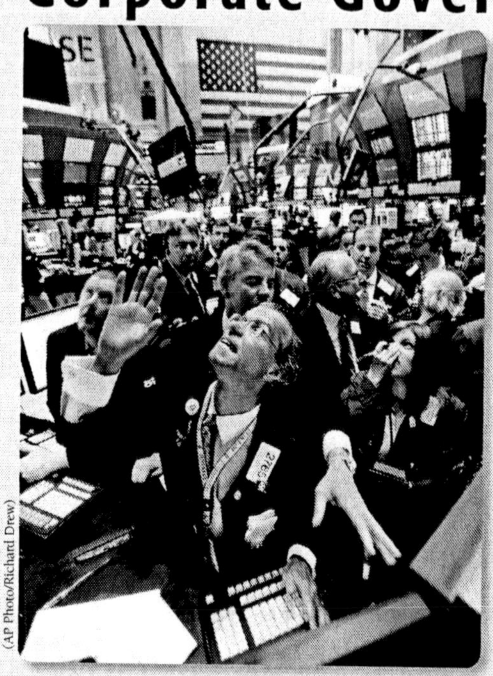
(AP Photo/Richard Drew)

Learning Objectives

After reading this chapter, you should be able to answer the following questions:

1. What is meant by the term *securities?*
2. What are the two major statutes regulating the securities industry?
3. What is insider trading? Why is it prohibited?
4. What are some of the features of state securities laws?
5. What certification requirements does the Sarbanes-Oxley Act impose on corporate executives?

Security Generally, a stock certificate, bond, note, debenture, warrant, or other document or record evidencing an ownership interest in a corporation or a promise of repayment of debt by a corporation.

After the stock market crash of 1929, Congress enacted legislation to regulate securities markets. **Securities** generally are defined as any documents or records evidencing corporate ownership (stock) or debts (bonds). The goal of regulation was to provide investors with more information to help them make buying and selling decisions about securities and to prohibit deceptive, unfair, and manipulative practices. Today, the sale and transfer of securities are heavily regulated by federal and state statutes and by government agencies, and the Obama administration has proposed even more regulations. As we have seen in recent years, General MacArthur's observation in the chapter-opening quotation that people are remembered for the rules that they break certainly holds true with regard to securities law violations.

This chapter discusses the nature of federal securities regulation and its effect on the business world. We first examine the major traditional laws governing securities offerings and trading. We then discuss corporate governance and the Sarbanes-Oxley Act of 2002,[1]

1. 15 U.S.C. Sections 7201 *et seq.*

which affects certain types of securities transactions. Finally, we look at the problem of online securities fraud. Before we begin, though, the important role played by the Securities and Exchange Commission (SEC) in the regulation of federal securities laws requires some attention. We examine the origin and functions of the SEC in this chapter's *Landmark in the Law* feature on the following page.

Securities Act of 1933

The Securities Act of 1933[2] governs initial sales of stock by businesses. The act was designed to prohibit various forms of fraud and to stabilize the securities industry by requiring that all essential information concerning the issuance of securities be made available to the investing public. Basically, the purpose of this act is to require disclosure. The 1933 act provides that all securities transactions must be registered with the SEC or be exempt from registration requirements.

During the stock market crash of 1929, hordes of investors crowded Wall Street to find out the latest news. How did the "crash" affect stock trading in the years thereafter?

(National Archives)

What Is a Security?

Section 2(1) of the Securities Act of 1933 contains a broad definition of securities, which generally include the following:[3]

1. Instruments and interests commonly known as securities, such as preferred and common stocks, treasury stocks, bonds, debentures, and stock warrants.
2. Any interests in securities, such as stock options, puts, calls, or other types of privilege on a security or on the right to purchase a security or a group of securities in a national security exchange.
3. Notes, instruments, or other evidence of indebtedness, including certificates of interest in a profit-sharing agreement and certificates of deposit.
4. Any fractional undivided interest in oil, gas, or other mineral rights.
5. Investment contracts, which include interests in limited partnerships and other investment schemes.

Investment Contract In securities law, a transaction in which a person invests in a common enterprise reasonably expecting profits that are derived primarily from the efforts of others.

In interpreting the act, the United States Supreme Court has held that an **investment contract** is any transaction in which a person (1) invests (2) in a common enterprise (3) reasonably expecting profits (4) derived *primarily* or *substantially* from others' managerial or entrepreneurial efforts. Known as the *Howey* test, this definition continues to guide the determination of what types of contracts can be considered securities.[4]

For our purposes, it is probably convenient to think of securities in their most common forms—stocks and bonds issued by corporations. Bear in mind, though, that securities can take many forms, including interests in whiskey, cosmetics, worms, beavers, boats, vacuum cleaners, muskrats, and cemetery lots. Almost any stake in the ownership or debt of a company can be considered a security. Investment contracts in condominiums, franchises, limited partnerships in real estate, and oil or gas or other mineral rights have qualified as securities. **CASE EXAMPLE 31.1** Alpha Telcom sold, installed, and maintained pay-phone systems. As part of its pay-phone program, Alpha guaranteed buyers a 14 percent return on the amount of their purchase. Alpha was operating at a net loss,

2. 15 U.S.C. Sections 77–77aa.
3. 15 U.S.C. Section 77b(1). Amendments in 1982 added stock options.
4. *SEC v. W. J. Howey Co.*, 328 U.S. 293, 66 S.Ct. 1100, 90 L.Ed. 1244 (1946).

Landmark in the Law The Securities and Exchange Commission

In 1931, the U.S. Senate passed a resolution calling for an extensive investigation of securities trading. The investigation led, ultimately, to the passage by Congress of the Securities Act of 1933, which is also known as the *truth-in-securities* bill. In the following year, Congress passed the Securities Exchange Act. This 1934 act created the Securities and Exchange Commission (SEC).

Major Responsibilities of the SEC The SEC was created as an independent regulatory agency with the function of administering the 1933 and 1934 acts. Its major responsibilities in this respect are as follows:

1. Interprets federal securities laws and investigates securities law violations.
2. Issues new rules and amends existing rules.
3. Oversees the inspection of securities firms, brokers, investment advisers, and ratings agencies.
4. Oversees private regulatory organizations in the securities, accounting, and auditing fields.
5. Coordinates U.S. securities regulation with federal, state, and foreign authorities.

The SEC's Expanding Regulatory Powers Since its creation, the SEC's regulatory functions have gradually been increased by legislation granting it authority in different areas. For example, to curb further securities fraud, the Securities Enforcement Remedies and Penny Stock Reform Act of 1990[a] was enacted to expand the SEC's enforcement options and allow SEC administrative law judges to hear cases involving more types of alleged securities law violations. In addition, the act provides that courts can prevent persons who have engaged in securities fraud from serving as officers and directors of publicly held corporations. The Securities Acts Amendments of 1990 authorized the SEC to seek sanctions against those who violate foreign securities laws.[b]

IN TODAY'S MARKET NEWS, GREED ROARED BACK.
SCHWADRON

(©Harley Schwadron)

The National Securities Markets Improvement Act of 1996 expanded the power of the SEC to exempt persons, securities, and transactions from the requirements of the securities laws.[c] (This part of the act is also known as the Capital Markets Efficiency Act.) The act also limited the authority of the states to regulate certain securities transactions and particular investment advisory firms.[d] The Sarbanes-Oxley Act of 2002,[e] which you will read about later in this chapter, further expanded the authority of the SEC by directing the agency to issue new rules relating to corporate disclosure requirements and by creating an oversight board to regulate public accounting firms.

• **Application to Today's World** *The SEC is working to make the regulatory process more efficient and more relevant to today's securities trading practices. To this end, the SEC has embraced modern technology and communications methods, especially the Internet, more completely than many other federal agencies have. For example, the agency now requires—not just allows—companies to file certain information electronically so that it can be posted on the SEC's EDGAR (Electronic Data Gathering, Analysis, and Retrieval) database.*

• **Relevant Web Sites** *To locate information on the Web concerning the SEC, go to this text's Web site at* www.cengage.com/blaw/blt*, select "Chapter 31," and click on "URLs for Landmarks."*

a. 15 U.S.C. Section 77g.
b. 15 U.S.C. Section 78a.
c. 15 U.S.C. Sections 77z-3, 78mm.
d. 15 U.S.C. Section 80b-3a.
e. 15 U.S.C. Sections 7201 *et seq.*

however, and continually borrowed funds to pay investors the fixed rate of return it had promised. Eventually, the company filed for bankruptcy, and the SEC brought an action alleging that Alpha had violated the Securities Act of 1933. In this situation, a federal court concluded that the pay-phone program was a security because it involved an investment contract.[5] ●

5. *SEC v. Alpha Telcom, Inc.*, 187 F.Supp.2d 1250 (2002). See also *SEC v. Edwards*, 540 U.S. 389, 124 S.Ct. 892, 157 L.Ed.2d 813 (2004), in which the United States Supreme Court held that an investment scheme offering contractual entitlement to a fixed rate of return can be an investment contract and therefore can be considered a security under federal law.

Preventing Legal Disputes

Securities are not limited to stocks and bonds but can encompass a wide variety of legal claims. The analysis hinges on the nature of the transaction rather than on the particular instrument or rights involved. Because Congress enacted securities laws to regulate investments, in whatever form and by whatever name they are called, almost any type of security that might be sold as an investment can be subject to securities laws. When in doubt about whether an investment transaction involves securities, seek the advice of a specialized attorney.

Registration Statement

Section 5 of the Securities Act of 1933 broadly provides that a security must be *registered* before being offered to the public unless it qualifies for an exemption. The issuing corporation must file a *registration statement* with the SEC and must provide all investors with a *prospectus*. A **prospectus** is a written disclosure document that describes the security being sold, the financial operations of the issuing corporation, and the investment or risk attaching to the security. The prospectus also serves as a selling tool for the issuing corporation. The SEC now allows an issuer to deliver its prospectus to investors electronically via the Internet.[6] In principle, the registration statement and the prospectus supply sufficient information to enable unsophisticated investors to evaluate the financial risk involved.

Prospectus A written document, required by securities laws, that describes the security being sold, the financial operations of the issuing corporation, and the investment or risk attaching to the security. It is designed to provide sufficient information to enable investors to evaluate the risk involved in purchasing the security.

Contents of the Registration Statement The registration statement must be written in plain English and fully describe the following:

1. The securities being offered for sale, including their relationship to the registrant's other capital securities.
2. The corporation's properties and business (including a financial statement certified by an independent public accounting firm).
3. The management of the corporation, including managerial compensation, stock options, pensions, and other benefits. Any interests of directors or officers in any material transactions with the corporation must be disclosed.
4. How the corporation intends to use the proceeds of the sale.
5. Any pending lawsuits or special risk factors.

DON'T FORGET The purpose of the Securities Act of 1933 is disclosure—the SEC does not consider whether a security is worth the investment price.

All companies, both domestic and foreign, must file their registration statements electronically so that they can be posted on the SEC's EDGAR (Electronic Data Gathering, Analysis, and Retrieval) database. The EDGAR database includes material on initial public offerings, proxy statements, corporations' annual reports, registration statements, and other documents that have been filed with the SEC. Investors can access the database via the Internet to obtain information that can be used to make investment decisions.

ON THE WEB The SEC's EDGAR system contains information about the SEC's operations, the statutes it implements, its proposed and final rules, and its enforcement actions, as well as corporate financial information. Go to www.sec.gov/edgar.shtml.

Registration Process The registration statement does not become effective until after it has been reviewed and approved by the SEC (unless it is filed by a *well-known seasoned issuer*, as will be discussed shortly). The 1933 act restricted the types of activities that an issuer can engage in at each stage in the registration process. During the *prefiling period* (before filing the registration statement), the issuer normally cannot either sell or offer to sell the securities. Once the registration statement has been filed, a waiting period begins while the SEC reviews the registration statement for completeness.[7]

6. Basically, an electronic prospectus must meet the same requirements as a printed prospectus. The SEC has special rules that address situations in which the graphics, images, or audio files in a printed prospectus cannot be reproduced in an electronic form. 17 C.F.R. Section 232.304.
7. The waiting period must last at least twenty days but always extends much longer because the SEC inevitably requires numerous changes and additions to the registration statement.

During the *waiting period,* the securities can be offered for sale but cannot be sold by the issuing corporation. Only certain types of offers are allowed. All issuers can distribute a *preliminary prospectus,* which contains most of the information that will be included in the final prospectus but often does not include a price. Most issuers can also use a *free-writing prospectus* during this period (although some inexperienced issuers will need to file a preliminary prospectus first).[8] A **free-writing prospectus** is any type of written, electronic, or graphic offer that describes the issuer or its securities and includes a legend indicating that the investor may obtain the prospectus at the SEC's Web site.

Free-Writing Prospectus A free-writing prospectus is any type of written, electronic, or graphic offer that describes the issuing corporation or its securities and includes a legend indicating that the investor may obtain the prospectus at the Securities and Exchange Commission's Web site.

Once the SEC has reviewed and approved the registration statement and the waiting period is over, the registration is effective, and the *posteffective period* begins. The issuer can now offer and sell the securities without restrictions. If the company issued a preliminary or free-writing prospectus to investors, it must provide those investors with a final prospectus either before or at the time they purchase the securities. The issuer can require investors to download the final prospectus from a Web site if it notifies them of the appropriate Internet address.

Restrictions Relaxed for Well-Known Seasoned Issuers In 2005, the SEC revised the registration process and loosened some of the restrictions on large experienced issuers.[9] The rules created new categories of issuers depending on their size and presence in the market and provided a simplified registration process for these issuers. The large, well-known securities firms that issue most securities have the greatest flexibility. A *well-known seasoned issuer* (WKSI) is a firm that has issued at least $1 billion in securities in the previous three years or has at least $700 million of value of outstanding stock in the hands of the public. WKSIs can file registration statements the day they announce a new offering and are not required to wait for SEC review and approval. They can also use a free-writing prospectus at any time, even during the prefiling period.

Exempt Securities and Transactions

Certain types of securities are exempt from the registration requirements of the Securities Act of 1933. These securities—which generally can also be resold without being registered—are summarized in Exhibit 31–1 under the "Exempt Securities" heading.[10] The exhibit also lists and describes certain transactions that are exempt from registration requirements under various SEC regulations.

ON THE WEB The Center for Corporate Law at the University of Cincinnati College of Law offers a Securities Lawyer's Deskbook online that examines all of the laws and legal terms discussed in this chapter. Go to www.law.uc.edu/CCL.

The transaction exemptions are the most important because they are very broad and can enable an issuer to avoid the high cost and complicated procedures associated with registration. Because the coverage of the exemptions overlaps somewhat, an offering may qualify for more than one. Therefore, many sales of securities occur without registration. Even when a transaction is exempt from the registration requirements, the offering is still subject to the antifraud provisions of the 1933 act (as well as those of the 1934 act, to be discussed later in this chapter).

Regulation A Offerings Securities issued by an issuer that has offered less than $5 million in securities during any twelve-month period are exempt from registration.[11] Under Regulation A,[12] the issuer must file with the SEC a notice of the issue and an offering circular, which must also be provided to investors before the sale. This is a much simpler and less expensive process than the procedures associated with full registration. Companies are

BE AWARE The issuer of an exempt security does not have to disclose the same information that other issuers do.

8. See SEC Rules 164 and 433.
9. Securities Offering Reform, codified at 17 C.F.R. Sections 200, 228, 229, 230, 239, 240, 243, 249, and 274.
10. 15 U.S.C. Section 77c.
11. 15 U.S.C. Section 77c(b).
12. 17 C.F.R. Sections 230.251–230.263.

Exhibit 31–1 **Exemptions for Securities Offerings under the 1933 Securities Act**

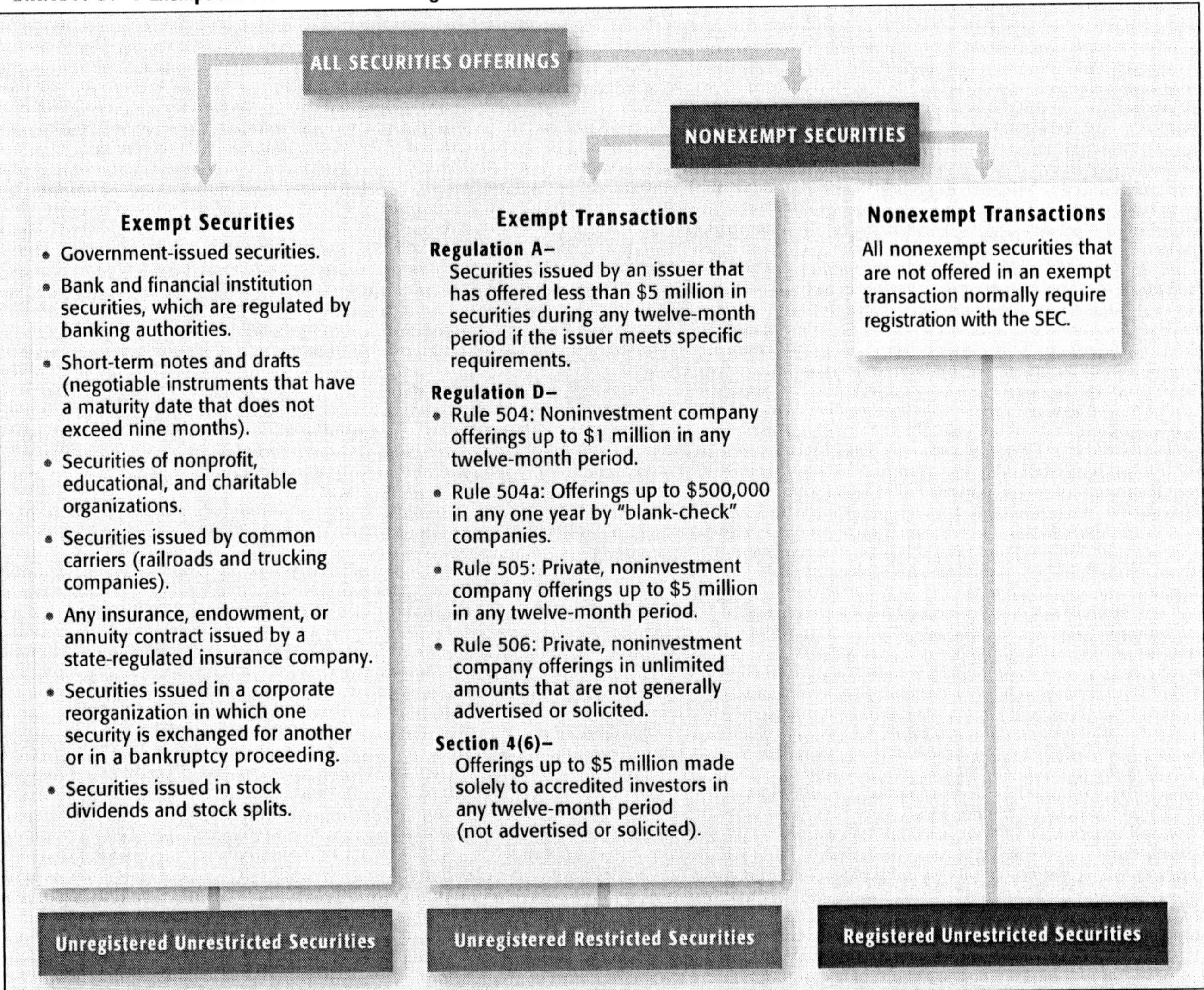
ALL SECURITIES OFFERINGS
NONEXEMPT SECURITIES
Exempt Securities
• Government-issued securities.
• Bank and financial institution securities, which are regulated by banking authorities.
• Short-term notes and drafts (negotiable instruments that have a maturity date that does not exceed nine months).
• Securities of nonprofit, educational, and charitable organizations.
• Securities issued by common carriers (railroads and trucking companies).
• Any insurance, endowment, or annuity contract issued by a state-regulated insurance company.
• Securities issued in a corporate reorganization in which one security is exchanged for another or in a bankruptcy proceeding.
• Securities issued in stock dividends and stock splits.
Exempt Transactions
Regulation A–
Securities issued by an issuer that has offered less than $5 million in securities during any twelve-month period if the issuer meets specific requirements.
Regulation D–
• Rule 504: Noninvestment company offerings up to $1 million in any twelve-month period.
• Rule 504a: Offerings up to $500,000 in any one year by "blank-check" companies.
• Rule 505: Private, noninvestment company offerings up to $5 million in any twelve-month period.
• Rule 506: Private, noninvestment company offerings in unlimited amounts that are not generally advertised or solicited.
Section 4(6)–
Offerings up to $5 million made solely to accredited investors in any twelve-month period (not advertised or solicited).
Nonexempt Transactions
All nonexempt securities that are not offered in an exempt transaction normally require registration with the SEC.
Unregistered Unrestricted Securities
Unregistered Restricted Securities
Registered Unrestricted Securities

allowed to "test the waters" for potential interest before preparing the offering circular. To *test the waters* means to determine potential interest without actually selling any securities or requiring any commitment on the part of those who express interest. Small-business issuers (companies with annual revenues of less than $25 million) can also use an integrated registration and reporting system that uses simpler forms than the full registration system.

ON THE WEB The SEC provides a list of downloadable forms pertinent to securities filings. Go to www.sec.gov/about/forms/secforms.htm.

Some companies have sold their securities via the Internet using Regulation A. **EXAMPLE 31.2** The Spring Street Brewing Company became the first company to sell securities via an online initial public offering (IPO). Spring Street raised about $1.6 million—without having to pay any commissions to brokers or underwriters. ● Such online IPOs are particularly attractive to small companies and start-up ventures that may find it difficult to raise capital from institutional investors or through underwriters.

Small Offerings—Regulation D The SEC's Regulation D contains several exemptions from registration requirements (Rules 504, 504a, 505, and 506) for offers that either involve a small dollar amount or are made in a limited manner. Rule 504 is the exemption used by most small businesses. It provides that noninvestment company offerings up to $1 million in any twelve-month period are exempt. Noninvestment companies are firms that are not engaged primarily in the business of investing or trading in securities. (In contrast, an **investment company** is a firm that buys a large portfolio of securities and professionally manages it on behalf of many smaller shareholders/owners. A **mutual fund** is a type of investment company.)

Investment Company A company that acts on the behalf of many smaller shareholders/owners by buying a large portfolio of securities and professionally managing that portfolio.

Mutual Fund A specific type of investment company that continually buys or sells to investors shares of ownership in a portfolio.

EXAMPLE 31.3 Zeta Enterprises is a limited partnership that develops commercial property. Zeta intends to offer $600,000 of its limited partnership interests for sale between June 1 and next May 31. Because an interest in a limited partnership meets the definition of a security (discussed earlier in this chapter), its sale would be subject to the registration and prospectus requirements of the Securities Act of 1933. Under Rule 504, however, the sales of Zeta's interests are exempt from these requirements because Zeta is a noninvestment company making an offering of less than $1 million in a twelve-month period. Therefore, Zeta can sell its limited partnership interests without filing a registration statement with the SEC or issuing a prospectus to any investor. ●

Another exemption is available under Rule 505 for private, noninvestment company offerings up to $5 million in any twelve-month period. The offer may be made to an unlimited number of *accredited investors* and up to thirty-five unaccredited investors. **Accredited investors** include banks, insurance companies, investment companies, employee benefit plans, the issuer's executive officers and directors, and persons whose income or net worth exceeds a certain threshold. The SEC must be notified of the sales, and precautions must be taken because these restricted securities may be resold only by registration or in an exempt transaction. No general solicitation or advertising is allowed. The issuer must provide any unaccredited investors with disclosure documents that generally are the same as those used in registered offerings.

Accredited Investor In the context of securities offerings, "sophisticated" investors, such as banks, insurance companies, investment companies, the issuer's executive officers and directors, and persons whose income or net worth exceeds certain limits.

PRIVATE PLACEMENT EXEMPTION Private, noninvestment company offerings in unlimited amounts that generally are not solicited or advertised are exempt under Rule 506. This exemption is often referred to as the *private placement* exemption because it exempts "transactions not involving any public offering."[13] To qualify for the exemption, the issuer must believe that each unaccredited investor has sufficient knowledge or experience in financial matters to be capable of evaluating the investment's merits and risks.[14]

KEEP IN MIND An investor can be "sophisticated" by virtue of his or her education and experience or by investing through a knowledgeable, experienced representative.

The private placement exemption is perhaps most important to firms that want to raise funds through the sale of securities without registering them. **EXAMPLE 31.4** Citco Corporation needs to raise capital to expand its operations. Citco decides to make a private $10 million offering of its common stock directly to two hundred accredited investors and thirty highly sophisticated, but unaccredited, investors. Citco provides all of these investors with a prospectus and material information about the firm, including its most recent financial statements. As long as Citco notifies the SEC of the sale, this offering will likely qualify for the private placement exemption. The offering is nonpublic and not generally advertised. There are fewer than thirty-five unaccredited investors, and each of them possesses sufficient knowledge and experience to evaluate the risks involved. The issuer has provided all purchasers with the material information. Thus, Citco will *not* be required to comply with the registration requirements of the Securities Act of 1933. ●

RESALES Most securities can be resold without registration. The Securities Act of 1933 provides exemptions for resales by most persons other than issuers or underwriters. The average investor who sells shares of stock does not have to file a registration statement with the SEC. Resales of restricted securities, however, trigger the registration requirements

13. 15 U.S.C. Section 77d(2).

14. 7 C.F.R. Section 230.506.

unless the party selling them complies with Rule 144 or Rule 144A. These rules are sometimes referred to as "safe harbors."

Rule 144. Rule 144 exempts restricted securities from registration on resale if all of the following conditions are met:

1. There is adequate current public information about the issuer. ("Adequate current public information" refers to the reports that certain companies are required to file under the Securities Exchange Act of 1934.)
2. The person selling the securities has owned them for at least six months if the issuer is subject to the reporting requirements of the 1934 act.[15] If the issuer is not subject to the 1934 act's reporting requirements, the seller must have owned the securities for at least one year.
3. The securities are sold in certain limited amounts in unsolicited brokers' transactions.
4. The SEC is notified of the resale.[16]

Exhibit 31–2 **A Sample Restricted Stock Certificate**

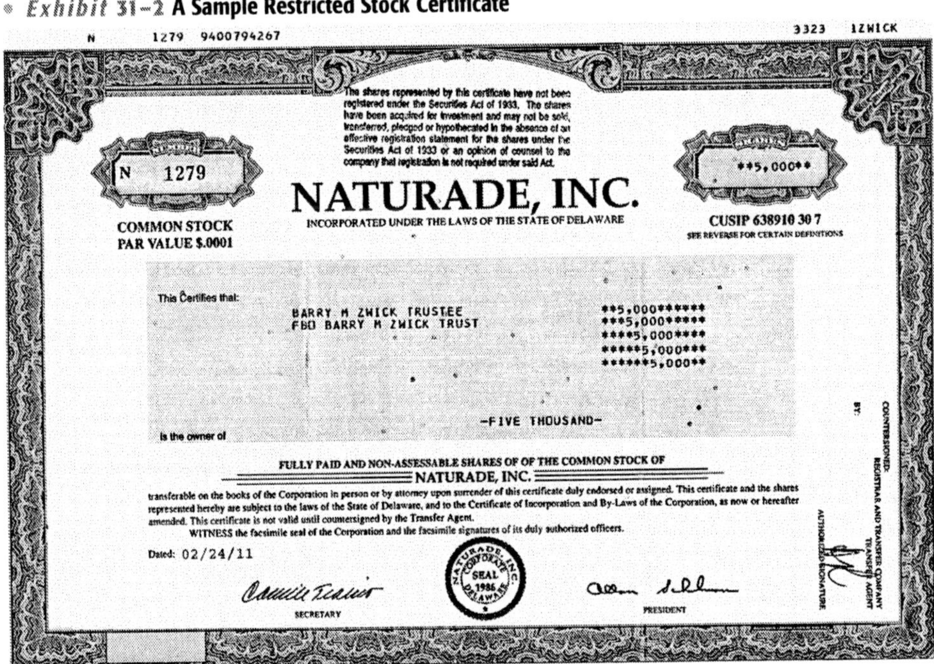

N 1279 9400794267 3323 1ZWICK

The shares represented by this certificate have not been registered under the Securities Act of 1933. The shares have been acquired for investment and may not be sold, transferred, pledged or hypothecated in the absence of an effective registration statement for the shares under the Securities Act of 1933 or an opinion of counsel to the company that registration is not required under said Act.

N 1279

5,000

NATURADE, INC.

INCORPORATED UNDER THE LAWS OF THE STATE OF DELAWARE

COMMON STOCK
PAR VALUE $.0001

CUSIP 638910 30 7
SEE REVERSE FOR CERTAIN DEFINITIONS

This Certifies that:

BARRY M ZWICK TRUSTEE
FBO BARRY M ZWICK TRUST

5,000****
5,000**
****5,000****
*****5,000***
******5,000**

is the owner of

-FIVE THOUSAND-

FULLY PAID AND NON-ASSESSABLE SHARES OF OF THE COMMON STOCK OF
NATURADE, INC.

transferable on the books of the Corporation in person or by attorney upon surrender of this certificate duly endorsed or assigned. This certificate and the shares represented hereby are subject to the laws of the State of Delaware, and to the Certificate of Incorporation and By-Laws of the Corporation, as now or hereafter amended. This certificate is not valid until countersigned by the Transfer Agent.

WITNESS the facsimile seal of the Corporation and the facsimile signatures of its duly authorized officers.

Dated: 02/24/11

NATURADE, INC. CORPORATE SEAL 1986 DELAWARE

SECRETARY

PRESIDENT

COUNTERSIGNED:
REGISTRAR AND TRANSFER COMPANY
TRANSFER AGENT
BY:
AUTHORIZED SIGNATURE

Rule 144A. Securities that at the time of issue are not of the same class as securities listed on a national securities exchange or quoted in a U.S. automated interdealer quotation system may be resold under Rule 144A.[17] They may be sold only to a qualified institutional buyer (an institution, such as an insurance company or a bank that owns and invests at least $100 million in securities). The seller must take reasonable steps to ensure that the buyer knows that the seller is relying on the exemption under Rule 144A. A sample restricted stock certificate is shown in Exhibit 31–2.

Violations of the 1933 Act

It is a violation of the Securities Act of 1933 to intentionally defraud investors by misrepresenting or omitting facts in a registration statement or prospectus. Liability is also imposed on those who are negligent for not discovering the fraud. Selling securities before the effective date of the registration statement or under an exemption for which the securities do not qualify results in liability.

CONTRAST Securities do not have to be held for a specific period (six months or one year) to be exempt from registration on a resale under Rule 144A, as they do under Rule 144.

Criminal violations are prosecuted by the U.S. Department of Justice. Violators may be fined up to $10,000, imprisoned for up to five years, or both. The SEC is authorized

15. Before 2008, when amendments to Rule 144 became effective, the holding period was one year if the issuer was subject to the reporting requirements of the 1934 act. See the revised SEC Rules and Regulations at 72 Federal Rules 71546-01, 2007 WL 4368599, Release No. 33-8869. This reduced holding period allows nonpublic issuers to raise capital electronically from private and overseas sources more quickly.

16. 17 C.F.R. Section 230.144.

17. 17 C.F.R. Section 230.144A.

to seek civil sanctions against those who willfully violate the 1933 act. It can request an injunction to prevent further sales of the securities involved or ask the court to grant other relief, such as an order to a violator to refund profits. Parties who purchase securities and suffer harm as a result of false or omitted statements may also bring suits in a federal court to recover their losses and other damages.

"The way to stop financial 'joy-riding' is to arrest the chauffeur, not the automobile."

Woodrow Wilson, 1856–1924
(Twenty-eighth president of the United States, 1913–1921)

There are three basic defenses to charges of violations under the 1933 act. A defendant can avoid liability by proving that (1) the statement or omission was not material, (2) the plaintiff knew about the misrepresentation at the time of purchasing the stock, or (3) the defendant exercised *due diligence* in preparing the registration and reasonably believed at the time that the statements were true.

Securities Exchange Act of 1934

The Securities Exchange Act of 1934 provides for the regulation and registration of securities exchanges, brokers, dealers, and national securities associations, such as the National Association of Securities Dealers (NASD). Unlike the 1933 act, which is a one-time disclosure law, the 1934 act provides for continuous periodic disclosures by publicly held corporations to enable the SEC to regulate subsequent trading. For a discussion of how the Securities Exchange Act applies in the online context, see the *Adapting the Law to the Online Environment* feature.

The Securities Exchange Act of 1934 applies to companies that have assets in excess of $10 million and five hundred or more shareholders. These corporations are referred to as Section 12 companies because they are required to register their securities under Section 12 of the 1934 act. Section 12 companies are required to file reports with the SEC annually and quarterly, and sometimes even monthly if specified events occur (such as a merger). Other provisions in the 1934 act require all securities brokers and dealers to be registered, to keep detailed records of their activities, and to file annual reports with the SEC.

SEC Rule 10b-5 A rule of the Securities and Exchange Commission that makes it unlawful, in connection with the purchase or sale of any security, to make any untrue statement of a material fact or to omit a material fact if such omission causes the statement to be misleading.

The act also authorizes the SEC to engage in market surveillance to deter undesirable market practices such as fraud, market manipulation (attempts at illegally influencing stock prices), and misrepresentation. In addition, the act provides for the SEC's regulation of proxy solicitations for voting (discussed in Chapter 30).

FBI agents escort Joseph Contorinis from FBI headquarters in New York in 2009. He was accused of making several million dollars from insider tips provided by an investment banker.

(AP Photo/Louis Lanzano)

Section 10(b), SEC Rule 10b-5, and Insider Trading

Section 10(b) is one of the more important sections of the Securities Exchange Act of 1934. This section proscribes the use of any manipulative or deceptive device in violation of SEC rules and regulations. Among the rules that the SEC has promulgated pursuant to the 1934 act is **SEC Rule 10b-5,** which prohibits the commission of fraud in connection with the purchase or sale of any security.

APPLICABILITY OF SEC RULE 10B-5 SEC Rule 10b-5 applies to almost all trading of securities, whether on organized exchanges, in over-the-counter markets, or in private transactions. Generally, the rule covers just about any form of security, including, among other things, notes, bonds, agreements to form a corporation, and joint-venture agreements. The securities need not be registered under the 1933 act for the 1934 act to apply.

SEC Rule 10b-5 applies only when the requisites of federal jurisdiction—such as the use of stock exchange facilities, U.S. mail, or any means of interstate commerce—are present, but this requirement is easily met because almost every commercial transaction involves interstate contacts. In addition, the states have corporate securities laws, many of which include provisions similar to SEC Rule 10b-5.

Adapting the Law to the Online Environment

Corporate Blogs and Tweets Must Comply with the Securities Exchange Act

In the fast-paced world of securities trading, there is great demand for the latest information about companies, earnings, and market conditions. Corporations are meeting this demand by establishing Web sites and blogs, and using other interactive online media, such as Twitter and online shareholder forums. Nearly 20 percent of Fortune 500 companies now sponsor blogs. Corporations that use the Internet to distribute information to investors, however, must make sure that they comply with SEC regulations. For purposes of federal securities laws, the SEC treats statements by employees on online media, such as blogs and Twitter, the same as any other company statements.

Beware of Tweets Containing Financial Information

Some corporate blogs include links to corporate employees' Twitter accounts so that readers can communicate directly with, and get updates from, the individual who posted the information. For example, eBay, Inc., launched its corporate blog in 2008. A few months later, Richard Brewer-Hay, a seasoned blogger whom eBay hired to report online about the company, began *tweeting* (posting updates on Twitter) about eBay's quarterly earnings and what took place at Silicon Valley technology conferences. Brewer-Hay's tweets gained him a following, but then eBay's lawyers required him to include a regulatory disclaimer with certain posts to avoid problems with the SEC. Many members of his audience were disappointed by the company's supervision, which curbed his spontaneity. Brewer-Hay is now much more reserved in his tweets on financial matters and often simply repeats eBay executives' statements verbatim.[a]

A 2008 SEC Release Provides Guidance

The reaction of eBay's lawyers to Brewer-Hay's tweets was prompted, in part, by an interpretive release issued by the SEC in August 2008. As noted earlier in this chapter, the SEC generally embraces new technology and encourages companies to use it. In the release, the SEC noted that, in some circumstances, posting information on a company's Web site may be a "sufficient method of public disclosure."

The release also acknowledged that company-sponsored blogs, electronic shareholders' forums, and other interactive Web features can be a useful means of ongoing communications among companies, their shareholders, and other stakeholders. The SEC cautioned, though, that all communications made by or on behalf of a company are subject to the antifraud provisions of federal securities laws. "While blogs or forums can be informal and conversational in nature, statements made there . . . will not be treated differently from other company statements." In addition, the release stated that companies cannot require investors to waive protections under federal securities laws as a condition of participating in a blog or forum. The release also warned companies that they can, in some situations, be liable for providing hyperlinks to third party information or inaccurate summaries of financial information on their Web sites.[b]

FOR CRITICAL ANALYSIS

Would Brewer-Hay's tweets about what had transpired at technology conferences require SEC disclosures? Why or why not?

a. Cari Tuna, "Corporate Blogs and 'Tweets' Must Keep SEC in Mind," *Wall Street Journal Online*, April 27, 2009.

b. SEC Release Nos. 34-58288, IC-28351, File No. S7-23-08, Commission Guidance on the Use of Company Web Sites.

Insider Trading The purchase or sale of securities on the basis of information that has not been made available to the public.

INSIDER TRADING One of the major goals of Section 10(b) and SEC Rule 10b-5 is to prevent so-called **insider trading**, which occurs when persons buy or sell securities on the basis of information that is not available to the public. Corporate directors, officers, and others such as majority shareholders, for instance, often have advance inside information that can affect the future market value of the corporate stock. Obviously, if they act on this information, their positions give them a trading advantage over the general public and other shareholders. The 1934 Securities Exchange Act defines inside information and extends liability to those who take advantage of such information in their personal transactions when they know that the information is unavailable to those with whom they are dealing. Section 10(b) of the 1934 act and SEC Rule 10b-5 apply to anyone who has access to or receives information of a nonpublic nature on which trading is based—not just to corporate "insiders."

DISCLOSURE UNDER SEC RULE 10B-5 Any material omission or misrepresentation of material facts in connection with the purchase or sale of a security may violate not only the Securities Act of 1933 but also the antifraud provisions of Section 10(b) of the 1934 act and SEC Rule 10b-5. The key to liability (which can be civil or criminal) under Section 10(b) and SEC Rule 10b-5 is whether the insider's information is *material*.

The following are some examples of material facts calling for disclosure under SEC Rule 10b-5:

1. Fraudulent trading in the company stock by a broker-dealer.
2. A dividend change (whether up or down).
3. A contract for the sale of corporate assets.
4. A new discovery, a new process, or a new product.
5. A significant change in the firm's financial condition.
6. Potential litigation against the company.

Note that any one of these facts, by itself, is not *automatically* considered a material fact. Rather, it will be regarded as a material fact if it is significant enough that it would likely affect an investor's decision as to whether to purchase or sell the company's securities. **EXAMPLE 31.5** Sheen, Inc., is the defendant in a class-action product liability suit that its attorney, Paula Frasier, believes that the company will lose. Frasier has advised Sheen's directors, officers, and accountants that the company will likely have to pay a substantial damages award. Sheen plans to make a $5 million offering of newly issued stock before the date when the trial is expected to end. Sheen's potential liability and the financial consequences to the firm are material facts that must be disclosed because they are significant enough to affect an investor's decision as to whether to purchase the stock. ●

The following is one of the classic cases interpreting materiality under SEC Rule 10b-5.

Classic Case 31.1 Securities and Exchange Commission v. Texas Gulf Sulphur Co.

United States Court of Appeals, Second Circuit, 401 F.2d 833 (1968).

HISTORICAL AND ENVIRONMENTAL SETTING *In 1957, the Texas Gulf Sulphur Company (TGS) began exploring for minerals in eastern Canada. In March 1959, aerial geophysical surveys were conducted over more than fifteen thousand square miles of the area. The operations revealed numerous variations in the conductivity of the rock, which indicated a remarkable concentration of commercially exploitable minerals. One site of such variations was near Timmins, Ontario. On October 29 and 30, 1963, a ground survey of the site near Timmins indicated a need to drill for further evaluation.*

(©Dmitri Melnik, 2009. Used under license from Shutterstock.com)

After sample drilling revealed potential mineral deposits, company executives made substantial stock purchases. Did they violate insider-trading laws?

FACTS On November 12, 1963, the Texas Gulf Sulphur Company drilled a hole that appeared to yield a core with an exceedingly high mineral content, although further drilling would be necessary to establish whether there was enough ore to be mined commercially. TGS kept secret the results of the core sample. After learning of the ore discovery, officers and employees of the company made substantial purchases of TGS's stock or accepted stock options (rights to purchase stock). On April 11, 1964, an unauthorized report of the mineral find appeared in the newspapers. On the following day, April 12, TGS issued a press release that played down the discovery and stated that it was too early to tell whether the ore find would be significant. Later on, TGS announced a strike of at least 25 million tons of ore. The news led to a substantial increase in the price of TGS stock. The Securities and Exchange Commission (SEC) brought a suit in a federal district court against the officers and employees of TGS for violating the insider-trading prohibition of SEC Rule 10b-5. The officers and employees argued that the prohibition did not apply. They reasoned that the information on which they had traded was not material, as the find had not been commercially proved. The trial court held that most of the defendants had not violated SEC Rule 10b-5, and the SEC appealed.

ISSUE Did the officers and employees of TGS violate SEC Rule 10b-5 by buying the stock, even though they did not know the full extent and profit potential of the ore discovery at the time of their purchases?

DECISION Yes. The U.S. Court of Appeals for the Second Circuit reversed the lower court's decision and remanded the case for further proceedings, holding that the employees and officers had violated SEC Rule 10b-5's prohibition against insider trading.

REASON For SEC Rule 10b-5 purposes, the test of materiality is whether the information would affect the judgment of reasonable investors. Reasonable investors include speculative as well as conservative investors. "A major factor in determining whether the * * * discovery [of the ore] was a material fact is the importance attached to the drilling results by those who knew about it. * * * The timing by those who knew of it of their stock purchases and their purchases of short-term calls [rights to buy shares at a specified price within a specified time period]—purchases in

Case 31.1—Continued

some cases by individuals who had never before purchased calls or even TGS stock—virtually compels the inference that the insiders were influenced by the drilling results. * * * We hold, therefore, that all transactions in TGS stock or calls by individuals apprised of the drilling results * * * were made in violation of Rule 10b-5."

IMPACT OF THIS CASE ON TODAY'S LAW *This landmark case affirmed the principle that the test of whether information is "material," for SEC Rule 10b-5 purposes, is whether it would affect the judgment of reasonable investors. The corporate insiders' purchases of stock and stock options indicated that they were influenced by the results and that the information about the results was material. The courts continue to cite this case when applying SEC Rule 10b-5 to other cases of alleged insider trading.*

RELEVANT WEB SITES *To locate information on the Web concerning the* Securities and Exchange Commission v. Texas Gulf Sulphur Co. *decision, go to this text's Web site at* www.cengage.com/blaw/blt. *Select "Chapter 31" and click on "Classic Cases."*

THE PRIVATE SECURITIES LITIGATION REFORM ACT OF 1995 One of the unintended effects of SEC Rule 10b-5 was to deter the disclosure of forward-looking information. To understand why, consider an example. **EXAMPLE 31.6** QT Company announces that its projected earnings in a future time period will be a certain amount, but the forecast turns out to be wrong. The earnings are in fact much lower, and the price of QT's stock is affected—negatively. The shareholders then bring a class-action suit against the company, alleging that the directors violated SEC Rule 10b-5 by disclosing misleading financial information. ●

In an attempt to rectify this problem and promote disclosure, Congress passed the Private Securities Litigation Reform Act of 1995. The act provides a "safe harbor" for publicly held companies that make forward-looking statements, such as financial forecasts. Those who make such statements are protected against liability for securities fraud as long as the statements are accompanied by "meaningful cautionary statements identifying important factors that could cause actual results to differ materially from those in the forward-looking statement."[18]

After the 1995 act was passed, a number of securities class-action suits were filed in state courts to skirt the requirements of the 1995 federal act. In response to this problem, Congress passed the Securities Litigation Uniform Standards Act of 1998 (SLUSA).[19] The act placed stringent limits on the ability of plaintiffs to bring class-action suits in state courts against firms whose securities are traded on national stock exchanges. SLUSA not only prevents the purchasers and sellers of securities from bringing class-action fraud claims under state securities laws, but also applies to investors who are fraudulently induced to hold on to their securities.[20]

OUTSIDERS AND SEC RULE 10B-5 The traditional insider-trading case involves true insiders—corporate officers, directors, and majority shareholders who have access to (and trade on) inside information. Increasingly, liability under Section 10(b) of the 1934 act and SEC Rule 10b-5 is being extended to certain "outsiders"—those persons who trade on inside information acquired indirectly. As will be discussed shortly, two theories have been developed under which outsiders may be held liable for insider trading: the *tipper/tippee theory* and the *misappropriation theory*.

In the following case, the plaintiffs attempted to assert a third theory—scheme liability. Can Section 10(b) and SEC Rule 10b-5 apply to outsiders—suppliers and customers—who seemingly "aid and abet" a scheme to show inflated sales revenue figures for a publicly traded company?

18. 15 U.S.C. Sections 77z-2, 78u-5.
19. Pub. L. No. 105-353. This act amended many sections of Title 15 of the *United States Code*.
20. *Merrill Lynch, Pierce, Fenner & Smith, Inc. v. Dabit*, 547 U.S. 71, 126 S.Ct. 1503, 164 L.Ed.2d 179 (2006). This Supreme Court decision forms the basis of the *Case Analysis Question* on page 807.

Case 31.2 Stoneridge Investment Partners, LLC v. Scientific-Atlanta, Inc.

Supreme Court of the United States, 552 U.S. 148, 128 S.Ct. 761, 169 L.Ed.2d 627 (2008).
www.supremecourtus.gov/opinions/opinions.html[a]

A cable TV operator, in a scheme to report higher earnings, asked its set-top box suppliers to overcharge them. Can investors in the cable company sue the set-top box suppliers for their role in the scheme?

FACTS In 2000, the cable operator Charter Communications wanted to satisfy stock analysts' expectations about its revenue growth and thereby keep its stock price high. When it became apparent that revenues were not growing as projected, Charter's management devised an accounting scheme that would artificially inflate its reported revenues. The scheme involved Charter's digital cable converter (set top) box suppliers, Scientific-Atlanta and Motorola. They agreed to overcharge Charter for the cable boxes in exchange for additional advertising on Charter's cable network. A group of investors, represented in this case by Stoneridge Investment Partners, sued Scientific-Atlanta and Motorola, alleging violation of Section 10(b) of the Securities Exchange Act of 1934 and of SEC Rule 10b-5. At trial, the district court dismissed the case. On appeal, the U.S. Court of Appeals for the Eighth Circuit upheld this ruling. Stoneridge then appealed to the United States Supreme Court.

ISSUE Can Charter investors sue third-party suppliers and customers (Scientific-Atlanta and Motorola) for participating in a scheme to overcharge Charter for cable boxes so that Charter could report inflated sales revenue figures?

a. Click on "2007 Term Opinions of the Court" and scroll down to "1/15/08" to access this case's opinion.

DECISION No. The United States Supreme Court affirmed the federal appellate court's decision that dismissed the case against Scientific-Atlanta and Motorola. Section 10(b)'s private right of action cannot be applied to a supplier or customer. Investors did not rely on Scientific-Atlanta's and Motorola's statements or representations.

REASON The Court pointed out that Scientific-Atlanta and Motorola had no role in preparing or disseminating Charter's financial statements. The financial statements of both Scientific-Atlanta and Motorola were correct. The $20 per cable set top box that they received from Charter was offset by their agreeing to spend the equivalent of $20 per cable set-top box in additional advertising. They "booked the transactions as a wash, under generally accepted accounting practices." To bring a Section 10(b) private action, the plaintiff must have relied on the defendant's deceptive acts. There has to be the "requisite causal connection between a defendant's misrepresentation and a plaintiff's injury" in order to assess liability against the defendant. But in this case, neither Scientific-Atlanta nor Motorola had a duty to disclose, and their deceptive acts were not communicated to the public. "No member of the investing public had knowledge, either actual or presumed, of [their] deceptive acts during the relevant times." Consequently, Stoneridge was unable to show reliance upon any of the actions of Scientific-Atlanta and Motorola "except in an indirect chain" that the Court found too remote to justify liability.

FOR CRITICAL ANALYSIS—Global Consideration *The Court noted that a ruling in favor of the investors bringing the suit would have had negative effects on foreign companies doing business within the United States. Explain the logic behind this line of reasoning.*

Tippee A person who receives inside information.

Tipper/Tippee Theory. Anyone who acquires inside information as a result of a corporate insider's breach of his or her fiduciary duty can be liable under SEC Rule 10b-5. This liability extends to **tippees** (those who receive "tips" from insiders) and even remote tippees (tippees of tippees).

The key to liability under this theory is that the inside information must be obtained as a result of someone's breach of a fiduciary duty to the corporation whose shares are involved in the trading. The tippee is liable under this theory only if (1) there is a breach of a duty not to disclose inside information, (2) the disclosure is in exchange for personal benefit, and (3) the tippee knows (or should know) of this breach and benefits from it.[21]

Misappropriation Theory. Liability for insider trading may also be established under the misappropriation theory. This theory holds that an individual who wrongfully obtains (misappropriates) inside information and trades on it for her or his personal gain should be held liable because, in essence, she or he stole information rightfully belonging to another.

21. See, for example, *Chiarella v. United States*, 445 U.S. 222, 100 S.Ct. 1108, 63 L.Ed.2d 348 (1980); and *Dirks v. SEC*, 463 U.S. 646, 103 S.Ct. 3255, 77 L.Ed.2d 911 (1983).

The misappropriation theory has been controversial because it significantly extends the reach of SEC Rule 10b-5 to outsiders who ordinarily would *not* be deemed fiduciaries of the corporations in whose stock they trade. The United States Supreme Court, however, has held that liability under SEC Rule 10b-5 can be based on the misappropriation theory.[22]

It is not always wrong to disclose material, nonpublic information about a company to another person. Nevertheless, a person who obtains the information and trades securities on it can be liable. **CASE EXAMPLE 31.7** Patricia Rocklage was the wife of Scott Rocklage, the chair and chief executive officer of Cubist Pharmaceuticals, Inc. Scott had sometimes disclosed material, nonpublic information about Cubist to Patricia, and she had always kept the information confidential. In December 2001, however, when Scott told Patricia that one of Cubist's key drugs had failed its clinical trial and reminded her not to tell anyone, Patricia refused to keep the information secret. She then warned her brother, William Beaver, who owned Cubist stock. William sold his 5,583 Cubist shares and tipped his friend David Jones, who sold his 7,500 shares.

On January 16, 2002, Cubist publicly announced the trial results, and the price of its stock dropped. William and David had avoided losses of $99,527 and $133,222, respectively, by selling when they did. The SEC filed a lawsuit against Patricia, William, and David, alleging insider trading. The defendants claimed that because Patricia had told Scott that she was going to tell William about the failed trial, they had not "misappropriated" the information. The court, however, determined that Patricia had "engaged in deceptive devices," because she "tricked her husband into revealing confidential information to her so that she could, and did, assist her brother with the sale of his Cubist stock." The court therefore found all three defendants guilty of insider trading under the misappropriation theory.[23] •

Short-Swing Profits Profits earned by a purchase and sale, or sale and purchase, of the same security within a six-month period; under Section 16(b) of the 1934 Securities Exchange Act, must be returned to the corporation if earned by company insiders from transactions in the company's stock.

ON THE WEB For information on investor protection, including answers to frequently asked questions on the topic of securities fraud, go to www.securitieslaw.com.

INSIDER REPORTING AND TRADING—SECTION 16(B) Section 16(b) of the 1934 act provides for the recapture by the corporation of all profits realized by an insider on any purchase and sale or sale and purchase of the corporation's stock within any six-month period.[24] It is irrelevant whether the insider actually uses inside information; *all such* **short-swing profits** *must be returned to the corporation.* In this context, *insiders* means officers, directors, and large stockholders of Section 12 corporations (those owning at least 10 percent of the class of equity securities registered under Section 12 of the 1934 act). To discourage such insiders from using nonpublic information about their companies for their personal benefit in the stock market, they must file reports with the SEC concerning their ownership and trading of the corporation's securities.

Section 16(b) applies not only to stock but also to warrants, options, and securities convertible into stock. In addition, the courts have fashioned complex rules for determining profits. Note that the SEC exempts a number of transactions under Rule 16b-3.[25] For all of these reasons, corporate insiders are wise to seek specialized counsel before trading in the corporation's stock. Exhibit 31–3 on the following page compares the effects of SEC Rule 10b-5 and Section 16(b).

Regulation of Proxy Statements

Section 14(a) of the Securities Exchange Act of 1934 regulates the solicitation of proxies (see Chapter 30) from shareholders of Section 12 companies. The SEC regulates the content of proxy statements. Whoever solicits a proxy must fully and accurately disclose in the proxy statement all of the facts that are pertinent to the matter on which the shareholders

22. *United States v. O'Hagan*, 521 U.S. 642, 117 S.Ct. 2199, 138 L.Ed.2d 724 (1997).
23. *SEC v. Rocklage*, 470 F.3d 1 (1st Cir. 2006).
24. A person who expects the price of a particular stock to decline can realize profits by "selling short"—selling at a high price and repurchasing later at a lower price to cover the "short sale."
25. 17 C.F.R. Section 240.16b-3.

Exhibit 31–3 Comparison of Coverage, Application, and Liability under SEC Rule 10b-5 and Section 16(b)

AREA OF COMPARISON	SEC RULE 10b-5	SECTION 16(b)
What is the subject matter of the transaction?	Any security (does not have to be registered).	Any security (does not have to be registered).
What transactions are covered?	Purchase or sale.	Short-swing purchase and sale or short-swing sale and purchase.
Who is subject to liability?	Almost anyone with inside information under a duty to disclose—including officers, directors, controlling shareholders, and tippees.	Officers, directors, and certain shareholders who own 10 percent or more.
Is omission or misrepresentation necessary for liability?	Yes.	No.
Are there any exempt transactions?	No.	Yes, there are a number of exemptions.
Who may bring an action?	A person transacting with an insider, the SEC, or a purchaser or seller damaged by a wrongful act.	A corporation or a shareholder by derivative action.

are to vote. SEC Rule 14a-9 is similar to the antifraud provisions of SEC Rule 10b-5. Remedies for violations are extensive, ranging from injunctions to prevent a vote from being taken to monetary damages.

Violations of the 1934 Act

As mentioned earlier, violations of Section 10(b) of the Securities Exchange Act of 1934 and SEC Rule 10b-5, including insider trading, may be subject to criminal or civil liability. For either criminal or civil sanctions to be imposed, however, *scienter* must exist—that is, the violator must have had an intent to defraud or knowledge of her or his misconduct (see Chapter 11). *Scienter* can be proved by showing that the defendant made false statements or wrongfully failed to disclose material facts.

Violations of Section 16(b) include the sale by insiders of stock acquired less than six months before the sale (or less than six months after the sale if selling short). These violations are subject to civil sanctions. Liability under Section 16(b) is strict liability. Neither *scienter* nor negligence is required.

When a company is held liable for a Section 10(b) violation, should its accounting firm also be held liable? Royal Ahold, N.V., a Dutch corporation, and its Maryland-based subsidiary, U.S. Foodservice, Inc. (USF), own and operate food service companies in the United States and elsewhere. From 1990 through 2003, Ahold perpetrated two frauds that resulted in its earnings being overstated by at least $500 million. Ahold and USF were later found liable for securities fraud, and Ahold shareholders brought a class-action suit against Deloitte & Touche, LLP, the accounting firm that had advised Ahold and USF.

One of Ahold's frauds had involved the accounting treatment of income from various joint ventures. Deloitte had been involved with Ahold since 1992 and had provided advice on the consolidation of the financial reports of joint ventures before the first venture was formed. None of Ahold's joint-venture agreements gave it the control necessary to consolidate their financial reports, but Ahold represented to Deloitte that it had sufficient control. Deloitte did not verify Ahold's control and only later discovered that Ahold's stake in the ventures was insufficient for consolidation. The second fraud involved USF's internal system for promotional allowances (PAs). Before Ahold had acquired USF in 2000, Deloitte performed a due diligence investigation and reported that USF's internal system for PAs was fraudulent and required a restatement of $11 million of PA income. In a 2001 audit, Deloitte reported that it "was unable to obtain supporting documentation" for some of the PA statistical samples. By 2003, Deloitte concluded that USF's system had been fraudulently inflating its PA income.

The class-action plaintiffs argued that Deloitte should be liable for the fraudulent accounting practices because of the "red flags" raised by the treatment of the joint-venture revenues and the PA income. The court, however, dismissed the suit. The court said that to establish liability for securities fraud, there must be evidence that leads to a strong inference of *scienter* on the part of the defendant. Here, such evidence was lacking. Instead, said the court, "the stronger and more plausible inference" is that the acountants "were, like the plaintiffs, victims of Ahold's fraud rather than its enablers."[26]

CRIMINAL PENALTIES For violations of Section 10(b) and Rule 10b-5, an individual may be fined up to $5 million, imprisoned for up to twenty years, or both. A partnership or a corporation may be fined up to $25 million. Under Section 807 of the Sarbanes-Oxley Act of 2002, for a *willful* violation of the 1934 act the violator may, in addition to being subject to a fine, be imprisoned for up to twenty-five years.

For a defendant to be convicted in a criminal prosecution under the securities laws, there can be no reasonable doubt that the defendant knew he or she was acting wrongfully—a jury is not allowed merely to speculate that the defendant may have acted willfully. **CASE EXAMPLE 31.8** Martha Stewart, founder of a well-known media and homemaking empire, was once charged with intentionally deceiving investors based on statements she made at a Martha Stewart Living Omnimedia (MSLO) conference. In December 2001, Stewart's stockbroker allegedly had informed Stewart that the head of ImClone Systems, Inc., was selling his shares in that company. Stewart then sold her ImClone shares. The next day, ImClone announced that the U.S. Food and Drug Administration had failed to approve Erbitux, the company's greatly anticipated medication.

The government began to investigate Stewart's ImClone trades, the media began to report on the investigation, and the value of MSLO stock began to fall. In June 2002, Stewart publicly stated at an MSLO conference that she had previously instructed her stockbroker to sell her ImClone stock if the price fell to $60 per share. The government filed a lawsuit and argued that Stewart's statement represented an intent to deceive because it was deliberately directed to investors at a time when she was aware that the negative publicity was affecting the market value of MSLO securities. The court, however, acquitted Stewart on this charge because "to find the essential element of criminal intent beyond a reasonable doubt, a rational juror would have to speculate."[27] Stewart was later convicted on other charges relating to her ImClone trading that did not require proof of intent. ●

CIVIL SANCTIONS The SEC can also bring suit in a federal district court against anyone violating or aiding in a violation of the 1934 act or SEC rules by purchasing or selling a security while in the possession of material nonpublic information.[28] The violation must occur on or through the facilities of a national securities exchange or from or through a broker or dealer. The court may assess a penalty for as much as triple the profits gained or the

26. *Public Employees' Retirement Association of Colorado v. Deloitte & Touche, LLP,* 551 F.3d 305 (4th Cir. 2009).
27. *United States v. Stewart,* 305 F.Supp.2d 368 (S.D.N.Y. 2004).
28. The Insider Trading Sanctions Act of 1984, 15 U.S.C. Section 78u(d)(2)(A).

loss avoided by the guilty party.[29] The Insider Trading and Securities Fraud Enforcement Act of 1988 enlarged the class of persons who may be subject to civil liability for insider trading and gave the SEC authority to give monetary rewards to informants.[30]

Private parties may also sue violators of Section 10(b) and Rule 10b-5. A private party may obtain rescission (cancellation) of a contract to buy securities or damages to the extent of the violator's illegal profits. Those found liable have a right to seek contribution from those who share responsibility for the violations, including accountants, attorneys, and corporations. For violations of Section 16(b), a corporation can bring an action to recover the short-swing profits.

Recall from Chapter 12 that a required element of fraud is reliance; the innocent party must justifiably have relied on the misrepresentation. If an investor is aware of misrepresentations by corporate management and purchases shares in the firm anyway, can the investor still bring a lawsuit against the corporation for a violation of Rule 10b-5? That was the question in the following case.

29. Profit or loss is defined as "the difference between the purchase or sale price of the security and the value of that security as measured by the trading price of the security at a reasonable period of time after public dissemination of the nonpublic information." 15 U.S.C. Section 78u(d)(2)(C).

30. 15 U.S.C. Section 78u-1.

Case 31.3 Stark Trading v. Falconbridge, Ltd.

United States Court of Appeals, Seventh Circuit, 552 F.3d 568 (2009).
www.ca7.uscourts.gov[a]

COMPANY PROFILE *Brian Stark's interest in investing began in high school when he worked for his father, an independent accountant. Together, they invested in the financial markets. Stark tested his own investment theories throughout college and law school, where he met Mike Roth. In 1992, Stark and Roth formed Stark Trading. Known today as Stark Investments (www.starkinvestments.com), the firm invests in commodities, real estate, equity, and other markets. Its principals apply hedging and portfolio management techniques on behalf of their investors, including institutions, investment funds, and wealthy individuals. The firm has offices in cities around the world, including Hong Kong, London, Singapore, and Toronto.*

In the first decade of the 2000s, many mining companies bought out their competitors.

FACTS Stark Trading was a minority shareholder in Falconbridge, Inc. Noranda, Inc., owned 59 percent of Falconbridge. Both were Canadian mining companies. Noranda offered its common stockholders preferred stock for their common stock. Noranda also offered to redeem the preferred stock for $25 per share, which exceeded the market value of the common stock. On the same day, Noranda offered minority shareholders in Falconbridge 1.77 shares of Noranda common stock for each share of Falconbridge common stock. Stark knew that Noranda's value was overstated in the offer to its common stockholders. Stark thought that the Falconbridge stock was undervalued in the market. This meant that Noranda was buying out Falconbridge's shareholders at a reduced price. Stark sent a letter explaining this to the Ontario Securities Commission. Nonetheless, Stark exchanged its Falconbridge shares for Noranda stock. Later, Noranda and Falconbridge merged to become Falconbridge, Ltd. Stark and others filed a suit in a federal district court against the new firm, alleging a violation of Rule 10b-5. The court dismissed the suit. The plaintiffs appealed.

a. In the left-hand column, click on "Opinions." On that page, in the "Case Number:" boxes, type "08" and "1327," and click on "List Case(s)." In the result, click on the appropriate link to access the opinion.

ISSUE Should the investors' claim under Rule 10b-5 be dismissed if the investors were not deceived by a purported dishonest tender offer?

DECISION Yes. The U.S. Court of Appeals for the Seventh Circuit upheld the lower court's decision. "So implausible is an inference of reliance from the complaint in this case * * * that the dismissal of the 10b-5 claim must be affirmed."

REASON A suit can be brought under Rule 10b-5 if a party buys stock at a price inflated by the misrepresentations of its issuer and sells the stock at a loss when the truth is revealed and the price drops. In this case, the plaintiffs argued that Noranda's offer to trade its stock for Falconbridge's stock inflated the value of Noranda's stock. But the plaintiffs were not fooled. As they explained in their letter to the Ontario Securities Commission, they were aware of what Noranda was trying to do. Thus, reliance is missing from the plaintiffs' claim for fraud as a violation of Rule 10b-5. "Sophisticated investors, they must have considered the combination of the tender offer and a later suit (this suit) against the defendants a better

Case 31.3–Continued

deal than holding on to their shares"–because Canadian law might have applied and would not have provided the same remedy as U.S. law–but "this is not a strategy that the courts should reward in the name of rectifying securities fraud."

FOR CRITICAL ANALYSIS—Global Consideration *Noranda and Falconbridge were Canadian companies. Falconbridge, Ltd., was later bought by Xstrata, a Swiss mining company. On what basis could a U.S. court exercise jurisdiction in this case?*

State Securities Laws

BE AWARE Federal securities laws do not take priority over state securities laws.

Today, every state has its own corporate securities laws, or "blue sky laws," that regulate the offer and sale of securities within its borders. (As mentioned in Chapter 11, the phrase *blue sky laws* dates to a 1917 decision by the United States Supreme Court in which the Court declared that the purpose of such laws was to prevent "speculative schemes which have no more basis than so many feet of 'blue sky.'")[31] Article 8 of the Uniform Commercial Code, which has been adopted by all of the states, also imposes various requirements relating to the purchase and sale of securities.

Requirements under State Securities Laws

Typically, state laws have disclosure requirements and antifraud provisions, many of which are patterned after Section 10(b) of the Securities Exchange Act of 1934 and SEC Rule 10b-5. State laws also provide for the registration of securities offered or issued for sale within the state and impose disclosure requirements. Methods of registration, required disclosures, and exemptions from registration vary among states. Unless an exemption from registration is applicable, issuers must register or qualify their stock with the appropriate state official, often called a *corporations commissioner.* Additionally, most state securities laws regulate securities brokers and dealers.

Concurrent Regulation

State securities laws apply mainly to intrastate transactions. Since the adoption of the 1933 and 1934 federal securities acts, the state and federal governments have regulated securities concurrently. Issuers must comply with both federal and state securities laws, and exemptions from federal law are not exemptions from state laws.

The dual federal and state system has not always worked well, particularly during the early 1990s, when the securities markets underwent considerable expansion. In response, Congress passed the National Securities Markets Improvement Act of 1996, which eliminated some of the duplicate regulations and gave the SEC exclusive power to regulate most national securities activities. The National Conference of Commissioners on Uniform State Laws then substantially revised the Uniform Securities Act to coordinate state and federal securities regulation and enforcement efforts. The new version was offered to the states for adoption in 2002. Seventeen states have adopted the Uniform Securities Act, and other states are considering adoption.[32]

31. *Hall v. Geiger-Jones Co.*, 242 U.S. 539, 37 S.Ct. 217, 61 L.Ed. 480 (1917).

32. At the time this book went to press, the Uniform Securities Act had been adopted in Georgia, Hawaii, Idaho, Indiana, Iowa, Kansas, Maine, Michigan, Minnesota, Mississippi, Missouri, New Mexico, Oklahoma, South Carolina, South Dakota, Vermont, and Wisconsin, as well as in the U.S. Virgin Islands. Adoption legislation was pending in Indiana and Washington State. You can find current information on state adoptions at www.nccusl.com.

Corporate Governance

Corporate Governance A set of policies or procedures affecting the way a corporation is directed or controlled.

Corporate governance can be narrowly defined as the relationship between a corporation and its shareholders. Some argue for a broader definition—that corporate governance specifies the rights and responsibilities among different participants in the corporation, such as the board of directors, managers, shareholders, and other stakeholders, and spells out the rules and procedures for making decisions on corporate affairs. Regardless of the way it is defined, effective corporate governance requires more than just compliance with laws and regulations. (For a discussion of corporate governance in other nations, see this chapter's *Beyond Our Borders* feature.)

Effective corporate governance is essential in large corporations because corporate ownership (by shareholders) is separated from corporate control (by officers and managers). Under these circumstances, officers and managers may attempt to advance their own interests at the expense of the shareholders. The well-publicized corporate scandals in the early 2000s clearly illustrate the reasons for concern about managerial opportunism.

Attempts at Aligning the Interests of Officers with Those of Shareholders

Stock Option A right to buy a given number of shares of stock at a set price, usually within a specified time period.

Some corporations have sought to align the financial interests of their officers with those of the company's shareholders by providing the officers with **stock options,** which enable them to purchase shares of the corporation's stock at a set price. When the market price rises above that level, the officers can sell their shares for a profit. Because a stock's market price generally increases as the corporation prospers, the options give the officers a financial stake in the corporation's well-being and supposedly encourage them to work hard for the benefit of the shareholders.

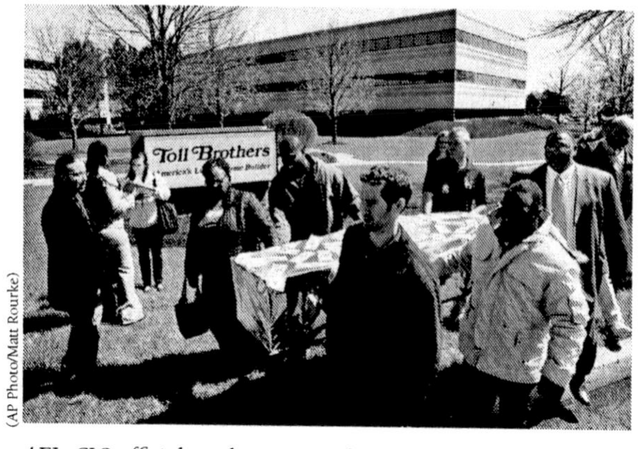

(AP Photo/Matt Rourke)

AFL-CIO officials and union members carry a decorated coffin as they conclude a mock funeral at the headquarters of Toll Brothers, Inc. The protesters were demonstrating against benefits and stock options granted to Toll Brothers, Inc., founding chairman and chief executive Robert Toll.

Options have turned out to be an imperfect device for providing effective governance, however. Executives in some companies have been tempted to "cook" the company's books in order to keep share prices higher so that they could sell their stock for a profit. Executives in other corporations have experienced no losses when share prices dropped; instead, their options were "repriced" so that they did not suffer from the share price decline and could still profit from future increases above the lowered share price. Thus, although stock options theoretically can motivate officers to protect shareholder interests, stock option plans have often become a way for officers to take advantage of shareholders.

With stock options generally failing to work as planned and numerous headline-making scandals occurring within major corporations, there has been an outcry for more "outside" directors (those with no formal employment affiliation with the company). The theory is that independent directors will more closely monitor the actions of corporate officers. Hence, today we see more boards with outside directors. Note, though, that outside directors may not be truly independent of corporate officers; they may be friends or business associates of the leading officers.

Corporate Governance and Corporate Law

Effective corporate governance standards are designed to address problems (such as those briefly discussed above) and to motivate officers to make decisions that promote the financial interests of the company's shareholders. Generally, corporate governance entails corporate decision-making structures that monitor employees (particularly officers) to ensure that they are acting for the benefit of the shareholders. Thus, corporate governance involves, at a minimum:

Beyond Our Borders — Corporate Governance in Other Nations

Corporate governance has become an issue of concern not only for U.S. corporations, but also for corporate entities around the world. With the globalization of business, a corporation's bad acts (or lack of control systems) can have far-reaching consequences. Different models of corporate governance exist, often depending on the degree of capitalism in the particular nation. In the United States, corporate governance tends to give priority to shareholders' interests. This approach encourages significant innovation and cost and quality competition. In contrast, the coordinated model of governance that prevails in continental Europe and Japan considers the interests of so-called stakeholders–employees, managers, suppliers, customers, and the community–to be a priority. The coordinated model still encourages innovation and cost and quality competition, but not to the same extent as the U.S. model.

For Critical Analysis

Why does the presence of a capitalist system affect a nation's perspective on corporate governance?

1. The audited reporting of financial progress at the corporation, so managers can be evaluated.
2. Legal protections for shareholders, so violators of the law, who attempt to take advantage of shareholders, can be punished for misbehavior and victims may recover damages for any associated losses.

The Practical Significance of Good Corporate Governance Effective corporate governance may have considerable practical significance. A study by researchers at Harvard University and the Wharton School of Business found that firms providing greater shareholder rights had higher profits, higher sales growth, higher firm value, and other economic advantages.[33] Thus, a corporation that provides better corporate governance in the form of greater accountability to investors may also have a higher valuation than a corporation that is less concerned about governance.

"Honesty is the single most important factor having a direct bearing on the final success of an individual, corporation, or product."

Ed McMahon, 1923–2009
(American entertainer)

Governance and Corporation Law Corporate governance is the essential purpose of corporation law in the United States. These statutes set up the legal framework for corporate governance. Under the corporate law of Delaware, where most major companies incorporate, all corporations must have in place certain structures of corporate governance. The key structure of corporate law is, of course, the board of directors.

The Board of Directors Some argue that shareholder democracy is key to improving corporate governance. If shareholders could vote on major corporate decisions, shareholders could presumably have more control over the corporation. Essential to shareholder democracy is the election of the board of directors, usually at the corporation's annual meeting. Under corporate law, a corporation must have a board of directors elected by the shareholders. Almost anyone can become a director, though some organizations, such as the New York Stock Exchange, require certain standards of service for directors of their listed corporations.

Directors are responsible for ensuring that the corporation's officers are operating wisely and in the exclusive interest of shareholders. The directors receive reports from the officers and give them managerial directions. In reality, though, corporate directors devote a relatively small amount of time to monitoring officers.

Ideally, shareholders would monitor the directors' supervision of the officers. As one leading board monitor commented, "Boards of directors are like subatomic particles—

33. Paul A. Gompers, Joy L. Ishii, and Andrew Metrick, "Corporate Governance and Equity Prices," *Quarterly Journal of Economics*, Vol. 118 (2003), p. 107.

they behave differently when they are observed." In practice, however, it can be difficult for shareholders to monitor directors and hold them responsible for corporate failings. Although the directors can be sued for failing to do their jobs effectively, directors are rarely held personally liable (as discussed in Chapter 30's *Ethical Issue* on page 759).

IMPORTANCE OF THE AUDIT COMMITTEE One crucial board committee is the *audit committee,* which oversees the corporation's accounting and financial reporting processes, including both internal and outside auditors. Unless the committee members have sufficient expertise and are willing to spend the time to carefully examine the corporation's bookkeeping methods, however, the audit committee may be ineffective.

The audit committee also oversees the corporation's "internal controls." These are the measures taken to ensure that reported results are accurate; they are carried out largely by the company's internal auditing staff. As an example, these controls help to determine whether a corporation's debts are collectible. If the debts are not collectible, it is up to the audit committee to make sure that the corporation's financial officers do not simply pretend that payment will eventually be made. (The *Linking the Law to Taxation* feature on pages 802 and 803 discusses how corporations, at least during the next few years, might benefit from *deleveraging,* or repurchasing, their debts.)

THE ROLE OF THE COMPENSATION COMMITTEE Another important committee of the board of directors is the *compensation committee.* This committee monitors and determines the compensation the company's officers are paid. As part of this process, it is responsible for assessing the officers' performance and for designing a compensation system that will better align the officers' interests with those of shareholders.

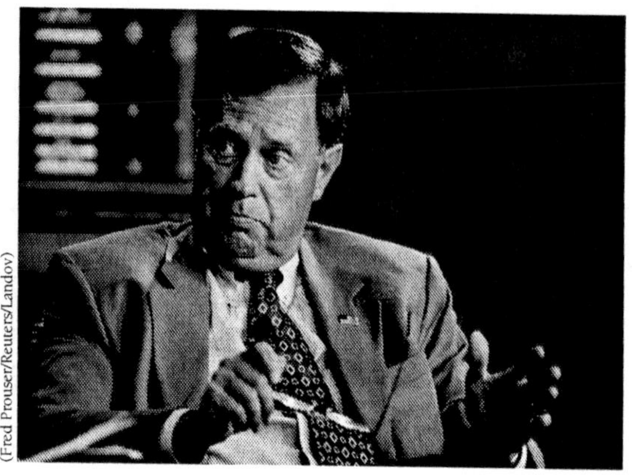

(Fred Prouser/Reuters/Landov)

Michael Oxley is a former member of the U.S. House of Representatives and vice president of NASDAQ, the over-the-counter stock exchange. When in Congress, he cosponsored legislation that imposed large compliance costs on publicly held companies. What is the name of that legislation?

The Sarbanes-Oxley Act of 2002

As discussed in Chapter 8, in 2002 following a series of corporate scandals, Congress passed the Sarbanes-Oxley Act. The act separately addresses certain issues relating to corporate governance. Generally, the act attempts to increase corporate accountability by imposing strict disclosure requirements and harsh penalties for violations of securities laws. Among other things, the act requires chief corporate executives to take responsibility for the accuracy of financial statements and reports that are filed with the SEC.

Additionally, the act requires that certain financial and stock-transaction reports be filed with the SEC earlier than was required under the previous rules. The act also created a new entity, called the Public Company Accounting Oversight Board, which regulates and oversees public accounting firms. Other provisions of the act establish private civil actions and expand the SEC's remedies in administrative and civil actions.

Because of the importance of this act for corporate leaders and for those dealing with securities transactions, we present excerpts and explanatory comments in Appendix D at the end of this text. We also highlight some of its key provisions relating to corporate accountability in Exhibit 31–4.

MORE INTERNAL CONTROLS AND ACCOUNTABILITY The Sarbanes-Oxley Act includes some traditional securities law provisions but also introduces direct *federal* corporate governance requirements for public companies (companies whose shares are traded in the public securities markets). The law addresses many of the corporate governance procedures just discussed and creates new requirements in an attempt to make the system work more effectively. The requirements deal with independent monitoring of company officers by both the board of directors and auditors.

Exhibit 31–4 Some Key Provisions of the Sarbanes-Oxley Act of 2002 Relating to Corporate Accountability

Certification Requirements—Under Section 906 of the Sarbanes-Oxley Act, the chief executive officers (CEOs) and chief financial officers (CFOs) of most major companies listed on public stock exchanges must certify financial statements that are filed with the SEC. CEOs and CFOs have to certify that filed financial reports "fully comply" with SEC requirements and that all of the information reported "fairly represents in all material respects, the financial conditions and results of operations of the issuer."

Under Section 302 of the act, CEOs and CFOs of reporting companies are required to certify that a signing officer reviewed each quarterly and annual filing with the SEC and that it contains no untrue statements of material fact. Also, the signing officer or officers must certify that they have established an internal control system to identify all material information and that any deficiencies in the system were disclosed to the auditors.

Loans to Directors and Officers—Section 402 prohibits any reporting company, as well as any private company that is filing an initial public offering, from making personal loans to directors and executive officers (with a few limited exceptions, such as for certain consumer and housing loans).

Protection for Whistleblowers—Section 806 protects "whistleblowers"—employees who report ("blow the whistle" on) securities violations by their employers—from being fired or in any way discriminated against by their employers.

Blackout Periods—Section 306 prohibits certain types of securities transactions during "blackout periods"—periods during which the issuer's ability to purchase, sell, or otherwise transfer funds in individual account plans (such as pension funds) is suspended.

Enhanced Penalties for—

- *Violations of Section 906 Certification Requirements*—A CEO or CFO who certifies a financial report or statement filed with the SEC knowing that the report or statement does not fulfill all of the requirements of Section 906 will be subject to criminal penalties of up to $1 million in fines, ten years in prison, or both. *Willful* violators of the certification requirements may be subject to $5 million in fines, twenty years in prison, or both.
- *Violations of the Securities Exchange Act of 1934*—Penalties for securities fraud under the 1934 act were also increased (as discussed earlier in this chapter). Individual violators may be fined up to $5 million, imprisoned for up to twenty years, or both. *Willful* violators may be imprisoned for up to twenty-five years in addition to being fined.
- *Destruction or Alteration of Documents*—Anyone who alters, destroys, or conceals documents or otherwise obstructs any official proceeding will be subject to fines, imprisonment for up to twenty years, or both.
- *Other Forms of White-Collar Crime*—The act stiffened the penalties for certain criminal violations, such as federal mail and wire fraud, and ordered the U.S. Sentencing Commission to revise the sentencing guidelines for white-collar crimes (see Chapter 6).

Statute of Limitations for Securities Fraud—Section 804 provides that a private right of action for securities fraud may be brought no later than two years after the discovery of the violation or five years after the violation, whichever is earlier.

Sections 302 and 404 of Sarbanes-Oxley require high-level managers (the most senior officers) to establish and maintain an effective system of internal controls. Moreover, senior management must reassess the system's effectiveness annually. Some companies already had strong and effective internal control systems in place before the passage of the act, but others had to take expensive steps to bring their internal controls up to the new federal standard. These include "disclosure controls and procedures" to ensure that company financial reports are accurate and timely. Assessment must involve the documenting of financial results and accounting policies before reporting the results. After the act was passed, hundreds of companies reported that they had identified and corrected shortcomings in their internal control systems.

Certification and Monitoring Requirements Section 906 requires that chief executive officers (CEOs) and chief financial officers (CFOs) certify that the information in the corporate financial statements "fairly represents in all material respects, the financial conditions and results of operations of the issuer." These corporate officers are subject to both civil and criminal penalties for violation of this section. This requirement makes officers directly accountable for the accuracy of their financial reporting and avoids any "ignorance defense" if shortcomings are later discovered.

Sarbanes-Oxley also includes requirements to improve directors' monitoring of officers' activities. All members of the corporate audit committee for public companies must be outside directors. The New York Stock Exchange (NYSE) has a similar rule that also extends to the board's compensation committee. The audit committee must have a written charter that sets out its duties and provides for performance appraisal. At least one "financial expert" must serve on the audit committee, which must hold executive meetings without company officers being present. The audit committee must establish procedures to encourage "whistleblowers" to report violations. In addition to reviewing the internal controls, the committee also monitors the actions of the outside auditor.

Online Securities Fraud

A major problem facing the SEC today is how to enforce the antifraud provisions of the securities laws in the online environment. In 1999, in the first cases involving illegal online securities offerings, the SEC filed suit against three individuals for illegally offering securities on an Internet auction site.[34] In essence, all three indicated that their companies would go public soon and attempted to sell unregistered securities via the Web auction site. All of these actions were in violation of Sections 5, 17(a)(1), and 17(a)(3) of the 1933 Securities Act. Since then, the SEC has brought a variety of Internet-related fraud cases and regularly issues interpretive releases to explain how securities laws apply in the online environment.

Investment Scams

"Make money your God and it will plague you like the devil."

Henry Fielding, 1707–1754
(English author)

An ongoing problem is how to curb online investment scams. As discussed in Chapter 7, the Internet has created a new vehicle for criminals to use to commit fraud and has provided them with new ways of targeting innocent investors. The criminally inclined can use spam, online newsletters and bulletin boards, chat rooms, blogs, and tweets to spread false information and perpetrate fraud. For a relatively small cost, criminals can even build sophisticated Web pages to facilitate their investment scams.

There are countless variations of investment scams, most of which promise spectacular returns for small investments. A person might receive spam e-mail, for example, that falsely claims the earnings potential of a home business can "turn $5 into $60,000 in just three to six weeks." Another popular investment scam claims "your stimulus package has arrived" and promises you can make $100,000 a year using your home computer. Although most people today are dubious of the bogus claims made in spam messages, such offers can be more attractive during times of economic recession. Often, investment scams are simply the electronic version of pyramid schemes in which the participants attempt to profit solely by recruiting new participants.

Online Investment Newsletters and Forums

Hundreds of online investment newsletters provide free information on stocks. Legitimate online newsletters can help investors gather valuable information, but some of these newsletters are used for fraud. The law allows companies to pay people who write these newsletters to tout their securities, but the newsletters are required to disclose who paid for the advertising. Many fraudsters either fail to disclose or lie about who paid them. Thus, an investor reading an online newsletter may believe that the information is unbiased, when in fact the fraudsters will directly profit by convincing investors to buy or sell particular stocks.

---

34. *In re Davis,* SEC Administrative File No. 3-10080 (October 20, 1999); *In re Haas,* SEC Administrative File No. 3-10081 (October 20, 1999); *In re Sitaras,* SEC Administrative File No. 3-10082 (October 20, 1999).

The same deceptive tactics can be used on online bulletin boards (such as newsgroups and usenet groups), blogs, and social networking sites, including Twitter. While hiding their true identity, fraudsters may falsely pump up a company or reveal some "inside" information about a new product or lucrative contract to convince people to invest. By using multiple aliases on an online forum, a single person can easily create the illusion of widespread interest in a small stock.

Ponzi Schemes

In recent years, the SEC has filed an increasing number of enforcement actions against perpetrators of Ponzi schemes. In these scams, named after swindler Charles Ponzi, the fraudster promises high returns to investors and then uses their funds to pay previous investors.

OFFSHORE FRAUD Ponzi schemes sometimes target U.S. residents and convince them to invest in offshore companies or banks. **EXAMPLE 31.9** In 2009, Texas billionaire R. Allen Stanford, of the Stanford Financial Group, was indicted for allegedly orchestrating a $7 billion scheme to defraud more than five thousand investors. For about ten years, Stanford advised clients to buy certificates of deposit with improbably high interest rates from his Antigua-based Stanford International Bank. Some early investors were paid returns from the funds provided by later investors, but Stanford allegedly used $1.6 billion of the funds for personal purchases. He also falsified financial statements that were filed with the SEC and reportedly paid more than $100,000 in bribes to an Antigua official to ensure that the bank would not be audited. ●

"RISK-FREE" FRAUD Another type of online fraud scheme offers risk-free or low-risk investments to lure investors. **CASE EXAMPLE 31.10** Michael C. Regan used his firm, Regan & Company, to fraudulently obtain at least $15.9 million from dozens of investors by selling securities in his River Stream Fund. Regan told investors that he had a "proven track record" of successful securities trading and showed them falsified account statements and tax returns that showed artificially high account balances.

In reality, Regan was not a registered investment adviser, had not traded any securities for several years, and had suffered substantial losses on investments he did make. Regan promised investors returns averaging 20 percent with minimal risk to their principal and claimed to be using an investment strategy based on "short-term price trends." He used less than half of the funds entrusted to him for trading purposes and spent at least $2.4 million for his personal and family expenses. In 2009, the SEC filed a complaint alleging that Regan and his company had engaged in a multimillion-dollar Ponzi scheme. Regan agreed to settle the case and return more than $8.7 million (plus interest) of the wrongfully acquired funds.[35] ●

Hacking into Online Stock Accounts

Millions of people now buy and sell investments online through online brokerage companies such as E*Trade and TD Ameritrade. Sophisticated hackers have learned to use online investing to their advantage. By installing keystroke-monitoring software on computer terminals in public places, such as hotels, libraries, and airports, hackers can gain access to online account information. All they have to do is wait for a person to access an online trading account and then monitor the next several dozen keystrokes to determine the customer's account number and password. Once they have the log-in information, they can access the customer's account and liquidate her or his existing stock holdings.

35. You can read the SEC's complaint against Regan at www.sec.gov/litigation/complaints/2009/comp21102.pdf.

The hackers then use the customer's funds to purchase thinly traded, microcap securities, also known as penny stocks. The goal is to boost the price of a stock that the hacker has already purchased at a lower price. Then, when the stock price goes up, the hacker sells all the stock and wires the funds to either an offshore account or a dummy corporation, making it difficult for the SEC to trace the transactions and prosecute the offender.

EXAMPLE 31.11 Aleksey Kamardin, a twenty-one-year-old Florida college student, purchased 55,000 shares of stock in Fuego Entertainment using an E*Trade account in his own name. Kamardin then hacked into other customers' accounts at E*Trade, TD Ameritrade, Charles Schwab, and other brokerage companies, and used their funds to purchase a total of 458,000 shares of Fuego stock. When the stock price rose from $0.88 per share to $1.28 per share, Kamardin sold all of his shares of Fuego, making a profit of $9,164.28 in about three hours. Kamardin did this with other thinly traded stocks as well, allegedly making $82,960 in about five weeks. The SEC filed charges against him in 2007, and he was later ordered to return the profits, plus interest.[36] ●

36. You can read about the judgment against Kamardin by going to the SEC's Web site at www.sec.gov, clicking on the link to litigation releases, and selecting "LR-20190."

Reviewing . . . Investor Protection, Insider Trading, and Corporate Governance

Dale Emerson served as the chief financial officer for Reliant Electric Company, a distributor of electricity serving portions of Montana and North Dakota. Reliant was in the final stages of planning a takeover of Dakota Gasworks, Inc., a natural gas distributor that operated solely within North Dakota. Emerson went on a weekend fishing trip with his uncle, Ernest Wallace. Emerson mentioned to Wallace that he had been putting in a lot of extra hours at the office planning a takeover of Dakota Gasworks. When he returned from the fishing trip, Wallace purchased $20,000 worth of Reliant stock. Three weeks later, Reliant made a tender offer to Dakota Gasworks stockholders and purchased 57 percent of Dakota Gasworks stock. Over the next two weeks, the price of Reliant stock rose 72 percent before leveling out. Wallace then sold his Reliant stock for a gross profit of $14,400. Using the information presented in the chapter, answer the following questions.

1. Would registration with the SEC be required for Dakota Gasworks securities? Why or why not?
2. Did Emerson violate Section 10(b) of the Securities Exchange Act of 1934 and SEC Rule 10b-5? Why or why not?
3. What theory or theories might a court use to hold Wallace liable for insider trading?
4. Under the Sarbanes-Oxley Act of 2002, who would be required to certify the accuracy of financial statements filed with the SEC?

Linking the Law *to Taxation*

The Tax Consequences of Deleveraging during an Economic Crisis

Part of corporate governance involves making sure that the corporation effectively examines trade-offs involved in any future action. When corporate boards or upper management makes decisions, those decisions affect employees, customers, and shareholders. In a time of economic crisis, *deleveraging,* or repurchasing debt, is one possible action that a corporation may take to reduce its debt.

Why Companies Leverage

Corporations engage in leveraging—borrowing on a large scale in order to make additional investments—particularly in boom times. Leverage in capital structure is neither good nor bad. Companies in volatile industries avoid taking on too much debt, but other companies have found that debt is an important part of their capital structure. In any event, corporations have to be flexible in their ratio of debt to equity as market conditions change.

Recessions, such as the one that may still be going on as you read this, create uncertainty. Uncertainty is the enemy of capital markets. Formerly routine credit transactions become unavailable, even to solvent firms, and companies that have leveraged—have large debt loads—may find that credit has disappeared altogether. Suppliers may refuse to ship goods to such corporations unless they agree to pay cash on delivery. This pessimism ripples through the economy. Today, not only have auto manufacturers suffered, but so too have community hospitals, restaurants, hotels, and a host of firms in other industries.

The Downside of Deleveraging

Many corporations' publicly traded debt instruments have been selling at very deep discounts. One way for a company to improve its balance sheet and to reassure suppliers that it will be able to pay its bills is to retire that debt (at deep discounts). Some corporations could do this by issuing additional shares of stock to obtain the financing for such debt retirement. Moreover, repurchasing corporate debt may be a beneficial use of cash for corporations when consumer demand slows and alternative capital investments do not offer immediate returns.

Until 2009, however, corporate finance officers faced a daunting cost for such debt retirement plans. Under tax code and regulatory changes made in the 1980s, the difference between the original issue price of debt and the lower price for which it was repurchased was treated as taxable income. Finance managers call this a tax liability on "phantom income" (calculated as the difference between the issued price and the repurchase price of corporate debt). Such tax liabilities have prevented many corporations from necessary capital restructuring. Additionally, the tax liability on phantom income helped to create a perverse preference for bankruptcy. To avoid the tax liability, a heavily leveraged firm might choose bankruptcy over debt retirement even though bankruptcy destroys asset values, customer relations, and, most of all, jobs.

A New Tax Incentive for Finance Managers to Consider

In 2009, as part of the economic stimulus bill, the Obama administration created a new tax break that applies to the retirement of heavily discounted debt instruments by corporations. Under this provision, tax liabilities on phantom income will not trigger corporate income taxes until 2014. At that time, corporations that have retired discounted debt will be able to spread out their tax liabilities over a five-year period.

Immediately, homebuilder Hovnanian Enterprises paid $105 million to repurchase $315 million of its unsecured debt. That $210 million of phantom income will not be taxable until 2014. At about the same time, GE Capital, a unit of General Electric, offered to buy back $1.46 billion of its bonds.

FOR CRITICAL ANALYSIS

If you were a finance manager in a large corporation, under what circumstances might you argue that the corporation should deleverage?

Key Terms

accredited investor 784
corporate governance 796
free-writing prospectus 782
insider trading 787
investment company 784
investment contract 779
mutual fund 784
prospectus 781
SEC Rule 10b-5 786
security 778
short-swing profits 791
stock option 796
tippee 790

Chapter Summary: Investor Protection, Insider Trading, and Corporate Governance

Securities Act of 1933 (See pages 779–786.)	Prohibits fraud and stabilizes the securities industry by requiring disclosure of all essential information relating to the issuance of securities to the investing public. 1. *Registration requirements*—Securities, unless exempt, must be registered with the SEC before being offered to the public. The *registration statement* must include detailed financial information about the issuing corporation; the intended use of the proceeds of the securities being issued; and certain disclosures, such as interests of directors or officers and pending lawsuits. 2. *Prospectus*—The issuer must provide investors with a *prospectus* that describes the security being sold, the issuing corporation, and the risk attaching to the security.

Continued

Chapter Summary: Investor Protection, Insider Trading, and Corporate Governance—Continued

Securities Act of 1933—Continued	3. *Exemptions*—The SEC has exempted certain offerings from the requirements of the Securities Act of 1933. Exemptions may be determined on the basis of the size of the issue, whether the offering is private or public, and whether advertising is involved. Exemptions are summarized in Exhibit 31–1 on page 783.
Securities Exchange Act of 1934 (See pages 786–795.)	Provides for the regulation and registration of securities exchanges, brokers, dealers, and national securities associations (such as the NASD). Maintains a continuous disclosure system for all corporations with securities on the securities exchanges and for those companies that have assets in excess of $10 million and five hundred or more shareholders (Section 12 companies). 1. *SEC Rule 10b-5 [under Section 10(b) of the 1934 act]*— a. Applies to almost all trading of securities—a firm's securities do not have to be registered under the 1933 act for the 1934 act to apply. b. Applies only when the requisites of federal jurisdiction (such as use of the mails, stock exchange facilities, or any facility of interstate commerce) are present. c. Applies to insider trading by corporate officers, directors, majority shareholders, and any persons receiving inside information (information not available to the public) who base their trading on this information. d. Liability for violations can be civil or criminal. e. May be violated by failing to disclose "material facts" that must be disclosed under this rule. f. Liability may be based on the tipper/tippee or the misappropriation theory. 2. *Insider trading [under Section 16(b) of the 1934 act]*—To prevent corporate insiders from taking advantage of inside information, the 1934 act requires officers, directors, and shareholders owning 10 percent or more of the issued stock of a corporation to turn over to the corporation all short-term profits (called *short-swing profits*) realized from the purchase and sale or sale and purchase of corporate stock within any six-month period. 3. *Regulation of proxies*—The SEC regulates the content of proxy statements sent to shareholders of Section 12 companies. Section 14(a) is essentially a disclosure law, with provisions similar to the antifraud provisions of SEC Rule 10b-5.
State Securities Laws (See page 795.)	All states have corporate securities laws *(blue sky laws)* that regulate the offer and sale of securities within state borders; these laws are designed to prevent "speculative schemes which have no more basis than so many feet of 'blue sky.'" States regulate securities concurrently with the federal government. The Uniform Securities Act of 2002, which has been adopted by seventeen states and is being considered by several others, is designed to promote coordination and reduce duplication between state and federal securities regulation.
Corporate Governance (See pages 796–800.)	1. *Definition*—Corporate governance is the system by which business corporations are governed, including policies and procedures for making decisions on corporate affairs. 2. *The need for corporate governance*—Corporate governance is necessary in large corporations because corporate ownership (by the shareholders) is separated from corporate control (by officers and managers). This separation of corporate ownership and control can often result in conflicting interests. Corporate governance standards address such issues. 3. *Sarbanes-Oxley Act of 2002*—This act attempts to increase corporate accountability by imposing strict disclosure requirements and harsh penalties for violations of securities laws.
Online Securities Fraud (See pages 800–802.)	A major problem facing the SEC today is how to enforce the antifraud provisions of the securities laws in the online environment. Internet-related forms of securities fraud include numerous types of investment scams, Ponzi schemes, pumping and dumping, and hacking into online trading accounts.

ExamPrep

ISSUE SPOTTERS

1 When a corporation wishes to issue certain securities, it must provide sufficient information for an unsophisticated investor to evaluate the financial risk involved. Specifically, the law imposes liability for making a false statement or omission that is "material." What sort of information would an investor consider material?

2 Lee is an officer of Magma Oil, Inc. Lee knows that a Magma geologist has just discovered a new deposit of oil. Can Lee take advantage of this information to buy and sell Magma stock? Why or why not?

BEFORE THE TEST

Check your answers to the Issue Spotters, and at the same time, take the interactive quiz for this chapter. Go to www.cengage.com/blaw/blt and click on "Chapter 31." First, click on "Answers to Issue Spotters" to check your answers. Next, click on "Interactive Quiz" to assess your mastery of the concepts in this chapter. Then click on "Flashcards" to review this chapter's Key Term definitions.

For Review

Answers for the even-numbered questions in this For Review section can be found on this text's accompanying Web site at www.cengage.com/blaw/blt. ***Select "Chapter 31" and click on "For Review."***

1 What is meant by the term *securities?*
2 What are the two major statutes regulating the securities industry?
3 What is insider trading? Why is it prohibited?
4 What are some of the features of state securities laws?
5 What certification requirements does the Sarbanes-Oxley Act impose on corporate executives?

Hypothetical Scenarios and Case Problems

31–1 **Registration Requirements.** Langley Brothers, Inc., a corporation incorporated and doing business in Kansas, decides to sell common stock worth $1 million to the public. The stock will be sold only within the state of Kansas. Joseph Langley, the chairman of the board, says the offering need not be registered with the Securities and Exchange Commission. His brother, Harry, disagrees. Who is right? Explain.

31–2 **Hypothetical Question with Sample Answer** Huron Corp. has 300,000 common shares outstanding. The owners of these outstanding shares live in several different states. Huron has decided to split the 300,000 shares two for one. Will Huron Corp. have to file a registration statement and prospectus on the 300,000 new shares to be issued as a result of the split? Explain.

—For a sample answer to Question 31–2, go to Appendix E at the end of this text.

31–3 **Insider Trading.** David Gain was chief executive officer (CEO) of Forest Media Corp., which became interested in acquiring RS Communications, Inc., in 2010. To initiate negotiations, Gain met with RS's CEO, Gill Raz, on Friday, July 12. Two days later, Gain phoned his brother Mark, who, on Monday, bought 3,800 shares of RS stock. Mark discussed the deal with their father, Jordan, who bought 20,000 RS shares on Thursday. On July 25, the day before the RS bid was due, Gain phoned his parents' home, and Mark bought another 3,200 RS shares. The same routine was followed over the next few days, with Gain periodically phoning Mark or Jordan, both of whom continued to buy RS shares. Forest's bid was refused, but on August 5, RS announced its merger with another company. The price of RS stock rose 30 percent, increasing the value of Mark and Jordan's shares by $664,024 and $412,875, respectively. Did Gain engage in insider trading? What is required to impose sanctions for this offense? Could a court hold Gain liable? Why or why not?

31–4 **Securities Trading.** Between 1994 and 1998, Richard Svoboda, a credit officer for NationsBank N.A., in Dallas, Texas, evaluated and approved his employer's extensions of credit to clients. These responsibilities gave Svoboda access to nonpublic information about the clients' earnings, performance, acquisitions, and business plans in confidential memos, e-mail, credit applications, and other sources. Svoboda devised a scheme with Michael Robles, an independent accountant, to use this information to trade securities. Pursuant to their scheme, Robles traded in the securities of more than twenty different companies and profited by more than $1 million. Svoboda also executed trades for his own profit of more than $200,000, despite their agreement that Robles would do all of the trading. Aware that their scheme violated NationsBank's policy, they attempted to conduct their trades to avoid suspicion. When NationsBank questioned Svoboda about his actions, he lied, refused to cooperate, and was fired. Did Svoboda or Robles commit any crimes? Are they subject to civil liability? If so, who could file a suit and on what ground? What are the possible sanctions? What might be a defense? How should a court rule? Discuss. [*SEC v. Svoboda*, 409 F.Supp.2d 331 (S.D.N.Y. 2006)]

31–5 **Case Problem with Sample Answer** In 1997, WTS Transnational, Inc., required financing to develop a prototype of an unpatented fingerprint-verification system. At the time, WTS had no revenue, $655,000 in liabilities, and only $10,000 in assets. Thomas Cavanagh and Frank Nicolois, who operated an investment banking company called U.S. Milestone (USM), arranged the financing using Curbstone Acquisition Corp. Curbstone had no assets but had registered approximately 3.5 million shares of stock with the Securities and Exchange Commission (SEC). Under the terms of the deal, Curbstone acquired WTS, and the resulting entity was named Electro-Optical Systems Corp. (EOSC). New EOSC shares were issued to all of the WTS shareholders. Only Cavanagh and others affiliated with USM could sell EOSC stock to the public, however. Over the next few months, these individuals issued false press releases, made small deceptive purchases of EOSC shares at high prices, distributed hundreds of thousands of shares to friends and relatives, and sold their own shares at inflated prices through third party companies they owned. When the SEC began to investigate, the share price fell to its actual value, and innocent investors lost more than $15 million. Were any securities laws violated in this case? If so, what might be an appropriate remedy? [*SEC v. Cavanagh*, 445 F.3d 105 (2d Cir. 2006)]

—**After you have answered Problem 31–5, compare your answer with the sample answer given on the Web site that accompanies this text. Go to www.cengage.com/blaw/blt, select "Chapter 31," and click on "Case Problem with Sample Answer."**

31–6 **Duty to Disclose.** Orphan Medical, Inc., was a pharmaceutical company that focused on central nervous system disorders. Its major product was the drug Xyrem. In June 2004, Orphan merged with Jazz, and Orphan shareholders received $10.75 per share for their stock. Before the merger was final, Orphan completed a phase of testing of Xyrem that indicated that the U.S. Food and Drug Administration (FDA) would allow the drug to go to the next stage of testing, which was necessary for the drug to be widely marketed. If that happened, the value of the drug and Orphan would go up, and the stock would have been worth more than $10.75. Little Gem Life Sciences, LLC, was an Orphan shareholder that received $10.75 a share. It sued, claiming violations of federal securities laws because shareholders were not told, during the merger process, that the current stage of FDA tests had been successful. Little Gem claimed that if the information had been public, the stock price would have been higher. The district court dismissed the suit, holding that it did not meet the standards required by the Private Securities Litigation Reform Act. Little Gem appealed. Did Orphan's directors have a duty to reveal all relevant drug-testing information to shareholders? Why or why not? [*Little Gem Life Sciences, LLC v. Orphan Medical, Inc.*, 537 F.3d 913 (8th Cir. 2008)]

31–7 **Violations of the 1934 Act.** To comply with accounting principles, a company that engages in software development must either "expense" the cost (record it immediately on the company's financial statement) or "capitalize" it (record it as a cost incurred in increments over time). If the project is in the pre- or post-development stage, the cost must be expensed. Otherwise it may be capitalized. Capitalizing a cost makes a company look more profitable in the short term. Digimarc Corp., which provides secure personal identification documents such as drivers' licenses using digital watermark technology, announced that it had improperly capitalized software development costs over at least the previous eighteen months. The errors resulted in $2.7 million in overstated earnings, requiring a restatement of prior financial statements. Zucco Partners, LLC, which had bought Digimarc stock within the relevant period, filed a suit in a federal district court against the firm. Zucco claimed that it could show that there had been disagreements within Digimarc over its accounting. Is this sufficient to establish a violation of SEC Rule 10b-5? Why or why not? [*Zucco Partners, LLC v. Digimarc Corp.*, 552 F.3d 981 (9th Cir. 2009)]

31–8 **A Question of Ethics** *Melvin Lyttle told John Montana and Paul Knight about a "Trading Program" that purportedly would buy and sell securities in deals that were fully insured, as well as monitored and controlled by the Federal Reserve Board. Without checking the details or even verifying whether the Program existed, Montana and Knight, with Lyttle's help, began to sell interests in the Program to investors. For a minimum investment of $1 million, the investors were promised extraordinary rates of return—from 10 percent to as much as 100 percent per week—without risk. They were told, among other things, that the Program would "utilize banks that can ensure full bank integrity of The Transaction whose undertaking[s] are in complete harmony with international banking rules and protocol and who [sic] guarantee maximum security of a Funder's Capital Placement Amount." Nothing was required but the investors' funds and their silence—the Program was to be kept secret. Over a four-month period in 1999, Montana raised approximately $23 million from twenty-two investors. The promised gains did not accrue, however. Instead, Montana, Lyttle, and Knight depleted the investors' funds in high-risk trades or spent the funds on themselves. [*SEC v. Montana, *464 F.Supp.2d 772 (S.D.Ind. 2006)]*

1 The Securities and Exchange Commission (SEC) filed a suit in a federal district court against Montana and the others, seeking an injunction, civil penalties, and disgorgement with interest. The SEC alleged, among other things, violations of Section 10(b) of the Securities Exchange Act of 1934 and SEC Rule 10b-5. What is required to establish a violation of these laws? Explain how and why the facts in this case meet, or fail to meet, these requirements.

2 It is often remarked, "There's a sucker born every minute!" Does that phrase describe the Program's investors? Ultimately, about half of the investors recouped the amount they invested. Should the others be considered at least partly responsible for their own losses? Why or why not?

Critical Thinking and Writing Assignments

31–9 **Critical Thinking and Writing Assignment for Business.** Insider trading, as you learned, is illegal. Not everyone agrees that it should be, though. A small group of legal scholars believes that insider trading should be completely legal. They argue that if insider trading was more widespread, it would cause stock prices to adjust almost instantly to new information. They further argue that insiders, if able to make profits from insider trading, would therefore accept lower salaries and benefits.

1 Why is insider trading illegal in the first place? Who is supposed to be protected and why?

2 What is wrong with the argument advanced by the legal scholars who want insider trading made legal? Or are they right? Explain your answer.

31–10 **Case Analysis Question** Go to Appendix F at the end of this text and examine Case No. 6 [*Merrill Lynch, Pierce, Fenner & Smith, Inc. v. Dabit,* 547 U.S. 71, 126 S.Ct. 1503, 164 L.Ed.2d 179 (2006)]. This case has been excerpted there in great detail. Review and then brief the case, making sure that your brief answers the following questions.

1 **Issue:** The dispute in this case centered on whether a certain federal statute covered the claims of a certain class of investors who had allegedly been the victims of fraud. What was the statute, who were the investors, and how were they allegedly defrauded?

2 **Rule of Law:** On what "requisite showing" did the United States Supreme Court base its decision?

3 **Applying the Rule of Law:** What were the reasons for the Court's conclusion? What rule of statutory interpretation supported this reasoning? How did the purpose of the statute influence its application?

4 **Conclusion:** How did the Court's ruling affect the investors' claims?

31–11 **Video Question Go to this text's Web site at www.cengage.com/blaw/blt and select "Chapter 31." Click on "Video Questions" and view the video titled *Mergers and Acquisitions*. Then answer the following questions.**

1 Analyze whether the purchase of Onyx Advertising is a material fact that the Quigley Company had a duty to disclose under SEC Rule 10b-5.

2 Does it matter whether Quigley personally knew about or authorized the company spokesperson's statements? Why or why not?

3 Who else might be able to bring a suit against the Quigley Company for insider trading under SEC Rule 10b-5?

Practical Internet Exercises

Go to this text's Web site at www.cengage.com/blaw/blt, select "Chapter 31," and click on "Practical Internet Exercises." There you will find the following Internet research exercises that you can perform to learn more about the topics covered in this chapter.

Practical Internet Exercise 31–1: LEGAL PERSPECTIVE—Electronic Delivery

Practical Internet Exercise 31–2: MANAGEMENT PERSPECTIVE—The SEC's Role

Unit Five Cumulative Business Hypothetical

John leases an office and buys computer equipment. Initially, to pay for the lease and the equipment, he goes into the business of designing Web pages. He also has an idea for a new software product that he hopes will be more profitable than designing Web pages. Whenever he has time, he works on the software.

1. After six months, Mary and Paul come to work in the office to help develop John's idea. John continues to pay the rent and other expenses, including salaries for Mary and Paul. John does not expect to make a profit until the software is developed, which could take months; even then, there may be very little profit unless the product is marketed successfully. If the software is successful, though, John believes that the firm will be able to follow up with other products. In choosing a form of business organization for this firm, what are the important considerations? What are the advantages and disadvantages of each basic option?
2. It is decided that the organizational form for this firm should provide limited liability for the owners. The owners will include John, Mary, Paul, and some members of their respective families. One of the features of the corporate form is limited liability. Ordinarily, however, corporate income is taxed at both the corporate level and the shareholder level. Which corporate form could the firm use to avoid this double taxation? Which other forms of business organization provide limited liability? What factors, other than liability and taxation, influence a firm's choice among these forms?
3. The firm is incorporated as Digital Software, Inc. (DSI). The software is developed and marketed successfully, and DSI prospers. John, Mary, and Paul become directors of DSI. At a board meeting, Paul proposes a marketing strategy for DSI's next product, and John and Mary approve it. Implementing the strategy causes DSI's profits to drop. If the shareholders accuse Paul of breaching his fiduciary duty to DSI, what is Paul's most likely defense? If the shareholders accuse John and Mary of the same breach, what is their best defense? In either case, if the shareholders file a suit, how is a court likely to rule?
4. International Investments, Inc., makes a public offer to buy the stock of DSI. The price of the offer is higher than the market price of the stock, but DSI's board believes that the offer should not be accepted and that International's attempt to take over DSI should be resisted. What steps can DSI take to resist the takeover?
5. Mary and Paul withdraw from DSI to set up their own firm. To obtain operating capital, they solicit investors who agree to become "general partners." Mary and Paul designate themselves "managing partners." The investors are spread over a wide area geographically and do not know anything about Mary and Paul's business until they are contacted. Are Mary and Paul truly soliciting partners, or are they selling securities? What are the criteria for determining whether an investment is a security? What are the advantages and disadvantages of selling securities versus soliciting partners?

Unit Five Extended Case Study: *Notz v. Everett Smith Group, Ltd.*

This Extended Case Study examines Notz v. Everett Smith Group, Ltd.,[1] *in which a minority shareholder was allegedly excluded from some of the benefits of participating in the corporation. The shareholder claimed that the majority shareholder and the board of directors, which was controlled by the majority shareholder, had breached their fiduciary duties to the minority shareholder and to the firm (see Chapter 30 on the fiduciary duties of majority shareholders and directors). The court had to decide, among other things, whether the minority shareholder could bring a suit directly to recover personally from the directors or whether he was limited to bringing a shareholder's derivative suit on behalf of the corporation (see the discussion of the options of shareholders with respect to appraisal rights in Chapter 29, as well as the discussion of shareholders' derivative suits in Chapter 30).*

1. 316 Wis.2d 640, 764 N.W.2d 904 (2009). To read this case online, go to www.wicourts.gov. In the "opinions & rules" pull-down menu, click on "Supreme Court." In the result, in the "Opinions and dispositional orders" section, click on "Search for opinions and dispositional orders." On that page, in the "Docket number:" box, type "2006AP3156" and click on "Search." In that result, select the appropriate "view" and click on the link to read the case. The Wisconsin court system maintains this Web site.

CASE BACKGROUND

Albert Trostel & Sons (ATS) began as a tannery in Milwaukee, Wisconsin, in the 1800s. Over the decades, ATS acquired subsidiaries and expanded into the production of rubber and plastics. Everett Smith came to work for ATS in 1938, later became its president, and eventually gained control of the company. Smith formed Everett Smith Group, Ltd., which owned 88.9 percent of ATS by 2003. Edward Notz owned 5.5 percent, and others owned the rest. All of the members of ATS's board of directors were either officers or directors of the Smith Group.

In 2004, ATS had an opportunity to acquire Dickten & Masch, a competing thermoplastics maker. The ATS board chose not to act. Instead, the Smith Group, which had no direct holdings in the plastics field, acquired Dickten & Masch. Within months, the Smith Group's new affiliate bought the assets of ATS's plastics subsidiary, Trostel Specialty Elastomers Group, Inc. (Trostel SEG), from ATS.

Notz filed a suit in a Wisconsin state court against the Smith Group, alleging breach of fiduciary duty for stripping ATS of its most important assets and diverting the corporate opportunity to buy Dickten & Masch. The court dismissed the claim, and a state intermediate appellate court affirmed. Notz appealed to the Wisconsin Supreme Court.

MAJORITY OPINION

N. PATRICK CROOKS, J.:

* * * *

Notz's claims of breach of fiduciary duty are primarily based on the series of transactions in which the Smith Group acquired two plastics companies. The allegations are that the Smith Group, as ATS's majority shareholder, rejected the opportunity ATS had to buy Dickten & Masch; the Smith Group subsequently bought Dickten & Masch itself; and the Smith Group, in its capacity as majority shareholder, orchestrated the sale of ATS's valuable plastics group, Trostel SEG, to its own new acquisition.

The question is whether those allegations support direct claims for breach of fiduciary duty to a minority shareholder. * * * The Smith Group argues that * * * these are derivative claims; Notz argues that * * * these are direct claims.

* * * *Though each shareholder has an individual right to be treated fairly by the board of directors, when the injury from such actions is primarily to the corporation, there can be no direct claim by minority shareholders.* [Emphasis added.]

* * * It is true the fiduciary duty of a director is owed to the individual stockholders as well as to the corporation. Directors in this state may not use their position of trust to further their private interests. Thus, where some individual right of a stockholder is being impaired by the improper acts of a director, the stockholder can bring a direct suit on his own behalf because it is his individual right that is being violated. However, a right of action that belongs to the corporation cannot be pursued as a direct claim by an individual stockholder. * * * *Even where the injury to the corporation results in harm to a shareholder, it won't transform an action from a derivative to a direct one* * * *. That such primary and direct injury to a corporation may have a subsequent impact on the value of the stockholders' shares is clear, but that is not enough to create a right to bring a direct, rather than derivative, action. Where the injury to the corporation is the primary injury, and any injury to stockholders secondary, it is the derivative action alone that can be brought and maintained. That is the general rule, and, if it were to be abandoned, there would be no reason left for the concept of derivative actions for the redress of wrongs to a corporation. [Emphasis added.]

* * * *

Notz alleges self-dealing on the part of the majority shareholder, but * * * a shareholder-director's self-dealing [does not] transform an action that primarily injures the corporation into one that primarily injures a shareholder.

We agree with the Smith Group that breach of fiduciary duty claims, based on the lost opportunity to purchase one company and the sale of a subsidiary with great growth potential, are [derivative claims]. Our analysis * * * centers on a determination of whether the primary injury is to the corporation or to the shareholder. * * * An injury primarily * * * to an individual shareholder [is] one which affects a shareholder's rights in a manner distinct from the effect upon other shareholders. We agree with the court of appeals that the allegations here are essentially that the Smith Group stripped ATS of its most important assets and engaged in various acts of self-dealing, and that those are allegations of injury primarily to ATS. * * * All of the shareholders of ATS were affected equally by the loss of the opportunity to acquire Dickten & Masch and by the sale of Trostel SEG, the plastics division.

* * * *

* * * We agree with the court of appeals that the claims of harm alleged—the loss of a corporate opportunity and the sale of a subsidiary with high growth potential—caused harm primarily to the corporation, and thus we affirm the dismissal of Notz's direct claim of breach of fiduciary duty as to those allegations.

DISSENTING OPINION

***ANN WALSH BRADLEY, J.* (* * * dissenting * * *).**

* * * *

* * * I disagree with the majority * * * that Notz's claim for breach of fiduciary duty arising out of corporate usurpation is a derivative rather than a direct claim and that it thus must be dismissed.

Continued

Instead, * * * I conclude that Notz states a direct claim for breach of fiduciary duty arising out of the defendants' usurpation of a corporate opportunity.

* * * *

* * * Officers and directors owe a fiduciary duty to shareholders to act in good faith and to treat each shareholder fairly. The directors and officers of a corporation owe a fiduciary duty to not use their positions for their own personal advantage * * * to the detriment of the interests of the stockholders of the corporation.

That same fiduciary duty is also owed by majority shareholders to minority shareholders.

Officers, directors, and controlling shareholders breach their fiduciary duties when they treat minority shareholders differently, and inequitably, or when they use their position of trust to further their private interests. If through that control a sale of the corporate property is made and the property acquired by the majority, the minority may not be excluded from a fair participation in the fruits of the sale.

* * * *

[The majority's] conclusion is antithetical to the facts. It is true that all shareholders suffered a common injury in that the value of their investment in ATS depreciated. Nonetheless, Notz suffered an additional injury that was unique to the minority shareholders. The Smith Group who planned and executed these transactions received a net gain, but Notz suffered a net loss. * * * Notz's injury was distinct from the injury to the controlling shareholder—unlike the defendants, Notz was denied continued participation in a thriving growth industry.

QUESTIONS FOR ANALYSIS

1. **Law.** What did the majority rule with respect to the dispute before the court? On what reasoning did the majority base its ruling?
2. **Law.** What was the dissent's interpretation of the facts in this case? How would the dissent have applied the law to these facts? Why?
3. **Ethics.** From an ethical perspective, should ATS's directors have made different decisions on the choices that came before the board? Discuss.
4. **Economic Dimensions.** Could a shareholder in the position of the minority shareholder in this case seek a judicial dissolution? If so, what would be the likely result?
5. **Implications for the Shareholder.** Can a shareholder pursue a derivative claim on behalf of a corporation? If so, what steps must the shareholder take? Why might a shareholder be reluctant to take these steps?

Chapter 33

Consumer and Environmental Law

"The good of the people is the greatest law."

—Marcus Tullius Cicero, 106–43 B.C.E. (Roman politician and orator)

Chapter Outline

- Consumer Law
- Environmental Law

(©SergoZ, 2009. Used under license from Shutterstock.com)

Learning Objectives

After reading this chapter, you should be able to answer the following questions:

1. When will advertising be deemed deceptive?
2. What are the major federal statutes providing for consumer protection in credit transactions?
3. Under what common law theories can polluters be held liable?
4. What is contained in an environmental impact statement, and who must file one?
5. What major federal statutes regulate air and water pollution? What is Superfund, and who is potentially liable under Superfund?

During the heyday of the consumer movement in the 1960s and 1970s, Congress enacted a substantial amount of legislation to protect "the good of the people," to borrow a phrase from Marcus Tullius Cicero. All statutes, agency rules, and common law judicial decisions that serve to protect the interests of consumers are classified as *consumer law.* While the consumer movement has abated somewhat in recent years, efforts to protect the environment have taken on increasing importance in the global community. In the first part of this chapter, we examine some of the major laws and regulations protecting consumers. We then turn to a discussion of *environmental law,* which consists of all of the laws and regulations designed to protect and preserve our environmental resources.

Consumer Law

Sources of consumer protection exist at all levels of government. At the federal level, a number of laws have been passed to define the duties of sellers and the rights of consumers. Exhibit 33–1 on the next page indicates many of the areas of consumer law that are regulated by statutes. Federal administrative agencies, such as the Federal Trade Commission (FTC), also provide an important source of consumer protection. Nearly every agency and

Exhibit 33–1 Selected Areas of Consumer Law Regulated by Statutes

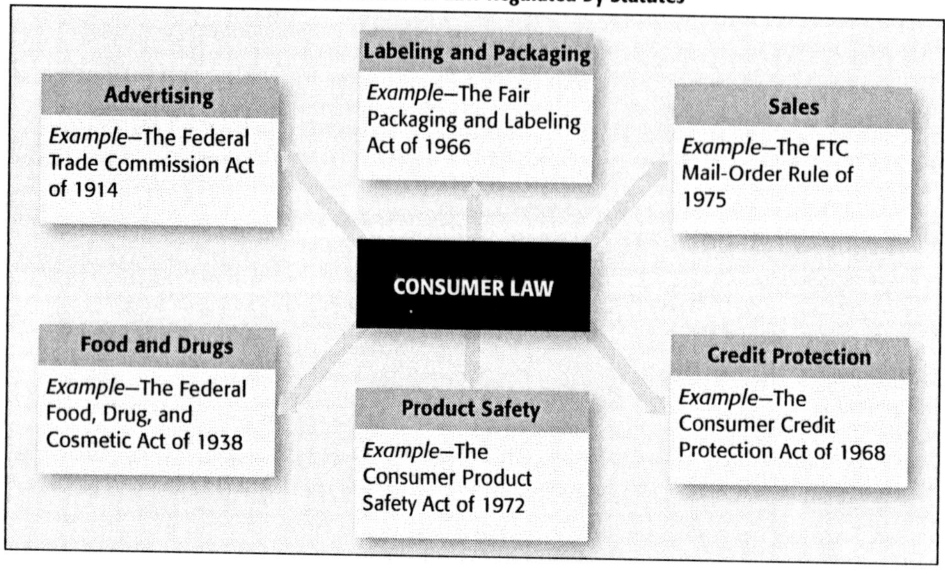

department of the federal government has an office of consumer affairs, and most states have one or more such offices, including the offices of state attorneys general, to assist consumers.

Because of the wide variation among state consumer protection laws, our primary focus here will be on federal legislation—specifically, on legislation governing deceptive advertising, telemarketing and electronic advertising, labeling and packaging, sales, health protection, product safety, and credit protection. Realize, though, that state laws often provide more sweeping and significant protections for the consumer than do federal laws.

Deceptive Advertising

Deceptive Advertising Advertising that misleads consumers, either by making unjustified claims concerning a product's performance or by omitting a material fact concerning the product's composition or performance.

One of the earliest—and still one of the most important—federal consumer protection laws is the Federal Trade Commission Act of 1914 (mentioned in Chapter 32). The act created the FTC to carry out the broadly stated goal of preventing unfair and deceptive trade practices, including deceptive advertising, within the meaning of Section 5 of the act.

Generally, **deceptive advertising** occurs if a reasonable consumer would be misled by the advertising claim. Vague generalities and obvious exaggerations are permissible. These claims are known as puffery. Recall from the discussion of warranties on page 416 in Chapter 17 that puffery consists of statements about a product that a reasonable person would not believe to be literally true. When a claim takes on the appearance of literal authenticity, however, it may create problems. Advertising that *appears* to be based on factual evidence but that in fact cannot be scientifically supported will be deemed deceptive. A classic example occurred in a 1944 case in which the claim that a skin cream would restore youthful qualities to aged skin was deemed deceptive.[1]

When Campbell's advertised that its soups helped fight heart disease, what important fact did the ads not include?

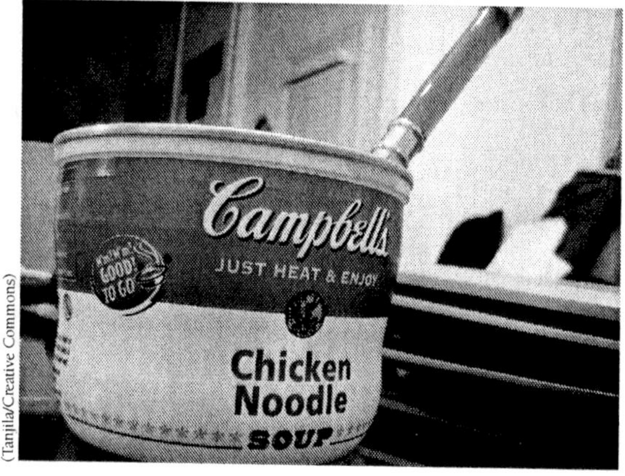

(Tanjila/Creative Commons)

Some advertisements contain "half-truths," meaning that the presented information is true but incomplete and, therefore, leads consumers to a false conclusion. **EXAMPLE 33.1** The maker of Campbell's soups advertised that "most" Campbell's soups were low in fat and cholesterol and thus were helpful in fighting heart disease. What the ad did not say was that Campbell's soups were also high in sodium and that high-sodium diets may increase the risk of heart disease. Hence, the FTC ruled that the company's claims were deceptive. ● Advertising featuring an endorsement by a celebrity may be deemed deceptive if the celebrity does not actually use the product.

Even before the FTC brought the following case, *Wired* magazine had already put the product in question on its list of the top ten "snake-oil gadgets."

1. *Charles of the Ritz Distributors Corp. v. Federal Trade Commission*, 143 F.2d 676 (2d Cir. 1944).

Case 33.1 Federal Trade Commission v. QT, Inc.

United States Court of Appeals, Seventh Circuit, 512 F.3d 858 (2008).
www.ca7.uscourts.gov[a]

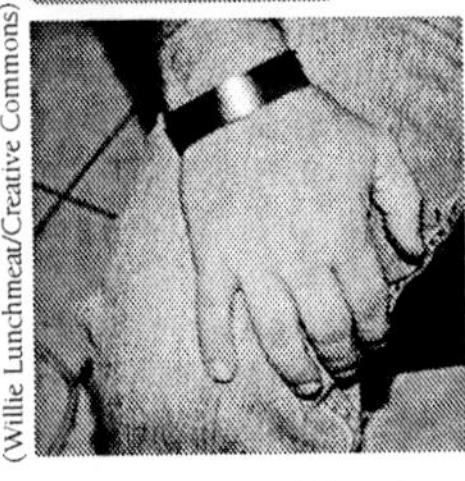

(Willie Lunchmeat/Creative Commons)

Did a company's claims that a metal bracelet cured chronic pain constitute deceptive advertising?

FACTS QT, Inc., heavily promoted the Q-Ray Ionized Bracelet on television infomercials and on its Web site. In its promotions, the company claimed that the bracelets offered immediate and significant or complete pain relief and could cure chronic pain. At trial, the U.S. district court labeled all such claims fraudulent, forbade further promotional claims, and ordered the company to pay $16 million, plus interest, into a fund to be distributed to customers. QT appealed to the U.S. Court of Appeals for the Seventh Circuit.

ISSUE Was the lower court correct in finding that the defendant's advertising of the Ionized Bracelet was deceptive?

a. Click on "Opinions" in the left-hand column. In the boxes for the case number, type "07" and "1662," and then click on "List Case." Follow the links to access this case opinion. The U.S. Court of Appeals for the Seventh Circuit maintains this Web site.

DECISION Yes. The U.S. Court of Appeals for the Seventh Circuit affirmed the district court's decision. QT, Inc., was required to stop its deceptive advertising and to pay the $16 million, plus interest, so that its customers could be reimbursed. The appellate court stated that "almost everything that defendants have said about the bracelet is false." It had no therapeutic effect. No bracelet had a memory cycle specific to each individual wearer, as the company had claimed. The judge presiding over the trial "did not commit a clear error, or abuse his discretion, in concluding that the defendants set out to bilk unsophisticated persons who found themselves in pain from arthritis and other chronic conditions." All statements about how the product worked were pure fiction. "Proof is what separates an effect new to science from a swindle." Although the defendants told customers that the bracelet's efficiency had been "test proven," it had not. What remained were testimonials, which are not a form of proof. "Physicians know how to treat pain. Why pay $200 for a Q-Ray Ionized Bracelet when you can get relief from an aspirin tablet that costs [one cent]?"

WHAT IF THE FACTS WERE DIFFERENT? *Assume that the defendant had actually conducted scientific studies, but the results were inconclusive. How might the judge have ruled in that situation?*

Bait-and-Switch Advertising Advertising a product at a very attractive price (the bait) and then, once the consumer is in the store, saying that the advertised product either is not available or is of poor quality. The customer is then urged to purchase (switched to) a more expensive item.

BAIT-AND-SWITCH ADVERTISING The FTC has issued rules that govern specific advertising techniques. One of the more important rules is contained in the FTC's "Guides Against Bait Advertising."[2] The rule is designed to prevent **bait-and-switch advertising**—that is, advertising a very low price for a particular item that will likely be unavailable to the consumer and then encouraging him or her to purchase a more expensive item. The low price is the "bait" to lure the consumer into the store. The salesperson is instructed to "switch" the consumer to a different, more expensive item. According to the FTC guidelines, bait-and-switch advertising occurs if the seller refuses to show the advertised item, fails to have reasonable quantities of it available, fails to promise to deliver the advertised item within a reasonable time, or discourages employees from selling the item.

"Ads are the cave art of the twentieth century."
Marshall McLuhan, 1911–1980
(Canadian academic and commentator)

ONLINE DECEPTIVE ADVERTISING Deceptive advertising can occur in the online environment as well. The FTC actively monitors online advertising and has identified hundreds of Web sites that have made false or deceptive claims for products ranging from medical treatments for various diseases to exercise equipment and weight-loss aids.

The FTC has issued guidelines to help online businesses comply with existing laws prohibiting deceptive advertising.[3] These guidelines include the following three basic requirements:

1. All ads—both online and offline—must be truthful and not misleading.
2. The claims made in an ad must be substantiated; that is, advertisers must have evidence to back up their claims.

2. 16 C.F.R. Section 288.
3. *Advertising and Marketing on the Internet: Rules of the Road*, September 2000, available at www.ftc.gov/bcp/conline/pubs/buspubs/ruleroad.htm. Also see the FTC's guidelines on behavioral advertising, which targets specific individuals based on their Web-browsing behavior, at www.ftc.gov/opa/2009/02/behavad.shtm.

"A consumer is a shopper who is sore about something."
Harold Coffin, 1905–1981
(American humorist)

3. Ads cannot be unfair, which the FTC defines as "likely to cause substantial consumer injury that consumers could not reasonably avoid and that is not outweighed by the benefit to consumers or competition."

The guidelines also call for "clear and conspicuous" disclosure of any qualifying or limiting information. The overall impression of the ad is important in meeting this requirement. The FTC suggests that advertisers should assume that consumers will not read an entire Web page. Therefore, to satisfy the "clear and conspicuous" requirement, advertisers should place the disclosure as close as possible to the claim being qualified or include the disclosure within the claim itself. If such placement is not feasible, the next-best location is on a section of the page to which a consumer can easily scroll. Generally, hyperlinks to a disclosure are recommended only for lengthy disclosures or for disclosures that must be repeated in a variety of locations on the Web page.

FTC ACTIONS AGAINST DECEPTIVE ADVERTISING The FTC receives complaints from many sources, including competitors of alleged violators, consumers, consumer organizations, trade associations, Better Business Bureaus, government organizations, and state and local officials. If it receives numerous and widespread complaints about a problem, the FTC will investigate. If the FTC concludes that a given advertisement is unfair or deceptive, it sends a formal complaint to the alleged offender. The company may agree to settle the complaint without further proceedings; if not, the FTC can conduct a hearing before an administrative law judge (discussed in Chapter 1) in which the company can present its defense.

If the FTC succeeds in proving that an advertisement is unfair or deceptive, it usually issues a **cease-and-desist order** requiring the company to stop the challenged advertising. In some circumstances, it may also require **counteradvertising** in which the company advertises anew—in print, on the Internet, on radio, and on television—to inform the public about the earlier misinformation. The FTC sometimes institutes a **multiple product order**, which requires a firm to cease and desist from false advertising in regard to all of its products, not just the product that was the subject of the action.

Cease-and-Desist Order An administrative or judicial order prohibiting a person or business firm from conducting activities that an agency or court has deemed illegal.

Counteradvertising New advertising that is undertaken pursuant to a Federal Trade Commission order for the purpose of correcting earlier false claims that were made about a product.

Multiple Product Order An order issued by the Federal Trade Commission to a firm that has engaged in deceptive advertising by which the firm is required to cease and desist from false advertising not only in regard to the product that was the subject of the action but also in regard to all the firm's other products.

When a company's deceptive ad involves wrongful charges to consumers, the FTC may seek other remedies, including restitution. **CASE EXAMPLE 33.2** Verity International, Ltd., billed phone-line subscribers who accessed certain online pornography sites at the rate for international calls to Madagascar. When consumers complained about the charges, Verity employees told them that the charges were valid and had to be paid, or the consumers would face further collection activity. A federal appellate court held that this representation of "uncontestability" was deceptive and a violation of the FTC Act and ordered Verity to pay nearly $18 million in restitution to consumers.[4] ●

Telemarketing and Fax Advertising

The pervasive use of telemarketing led Congress to pass the Telephone Consumer Protection Act (TCPA) of 1991.[5] The act prohibits telephone solicitation using an automatic telephone dialing system or a prerecorded voice. Most states also have laws regulating telephone solicitation. The TCPA also makes it illegal to transmit ads via fax without first obtaining the recipient's permission.

The Federal Communications Commission (FCC) enforces the act. The FCC imposes substantial fines ($11,000 each day) on companies that violate the junk fax provisions of the TCPA and has fined one company as much as $5.4 million for violations.[6] The TCPA

4. *Federal Trade Commission v. Verity International, Ltd.*, 443 F.3d 48 (2d Cir. 2006).
5. 47 U.S.C. Sections 227 *et seq.*, as modified by the Junk Fax Protection Act of 2005.
6. See *Missouri ex rel. Nixon v. American Blast Fax, Inc.*, 323 F.3d 649 (8th Cir. 2003); *cert.* denied, 540 U.S. 1104, 124 S.Ct. 1043, 157 L.Ed.2d 888 (2004). The term *ex rel.* in the case title means that the government brought this action on behalf of an individual (Nixon).

also gives consumers a right to sue for either the actual monetary loss resulting from a violation of the act or $500 in damages for each violation, whichever is greater. If a court finds that a defendant willfully or knowingly violated the act, the court has the discretion to triple the damages that are awarded.

REMEMBER Changes in technology often require changes in the law.

The Telemarketing and Consumer Fraud and Abuse Prevention Act of 1994[7] directed the FTC to establish rules governing telemarketing and to bring actions against fraudulent telemarketers. The FTC's Telemarketing Sales Rule of 1995[8] requires a telemarketer to identify the seller; describe the product being sold; and disclose all material facts related to the sale, including the total cost of the goods being sold, any restrictions on obtaining or using the goods, and whether a sale will be considered final and nonrefundable. The act makes it illegal for telemarketers to misrepresent information (including facts about their goods or services and earnings potential, for example). A telemarketer must also remove a consumer's name from its list of potential contacts if the consumer so requests. (For a discussion of how this rule applies to foreign telemarketers, see this chapter's *Beyond Our Borders* feature on the following page.) An amendment to the Telemarketing Sales Rule established the national Do Not Call Registry. Telemarketers must refrain from calling consumers who have placed their names on the list.

Preventing Legal Disputes

Advertising is essential to business. Before you advertise via faxes, however, you should know the applicable rules and be aware that the FCC aggressively enforces these rules. Make sure that all fax advertisements comply with the Telephone Consumer Protection Act and any state laws on faxes. Educate and train your employees about these laws. Do not send faxes without first obtaining the recipient's permission, and develop effective opt-out procedures so that anyone who no longer wants to receive faxes can notify you. Keep reliable records of the faxes you send and maintain these records for at least four years. Do not purchase lists of fax numbers from outsiders. Avoiding consumer complaints about unwanted faxes and phone calls is the best way to avoid potentially significant liability.

Why would some consumer legislation require that the fiber content of certain products be clearly stated?

Labeling and Packaging

A number of federal and state laws deal specifically with the information given on labels and packages. In general, labels must be accurate, and they must use words that are understood by the ordinary consumer. In some instances, labels must specify the raw materials used in the product, such as the percentage of cotton, nylon, or other fibers used in a garment. In other instances, the products must carry a warning, such as those required on cigarette packages and advertising.[9]

The Fair Packaging and Labeling Act requires that food product labels identify (1) the product; (2) the net quantity of the contents and, if the number of servings is stated, the size of a serving; (3) the manufacturer; and (4) the packager or distributor.[10] The act also provides for additional requirements concerning descriptions on packages, savings claims, components of nonfood products, and standards for the partial filling of packages.

The Nutrition Labeling and Education Act of 1990 requires food labels to provide standard nutrition facts (including the amount and type of fat that the food contains) and regulates the use of such terms as *fresh* and *low fat*. The U.S. Food and Drug Administration and the U.S. Department of Agriculture (USDA) are the primary agencies that publish regulations on food labeling in the *Federal Register*. These rules are updated annually. New rules that became effective in 2009 require the labels on fresh meats, vegetables,

7. 15 U.S.C. Sections 6101–6108.
8. 16 C.F.R. Sections 310.1–310.8.
9. 15 U.S.C. Sections 1331 *et seq.*
10. 15 U.S.C. Sections 4401–4408.

Beyond Our Borders — Protecting U.S. Consumers from Cross-Border Telemarketers

One of the problems that the Federal Trade Commission (FTC) faces in protecting consumers from scams is that those involved in the illegal operations frequently are located outside the United States. Nevertheless, the FTC has had some success in bringing cases under the Telemarketing Sales Rule (TSR) against telemarketers who violate the law from foreign locations. As discussed in the text, the TSR requires telemarketers to disclose all material facts about the goods or services being offered and prohibits the telemarketers from misrepresenting information. Significantly, the TSR applies to any offer made to consumers in the United States—even if the offer comes from a foreign firm.

"I just got home. Can you call back tomorrow when I'm still at work?"

A Telemarketing Scam from Canada

Oleg Oks and Aleksandr Oks, along with several other residents of Canada, set up a number of sham corporations in Ontario. Through these businesses, they placed unsolicited outbound telephone calls to consumers in the United States. The telemarketers offered preapproved Visa or MasterCard credit cards to consumers who agreed to permit their bank accounts to be electronically debited for an advance fee of $319.

The telemarketers frequently promised that the consumers would receive other items—such as a cell phone, satellite dish system, vacation package, or home security system—at no additional cost. In fact, *no consumers* who paid the advance fee received either a credit card or any of the promised gifts. Instead, consumers received a "member benefits" package that included items such as booklets on how to improve their creditworthiness or merchandise cards that could be used only to purchase goods from the catalogue provided.

Joint Cooperation to Prosecute the Telemarketers

The FTC, working in conjunction with the U.S. Postal Service and various Canadian government and law enforcement agencies, conducted an investigation that lasted several years. Ultimately, in 2007 Oleg and Aleksandr Oks pleaded guilty in Canada to criminal charges for deceptive advertising. They were barred from telemarketing for ten years.[a]

In addition, the FTC filed a civil lawsuit against the Okses and other Canadian defendants in a federal court in Illinois. The court found that the defendants had violated the FTC Act and the TSR and ordered them to pay nearly $5 million in damages.[b]

• For Critical Analysis

Suppose that this scam had originated in a country that was not as friendly and cooperative as Canada is with the United States. In that situation, how would the FTC obtain sufficient evidence to prosecute the foreign telemarketers? Is the testimony of U.S. consumers regarding the phone calls that they received sufficient proof? Why or why not?

a. Oleg was also sentenced to a year in jail and two years' probation.
b. *Federal Trade Commission v. Oks*, 2007 WL 3307009 (N.D.Ill. 2007). The court entered its final judgment on March 18, 2008.

ON THE WEB You can find current articles concerning consumer issues at the "Consumer Law Page" of the law firm Alexander Hawes, LLP. Go to consumerlawpage.com.

and fruits to indicate where the food originated so that consumers can know whether it was imported.

Sales

A number of statutes protect consumers by requiring the disclosure of certain terms in sales transactions and providing rules governing home or door-to-door sales, mail-order transactions, referral sales, and unsolicited merchandise. The Federal Reserve Board of Governors, for example, has issued **Regulation Z**, which governs credit provisions associated with sales contracts (discussed later in this chapter). Many states and the FTC have **"cooling-off" laws** that permit the buyers of goods sold door to door to cancel their contracts within three business days. The FTC rule further requires that consumers be notified in Spanish of this right if the oral negotiations for the sale were in that language.

Regulation Z A set of rules issued by the Federal Reserve Board of Governors to implement the provisions of the Truth-in-Lending Act.

"Cooling-off" Laws Laws that allow buyers a period of time, such as three business days, in which to cancel door-to-door sales contracts.

TELEPHONE AND MAIL-ORDER SALES The FTC's Mail or Telephone Order Merchandise Rule of 1993 amended the FTC's Mail-Order Rule of 1975.[11] The rule provides specific

11. 16 C.F.R. Sections 435.1–435.2.

(©Stephen Coburn, 2009. Used under license from Shutterstock.com)

What are the FTC's Mail-Order Rule requirements with respect to when merchants must ship goods?

protections for consumers who purchase goods over the phone, through the mail, or via a computer (Internet) or fax machine. For instance, merchants are required to ship orders within the time promised in their advertisements and to notify consumers when orders cannot be shipped on time. The rule also requires merchants to issue a refund within a specified period of time when a consumer cancels an order.

In addition, under the Postal Reorganization Act of 1970[12] a consumer who receives *unsolicited* merchandise sent by U.S. mail can keep it, throw it away, or dispose of it in any manner that she or he sees fit. The recipient will not be obligated to the sender.

ONLINE SALES The FTC and other federal agencies have brought numerous enforcement actions against those who perpetrate online fraud. Nonetheless, protecting consumers from fraudulent and deceptive sales practices conducted via the Internet has proved to be a challenging task. Faced with economic recession, job losses, mounting debt, and dwindling savings, many consumers are looking for any source of income. The number of consumers who have fallen prey to Internet fraud has actually grown in recent years. Complaints to the FTC about the sale of business opportunities, such as work-at-home offers, nearly doubled from 2007 to 2008 and tripled in the first six months of 2009.

ON THE WEB The federal government provides practical tips to guard against online fraud and protect a consumer's personal information at the following Web site: www.onguardonline.gov/default.aspx.

Health and Safety

Although labeling and packaging laws (discussed earlier) promote consumer health and safety, there is a significant distinction between regulating the information dispensed about a product and regulating the actual content of the product. The classic example is tobacco products. Producers of tobacco products are required to warn consumers about the hazards associated with the use of their products, but the sale of tobacco products has not been subjected to significant restrictions or banned outright despite the obvious dangers to health. We now examine various laws that regulate the actual products made available to consumers.

FOOD AND DRUGS The first federal legislation regulating food and drugs was enacted in 1906 as the Pure Food and Drugs Act.[13] That law, as amended in 1938, exists now as the Federal Food, Drug, and Cosmetic Act (FDCA).[14] The act protects consumers against adulterated and misbranded foods and drugs. As to foods, the act establishes food standards, specifies safe levels of potentially hazardous food additives, and sets classifications of food and food advertising. Most of these statutory requirements are monitored and enforced by the U.S. Food and Drug Administration (FDA).

BE AWARE The U.S. Food and Drug Administration is authorized to obtain, among other things, orders for the recall and seizure of certain products.

The FDCA also charges the FDA with the responsibility of ensuring that drugs are safe before they are marketed to the public. Under an extensive set of procedures established by the FDA, drugs must be shown to be safe, as well as effective, before they may be marketed to the public. **CASE EXAMPLE 33.3** A group of terminally ill patients claimed that they were entitled, under the U.S. Constitution, to better access to experimental drugs before the FDA completed its clinical tests. The court, however, found that the FDA's policy of limiting access to drugs that were undergoing tests was rationally related to protecting patients from potentially unsafe drugs. Therefore, the court held that terminally ill patients do not have a fundamental constitutional right of access to experimental drugs.[15] ● A 1976

12. 39 U.S.C. Section 3009.

13. 21 U.S.C. Sections 1–5, 7–15.

14. 21 U.S.C. Section 301.

15. *Abigail Alliance for Better Access to Developmental Drugs v. von Eschenbach*, 495 F.3d 695 (D.C.Cir. 2007).

amendment to the FDCA[16] authorizes the FDA to regulate medical devices, such as pacemakers, and to withdraw from the market any such device that is mislabeled.

ON THE WEB The Web site of the Consumer Product Safety Commission offers a business information page that provides the text of regulations and laws, notices in the *Federal Register*, and other information. Go to www.cpsc.gov/businfo/businfo.html.

CONSUMER PRODUCT SAFETY In 1972, Congress enacted the Consumer Product Safety Act,[17] which created the first comprehensive scheme of regulation over matters concerning consumer safety. The act also established the Consumer Product Safety Commission (CPSC) and gave it far-reaching authority over consumer safety.

The CPSC's Authority. The CPSC conducts research on the safety of individual products and maintains a clearinghouse on the risks associated with various products. The Consumer Product Safety Act authorizes the CPSC to do the following:

1. Set safety standards for consumer products.
2. Ban the manufacture and sale of any product that the commission believes poses an "unreasonable risk" to consumers. (Products banned by the CPSC have included various types of fireworks, cribs, and toys, as well as many products containing asbestos or vinyl chloride.)
3. Remove from the market any products it believes to be imminently hazardous. The CPSC frequently works in conjunction with manufacturers to voluntarily recall defective products from stores. **EXAMPLE 33.4** In 2009, in cooperation with the CPSC, Kolcraft Enterprises, Inc., recalled one million infant play yards because of a defective latch that could cause a rail to fall, posing a risk to children. ●
4. Require manufacturers to report on any products already sold or intended for sale if the products have proved to be hazardous.
5. Administer other product-safety legislation, including the Child Protection and Toy Safety Act of 1969[18] and the Federal Hazardous Substances Act of 1960.[19]

(AP Photo/Kelley McCall)

The CPSC passed a rule requiring that any product sold to children cannot contain lead. How could children be harmed if some lead was used in the manufacturing of dirt bikes?

Notification Requirements. The Consumer Product Safety Act imposes notification requirements on distributors of consumer products. Distributors must immediately notify the CPSC when they receive information that a product "contains a defect which . . . creates a substantial risk to the public" or "an unreasonable risk of serious injury or death."

CASE EXAMPLE 33.5 A company that sold juicers began receiving letters from customers complaining that during operation the juicer suddenly exploded, sending pieces of glass and razor-sharp metal across the room. The company received twenty-three letters from angry consumers about the exploding juicer but waited more than six months before notifying the CPSC that the product posed a significant risk to the public. In a case filed by the federal government, the court held that when a company first receives information regarding a threat, the company is required to report the problem within twenty-four hours to the CPSC. Even if the company had to investigate the allegations, it should not have taken more than ten days to verify the information and report the problem. The court therefore found that the company had violated the law and ordered it to pay damages.[20] ●

Credit Protection

Credit protection is one of the most important aspects of consumer protection legislation. Nearly 80 percent of U.S. consumers have credit cards, and most carry a balance on these cards, amounting to about $2.5 trillion of debt nationwide.

16. 21 U.S.C. Sections 352(o), 360(j), 360(k), and 360c–360k.
17. 15 U.S.C. Section 2051.
18. 15 U.S.C. Section 1262(e).
19. 15 U.S.C. Sections 1261–1273.
20. *United States v. Mirama Enterprises, Inc.*, 185 F.Supp.2d 1148 (S.D.Cal. 2002).

A key statute regulating the credit and credit-card industries is the Truth-in-Lending Act (TILA), the name commonly given to Title 1 of the Consumer Credit Protection Act (CCPA),[21] which was passed by Congress in 1968. The TILA has been amended several times, most recently in 2009, when Congress passed sweeping reforms to strengthen its consumer protections.[22]

Truth in Lending The TILA is basically a *disclosure law.* It is administered by the Federal Reserve Board and requires sellers and lenders to disclose credit terms or loan terms so that individuals can shop around for the best financing arrangements. TILA requirements apply only to persons who, in the ordinary course of business, lend funds, sell on credit, or arrange for the extension of credit. Thus, sales or loans made between two consumers do not come under the protection of the act. Additionally, this law protects only debtors who are *natural* persons (as opposed to the artificial "person" of a corporation); it does not extend to other legal entities.

The disclosure requirements are found in Regulation Z. If the contracting parties are subject to the TILA, the requirements of Regulation Z apply to any transaction involving an installment sales contract that calls for payment to be made in more than four installments. Transactions subject to Regulation Z typically include installment loans, retail and installment sales, car loans, home-improvement loans, and certain real estate loans if the amount of financing is less than $25,000.

NOTE **The Federal Reserve Board is part of the Federal Reserve System, which influences the lending and investing activities of commercial banks and the cost and availability of credit.**

Under the provisions of the TILA, all of the terms of a credit instrument must be clearly and conspicuously disclosed. A lender must disclose the annual percentage rate (APR), finance charge, amount financed, and total payments (the sum of the amount loaned, plus any fees, finance charges, and interest at the end of the loan). The TILA provides for contract rescission (cancellation) if a creditor fails to follow the exact procedures required by the act.[23]

Equal Credit Opportunity. In 1974, Congress enacted, as an amendment to the TILA, the Equal Credit Opportunity Act (ECOA). The ECOA prohibits the denial of credit solely on the basis of race, religion, national origin, color, gender, marital status, or age. The act also prohibits credit discrimination on the basis of whether an individual receives certain forms of income, such as public-assistance benefits.

"Credit is a system whereby a person who can't pay gets another person who can't pay to guarantee that he can pay."

Charles Dickens, 1812–1870
(English novelist)

Under the ECOA, a creditor may not require the signature of an applicant's spouse, or a cosigner, on a credit instrument if the applicant qualifies under the creditor's standards of creditworthiness for the amount requested. **CASE EXAMPLE 33.6** Tonja, an African American, applied for financing with a used-car dealer. The dealer reviewed Tonja's credit report and, without submitting the application to the lender, decided that she would not qualify. Instead of informing Tonja that she did not qualify, the dealer told her that she needed a cosigner on the loan to purchase the car. According to a federal appellate court, the dealership qualified as a creditor in this situation because it unilaterally denied credit. Thus, the dealer could be held liable under the ECOA.[24] ●

---

21. 15 U.S.C. Sections 1601–1693r.
22. The TILA was amended in 1980 by the Truth-in-Lending Simplification and Reform Act; and significantly amended again in 2009 by the Credit Card Accountability Responsibility and Disclosure Act of 2009, Pub. L. No. 111-24, 123 Stat. 1734, enacting 15 U.S.C. Sections 1616, 1651, 1665c to 1665e, 1666i-1, 1666i-2, 1666b, and 1693l-1, and 16 U.S.C. Section 1a-7b, as well as amending many other provisions of the TILA.
23. Note, though, that amendments to the TILA enacted in 1995 prevent borrowers from rescinding loans because of minor clerical errors in the final documents that were signed [15 U.S.C. Sections 1605, 1631, 1635, 1640, and 1641].
24. *Treadway v. Gateway Chevrolet Oldsmobile, Inc.*, 362 F.3d 971 (7th Cir. 2004).

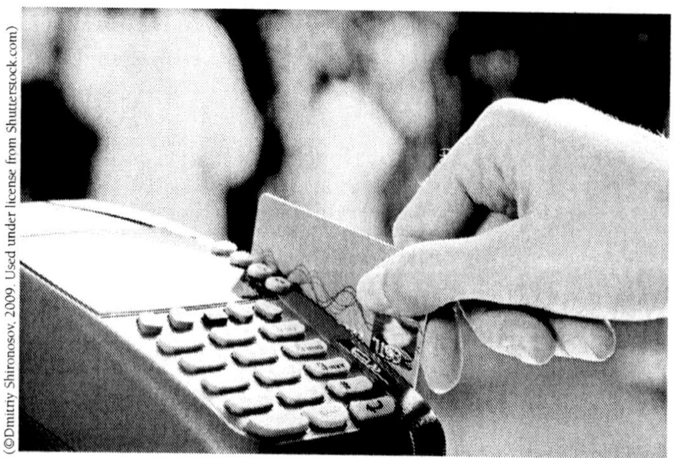
(©Dmitriy Shironosov, 2009. Used under license from Shutterstock.com)

Assume that your credit card is stolen, but you do not report the theft to the credit-card issuer. What is the maximum dollar liability you face?

Credit-Card Rules. The TILA also contains provisions regarding credit cards. One provision limits the liability of a cardholder to $50 per card for unauthorized charges made before the creditor is notified that the card has been lost. If a consumer received an *unsolicted* credit card in the mail that is later stolen, the company that issued the card cannot charge the consumer for any unauthorized charges. Another provision requires credit-card companies to disclose the balance computation method that is used to determine the outstanding balance, and to state when finance charges begin to accrue. Other provisions set forth procedures for resolving billing disputes with the credit-card company. These procedures may be used if, for example, a cardholder thinks that an error has occurred in billing or wishes to withhold payment for a faulty product purchased by credit card.

In 2009, President Barack Obama signed into law amendments to the credit-card protections of the TILA that became effective in 2010. The most significant provisions of the new rules are as follows:

1. Protect consumers from retroactive increases in interest rates on existing card balances unless the account is sixty days delinquent.
2. Require companies to provide forty-five days' advance notice to consumers before making changes to the credit-card terms.
3. Require companies to send out monthly bills to cardholders twenty-one days before the due date.
4. Prevent companies from increasing the interest rate charged on a customer's credit-card balance except in specific situations, such as when a promotional rate ends.
5. Prevent companies from charging over-limit fees except in specified situations.
6. Require companies to apply payments in excess of the minimum amount due to the customer's higher-interest balances first when the borrower has balances with different rates (such as the higher interest rates commonly charged for cash advances).
7. Prevent companies from computing finance charges based on the previous billing cycle (known as double-cycle billing, which hurts consumers because they are charged interest for the previous cycle even though they have paid the bill in full).

ON THE WEB The Consumer Action Web site offers useful information and links to consumer protection agencies at the city, county, and state level. Go to www.consumeraction.gov.

Consumer Leases. The Consumer Leasing Act (CLA) of 1988[25] amended the TILA to provide protection for consumers who lease automobiles and other goods. The CLA applies to those who lease or arrange to lease consumer goods in the ordinary course of their business. The act applies only if the goods are priced at $25,000 or less and if the lease term exceeds four months. The CLA and its implementing regulation, Regulation M,[26] require lessors to disclose in writing all of the material terms of the lease.

FAIR CREDIT REPORTING In 1970, to protect consumers against inaccurate credit reporting, Congress enacted the Fair Credit Reporting Act (FCRA).[27] The act provides that consumer credit reporting agencies may issue credit reports to users only for specified purposes, including the extension of credit, the issuance of insurance policies, compliance with a court order, and compliance with a consumer's request for a copy of her or his own credit report. Any time a consumer is denied credit or insurance on the basis of his or her credit report, the consumer must be notified of that fact and of the name

25. 15 U.S.C. Sections 1667–1667e.
26. 12 C.F.R. Part 213.
27. 15 U.S.C. Sections 1681 *et seq.*

and address of the credit reporting agency that issued the report. The same notice must be sent to consumers who are charged more than others ordinarily would be for credit or insurance because of their credit reports.

Under the FCRA, consumers can request the source of any information used by the credit agency, as well as the identity of anyone who has received an agency's report. Consumers are also permitted to have access to the information contained about them in a credit reporting agency's files. If a consumer discovers that the agency's files contain inaccurate information about his or her credit standing, the agency, on the consumer's written request, must investigate the disputed information. Any unverifiable or erroneous information must be deleted within a reasonable period of time.

An agency that fails to comply with the act is liable for actual damages, plus additional damages not to exceed $1,000 and attorneys' fees.[28] The FCRA also allows a court to award punitive damages for a "willful" violation. In 2007, the United States Supreme Court held that an insurance company's failure to notify new customers that they were paying higher insurance rates as a result of their credit scores was a *willful* violation of the FCRA.[29]

FAIR AND ACCURATE CREDIT TRANSACTIONS ACT In an effort to combat rampant identity theft (discussed in Chapter 7), Congress passed the Fair and Accurate Credit Transactions (FACT) Act of 2003.[30] The act established a national fraud alert system so that consumers who suspect that they have been or may be victimized by identity theft can place an alert in their credit files. The FACT Act also requires the major credit reporting agencies to provide consumers with a free copy of their credit reports every twelve months. Another provision requires account numbers on credit-card receipts to be truncated (shortened) so that merchants, employees, and others who have access to the receipts cannot obtain a consumer's name and full credit-card number. The act also mandates that financial institutions work with the FTC to identify "red flag" indicators of identity theft and to develop rules for disposing of sensitive credit information.

ON THE WEB For information on the Fair and Accurate Credit Transactions Act, including transcripts of congressional hearings concerning the act, go to www.ftc.gov/opa/2004/06/factaidt.htm.

The FACT Act also gives consumers who have been victimized by identity theft some assistance in rebuilding their credit reputations. For example, credit reporting agencies must stop reporting allegedly fraudulent account information once the consumer establishes that identify theft has occurred. Business owners and creditors are required to provide a consumer with copies of any records that can help the consumer prove that a particular account or transaction is fraudulent (records showing that an account was created with a fraudulent signature, for example). In addition, to help prevent the spread of erroneous credit information, the act allows consumers to report the accounts affected by identity theft directly to the creditors.

FAIR DEBT-COLLECTION PRACTICES In 1977, Congress enacted the Fair Debt Collection Practices Act (FDCPA)[31] in an attempt to curb what were perceived to be abuses by collection agencies. The act applies only to specialized debt-collection agencies and attorneys who regularly attempt to collect debts on behalf of someone else, usually for a percentage of the amount owed. Creditors attempting to collect debts are not covered by the act unless, by misrepresenting themselves, they cause the debtors to believe that they are collection agencies.

The act prohibits a collection agency from using certain offensive tactics to collect the debt. For instance, a collection agency may not contact the debtor at his or her place of employment if the employer objects and may not contact the debtor's family members or other third parties about payment. The agency also may not harass or intimidate the

28. 15 U.S.C. Section 1681n.
29. *Safeco Insurance Co. of America v. Burr,* 551 U.S. 47, 127 S.Ct. 2201, 167 L.Ed.2d 1045 (2007).
30. Pub. L. No. 108-159, 117 Stat. 1952 (December 4, 2003).
31. 15 U.S.C. Section 1692.

debtor, or make false or misleading statements (such as posing as a police officer). A debt collector who fails to comply with the act is liable for actual damages, plus additional damages not to exceed $1,000[32] and attorneys' fees.

 Environmental Law

To this point, this chapter has dealt with government regulation of business in the interest of protecting consumers. We now turn to a discussion of the various ways in which businesses are regulated by the government in the interest of protecting the environment. Concern over the degradation of the environment has increased over time in response to the environmental effects of population growth, urbanization, and industrialization. Environmental protection is not without a price, however. For many businesses, the costs of complying with environmental regulations are high, and for some they may seem too high. (See the *Business Application* feature at the end of this chapter for information on how to avoid facing penalties for violating environmental laws.) A constant tension exists between the desirability of increasing profits and productivity and the need to protect the environment.

To a great extent, environmental law consists of statutes passed by federal, state, or local governments and regulations issued by administrative agencies. Before examining statutory and regulatory environmental laws, however, we look at the remedies against environmental pollution that are available under the common law.

Common Law Actions

Common law remedies against environmental pollution originated centuries ago in England. Those responsible for operations that created dirt, smoke, noxious odors, noise, or toxic substances were sometimes held liable under common law theories of nuisance or negligence. Today, injured individuals continue to rely on the common law to obtain damages and injunctions against business polluters.

Nuisance A common law doctrine under which persons may be held liable for using their property in a manner that unreasonably interferes with others' rights to use or enjoy their own property.

NUISANCE Under the common law doctrine of **nuisance**, persons may be held liable if they use their property in a manner that unreasonably interferes with others' rights to use or enjoy their own property. In these situations, the courts commonly balance the harm caused by the pollution against the costs of stopping it.

Courts have often denied injunctive relief on the ground that the hardships that would be imposed on the polluter and on the community are relatively greater than the hardships suffered by the plaintiff. **EXAMPLE 33.7** A factory that causes neighboring landowners to suffer from smoke, soot, and vibrations may be left in operation if it is the core of the local economy. The injured parties may be awarded only monetary damages, which may include compensation for the decrease in the value of their property caused by the factory's operation. ●

A property owner may be given relief from pollution if she or he can identify a distinct harm separate from that affecting the general public. This harm is referred to as a "private" nuisance. Under the common law, individuals were denied standing (access to the courts—see Chapter 3) unless they suffered a harm distinct from the harm suffered by the public at large. Some states still require this. A public authority (such as a state's attorney general), though, can sue to abate a "public" nuisance.

NEGLIGENCE AND STRICT LIABILITY An injured party may sue a business polluter in tort under the negligence and strict liability theories discussed in Chapter 4. The basis for a negligence action is the business's alleged failure to use reasonable care toward the party

32. According to the U.S. Court of Appeals for the Sixth Circuit, the $1,000 limit on damages applies to each lawsuit, not to each violation. See *Wright v. Finance Service of Norwalk, Inc.*, 22 F.3d 647 (6th Cir. 1994).

whose injury was foreseeable and, of course, caused by the lack of reasonable care. For instance, employees might sue an employer whose failure to use proper pollution controls contaminated the air and caused the employees to suffer respiratory illnesses. Lawsuits for personal injuries caused by exposure to a toxic substance, such as asbestos, radiation, or hazardous waste, have given rise to a growing body of tort law known as **toxic torts.**

Toxic Tort A civil wrong arising from exposure to a toxic substance, such as asbestos, radiation, or hazardous waste.

Businesses that engage in ultrahazardous activities—such as the transportation of radioactive materials—are strictly liable for any injuries the activities cause. In a strict liability action, the injured party does not need to prove that the business failed to exercise reasonable care.

State and Local Regulation

In addition to the federal regulation to be discussed shortly, many states have enacted laws to protect the environment. State laws may restrict a business's discharge of chemicals into the air or water or regulate its disposal of toxic wastes. States may also regulate the disposal or recycling of other wastes, including glass, metal, plastic containers, and paper. Additionally, states may restrict emissions from motor vehicles.

City, county, and other local governments also regulate some aspects of the environment. For instance, local zoning laws may be designed to inhibit or regulate the growth of cities and suburbs or to protect the natural environment. In the interest of safeguarding the environment, such laws may prohibit certain land uses. Even when zoning laws permit a business's proposed development, the proposal may have to be altered to lessen the development's impact on the environment. In addition, cities and counties may impose rules regulating methods of waste removal, the appearance of buildings, the maximum noise level, and other aspects of the local environment.

State and local regulatory agencies also play a significant role in implementing federal environmental legislation. Typically, the federal government relies on state and local governments to enforce federal environmental statutes and regulations such as those regulating air quality.

Federal Regulation

Congress has enacted a number of statutes to control the impact of human activities on the environment. Some of these laws have been passed in an attempt to improve the quality of air and water. Other laws specifically regulate toxic chemicals, including pesticides, herbicides, and hazardous wastes.

Environmental Regulatory Agencies The primary agency regulating environmental law is, of course, the Environmental Protection Agency (EPA), which was created in 1970 to coordinate federal environmental responsibilities. Other federal agencies with authority to regulate specific environmental matters include the Department of the Interior, the Department of Defense, the Department of Labor, the Food and Drug Administration, and the Nuclear Regulatory Commission. All agencies of the federal government must take environmental factors into consideration when making significant decisions. In addition, as mentioned, state and local agencies play an important role in enforcing federal environmental legislation.

Most federal environmental laws provide that private parties can sue to enforce environmental regulations if government agencies fail to do so—or if agencies go too far in their enforcement actions. Typically, a threshold hurdle in such suits is meeting the requirements for standing to sue.

Environmental Impact Statement (EIS) A statement required by the National Environmental Policy Act for any major federal action that will significantly affect the quality of the environment. The statement must analyze the action's impact on the environment and explore alternative actions that might be taken.

Environmental Impact Statements The National Environmental Policy Act (NEPA) of 1969[33] requires that an **environmental impact statement (EIS)** be prepared for

33. 42 U.S.C. Sections 4321–4370d.

every major federal action that significantly affects the quality of the environment. An EIS must analyze (1) the impact on the environment that the action will have, (2) any adverse effects on the environment and alternative actions that might be taken, and (3) irreversible effects the action might generate.

An action qualifies as "major" if it involves a substantial commitment of resources (monetary or otherwise). An action is "federal" if a federal agency has the power to control it. Construction by a private developer of a ski resort on federal land, for example, may require an EIS. Building or operating a nuclear plant, which requires a federal permit, requires an EIS. If an agency decides that an EIS is unnecessary, it must issue a statement supporting this conclusion. Private individuals, consumer interest groups, businesses, and others who believe that a federal agency's actions threaten the environment often use EISs as a means of challenging those actions.

ON THE WEB For information on EPA standards, guidelines, and regulations, go to the EPA's Web site at www.epa.gov.

Air Pollution

Federal involvement with air pollution goes back to the 1950s and 1960s, when Congress authorized funds for air-pollution research and enacted the Clean Air Act to address multistate air pollution.[34] The Clean Air Act provides the basis for issuing regulations to control pollution coming both from mobile sources (such as automobiles and other vehicles) and from stationary sources (such as electric utilities and industrial plants).

"There's so much pollution in the air now that if it weren't for our lungs, there'd be no place to put it all."

Robert Orben, 1927–present
(American comedian)

Mobile Sources of Pollution Regulations governing air pollution from automobiles and other mobile sources specify pollution standards and establish time schedules for meeting the standards. Under the 1990 amendments to the Clean Air Act, automobile manufacturers were required to cut new automobiles' exhaust emissions of nitrogen oxide by 60 percent and of other pollutants by 35 percent by 1998. Beginning with 2004 model cars, regulations required nitrogen oxide tailpipe emissions to be cut nearly 10 percent by 2007. For the first time, sport utility vehicles (SUVs) and light trucks had to meet the same standards as automobiles. The amendments also required service stations to sell gasoline with a higher oxygen content in certain cities and to sell even cleaner-burning gasoline in the most polluted urban areas. In 2009, the Obama administration announced that it will seek to amend these standards to reduce emissions by 80 percent by 2050.

Updating Pollution-Control Standards The EPA attempts to update pollution-control standards when new scientific information becomes available. For instance, studies conducted in the 1990s showed that very small particles (2.5 microns, or about one-thirtieth the width of a human hair) of soot might affect our health as significantly as larger particles. Based on this evidence, in 1997 the EPA issued new particulate standards for motor vehicle exhaust systems and other sources of pollution. The EPA also instituted a more rigorous standard for ozone (the basic ingredient of smog), which is formed when sunlight combines with pollutants from cars and other sources. The United States Supreme Court has upheld the EPA's authority to issue emission standards under the Clean Air Act without taking economic costs into account when creating new rules.[35]

In 2006, the EPA again re-evaluated its particulate standards and found that more than two hundred counties were not meeting the standards set in 1997. The EPA issued new regulations for daily (twenty-four-hour) exposure to particles of soot but did not change the annual particulate standards.[36]

---

34. 42 U.S.C. Sections 7401 *et seq.*

35. *Whitman v. American Trucking Associations*, 531 U.S. 457, 121 S.Ct. 903, 149 L.Ed.2d 1 (2001).

36. 40 C.F.R. Part 50.

The most common stationary sources of air pollution are factories and electricity-generating facilities. For the application of the EPA's ambient standards, does it matter where the factory or electricity-generating facility is located? Why or why not?

STATIONARY SOURCES OF POLLUTION The Clean Air Act authorizes the EPA to establish air-quality standards for stationary sources (such as manufacturing plants) but recognizes that the primary responsibility for preventing and controlling air pollution rests with state and local governments. The standards are aimed at controlling hazardous air pollutants—those likely to cause death or serious irreversible or incapacitating illness such as cancer or neurological and reproductive damage. In all, 189 substances, including asbestos, benzene, beryllium, cadmium, and vinyl chloride, have been classified as hazardous. They are emitted from stationary sources by a variety of business activities, including smelting (melting ore to produce metal), dry cleaning, house painting, and commercial baking.

Mercury was added to the list of hazardous substances in 2000. **CASE EXAMPLE 33.8** In 2005, the EPA published a rule (the Delisting Rule) stating that it was removing mercury from its list of hazardous emissions from steam-generated electricity plants. New Jersey and fourteen other states filed a lawsuit challenging the EPA's action. The EPA argued that it had the authority to remove mercury from the list because its inclusion on the list was not a final agency action and because mercury was more appropriately regulated under other provisions. In 2008, a federal appellate court ruled that the EPA had exceeded its authority and required it to return mercury to the list of hazardous air pollutants.[37] •

The EPA sets primary and secondary levels of ambient standards—that is, the maximum levels of certain pollutants—and the states formulate plans to achieve those standards. Different standards apply depending on whether the sources of pollution are located in clean areas or polluted areas and whether they are already existing sources or major new sources. Major new sources include existing sources modified by a change in a method of operation that increases emissions. Performance standards for major sources require the use of the *maximum achievable control technology*, or MACT, to reduce emissions. The EPA issues guidelines as to what equipment meets this standard.[38]

VIOLATIONS OF THE CLEAN AIR ACT For violations of emission limits under the Clean Air Act, the EPA can assess civil penalties of up to $25,000 per day. Additional fines of up to $5,000 per day can be assessed for other violations, such as failing to maintain the required records. To penalize those who find it more cost-effective to violate the act than to comply with it, the EPA is authorized to obtain a penalty equal to the violator's economic benefits from noncompliance. Persons who provide information about violators may be paid up to $10,000. Private individuals can also sue violators.

Those who knowingly violate the act may be subject to criminal penalties, including fines of up to $1 million and imprisonment for up to two years (for false statements or failures to report violations). Corporate officers are among those who may be subject to these penalties.

Water Pollution

Water pollution stems mostly from industrial, municipal, and agricultural sources. Pollutants entering streams, lakes, and oceans include organic wastes, heated water, sediments from soil runoff, nutrients (including fertilizers and human and animal wastes), and toxic chemicals and other hazardous substances. We look here at laws and regulations governing water pollution.

Federal regulations governing the pollution of water can be traced back to the Rivers and Harbors Appropriations Act of 1899.[39] These regulations prohibited ships and manufacturers from discharging or depositing refuse in navigable waterways without a permit. In

37. *New Jersey v. Environmental Protection Agency,* 517 F.3d 574 (D.C.Cir. 2008).
38. The EPA has also issued rules to regulate hazardous air pollutants emitted by landfills. See 40 C.F.R. Sections 60.750–60.759.
39. 33 U.S.C. Sections 401–418.

1948, Congress passed the Federal Water Pollution Control Act (FWPCA),[40] but its regulatory system and enforcement powers proved to be inadequate.

"*Among the treasures of our land is water—fast becoming our most valuable, most prized, most critical resource.*"

Dwight D. Eisenhower, 1890–1969
(Thirty-fourth president of the United States, 1953–1961)

THE CLEAN WATER ACT In 1972, amendments to the FWPCA—known as the Clean Water Act (CWA)—established the following goals: (1) make waters safe for swimming, (2) protect fish and wildlife, and (3) eliminate the discharge of pollutants into the water. The amendments set specific time schedules, which were extended by amendment in 1977 and by the Water Quality Act of 1987.[41] Under these schedules, the EPA limits the discharge of various types of pollutants based on the technology available for controlling them.

The CWA established a permit system, called the *National Pollutant Discharge Elimination System* (NPDES), for regulating discharges from "point sources" of pollution that include industrial, municipal (such as pipes and sewage treatment plants), and agricultural facilities.[42] Under this system, industrial, municipal, and agricultural polluters must apply for permits before discharging wastes into surface waters. NPDES permits can be issued by the EPA and authorized state agencies and Indian tribes, but only if the discharge will not violate water-quality standards. NPDES permits must be reissued every five years. Although initially the NPDES system focused mainly on industrial wastewater, it was later expanded to cover storm water discharges.

The EPA must take into account many factors when issuing and updating the rules that impose standards to attain the goals of the CWA. Some provisions of the act instruct the EPA to weigh the cost of the technology applied against the benefits achieved. The statute that covers power plants, however, neither requires nor prohibits a comparison of the economic costs and benefits. The question in the following case was whether the EPA could make this comparison anyway.

40. 33 U.S.C. Sections 1251–1387.
41. This act amended 33 U.S.C. Section 1251.
42. 33 U.S.C. Section 1342.

Case 33.2 Entergy Corp. v. Riverkeeper, Inc.

Supreme Court of the United States, __ U.S. __, 129 S.Ct. 1498, 173 L.Ed.2d 369 (2009).
www.findlaw.com/casecode/supreme.html[a]

HISTORICAL AND ENVIRONMENTAL SETTING *In generating electricity, a power plant produces heat. To cool the operating machinery, the plant can use water pulled from a nearby source through a cooling water intake structure. The structure affects the environment by squashing aquatic organisms against intake screens or sucking the organisms into the cooling system. The Clean Water Act mandates that "cooling water intake structures reflect the best technology available for minimizing adverse environmental impact." For more than thirty years, the EPA made the "best technology available" determination on a case-by-case basis. In 2001 and 2004, the EPA adopted "Phase I" and "Phase II" rules for power plants.*

(Jason Tessmann/Creative Commons)

Can the EPA use cost-versus-benefit analyses to determine whether power plants are implementing the best technological method for minimal environmental impact when cooling water?

FACTS Phase I rules require new power plants to restrict their inflow of water "to a level commensurate with that which can be attained by a closed-cycle recirculating cooling water system." Phase II rules apply "national performance standards" to more than five hundred existing plants but do not require closed-cycle cooling systems. The EPA found that converting these facilities to closed-cycle operations would cost $3.5 billion per year. The facilities would then produce less power while burning the same amount of coal. Moreover, other technologies can attain nearly the same results as closed-cycle systems. Phase II rules also allow a variance from the national performance standards if a facility's cost of compliance "would be significantly greater than the benefits." Environmental organizations, including Riverkeeper, Inc., challenged the Phase II regulations, arguing that existing plants should be required to convert to closed-cycle systems. The U.S. Court of Appeals for the Second Circuit issued a ruling in the plaintiffs' favor. Power-generating companies, including Entergy Corporation, appealed.

ISSUE Can the EPA compare costs with benefits to determine the "best technology available for minimizing adverse environmental impact" at cooling water intake structures?

a. In the "Browse Supreme Court Opinions" section, click on "2009." On that page, scroll to the name of the case and click on it to access the opinion.

Case 33.2–Continued

DECISION Yes. The United States Supreme Court reversed the lower court's decision. The EPA can rely on a cost-benefit analysis to set national performance standards and allow for variances from those standards as part of the Phase II regulations.

REASON "Best technology" can mean the technology that achieves the greatest reduction in adverse environmental impacts, but it can also describe the technology that "most efficiently" achieves a reduction, even if the result is less than other technologies might achieve. The use of the word *minimizing* in the controlling statute indicates that the intended objective was not the greatest possible reduction. When Congress wanted to set that as the goal in other parts of the Clean Water Act, it did so in "plain language." This suggests that the EPA has some discretion to determine the extent of the reduction under this provision. Other provisions order the EPA to consider costs and benefits in some situations. This shows that "cost-benefit analysis is not categorically forbidden." Also, in imposing standards on power plants, the EPA has been weighing costs against benefits for more than thirty years. This suggests that the practice is "reasonable and hence legitimate."

FOR CRITICAL ANALYSIS—Political Consideration *Is a comparison of costs and benefits always an effective method for choosing among alternatives? Why or why not?*

VIOLATIONS OF THE CLEAN WATER ACT Under the CWA, violators are subject to a variety of civil and criminal penalties. Depending on the violation, civil penalties range from $10,000 per day to $25,000 per day, but not more than $25,000 per violation. Criminal penalties, which apply only if a violation was intentional, range from a fine of $2,500 per day and imprisonment for up to one year to a fine of $1 million and fifteen years' imprisonment. Injunctive relief and damages can also be imposed. The polluting party can be required to clean up the pollution or pay for the cost of doing so.

Wetlands Water-saturated areas of land that are designated by a government agency (such as the Army Corps of Engineers or the Environmental Protection Agency) as protected areas that support wildlife and therefore cannot be filled in or dredged by private contractors or parties without a permit.

WETLANDS The Clean Water Act prohibits the filling or dredging of **wetlands** unless a permit is obtained from the Army Corps of Engineers. The EPA defines *wetlands* as "those areas that are inundated or saturated by surface or ground water at a frequency and duration sufficient to support . . . vegetation typically adapted for life in saturated soil conditions." Wetlands are thought to be vital to the ecosystem because they filter streams and rivers and provide habitat for wildlife. Although in the past the EPA's broad interpretation of what constitutes a wetland generated substantial controversy, the courts have considerably scaled back the CWA's protection of wetlands in recent years.[43]

DRINKING WATER The Safe Drinking Water Act of 1974[44] requires the EPA to set maximum levels for pollutants in public water systems. Public water system operators must come as close as possible to meeting the EPA's standards by using the best available technology that is economically and technologically feasible. The EPA is particularly concerned about contamination from underground sources, such as pesticides and wastes leaked from landfills or disposed of in underground injection wells. Many of these substances are associated with cancer and may cause damage to the central nervous system, liver, and kidneys.

The act was amended in 1996 to give the EPA more flexibility in setting regulatory standards. These amendments also imposed requirements on suppliers of drinking water. Each supplier must send to every household it supplies with water an annual statement describing the source of its water, the level of any contaminants contained in the water, and any possible health concerns associated with the contaminants.

Ethical Issue

Should the government begin regulating the presence of pharmaceuticals in drinking water? **The amount of pharmaceuticals used by the American public and in agriculture (antibiotics and hormones given to livestock) has grown substantially in recent years. Now trace amounts of many drugs have been detected in our nation's water supply. In 2008, for example, the drinking water of**

43. See, for example, *Rapanos v. United States,* 547 U.S. 715, 126 S.Ct. 2208, 165 L.Ed.2d 159 (2006).
44. 42 U.S.C. Sections 300f to 300j-25.

at least 41 million Americans in twenty-four regions across the country was found to contain small amounts of prescription drugs. Some of these trace amounts came from unmetabolized drugs that had passed through the humans and animals that ingested them, but the rest had been flushed down the toilet. For years, pharmacists, physicians, and the federal government have recommended that people dispose of unused medications by flushing them away. This prevents children from accidentally ingesting the drugs and keeps controlled substances, such as the painkillers oxycodone and morphine, from falling into the hands of people who might abuse them. In making these recommendations, however, no one considered the long-term effect on the environment of adding pharmaceuticals to the water supply.

Clearly, the quantities present in water now are far below medicinal doses, but no one knows how long-term exposure to random combinations of drugs will affect humans or wildlife. As yet there is little scientific evidence about the long-term effects. The federal government does not require drinking water to be tested for drugs, so Americans do not know whether their drinking water is contaminated. Requiring that water be tested and that all traces of drugs be filtered from it would be enormously expensive. In a time of economic recession, should the government wait until there is scientific proof of the harmful effects on humans and wildlife before regulating? Or should the government enact legislation to address the problem now—before it becomes worse?

OCEAN DUMPING The Marine Protection, Research, and Sanctuaries Act of 1972[45] (popularly known as the Ocean Dumping Act), as amended in 1983, regulates the transportation and dumping of material into ocean waters. It prohibits entirely the ocean dumping of radiological, chemical, and biological warfare agents and high-level radioactive waste. The act also established a permit program for transporting and dumping other materials, and designated certain areas as marine sanctuaries. Each violation of any provision in the Ocean Dumping Act may result in a civil penalty of up to $50,000. A knowing violation is a criminal offense that may result in a $50,000 fine, imprisonment for not more than a year, or both. A court may also grant an injunction to prevent an imminent or continuing violation of the Ocean Dumping Act.

OIL POLLUTION In response to the worst oil spill in North American history—more than 10 million gallons of oil that leaked into Alaska's Prince William Sound from the *Exxon Valdez* supertanker—Congress passed the Oil Pollution Act of 1990.[46] Under this act, any onshore or offshore oil facility, oil shipper, vessel owner, or vessel operator that discharges oil into navigable waters or onto an adjoining shore can be liable for clean-up costs, as well as damages.

Under the act, damage to natural resources, private property, and the local economy, including the increased cost of providing public services, is compensable. The penalties range from $2 million to $350 million, depending on the size of the vessel and on whether the oil spill came from a vessel or an offshore facility. The party held responsible for the clean-up costs can bring a civil suit for contribution from other potentially liable parties. The act also mandated that by the year 2011, oil tankers using U.S. ports must be double hulled to limit the severity of accidental spills.

Toxic Chemicals

Originally, most environmental clean-up efforts were directed toward reducing smog and making water safe for fishing and swimming. Today, the control of toxic chemicals used in agriculture and in industry has become increasingly important.

---

45. 16 U.S.C. Sections 1401–1445.

46. 33 U.S.C. Sections 2701–2761.

Pesticides and Herbicides The Federal Insecticide, Fungicide, and Rodenticide Act (FIFRA) of 1947 regulates pesticides and herbicides.[47] Under FIFRA, pesticides and herbicides must be (1) registered before they can be sold, (2) certified and used only for approved applications, and (3) used in limited quantities when applied to food crops. The EPA can cancel or suspend registration of substances that are identified as harmful and may also inspect factories where the chemicals are made. Under 1996 amendments to FIFRA, there must be no more than a one-in-a-million risk to people of developing cancer from any kind of exposure to the substance, including eating food that contains pesticide residues.[48]

It is a violation of FIFRA to sell a pesticide or herbicide that is either unregistered or has had its registration canceled or suspended. It is also a violation to sell a pesticide or herbicide with a false or misleading label or to destroy or deface any labeling required under the act. Penalties for commercial dealers include imprisonment for up to one year and a fine of no more than $25,000. Farmers and other private users of pesticides or herbicides who violate the act are subject to a $1,000 fine and incarceration for up to thirty days.

Note that a state can also regulate the sale and use of federally registered pesticides. **CASE EXAMPLE 33.9** The EPA conditionally registered Strongarm, a weed-killing pesticide, in 2000. Dow Agrosciences, LLC, immediately sold Strongarm to Texas peanut farmers. When the farmers applied it, however, Strongarm damaged their crops while failing to control the growth of weeds. The farmers sued Dow, but the lower courts ruled that FIFRA preempted their claims. The farmers appealed to the United States Supreme Court. The Supreme Court held that under a specific provision of FIFRA, a state can regulate the sale and use of federally registered pesticides so long as the regulation does not permit anything that FIFRA prohibits.[49] ●

Toxic Substances The first comprehensive law covering toxic substances was the Toxic Substances Control Act of 1976.[50] The act was passed to regulate chemicals and chemical compounds that are known to be toxic—such as asbestos and polychlorinated biphenyls, popularly known as PCBs—and to institute investigation of any possible harmful effects from new chemical compounds. The regulations authorize the EPA to require that manufacturers, processors, and other organizations planning to use chemicals first determine their effects on human health and the environment. The EPA can regulate substances that potentially pose an imminent hazard or an unreasonable risk of injury to health or the environment. The EPA may require special labeling, limit the use of a substance, set production quotas, or prohibit the use of a substance altogether.

Hazardous Waste Disposal

Some industrial, agricultural, and household wastes pose more serious threats than others. If not properly disposed of, these toxic chemicals may present a substantial danger to human health and the environment. If released into the environment, they may contaminate public drinking water resources.

Resource Conservation and Recovery Act In 1976, Congress passed the Resource Conservation and Recovery Act (RCRA)[51] in reaction to concern over the effects of hazardous waste materials on the environment. The RCRA required the EPA to determine which forms of solid waste should be considered hazardous and to establish regulations

47. 7 U.S.C. Sections 135–136y.
48. 21 U.S.C. Section 346a.
49. *Bates v. Dow Agrosciences, LLC*, 544 U.S. 431, 125 S.Ct. 1788, 161 L.Ed.2d 687 (2005).
50. 15 U.S.C. Sections 2601–2692.
51. 42 U.S.C. Sections 6901 *et seq.*

to monitor and control hazardous waste disposal. The act also requires all producers of hazardous waste materials to label and package properly any hazardous waste to be transported. The RCRA was amended in 1984 and 1986 to decrease the use of land containment in the disposal of hazardous waste and to require smaller generators of hazardous waste to comply with the act.

Under the RCRA, a company may be assessed a civil penalty of up to $25,000 for each violation.[52] Penalties are based on the seriousness of the violation, the probability of harm, and the extent to which the violation deviates from RCRA requirements. Criminal penalties include fines of up to $50,000 for each day of violation, imprisonment for up to two years (in most instances), or both.[53] Criminal fines and the period of imprisonment can be doubled for certain repeat offenders.

SUPERFUND In 1980, Congress passed the Comprehensive Environmental Response, Compensation, and Liability Act (CERCLA),[54] commonly known as Superfund, to regulate the clean-up of leaking hazardous waste–disposal sites. A special federal fund was created for that purpose.

CERCLA, as amended in 1986, has four primary elements:

1. It established an information-gathering and analysis system that enables the government to identify chemical dump sites and determine the appropriate action.
2. It authorized the EPA to respond to hazardous substance emergencies and to arrange for the clean-up of a leaking site directly if the persons responsible for the problem fail to clean up the site.
3. It created a Hazardous Substance Response Trust Fund (Superfund) to pay for the clean-up of hazardous sites using funds obtained through taxes on certain businesses.
4. It allowed the government to recover the cost of clean-up from the persons who were (even remotely) responsible for hazardous substance releases.

Potentially Responsible Parties under Superfund. Superfund provides that when a release or a threatened release of hazardous chemicals from a site occurs, the EPA can clean up the site and recover the cost of the clean-up from the following persons: (1) the person who generated the wastes disposed of at the site, (2) the person who transported the wastes to the site, (3) the person who owned or operated the site at the time of the disposal, or (4) the current owner or operator. A person falling within one of these categories is referred to as a **potentially responsible party (PRP).**

Potentially Responsible Party (PRP) A party liable for the costs of cleaning up a hazardous waste-disposal site under the Comprehensive Environmental Response, Compensation, and Liability Act. Any person who generated the hazardous waste, transported it, owned or operated the waste site at the time of disposal, or owns or operates the site at the present time may be responsible for some or all of the clean-up costs.

Joint and Several Liability under Superfund. Liability under Superfund is usually joint and several—that is, a person who generated *only a fraction of the hazardous waste* disposed of at the site may nevertheless be liable for *all* of the clean-up costs. CERCLA authorizes a party who has incurred clean-up costs to bring a "contribution action" against any other person who is liable or potentially liable for a percentage of the costs.

52. 42 U.S.C. Section 6928(a).
53. 42 U.S.C. Section 6928(d).
54. 42 U.S.C. Sections 9601–9675.

Reviewing . . . Consumer and Environmental Law

Leota Sage saw a local motorcycle dealer's advertisement in a newspaper offering a MetroRider EZ electric scooter for $1,699. When she went to the dealership, however, she learned that the EZ model was sold out. The salesperson told Sage that he still had the higher-end MetroRider FX model in stock for $2,199 and would sell her one for $1,999. Sage was disappointed but decided to purchase the FX model. Sage told the sales representative that she wished to purchase the scooter on credit and was directed to the dealer's credit department. As she filled out the credit forms, the clerk told Sage, an African American, that she would need a cosigner. Sage could not understand why she would need a cosigner and asked to speak to the manager. The manager apologized, told her that the clerk was mistaken, and said that he would "speak to" the clerk. The manager completed Sage's credit application, and Sage then rode the scooter home. Seven months later, Sage received a letter from the Federal Trade Commission (FTC) asking questions about her transaction with the motorcycle dealer and indicating that it had received complaints from other consumers. Using the information presented in the chapter, answer the following questions.

1. Did the dealer engage in deceptive advertising? Why or why not?
2. Suppose that Sage had ordered the scooter through the dealer's Web site but the dealer had been unable to deliver it by the date promised. What would the FTC have required the merchant to do in that situation?
3. Assuming that the clerk required a cosigner based on Sage's race or gender, what act prohibits such credit discrimination?
4. What organization has the authority to ban the sale of scooters based on safety concerns?

Business Application

How Can You Keep Abreast of Environmental Laws?*

Businesspersons today increasingly face the threat of severe civil or criminal penalties if they violate environmental laws and regulations. Thus, it is crucial to be aware of what those laws and regulations are, how to monitor changes in them, and when to consult with an attorney during the normal course of business. Consider some areas of concern that affect businesses.

Factors to Consider When Purchasing Business Property

When purchasing business property, keep in mind the environmental problems that may arise. Realize that it is up to you as a purchaser of the property to raise environmental issues—sellers, title insurance companies, and real estate brokers will rarely pursue such matters. (A bank financing the property may worry about the potential environmental hazards of the property, however.)

As a purchaser of business property, you should find out whether there are any restrictions on the use of the land, such as whether it can be cleared of trees for construction purposes. The most important environmental concern, though, is whether the property has been contaminated by hazardous wastes created by the previous owners.

Investigate Land-Use History

Purchasers of property can be held liable under Superfund for the clean-up of hazardous wastes dumped by previous property owners. Although current property owners who pay clean-up costs can sue the previous owners for contribution, such litigation is expensive and the outcome uncertain. Clearly, a more prudent course is to investigate the history of the use of the land before purchasing the property. You might even want to hire a private environmental site inspector to determine, at a minimum, whether the land has any obvious signs of former contamination.

Investigate and Correct Environmental Violations

Today's companies have an incentive to discover their own environmental wrongdoings. As mentioned in Chapter 6, the federal sentencing guidelines encourage companies to promptly detect, disclose, and correct wrongdoing, including environmental crimes. Companies that do so are subject to lighter penalties for violations of environmental laws. Thus, a company would be well advised to conduct environmental compliance audits regularly.

Small businesses (those with up to one hundred employees) will find it particularly advantageous to investigate and correct environmental violations. Under EPA guidelines, the EPA will waive all fines if a small company corrects environmental violations within 180 days after being notified of the violations (or 360 days if pollution-prevention techniques are involved). The policy does not apply to criminal violations of environmental laws or to actions that pose a significant threat to public health, safety, or the environment.

CHECKLIST FOR THE BUSINESSPERSON

1. **If you are going to purchase real estate, consult your attorney to find out whether there are any restrictions on the use of the property and investigate its history to check for previous contamination.**
2. **If you want to avoid liability for violating environmental regulations or statutes, conduct environmental compliance audits on a regular basis.**
3. **If you are ever charged with violating an environmental regulation or law, immediately cease the activity you are being charged with and contact your attorney.**
4. **In general, environmental law is sufficiently complex that you should never attempt to deal with it without the help of an attorney.**

* This *Business Application* is not meant to substitute for the services of an attorney who is licensed to practice law in your state.

Key Terms

bait-and-switch advertising 837
cease-and-desist order 838
"cooling-off" laws 840
counteradvertising 838
deceptive advertising 836
environmental impact statement (EIS) 847
multiple product order 838
nuisance 846
potentially responsible party (PRP) 854
Regulation Z 840
toxic tort 847
wetlands 851

Chapter Summary: Consumer and Environmental Law

CONSUMER LAW	
Deceptive Advertising (See pages 836–838.)	1. *Definition of deceptive advertising*—Generally, an advertising claim will be deemed deceptive if it would mislead a reasonable consumer. 2. *Bait-and-switch advertising*—Advertising a lower-priced product (the bait) when the intention is not to sell the advertised product but to lure consumers into the store and convince them to buy a higher-priced product (the switch) is prohibited by the FTC. 3. *Online deceptive advertising*—The FTC has issued guidelines to help online businesses comply with existing laws prohibiting deceptive advertising. 4. *FTC actions against deceptive advertising*— a. Cease-and-desist orders—Requiring the advertiser to stop the challenged advertising. b. Counteradvertising—Requiring the advertiser to advertise to correct the earlier misinformation.
Telemarketing and Fax Advertising (See pages 838–839.)	The Telephone Consumer Protection Act of 1991 prohibits telephone solicitation using an automatic telephone dialing system or a prerecorded voice, as well as the transmission of advertising materials via fax without first obtaining the recipient's permission.
Labeling and Packaging (See pages 839–840.)	Manufacturers must comply with the labeling or packaging requirements for their specific products. In general, all labels must be accurate and not misleading.
Sales (See pages 840–841.)	1. *Telephone and mail-order sales*—Federal and state statutes and regulations govern certain practices of sellers who solicit over the telephone or through the mails and prohibit the use of the mails to defraud individuals. 2. *Online sales*—Both state and federal laws protect consumers to some extent against fraudulent and deceptive online sales practices.
Health and Safety (See pages 841–842.)	1. *Food and drugs*—The Federal Food, Drug, and Cosmetic Act of 1916, as amended in 1938, protects consumers against adulterated and misbranded foods and drugs. The act establishes food standards, specifies safe levels of potentially hazardous food additives, and sets classifications of food and food advertising. 2. *Consumer product safety*—The Consumer Product Safety Act of 1972 seeks to protect consumers from risk of injury from hazardous products. The Consumer Product Safety Commission has the power to remove products that are deemed imminently hazardous from the market and to ban the manufacture and sale of hazardous products.
Credit Protection (See pages 842–846.)	1. *Consumer Credit Protection Act, Title I (Truth-in-Lending Act, or TILA)*—A disclosure law that requires sellers and lenders to disclose credit terms or loan terms in certain transactions, including retail and installment sales and loans, car loans, home-improvement loans, and certain real estate loans. Additionally, the TILA provides for the following: a. Equal credit opportunity—Creditors are prohibited from discriminating on the basis of race, religion, marital status, gender, national origin, color, or age. b. Credit-card protection—Liability of cardholders for unauthorized charges is limited to $50, providing notice requirements are met; consumers are not liable for unauthorized charges made on unsolicited credit cards. The act also sets out procedures to be used in settling disputes between credit-card companies and their cardholders. c. Consumer leases—The Consumer Leasing Act (CLA) of 1988 protects consumers who lease automobiles and other goods priced at $25,000 or less if the lease term exceeds four months.

Chapter Summary: Consumer and Environmental Law—Continued

Credit Protection—Continued	2. *Fair Credit Reporting Act*—Entitles consumers to request verification of the accuracy of a credit report and to have unverified or false information removed from their files. 3. *Fair and Accurate Credit Transaction Act*—Attempts to combat identity theft by establishing a national fraud alert system. Requires account numbers to be truncated and credit reporting agencies to provide one free credit report per year to consumers. Assists victims of identity theft in rebuilding their credit. 4. *Fair Debt Collection Practices Act*—Prohibits debt collectors from using unfair debt-collection practices, such as contacting the debtor at his or her place of employment if the employer objects or at unreasonable times, contacting third parties about the debt, and harassing the debtor.
	ENVIRONMENTAL LAW
Common Law Actions (See pages 846–847.)	1. *Nuisance*—A common law doctrine under which actions against pollution-causing activities may be brought. An action is permissible only if an individual suffers a harm separate and distinct from that of the general public. 2. *Negligence and strict liability*—Parties may recover damages for injuries sustained as a result of a firm's pollution-causing activities if they can demonstrate that the harm was a foreseeable result of the firm's failure to exercise reasonable care (negligence); businesses engaging in ultrahazardous activities are liable for whatever injuries the activities cause, regardless of whether the firms exercise reasonable care.
State and Local Regulation (See page 847.)	Activities affecting the environment are controlled at the local and state levels through regulations relating to land use, the disposal and recycling of garbage and waste, and pollution-causing activities in general.
Federal Regulation (See pages 847–854.)	1. *Environmental protection agencies*—The primary agency regulating environmental law is the federal Environmental Protection Agency (EPA), which was created in 1970 to coordinate federal environmental programs. The EPA administers most federal environmental policies and statutes. 2. *Assessing environmental impact*—The National Environmental Policy Act of 1969 imposes environmental responsibilities on all federal agencies and requires the preparation of an environmental impact statement (EIS) for every major federal action. An EIS must analyze the action's impact on the environment, its adverse effects and possible alternatives, and its irreversible effects on environmental quality. 3. *Important areas regulated by the federal government*—Important areas regulated by the federal government include the following: a. Air pollution—Regulated under the authority of the Clean Air Act and its amendments. b. Water pollution—Regulated under the authority of the Rivers and Harbors Appropriations Act of 1899, as amended, and the Federal Water Pollution Control Act of 1948, as amended by the Clean Water Act of 1972. c. Toxic chemicals and hazardous waste—Pesticides and herbicides, toxic substances, and hazardous waste are regulated under the authority of the Federal Insecticide, Fungicide, and Rodenticide Act of 1947, the Toxic Substances Control Act of 1976, and the Resource Conservation and Recovery Act of 1976, respectively. The Comprehensive Environmental Response, Compensation, and Liability Act (CERCLA) of 1980, as amended, regulates the clean-up of hazardous waste-disposal sites.

ExamPrep

ISSUE SPOTTERS

1 Gert buys a notebook computer from EZ Electronics. She pays for it with her credit card. When the computer proves defective, she asks EZ to repair or replace it, but EZ refuses. What can Gert do?

2 Resource Refining Company's plant emits smoke and fumes. Resource's operation includes a short railway system, and trucks enter and exit the grounds continuously. Constant vibrations from the trains and trucks rattle nearby residential neighborhoods. The residents sue Resource. Are there any reasons that the court might refuse to enjoin Resource's operation? Explain.

BEFORE THE TEST

Check your answers to the Issue Spotters, and at the same time, take the interactive quiz for this chapter. Go to www.cengage.com/blaw/blt and click on "Chapter 33." First, click on "Answers to Issue Spotters" to check your answers. Next, click on "Interactive Quiz" to assess your mastery of the concepts in this chapter. Then click on "Flashcards" to review this chapter's Key Term definitions.

For Review

Answers for the even-numbered questions in this For Review *section can be found on this text's accompanying Web site at* www.cengage.com/blaw/blt. *Select "Chapter 33" and click on "For Review."*

1 When will advertising be deemed deceptive?
2 What are the major federal statutes providing for consumer protection in credit transactions?
3 Under what common law theories can polluters be held liable?
4 What is contained in an environmental impact statement, and who must file one?
5 What major federal statutes regulate air and water pollution? What is Superfund, and who is potentially liable under Superfund?

Hypothetical Scenarios and Case Problems

33–1 **Clean Air Act.** Current scientific knowledge indicates that there is no safe level of exposure to a cancer-causing agent. In theory, even one molecule of such a substance has the potential for causing cancer. Section 112 of the Clean Air Act requires that all cancer-causing substances be regulated to ensure a margin of safety. Some environmental groups have argued that all emissions of such substances must be eliminated if a margin of safety is to be reached. Such a total elimination would likely shut down many major U.S. industries. Should the Environmental Protection Agency totally eliminate all emissions of cancer-causing chemicals? Discuss.

33–2 **Hypothetical Question with Sample Answer** Maria Ochoa receives two new credit cards on May 1. She had solicited one of them from Midtown Department Store, and the other arrived unsolicited from High-Flying Airlines. During the month of May, Ochoa makes numerous credit-card purchases from Midtown Department Store, but she does not use the High-Flying Airlines card. On May 31, a burglar breaks into Ochoa's home and steals both credit cards, along with other items. Ochoa notifies Midtown Department Store of the theft on June 2, but she fails to notify High-Flying Airlines. Using the Midtown credit card, the burglar makes a $500 purchase on June 1 and a $200 purchase on June 3. The burglar then charges a vacation flight on the High-Flying Airlines card for $1,000 on June 5. Ochoa receives the bills for these charges and refuses to pay them. Discuss Ochoa's liability in these situations.

—For a sample answer to Question 33–2, go to Appendix E at the end of this text.

33–3 **Environmental Laws.** Fruitade, Inc., is a processor of a soft drink called Freshen Up. Fruitade uses returnable bottles, which it cleans with a special acid to allow for further beverage processing. The acid is diluted with water and then allowed to pass into a navigable stream. Fruitade crushes its broken bottles and throws the crushed glass into the stream. Discuss fully any environmental laws that Fruitade has violated.

33–4 **Clean Water Act.** The Anacostia River, which flows through Washington, D.C., is one of the ten most polluted rivers in the country. For bodies of water such as the Anacostia, the Clean Water Act requires states (which, under the act, include the District of Columbia) to set a "total maximum daily load" (TMDL) for pollutants. A TMDL is to be set "at a level necessary to implement the applicable water-quality standards with seasonal variations." The Anacostia contains biochemical pollutants that consume oxygen, putting the river's aquatic life at risk for suffocation. In addition, the river is murky, stunting the growth of plants that rely on sunlight and impairing recreational use. The Environmental Protection Agency (EPA) approved one TMDL limiting the *annual* discharge of oxygen-depleting pollutants and a second limiting the *seasonal* discharge of pollutants contributing to turbidity. Neither TMDL limited daily discharges. Friends of the Earth, Inc. (FoE), asked a federal district court to review the TMDLs. What is FoE's best argument in this dispute? What is the EPA's likely response? What should the court rule, and why? [*Friends of the Earth, Inc. v. Environmental Protection Agency,* 446 F.3d 140 (D.C.Cir. 2006)]

33–5 **Environmental Impact Statement.** The fourth largest crop in the United States is alfalfa, of which 5 percent is exported to Japan. RoundUp Ready alfalfa is genetically engineered to resist glyphosate, the active ingredient in the herbicide RoundUp. The U.S. Department of Agriculture (USDA) regulates genetically engineered agricultural products through the Animal and Plant Health Inspection Service (APHIS). APHIS concluded that RoundUp Ready alfalfa does not have any harmful effects on the health of humans or livestock and deregulated it. Geertson Seed Farms and others filed a suit in a federal district court against Mike Johanns (the secretary of the USDA) and others, asserting that APHIS's decision required the preparation of an environmental impact statement (EIS). The plaintiffs argued, among other things, that the introduction of RoundUp Ready alfalfa might significantly decrease the availability of, or even eliminate, all nongenetically engineered varieties. The plaintiffs were concerned that the RoundUp Ready alfalfa might contaminate standard alfalfa because alfalfa is pollinated by bees, which can travel as far as two miles from a pollen source. If contamination occurred, farmers would not be able to market "contaminated" varieties as "organic," which would affect the sales of "organic" livestock and exports to Japan, which does not allow the import of glyphosate-resistant alfalfa. Should an EIS be prepared in this case? Why or why not? [*Geertson Seed Farms v. Johanns,* __ F.Supp.2d __ (N.D.Cal. 2007)]

33–6 **Case Problem with Sample Answer** The Nutrition Labeling and Education Act (NLEA) requires packaged food to have a "Nutrition Facts" panel that sets out "nutrition information," including "the total number of calories" per serving. Restaurants are exempt from this requirement. The NLEA also regulates nutrition-content claims, such as "low sodium," that a purveyor might choose to add to a label. The NLEA permits a state or local law to require restaurants to disclose nutrition information about the food they serve, but expressly preempts state or local attempts to regulate nutrition-content claims. New York City Health Code Section 81.50 requires 10 percent of the restaurants in the city, including McDonald's, Burger King, and Kentucky Fried Chicken, to post calorie content information on their menus. The New York State Restaurant Association (NYSRA) filed a suit in a federal district court, contending that the NLEA preempts Section 81.50. (Under the U.S. Constitution, state or local laws that conflict with federal laws are preempted.) Is the NYSRA correct? Explain. [*New York State Restaurant Association v. New York City Board of Health*, 556 F.3d 114 (2d Cir. 2009)]

—After you have answered Problem 33–6, compare your answer with the sample answer given on the Web site that accompanies this text. Go to www.cengage.com/blaw/blt, select "Chapter 33," and click on "Case Problem with Sample Answer."

33–7 **A Question of Ethics** *In the Clean Air Act, Congress allowed California, which has particular problems with clean air, to adopt its own standard for emissions from cars and trucks, subject to the approval of the Environmental Protection Agency (EPA) according to certain criteria. Congress also allowed other states to adopt California's standard after the EPA's approval. In 2004, in an effort to address global warming, the California Air Resources Board amended the state's standard to attain "the maximum feasible and cost-effective reduction of GHG [greenhouse gas] emissions from motor vehicles." The regulation, which applies to new passenger vehicles and light-duty trucks for 2009 and later, imposes decreasing limits on emissions of carbon dioxide through 2016. While EPA approval was pending, Vermont and other states adopted similar standards. Green Mountain Chrysler Plymouth Dodge Jeep and other auto dealers, automakers, and associations of automakers filed a suit in a federal district court against George Crombie (secretary of the Vermont Agency of Natural Resources) and others, seeking relief from the state regulations.* [Green Mountain Chrysler Plymouth Dodge Jeep v. Crombie, __ *F.Supp.2d* __ *(D.Vt. 2007)*]

1. Under the Environmental Policy and Conservation Act (EPCA) of 1975, the National Highway Traffic Safety Administration sets fuel economy standards for new cars. The plaintiffs argued, among other things, that the EPCA, which prohibits states from adopting fuel economy standards, preempts Vermont's GHG regulation. Do the GHG rules equate to the fuel economy standards? Discuss.
2. Do Vermont's rules tread on the efforts of the federal government to address global warming internationally? Who should regulate GHG emissions? The federal government? The state governments? Both? Neither? Why?
3. The plaintiffs claimed that they would go bankrupt if they were forced to adhere to the state's GHG standards. Should they be granted relief on this basis? Does history support their claim? Explain.

Critical Thinking and Writing Assignments

33–8 **Critical Legal Thinking.** It has been estimated that for every dollar spent cleaning up hazardous waste sites, administrative agencies spend seven dollars in overhead. Can you think of any way to trim these administrative costs? Explain.

33–9 **Critical Thinking and Writing Assignment for Business.** Many states have enacted laws that go even further than federal law to protect consumers. These laws vary tremendously from state to state. Generally, is having different laws fair to sellers who may be prohibited from engaging in a practice in one state that is legal in another? How might these different laws affect a business? Is it fair that residents of one state have more protection than residents of another?

33–10 

Video Question Go to this text's Web site at www.cengage.com/blaw/blt **and select "Chapter 33." Click on "Video Questions" and view the video titled *Advertising Communication Law: Bait and Switch.* Then answer the following questions.**

1. Is the auto dealership's advertisement for the truck in the video deceptive? Why or why not?
2. Is the advertisement for the truck an offer to which the dealership is bound? Does it matter if Betty detrimentally relied on the advertisement?
3. Is Tony committed to buying Betty's trade-in truck for $3,000 because that is what he told her over the phone?

Practical Internet Exercises

Go to this text's Web site at www.cengage.com/blaw/blt, select "Chapter 33," and click on "Practical Internet Exercises." There you will find the following Internet research exercises that you can perform to learn more about the topics covered in this chapter.

Practical Internet Exercise 33–1: LEGAL PERSPECTIVE—**The Food and Drug Administration**
Practical Internet Exercise 33–2: SOCIAL PERSPECTIVE—**Nuisance Law**
Practical Internet Exercise 33–3: MANAGEMENT PERSPECTIVE—**Complying with Environmental Regulations**

Chapter 34

Liability of Accountants and Other Professionals

Chapter Outline

- Potential Common Law Liability to Clients
- Potential Liability to Third Parties
- The Sarbanes-Oxley Act of 2002
- Potential Statutory Liability of Accountants under Securities Laws
- Potential Criminal Liability
- Confidentiality and Privilege

"A member should observe the profession's technical and ethical standard . . . and discharge professional responsibility to the best of the member's ability."

—Article V, *Code of Professional Conduct*, American Institute of Certified Public Accountants

Learning Objectives

After reading this chapter, you should be able to answer the following questions:

1. Under what common law theories may professionals be liable to clients?
2. What are the rules concerning an auditor's liability to third parties?
3. How might an accountant violate federal securities laws?
4. What crimes might an accountant commit under the Internal Revenue Code?
5. What constrains professionals to keep communications with their clients confidential?

The standard of due care to which the members of the American Institute of Certified Public Accountants are expected to adhere is set out in the chapter-opening quotation. Accountants, attorneys, physicians, and other professionals have found themselves increasingly subject to liability in the past decade or so. This more extensive liability has resulted in large part from a greater public awareness of the fact that professionals are required to deliver competent services and are obligated to adhere to standards of performance commonly accepted within their professions.

Certainly, the dizzying collapse of Enron Corporation and the failure of other major companies, including WorldCom, Inc., in the early 2000s called attention to the importance of abiding by professional accounting standards. Arthur Andersen, LLP, one of the world's leading public accounting firms, ended up being indicted on criminal charges for its role in thwarting the government's investigation into Enron's accounting practices.[1] As a result, Arthur Andersen ceased to exist and roughly 85,000 employees lost their jobs. Moreover, under the Sarbanes-Oxley Act of 2002, which Congress passed in response to these events, public accounting firms throughout the nation will feel the effects for years to

1. Although Arthur Andersen, LLP, was subsequently convicted in a federal district court on the charge of obstructing justice, the United States Supreme Court reversed and remanded the case in 2005 due to erroneous jury instructions. *Arthur Andersen, LLP v. United States,* 544 U.S. 696, 125 S.Ct. 2129, 161 L.Ed.2d 1008 (2005).

come. Among other things, the act imposed stricter regulation and oversight on the public accounting industry.

Considering the many potential sources of legal liability that they face, accountants, attorneys, and other professionals should be very aware of their legal obligations. In this chapter, we look at the potential common law liability of professionals and then examine the potential liability of accountants under securities laws and the Internal Revenue Code. The chapter concludes with a brief examination of the relationship of professionals, particularly accountants and attorneys, with their clients.

Potential Common Law Liability to Clients

Under the common law, professionals may be liable to clients for breach of contract, negligence, or fraud.

Liability for Breach of Contract

Accountants and other professionals face liability under the common law for any breach of contract. A professional owes a duty to his or her client to honor the terms of their contract and to perform the contract within the stated time period. If the professional fails to perform as agreed in the contract, then he or she has breached the contract, and the client has the right to recover damages from the professional. A professional may be held liable for expenses incurred by the client in securing another professional to provide the contracted-for services, for penalties imposed on the client for failure to meet time deadlines, and for any other reasonable and foreseeable monetary losses that arise from the professional's breach.

Liability for Negligence

Accountants and other professionals may also be held liable under the common law for negligence in the performance of their services. The elements that must be proved to establish negligence on the part of a professional are as follows:

1. A duty of care existed.
2. That duty of care was breached.
3. The plaintiff suffered an injury.
4. The injury was proximately caused by the defendant's breach of the duty of care.

All professionals are subject to standards of conduct established by codes of professional ethics, by state statutes, and by judicial decisions. They are also governed by the contracts they enter into with their clients. In their performance of contracts, professionals must exercise the established standards of care, knowledge, and judgment generally accepted by members of their professional group. Here, we look at the duty of care owed by two groups of professionals that frequently perform services for business firms: accountants and attorneys.

Generally Accepted Accounting Principles (GAAP) The conventions, rules, and procedures that define accepted accounting practices at a particular time. The source of the principles is the Financial Accounting Standards Board.

Generally Accepted Auditing Standards (GAAS) Standards concerning an auditor's professional qualities and the judgment exercised by him or her in the performance of an audit and report. The source of the standards is the American Institute of Certified Public Accountants.

ACCOUNTANT'S DUTY OF CARE Accountants play a major role in a business's financial system. Accountants have the necessary expertise and experience to establish and maintain accurate financial records; design, control, and audit record-keeping systems; prepare reliable statements that reflect an individual's or a business's financial status; and give tax advice and prepare tax returns.

GAAP and GAAS. In the performance of their services, accountants must comply with **generally accepted accounting principles (GAAP)** and **generally accepted auditing standards (GAAS).** The Financial Accounting Standards Board (FASB, usually pronounced "faz-bee") determines what accounting conventions, rules, and procedures constitute GAAP at a given point in time. GAAS are standards concerning an auditor's professional qualities and the judgment that he or she exercises in performing an audit and report. GAAS are established by the American Institute of Certified Public Accountants. As long as an accountant conforms to GAAP and acts in good faith, he or she normally will not be held liable to the client for incorrect judgment. (For a discussion of how GAAP will be replaced by global accounting rules in the future, see this chapter's *Landmark in the Law* feature.)

Defalcation Embezzlement; the misappropriation of funds by a party, such as a corporate officer or public official, in a fiduciary relationship with another.

As a general rule, an accountant is not required to discover every impropriety, **defalcation**[2] (embezzlement), or fraud, in her or his client's books. If, however, the impropriety, defalcation, or fraud has gone undiscovered because of the accountant's negligence or failure to perform an express or implied duty, the accountant will be liable for any resulting losses suffered by the client. Therefore, an accountant who uncovers suspicious financial transactions and fails to investigate the matter fully or to inform the client of the discovery can be held liable to the client for the resulting loss.

A violation of GAAP and GAAS is considered *prima facie* evidence of negligence on the part of the accountant. Compliance with GAAP and GAAS, however, does not *necessarily* relieve an accountant from potential legal liability. An accountant may be held to a higher standard of conduct established by state statute and by judicial decisions.

Audits, Qualified Opinions, and Disclaimers. One of the most important tasks that an accountant may perform for a business is an audit. An *audit* is a systematic inspection, by analyses and tests, of a business's financial records. (For a discussion of the use of statistical sampling in audits, see this chapter's *Linking the Law to Business Statistics* feature on page 875.)

"Never call an accountant a credit to his profession; a good accountant is a debit to his profession."

Attributed to Charles J. C. Lyall, 1943–1996
(American commentator)

The purpose of an audit is to provide the auditor with evidence to support an opinion on the reliability of the business's financial statements. A normal audit is not intended to uncover fraud or other misconduct. Nevertheless, an accountant may be liable for failing to detect misconduct if a normal audit would have revealed it. Also, if the auditor agreed to examine the records for evidence of fraud or other obvious misconduct and then failed to detect it, he or she may be liable. After performing an audit, the auditor issues an opinion letter stating whether, in his or her opinion, the financial statements fairly present the business's financial position.

In issuing an opinion letter, an auditor may *qualify* the opinion or include a disclaimer. An opinion that disclaims any liability for false or misleading financial statements is too general, however. A qualified opinion or a disclaimer must be specific and identify the reason for the qualification or disclaimer. **EXAMPLE 34.1** Richard Zehr performs an audit of Lacey Corporation. In the opinion letter, Zehr qualifies his opinion by stating that there is uncertainty about how a lawsuit against the firm will be resolved. In this situation, Zehr will not be liable if the outcome of the suit is unfavorable for the firm. Zehr could still be liable, however, for failing to discover other problems that an audit in compliance with GAAS and GAAP would have revealed. ● In a disclaimer, the auditor basically is stating that she or he does not have sufficient information to issue an opinion. Again, the auditor must identify the problem and indicate what information is lacking.

Unaudited Financial Statements. Sometimes, accountants are hired to prepare unaudited financial statements. (A financial statement is considered unaudited if incomplete auditing procedures have been used in its preparation or if insufficient procedures have been used to justify an opinion.) Accountants may be subject to liability for failing, in accor-

2. This term, pronounced deh-fal-*kay*-shun, is derived from the Latin *de* ("off") and *falx* ("sickle"—a tool for cutting grain or tall grass). In law, the term refers to the act of a defaulter or of an embezzler. As used here, it means embezzlement.

Landmark in the Law The SEC Adopts Global Accounting Rules

At one time, investors and companies considered the U.S. accounting rules, known as generally accepted accounting principles (GAAP), to be the gold standard–the best system for reporting earnings and other financial information. Then came the subprime mortgage meltdown and the global economic crisis, which caused many to question the effectiveness and superiority of GAAP.

In 2008, the Securities and Exchange Commission (SEC) unanimously approved a plan to require U.S. companies to use a set of global accounting rules, known as International Financial Reporting Standards (IFRS), for all of the financial reports that they must file with the Commission. Under the plan, the use of GAAP will be phased out, with final approval of rules implementing the IFRS scheduled for 2011.

Why Shift to Global Accounting Standards? The SEC decided to replace the rules-based GAAP with the principles-based IFRS for several reasons. GAAP rules are detailed and fill nearly 25,000 pages. The IFRS are simpler and more straightforward, spanning only 2,500 pages, and they focus more on overrriding principles than on specific rules.

Consequently, companies should eventually find it less difficult to comply with the international rules, and this should lead to cost savings. Another benefit is that investors will find it easier to make cross-country comparisons between, say, a technology company in the Silicon Valley and one in Germany or Japan.

Furthermore, having uniform accounting rules that apply to all nations makes sense in a global economy. The European Union and 113 other nations, including Australia, Canada, China, India, and Mexico, have already adopted the IFRS. In fact, most of the United States' trading partners use the global rules. The widespread use of the IFRS is why some large multinational firms embraced the SEC's decision. By switching to the IFRS, multinational companies will no longer have to prepare different financial reports for their subsidiaries located in various countries around the world.

The Downside to Adopting Global Rules Despite these benefits, the shift to the global rules has some drawbacks. For one thing, the switch will be both costly and time consuming. Companies will have to upgrade their communications and software systems, study and implement the new rules, and train their employees, accountants, and tax attorneys. To ease the transition, the SEC has set up a multiyear timetable for converting to the IFRS. Although 110 of the largest multinational companies began using the IFRS in 2009, they are not legally required to do so until 2014. Smaller firms will make the change in 2015, and the smallest publicly reporting companies will be required to shift by 2016. Nonetheless, some of the smaller U.S. firms may find it difficult to absorb the costs of converting to the IFRS.

Another issue is that although the IFRS rules are simpler, they may not be better than GAAP. Because the global rules are broader and less detailed, they give companies more leeway in reporting, so less financial information may be disclosed. Reports have also indicated that using the IFRS can lead to wide variances in profit reporting and tends to boost earnings above what they would have been under GAAP. Finally, the role of the U.S. Financial Accounting Standards Board and the SEC in shaping and overseeing accounting standards will necessarily be reduced because the London-based International Accounting Standards Board sets the IFRS.

• **Application to Today's World** *The shift to the IFRS has received broad bipartisan political support even in the face of the current economic crisis. Nevertheless, it will take years for U.S. companies to completely implement the global accounting rules. Business students should study and understand the global accounting rules so that they will be prepared to use these rules in their future careers.*

• **Relevant Web Sites** To locate information on the Web concerning the SEC's adoption of the International Financial Reporting Standards, go to this text's Web site at www.cengage.com/blaw/blt, select "Chapter 34," and click on "URLs for Landmarks."

dance with standard accounting procedures, to designate a balance sheet as "unaudited." An accountant will also be held liable for failure to disclose to a client the facts or circumstances that give reason to believe that misstatements have been made or that a fraud has been committed.

Defenses to Negligence. If an accountant is found guilty of negligence, the client can collect damages for losses that arose from the accountant's negligence. An accountant facing a claim of negligence, however, has several possible defenses, including the following:

1. The accountant was not negligent.
2. If the accountant was negligent, this negligence was not the proximate cause of the client's losses.
3. The client was also negligent (depending on whether state law allows contributory negligence as a defense).

Attorney's Duty of Care The conduct of attorneys is governed by rules established by each state and by the American Bar Association's Code of Professional Responsibility and Model Rules of Professional Conduct. All attorneys owe a duty to provide competent and diligent representation. Attorneys are required to be familiar with well-settled principles of law applicable to a case and to discover law that can be found through a reasonable amount of research. The lawyer must also investigate and discover facts that could materially affect the client's legal rights.

In judging an attorney's performance, the standard used will normally be that of a reasonably competent general practitioner of ordinary skill, experience, and capacity. If the attorney holds himself or herself out as having expertise in a particular area of law, the standard is that of a reasonably competent specialist of ordinary skill, experience, and capacity in that area of the law.

When an attorney fails to exercise reasonable care and professional judgment, she or he breaches the duty of care. The plaintiff must then prove that the breach actually caused him or her some injury. **EXAMPLE 34.2** Attorney Lynette Boehmer allows the statute of limitations to lapse on the claim of Karen Anderson, a client. Boehmer can be held liable for **malpractice** (professional negligence) because Anderson can no longer pursue her claim and has lost a potential award of damages. •

Malpractice Professional misconduct or unreasonable lack of skill; the failure of a professional to use the skills and learning common to the average reputable members of the profession or the skills and learning the professional claims to possess, resulting in injury, loss, or damage to those relying on the professional.

Liability for Fraud

An accountant may be found liable for either actual fraud or constructive fraud. Recall from Chapter 12 that fraud, or misrepresentation, involves the following elements:

1. A misrepresentation of a material fact has occurred.
2. There is an intent to deceive.
3. The innocent party has justifiably relied on the misrepresentation.
4. To obtain damages, the innocent party must have been injured.

A professional may be held liable for *actual fraud* when he or she intentionally misstates a material fact to mislead a client and the client is injured as a result of her or his justifiable reliance on the misstated fact. A material fact is one that a reasonable person would consider important in deciding whether to act.

In contrast, a professional may be held liable for *constructive* fraud whether or not he or she acted with fraudulent intent. **EXAMPLE 34.3** Paula, an accountant, is conducting an audit of National Computing Company (NCC). Paula accepts the explanations of Ron, an NCC officer, regarding certain financial irregularities, despite evidence that contradicts those explanations and indicates that the irregularities may be illegal. Paula's conduct could be characterized as an intentional failure to perform a duty in reckless disregard of the consequences of such failure. This would constitute gross negligence and could be held to be constructive fraud. • Both actual and constructive fraud are potential sources of legal liability for an accountant or other professional.

For fraudulent conduct, an accountant may also suffer penalties imposed by a state board of accountancy, as the following case illustrates.

Case 34.1 Walsh v. State

Nebraska Supreme Court, 276 Neb. 1034, 759 N.W.2d 100 (2009).

FACTS Stephen Teiper wrote a letter to the Nebraska Board of Public Accountancy to accuse his brother-in-law, Michael Walsh, a certified public accountant (CPA), of impersonating Teiper on the phone to obtain financial information from Teiper's insurance company. The board filed a complaint against Walsh for a violation of its rules. At a hearing, Walsh admitted that he had impersonated Teiper, but argued that Teiper had provided his personal

Case 34.1—Continued

Did a CPA who impersonated someone on the phone to obtain financial information breach his professional standards?

information to Walsh for this purpose. The board found that Walsh had committed a "discreditable act" and concluded that his conduct was reprehensible and reflected adversely on his fitness to engage in the practice of public accountancy. As sanctions, the board reprimanded Walsh, placed him on probation for three months, and ordered him to attend four hours of continuing education in ethics. The board also ordered him to pay the costs of the hearing. Walsh petitioned a Nebraska state court, which affirmed the orders. Walsh appealed.

ISSUE Is there a sufficient connection between the practice of public accountancy and Walsh's conduct to allow the board to discipline him?

DECISION Yes. The Nebraska Supreme Court affirmed the lower court's decision. Walsh's actions reflected adversely on the accountancy profession, which demands a high level of honesty and integrity.

REASON A CPA cannot impersonate another person and "make false statements," or otherwise commit fraud, without "tainting" the CPA's reputation and the reputation of the accountancy profession. Like attorneys and other professionals, CPAs are held to "a high degree of moral and ethical integrity" because laypersons depend on their "honesty, integrity, sound professional judgment, and compliance with government regulations." The Nebraska Board of Public Accountancy has the authority to issue rules to "establish and maintain a high standard of integrity and dignity in the profession of public accountancy." Under these rules, a CPA "shall not commit an act that reflects adversely" on his or her fitness to practice the profession. The board can discipline CPAs who do not follow these standards and can impose various sanctions, including those levied on Walsh.

FOR CRITICAL ANALYSIS—Ethical Consideration *Was the specific reason for Walsh's impersonation significant to the result in this case? Why or why not?*

Potential Liability to Third Parties

Traditionally, an accountant or other professional did not owe any duty to a third person with whom she or he had no direct contractual relationship—that is, to any person not in *privity of contract.* A professional's duty was only to her or his client. Violations of statutory laws, fraud, and other intentional or reckless acts of wrongdoing were the only exceptions to this general rule.

Today, numerous third parties—including investors, shareholders, creditors, corporate managers and directors, and regulatory agencies—rely on professional opinions, such as those of auditors, when making decisions. In view of this extensive reliance, many courts have all but abandoned the privity requirement in regard to accountants' liability to third parties.

In this section, we focus primarily on the potential liability of auditors to third parties. Understanding an auditor's common law liability to third parties is critical because often, when a business fails, its independent auditor (accountant) is one of the few potentially solvent defendants. The majority of courts now hold that auditors can be held liable to third parties for negligence, but the standard for the imposition of this liability varies. There generally are three different views of accountants' liability to third parties, each of which we discuss below.

The *Ultramares* Rule

The traditional rule regarding an accountant's liability to third parties was enunciated by Chief Judge Benjamin Cardozo in *Ultramares Corp. v. Touche,* a case decided in 1931.[3] **CASE EXAMPLE 34.4** Fred Stern & Company hired the public accounting firm of Touche, Niven & Company to review Stern's financial records and prepare a balance sheet for the year ending December 31, 1923.[4] Touche prepared the balance sheet and supplied Stern with thirty-two certified copies. According to the certified balance sheet, Stern had a net worth (assets less

3. 255 N.Y. 170, 174 N.E. 441 (1931).

4. Banks, creditors, stockholders, purchasers, or sellers often rely on a balance sheet as a basis for making decisions relating to a company's business.

liabilities) of $1,070,715.26. In reality, however, Stern's liabilities exceeded its assets—the company's records had been falsified by insiders at Stern to reflect a positive net worth (assets exceed liabilities). In reliance on the certified balance sheets, Ultramares Corporation loaned substantial amounts to Stern. After Stern was declared bankrupt, Ultramares brought an action against Touche for negligence in an attempt to recover damages. ●

THE REQUIREMENT OF PRIVITY The New York Court of Appeals (that state's highest court) refused to impose liability on the Touche accountants and concluded that they owed a duty of care only to those persons for whose "primary benefit" the statements were intended. In this case, Stern was the only person for whose primary benefit the statements were intended. The court held that in the absence of privity or a relationship "so close as to approach that of privity," a party could not recover from an accountant. The court's requirement of privity has since been referred to as the *Ultramares* rule, or the New York rule.

CASE EXAMPLE 34.5 Toro Company supplied equipment and credit to Summit Power Equipment Distributors and required Summit to submit audited reports so that Toro could evaluate the distributor's financial condition. Summit supplied Toro with reports prepared by accountants at Krouse, Kern & Company, which allegedly contained mistakes and omissions regarding Summit's financial condition. Toro extended and renewed large amounts of credit to Summit in reliance on the audited reports, but Summit was unable to repay these amounts. Toro brought a negligence action against the accounting firm and proved that accountants at Krouse knew the reports it furnished would be used by Summit to induce Toro to extend credit. Nevertheless, under the *Ultramares* rule, the court refused to hold the accounting firm liable because the firm was not in privity with Toro.[5] ●

MODIFIED TO ALLOW "NEAR PRIVITY" The *Ultramares* rule was restated and somewhat modified in a 1985 New York case, *Credit Alliance Corp. v. Arthur Andersen & Co.*[6] In that case, the court held that if a third party has a sufficiently close relationship or nexus (link or connection) with an accountant, then the *Ultramares* privity requirement may be satisfied even if no accountant-client relationship is established. The rule enunciated in the *Credit Alliance* case is often referred to as the "near privity" rule. Only a minority of states have adopted this rule of accountants' liability to third parties.

The *Restatement* Rule

The *Ultramares* rule has been severely criticized because much of the work performed by auditors is intended for use by persons who are not parties to the contract. Thus, it is asserted that the auditors owe a duty to these third parties. Consequently, there has been an erosion of the *Ultramares* rule, and accountants have increasingly been exposed to potential liability to third parties. The majority of courts have adopted the position taken by the *Restatement (Second) of Torts,* which states that accountants are subject to liability for negligence not only to their clients but also to foreseen, or *known,* users—or classes of users—of their reports or financial statements.

Under Section 552(2) of the *Restatement (Second) of Torts,* an accountant's liability extends to

1. Persons for whose benefit and guidance the accountant intends to supply the information or knows that the recipient intends to supply it, and
2. Persons whom the accountant intends the information to influence or knows that the recipient so intends.

5. *Toro Co. v. Krouse, Kern & Co.*, 827 F.2d 155 (7th Cir. 1987).
6. 65 N.Y.2d 536, 483 N.E.2d 110 (1985). A "relationship sufficiently intimate to be equated with privity" is enough for a third party to sue another's accountant for negligence.

EXAMPLE 34.6 Steve, an accountant, prepares a financial statement for Tech Software, Inc., a client, knowing that the client will submit that statement to First National Bank to secure a loan. If Steve makes negligent misstatements or omissions in the statement, he may be held liable by the bank because he knew that the bank would rely on his work product when deciding whether to make the loan. •

Liability to Reasonably Foreseeable Users

A small minority of courts hold accountants liable to any users whose reliance on an accountant's statements or reports was *reasonably foreseeable*. This standard has been criticized as extending liability too far and exposing accountants to massive liability.

The majority of courts have concluded that the *Restatement*'s approach is more reasonable because it allows accountants to control their exposure to liability. Liability is "fixed by the accountants' particular knowledge at the moment the audit is published," not by the foreseeability of the harm that might occur to a third party after the report is released.

Liability of Attorneys

Like accountants, attorneys may be held liable under the common law to third parties who rely on legal opinions to their detriment. Generally, an attorney is not liable to a nonclient unless there is fraud (or malicious conduct) by the attorney. The liability principles stated in Section 552 of the *Restatement (Second) of Torts,* however, may apply to attorneys as well as to accountants.

The Sarbanes-Oxley Act of 2002

As previously mentioned, in 2002 Congress enacted the Sarbanes-Oxley Act. The act imposes a number of strict requirements on both domestic and foreign public accounting firms that provide auditing services to companies ("issuers") whose securities are sold to public investors. The act defines the term *issuer* as a company that has securities that are registered under Section 12 of the Securities Exchange Act of 1934, that is required to file reports under Section 15(d) of the 1934 act, or that files—or has filed—a registration statement that has not yet become effective under the Securities Act of 1933 (see Chapter 31).

To the extent that Deloitte & Touche engages in auditing public companies, its procedures are overseen by the Public Company Accounting Oversight Board.

(Photo by Tim Boyle/Getty Images)

The Public Company Accounting Oversight Board

Among other things, the Sarbanes-Oxley Act increased the degree of government oversight of public accounting practices by creating the Public Company Accounting Oversight Board, which reports to the Securities and Exchange Commission. The board consists of a chair and four other members. The purpose of the board is to oversee the audit of public companies that are subject to securities laws. The goal is to protect public investors and to ensure that public accounting firms comply with the provisions of the Sarbanes-Oxley Act.

Applicability to Public Accounting Firms

Titles I and II of the act set forth the key provisions relating to the duties of the oversight board and the requirements relating to *public accounting firms*—defined by the act as firms and associated persons that are "engaged in the practice of public accounting or preparing or issuing audit reports." These provisions are summarized in Exhibit 34–1 on the next page. (Provisions relating to corporate fraud and the responsibilities of corporate officers and directors were described in Chapter 31 and listed in Exhibit 31–4 on page 799.)

Exhibit 34–1 Key Provisions of the Sarbanes-Oxley Act of 2002 Relating to Public Accounting Firms

AUDITOR INDEPENDENCE

To help ensure that auditors remain independent of the firms that they audit, Title II of the Sarbanes-Oxley Act does the following:

- Makes it unlawful for Registered Public Accounting Firms (RPAFs) to perform both audit and nonaudit services for the same company at the same time. Nonaudit services include the following:
  1. Bookkeeping or other services related to the accounting records or financial statements of the audit client.
  2. Financial information systems design and implementation.
  3. Appraisal or valuation services.
  4. Fairness opinions.
  5. Management functions.
  6. Broker or dealer, investment adviser, or investment banking services.
- Requires preapproval for most auditing services from the issuer's (the corporation's) audit committee.
- Requires audit partner rotation by prohibiting RPAFs from providing audit services to an issuer if either the lead audit partner or the audit partner responsible for reviewing the audit has provided such services to that corporation in each of the prior five years.
- Requires RPAFs to make timely reports to the audit committees of the corporations. The report must indicate all critical accounting policies and practices to be used; all alternative treatments of financial information within generally accepted accounting principles that have been discussed with the corporation's management officials, the ramifications of the use of such alternative treatments, and the treatment preferred by the auditor; and other material written communications between the auditor and the corporation's management.
- Makes it unlawful for an RPAF to provide auditing services to an issuer if the corporation's chief executive officer, chief financial officer, chief accounting officer, or controller was previously employed by the auditor and participated in any capacity in the audit of the corporation during the one-year period preceding the date that the audit began.

DOCUMENT RETENTION AND DESTRUCTION

- The Sarbanes-Oxley Act provides that anyone who destroys, alters, or falsifies records with the intent to obstruct or influence a federal investigation or in relation to bankruptcy proceedings can be criminally prosecuted and sentenced to a fine, imprisonment for up to twenty years, or both.
- The act also requires accountants who audit or review publicly traded companies to retain all working papers related to the audit or review for a period of five years (now amended to seven years). Violators can be sentenced to a fine, imprisonment for up to ten years, or both.

Requirements for Maintaining Working Papers

Working Papers The various documents used and developed by an accountant during an audit. Working papers include notes, computations, memoranda, copies, and other papers that make up the work product of an accountant's services to a client.

Performing an audit for a client involves an accumulation of **working papers**—the various documents used and developed during the audit. These include notes, computations, memoranda, copies, and other papers that make up the work product of an accountant's services to a client. Under the common law, which in this instance has been codified in a number of states, working papers remain the accountant's property. It is important for accountants to retain such records in the event that they need to defend against lawsuits for negligence or other actions in which their competence is challenged. The client also has a right to access an accountant's working papers because they reflect the client's financial situation. On a client's request, an accountant must return to the client any of the client's records or journals, and failure to do so may result in liability.

"Destroy the old files, but make copies first."
Samuel Goldwyn, 1879–1974
(American motion picture producer)

Section 802(a)(1) of the Sarbanes-Oxley Act provides that accountants must maintain working papers relating to an audit or review for five years—subsequently increased to seven years—from the end of the fiscal period in which the audit or review was concluded. A knowing violation of this requirement will subject the accountant to a fine, imprisonment for up to ten years, or both.

Ethical Issue

Are the high costs of complying with the Sarbanes-Oxley Act justified by more ethical conduct? Since its enactment, critics have complained that the costs of complying with the Sarbanes-Oxley Act greatly outweigh the perceived benefits. In fact, studies estimate that a public company spends, on average, at least $2.9 million annually complying with the act's provisions. These funds could otherwise have been distributed as dividends to shareholders or reinvested to finance the company's growth and thereby provide more jobs. The burdens of complying with the Sarbanes-Oxley Act have also led many companies to go private, turning over control to private equity firms (businesses that own shares in companies that are not listed on a public stock exchange). There is also some doubt as to whether the act has been effective in improving corporate ethics and accountability.

Potential Statutory Liability of Accountants under Securities Laws

Both civil and criminal liability may be imposed on accountants under the Securities Act of 1933, the Securities Exchange Act of 1934, and the Private Securities Litigation Reform Act of 1995.[7]

Liability under the Securities Act of 1933

The Securities Act of 1933 requires registration statements to be filed with the Securities and Exchange Commission (SEC) prior to an offering of securities (see Chapter 31).[8] Accountants frequently prepare and certify the issuer's financial statements that are included in the registration statement.

Liability under Section 11 Section 11 of the Securities Act of 1933 imposes civil liability on accountants for misstatements and omissions of material facts in registration statements. An accountant may be liable if he or she prepared any financial statements included in the registration statement that "contained an untrue statement of a material fact or omitted to state a material fact required to be stated therein or necessary to make the statements therein not misleading."[9]

Under Section 11, an accountant's liability for a misstatement or omission of a material fact in a registration statement extends to anyone who acquires a security covered by the registration statement. A purchaser of a security need only demonstrate that she or he has suffered a loss on the security. Proof of reliance on the materially false statement or misleading omission ordinarily is not required. Nor is there a requirement of privity between the accountant and the security purchasers.

Due Diligence A required standard of care that certain professionals, such as accountants, must meet to avoid liability for securities violations.

The Due Diligence Standard. Section 11 imposes a duty on accountants to use **due diligence** in preparing the financial statements included in the filed registration statements. After a purchaser has proved a loss on the security, the accountant has the burden of showing that he or she exercised due diligence in preparing the financial statements. To avoid liability, the accountant must show that he or she had, "after reasonable investigation, reasonable grounds to believe and did believe, at the time such part of the registration statement became effective, that the statements therein were true and that there was no omission of a material fact required to be stated therein or necessary to make the statements therein not misleading."[10] Failure to follow GAAP and GAAS is also proof of a lack of due diligence.

7. Civil and criminal liability may also be imposed on accountants and other professionals under other statutes, including the Racketeer Influenced and Corrupt Organizations Act (RICO). RICO was discussed in Chapter 6.
8. Many securities and transactions are expressly exempted from the 1933 act.
9. 15 U.S.C. Section 77k(a).
10. 15 U.S.C. Section 77k(b)(3).

In particular, the due diligence standard places a burden on accountants to verify information furnished by a corporation's officers and directors. The burden of proving due diligence requires an accountant to demonstrate that she or he is free from negligence or fraud. Merely asking questions is not always sufficient to satisfy the requirement. Accountants can be held liable for failing to detect danger signals in documents furnished by corporate officers that, under GAAS, require further investigation under the circumstances.[11]

Preventing Legal Disputes

When "danger signals" exist, you must investigate the situation further. Remember that persons other than accountants, such as corporate directors, officers, and managers, can also be liable for failing to perform due diligence. Courts are more likely to impose liability when someone has ignored warning signs or red flags that suggest accounting errors or misstatements are present. To avoid liability, always investigate the facts underlying financial statements that appear "too good to be true." Compare recent financial statements with earlier ones, read minutes of shareholders' and directors' meetings, and inspect changes in material contracts, bad debts, and newly discovered liabilities. Know what is required to meet due diligence standards in the particular jurisdiction and conduct yourself in a manner that is above reproach.

Defenses to Liability. Besides proving that he or she has acted with due diligence, an accountant can raise the following defenses to Section 11 liability:

1. There were no misstatements or omissions.
2. The misstatements or omissions were not of material facts.
3. The misstatements or omissions had no causal connection to the plaintiff's loss.
4. The plaintiff-purchaser invested in the securities knowing of the misstatements or omissions.

LIABILITY UNDER SECTION 12(2) Section 12(2) of the Securities Act of 1933 imposes civil liability for fraud in relation to offerings or sales of securities.[12] Liability is based on communication to an investor, whether orally or in the written prospectus,[13] of an untrue statement or omission of a material fact.

PENALTIES AND SANCTIONS FOR VIOLATIONS Those who purchase securities and suffer harm as a result of a false or omitted statement, or some other violation, may bring a suit in a federal court to recover their losses and other damages. The U.S. Department of Justice brings criminal actions against those who commit willful violations. The penalties include fines of up to $10,000, imprisonment for up to five years, or both. The SEC is authorized to seek an injunction against a willful violator to prevent further violations. The SEC can also ask a court to grant other relief, such as an order to a violator to refund profits derived from an illegal transaction.

Liability under the Securities Exchange Act of 1934

Under Sections 18 and 10(b) of the Securities Exchange Act of 1934 and SEC Rule 10b-5, an accountant may be found liable for fraud. A plaintiff has a substantially heavier burden of proof under the 1934 act than under the 1933 act, because under the 1934 act an accountant does not have to prove due diligence to escape liability.

11. See *In re Cardinal Health, Inc. Securities Litigation*, 426 F.Supp.2d 688 (S.D. Ohio 2006); and *In re WorldCom, Inc. Securities Litigation*, 352 F.Supp.2d 472 (S.D.N.Y. 2005).
12. 15 U.S.C. Section 77l.
13. As discussed in Chapter 31, a *prospectus* contains financial disclosures about the corporation for the benefit of potential investors.

LIABILITY UNDER SECTION 18 Section 18 of the 1934 act imposes civil liability on an accountant who makes or causes to be made in any application, report, or document a statement that at the time and in light of the circumstances was false or misleading with respect to any material fact.[14]

Section 18 liability is narrow in that it applies only to applications, reports, documents, and registration statements filed with the SEC. This remedy is further limited in that it applies only to sellers and purchasers. Under Section 18, a seller or purchaser must prove one of the following:

1. That the false or misleading statement affected the price of the security.
2. That the purchaser or seller relied on the false or misleading statement in making the purchase or sale and was not aware of the inaccuracy of the statement.

An accountant will not be liable for violating Section 18 if he or she acted in good faith in preparing the financial statement. To demonstrate good faith, an accountant must show that he or she had no knowledge that the financial statement was false and misleading. Acting in good faith also requires that the accountant lacked any intent to deceive, manipulate, defraud, or seek unfair advantage over another party. (Note that "mere" negligence in preparing a financial statement does not lead to liability under the 1934 act. This differs from the 1933 act, under which an accountant is liable for *all* negligent acts.)

In addition to the good faith defense, accountants can escape liability by proving that the buyer or seller of the security in question knew the financial statement was false and misleading. Sellers and purchasers must bring a cause of action "within one year after the discovery of the facts constituting the cause of action and within three years after such cause of action accrued."[15] A court also has the discretion to assess reasonable costs, including attorneys' fees, against accountants who violate this section.

LIABILITY UNDER SECTION 10(B) AND RULE 10B-5 Accountants additionally face potential legal liability under the antifraud provisions contained in the Securities Exchange Act of 1934 and SEC Rule 10b-5. The scope of these antifraud provisions is very broad and allows private parties to bring civil actions against violators.

Section 10(b) makes it unlawful for any person, including accountants, to use, in connection with the purchase or sale of any security, any manipulative or deceptive device or contrivance in contravention of SEC rules and regulations.[16] Rule 10b-5 further makes it unlawful for any person, by use of any means or instrumentality of interstate commerce, to do the following:

1. Employ any device, scheme, or artifice (pretense) to defraud.
2. Make any untrue statement of a material fact or omit to state a material fact necessary to make the statements made, in light of the circumstances, not misleading.
3. Engage in any act, practice, or course of business that operates or would operate as a fraud or deceit on any person, in connection with the purchase or sale of any security.[17]

Accountants may be held liable only to sellers or purchasers of securities under Section 10(b) and Rule 10b-5. Privity is not necessary for a recovery. An accountant may be found liable not only for fraudulent misstatements of material facts in written material filed with the SEC, but also for any fraudulent oral statements or omissions made in connection with the purchase or sale of any security.

14. 15 U.S.C. Section 78r(a).
15. 15 U.S.C. Section 78r(c).
16. 15 U.S.C. Section 78j(b)
17. 17 C.F.R. Section 240.10b-5.

For a plaintiff to succeed in recovering damages under these antifraud provisions, however, he or she must prove intent (*scienter*) to commit the fraudulent or deceptive act. Ordinary negligence is not enough.

Do accountants have a duty to correct misstatements that they discover in *previous* financial statements? What if they know that potential investors are relying on those statements? Those were the questions in the following case.

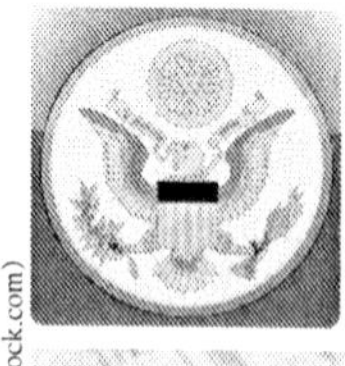

Case 34.2 Overton v. Todman & Co., CPAs, P.C.

United States Court of Appeals, Second Circuit, 478 F.3d 479 (2007).

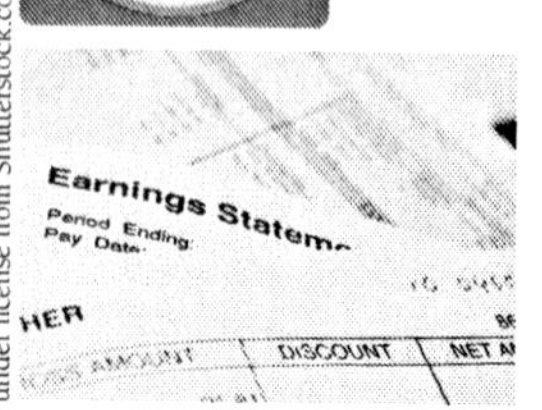

Must an accounting firm make public its new knowledge of prior misstatements?

FACTS From 1999 through 2002, Todman & Company, CPAs, P.C., audited the financial statements of Direct Brokerage, Inc. (DBI), a broker-dealer in New York registered with the Securities and Exchange Commission (SEC). Each year, Todman issued an unqualified opinion that DBI's financial statements were accurate. DBI filed its statements and Todman's opinions with the SEC. Despite the certifications of accuracy, Todman made significant errors that concealed DBI's largest liability—its payroll taxes—in the 1999 and 2000 audits. The errors came to light in 2003 when the New York State Division of Taxation subpoenaed DBI's payroll records, and it became clear that the company had not filed or paid its payroll taxes for 1999 and 2000. This put DBI in a precarious financial position, owing the state more than $3 million in unpaid taxes, interest, and penalties. To meet its needs, DBI sought outside investors, including David Overton, who relied on DBI's statements and Todman's opinion for 2002 to invest in DBI. When DBI collapsed under the weight of its liabilities in 2004, Overton and others filed a suit in a federal district court against Todman, asserting, among other things, fraud under Section 10(b) and Rule 10b-5. The court dismissed the complaint. The plaintiffs appealed to the U.S. Court of Appeals for the Second Circuit.

ISSUE Is an accountant liable for securities fraud if the accountant certified a financial statement containing a misstatement and later learned of the misstatement but failed to correct it, even though the accountant knew that investors were relying on the statement?

DECISION Yes. The U.S. Court of Appeals for the Second Circuit held that an accountant is liable in these circumstances under Section 10(b) and Rule 10b-5. The court vacated the lower court's dismissal and remanded the case "for further proceedings consistent with this opinion."

REASON The appellate court pointed out that "[a]ny person or entity," including an accountant, "who employs a manipulative device or makes a material misstatement (or omission) on which a purchaser or seller of securities relies may be liable as a primary violator under [Section] 10b-5, assuming all of the requirements for primary liability under Rule 10b-5 are met." To be liable, one of the requirements is a "duty to speak." Such a duty arises "when one party has information that the other party is entitled to know because of a fiduciary or other similar relation of trust and confidence between them." When accountants issue a certified opinion, they create the required special relationship with investors. Thus, accountants have a duty to take reasonable steps to correct misstatements that they discover in previous financial statements on which they know the public is relying. Silence in this situation can constitute a false or misleading statement under Section 10(b) and Rule 10b-5. Among other authorities, the court cited Section 10(b), which covers "any person," and a United States Supreme Court decision that "labeled a critical element under [Section] 10(b) and Rule 10b-5: reliance by potential investors on the accountant's omission."[a]

WHAT IF THE FACTS WERE DIFFERENT? *If Todman had conducted an audit for DBI but had not issued a certified opinion about DBI's financial statements, would the result in this case have been the same? Explain.*

a. *Central Bank of Denver v. First Interstate Bank of Denver*, 511 U.S. 164, 114 S.Ct. 1439, 128 L.Ed.2d 119 (1994).

The Private Securities Litigation Reform Act of 1995

The Private Securities Litigation Reform Act of 1995 made some changes to the potential liability of accountants and other professionals in securities fraud cases. Among other things, the act imposed a new statutory obligation on accountants. An auditor must use adequate procedures in an audit to detect any illegal acts of the company being audited. If something illegal is detected, the auditor must disclose it to the company's board of directors, the audit committee, or the SEC, depending on the circumstances.[18]

18. 15 U.S.C. Section 78j-1.

The 1995 act also provides that, in most situations, a party is liable only for the proportion of damages for which he or she is responsible.[19] An accountant who participates in, but is unaware of, illegal conduct may not be liable for the entire loss caused by the illegality.

EXAMPLE 34.7 Nina, an accountant, helps the president and owner of Midstate Trucking Company draft financial statements that misrepresent Midstate's financial condition, but Nina is not actually aware of the fraud. Nina might be held liable, but the amount of her liability could be proportionately less than the entire loss. ●

If an accountant knowingly aids and abets a primary violator, the SEC can seek an injunction or monetary damages. **EXAMPLE 34.8** Smith & Jones, an accounting firm, performs an audit for ABC Sales Company that is so inadequate as to constitute gross negligence. ABC uses the materials provided by Smith & Jones as part of a scheme to defraud investors. When the scheme is uncovered, the SEC can bring an action against Smith & Jones for aiding and abetting on the ground that the firm knew or should have known of the material misrepresentations that were in its audit and on which investors were likely to rely. ●

Potential Criminal Liability

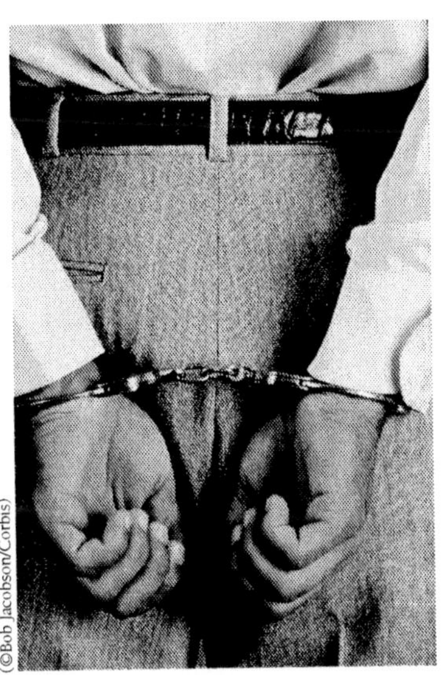

(©Bob Jacobson/Corbis)

The Securities and Exchange Acts of 1933 and 1934 created accountants' violations that can be criminally prosecuted.

An accountant may be found criminally liable for violations of the Securities Act of 1933, the Securities Exchange Act of 1934, the Internal Revenue Code, and both state and federal criminal codes. Under both the 1933 act and the 1934 act, accountants may be subject to criminal penalties for *willful* violations—imprisonment for up to five years and/or a fine of up to $10,000 under the 1933 act and imprisonment for up to ten years and a fine of $100,000 under the 1934 act. Under the Sarbanes-Oxley Act of 2002, for a securities filing that is accompanied by an accountant's false or misleading certified audit statement, the accountant may be fined up to $5 million, imprisoned for up to twenty years, or both.

The Internal Revenue Code makes aiding or assisting in the preparation of a false tax return a felony punishable by a fine of $100,000 ($500,000 in the case of a corporation) and imprisonment for up to three years.[20] This provision applies to anyone who prepares tax returns for others for compensation, and not just to accountants.[21] A penalty of $250 per tax return is levied on tax preparers for negligent understatement of the client's tax liability. For willful understatement of tax liability or reckless or intentional disregard of rules or regulations, a penalty of $1,000 is imposed.[22]

A tax preparer may also be subject to penalties for failing to furnish the taxpayer with a copy of the return, failing to sign the return, or failing to furnish the appropriate tax identification numbers.[23] In addition, those who prepare tax returns for others may be fined $1,000 per document for aiding and abetting another's understatement of tax liability (the penalty is increased to $10,000 in corporate cases).[24] The tax preparer's liability is limited to one penalty per taxpayer per tax year.

In most states, criminal penalties may be imposed for such actions as knowingly certifying false or fraudulent reports; falsifying, altering, or destroying books of account; and obtaining property or credit through the use of false financial statements.

19. 15 U.S.C. Section 78u-4(g).
20. 26 U.S.C. Section 7206(2).
21. 26 U.S.C. Section 7701(a)(36).
22. 26 U.S.C. Section 6694.
23. 26 U.S.C. Section 6695.
24. 26 U.S.C. Section 6701.

 Confidentiality and Privilege

Professionals are restrained by the ethical tenets of their professions to keep all communications with their clients confidential.

Attorney-Client Relationships

The confidentiality of attorney-client communications is protected by law, which confers a privilege on such communications. This privilege is granted because of the need for full disclosure to the attorney of the facts of a client's case. To encourage frankness, confidential attorney-client communications relating to representation are normally held in strictest confidence and protected by law. The attorney and her or his employees may not discuss the client's case with anyone—even under court order—without the client's permission. The client holds the privilege, and only the client may waive it—by disclosing privileged information to someone outside the privilege, for example.

Note, however, that since the Sarbanes-Oxley Act was enacted in 2002, the SEC has implemented new rules requiring attorneys who become aware that a client has violated securities laws to report the violation to the SEC. Reporting a client's misconduct could be a breach of the attorney-client privilege, however, an issue that has caused controversy in the legal community.

Accountant-Client Relationships

In a few states, accountant-client communications are privileged by state statute. In these states, accountant-client communications may not be revealed even in court or in court-sanctioned proceedings without the client's permission. The majority of states, however, abide by the common law, which provides that, if a court so orders, an accountant must disclose information about his or her client to the court. Physicians and other professionals may similarly be compelled to disclose in court information given to them in confidence by patients or clients.

Communications between professionals and their clients—other than those between an attorney and her or his client—are not privileged under federal law. In cases involving federal law, state-provided rights to confidentiality of accountant-client communications are not recognized. Thus, in those cases, in response to a court order, an accountant must provide the information sought.

 Reviewing . . . Liability of Accountants and Other Professionals

Superior Wholesale Corporation planned to purchase Regal Furniture, Inc., and wished to determine Regal's net worth. Superior hired Lynette Shuebke, of the accounting firm Shuebke Delgado, to review an audit that had been prepared by Norman Chase, the accountant for Regal. Shuebke advised Superior that Chase had performed a high-quality audit and that Regal's inventory on the audit dates was stated accurately on the general ledger. As a result of these representations, Superior went forward with its purchase of Regal. After the purchase, Superior discovered that the audit by Chase had been materially inaccurate and misleading, primarily because the inventory had been grossly overstated on the balance sheet. Later, a former Regal employee who had begun working for Superior exposed an e-mail exchange between Chase and former Regal chief executive officer Buddy Gantry. The exchange revealed that Chase had cooperated in overstating the inventory and understating Regal's tax liability. Using the information presented in the chapter, answer the following questions.

1. If Shuebke's review was conducted in good faith and conformed to generally accepted accounting principles, could Superior hold Shuebke Delgado liable for negligently failing to detect material omissions in Chase's audit? Why or why not?

2. According to the rule adopted by the majority of courts to determine accountants' liability to third parties, could Chase be liable to Superior?
3. Generally, what requirements must be met before Superior can recover damages under Section 10(b) of the Securities Exchange Act of 1934 and SEC Rule 10b-5? Can Superior meet these requirements?
4. Suppose that a court determined that Chase had aided Regal in willfully understating its tax liability. What is the maximum penalty that could be imposed on Chase?

Linking the Law to Business Statistics

Statistical Sampling When Conducting Audits

Some of you taking this business law or legal environment course are doing so as part of your business school curriculum to become certified public accountants (CPAs). Eventually, you may be part of an audit team that regularly examines company statistics to determine whether generally accepted accounting principles have been used to state each firm's net income and net worth. Even if you do not become part of an auditing team, it will be helpful for you to understand how auditors use statistical sampling in their work.

What Statistical Sampling Means

Most of you are familiar with opinion polls, particularly during presidential campaigns. Obviously, pollsters cannot query every potential voter. Instead, they take a statistical sample of potential voters to determine the likely outcome of an election. Such samples are supposed to be random–they should not prejudice the outcome of the poll. Pollsters attempt to sample all types of demographic groups–rural, urban, poor, middle class, rich, African American, Hispanic, white, and more.

Many of the "facts" that are reported about businesses are also based on statistical sampling. If you read that the average automotive cash rebate last year was $4,000 per vehicle, you can be sure that the person citing that number did not examine every single cash rebate in the industry. Rather, a random sampling of rebates was used to arrive at the number.

How Public Accounting Firms Use Statistical Sampling

Public accountants use statistical sampling. Assume that you are working with an audit team and you wish to determine whether the total accounts receivable shown on a client's balance sheet are accurate. Of course, if the business is very small, you could actually look at every single accounts receivable. In large corporations, however, statistical sampling must be used. As an auditor, you would select a subset of accounts receivable and check the validity of each actual account within that small sample. You might take additional samples to confirm your results. In any event, you would draw a conclusion as to whether the amount shown for total accounts receivable on the client's balance sheet was acceptably accurate.

Your Work as an Internal Auditor

As a CPA, you may be hired by a large corporation to be an internal auditor. Your job would involve regular reviews of the same types of financial data that external auditors examine. Thus, you too would have to engage in statistical sampling to make sure that the company's books were accurate.

Assume that your company extends equipment leases to tens of thousands of businesses. Of course, you could access every lease record to determine what percentage of lease payments are being timely paid. Such a task could take more time than you have allocated, however. Instead, you could take a random sample of lease payment data to come up with a relatively accurate estimate of the percentage of lease payments that are being made on time.

In all statistical sampling, assuming that it is random, the larger the sample size, the greater the accuracy. The most accurate sample is not a sample at all–it is the entire universe of whatever you are studying.

FOR CRITICAL ANALYSIS

How does an auditor determine the appropriate size of the sample?

Key Terms

defalcation 862
due diligence 869
generally accepted accounting principles (GAAP) 861
generally accepted auditing standards (GAAS) 861
malpractice 864
working papers 868

Chapter Summary: Liability of Accountants and Other Professionals

	COMMON LAW LIABILITY
Potential Common Law Liability to Clients (See pages 861–865.)	1. *Breach of contract*—An accountant or other professional who fails to perform according to his or her contractual obligations can be held liable for breach of contract and resulting damages. 2. *Negligence*—An accountant, attorney, or other professional, in performance of her or his duties, must use the care, knowledge, and judgment generally used by professionals in the same or similar circumstances. Failure to do so is negligence. An accountant's violation of generally accepted accounting principles and generally accepted auditing standards is *prima facie* evidence of negligence. 3. *Fraud*—Intentionally misrepresenting a material fact to a client, when the client relies on the misrepresentation, is actual fraud. Gross negligence in performance of duties is constructive fraud.
Potential Liability to Third Parties (See pages 865–867.)	An accountant may be liable for negligence to any third person the accountant knows or should have known will benefit from the accountant's work. The standard for imposing this liability varies, but generally courts follow one of the following rules: 1. *Ultramares rule*—Liability will be imposed only if the accountant is in privity, or near privity, with the third party. 2. *Restatement rule*—Liability will be imposed only if the third party's reliance is foreseen, or known, or if the third party is among a class of foreseen, or known, users. The majority of courts have adopted this rule. 3. *"Reasonably foreseeable user" rule*—Liability will be imposed if the third party's use was reasonably foreseeable.
	STATUTORY LIABILITY
The Sarbanes-Oxley Act of 2002 (See pages 867–869.)	1. *Purpose*—This act imposed requirements on public accounting firms that provide auditing services to companies whose securities are sold to public investors. 2. *Government oversight*—Among other things, the act created the Public Company Accounting Oversight Board to provide government oversight over public accounting practices. 3. *Working papers*—The act requires accountants to maintain working papers relating to an audit or review for seven years from the end of the fiscal period in which the audit or review was concluded. 4. *Other requirements*—See Exhibit 34–1 on page 868.
Securities Act of 1933, Section 11 (See pages 869–870.)	An accountant who makes a false statement or omits a material fact in audited financial statements required for registration of securities under the law may be liable to anyone who acquires securities covered by the registration statement. The accountant's defense is basically the use of due diligence and the reasonable belief that the work was complete and correct. The burden of proof is on the accountant. Willful violations of this act may be subject to criminal penalties.
Securities Act of 1933, Section 12(2) (See page 870.)	An accountant may be liable for aiding and abetting the seller or offeror of securities when a prospectus or communication presented to an investor contained an untrue statement or omission of a material fact. To be liable, the accountant must have known, or at least should have known, that an untrue statement or omission of material fact existed in the offer to sell the security.
Securities Exchange Act of 1934, Sections 10(b) and 18 (See pages 870–873.)	Accountants may be held liable for false and misleading applications, reports, and documents required under the act. The burden is on the plaintiff, and the accountant has numerous defenses, including good faith and lack of knowledge that what was submitted was false.
Potential Criminal Liability (See page 873.)	1. Willful violations of the Securities Act of 1933 and the Securities Exchange Act of 1934 may be subject to criminal penalties. 2. Aiding or assisting in the preparation of a false tax return is a felony. Aiding and abetting an individual's understatement of tax liability is a separate crime. 3. Tax preparers who negligently or willfully understate a client's tax liability or who recklessly or intentionally disregard Internal Revenue rules or regulations are subject to criminal penalties. 4. Tax prepares who fail to provide a taxpayer with a copy of the return, fail to sign the return, or fail to furnish the appropriate tax identification numbers may also be subject to criminal penalties.

ExamPrep

ISSUE SPOTTERS

1 Dave, an accountant, prepares a financial statement for Excel Company, a client, knowing that Excel will use the statement to obtain a loan from First National Bank. Dave makes negligent omissions in the statement that result in a loss to the bank. Can the bank successfully sue Dave? Why or why not?

2 Nora, an accountant, prepares a financial statement as part of a registration statement that Omega, Inc., files with the Securities and Exchange Commission before making a public offering of securities. The statement contains a misstatement of material fact that is not attributable to Nora's fraud or negligence. Pat relies on the misstatement, buys some of the securities, and suffers a loss. Can Nora be held liable to Pat? Explain.

BEFORE THE TEST

Check your answers to the Issue Spotters, and at the same time, take the interactive quiz for this chapter. Go to www.cengage.com/blaw/blt and click on "Chapter 34." First, click on "Answers to Issue Spotters" to check your answers. Next, click on "Interactive Quiz" to assess your mastery of the concepts in this chapter. Then click on "Flashcards" to review this chapter's Key Term definitions.

For Review

Answers for the even-numbered questions in this* For Review *section can be found on this text's accompanying Web site at* www.cengage.com/blaw/blt. *Select "Chapter 34" and click on "For Review."

1 Under what common law theories may professionals be liable to clients?
2 What are the rules concerning an auditor's liability to third parties?
3 How might an accountant violate federal securities laws?
4 What crimes might an accountant commit under the Internal Revenue Code?
5 What constrains professionals to keep communications with their clients confidential?

Hypothetical Scenarios and Case Problems

34–1 The *Ultramares* Rule. Larkin, Inc., retains Howard Perkins to manage its books and prepare its financial statements. Perkins, a certified public accountant, lives in Indiana and practices there. After twenty years, Perkins has become a bit bored with generally accepted accounting principles (GAAP) and has adopted more creative accounting methods. Now, though, Perkins has a problem, as he is being sued by Molly Tucker, one of Larkin's creditors. Tucker alleges that Perkins either knew or should have known that Larkin's financial statements would be distributed to various individuals. Furthermore, she asserts that these financial statements were negligently prepared and seriously inaccurate. What are the consequences of Perkins's failure to follow GAAP? Under the traditional *Ultramares* rule, can Tucker recover damages from Perkins? Explain.

34–2 Hypothetical Question with Sample Answer The accounting firm of Goldman, Walters, Johnson & Co. prepared financial statements for Lucy's Fashions, Inc. After reviewing the various financial statements, Happydays State Bank agreed to loan Lucy's Fashions $35,000 for expansion. When Lucy's Fashions declared bankruptcy under Chapter 11 six months later, Happydays State Bank promptly filed an action against Goldman, Walters, Johnson & Co., alleging negligent preparation of financial statements. Assuming that the court has abandoned the *Ultramares* approach, what is the result? What are the policy reasons for holding accountants liable to third parties with whom they are not in privity?

—For a sample answer to Question 34–2, go to Appendix E at the end of this text.

34–3 Accountant's Liability under Rule 10b-5. In early 2010, Bennett, Inc., offered a substantial number of new common shares to the public. Harvey Helms had a long-standing interest in Bennett because his grandfather had once been president of the company. On receiving a prospectus prepared and distributed by Bennett, Helms was dismayed by the pessimism it embodied. Helms decided to delay purchasing stock in the company. Later, Helms asserted that the prospectus prepared by the accountants was overly pessimistic and contained materially misleading statements. Discuss fully how successful Helms would be in bringing a cause of action under Rule 10b-5 against the accountants of Bennett, Inc.

34–4 **Case Problem with Sample Answer** In October 1993, Marilyn Greenen, a licensed certified public accountant (CPA), began working at the Port of Vancouver, Washington (the Port), as an account manager. She was not directly engaged in public accounting at the Port, but she oversaw the preparation of financial statements and supervised employees with accounting duties. At the start of her employment, she enrolled her husband for benefits under the Port's medical plan. Her marriage was dissolved in November, but she did not notify the Port of the change. In May 1998 and April 1999, the Port confronted her about the divorce, but she did not update her insurance information. After she was terminated, she reimbursed the Port for the additional premiums it had paid for unauthorized coverage for her former spouse. The Washington State Board of Accountancy imposed sanctions on Greenen for "dishonesty and misleading representations" while, in the words of an applicable state statute, "representing oneself as a CPA." Greenen asked a Washington state court to review the case. What might be an appropriate sanction in this case? What might be Greenen's best argument against the board's action? On what reasoning might the court uphold the decision? [*Greenen v. Washington State Board of Accountancy,* 824 Wash. App. 126, 110 P.3d 224 (Div. 2 2005)]

—After you have answered Problem 34–4, compare your answer with the sample answer given on the Web site that accompanies this text. Go to www.cengage.com/blaw/blt, select "Chapter 34," and click on "Case Problem with Sample Answer."

34–5 **Confidentiality and Privilege.** Napster, Inc., offered a service that allowed its users to browse digital music files on other users' computers and download selections for free. Music industry principals filed a suit in a federal district court against Napster, alleging copyright infringement. The court ordered Napster to remove from its service files that were identified as infringing. Napster failed to comply and was shut down in July 2001. In October, Bertelsmann AG, a German corporation, loaned Napster $85 million to fund its anticipated transition to a licensed digital music distribution system. The terms allowed Napster to spend the loan on "general, administrative and overhead expenses." In an e-mail, Hank Barry, Napster's chief executive officer, referred to a "side deal" under which Napster could use up to $10 million of the loan to pay litigation expenses. Napster failed to launch the new system before declaring bankruptcy in June 2002. Some of the plaintiffs filed a suit in a federal district court against Bertelsmann, charging that by its loan, it prolonged Napster's infringement. The plaintiffs asked the court to order the disclosure of all attorney-client communications related to the loan. What principle could Bertelsmann assert to protect these communications? What is the purpose of this protection? Should this principle protect a client who consults an attorney for advice that will help the client commit fraud? Should the court grant the plaintiffs' request? Discuss. [*In re Napster, Inc. Copyright Litigation,* 479 F.3d 1078 (9th Cir. 2007)]

34–6 **Accountant's Liability for Audit.** A West Virginia bank ran its asset value from $100 million to $1 billion over seven years by aggressively marketing subprime loans. The Office of the Comptroller of the Currency, a federal regulator, audited the bank and discovered that the books had been falsified for several years and that the bank was insolvent. The Comptroller closed the bank and brought criminal charges against its managers. The Comptroller fined Grant Thornton, the bank's accounting firm, $300,000 for recklessly failing to meet generally accepted auditing standards during the years it audited the bank. The Comptroller claimed Thornton violated federal law by "participating in . . . unsafe and unsound banking practice." Thornton appealed, contending that it was not involved in bank operations to that extent based on its audit function. What would be the key to determining if the accounting firm could be held liable for that violation of federal law? [*Grant Thornton, LLP v. Office of the Comptroller of the Currency,* 514 F.3d 1328 (D.C.Cir. 2008)]

34–7 **Professional's Liability.** Soon after Teresa DeYoung's husband died, her mother-in-law also died, leaving an inheritance of more than $400,000 for DeYoung's children. DeYoung hired John Ruggerio, an attorney, to ensure that her children would receive it. Ruggerio advised her to invest the funds in his real estate business. She declined. A few months later, $300,000 of the inheritance was sent to Ruggerio. Without telling DeYoung, he deposited the $300,000 in his account and began to use the funds in his real estate business. Nine months later, $109,000 of the inheritance was sent to Ruggerio. He paid this to DeYoung. She asked about the remaining amount. Ruggerio lied to hide his theft. Unable to access these funds, DeYoung's children changed their college plans to attend less expensive institutions. Nearly three years later, DeYoung learned the truth. Can she bring a suit against Ruggerio? If so, on what ground? If not, why not? Did Ruggerio violate any standard of professional ethics? Discuss. [*DeYoung v. Ruggerio,* 2009 VT 9, 971 A.2d 627 (2009)]

34–8 **A Question of Ethics** *Portland Shellfish Co. processes live shellfish in Maine. As one of the firm's two owners, Frank Wetmore held 300 voting and 150 nonvoting shares of the stock. Donna Holden held the other 300 voting shares. Donna's husband, Jeff, managed the company's daily operations, including production, procurement, and sales. The board of directors consisted of Frank and Jeff. In 2001, disagreements arose over the company's management. The Holdens invoked the "Shareholders' Agreement," which provided that "[i]n the event of a deadlock, the directors shall hire an accountant at [MacDonald, Page, Schatz, Fletcher & Co., LLC] to determine the value of the outstanding shares. . . . [E]ach shareholder shall have the right to buy out the other shareholder(s)' interest." MacDonald Page estimated the stock's "fair market value" to be $1.09 million. Donna offered to buy Frank's shares at a price equal to his proportionate share. Frank countered by offering $1.25 million for Donna's shares. Donna rejected Frank's offer and insisted* *that he sell his shares to her or she would sue. In the face of this threat, Frank sold his shares to Donna for $750,705. Believing the stock to be worth more than twice MacDonald Page's estimate, Frank filed a suit in a federal district court against the accountant. [*Wetmore v. MacDonald, Page, Schatz, Fletcher & Co., LLC, *476 F.3d 1 (1st Cir. 2007)]*

1 Frank claimed that in valuing the stock, the accountant disregarded "commonly accepted and reliable methods of valuation in favor of less reliable methods." He alleged negligence, among other things. MacDonald Page filed a motion to dismiss the complaint. What are the elements that establish negligence? Which is the most critical element in this case?
2 MacDonald Page evaluated the company's stock by identifying its "fair market value," defined as "[t]he price at which the property would change hands between a willing buyer and a willing seller, neither being under a compulsion to buy or sell and both having reasonable knowledge of relevant facts." The accountant knew that the shareholders would use its estimate to determine the price that one would pay to the other. Under these circumstances, was Frank's injury foreseeable? Explain.
3 What factor might have influenced Frank to sell his shares to Donna even if he thought that MacDonald Page's "fair market value" figure was less than half what it should have been? Does this factor represent an unfair, or unethical, advantage? Why or why not?

Critical Thinking and Writing Assignments

34–9 Critical Legal Thinking. In cases involving third parties who have suffered losses in reliance on negligent misrepresentations in accountants' financial reports, the courts apply different standards to assess liability. Some courts impose liability only when there is privity between the accountant and the party seeking recovery. Other courts impose liability under a foreseeability rule. What are the implications of imposing liability on accountants for losses suffered by third parties on the basis of foreseeability rather than privity?

34–10 

Video Question Go to this text's Web site at www.cengage.com/blaw/blt and select "Chapter 34." Click on "Video Questions" and view the video titled *Accountant's Liability.* Then answer the following questions.

1 Should Ray prepare a financial statement that values a list of assets provided by the advertising firm without verifying that the firm actually owns these assets?
2 Discuss whether Ray is in privity with the company interested in buying Laura's advertising firm.
3 Under the *Ultramares* rule, to whom does Ray owe a duty?
4 Assume that Laura did not tell Ray that she intended to give the financial statement to the potential acquirer. Would this fact change Ray's liability under the *Ultramares* rule? Explain.

Practical Internet Exercises

Go to this text's Web site at www.cengage.com/blaw/blt, select "Chapter 34," and click on "Practical Internet Exercises." There you will find the following Internet research exercises that you can perform to learn more about the topics covered in this chapter.

Practical Internet Exercise 34–1: LEGAL PERSPECTIVE—**The Sarbanes-Oxley Act of 2002**
Practical Internet Exercise 34–2: MANAGEMENT PERSPECTIVE—**Avoiding Legal Liability**

Unit Six Cumulative Business Hypothetical

Alpha Software, Inc., and Beta Products Corporation—both small firms—are competitors in the business of software research, development, and production.

1. Alpha and Beta form a joint venture to research, develop, and produce new software for a particular line of computers. Does this business combination violate the antitrust laws? If so, is it a per se violation, or is it subject to the rule of reason? Alpha and Beta decide to merge. After the merger, Beta is the surviving firm. What aspect of this firm's presence in the market will be assessed to decide whether this merger is in violation of any antitrust laws?
2. To market its products profitably, Beta considers a number of advertising and labeling proposals. One proposal is that Beta suggest in its advertising that one of its software products has a certain function even though the product does not actually have that capability. Another suggestion is that Beta sell half of a certain program in packaging that misleads the buyer into believing the entire program is included. To obtain the entire program, customers would need to buy a second product. Can Beta implement these suggestions or otherwise market its products in any way it likes? If not, why not?
3. The production part of Beta's operations generates hazardous waste. Gamma Transport Company transports the waste to Omega Waste Corporation, which owns and operates a hazardous waste–disposal site. At the site, some containers leak hazardous waste, and the Environmental Protection Agency (EPA) cleans it up. From whom can the EPA recover the cost of the clean-up?
4. Beta hires a certified public accountant, Aaron Schleger, to prepare its financial reports and issue opinion letters based on those reports. One year, Beta falls into serious financial trouble, but this is not reflected in Schleger's reports and opinion letters. Relying on Schleger's portrayal of the company's fiscal health, Beta borrows substantial amounts to develop a new product. The bank, in lending funds to Beta, relies on an opinion letter from Schleger, and Schleger is aware of the bank's reliance. Assuming that Schleger was negligent but did not engage in intentional fraud, what is his potential liability in this situation? Discuss fully.

Unit Six Extended Case Study: *McCoy v. Chase Manhattan Bank, USA*

As Chapter 33 described, credit-card agreements are governed by the Truth-in-Lending Act (TILA) and by Regulation Z, which was adopted by the Federal Reserve Board to implement the TILA. An important part of any credit-card agreement is the rate of interest that will be charged. In this Extended Case Study, we look at McCoy v. Chase Manhattan Bank, USA,[1] *in which a cardholder challenged the credit-card issuer's rate increase, claiming that he had not been notified as required by the TILA. The issuer claimed that its "Cardmember Agreement" provided advance notice of the rate increase. The issue for the court was whether the increase also required contemporaneous notice under the TILA and Regulation Z.*

1. 559 F.3d 963 (9th Cir. 2009). To read this case online, go to www.ca9.uscourts.gov. In the left-hand column, in the "Decisions" pull-down menu, click on "Opinions." On that page, click on "Advanced Search"; then, in the "by Case No.:" box, type "06-56278" and click on "Search." In the result, click on the appropriate link to access the opinion.

CASE BACKGROUND

James McCoy held a credit card issued by Chase Manhattan Bank, USA, N.A., a national bank located in Delaware. Chase closed McCoy's account to new transactions after he made a late payment. Chase also increased the interest rate on McCoy's card retroactively to the beginning of his payment cycle. The bank did not notify him of the increase, however, until the following periodic statement, after the increase had already taken effect.

McCoy filed a suit in a federal district court against Chase, on behalf of himself and other cardholders similarly situated, claiming that the rate increase without notice violated the TILA. The court dismissed McCoy's complaint, holding that no notice was required. McCoy appealed to the U.S. Court of Appeals for the Ninth Circuit.

MAJORITY OPINION

HAWKINS, **Circuit Judge:**

* * * *

Congress enacted TILA to "assure a meaningful disclosure of credit terms * * * ." Regulation Z * * * addresses when and how notice of changes in terms must be given:

> * * * Whenever any term required to be disclosed under [12 Code of Federal Regulations] Section 226.6 is changed or the required minimum periodic payment is increased, the creditor shall mail or deliver written notice of the change to each consumer who may be affected. * * *

Section 226.6 requires that a creditor disclose * * * "each periodic rate that may be used to compute the finance charge."

The parties dispute the meaning of the phrase "any term required to be disclosed under Section 226.6." Chase argues that the phrase applies only to the contractual terms of Chase's Card-member Agreement. McCoy suggests the phrase also applies to the list of specific "items" Section 226.6(a)(2) requires be disclosed, which includes the interest rate that may be used.

* * * *

Chase argues that the Federal Reserve Board ("FRB")'s Official Staff Commentary interprets Regulation Z to require no notice in this case.

Comment 3 is the most salient [important] Official Staff Commentary to [Regulation Z] and, when describing the amount of notice required for different kinds of changes, provides that "a notice of change in terms is required, but may be mailed or delivered as late as the effective date of the change * * * if there is an increased periodic rate or any other finance charge attributable to the consumer's delinquency or default." The plain-meaning of Comment 3 is to require notice when a cardholder's interest rates increase because of a default * * * . Under Comment 3, McCoy has stated a claim.

Chase argues that * * * a different portion of the Official Staff Commentary, Comment 1, should govern instead. Comment 3's specific reference to interest rate increases attributable to the consumer's delinquency or default is directly on point and therefore governs.

Comment 1 * * * describes the circumstances in which Regulation Z requires no notice of a change in terms:

> * * * No notice of a change in terms need be given if the specific change is set forth initially * * * . In contrast, notice must be given if the contract allows the creditor to increase the rate at its discretion but does not include specific terms for an increase.

* * * *

* * * Chase's "contract allows the creditor to increase the rate at its discretion" and does not specify the relevant terms, including the conditions that are necessary and sufficient for an increase to occur and the actual amount of the increase that will occur. * * * *An interpretation of Comment 1 as eliminating Regulation Z's notice requirement even where consumers do not have sufficient information to determine whether their interest rate will be raised, or by how much, dilutes the meaning of the word "specific" beyond recognition.* [Emphasis added.]

Chase argues that we must nevertheless interpret Regulation Z to require no notice in this case because we must defer to [an] Advance Notice of Proposed Rule-making, [ANPR] promulgated * * * by the Federal Reserve in 2007, which briefly characterizes existing law in the process of explaining a proposal to amend Regulation Z. [The final rule amended Regulation Z to require forty-five days' notice for interest rate increases effective July 1, 2010.]

Consideration of the 2007 ANPR does not lead us to change our interpretation of the FRB's Official Staff Commentary. Chase observes that the 2007 ANPR includes as an example of when a "change-in-terms notice" is not required, "some credit card account agreements that permit the card issuer to increase the periodic rate if the consumer makes a late payment" * * * . The effect of this language is ambiguous, however, because the term "change-in-terms notice" could * * * refer to contemporaneous notice required for changes in interest rates, but might instead refer only to the * * * advance notice required for changes in contractual terms.

* * * FRB chose to remove the ambiguous language entirely when it issued a Final Rule and Supplementary Information amending Regulation Z.

* * * The primary purpose of the 2007 ANPR * * * was to announce proposed amendments to Regulation Z and solicit comment, not to offer additional staff commentary on Regulation Z's current requirements.

* * * Our own consideration of the FRB's Official Staff Commentary, unofficial [ANPR], and the Supplementary

Continued

Unit Six Extended Case Study: *McCoy v. Chase Manhattan Bank, USA*—Continued

Information accompanying its recent amendment of Regulation Z *leaves us firmly convinced of the FRB's intent to require contemporaneous notice when rates are raised because of a consumer's delinquency or default,* as McCoy alleges occurred in this case. [Emphasis added.]

* * * *

* * * Having concluded that McCoy has stated a claim * * *, we reverse and remand to the district court.

DISSENTING OPINION

***CUDAHY*, Circuit Judge, dissenting:**

* * * *

The claims made by Mr. McCoy have been raised in many other forums * * *. In all of those cases the result was the opposite of the one reached here. In one case the court did at first indicate that it was inclined to rule in favor of the plaintiffs but reversed course when it was made aware of the Advance Notice of Proposed Rulemaking (ANPR) issued by the expert agency, the Federal Reserve Board (FRB or the Board), which quite clearly showed that the Board disagreed with their interpretation.

* * * So the question becomes the following: did [Regulation Z] require Chase to provide contemporaneous notice to McCoy of an increase in his interest rate due to his default when that increase was an implementation of the existing terms of his agreement with Chase? The majority says that * * * the FRB's Official Staff Commentary to [Regulation Z] makes the answer a clear "yes." The majority feels no need to give any deference to the Board's views expressed in its [ANPR], which [leads] to the opposite conclusion and which [is] reinforced by every other court that has considered the question.

* * * *

* * * I would find that McCoy has not stated a claim for a violation of TILA.

QUESTIONS FOR ANALYSIS

1. **Law.** What conclusion did the majority reach on the question in this case? What points supported this conclusion?
2. **Law.** What was the dissent's view with regard to the majority's analysis?
3. **Ethics.** Suppose that Chase's card-member agreement was written by an accountant or an attorney. Could that individual be found to be in breach of her or his profession's ethics? Why or why not?
4. **Social Dimensions.** Under the TILA, credit terms must be clearly disclosed. Can any credit-card agreement meet this requirement? Explain.
5. **Implications for the Consumer.** What do the circumstances of this case suggest to current and potential cardholders concerning the management of their personal finances? Discuss.

Appendix A

How to Brief Cases and Analyze Case Problems

How to Brief Cases

To fully understand the law with respect to business, you need to be able to read and understand court decisions. To make this task easier, you can use a method of case analysis that is called *briefing*. There is a fairly standard procedure that you can follow when you "brief" any court case. You must first read the case opinion carefully. When you feel you understand the case, you can prepare a brief of it.

Although the format of the brief may vary, typically it will present the essentials of the case under headings such as those listed below.

1. **Citation.** Give the full citation for the case, including the name of the case, the date it was decided, and the court that decided it.
2. **Facts.** Briefly indicate (a) the reasons for the lawsuit; (b) the identity and arguments of the plaintiff(s) and defendant(s), respectively; and (c) the lower court's decision—if appropriate.
3. **Issue.** Concisely phrase, in the form of a question, the essential issue before the court. (If more than one issue is involved, you may have two—or even more—questions here.)
4. **Decision.** Indicate here—with a "yes" or "no," if possible—the court's answer to the question (or questions) in the Issue section above.
5. **Reason.** Summarize as briefly as possible the reasons given by the court for its decision (or decisions) and the case or statutory law relied on by the court in arriving at its decision.

For a case-specific example of what should be included under each of the above headings when briefing a case, see the review of the sample court case presented in the appendix to Chapter 1 of this text on pages 30 and 31.

Analyzing Case Problems

In addition to learning how to brief cases, students of business law and the legal environment also find it helpful to know how to analyze case problems. Part of the study of business law and the legal environment usually involves analyzing case problems, such as those included in this text at the end of each chapter.

For each case problem in this book, we provide the relevant background and facts of the lawsuit and the issue before the court. When you are assigned one of these problems, your job will be to determine how the court should decide the issue, and why. In other words, you will need to engage in legal analysis and reasoning. Here, we offer some suggestions on how to make this task less daunting. We begin by presenting a sample case problem:

> While Janet Lawson, a famous pianist, was shopping in Quality Market, she slipped and fell on a wet floor in one of the aisles. The floor had recently been mopped by one of the store's employees, but there were no signs warning customers that the floor in that area was wet. As a result of the fall, Lawson injured her right arm and was unable to perform piano concerts for the next six months. Had she been able to perform the scheduled concerts, she would have earned approximately $60,000 over that period of time. Lawson sued Quality Market for this amount, plus another $10,000 in medical expenses. She claimed that the store's failure to warn customers of the wet floor constituted negligence and therefore the market was liable for her injuries. Will the court agree with Lawson? Discuss.

Understand the Facts

This may sound obvious, but before you can analyze or apply the relevant law to a specific set of facts, you must clearly understand those facts. In other words, you should read through the case problem carefully—more than once, if necessary—to make sure you understand the identity of the plaintiff(s) and defendant(s) in the case and the progression of events that led to the lawsuit.

In the sample case problem just given, the identity of the parties is fairly obvious. Janet Lawson is the one bringing the suit; therefore, she is the plaintiff. Lawson is bringing the suit against Quality Market, so it is the defendant. Some of the case problems you may work on have multiple plaintiffs or defendants. Often, it is helpful to use abbreviations for the parties. To indicate a reference to a plaintiff, for example, the *pi* symbol—π—is often used, and a defendant is denoted by a *delta*—Δ—a triangle.

The events leading to the lawsuit are also fairly straightforward. Lawson slipped and fell on a wet floor, and she contends that Quality Market should be liable for her injuries because it was negligent in not posting a sign warning customers of the wet floor.

When you are working on case problems, realize that the facts should be accepted as they are given. For instance, in our sample problem, it should be accepted that the floor was wet and that there was no sign. In other words, avoid making conjectures, such as "Maybe the floor wasn't too wet," or "Maybe an employee was getting a sign to put up," or "Maybe someone stole the sign." Questioning the facts as they are presented only adds confusion to your analysis.

Legal Analysis and Reasoning

Once you understand the facts given in the case problem, you can begin to analyze the case. Recall from Chapter 1 that the **IRAC method** is a helpful tool to use in the legal analysis and reasoning process. IRAC is an acronym for **I**ssue, **R**ule, **A**pplication, **C**onclusion. Applying this method to our sample problem would involve the following steps:

1. First, you need to decide what legal **issue** is involved in the case. In our sample case, the basic issue is whether Quality Market's failure to warn customers of the wet floor constituted negligence. As discussed in Chapter 4 negligence is a *tort*—a civil wrong. In a tort lawsuit, the plaintiff seeks to be compensated for another's wrongful act. A defendant will be deemed negligent if he or she breached a duty of care owed to the plaintiff and the breach of that duty caused the plaintiff to suffer harm.
2. Once you have identified the issue, the next step is to determine what **rule of law** applies to the issue. To make this determination, you will want to carefully review the text discussion relating to the issue involved in the problem. Our sample case problem involves the tort of negligence, which is covered in Chapter 4. The applicable rule of law is the tort law principle that business owners owe a duty to exercise reasonable care to protect their customers *(business invitees)*. Reasonable care, in this context, includes either removing—or warning customers of—*foreseeable* risks about which the owner *knew* or *should have known*. Business owners need not warn customers of "open and obvious" risks, however. If a business owner breaches this duty of care (fails to exercise the appropriate degree of care toward customers), and the breach of duty causes a customer to be injured, the business owner will be liable to the customer for the customer's injuries.
3. The next—and usually the most difficult—step in analyzing case problems is the **application** of the relevant rule of law to the specific facts of the case you are studying. In our sample problem, applying the tort law principle just discussed presents few difficulties. An employee of the store had mopped the floor in the aisle where Lawson slipped and fell, but no sign was present indicating that the floor was wet. That a customer might fall on a wet floor is clearly a foreseeable risk. Therefore, the failure to warn customers about the wet floor was a breach of the duty of care owed by the business owner to the store's customers.
4. Once you have completed Step 3 in the IRAC method, you should be ready to draw your **conclusion.** In our sample problem, Quality Market is liable to Lawson for her injuries because the market's breach of its duty of care caused Lawson's injuries.

The fact patterns in the case problems presented in this text are not always as simple as those presented in our sample problem. Often, a case has more than one plaintiff or defendant. A case may also involve more than one issue and have more than one applicable rule of law. Furthermore, in some case problems the facts may indicate that the general rule of law should not apply. Suppose that a store employee told Lawson about the wet floor and advised her not to walk in that aisle, but Lawson decided to walk there anyway. This fact could alter the outcome of the case because the store could then raise the defense of *assumption of risk* (see Chapter 4). Nonetheless, a careful review of the chapter should always provide you with the knowledge you need to analyze the problem thoroughly and arrive at accurate conclusions.

Appendix E

Sample Answers for End-of-Chapter *Hypothetical Questions with Sample Answer*

1–4A HYPOTHETICAL QUESTION WITH SAMPLE ANSWER

1 The U.S. Constitution—The U.S. Constitution is the supreme law of the land. A law in violation of the Constitution, no matter what its source, will be declared unconstitutional and will not be enforced.

2 The federal statute—Under the U.S. Constitution, when there is a conflict between federal law and state law, federal law prevails.

3 The state statute—State statutes are enacted by state legislatures. Areas not covered by state statutory law are governed by state case law.

4 The U.S. Constitution—State constitutions are supreme within their respective borders unless they conflict with the U.S. Constitution, which is the supreme law of the land.

5 The federal administrative regulation—Under the U.S. Constitution, when there is a conflict between federal law and state law, federal law prevails.

2–2A HYPOTHETICAL QUESTION WITH SAMPLE ANSWER

As the text points out, Thomas has a constitutionally protected right to his religion and the free exercise of it. In denying his unemployment benefits, the state violated these rights. Employers are obligated to make reasonable accommodations for their employees' beliefs, right or wrong, that are openly and sincerely held. Thomas's beliefs were openly and sincerely held. By placing him in a department that made military goods, his employer effectively put him in a position of having to choose between his job and his religious principles. This unilateral decision on the part of the employer was the reason Thomas left his job and why the company was required to compensate Thomas for his resulting unemployment.

3–2A HYPOTHETICAL QUESTION WITH SAMPLE ANSWER

Marya can bring suit in all three courts. The trucking firm did business in Florida, and the accident occurred there. Thus, the state of Florida would have jurisdiction over the defendant. Because the firm was headquartered in Georgia and had its principal place of business in that state, Marya could also sue in a Georgia court. Finally, because the amount in controversy exceeds $75,000, the suit could be brought in federal court on the basis of diversity of citizenship.

4–2A HYPOTHETICAL QUESTION WITH SAMPLE ANSWER

To answer this question, you must first decide if there is a legal theory under which Harley may be able to recover. A possibility is the intentional tort of wrongful interference with a contractual relationship. To recover damages under this theory, Harley would need to show (1) that he and Martha had a valid contract, (2) that Lothar knew of this contractual relationship, and (3) that Lothar intentionally convinced Martha to break her contract with Harley. Even though Lothar hoped that his advertisements would persuade Martha to break her contract with Harley, the question states that Martha's decision to change bakers was based solely on the advertising and not on anything else that Lothar did. Lothar's advertisements did not constitute a tort. Note, though, that while Harley cannot collect from Lothar for Martha's actions, he does have a cause of action against Martha for her breach of their contract.

5–2A HYPOTHETICAL QUESTION WITH SAMPLE ANSWER

1 Making a photocopy of an article in a scholarly journal "for purposes such as . . . scholarship, or research, is not an infringement of copyright" under Section 107 of the Copyright Act (the fair use exception).

2 This is an example of trademark infringement rather than copyright infringement. Whenever a trademark is copied to a substantial degree or used in its entirety by one who is not entitled to its use, the trademark has been infringed.

3 This is the most likely example of copyright infringement. Generally, determining whether the reproduction of copyrighted material constitutes copyright infringement is made on a case-by-case basis under the "fair use" doctrine, as expressed in Section 107 of the Copyright Act. Courts look at such factors as the "purpose and character" of a use, such as whether it is "of a commercial nature"; "the amount and substantiality of the portion used in relation to the copyrighted work as a whole"; and "the effect of the use on the potential market" for the copied work. In this question, the DVD store owner is copying copyright-protected works in their entirety for commercial purposes, thereby affecting the market for the works.

4 Recording a television program "for purposes such as . . . teaching . . . is not an infringement of copyright" under Section 107 of the Copyright Act.

6–2A HYPOTHETICAL QUESTION WITH SAMPLE ANSWER

1 Sarah has wrongfully taken and carried away the personal property of another with the intent to permanently deprive the owner of such property. She has committed the crime of larceny.

2 Sarah has unlawfully and forcibly taken the personal property of another. She has committed the crime of robbery.

3 Sarah has broken and entered a dwelling with the intent to commit a felony. She has committed the crime of burglary. (Most states have dispensed with the requirement that the act take place at night.)

Note the basic differences: Burglary requires breaking and entering into a building without the use of force against a person. Robbery does not involve any breaking and entering, but force is required. Larceny is the taking of personal property without force and without breaking and entering into a building. Generally, because force is used, robbery is considered the most serious of these crimes and carries the most severe penalties. Larceny involves no force or threat to human life; therefore, it carries the least severe penalty of the three. Burglary, because it involves breaking and entering, frequently where people live, carries a lesser penalty than robbery but a greater penalty than larceny.

7–3A HYPOTHETICAL QUESTION WITH SAMPLE ANSWER

The perpetrator in this set of facts is a hacker—someone who uses one computer to break into another. Computers can be hacked, or broken into, in various ways to commit a multitude of crimes. In this problem, the hacker created a *botnet* by appropriating others' computers to forward transmissions to the creditor's system. Here, the crime of altering the figures to show that a debt has been paid is theft (wrongfully taking and carrying away another's property with the intent of depriving the owner permanently of it). "Carrying away" can be done by any act that removes something of value from its owner's possession, and the "property" may be any type of tangible or intangible item. In this problem, the hacker accomplished "carrying away" by altering the figures, and the property taken was the creditor's right to receive payment.

8–2A HYPOTHETICAL QUESTION WITH SAMPLE ANSWER

Ethical and other dilemmas faced by businesspersons are rarely clear-cut choices between good and bad alternatives. This problem is no exception. The questions in the problem indicate some of the issues that businesspersons in such situations should consider. But potentially higher profits and possible negative publicity are not the only considerations—decisions made by businesspersons can have wide-ranging implications. When a firm takes advantage of cheaper overseas labor, it must lay off domestic workers or even close a domestic operation. When workers are laid off, there are repercussions throughout the local economy. Closing an operation reduces the local tax base—property taxes, business taxes, and income taxes—which funds the local infrastructure. Thus, the firm must determine to whom it owes duties (shareholders, employees, or others) and to what degree each group is owed. In addition, all of the factors that exist when business is done internationally must be considered. These include the foreign economic and political situation, and other costs (materials, equipment, foreign taxes, domestic import duties) besides cheap labor. These and other considerations require a balancing known as a trade-off.

9–2A HYPOTHETICAL QUESTION WITH SAMPLE ANSWER

According to the question, Janine was apparently unconscious or otherwise unable to agree to a contract for the nursing services she received while she was in the hospital. As you read in the chapter, however, sometimes the law will create a fictional contract in order to prevent one party from unjustly receiving a benefit at the expense of another. This is known as a quasi contract and provides a basis for Nursing Services to recover the value of the services it provided while Janine was in the hospital. As for the at-home services that were provided to Janine, because Janine was aware that those services were being provided for her, Nursing Services can recover for those services under an implied-in-fact contract. Under this type of contract, the conduct of the parties creates and defines the terms. Janine's acceptance of the services constitutes her agreement to form a contract, and she will probably be required to pay Nursing Services in full.

10–3A HYPOTHETICAL QUESTION WITH SAMPLE ANSWER

1 Death of either the offeror or the offeree prior to acceptance automatically terminates a revocable offer. The basic legal reason is that the offer is personal to the parties and cannot be passed on to others, not even to the estate of the deceased. This rule applies even if the other party is unaware of the death. Thus, Cherneck's offer terminates on Cherneck's death, and Bollow's later acceptance does not constitute a contract.

2 An offer is automatically terminated by the destruction of the specific subject matter of the offer prior to acceptance. Thus, Bollow's acceptance after the fire does not constitute a contract.

3 When the offer is irrevocable, under an option contract, death of the offeror does not terminate the option contract, and the offeree can accept the offer to sell the equipment, binding the offeror's estate to performance. Performance is not personal to Cherneck, as the estate can transfer title to the equipment. Knowledge of the death is immaterial to the offeree's right of acceptance. Thus, Bollow can hold Cherneck's estate to a contract for the purchase of the equipment.

4 When the offer is irrevocable, under an option contract, death of the offeree also does not terminate the offer. Because the option is a separate contract, the contract survives and passes to the offeree's estate, which can exercise the option by acceptance within the option period. Thus, acceptance by Bollow's estate binds Cherneck to a contract for the sale of the equipment.

11–3A HYPOTHETICAL QUESTION WITH SAMPLE ANSWER

Contracts in restraint of trade are usually illegal and unenforceable. An exception to this rule applies to a covenant not to compete that is ancillary to certain types of business contracts in which some fair protection is deemed appropriate (such as in the sale of a business). To be legally enforceable, however, the covenant must be reasonable in terms of time and area. If either term is excessive, the court can declare that the restraint goes beyond what is necessary for reasonable protection. In this event, the court can either declare the covenant illegal, or it can reform the covenant to make the terms of time and area reasonable and then enforce it. Suppose the court declares the covenant illegal and unenforceable. Because the covenant is ancillary and severable from the primary contract, the primary contract is not affected by such a ruling. In the case of Hotel Lux, the primary contract concerns employment; the covenant is ancillary and desirable for the protection of the hotel. The time period of one year may be considered reasonable for a chef with an international reputation. The reasonableness of the three-state area restriction may be questioned, however. If it is found to be reasonable, the covenant probably will be enforced. If it is not found to be reasonable, the court could declare the entire covenant illegal, allowing Perlee to be employed by any restaurant or hotel, including one in direct competition with Hotel Lux. Alternatively, the court could reform the covenant, making its terms reasonable for protecting Hotel Lux's normal customer market area.

12–2A HYPOTHETICAL QUESTION WITH SAMPLE ANSWER

In this situation, Gemma becomes what is known as a *guarantor* on the loan. That is, she guarantees the hardware store that she will pay for the mower if her brother fails to do so. This kind of collateral promise, in which the guarantor states that he or she will become responsible *only* if the primary party does not perform, must be in writing to be enforceable. There is an exception, however. If the main purpose in accepting secondary liability is to secure a personal benefit—for example, if Gemma's brother bought the mower for her—the contract need not be in writing. The assumption is that a court can infer from the circumstances of the case whether the main purpose was to secure a personal benefit and thus, in effect, to answer for the guarantor's own debt.

13–3A HYPOTHETICAL QUESTION WITH SAMPLE ANSWER

As a general rule, any right(s) flowing from a contract can be assigned. There are, however, exceptions, such as when the contract expressly and specifically prohibits or limits the right of assignment. Because of the principle of freedom of contract, this type of prohibition is enforced—unless it is deemed contrary to public policy. Authorities differ on how a case like Aron's should be decided. Some courts would enforce the prohibition completely, holding that Aron's assignment to Erica is completely ineffective without the landlord's consent. Others would permit the assignment to be effective and would limit the landlord's remedies to the normal contract remedies ensuing from Aron's breach.

14–2A HYPOTHETICAL QUESTION WITH SAMPLE ANSWER

Generally, the equitable remedy of specific performance will be granted only if two criteria are met: monetary damages (under the circumstances) must be inadequate as a remedy, and the subject matter of the contract must be unique.

1 In the sale of land, the buyer's contract is for a specific piece of real property. The land under contract is unique because no two pieces of real property have the same legal description. In addition, monetary damages would not compensate a buyer adequately, as the same land cannot be purchased elsewhere. Specific performance is an appropriate remedy.

2 The basic criteria for specific performance do not apply well to personal-service contracts. If the identical service contracted for is readily available from others, the service is not unique and monetary damages for nonperformance are adequate. If, however, the services are so personal that only the contracted party can perform them, the contract meets the test of uniqueness; but the courts will refuse to decree specific performance based on either of two theories. First, the enforcement of specific performance requires involuntary servitude (prohibited by the Thirteenth Amendment to the U. S. Constitution). Second, it is impractical to attempt to force meaningful performance by someone against his or her will. In the case of Marita and Horace, specific performance is not an appropriate remedy.

3 A rare coin is unique, and monetary damages for breach are inadequate, as Juan cannot obtain a substantially identical substitute in the market. This is a typical case where specific performance is an appropriate remedy.

4 The key fact for consideration here is that this is a closely held corporation. Therefore, the stock is not available in the market, and the shares become unique. The uniqueness of these shares is enhanced by the fact that if Cary sells his 4 percent of the shares to De Valle, De Valle will have a controlling voice in the corporation. Because of this, monetary damages for De Valle are totally inadequate as a remedy. Specific performance is an appropriate remedy.

15–3A HYPOTHETICAL QUESTION WITH SAMPLE ANSWER

1 In a destination contract, the risk of loss passes to the buyer when the goods are tendered to the buyer at the specified destination—in this case, San Francisco.

2 In a shipment contract, if the seller is required or authorized to ship goods by carrier, but the contract does not specify a locale, the risk of loss passes to the buyer when the goods are duly delivered to the carrier.

3 If the seller is a merchant, risk of loss to goods held by the seller passes to the buyer when the buyer actually takes physical possession of the goods. If the seller is not a merchant, the risk of loss to goods held by the seller passes to the buyer on tender of delivery.

4 When a bailee is holding goods for a person who has contracted to sell them and the goods are to be delivered without being moved, risk of loss passes to the buyer when (a) the buyer receives a negotiable document of title for the goods, (b) the bailee acknowledges the buyer's right to possess the goods, or (c) the buyer receives a nonnegotiable document of title and has had a reasonable time to present the document to the bailee and demand the goods. (If the bailee refuses to honor the document, the risk of loss remains with the seller.) If the goods are to be delivered by being moved, but the contract does not specify whether it is a destination or a shipment contract, it is presumed to be a shipment contract. If no locale is specified in the contract, risk of loss passes to the buyer when the seller delivers the goods to the carrier.

16–2A HYPOTHETICAL QUESTION WITH SAMPLE ANSWER

No. Cummings had not breached the sales contract because the C.O.D. shipment had deprived him of his absolute right, in the absence of agreement, to inspect the goods before accepting them. Had Cummings requested or agreed to the C.O.D. method of shipment, the result would have been different. Because he had not agreed to the C.O.D. shipment, he was fully within his rights to refuse to accept the goods because he could not inspect them prior to acceptance. In this case, it was the seller who had breached the contract by shipping the goods C.O.D. without Cummings's consent.

17–2A HYPOTHETICAL QUESTION WITH SAMPLE ANSWER

Yes. To disclaim the implied warranty of fitness for a particular purpose, the disclaimer must be in writing and be conspicuous. Although the implied warranty of merchantability can be disclaimed orally, if the disclaimer is in writing it must be conspicuously written. This means that the disclaimer must—either by different color or type size or some other technique—stand out from the context in which it is printed so as to readily alert the reader of the document of the disclaimer. In this case, the disclaimer was printed in the same size and color of type as the rest of the contract and was not conspicuous. If this was the only warranty disclaimer, it is not effective and Tandy can recover.

18–2A HYPOTHETICAL QUESTION WITH SAMPLE ANSWER

For an instrument to be negotiable, it must meet the following requirements:

1. Be in writing.
2. Be signed by the maker or the drawer.
3. Be an unconditional promise or order to pay.
4. State a fixed amount of money.
5. Be payable on demand or at a definite time.
6. Be payable to order or to bearer, unless it is a check.

The instrument in this case meets the writing requirement in that it is handwritten and on something with a degree of permanence that is transferable. The instrument meets the requirement of being signed by the maker, as Muriel Evans's signature (her name in her handwriting) appears in the body of the instrument. The instrument's payment is not conditional and contains Muriel Evans's definite promise to pay. In addition, the sum of $100 is both a fixed amount and payable in money (U.S. currency). Because the instrument is payable on demand and to bearer (Karen Marvin or any holder), the instrument is negotiable.

19–2A HYPOTHETICAL QUESTION WITH SAMPLE ANSWER

Under the Home Mortgage Disclosure Act (HMDA) and the Community Reinvestment Act of 1977, which were passed to prevent discrimination in lending practices, a bank is required to define its market area. This area must be established contiguous to the bank's branch offices. It must be mapped using the existing boundaries of the counties or the standard metropolitan areas (SMAs) in which the offices are located. A bank must delineate the community served, and annually review this delineation. The issue here is how successful iBank, an Internet-only bank, could delineate its community. Does iBank have a physically limited market area or serve a physically distinct community? Will the Federal Reserve Board, the government agency charged with enforcing this law, allow a bank to describe its market area as a "cybercommunity"?

20–2A HYPOTHETICAL QUESTION WITH SAMPLE ANSWER

Mendez has a security interest in Arabian Knight and is a perfected secured party. He has met all the necessary criteria listed under UCC 9–203 to be a secured creditor. Mendez has given value of $5,000 and has taken possession of the collateral, Arabian Knight, owned by Marsh (who has rights in the collateral). Thus, he has a security interest even though Marsh did not sign a security agreement. Once a security interest attaches, a transfer of possession of the collateral to the secured party can perfect the party's security interest without a filing [UCC 9–310(b)(6); 9–313]. Thus, a security interest was created and perfected at the time Marsh transferred Arabian Knight to Mendez as security for the loan.

21–2A HYPOTHETICAL QUESTION WITH SAMPLE ANSWER

The Bankruptcy Code establishes the priority of payment of claims from the debtor's estate. Each class of debt in this priority list must be fully paid before the next class in priority is entitled to any of the proceeds. If insufficient funds remain to pay an entire class, the proceeds are distributed on a pro rata basis to each creditor within that class. The order of priority for claims listed in this problem is as follows:

1. Administrative bankruptcy costs (Martinez)—$500.
2. Claims for back wages, limited to $4,300 per claimant, provided wages were earned within ninety days of petition (Kohak)—$4,300.
3. Taxes and penalties due and owing (Micanopa County)—$1,000.
4. General creditors, $10,000 (First Bank of Sunny Acres—$5,000; Calvin—$2,500; balance of Kohak wages owed—$2,500).

Because the amount remaining after paying (a), (b), and (c) is only $1,200, the general creditors will share on a pro rata basis. First Bank of Sunny Acres will receive $600 ($5,000/$10,000 × $1,200 = $600), and Calvin and Kohak will each receive $300 ($2,500/$10,000 × $1,200 = $300).

22–2A HYPOTHETICAL QUESTION WITH SAMPLE ANSWER

Yes, it is a reasonable approach to rely on the producers' financial records, which are reasonably reflective of their costs because their normal allocation methodologies were used for a number of years. These records are historically relied on to present important financial information to shareholders, lenders, tax authorities, auditors, and other third parties. Provided that the producers' records and books comply with generally accepted accounting principles and were verified by independent auditors, it is reasonable to use them to determine the production costs and fair market value of canned pineapple in the United States.

23–2A HYPOTHETICAL QUESTION WITH SAMPLE ANSWER

Agency usually is a consensual relationship in that the principal and agent agree that the agent will have the authority to act for the principal, binding the principal to any contract with a third party. If no agency in fact exists, the purported agent's contracts with third parties are not binding on the principal. In this case, no agency by agreement was created. Brown may claim that an agency by estoppel was created; however, this argument will fail. Agency by estoppel is applicable only when a *principal* causes a third person to believe that another person is the principal's agent. Then the third party's actions in dealing with the agent are in reliance upon the principal's words or actions and the third party's reasonable belief that the agent has authority. This is said to estop the principal from claiming that in fact no agency existed. Acts and declarations of the *agent,* however, do not in and of themselves create an agency by estoppel, because such actions should not reasonably lead a third person to believe that the purported agent has authority. In this case, Wade's declarations and allegations alone led Brown to believe that Wade was an agent. Gett's actions were not involved. It is not reasonable to believe that someone is an agent solely because he or she is a friend of the principal. Therefore, Brown cannot hold Gett liable unless Gett ratifies Wade's contract—which is unlikely, as Wade has disappeared with the rare coin.

24–2A HYPOTHETICAL QUESTION WITH SAMPLE ANSWER

The Occupational Safety and Health Act (OSHA) requires employers to provide safe working conditions for employees. The act prohibits employers from discharging or discriminating against any employee who refuses to work when the employee believes in good faith that he or she will risk death or great bodily harm by undertaking the employment activity. Denton and Carlo had sufficient reason to believe that the maintenance job required of them by their employer involved great risk, and therefore, under OSHA, their discharge was wrongful. Denton and Carlo can turn to the Occupational Safety and Health Administration, which is part of the U.S. Department of Labor, for assistance.

25–2A HYPOTHETICAL QUESTION WITH SAMPLE ANSWER

Educational requirements can be legally imposed provided that the educational requirement is directly related to, and necessary for, performance of the job. The requirement of a high school diploma is not a direct, job-related requirement in this case. Chinawa obviously comes under the 1964 Civil Rights Act, Title VII, as amended, and the educational requirement under the circumstances is definitely discriminatory against minorities.

26–2A HYPOTHETICAL QUESTION WITH SAMPLE ANSWER

The court would likely consider the terms of any contracts between the parties and whether the parties were acting in good faith. One way to avoid conflicts such as those described in this problem is to institute a Web site in conjunction with a franchisor's franchisees. When a Web site directs interested parties to a franchisee, for example, all parties would seem to benefit. Because territorial conflicts can occur not only between a franchisor and its franchisees but also between competing franchisees, some companies have instituted specific "no compete" pledges.

27–2A HYPOTHETICAL QUESTION WITH SAMPLE ANSWER

1 A limited partner's interest is assignable. In fact, assignment allows the assignee to become a substituted limited partner with the consent of the remaining partners. The assignment, however, does not dissolve the limited partnership.
2 Bankruptcy of the limited partnership itself causes dissolution, but bankruptcy of one of the limited partners does not dissolve the partnership unless it causes the bankruptcy of the firm.
3 The retirement, death, or insanity of a general partner dissolves the partnership unless the business can be continued by the remaining general partners. Because Dorinda was the only general partner, her death dissolves the limited partnership.

28–2A HYPOTHETICAL QUESTION WITH SAMPLE ANSWER

Although a joint stock company has characteristics of a corporation, it is usually treated as a partnership. Therefore, although the joint stock company issues transferable shares of stock and is managed by directors and officers, the shareholders have personal liability. Unless the shareholders transfer their stock and ownership to a third party, not only are the joint stock company's assets available for damages caused by a breach, but the individual shareholders' estates are also subject to such liability. The business trust resembles and is treated like a corporation in many respects. One is the limited liability of the beneficiaries. Unless by state law the beneficiaries are treated as partners, making them liable to business trust creditors, Faraway Corp. can look to only business trust assets in the event of breach.

29–2A HYPOTHETICAL QUESTION WITH SAMPLE ANSWER

If Artel acquires the stocks and assets of Fox Express, a *merger* will take place. Artel will be the surviving corporation, and Fox Express will disappear as a corporation. If Artel and Fox Express combine so that both corporations cease to exist and a new corporation, A&F Enterprises, is formed, a *consolidation* will take place. In either situation, title to the property of the corporation that ceases to exist will pass automatically to the surviving or new corporation without a formal transfer being necessary. In addition, in a merger, the debt liabilities of Fox Express become the liabilities of Artel. Artel's articles of incorporation are deemed to be amended to include the terms stated in the articles of merger. If a consolidation takes place, A&F Enterprises will automatically acquire title to the properties of both Artel and Fox Express without a formal transfer being necessary. A&F Enterprises also will assume liability for the debts and obligations of Artel and Fox Express. The articles of consolidation take the place of the articles of incorporation of Artel and Fox Express, and they will be regarded thereafter as the articles of incorporation of A&F Enterprises.

30–2A HYPOTHETICAL QUESTION WITH SAMPLE ANSWER

Directors are personally answerable to the corporation and the shareholders for breach of their duty to exercise reasonable care in conducting the affairs of the corporation. Reasonable care is defined as being the degree of care that a reasonably prudent person would use in the conduct of personal business affairs. When directors delegate the running of the corporate affairs to officers, the directors are expected to use reasonable care in the selection and supervision of such officers. Failure to do so will make the directors liable for negligence or mismanagement. A director who dissents from an action by the board is not personally liable for losses resulting from that action. Unless the dissent is entered into the board meeting minutes, however, the director is presumed to have assented. Therefore, the first issue in the case of Starboard, Inc., is whether the board members failed to use reasonable care in the selection of the president, Tyson. If so, and particularly if the board failed to provide a reasonable amount of supervision (and openly embezzled funds indicate that failure), the directors will be personally liable. This liability will include Ellsworth unless she can prove that she dissented and that she tried to reasonably supervise Tyson. Considering the facts in this case, it is questionable that Ellsworth could prove this.

31–2A HYPOTHETICAL QUESTION WITH SAMPLE ANSWER

No. Under federal securities law, a stock split is exempt from registration requirements. This is because no *sale* of stock is involved. The existing shares are merely being split, and no consideration is received by the corporation for the additional shares created.

32–2A HYPOTHETICAL QUESTION WITH SAMPLE ANSWER

Yes. The major antitrust law being violated is the Sherman Act, Section 1. Allitron and Donovan are engaged in interstate commerce, and the agreement to divide marketing territories between them is a contract in restraint of trade. The U.S. Department of Justice could seek fines of up to $1 million from each corporation, and the officers or directors responsible could be imprisoned for up to three years. In addition, the U.S. Department of Justice could institute civil proceedings to restrain this conduct.

33–2A HYPOTHETICAL QUESTION WITH SAMPLE ANSWER

The Truth-in-Lending Act (TILA) deals specifically with lost or stolen credit cards and their unauthorized use. For credit cards *solicited* by the cardholder and then lost or stolen, the act limits the liability of the cardholder to $50 for unauthorized charges made prior to the time the creditor is notified. There is no liability for any unauthorized charges made after the date of notice. In the case of the Midtown Department Store credit card stolen on May 31, the $500 charge made on June 1, which is prior to Ochoa's notice, causes Ochoa to be liable for the $50 limit. For the June 3 charge of $200 made after the notification, Ochoa has no liability. TILA also deals with unsolicited credit cards. Unless a credit cardholder accepts an unsolicited card (such as by using it), the cardholder is not liable for any unauthorized charges. Moreover, the act prohibits the issuance of unsolicited credit cards. No notice by the cardholder of an unsolicited, unaccepted credit card is required to absolve the cardholder from liability for unauthorized charges. Therefore, Ochoa owes $50 to the Midtown Department Store and nothing to High-Flying Airlines.

34–2A HYPOTHETICAL QUESTION WITH SAMPLE ANSWER

Assuming that the circuit court has abandoned the *Ultramares* rule, it is likely that the accounting firm of Goldman, Walters, Johnson & Co. will be held liable to Happydays State Bank for negligent preparation of financial statements. This hypothetical scenario is partially derived from *Citizens State Bank v. Timm, Schmidt & Co.* In *Citizens State Bank,* the Supreme Court of Wisconsin enunciated various policy reasons for holding accountants liable to third parties even in the absence of privity. The court suggested that this potential liability would make accountants more careful in the preparation of financial statements. Moreover, in some situations the accountants may be the only solvent defendants, and hence, unless liability is imposed on accountants, third parties who reasonably rely on financial statements may go unprotected. The court further asserted that accountants, rather than third parties, are in a better position to spread the risks. If third parties such as banks have to absorb the costs of bad loans made as a result of negligently prepared financial statements, then the cost of credit to the public in general will increase. In contrast, the court suggests that accountants are in a better position to spread the risk by purchasing liability insurance.

35–3A HYPOTHETICAL QUESTION WITH SAMPLE ANSWER

For Curtis to recover against the hotel, he must first prove that a bailment relationship was created between himself and the hotel as to the car or the fur coat, or both. For a bailment to exist, there must be a delivery of the personal property that gives the bailee exclusive possession of the property, and the bailee must knowingly accept the bailed property. If either element is lacking, there is no bailment relationship and no liability on the part of the bailee hotel. The facts clearly indicate that the bailee hotel took exclusive possession and control of Curtis's car, and it knowingly accepted the car when the attendant took the car from Curtis and parked it in the underground guarded garage, retaining the keys. Thus, a bailment was created as to the car, and, because a mutual benefit bailment was created, the hotel owes Curtis the duty to exercise reasonable care over the property and to return the bailed car at the end of the bailment. Failure to return the car creates a presumption of negligence (lack of reasonable care), and unless the hotel can rebut this presumption, the hotel is liable to Curtis for the loss of the car. As to the fur coat, the hotel neither knew nor expected that the trunk contained an expensive fur coat. Thus, although the hotel knowingly took exclusive possession of the car, the hotel did not do so with the fur coat. (But the hotel would be liable for a regular coat and other items likely to be in the car.) Because no bailment of the expensive fur coat was created, the hotel has no liability for its loss.

36–2A HYPOTHETICAL QUESTION WITH SAMPLE ANSWER

Wiley understandably wants a general warranty deed, as this type of deed will give him the most extensive protection against any defects of title claimed against the property transferred. The general warranty would have Gemma warranting the following covenants:

1. Covenant of seisin and right to convey—a warranty that the seller has good title and power to convey.
2. Covenant against encumbrances—a guaranty by the seller that, unless stated, there are no outstanding encumbrances or liens against the property conveyed.
3. Covenant of quiet possession—a warranty that the grantee's possession will not be disturbed by others claiming a prior legal right. Gemma, however, is conveying only ten feet along a property line that may not even be accurately surveyed. Gemma therefore does not wish to make these warranties. Consequently, she is offering a quitclaim deed, which does not convey any warranties but conveys only whatever interest, if any, the grantor owns. Although title is passed by the quitclaim deed, the quality of the title is not warranted. Because Wiley really needs the property, it appears that he has three choices: he can accept the quitclaim deed; he can increase his offer price to obtain the general warranty deed he wants; or he can offer to have a title search made, which should satisfy both parties.

37–2A HYPOTHETICAL QUESTION WITH SAMPLE ANSWER

1. In most states, for a will to be valid, it must be in writing, signed by the testator, and witnessed (attested to) according to the statutes of the state. In some states, the testator is also required to publish (declare) that the document is his or her last will and testament. (This is not required under the Uniform Probate Code.) In the case of Benjamin, the will is unquestionably written (typewritten) and signed by the testator. The only problem is with the witnesses. Some states require three witnesses, and some invalidate a will if a named beneficiary is also a witness. The Uniform Probate Code provides that a will is valid even if attested to by an interested witness. Therefore, whether the will is valid depends on the state laws dealing with witness qualifications.
2. If the will is declared invalid, Benjamin's estate will pass in accordance with the state's intestacy laws. These statutes provide for distribution of an estate when there is no valid will. The intent of the statutes is to distribute the estate in the way that the deceased person would have wished. Generally, the estate is divided between a surviving spouse and all surviving children. Because Benjamin is a widower, if his only surviving child is Edward, the entire estate will go to Edward, and Benjamin's grandchildren, Perry and Paul, will receive nothing from the estate.
3. If the will is valid, the estate will be divided between Benjamin's two children, Patricia and Edward. Should either or both predecease Benjamin, leaving children (Benjamin's grandchildren), the grandchildren take *per stirpes* the share that would have gone to their parent. In this case Edward, as a surviving child of Benjamin, would receive one-half of the estate, and Perry and Paul, as grandchildren, would each receive *per stirpes* one-fourth of the estate (one-half of the share that would have gone to their deceased mother, Patricia).

Appendix F

Case Excerpts for Case Analysis Questions

CASE NO. 1 (FOR CHAPTER 4)

Lott v. Levitt, United States District Court, 469 F.Supp.2d 575 (E.D.Ill. 2007).

In 2005, well-known economist Steven Levitt ("Levitt") and journalist Stephen J. Dubner ("Dubner") coauthored the best-selling book *Freakonomics*[.] * * * In the book, Levitt and Dubner [discuss] * * * the theory for which fellow economist, * * * John R. Lott, Jr. ("Lott"), is known[:] * * * that laws permitting individuals to carry concealed weapons result in a statistically significant and provable reduction in serious crime rates. Lott filed the instant lawsuit against Levitt and [others] * * *. Lott claims [in part] that an email written by Levitt to another economist * * * constitutes defamation * * *. [Levitt filed a motion to dismiss this claim.]

* * * *

Lott is discussed in the following single paragraph in Chapter 4 of *Freakonomics,* entitled "Where Have All the Criminals Gone?":

> * * * There is an * * * argument—that we need more guns on the street, but in the hands of the right people * * *. The economist John R. Lott Jr. is the main champion of this idea. * * * [H]e argues that violent crime has decreased in areas where law abiding citizens are allowed to carry concealed weapons. His theory might be surprising, but it is sensible. If a criminal thinks his potential victim may be armed, he may be deterred from committing the crime. Handgun opponents call Lott a pro-gun ideologue * * *. There was the troubling allegation that Lott actually invented some of the survey data that support his more-guns/less-crime theory. Regardless of whether the data were faked, Lott's admittedly intriguing hypothesis doesn't seem to be true. When other scholars have tried to replicate his results, they found that right-to-carry laws simply don't bring down crime.

On May 24 or May 25, 2005, John McCall ("McCall"), described by Lott as an economist residing in Texas, sent Levitt an email regarding the above passage, stating:

> I * * * found the following citations—have not read any of them yet, but it appears they all replicate Lott's research. [McCall referred to a "Special Issue" of *The Journal of Law and Economics* published in October 2001 that contained a collection of articles delivered at an academic conference co-sponsored by the Center for Law, Economics and Public Policy at Yale Law School and the American Enterprise Institute, where Lott had recently been a resident scholar.] *The Journal of Law and Economics* is not chopped liver.

That same day, Levitt responded:

> It was not a peer refereed edition of the *Journal.* For $15,000 he was able to buy an issue and put in only work that supported him. My best friend was the editor and was outraged the press let Lott do this.

* * * *

A statement is considered defamatory if it tends to cause such harm to the reputation of another that it lowers that person in the eyes of the community or deters third persons from associating with that person. [Emphasis added.]

* * * *

* * * Lott contends that the statements about him in * * * the email * * * imply that his results were falsified or that his theories lack merit, and thus impute a lack of ability and integrity in his profession as an economist, academic, and researcher. Indeed, a claim that an academic or economist falsified his results and could only publish his theories by buying an issue of a journal and avoiding peer review would surely impute a lack of ability and prejudice that person in his profession.

* * * *

* * * *The First Amendment protects statements that cannot be reasonably interpreted as stating actual facts.* [Emphasis added.]

The test for whether a statement is a factual assertion is whether the statement is precise, readily understood, and susceptible of being verified as true or false. This test * * * is a reasonableness standard; whether a reasonable reader would understand the defendant to be informing him of a fact or opinion. Language that is loose, figurative, or hyperbolic negates the impression that a statement is asserting actual facts. Accordingly, *vague, unprovable statements and statements of opinion do not give rise to a defamation claim.* If it is plain that the speaker is expressing a subjective view, an interpretation, a theory, conjecture, or surmise, rather than claiming to be in possession of objectively verifiable facts, the statement is not actionable. [Emphasis added.]

In this case, however, Levitt's email sounds as if he was in possession of objectively verifiable facts. * * * First, it would be unreasonable to interpret Levitt's unqualified statement that the *Journal* edition was not "peer refereed" as Levitt [argues that he was] merely giving his opinion on the "peers" chosen to review, or referee, the Special Issue. Indeed, the editor of the *Journal* might be able to verify the truth or falsity of whether the Special Issue was reviewed by peers. * * * Second, a reasonable reader would not interpret Levitt's assertion that "For $15,000 [Lott] was able to buy an issue and put in only work that supported him" as simply a statement of Levitt's opinion. Levitt's email appears to state objectively verifiable facts: that Lott paid $15,000 to control the content of the Special Issue. The editor of the *Journal* again might be the source to verify the truth or falsity of this statement. Third, the same editor could verify whether he was "outraged" by the acts described in the foregoing statements. Therefore, the defamatory statements in Levitt's email to McCall are objectively verifiable * * *.

* * * *

* * * In his email to McCall, * * * Levitt made a string of defamatory assertions about Lott's involvement in the publication of the Special Issue of the *Journal* that—no matter how rash or short-sighted Levitt was when he made them—cannot be reasonably interpreted as innocent or mere opinion.

* * * Levitt's motion to dismiss [this part of Lott's] Complaint is denied.

CASE NO. 2 (FOR CHAPTER 10)

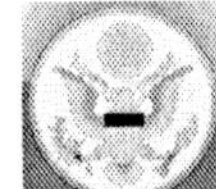

Feldman v. Google, Inc., 513 F.Supp.2d 229 (E.D.Pa. 2007).

Before the court is Defendant Google, Inc.'s Motion to * * * Transfer [the case to Santa Clara County]. Also before the court is Plaintiff Lawrence E. Feldman's Cross-Motion for Summary Judgment. The ultimate issues raised by the motions and determined by the court are whether a forum selection clause in an Internet "clickwrap" agreement is enforceable * * *.

Defendant's motion seeks to enforce the forum selection clause in an online "clickwrap" agreement, which provides for venue in Santa Clara County * * *.

On or about January 2003, Plaintiff, a lawyer with his own law firm, Lawrence E. Feldman & Associates, purchased advertising from Defendant Google, Inc.'s "AdWords" Program, to attract potential clients who may have been harmed by drugs under scrutiny by the U.S. Food and Drug Administration.

In the AdWords program, whenever an internet user searched on the internet search engine, Google.com, for keywords or "Adwords" purchased by Plaintiff, such as "Vioxx," "Bextra," and "Celebrex," Plaintiff's ad would appear. If the searcher clicked on Plaintiff's ad, Defendant would charge Plaintiff for each click made on the ad.

This procedure is known as "pay per click" advertising. The price per keyword is determined by a bidding process, wherein the highest bidder for a keyword would have its ad placed at the top of the list of results from a Google.com search by an Internet user.

Plaintiff claims that he was the victim of "click fraud." Click fraud occurs when entities or persons, such as competitors or pranksters, without any interest in Plaintiff's services, click repeatedly on Plaintiff's ad, the result of which drives up his advertising cost and discourages him from advertising. * * * Plaintiff alleges that twenty to thirty percent of all clicks for which he was charged were fraudulent. He claims that Google required him to pay for all clicks on his ads, including those which were fraudulent.

* * * *

The type of contract at issue here is commonly referred to as a "clickwrap" agreement. A clickwrap agreement appears on an Internet web page and requires that a user consent to any terms or conditions by clicking on a dialog box on the screen in order to proceed with the Internet transaction. *Even though they are electronic, clickwrap agreements are considered to be writings because they are printable and storable.* [Emphasis added.]

To determine whether a clickwrap agreement is enforceable, courts * * * apply traditional principles of contract law and focus on whether the plaintiffs had reasonable notice of and manifested assent to the clickwrap agreement. *Absent a showing of fraud, failure to read an enforceable clickwrap agreement, as with any binding contract, will not excuse compliance with its terms.* [Emphasis added.]

* * * *

Plaintiff [Feldman] claims he did not have notice or knowledge of the forum selection clause, and therefore that there was no "meeting of the minds" required for contract formation.

* * * *

* * * In order to activate an AdWords account, the user had to visit a Web page which displayed the Agreement in a scrollable text box. * * * The user did not have to scroll down to a submerged screen or click on a series of hyperlinks to view the Agreement. Instead, text of the AdWords Agreement was immediately visible to the user, as was a prominent admonition in boldface to read the terms and conditions carefully, and with instruction to indicate assent if the user agreed to the terms.

That the user would have to scroll through the text box of the Agreement to read it in its entirety does not defeat notice because there was sufficient notice of the Agreement itself and clicking "Yes" constituted assent to all of the terms. The preamble, which was immediately visible, also made clear that assent to the terms was binding. The Agreement was presented in readable 12-point font. It was only seven paragraphs long—not so long so as to render scrolling down to view all of the terms inconvenient or impossible. A printer-friendly, full-screen version was made readily available. The user had ample time to review the document.

* * * The user * * * had to take affirmative action and click the "Yes, I agree to the above terms and conditions" button in order to proceed to the next step. Clicking "Continue" without clicking the "Yes" button would have returned the user to the same Web page. If the user did not agree to all of the terms, he could not have activated his account, placed ads, or incurred charges.

* * * *

A reasonably prudent Internet user would have known of the existence of terms in the AdWords Agreement. Plaintiff had to have had reasonable notice of the terms. By clicking on "Yes, I agree to the above terms and conditions" button, Plaintiff indicated assent to the terms.

* * * *

For the foregoing reasons, * * * Defendant's motion to transfer is granted and Plaintiff's motion for summary judgment is denied.

CASE NO. 3 (FOR CHAPTER 15)

Spray-Tek, Inc. v. Robbins Motor Transportation, Inc., 426 F.Supp.2d 875 (W.D.Wis. 2006).

* * * *

Plaintiff Spray-Tek, Inc. is engaged in the business of commercial dehydration of food flavor, pharmaceutical and soft chemical products. In 2003 plaintiff entered into a contract with Niro, Inc. (hereinafter Niro) in which Niro was to design and manufacture a fourteen-foot diameter conebottom drying chamber * * * for plaintiff. Pursuant to the terms of the contract Niro was also responsible for shipping the drying chamber from its facility in Hudson, Wisconsin to plaintiff's facility in Bethlehem, Pennsylvania. The contract stated in relevant part:

* * * *

For one (1) Niro-Bowen * * * drying chamber, * * * F.O.B. points of manufacture in the U.S.A. * * * Price * * * $1,161,500.00

* * * *

IX. RISKS OF LOSS. The Purchaser shall bear the risk of loss of or damage to the equipment and parts after delivery of the equipment and parts to the job site or to the shipping point if delivery F.O.B. shipping point is specified.

On October 14, 2004, Niro's representative Mr. David Thoen contacted defendant Robbins Motor Transportation, Inc. to obtain an estimate for transporting the drying chamber to plaintiff. * * * Mr. Robert Kauffman, Jr. who serves as defendant's Southwest Regional Terminal Manager * * * prepared and sent an estimate to Niro. * * *

Mr.Thoen signed the estimate and faxed it back to defendant * * *.

On October 18, 2004, defendant arrived at Niro's facility in Hudson, Wisconsin and the drying chamber was loaded onto its trailer. Niro prepared a Bill of Lading * * *.

* * * *

On or about October 28, 2004 the drying chamber was damaged while it was in transit * * * when it struck an overpass and became dislodged from defendant's vehicle. It was inspected and declared a total loss. Accordingly, Niro manufactured a replacement drying chamber for plaintiff and invoiced it $233,100.00 in replacement costs.* * *

* * * *

[Spray-Tek filed a suit in a federal district court against Robbins under a federal statute known as the Carmack Amendment to recover the replacement cost and other expenses.] The Carmack Amendment * * * states in relevant part:

A carrier providing transportation or service * * * shall issue a receipt or bill of lading for property it receives for transportation under this part. That carrier * * * [is] liable to the person entitled to recover under the receipt or bill of lading. * * *

The purpose of the Carmack Amendment is to establish uniform federal guidelines designed in part to remove the uncertainty surrounding a carrier's liability when damage occurs to a shipper's interstate shipment.

Under the Carmack Amendment plaintiff bears the burden of establishing a *prima facie* [legally sufficient] case which requires it to demonstrate: (1) delivery to the carrier in good condition; (2) arrival in damaged condition; and (3) the amount of damages. * * * The excepted causes [relieving a carrier of liability] are: (1) acts of God; (2) the public enemy; (3) acts of the shipper himself; (4) public authority; or (5) the inherent vice or nature of the goods. * * *

Defendant concedes that it received the drying chamber in good condition. Accordingly, plaintiff's first element of its *prima facie* case is established. * * *

* * * *

It is undisputed that the drying chamber was damaged when it struck an overpass and became dislodged from defendant's vehicle. Additionally, it is undisputed that after the accident the drying chamber was inspected and declared a total loss. * * *

An * * * argument defendant asserts concerning plaintiff's second element of its *prima facie* case is that plaintiff cannot demonstrate it owned the drying chamber during transport. However, the contract plaintiff entered into with Niro establishes that it was the owner of the drying chamber when it was damaged. The contract provided that the terms of sale were "F.O.B. points of manufacture in the U.S.A." According to * * * plaintiff's vice president and general manager "F.O.B. points of manufacture" means that the drying chamber became plaintiff's property once it was "placed on board the delivery truck at its point of manufacture in Hudson, Wisconsin."

[This] assertion * * * is reinforced by the provision in the contract concerning risks of loss. * * * [T]he "F.O.B. points of manufacture" language * * * demonstrates that plaintiff bore the risk of loss once the drying chamber departed from Niro's Hudson, Wisconsin facility. * * * Accordingly, plaintiff established the second element of its *prima facie* case.

Finally, defendant asserts plaintiff cannot meet its burden of establishing the third element of its *prima facie* case because it failed to demonstrate what "it is obligated to pay for the dryer." However, * * * Niro invoiced plaintiff $233,100.00 for the replacement dryer. Accordingly, plaintiff established the third element of its *prima facie* case because its amount of damages is $233,100.00.

Plaintiff met its burden of establishing a *prima facie* case under the Carmack Amendment. * * * Defendant concedes it failed to produce any evidence establishing that damage to the shipment was due to one of the excepted causes. Accordingly, plaintiff is entitled to summary judgment on the issue of defendant's liability under the Carmack Amendment.

* * * *

[The court allowed the case to go to trial on another issue, however.]

CASE NO. 4 (FOR CHAPTER 19)

NBT Bank, N.A. v. First National Community Bank, 393 F.3d 404 (3d Cir. 2004).

* * * *

* * * [A] small group of Pennsylvania business entities arranged to write checks on one account, drawing on non-existent funds, and then cover these overdrafts with checks drawn on another account that also lacked sufficient funds. * * * The scheme collapsed when three checks initially deposited at [NBT Bank, N.A.,] and subsequently presented for payment to [First National Community Bank (FNCB)] were discovered by FNCB to have been drawn on an FNCB account that lacked sufficient funds. There is no dispute between the parties that two of these three checks were properly returned by FNCB to the [Federal Reserve Bank of Philadelphia] prior to the applicable midnight deadline.

* * * *

[On March 8, 2001, the third check (the "Disputed Check"), which was drawn on an FNCB account in the amount of $706,000, was deposited at NBT by an entity called PA Health.] After the Disputed Check was presented for deposit at NBT, the bank gave provisional credit to the depositor, PA Health, for the amount of the Disputed Check. NBT also transmitted the Disputed Check to the Reserve Bank for presentment to FNCB. * * * The Reserve Bank then forwarded the Disputed Check to FNCB, and FNCB received it on March 12, 2001. * * *

* * * *

On March 13, 2001, FNCB determined it would not pay the Disputed Check because of the absence of sufficient funds in the account on which the check was drawn. That same day, FNCB sought to return the Disputed Check to NBT through the Reserve Bank. * * * [T]he Disputed Check was physically delivered to the Reserve Bank prior to 11:59 P.M. on March 13.* * * FNCB also sent a notice of dishonor to NBT * * * in which FNCB indicated that it did not intend to pay the Disputed Check. NBT received this notice prior to the close of business on March 13. * * *

* * * *

When FNCB sent the Disputed Check to the Reserve Bank on March 13, 2001, FNCB * * * erroneously encoded [it] with the routing number for PNC Bank instead of the routing number for NBT [Bank].

* * * Because the Disputed Check was improperly encoded, NBT did not receive it back * * * until March 16, 2001. * * * NBT suffered no damages or actual loss as a result of the encoding error * * *.

* * * *

NBT instituted this action [in a federal district court] against FNCB on May 25, 2001. * * * NBT claimed that FNCB's encoding error meant FNCB had failed to return the Disputed Check prior to the midnight deadline as required by the UCC, and that FNCB was therefore accountable to NBT for the full amount of the Disputed Check. * * *

The District Court granted FNCB's motion [for summary judgment]. NBT appeals.

* * * *

* * * Federal law forms part of the legal framework within which check-processing activities take place. Of particular relevance to this appeal are the 1988 regulations adopted by the Federal Reserve implementing the Expedited Funds Availability Act. These regulations, referred to collectively as "Regulation CC," complement but do not necessarily replace the requirements of Article 4 of the UCC.

* * * *

* * * Regulation CC indisputably binds the parties, pursuant to both its own terms, as well as [13 Pennsylvania Consolidated Statutes Annotated Section 4103 (Pennsylvania's version of UCC 4–103)], which indicates that "Federal Reserve regulations" are to be treated as agreements that may vary the terms of the UCC.* * *

Because Regulation CC * * * is binding on the parties, and because Regulation CC is the source of the encoding requirement invoked by NBT, the extent of FNCB's liability for its encoding error must be measured by the standards set forth in Regulation CC. *Regulation CC states that a bank that fails to exercise ordinary care in complying with the [encoding] provisions of * * * Regulation CC * * * "may be liable" to the depositary bank.* Then, in broad, unrestricted language, Regulation CC states: [Emphasis added.]

> The measure of damages for failure to exercise ordinary care is the amount of the loss incurred, up to the amount of the check, reduced by the amount of the loss that the [plaintiff bank] would have incurred even if the [defendant] bank had exercised ordinary care.

This provision does not provide an exception to this standard for measuring damages in instances where noncompliance with Regulation CC is alleged to have resulted in noncompliance with the UCC's midnight deadline rule. Here, the parties have stipulated that NBT suffered no loss as a result of FNCB's encoding error. Thus, under the plain language of Regulation CC, NBT may not recover from FNCB for the amount of the Disputed Check.

* * * *

Accordingly,* * * we affirm the order of the District Court * * *.

CASE NO. 5 (FOR CHAPTER 25)

Burlington Northern and Santa Fe Railway Co. v. White, 548 U.S. 53, 126 S.Ct. 2405, 165 L.Ed.2d 345 (2006).

* * * *

* * * Sheila White [was] the only woman working in the Maintenance of Way department at [Burlington Northern & Santa Fe Railway Company's] Tennessee Yard. In September 1997, White complained to Burlington officials that her * * * supervisor, Bill Joiner, had repeatedly told her that women should not be working in the Maintenance of Way department. [Joiner was disciplined. White was reassigned from forklift duty to "track laborer" tasks.]

* * * *

On October 10, White filed a complaint with the Equal Employment Opportunity Commission (EEOC * * *).

[In December, White's supervisor, Percy Sharkey, complained to Burlington officials that White had been insubordinate. She was suspended without pay but reinstated after an investigation and awarded back pay for the period of the suspension. White filed a second charge with the EEOC.]

* * * *

* * * [Later] White filed this Title VII action against Burlington in federal [district] court. * * * [S]he claimed that Burlington's actions—(1) changing her job responsibilities, and (2) suspending her * * * without pay—amounted to unlawful retaliation in violation of Title VII. A jury found in White's favor * * * [and] awarded her $43,500 in * * * damages * * *.

* * * [On appeal, the U.S. Court of Appeals for the Sixth Circuit held that Title VII's antiretaliation ban is limited to acts that adversely affect the terms, conditions, or benefits of employment, and] affirmed the District Court's judgment in White's favor on both retaliation claims. [Burlington appealed to the United States Supreme Court.]

* * * *

* * * The language of the [antidiscrimination] provision differs from that of the antiretaliation provision in important ways.

The * * * words in the [antidiscrimination] provision—"hire," "discharge," "compensation, terms, conditions, or privileges of employment," "employment opportunities," and "status as an employee"—explicitly limit the scope of that provision to actions that affect employment or alter the conditions of the workplace. No such limiting words appear in the antiretaliation provision.

* * * The two provisions differ not only in language but in purpose as well. The antidiscrimination provision seeks a workplace where individuals are not discriminated against because of their racial, ethnic, religious, or gender-based status. *The anti-retaliation provision seeks to secure that primary objective by preventing an employer from interfering (through retaliation) with an employee's efforts to secure*

or advance enforcement of the Act's basic guarantees. The [antidiscrimination] provision seeks to prevent injury to individuals based on who they are, i.e., their status. *The antiretaliation provision seeks to prevent harm to individuals based on what they do, i.e., their conduct.* [Emphasis added.]

To secure the first objective, Congress did not need to prohibit anything other than employment related discrimination.

But one cannot secure the second objective by focusing only upon employer actions and harm that concern employment and the workplace. * * * *An employer can effectively retaliate against an employee by taking actions not directly related to his employment or by causing him harm outside the workplace.* [Emphasis added.]

* * * *

* * * We conclude that * * * the anti-retaliation provision extends beyond workplace related or employment-related retaliatory acts * * *.

* * * *

* * * A plaintiff must show that a reasonable employee would have found the challenged action materially adverse, which in this context means it well might have dissuaded a reasonable worker from making or supporting a charge of discrimination.

* * * *

* * * [In this case] the track labor duties were by all accounts more arduous and dirtier; * * * the forklift operator position required more qualifications, which is an indication of prestige; and * * * the forklift operator position was objectively considered a better job and the male employees resented White for occupying it. Based on this record, a jury could reasonably conclude that the reassignment of responsibilities would have been materially adverse to a reasonable employee.

* * * *

For these reasons, the judgment of the Court of Appeals is affirmed.

CASE NO. 6 (FOR CHAPTER 31)

Merrill Lynch, Pierce, Fenner & Smith, Inc. v. Dabit, 547 U.S. 71, 126 S.Ct. 1503, 164 L.Ed.2d 179 (2006).

* * * *

Petitioner Merrill Lynch, Pierce, Fenner & Smith, Inc. (Merrill Lynch), * * * offers research and brokerage services to investors.

Respondent, Shadi Dabit, is a former Merrill Lynch broker. He filed this class action in the United States District Court for the Western District of Oklahoma on behalf of himself and all other former or current brokers who, while employed by Merrill Lynch, purchased (for themselves and for their clients) certain stocks between December 1, 1999, and December 31, 2000. * * * Dabit * * * advanced his claims under Oklahoma state law.

* * * [Dabit's theory was that Merrill Lynch] research analysts * * * issued overly optimistic appraisals of the stocks' value; the brokers * * * relied on the analysts' reports in advising their investor clients * * * ; and the clients and brokers both continued to hold their stocks long beyond the point when, had the truth been known, they would have sold. * * * [W]hen the truth was actually revealed * * * , the stocks' prices plummeted.

* * * *

* * * [The case was transferred] to the United States District Court for the Southern District of New York * * * [which granted Merrill Lynch's motion to dismiss. The U.S. Court of Appeals for the Second Circuit reversed this ruling. Merrill Lynch appealed to the United States Supreme Court.]

* * * *

The magnitude of the federal interest in protecting the integrity and efficient operation of the market for nationally traded securities cannot be overstated. In response to the sudden and disastrous collapse in prices of listed stocks in 1929, and the Great Depression that followed, Congress enacted the Securities Act of 1933, and the Securities Exchange Act of 1934. Since their enactment, these two statutes have anchored federal regulation of vital elements of our economy.

* * * *

Policy considerations * * * prompted Congress, in 1995, to adopt [the Private Securities Litigation Reform Act] targeted at perceived abuses of the class-action vehicle in litigation involving nationally traded securities.

* * * *

* * * [P]laintiffs and their representatives began bringing class actions under state law, often in state court. * * * To stem this shift from Federal to State courts * * * , Congress enacted SLUSA.

* * * *

The core provision of SLUSA reads as follows:

> * * * No * * * class action based upon the * * * law of any State * * * may be maintained in any * * * court by any private party alleging—* * * a misrepresentation or omission of a material fact in connection with the purchase or sale of a * * * security * * * .

* * * *

* * * Under our precedents, it is enough that the fraud alleged "coincide" with a securities transaction—whether by the plaintiff or by someone else. *The requisite showing, in other words, is deception "in connection with the purchase or sale of any security," not deception of an identifiable purchaser or seller.* Notably, this broader interpretation of the statutory language comports [is consistent] with the longstanding views of the [Securities and Exchange Commission (SEC)]. [Emphasis added.]

Congress can hardly have been unaware of the broad construction adopted by both this Court and the SEC when it imported the key phrase—"in connection with the purchase or sale"—into SLUSA's core provision. *And when judicial interpretations have settled the meaning of an existing statutory provision, repetition of the same language in a new statute indicates * * * the intent to incorporate its * * * judicial interpretations as well.* [Emphasis added.]

* * * A narrow reading of the statute would undercut the effectiveness of the 1995 Reform Act and thus run contrary to SLUSA's stated purpose "to prevent certain State private securities class action lawsuits alleging fraud from being used to frustrate the objectives" of the 1995 Act.

* * * The prospect is raised, then, of parallel class actions proceeding in state and federal court, with different standards governing claims asserted on identical facts. That prospect * * * squarely conflicts with the congressional preference for national standards for securities class action lawsuits involving nationally traded securities.

* * * *

The judgment of the Court of Appeals for the Second Circuit is vacated, and the case is remanded * * * .

CASE NO. 7 (FOR CHAPTER 36)

Kelo v. City of New London, Connecticut, 545 U.S. 469, 125 S.Ct. 2655, 162 L.Ed.2d 439 (2005).

* * * *

The city of New London (hereinafter City) sits at the junction of the Thames River and the Long Island Sound in southeastern Connecticut. Decades of economic decline led a state agency in 1990 to designate the City a "distressed municipality." In 1996, the Federal Government closed the Naval Undersea Warfare Center, which had been located in the Fort Trumbull area of the City and had employed over 1,500 people. In 1998, the City's unemployment rate was nearly double that of the State, and its population of just under 24,000 residents was at its lowest since 1920.

These conditions prompted state and local officials to target New London * * * for economic revitalization. * * * In February [1998] the pharmaceutical company Pfizer Inc. announced that it would build a $300 million research facility on a site immediately adjacent to Fort Trumbull; local planners hoped that Pfizer would draw new business to the area * * *.

* * * *

The city council approved [a] plan in January 2000 [to redevelop the area that once housed the federal facility]. The [City] successfully negotiated the purchase of most of the real estate in the 90-acre area, but its negotiations with [some of the property owners] failed. As a consequence, in November 2000, the [City] initiated * * * condemnation proceedings * * *.

* * * *

* * * Susette Kelo has lived in the Fort Trumbull area since 1997. * * * [S]he prizes [her house] for its water view. * * *

In December 2000 [Kelo and others] brought this action in [a Connecticut state court against the City and others]. They claimed, among other things, that the taking of their properties would violate the "public use" restriction in the [U.S. Constitution's] Fifth Amendment. * * * [The court issued a ruling partly in favor of both sides].

* * * [B]oth sides took appeals to the Supreme Court of Connecticut [which] held * * * that all of the City's proposed takings were valid.* * *

* * * *

We granted *certiorari* to determine whether a city's decision to take property for the purpose of economic development satisfies the "public use" requirement of the Fifth Amendment.

* * * *

* * * [T]his Court long ago rejected any literal requirement that condemned property be put into use for the general public. * * * Not only was the "use by the public" test difficult to administer (e.g., what proportion of the public need have access to the property? at what price?), but it proved to be impractical given the diverse and always evolving needs of society. Accordingly, * * * *this Court* * * * *embraced the broader and more natural interpretation of public use as "public purpose."* * * * [Emphasis added.]

The disposition of this case therefore turns on the question whether the City's development plan serves a "public purpose." * * *

* * * *

Viewed as a whole, our jurisprudence has recognized that the needs of society have varied between different parts of the Nation, just as they have evolved over time in response to changed circumstances. * * * *For more than a century, our public use jurisprudence has wisely eschewed [avoided] rigid formulas and intrusive scrutiny in favor of affording legislatures broad latitude in determining what public needs justify the use of the takings power.* [Emphasis added.]

* * * *

Those who govern the City were not confronted with the need to remove blight in the Fort Trumbull area, but their determination that the area was sufficiently distressed to justify a program of economic rejuvenation is entitled to our deference. The City has carefully formulated an economic development plan that it believes will provide appreciable benefits to the community, including—but by no means limited to—new jobs and increased tax revenue. * * * To effectuate this plan, the City has invoked a state statute that specifically authorizes the use of eminent domain to promote economic development. Given the comprehensive character of the plan, the thorough deliberation that preceded its adoption, and the limited scope of our review, it is appropriate for us * * * to resolve the challenges of the individual owners, not on a piecemeal basis,but rather in light of the entire plan. *Because that plan unquestionably serves a public purpose, the takings challenged here satisfy the public use requirement of the Fifth Amendment.* [Emphasis added.]

* * * *

The judgment of the Supreme Court of Connecticut is affirmed.

Glossary

A

abandoned property • Property that has been discarded by the owner, with no intention of reclaiming it.
acceleration clause • A clause that allows a payee or other holder of a time instrument to demand payment of the entire amount due, with interest, if a certain event occurs, such as a default in the payment of an installment when due.
acceptance • A voluntary act by the offeree that shows assent, or agreement, to the terms of an offer; may consist of words or conduct. In negotiable instruments law, the drawee's signed agreement to pay a draft when it is presented.
acceptor • A drawee that is legally obligated to pay an instrument when it is presented later for payment.
accession • Occurs when an individual adds value to personal property by the use of either labor or materials. In some situations, a person may acquire ownership rights in another's property through accession.
accord and satisfaction • A common means of settling a disputed claim, whereby a debtor offers to pay a lesser amount than the creditor purports to be owed. The creditor's acceptance of the offer creates an accord (agreement), and when the accord is executed, satisfaction occurs.
accredited investors • In the context of securities offerings, "sophisticated" investors, such as banks, insurance companies, investment companies, the issuer's executive officers and directors, and persons whose income or net worth exceeds certain limits.
actionable • Capable of serving as the basis of a lawsuit. An actionable claim can be pursued in a lawsuit or other court action.
act of state doctrine • A doctrine providing that the judicial branch of one country will not examine the validity of public acts committed by a recognized foreign government within its own territory.
actual malice • The deliberate intent to cause harm, which exists when a person makes a statement either knowing that it is false or showing a reckless disregard for whether it is true. In a defamation suit, a statement made about a public figure normally must be made with actual malice for the plaintiff to recover damages.
actus reus • A guilty (prohibited) act. The commission of a prohibited act is one of the two essential elements required for criminal liability, the other element being the intent to commit a crime.
adhesion contract • A "standard-form" contract, such as that between a large retailer and a consumer, in which the stronger party dictates the terms.
adjudicate • To render a judicial decision. In the administrative process, adjudication is the trial-like proceeding in which an administrative law judge hears and decides issues that arise when an administrative agency charges a person or a firm with violating a law or regulation enforced by the agency.
administrative agency • A federal or state government agency established to perform a specific function. Administrative agencies are authorized by legislative acts to make and enforce rules in order to administer and enforce the acts.
administrative law • The body of law created by administrative agencies (in the form of rules, regulations, orders, and decisions) in order to carry out their duties and responsibilities.
administrative law judge (ALJ) • One who presides over an administrative agency hearing and has the power to administer oaths, take testimony, rule on questions of evidence, and make determinations of fact.
administrative process • The procedure used by administrative agencies in administering the law.
administrator • One who is appointed by a court to handle the probate (disposition) of a person's estate if that person dies intestate (without a valid will) or if the executor named in the will cannot serve.
adverse possession • The acquisition of title to real property by occupying it openly, without the consent of the owner, for a period of time specified by a state statute. The occupation must be actual, open, notorious, exclusive, and in opposition to all others, including the owner.
affirmative action • Job-hiring policies that give special consideration to members of protected classes in an effort to overcome present effects of past discrimination.
after-acquired property • Property that is acquired by the debtor after the execution of a security agreement.
agency • A relationship between two parties in which one party (the agent) agrees to represent or act for the other (the principal).
agreement • A meeting of two or more minds in regard to the terms of a contract; usually broken down into two events—an offer by one party to form a contract and an acceptance of the offer by the person to whom the offer is made.
alienation • The process of transferring land out of one's possession (thus "alienating" the land from oneself).
alien corporation • A designation in the United States for a corporation formed in another country but doing business in the United States.
alternative dispute resolution (ADR) • The resolution of disputes in ways other than those involved in the traditional judicial process. Negotiation, mediation, and arbitration are forms of ADR.
answer • Procedurally, a defendant's response to the plaintiff's complaint.
anticipatory repudiation • An assertion or action by a party indicating that he or she will not perform an obligation that the party is contractually obligated to perform at a future time.
antitrust law • Laws protecting commerce from unlawful restraints.
apparent authority • Authority that is only apparent, not real. In agency law, a person may be deemed to have had the power to act as an agent for another party if the other party's manifestations to a third party led the third party to believe that an agency existed when, in fact, it did not.
appraisal right • The right of a dissenting shareholder, who objects to an extraordinary transaction of the corporation (such as a merger or a consolidation), to have his or her shares appraised and to be paid the fair value of those shares by the corporation.
appropriation • In tort law, the use by one person of another person's name, likeness, or other identifying characteristic without permission and for the benefit of the user.
arbitration • The settling of a dispute by submitting it to a disinterested third party (other than a court), who renders a decision that is (most often) legally binding.
arbitration clause • A clause in a contract that provides that, in the event of a dispute, the parties will submit the dispute to arbitration rather than litigate the dispute in court.
arson • The intentional burning of another's building. Some statutes have expanded this to include any real property regardless of ownership and the destruction of property by other means—for example, by explosion.
articles of incorporation • The document filed with the appropriate governmental agency, usually the secretary of state, when a business is

incorporated. State statutes usually prescribe what kind of information must be contained in the articles of incorporation.

articles of organization • The document filed with a designated state official by which a limited liability company is formed.

articles of partnership • A written agreement that sets forth each partner's rights and obligations with respect to the partnership.

artisan's lien • A possessory lien given to a person who has made improvements and added value to another person's personal property as security for payment for services performed.

assault • Any word or action intended to make another person fearful of immediate physical harm; a reasonably believable threat.

assignee • A party to whom the rights under a contract are transferred, or assigned.

assignment • The act of transferring to another all or part of one's rights arising under a contract.

assignor • A party who transfers (assigns) his or her rights under a contract to another party (called the assignee).

assumption of risk • A doctrine under which a plaintiff may not recover for injuries or damage suffered from risks he or she knows of and has voluntarily assumed.

attachment • In a secured transaction, the process by which a secured creditor's interest "attaches" to the property of another (collateral) and the creditor's security interest becomes enforceable. In the context of judicial liens, a court-ordered seizure and taking into custody of property prior to the securing of a judgment for a past-due debt.

attempted monopolization • Any actions by a firm to eliminate competition and gain monopoly power.

authorization card • A card signed by an employee that gives a union permission to act on his or her behalf in negotiations with management.

automatic stay • In bankruptcy proceedings, the suspension of almost all litigation and other action by creditors against the debtor or the debtor's property. The stay is effective the moment the debtor files a petition in bankruptcy.

award • In litigation, the amount of monetary compensation awarded to a plaintiff in a civil lawsuit as damages. In the context of alternative dispute resolution, the decision rendered by an arbitrator.

B

bailee • One to whom goods are entrusted by a bailor. Under the UCC, a party who, by a bill of lading, warehouse receipt, or other document of title, acknowledges possession of goods and/or contracts to deliver them.

bailee's lien • A possessory lien, or claim, that a bailee entitled to compensation can place on the bailed property to ensure that he or she will be paid for the services provided. The lien is effective as long as the bailee retains possession of the bailed goods and has not agreed to extend credit to the bailor. Sometimes referred to as an artisan's lien.

bailment • A situation in which the personal property of one person (a bailor) is entrusted to another (a bailee), who is obligated to return the bailed property to the bailor or dispose of it as directed.

bailor • One who entrusts goods to a bailee.

bait-and-switch advertising • Advertising a product at a very attractive price (the bait) and then, once the consumer is in the store, saying that the advertised product either is not available or is of poor quality. The customer is then urged to purchase (switched to) a more expensive item.

bankruptcy court • A federal court of limited jurisdiction that handles only bankruptcy proceedings, which are governed by federal bankruptcy law.

battery • The unexcused, harmful or offensive, intentional touching of another.

bearer • A person in possession of an instrument payable to bearer or indorsed in blank.

bearer instrument • Any instrument that is not payable to a specific person, including instruments payable to the bearer or to "cash."

bequest • A gift of personal property by will (from the verb to bequeath).

beyond a reasonable doubt • The standard of proof used in criminal cases. If there is any reasonable doubt that a criminal defendant committed the crime with which she or he has been charged, then the verdict must be "not guilty."

bilateral contract • A type of contract that arises when a promise is given in exchange for a return promise.

Bill of Rights • The first ten amendments to the U.S. Constitution.

binder • A written, temporary insurance policy.

binding authority • Any source of law that a court must follow when deciding a case. Binding authorities include constitutions, statutes, and regulations that govern the issue being decided, as well as court decisions that are controlling precedents within the jurisdiction.

blank indorsement • An indorsement that specifies no particular indorsee and can consist of a mere signature. An order instrument that is indorsed in blank becomes a bearer instrument.

blue sky laws • State laws that regulate the offering and sale of securities for the protection of the public.

bona fide occupational qualification (BFOQ) • Identifiable characteristics reasonably necessary to the normal operation of a particular business. These characteristics can include gender, national origin, and religion, but not race.

bond • A security that evidences a corporate (or government) debt. It does not represent an ownership interest in the issuing entity.

bond indenture • A contract between the issuer of a bond and the bondholder.

botnet • A network of computers that have been appropriated without the knowledge of their owners and used to spread harmful programs via the Internet; short for robot network.

breach • The failure to perform a legal obligation.

breach of contract • The failure, without legal excuse, of a promisor to perform the obligations of a contract.

brief • A formal legal document prepared by a party's attorney for the appellant or the appellee (in answer to the appellant's brief) and submitted to an appellate court when a case is appealed. The appellant's brief outlines the facts and issues of the case, the judge's rulings or jury's findings that should be reversed or modified, the applicable law, and the arguments on the client's behalf.

browse-wrap term • A term or condition of use that is presented to an Internet user at the time certain products, such as software, are being downloaded but that need not be agreed to (by clicking "I agree," for example) before the user is able to install or use the product.

burglary • The unlawful entry or breaking into a building with the intent to commit a felony. (Some state statutes expand this to include the intent to commit any crime.)

business ethics • Ethics in a business context; a consensus as to what constitutes right or wrong behavior in the world of business and the application of moral principles to situations that arise in a business setting.

business invitee • A person, such as a customer or a client, who is invited onto business premises by the owner of those premises for business purposes.

business judgment rule • A rule that immunizes corporate management from liability for actions that result in corporate losses or damages if the actions are undertaken in good faith and are within both the power of the corporation and the authority of management to make.

business necessity • A defense to allegations of employment discrimination in which the employer demonstrates that an employment practice that discriminates against members of a protected class is related to job performance.

business tort • Wrongful interference with another's business rights.

business trust • A form of business organization in which investors (trust beneficiaries) transfer cash or property to trustees in exchange for trust certificates that represent their investment shares. The certificate holders share in the trust's profits but have limited liability.

buyout price • The amount payable to a partner on his or her dissociation from a partnership, based on the amount distributable to that partner if the firm were wound up on that date, and offset by any damages for wrongful dissociation.
bylaws • A set of governing rules adopted by a corporation or other association.

C

case law • The rules of law announced in court decisions. Case law includes the aggregate of reported cases that interpret judicial precedents, statutes, regulations, and constitutional provisions.
cashier's check • A check drawn by a bank on itself.
categorical imperative • A concept developed by the philosopher Immanuel Kant as an ethical guideline for behavior. In deciding whether an action is right or wrong, or desirable or undesirable, a person should evaluate the action in terms of what would happen if everybody else in the same situation, or category, acted the same way.
causation in fact • An act or omission without which an event would not have occurred.
cease-and-desist order • An administrative or judicial order prohibiting a person or business firm from conducting activities that an agency or court has deemed illegal.
certificate of deposit (CD) • A note issued by a bank in which the bank acknowledges the receipt of funds from a party and promises to repay that amount, with interest, to the party on a certain date.
certificate of limited partnership • The basic document filed with a designated state official by which a limited partnership is formed.
certification mark • A mark used by one or more persons, other than the owner, to certify the region, materials, mode of manufacture, quality, or other characteristic of specific goods or services.
certified check • A check that has been accepted in writing by the bank on which it is drawn. Essentially, the bank, by certifying (accepting) the check, promises to pay the check at the time the check is presented.
charging order • In partnership law, an order granted by a court to a judgment creditor that entitles the creditor to attach profits or assets of a partner on the dissolution of the partnership.
charitable trust • A trust in which the property held by the trustee must be used for a charitable purpose, such as the advancement of health, education, or religion.
chattel • All forms of personal property.
check • A draft drawn by a drawer ordering the drawee bank or financial institution to pay a certain amount of money to the holder on demand.
checks and balances • The principle under which the powers of the national government are divided among three separate branches—the executive, legislative, and judicial branches—each of which exercises a check on the actions of the others.
choice-of-language clause • A clause in a contract designating the official language by which the contract will be interpreted in the event of a future disagreement over the contract's terms.
choice-of-law clause • A clause in a contract designating the law (such as the law of a particular state or nation) that will govern the contract.
citation • A reference to a publication in which a legal authority—such as a statute or a court decision—or other source can be found.
civil law • The branch of law dealing with the definition and enforcement of all private or public rights, as opposed to criminal matters.
civil law system • A system of law derived from that of the Roman Empire and based on a code rather than case law; the predominant system of law in the nations of continental Europe and the nations that were once their colonies. In the United States, Louisiana, because of its historical ties to France, has, in part, a civil law system.
clearinghouse • A system or place where banks exchange checks and drafts drawn on each other and settle daily balances.
click-on agreement • An agreement that arises when a buyer, engaging in a transaction on a computer, indicates assent to be bound by the terms of an offer by clicking on a button that says, for example, "I agree"; sometimes referred to as a click-on license or a click-wrap agreement.
close corporation • A corporation whose shareholders are limited to a small group of persons, often only family members. In a close corporation, the shareholders' rights to transfer shares to others are usually restricted.
closed shop • A firm that requires union membership by its workers as a condition of employment. The closed shop was made illegal by the Labor-Management Relations Act of 1947.
cloud computing • A subscription-based or pay-per-use service that, in real time over the Internet, extends a computer's software or storage capabilities. By using the services of large companies with excess storage and computing capacity, a company can increase its information technology capabilities without investing in new infrastructure, training new personnel, or licensing new software.
codicil • A written supplement or modification to a will. A codicil must be executed with the same formalities as a will.
collateral • Under Article 9 of the UCC, the property subject to a security interest, including accounts and chattel paper that have been sold.
collateral promise • A secondary promise that is ancillary (subsidiary) to a principal transaction or primary contractual relationship, such as a promise made by one person to pay the debts of another if the latter fails to perform. A collateral promise normally must be in writing to be enforceable.
collecting bank • Any bank handling an item for collection, except the payor bank.
collective bargaining • The process by which labor and management negotiate the terms and conditions of employment, including working hours and workplace conditions.
collective mark • A mark used by members of a cooperative, association, union, or other organization to certify the region, materials, mode of manufacture, quality, or other characteristic of specific goods or services.
comity • The principle by which one nation defers to and gives effect to the laws and judicial decrees of another nation. This recognition is based primarily on respect.
commerce clause • The provision in Article I, Section 8, of the U.S. Constitution that gives Congress the power to regulate interstate commerce.
commercial impracticability • A doctrine under which a seller may be excused from performing a contract when (1) a contingency occurs, (2) the contingency's occurrence makes performance impracticable, and (3) the nonoccurrence of the contingency was a basic assumption on which the contract was made. Although UCC Section 2–615 expressly frees only sellers under this doctrine, courts have not distinguished between buyers and sellers in applying it.
commingle • To put funds or goods together into one mass so that they are mixed to such a degree that they no longer have separate identities. In corporate law, if personal and corporate interests are commingled to the extent that the corporation has no separate identity, a court may "pierce the corporate veil" and expose the shareholders to personal liability.
common law • The body of law developed from custom or judicial decisions in English and U.S. courts, not attributable to a legislature.
common stock • Shares of ownership in a corporation that give the owner of the stock a proportionate interest in the corporation with regard to control, earnings, and net assets. Shares of common stock are lowest in priority with respect to payment of dividends and distribution of the corporation's assets on dissolution.
community property • A form of concurrent ownership of property in which each spouse technically owns an undivided one-half interest in property acquired during the marriage. This form of joint ownership occurs in only ten states and Puerto Rico.

comparative negligence • A rule in tort law that reduces the plaintiff's recovery in proportion to the plaintiff's degree of fault, rather than barring recovery completely; used in the majority of states.
compensatory damages • A monetary award equivalent to the actual value of injuries or damage sustained by the aggrieved party.
complaint • The pleading made by a plaintiff alleging wrongdoing on the part of the defendant; the document that, when filed with a court, initiates a lawsuit.
computer crime • Any wrongful act that is directed against computers and computer parts or that involves the wrongful use or abuse of computers or software.
concentrated industry • An industry in which a large percentage of market sales is controlled by either a single firm or a small number of firms.
concurrent conditions • Conditions that must occur or be performed at the same time; they are mutually dependent. No obligations arise until these conditions are simultaneously performed.
concurrent jurisdiction • Jurisdiction that exists when two different courts have the power to hear a case. For example, some cases can be heard in a federal or a state court.
concurrent ownership • Joint ownership.
condemnation • The process of taking private property for public use through the government's power of eminent domain.
condition • A qualification, provision, or clause in a contractual agreement, the occurrence or nonoccurrence of which creates, suspends, or terminates the obligations of the contracting parties.
condition precedent • In a contractual agreement, a condition that must be met before a party's promise becomes absolute.
condition subsequent • A condition in a contract that, if it occurs, operates to terminate a party's absolute promise to perform.
confession of judgment • The act or agreement of a debtor permitting a judgment to be entered against him or her by a creditor, for an agreed sum, without the institution of legal proceedings.
confiscation • A government's taking of a privately owned business or personal property without a proper public purpose or an award of just compensation.
conforming goods • Goods that conform to contract specifications.
confusion • The mixing together of goods belonging to two or more owners to such an extent that the separately owned goods cannot be identified.
consequential damages • Special damages that compensate for a loss that does not directly or immediately result from the breach (for example, lost profits). For the plaintiff to collect consequential damages, they must have been reasonably foreseeable at the time the breach or injury occurred.
consideration • Generally, the value given in return for a promise; involves two elements—the giving of something of legally sufficient value and a bargained-for exchange. The consideration must result in a detriment to the promisee or a benefit to the promisor.
consolidation • A contractual and statutory process in which two or more corporations join to become a completely new corporation. The original corporations cease to exist, and the new corporation acquires all their assets and liabilities.
constitutional law • The body of law derived from the U.S. Constitution and the constitutions of the various states.
constructive delivery • An act equivalent to the actual, physical delivery of property that cannot be physically delivered because of difficulty or impossibility. For example, the transfer of a key to a safe constructively delivers the contents of the safe.
constructive discharge • A termination of employment brought about by making the employee's working conditions so intolerable that the employee reasonably feels compelled to leave.
constructive eviction • A form of eviction that occurs when a landlord fails to perform adequately any of the duties (such as providing heat in the winter) required by the lease, thereby making the tenant's further use and enjoyment of the property exceedingly difficult or impossible.
constructive trust • An equitable trust that is imposed in the interests of fairness and justice when someone wrongfully holds legal title to property. A court may require the owner to hold the property in trust for the person or persons who should rightfully own the property.
consumer-debtor • An individual whose debts are primarily consumer debts (debts for purchases made primarily for personal, family, or household use).
continuation statement • A statement that, if filed within six months prior to the expiration date of the original financing statement, continues the perfection of the original security interest for another five years. The perfection of a security interest can be continued in the same manner indefinitely.
contract • An agreement that can be enforced in court; formed by two or more competent parties who agree, for consideration, to perform or to refrain from performing some legal act now or in the future.
contractual capacity • The threshold mental capacity required by law for a party who enters into a contract to be bound by that contract.
contributory negligence • A rule in tort law that completely bars the plaintiff from recovering any damages if the damage suffered is partly the plaintiff's own fault; used in a minority of states.
conversion • Wrongfully taking or retaining possession of an individual's personal property and placing it in the service of another.
conveyance • The transfer of title to land from one person to another by deed; a document (such as a deed) by which an interest in land is transferred from one person to another.
"cooling-off" laws • Laws that allow buyers a period of time, such as three business days, in which to cancel door-to-door sales contracts.
cooperative • An association, which may or may not be incorporated, that is organized to provide an economic service to its members. Unincorporated cooperatives are often treated like partnerships for tax and other legal purposes. Examples of cooperatives include consumer purchasing cooperatives, credit cooperatives, and farmers' cooperatives.
copyright • The exclusive right of an author or originator of a literary or artistic production to publish, print, or sell that production for a statutory period of time. A copyright has the same monopolistic nature as a patent or trademark, but it differs in that it applies exclusively to works of art, literature, and other works of authorship (including computer programs).
corporate governance • A set of policies or procedures affecting the way a corporation is directed or controlled.
corporate social responsibility • The idea that corporations can and should act ethically and be accountable to society for their actions.
corporation • A legal entity formed in compliance with statutory requirements that is distinct from its shareholder-owners.
correspondent bank • A bank in which another bank has an account (and vice versa) for the purpose of facilitating fund transfers.
cost-benefit analysis • A decision-making technique that involves weighing the costs of a given action against the benefits of that action.
co-surety • A joint surety; a person who assumes liability jointly with another surety for the payment of an obligation.
counteradvertising • New advertising that is undertaken pursuant to a Federal Trade Commission order for the purpose of correcting earlier false claims that were made about a product.
counterclaim • A claim made by a defendant in a civil lawsuit against the plaintiff. In effect, the defendant is suing the plaintiff.
counteroffer • An offeree's response to an offer in which the offeree rejects the original offer and at the same time makes a new offer.
course of dealing • Prior conduct between the parties to a contract that establishes a common basis for their understanding.
course of performance • The conduct that occurs under the terms of a particular agreement. Such conduct indicates what the parties to an agreement intended it to mean.
covenant not to compete • A contractual promise of one party to refrain from conducting business similar to that of another party for a certain

period of time and within a specified geographic area. Courts commonly enforce such covenants if they are reasonable in terms of time and geographic area and are part of, or supplemental to, a contract for the sale of a business or an employment contract.

covenant not to sue • An agreement to substitute a contractual obligation for some other type of legal action based on a valid claim.

cover • Under the UCC, a remedy that allows the buyer or lessee, on the seller's or lessor's breach, to purchase the goods, in good faith and within a reasonable time, from another seller or lessor and substitute them for the goods due under the contract. If the cost of cover exceeds the cost of the contract goods, the breaching seller or lessor will be liable to the buyer or lessee for the difference, plus incidental and consequential damages.

cram-down provision • A provision of the Bankruptcy Code that allows a court to confirm a debtor's Chapter 11 reorganization plan even though only one class of creditors has accepted it.

creditors' composition agreement • An agreement formed between a debtor and his or her creditors in which the creditors agree to accept a lesser sum than that owed by the debtor in full satisfaction of the debt.

crime • A wrong against society proclaimed in a statute and, if committed, punishable by society through fines and/or imprisonment—and, in some cases, death.

criminal law • Law that defines and governs actions that constitute crimes. Generally, criminal law has to do with wrongful actions committed against society for which society demands redress.

cross-collateralization • The use of an asset that is not the subject of a loan to collateralize that loan.

cure • The right of a party who tenders nonconforming performance to correct that performance within the contract period [UCC 2–508(1)].

cyber crime • A crime that occurs online, in the virtual community of the Internet, as opposed to in the physical world.

cyber fraud • Any misrepresentation knowingly made over the Internet with the intention of deceiving another and on which a reasonable person would and does rely to his or her detriment.

cyberlaw • An informal term used to refer to all laws governing electronic communications and transactions, particularly those conducted via the Internet.

cyber mark • A trademark in cyberspace.

cybernotary • A legally recognized authority that can certify the validity of digital signatures.

cybersquatting • The act of registering a domain name that is the same as, or confusingly similar to, the trademark of another and then offering to sell that domain name back to the trademark owner.

cyberstalking • The crime of stalking committed in cyberspace though the use of the Internet, e-mail, or another form of electronic communication. Generally, stalking involves harassing a person and putting that person in reasonable fear for his or her safety or the safety of the person's immediate family.

cyberterrorist • A person who uses the Internet to attack or sabotage businesses and government agencies with the purpose of disrupting infrastructure systems.

cyber tort • A tort committed in cyberspace.

D

damages • Money sought as a remedy for a breach of contract or a tortious action.

debtor • Under Article 9 of the UCC, any party who owes payment or performance of a secured obligation, whether or not the party actually owns or has rights in the collateral.

debtor in possession (DIP) • In Chapter 11 bankruptcy proceedings, a debtor who is allowed to continue in possession of the estate in property (the business) and to continue business operations.

deceptive advertising • Advertising that misleads consumers, either by making unjustified claims concerning a product's performance or by omitting a material fact concerning the product's composition or performance.

deed • A document by which title to property (usually real property) is passed.

defalcation • Embezzlement; the misappropriation of funds by a party, such as a corporate officer or public official, in a fiduciary relationship with another.

defamation • Anything published or publicly spoken that causes injury to another's good name, reputation, or character.

default • Failure to observe a promise or discharge an obligation; commonly used to refer to failure to pay a debt when it is due.

default judgment • A judgment entered by a court against a defendant who has failed to appear in court to answer or defend against the plaintiff's claim.

defendant • One against whom a lawsuit is brought; the accused person in a criminal proceeding.

defense • A reason offered and alleged by a defendant in an action or lawsuit as to why the plaintiff should not recover or establish what she or he seeks.

deficiency judgment • A judgment against a debtor for the amount of a debt remaining unpaid after the collateral has been repossessed and sold.

delegatee • A party to whom contractual obligations are transferred, or delegated.

delegation of duties • The act of transferring to another all or part of one's duties arising under a contract.

delegator • A party who transfers (delegates) her or his obligations under a contract to another party (called the delegatee).

depositary bank • The first bank to receive a check for payment.

deposition • The testimony of a party to a lawsuit or a witness taken under oath before a trial.

destination contract • A contract for the sale of goods in which the seller is required or authorized to ship the goods by carrier and tender delivery of the goods at a particular destination. The seller assumes liability for any losses or damage to the goods until they are tendered at the destination specified in the contract.

devise • As a noun, a gift of real property by will; as a verb, to make a gift of real property by will.

devisee • One designated in a will to receive a gift of real property.

digital cash • Funds contained on computer software, in the form of secure programs stored on microchips and on other computer devices.

disaffirmance • The legal avoidance, or setting aside, of a contractual obligation.

discharge • The termination of an obligation. In contract law, discharge occurs when the parties have fully performed their contractual obligations or when events, conduct of the parties, or operation of law releases the parties from performance. In bankruptcy proceedings, the extinction of the debtor's dischargeable debts, thereby relieving the debtor of the obligation to pay the debts.

disclosed principal • A principal whose identity is known to a third party at the time the agent makes a contract with the third party.

discovery • A phase in the litigation process during which the opposing parties may obtain information from each other and from third parties prior to trial.

dishonor • To refuse to pay or accept a negotiable instrument, whichever is required, even though the instrument is presented in a timely and proper manner.

disparagement of property • An economically injurious falsehood made about another's product or property; a general term for torts that are more specifically referred to as slander of quality or slander of title.

disparate-impact discrimination • A form of employment discrimination that results from certain employer practices or procedures that, although not discriminatory on their face, have a discriminatory effect.

disparate-treatment discrimination • A form of employment discrimination that results when an employer intentionally discriminates against employees who are members of protected classes.
dissociation • The severance of the relationship between a partner and a partnership when the partner ceases to be associated with the carrying on of the partnership business.
dissolution • The formal disbanding of a partnership or a corporation. Dissolution of a corporation can take place by (1) an act of the state, (2) agreement of the shareholders and the board of directors, (3) the expiration of a time period stated in the certificate of incorporation, or (4) court order.
dissolution • The formal disbanding of a partnership or a corporation. It can take place by (1) acts of the partners or, in a corporation, acts of the shareholders and board of directors; (2) the subsequent illegality of the firm's business; (3) the expiration of a time period stated in a partnership agreement or a certificate of incorporation; or (4) judicial decree.
distributed network • A network that can be used by persons located (distributed) around the country or the globe to share computer files.
distribution agreement • A contract between a seller and a distributor of the seller's products setting out the terms and conditions of the distributorship.
diversity of citizenship • Under Article III, Section 2, of the U.S. Constitution, a basis for federal district court jurisdiction over a lawsuit between (1) citizens of different states, (2) a foreign country and citizens of a state or of different states, or (3) citizens of a state and citizens or subjects of a foreign country. The amount in controversy must be more than $75,000 before a federal district court can take jurisdiction in such cases.
divestiture • The act of selling one or more of a company's divisions or parts, such as a subsidiary or plant; often mandated by the courts in merger or monopolization cases.
dividend • A distribution to corporate shareholders of corporate profits or income, disbursed in proportion to the number of shares held.
docket • The list of cases entered on a court's calendar and thus scheduled to be heard by the court.
document of title • A paper exchanged in the regular course of business that evidences the right to possession of goods (for example, a bill of lading or a warehouse receipt).
domain name • The last part of an Internet address, such as "westlaw.com." The top level (the part of the name to the right of the period) indicates the type of entity that operates the site (com is an abbreviation for "commercial"). The second level (the part of the name to the left of the period) is chosen by the entity.
domestic corporation • In a given state, a corporation that does business in, and is organized under the law of, that state.
dominion • Ownership rights in property, including the right to possess and control the property.
double jeopardy • A situation occurring when a person is tried twice for the same criminal offense; prohibited by the Fifth Amendment to the U.S. Constitution.
draft • Any instrument drawn on a drawee that orders the drawee to pay a certain sum of money, usually to a third party (the payee), on demand or at a definite future time.
dram shop act • A state statute that imposes liability on the owners of bars and taverns, as well as those who serve alcoholic drinks to the public, for injuries resulting from accidents caused by intoxicated persons when the sellers or servers of alcoholic drinks contributed to the intoxication.
drawee • The party that is ordered to pay a draft or check. With a check, a bank or a financial institution is always the drawee.
drawer • The party that initiates a draft (such as a check), thereby ordering the drawee to pay.
due diligence • A required standard of care that certain professionals, such as accountants, must meet to avoid liability for securities violations.
due process clause • The provisions in the Fifth and Fourteenth Amendments to the U.S. Constitution that guarantee that no person shall be deprived of life, liberty, or property without due process of law. Similar clauses are found in most state constitutions.
dumping • The selling of goods in a foreign country at a price below the price charged for the same goods in the domestic market.
duress • Unlawful pressure brought to bear on a person, causing the person to perform an act that she or he would not otherwise perform.
duty of care • The duty of all persons, as established by tort law, to exercise a reasonable amount of care in their dealings with others. Failure to exercise due care, which is normally determined by the reasonable person standard, constitutes the tort of negligence.

E

e-agent • A computer program that by electronic or other automated means can independently initiate an action or respond to electronic messages or data without review by an individual.
easement • A nonpossessory right to use another's property in a manner established by either express or implied agreement.
e-contract • A contract that is formed electronically.
e-evidence • Evidence that consists of computer-generated or electronically recorded information, including e-mail, voice mail, spreadsheets, word-processing documents, and other data.
electronic fund transfer (EFT) • A transfer of funds through the use of an electronic terminal, a telephone, a computer, or magnetic tape.
emancipation • In regard to minors, the act of being freed from parental control; occurs when a child's parent or legal guardian relinquishes the legal right to exercise control over the child. Normally, a minor who leaves home to support himself or herself is considered emancipated.
embezzlement • The fraudulent appropriation of funds or other property by a person to whom the funds or property has been entrusted.
eminent domain • The power of a government to take land from private citizens for public use on the payment of just compensation.
e-money • Prepaid funds recorded on a computer or a card (such as a smart card or a stored-value card).
employment at will • A common law doctrine under which either party may terminate an employment relationship at any time for any reason, unless a contract specifies otherwise.
employment contract • A contract between an employer and an employee in which the terms and conditions of employment are stated.
employment discrimination • Treating employees or job applicants unequally on the basis of race, color, national origin, religion, gender, age, or disability; prohibited by federal statutes.
enabling legislation • A statute enacted by Congress that authorizes the creation of an administrative agency and specifies the name, composition, purpose, and powers of the agency being created.
encryption • The process by which a message is transmitted into a form or code that the sender and receiver intend not to be understandable by third parties.
entrapment • In criminal law, a defense in which the defendant claims that he or she was induced by a public official—usually an undercover agent or police officer—to commit a crime that he or she would otherwise not have committed.
entrepreneur • One who initiates and assumes the financial risk of a new business enterprise and undertakes to provide or control its management.
environmental impact statement (EIS) • A statement required by the National Environmental Policy Act for any major federal action that will significantly affect the quality of the environment. The statement must analyze the action's impact on the environment and explore alternative actions that might be taken.
equal dignity rule • In most states, a rule stating that express authority given to an agent must be in writing if the contract to be made on behalf of the principal is required to be in writing.

equal protection clause • The provision in the Fourteenth Amendment to the U.S. Constitution that guarantees that no state will "deny to any person within its jurisdiction the equal protection of the laws." This clause mandates that the state governments must treat similarly situated individuals in a similar manner.
equitable principles and maxims • General propositions or principles of law that have to do with fairness (equity).
e-signature • As defined by the Uniform Electronic Transactions Act, "an electronic sound, symbol, or process attached to or logically associated with a record and executed or adopted by a person with the intent to sign the record."
establishment clause • The provision in the First Amendment to the U.S. Constitution that prohibits the government from establishing any state-sponsored religion or enacting any law that promotes religion or favors one religion over another.
estate in property • In bankruptcy proceedings, all of the debtor's interests in property currently held, wherever located, together with certain jointly owned property, property transferred in transactions voidable by the trustee, proceeds and profits from the property of the estate, and certain property interests to which the debtor becomes entitled within 180 days after filing for bankruptcy.
estopped • Barred, impeded, or precluded.
estray statute • A statute defining finders' rights in property when the true owners are unknown.
ethical reasoning • A reasoning process in which an individual links his or her moral convictions or ethical standards to the particular situation at hand.
ethics • Moral principles and values applied to social behavior.
eviction • A landlord's act of depriving a tenant of possession of the leased premises.
exclusionary rule • In criminal procedure, a rule under which any evidence that is obtained in violation of the accused's constitutional rights guaranteed by the Fourth, Fifth, and Sixth Amendments to the U.S. Constitution, as well as any evidence derived from illegally obtained evidence, will not be admissible in court.
exclusive-dealing contract • An agreement under which a seller forbids a buyer to purchase products from the seller's competitors.
exclusive jurisdiction • Jurisdiction that exists when a case can be heard only in a particular court or type of court.
exculpatory clause • A clause that releases a contractual party from liability in the event of monetary or physical injury, no matter who is at fault.
executed contract • A contract that has been completely performed by both parties.
execution • An action to carry into effect the directions in a court decree or judgment.
executor • A person appointed by a testator in a will to see that her or his will is administered appropriately.
executory contract • A contract that has not as yet been fully performed.
export • The sale of goods and services by domestic firms to buyers located in other countries.
express contract • A contract in which the terms of the agreement are stated in words, oral or written.
express warranty • A seller's or lessor's oral or written promise or affirmation of fact ancillary (secondary) to an underlying sales or lease agreement, as to the quality, condition, description, or performance of the goods being sold or leased.
expropriation • The seizure by a government of a privately owned business or personal property for a proper public purpose and with just compensation.
extension clause • A clause in a time instrument that allows the instrument's date of maturity to be extended into the future.

F

family limited liability partnership (FLLP) • A type of limited liability partnership owned by family members or fiduciaries of family members.
federal form of government • A system of government in which the states form a union and the sovereign power is divided between the central government and the member states.
federal question • A question that pertains to the U.S. Constitution, acts of Congress, or treaties. A federal question provides a basis for federal jurisdiction.
Federal Reserve System • A network of twelve district banks and related branches located around the country and headed by the Federal Reserve Board of Governors. Most banks in the United States have Federal Reserve accounts.
fee simple • An absolute form of property ownership entitling the property owner to use, possess, or dispose of the property as he or she chooses during his or her lifetime. On death, the interest in the property descends to the owner's heirs.
fee simple absolute • An ownership interest in land in which the owner has the greatest possible aggregation of rights, privileges, and power. Ownership in fee simple absolute is limited absolutely to a person and her or his heirs.
felony • A crime—such as arson, murder, rape, or robbery—that carries the most severe sanctions, ranging from one year in a state or federal prison to the death penalty.
fictitious payee • A payee on a negotiable instrument whom the maker or drawer does not intend to have an interest in the instrument. Indorsements by fictitious payees are treated as authorized indorsements under Article 3 of the UCC.
fiduciary • As a noun, a person having a duty created by his or her undertaking to act primarily for another's benefit in matters connected with the undertaking. As an adjective, a relationship founded on trust and confidence.
filtering software • A computer program that is designed to block access to certain Web sites, based on their content. The software blocks the retrieval of a site whose URL or key words are on a list within the program.
financing statement • A document prepared by a secured creditor, and filed with the appropriate state or local official, to give notice to the public that the creditor has a security interest in collateral belonging to the debtor named in the statement. The financing statement must contain the names and addresses of both the debtor and the secured party and must describe the collateral by type or item.
firm offer • An offer (by a merchant) that is irrevocable without the necessity of consideration for a stated period of time or, if no definite period is stated, for a reasonable time (neither period to exceed three months). A firm offer by a merchant must be in writing and must be signed by the offeror.
fixed-term tenancy • A type of tenancy under which property is leased for a specified period of time, such as a month, a year, or a period of years; also called a tenancy for years.
fixture • An item thing that was once personal property but has become attached to real property in such a way that it takes on the characteristics of real property and becomes part of that real property.
floating lien • A security interest in proceeds, after-acquired property, or collateral subject to future advances by the secured party (or all three); a security interest in collateral that is retained even when the collateral changes in character, classification, or location.
forbearance • The act of refraining from an action that one has a legal right to undertake.
***force majeure* clause** • A provision in a contract stipulating that certain unforeseen events—such as war, political upheavals, or acts of God—will excuse a party from liability for nonperformance of contractual obligations.
foreign corporation • In a given state, a corporation that does business in the state without being incorporated therein.
foreign exchange market • A worldwide system in which foreign currencies are bought and sold.

forgery • The fraudulent making or altering of any writing in a way that changes the legal rights and liabilities of another.
formal contract • A contract that by law requires a specific form, such as being executed under seal, for its validity.
forum-selection clause • A provision in a contract designating the court, jurisdiction, or tribunal that will decide any disputes arising under the contract.
franchise • Any arrangement in which the owner of a trademark, trade name, or copyright licenses another to use that trademark, trade name, or copyright in the selling of goods or services.
franchisee • One receiving a license to use another's (the franchisor's) trademark, trade name, or copyright in the sale of goods and services.
franchisor • One licensing another (the franchisee) to use the owner's trademark, trade name, or copyright in the selling of goods or services.
fraudulent misrepresentation • Any misrepresentation, either by misstatement or by omission of a material fact, knowingly made with the intention of deceiving another and on which a reasonable person would and does rely to his or her detriment.
free exercise clause • The provision in the First Amendment to the U.S. Constitution that prohibits the government from interfering with people's religious practices or forms of worship.
free-writing prospectus • A free-writing prospectus is any type of written, electronic, or graphic offer that describes the issuing corporation or its securities and includes a legend indicating that the investor may obtain the prospectus at the Securities and Exchange Commission's Web site.
frustration of purpose • A court-created doctrine under which a party to a contract will be relieved of her or his duty to perform when the objective purpose for performance no longer exists (due to reasons beyond that party's control).
fungible goods • Goods that are alike by physical nature, by agreement, or by trade usage (for example, wheat, oil, and wine that are identical in type and quality). When owners hold fungible goods as tenants in common, title and risk can pass without actually separating the goods being sold from the larger mass.

G

garnishment • A legal process used by a creditor to collect a debt by seizing property of the debtor (such as wages) that is being held by a third party (such as the debtor's employer).
generally accepted accounting principles (GAAP) • The conventions, rules, and procedures that define accepted accounting practices at a particular time. The source of the principles is the Financial Accounting Standards Board.
generally accepted auditing standards (GAAS) • Standards concerning an auditor's professional qualities and the judgment exercised by him or her in the performance of an audit and report. The source of the standards is the American Institute of Certified Public Accountants.
general partner • In a limited partnership, a partner who assumes responsibility for the management of the partnership and liability for all partnership debts.
gift • Any voluntary transfer of property made without consideration, past or present.
gift *causa mortis* • A gift made in contemplation of death. If the donor does not die of that ailment, the gift is revoked.
gift *inter vivos* • A gift made during one's lifetime and not in contemplation of imminent death, in contrast to a gift causa mortis.
good faith purchaser • A purchaser who buys without notice of any circumstance that would cause a person of ordinary prudence to inquire as to whether the seller has valid title to the goods being sold.
Good Samaritan Statute • A state statute stipulating that persons who provide emergency services to, or rescue, someone in peril cannot be sued for negligence, unless they act recklessly, thereby causing further harm.
grand jury • A group of citizens called to decide, after hearing the state's evidence, whether a reasonable basis (probable cause) exists for believing that a crime has been committed and that a trial ought to be held.
group boycott • The refusal by a group of competitors to deal with a particular person or firm; prohibited by the Sherman Act.
guarantor • A person who agrees to satisfy the debt of another (the debtor) only after the principal debtor defaults. Thus, a guarantor's liability is secondary.

H

hacker • A person who uses one computer to break into another.
Herfindahl-Hirschman Index (HHI) • An index of market power used to calculate whether a merger of two businesses will result in sufficient monopoly power to violate antitrust laws.
historical school • A school of legal thought that emphasizes the evolutionary process of law and looks to the past to discover what the principles of contemporary law should be.
holder • Any person in possession of an instrument drawn, issued, or indorsed to him or her, to his or her order, to bearer, or in blank.
holder in due course (HDC) • A holder who acquires a negotiable instrument for value; in good faith; and without notice that the instrument is overdue, that it has been dishonored, that any person has a defense against it or a claim to it, or that the instrument contains unauthorized signatures, has been altered, or is so irregular or incomplete as to call into question its authenticity.
holding company • A company whose business activity is holding shares in another company.
holographic will • A will written entirely in the signer's handwriting and usually not witnessed.
homestead exemption • A law permitting a debtor to retain the family home, either in its entirety or up to a specified dollar amount, free from the claims of unsecured creditors or trustees in bankruptcy.
horizontal merger • A merger between two firms that are competing in the same marketplace.
horizontal restraint • Any agreement that in some way restrains competition between rival firms competing in the same market.
hot-cargo agreement • An agreement in which employers voluntarily agree with unions not to handle, use, or deal in other employers' goods that were not produced by union employees; a type of secondary boycott explicitly prohibited by the Labor-Management Reporting and Disclosure Act of 1959.

I

I-9 verification • A process that all employers in the United States must perform within three business days of hiring a new worker to verify the employment eligibility and identity of the worker by completing an I-9 Employment Eligibility Verification form.
I-551 Alien Registration Receipt • A document, commonly known as a green card, that shows that a foreign-born individual has been lawfully admitted for permanent residency in the United States. Persons seeking employment can prove to prospective employers that they are legally within the United States by showing this receipt.
identification • In a sale of goods, the express designation of the goods provided for in the contract.
identity theft • The theft of identity information, such as a person's name, driver's license number, or Social Security number. The information is then usually used to access the victim's financial resources.
implied-in-fact contract • A contract formed in whole or in part from the conduct of the parties (as opposed to an express contract).
implied warranty • A warranty that arises by law because of the circumstances of a sale rather than by the seller's express promise.
implied warranty of fitness for a particular purpose • A warranty that goods sold or leased are fit for a particular purpose. The warranty arises when

any seller or lessor knows the particular purpose for which a buyer or lessee will use the goods and knows that the buyer or lessee is relying on the skill and judgment of the seller or lessor to select suitable goods.

implied warranty of habitability • An implied promise by a seller of a new house that the house is fit for human habitation—that is, in a condition that is safe and suitable for people to live there. Also, the implied promise by a landlord that rented residential premises are habitable.

implied warranty of merchantability • A warranty that goods being sold or leased are reasonably fit for the general purpose for which they are sold or leased, are properly packaged and labeled, and are of proper quality. The warranty automatically arises in every sale or lease of goods made by a merchant who deals in goods of the kind sold or leased.

impossibility of performance • A doctrine under which a party to a contract is relieved of his or her duty to perform when performance becomes objectively impossible or totally impracticable (through no fault of either party).

imposter • One who, by use of the mails, Internet, telephone, or personal appearance, induces a maker or drawer to issue an instrument in the name of an impersonated payee. Indorsements by imposters are treated as authorized indorsements under Article 3 of the UCC.

incidental beneficiary • A third party who incidentally benefits from a contract but whose benefit was not the reason the contract was formed. An incidental beneficiary has no rights in a contract and cannot sue to have the contract enforced.

incidental damages • Damages awarded to compensate for expenses that are directly incurred because of a breach of contract—such as those incurred to obtain performance from another source.

incontestability clause • A clause within a life or health insurance policy that states after the policy has been in force for a specified length of time—most often two or three years—the insurer cannot contest statements made in the policyholder's application.

independent contractor • One who works for, and receives payment from, an employer but whose working conditions and methods are not controlled by the employer. An independent contractor is not an employee but may be an agent.

indictment • A charge by a grand jury that a named person has committed a crime.

indorsement • A signature placed on an instrument for the purpose of transferring one's ownership rights in the instrument.

informal contract • A contract that does not require a specified form or formality to be valid.

information • A formal accusation or complaint (without an indictment) issued in certain types of actions (usually criminal actions involving lesser crimes) by a government prosecutor.

information return • A tax return submitted by a partnership that only reports the income and losses earned by the business. The partnership as an entity does not pay taxes on the income received by the partnership.

inside director • A person on the board of directors who is also an officer of the corporation.

insider trading • The purchase or sale of securities on the basis of information that has not been made available to the public.

insolvent • Under the UCC, a term describing a person who ceases to pay "his [or her] debts in the ordinary course of business or cannot pay his [or her] debts as they become due or is insolvent within the meaning of federal bankruptcy law" [UCC 1–201(23)].

installment contract • Under the UCC, a contract that requires or authorizes delivery in two or more separate lots to be accepted and paid for separately.

insurable interest • An interest either in a person's life or well-being or in property that is sufficiently substantial that insuring against injury to (or the death of) the person or against damage to the property does not amount to a mere wagering (betting) contract. In regard to the sale or lease of goods, a property interest in the goods that is sufficiently substantial to permit a party to insure against damage to the goods.

insurance • A contract in which, for a stipulated consideration, one party agrees to compensate the other for loss on a specific subject by a specified peril.

intangible property • Property that cannot be seen or touched but exists only conceptually, such as corporate stocks and bonds, patents and copyrights, and ordinary contract rights. Article 2 of the UCC does not govern intangible property.

integrated contract • A written contract that constitutes the final expression of the parties' agreement. If a contract is integrated, evidence extraneous to the contract that contradicts or alters the meaning of the contract in any way is inadmissible.

intellectual property • Property resulting from intellectual, creative processes.

intended beneficiary • A third party for whose benefit a contract is formed. An intended beneficiary can sue the promisor if such a contract is breached.

intentional tort • A wrongful act knowingly committed.

intermediary bank • Any bank to which an item is transferred in the course of collection, except the depositary or payor bank.

international law • The law that governs relations among nations. International customs, treaties, and organizations are important sources of international law.

international organization • Any member-ship group that operates across national borders. These organizations can be governmental organizations, such as the United Nations, or nongovernmental organizations, such as the Red Cross.

interpretive rule • An administrative agency rule that is simply a statement or opinion issued by the agency explaining how it interprets and intends to apply the statutes it enforces. Such rules are not binding on private individuals or organizations.

interrogatories • A series of written questions for which written answers are prepared by a party to a lawsuit, usually with the assistance of the party's attorney, and then signed under oath.

***inter vivos* trust** • A trust created by the grantor (settlor) and effective during the grantor's lifetime; a trust not established by a will.

intestacy laws • State statutes that specify how property will be distributed when a person dies intestate (without a valid will); also called statutes of descent and distribution.

intestate • As a noun, one who has died without having created a valid will; as an adjective, the state of having died without a will.

investment company • A company that acts on the behalf of many smaller shareholders/owners by buying a large portfolio of securities and professionally managing that portfolio.

investment contract • In securities law, a transaction in which a person invests in a common enterprise reasonably expecting profits that are derived primarily from the efforts of others.

J

joint and several liability • In partnership law, a doctrine under which a plaintiff may sue, and collect a judgment from, all of the partners together (jointly) or one or more of the partners separately (severally, or individually). This is true even if one of the partners sued did not participate in, ratify, or know about whatever it was that gave rise to the cause of action.

joint liability • Shared liability. In partnership law, partners incur joint liability for partnership obligations and debts. For example, if a third party sues a partner on a partnership debt, the partner has the right to insist that the other partners be sued with him or her.

joint stock company • A hybrid form of business organization that combines characteristics of a corporation and a partnership. Usually, a joint stock company is regarded as a partnership for tax and other legal purposes.

joint tenancy • The joint ownership of property by two or more co-owners in which each co-owner owns an undivided portion of the property. On the death of one of the joint tenants, his or her interest automatically passes to the surviving joint tenant(s).

joint venture • A joint undertaking of a specific commercial enterprise by an association of persons. A joint venture normally is not a legal entity and is treated like a partnership for federal income tax purposes.

judicial review • The process by which a court decides on the constitutionality of legislative enactments and actions of the executive branch.

junior lienholder • A party that holds a lien that is subordinate to one or more other liens on the same property.

jurisdiction • The authority of a court to hear and decide a specific case.

jurisprudence • The science or philosophy of law.

justiciable controversy • A controversy that is not hypothetical or academic but real and substantial; a requirement that must be satisfied before a court will hear a case.

L

larceny • The wrongful taking and carrying away of another person's personal property with the intent to permanently deprive the owner of the property. Some states classify larceny as either grand or petit, depending on the property's value.

law • A body of enforceable rules governing relationships among individuals and between individuals and their society.

lease • Under Article 2A of the UCC, a transfer of the right to possess and use goods for a period of time in exchange for payment.

lease agreement • In regard to the lease of goods, an agreement in which one person (the lessor) agrees to transfer the right to the possession and use of property to another person (the lessee) in exchange for rental payments.

leasehold estate • An estate in realty held by a tenant under a lease. In every leasehold estate, the tenant has a qualified right to possess and/or use the land.

legacy • A gift of personal property under a will.

legal positivism • A school of legal thought centered on the assumption that there is no law higher than the laws created by a national government. Laws must be obeyed, even if they are unjust, to prevent anarchy.

legal realism • A school of legal thought of the 1920s and 1930s that generally advocated a less abstract and more realistic approach to the law, an approach that takes into account customary practices and the circumstances in which transactions take place. This school left a lasting imprint on American jurisprudence.

legatee • One designated in a will to receive a gift of personal property.

legislative rule • An administrative agency rule that carries the same weight as a congressionally enacted statute.

lessee • A person who acquires the right to the possession and use of another's goods in exchange for rental payments.

lessor • A person who transfers the right to the possession and use of goods to another in exchange for rental payments.

letter of credit • A written instrument, usually issued by a bank on behalf of a customer or other person, in which the issuer promises to honor drafts or other demands for payment by third parties in accordance with the terms of the instrument.

levy • The obtaining of funds by legal process through the seizure and sale of nonexempt property, usually done after a writ of execution has been issued.

libel • Defamation in writing or other form having the quality of permanence (such as a digital recording).

license • A revocable right or privilege of a person to come onto another person's land. In the context of intellectual property law, an agreement permitting the use of a trademark, copyright, patent, or trade secret for certain limited purposes.

lien • An encumbrance on a property to satisfy a debt or protect a claim for payment of a debt.

life estate • An interest in land that exists only for the duration of the life of some person, usually the holder of the estate.

limited liability company (LLC) • A hybrid form of business enterprise that offers the limited liability of a corporation and the tax advantages of a partnership.

limited liability limited partnership (LLLP) • A type of limited partnership in which the liability of all of the partners, including general partners, is limited to the amount of their investments.

limited liability partnership (LLP) • A hybrid form of business organization that is used mainly by professionals who normally do business in a partnership. An LLP is a pass-through entity for tax purposes, but the personal liability of the partners is limited.

limited partner • In a limited partnership, a partner who contributes capital to the partnership but has no right to participate in the management and operation of the business. The limited partner assumes no liability for partnership debts beyond the capital contributed.

limited partnership • A partnership consisting of one or more general partners (who manage the business and are liable to the full extent of their personal assets for debts of the partnership) and one or more limited partners (who contribute only assets and are liable only up to the extent of their contributions).

liquidated damages • An amount, stipulated in a contract, that the parties to the contract believe to be a reasonable estimation of the damages that will occur in the event of a breach.

liquidated debt • A debt for which the amount has been ascertained, fixed, agreed on, settled, or exactly determined. If the amount of the debt is in dispute, the debt is considered unliquidated.

liquidation • The sale of all of the nonexempt assets of a debtor and the distribution of the proceeds to the debtor's creditors. Chapter 7 of the Bankruptcy Code provides for liquidation bankruptcy proceedings.

litigation • The process of resolving a dispute through the court system.

long arm statute • A state statute that permits a state to obtain personal jurisdiction over nonresident defendants. A defendant must have certain "minimum contacts" with that state for the statute to apply.

lost property • Property with which the owner has involuntarily parted and then cannot find or recover.

M

mailbox rule • A rule providing that an acceptance of an offer becomes effective on dispatch (on being placed in an official mailbox), if mail is, expressly or impliedly, an authorized means of communication of acceptance to the offeror.

maker • One who promises to pay a fixed amount of money to the holder of a promissory note or a certificate of deposit (CD).

malpractice • Professional misconduct or unreasonable lack of skill; the failure of a professional to use the skills and learning common to the average reputable members of the profession or the skills and learning the professional claims to possess, resulting in injury, loss, or damage to those relying on the professional. Negligence—the failure to exercise due care—on the part of a professional, such as a physician, is commonly referred to as malpractice.

malware • Any program that is harmful to a computer or a computer user; for example, worms and viruses.

market concentration • The degree to which a small number of firms control a large percentage share of a relevant market; determined by calculating the percentages held by the largest firms in that market.

market power • The power of a firm to control the market price of its product. A monopoly has the greatest degree of market power.

market-share liability • A theory under which liability is shared among all firms that manufactured and distributed a particular product during a certain period of time. This form of liability sharing is used only when the true source of the harmful product is unidentifiable; it is not recognized in many jurisdictions.

mechanic's lien • A statutory lien on the real property of another to ensure payment for work performed and materials furnished in the repair or improvement of real property, such as a building.
mediation • A method of settling disputes outside the courts by using the services of a neutral third party, who acts as a communicating agent between the parties and assists them in negotiating a settlement.
member • A person who has an ownership interest in a limited liability company.
mens rea • Mental state, or intent. Normally, a wrongful mental state is as necessary as a wrongful act to establish criminal liability. What constitutes such a mental state varies according to the wrongful action. Thus, for murder, the *mens rea* is the intent to take a life.
merchant • A person who is engaged in the purchase and sale of goods. Under the UCC, a person who deals in goods of the kind involved in the sales contract or who holds herself or himself out as having skill or knowledge peculiar to the practices or goods being purchased or sold [UCC 2–104].
merger • A contractual and statutory process in which one corporation (the surviving corporation) acquires all of the assets and liabilities of another corporation (the merged corporation).
meta tag • A key word in a document that can serve as an index reference to the document. On the Web, search engines return results based, in part, on these tags in Web documents.
minimum wage • The lowest wage, either by government regulation or union contract, that an employer may pay an hourly worker.
mirror image rule • A common law rule that requires that the terms of the offeree's acceptance adhere exactly to the terms of the offeror's offer for a valid contract to be formed.
misdemeanor • A lesser crime than a felony, punishable by a fine or incarceration in jail for up to one year.
mislaid property • Property with which the owner has voluntarily parted and then cannot find or recover.
mitigation of damages • A rule requiring a plaintiff to do whatever is reasonable to minimize the damages caused by the defendant.
money laundering • Engaging in financial transactions to conceal the identity, source, or destination of illegally gained funds.
monopolization • The possession of monopoly power in the relevant market and the willful acquisition or maintenance of that power, as distinguished from growth or development as a consequence of a superior product, business acumen, or historic accident.
monopoly • A term generally used to describe a market in which there is a single seller or a very limited number of sellers.
monopoly power • The ability of a monopoly to dictate what takes place in a given market.
moral minimum • The minimum degree of ethical behavior expected of a business firm, which is usually defined as compliance with the law.
mortgage • A written instrument giving a creditor an interest in (lien on) the debtor's real property as security for payment of a debt.
mortgagee • Under a mortgage agreement, the creditor who takes a security interest in the debtor's property.
mortgagor • Under a mortgage agreement, the debtor who gives the creditor a security interest in the debtor's property in return for a mortgage loan.
motion for a directed verdict • In a jury trial, a motion for the judge to take the decision out of the hands of the jury and to direct a verdict for the party who filed the motion on the ground that the other party has not produced sufficient evidence to support her or his claim.
motion for a new trial • A motion asserting that the trial was so fundamentally flawed (because of error, newly discovered evidence, prejudice, or another reason) that a new trial is necessary to prevent a miscarriage of justice.
motion for judgment n.o.v. • A motion requesting the court to grant judgment in favor of the party making the motion on the ground that the jury's verdict against him or her was unreasonable and erroneous.
motion for judgment on the pleadings • A motion by either party to a lawsuit at the close of the pleadings requesting the court to decide the issue solely on the pleadings without proceeding to trial. The motion will be granted only if no facts are in dispute.
motion for summary judgment • A motion requesting the court to enter a judgment without proceeding to trial. The motion can be based on evidence outside the pleadings and will be granted only if no facts are in dispute.
motion to dismiss • A pleading in which a defendant asserts that the plaintiff's claim fails to state a cause of action (that is, has no basis in law) or that there are other grounds on which the suit should be dismissed. Although the defendant normally is the party requesting a dismissal, either the plaintiff or the court can also make a motion to dismiss the case.
multiple product order • An order issued by the Federal Trade Commission to a firm that has engaged in deceptive advertising by which the firm is required to cease and desist from false advertising not only in regard to the product that was the subject of the action but also in regard to all the firm's other products.
mutual fund • A specific type of investment company that continually buys or sells to investors shares of ownership in a portfolio.

N

national law • Law that pertains to a particular nation (as opposed to international law).
natural law • The belief that government and the legal system should reflect universal moral and ethical principles that are inherent in human nature. The natural law school is the oldest and one of the most significant schools of legal thought.
necessaries • Necessities required for life, such as food, shelter, clothing, and medical attention; may include whatever is believed to be necessary to maintain a person's standard of living or financial and social status.
negligence • The failure to exercise the standard of care that a reasonable person would exercise in similar circumstances.
negligence *per se* • An action or failure to act in violation of a statutory requirement.
negotiable instrument • A signed writing (record) that contains an unconditional promise or order to pay an exact sum on demand or at an exact future time to a specific person or order, or to bearer.
negotiation • A process in which parties attempt to settle their dispute informally, with or without attorneys to represent them. In the context of negotiable instruments, the transfer of an instrument in such form that the transferee (the person to whom the instrument is transferred) becomes a holder.
nominal damages • A small monetary award (often one dollar) granted to a plaintiff when no actual damage was suffered.
nonpossessory interest • In the context of real property, an interest in land that does not include any right to possess the property.
normal trade relations (NTR) status • A status granted by each member country of the World Trade Organization to other member countries. Each member is required to treat other members at least as well as it treats the country that receives its most favorable treatment with respect to trade.
notary public • A public official authorized to attest to the authenticity of signatures.
novation • The substitution, by agreement, of a new contract for an old one, with the rights under the old one being terminated. Typically, novation involves the substitution of a new person who is responsible for the contract and the removal of the original party's rights and duties under the contract.
nuisance • A common law doctrine under which persons may be held liable for using their property in a manner that unreasonably interferes with others' rights to use or enjoy their own property.

nuncupative will • An oral will (often called a deathbed will) made before witnesses; usually limited to transfers of personal property.

O

objective theory of contracts • A theory under which the intent to form a contract will be judged by outward, objective facts (what the party said when entering into the contract, how the party acted or appeared, and the circumstances surrounding the transaction) as interpreted by a reasonable person, rather than by the party's own secret, subjective intentions.

obligee • One to whom an obligation is owed.

obligor • One who owes an obligation to another.

offer • A promise or commitment to perform or refrain from performing some specified act in the future.

offeree • A person to whom an offer is made.

offeror • A person who makes an offer.

online dispute resolution (ODR) • The resolution of disputes with the assistance of organizations that offer dispute-resolution services via the Internet.

operating agreement • In a limited liability company, an agreement in which the members set forth the details of how the business will be managed and operated. State statutes typically give the members wide latitude in deciding for themselves the rules that will govern their organization.

option contract • A contract under which the offeror cannot revoke the offer for a stipulated time period. During this period, the offeree can accept or reject the offer without fear that the offer will be made to another person. The offeree must give consideration for the option (the irrevocable offer) to be enforceable.

order for relief • A court's grant of assistance to a complainant. In bankruptcy proceedings, the order relieves the debtor of the immediate obligation to pay the debts listed in the bankruptcy petition.

order instrument • A negotiable instrument that is payable "to the order of an identified person" or "to an identified person or order."

ordinance • A regulation enacted by a city or county legislative body that becomes part of that state's statutory law.

output contract • An agreement in which a seller agrees to sell and a buyer agrees to buy all or up to a stated amount of what the seller produces.

outside director • A person on the board of directors who does not hold a management position at the corporation.

overdraft • A check that is paid by the bank when the checking account on which the check is written contains insufficient funds to cover the check.

P

parol evidence rule • A substantive rule of contracts, as well as a procedural rule of evidence, under which a court will not receive into evidence the parties' prior negotiations, prior agreements, or contemporaneous oral agreements if that evidence contradicts or varies the terms of the parties' written contract.

partially disclosed principal • A principal whose identity is unknown by a third party, but the third party knows that the agent is or may be acting for a principal at the time the agent and the third party form a contract.

partnering agreement • An agreement between a seller and a buyer who frequently do business with each other concerning the terms and conditions that will apply to all subsequently formed electronic contracts.

partnership • An agreement by two or more persons to carry on, as co-owners, a business for profit.

pass-through entity • A business entity that has no tax liability. The entity's income is passed through to the owners, and the owners pay taxes on the income.

past consideration • An act that takes place before the contract is made and that ordinarily, by itself, cannot be consideration for a later promise to pay for the act.

patent • A government grant that gives an inventor the exclusive right or privilege to make, use, or sell his or her invention for a limited time period.

payee • A person to whom an instrument is made payable.

payor bank • The bank on which a check is drawn (the drawee bank).

peer-to-peer (P2P) networking • The sharing of resources (such as files, hard drives, and processing styles) among multiple computers without necessarily requiring a central network server.

penalty • A contractual clause that states that a certain amount of monetary damages will be paid in the event of a future default or breach of contract. The damages are a punishment for a default and not an accurate measure of compensation for the contract's breach. The agreement as to the penalty amount will not be enforced, and recovery will be limited to actual damages.

per capita • A Latin term meaning "per person." In the law governing estate distribution, a method of distributing the property of an intestate's estate so that each heir in a certain class (such as grandchildren) receives an equal share.

perfection • The legal process by which secured parties protect themselves against the claims of third parties who may wish to have their debts satisfied out of the same collateral; usually accomplished by filing a financing statement with the appropriate government official.

performance • In contract law, the fulfillment of one's duties arising under a contract with another; the normal way of discharging one's contractual obligations.

periodic tenancy • A lease interest in land for an indefinite period involving payment of rent at fixed intervals, such as week to week, month to month, or year to year.

***per se* violation** • A type of anticompetitive agreement that is considered to be so injurious to the public that there is no need to determine whether it actually injures market competition. Rather, it is in itself (*per se*) a violation of the Sherman Act.

personal defense • A defense that can be used to avoid payment to an ordinary holder of a negotiable instrument but not a holder in due course (HDC) or a holder with the rights of an HDC.

personal property • Property that is movable; any property that is not real property.

per stirpes • A Latin term meaning "by the roots." In the law governing estate distribution, a method of distributing an intestate's estate so that each heir in a certain class (such as grandchildren) takes the share to which her or his deceased ancestor (such as a mother or father) would have been entitled.

persuasive authority • Any legal authority or source of law that a court may look to for guidance but on which it need not rely in making its decision. Persuasive authorities include cases from other jurisdictions and secondary sources of law.

petition in bankruptcy • The document that is filed with a bankruptcy court to initiate bankruptcy proceedings. The official forms required for a petition in bankruptcy must be completed accurately, sworn to under oath, and signed by the debtor.

petty offense • In criminal law, the least serious kind of criminal offense, such as a traffic or building-code violation.

phishing • The attempt to acquire financial data, passwords, or other personal information from consumers by sending e-mail messages that purport to be from a legitimate business, such as a bank or a credit-card company.

piercing the corporate veil • An action in which a court disregards the corporate entity and holds the shareholders personally liable for corporate debts and obligations.

plaintiff • One who initiates a lawsuit.

plea bargaining • The process by which a criminal defendant and the prosecutor in a criminal case work out a mutually satisfactory disposition of the case, subject to court approval; usually involves the defendant's pleading guilty to a lesser offense in return for a lighter sentence.

pleadings • Statements made by the plaintiff and the defendant in a lawsuit that detail the facts, charges, and defenses involved in the litigation. The complaint and answer are part of the pleadings.
pledge • A common law security device (retained in Article 9 of the UCC) in which personal property is transferred into the possession of the creditor as security for the payment of a debt and retained by the creditor until the debt is paid.
police powers • Powers possessed by the states as part of their inherent sovereignty. These powers may be exercised to protect or promote the public order, health, safety, morals, and general welfare.
policy • In insurance law, a contract between the insurer and the insured in which, for a stipulated consideration, the insurer agrees to compensate the insured for loss on a specific subject by a specified peril.
potentially responsible party (PRP) • A party liable for the costs of cleaning up a hazardous waste-disposal site under the Comprehensive Environmental Response, Compensation, and Liability Act. Any person who generated the hazardous waste, transported it, owned or operated the waste site at the time of disposal, or owns or operates the site at the present time may be responsible for some or all of the clean-up costs.
power of attorney • A written document, which is usually notarized, authorizing another to act as one's agent; can be special (permitting the agent to do specified acts only) or general (permitting the agent to transact all business for the principal).
precedent • A court decision that furnishes an example or authority for deciding subsequent cases involving identical or similar facts.
predatory pricing • The pricing of a product below cost with the intent to drive competitors out of the market.
predominant-factor test • A test courts use to determine whether a contract is primarily for the sale of goods or for the sale of services.
preemption • A doctrine under which certain federal laws preempt, or take precedence over, conflicting state or local laws.
preemptive rights • Rights held by shareholders that entitle them to purchase newly issued shares of a corporation's stock, equal in percentage to shares already held, before the stock is offered to any outside buyers. Preemptive rights enable shareholders to maintain their proportionate ownership and voice in the corporation.
preference • In bankruptcy proceedings, property transfers or payments made by the debtor that favor (give preference to) one creditor over others. The bankruptcy trustee is allowed to recover payments made both voluntarily and involuntarily to one creditor in preference over another.
preferred creditor • In the context of bankruptcy, a creditor who has received a preferential transfer from a debtor.
preferred stock • Classes of stock that have priority over common stock as to both payment of dividends and distribution of assets on the corporation's dissolution.
premium • In insurance law, the price paid by the insured for insurance protection for a specified period of time.
prenuptial agreement • An agreement made before marriage that defines each partner's ownership rights in the other partner's property. Prenuptial agreements must be in writing to be enforceable.
presentment • The act of presenting an instrument to the party liable on the instrument in order to collect payment. Presentment also occurs when a person presents an instrument to a drawee for a required acceptance.
presentment warranties • Implied warranties, made by any person who presents an instrument for payment or acceptance, that (1) the person obtaining payment or acceptance is entitled to enforce the instrument or is authorized to obtain payment or acceptance on behalf of a person who is entitled to enforce the instrument, (2) the instrument has not been altered, and (3) the person obtaining payment or acceptance has no knowledge that the signature of the drawer of the instrument is unauthorized.
price discrimination • Setting prices in such a way that two competing buyers pay two different prices for an identical product or service.
price-fixing agreement • An agreement between competitors to fix the prices of products or services at a certain level.
***prima facie* case** • A case in which the plaintiff has produced sufficient evidence of his or her claim that the case can go to a jury; a case in which the evidence compels a decision for the plaintiff if the defendant produces no affirmative defense or evidence to disprove the plaintiff's assertion.
primary source of law • A document that establishes the law on a particular issue, such as a constitution, a statute, an administrative rule, or a court decision.
principle of rights • The principle that human beings have certain fundamental rights (to life, liberty, and the pursuit of happiness, for example). Those who adhere to this "rights theory" believe that a key factor in determining whether a business decision is ethical is how that decision affects the rights of various groups. These groups include the firm's owners, its employees, the consumers of its products or services, its suppliers, the community in which it does business, and society as a whole.
private equity capital • Private equity capital is a financing method by which a company sells equity in an existing business to a private or institutional investor.
privilege • A legal right, exemption, or immunity granted to a person or a class of persons. In the context of defamation, an absolute privilege immunizes the person making the statements from a lawsuit, regardless of whether the statements were malicious.
privity of contract • The relationship that exists between the promisor and the promisee of a contract.
probable cause • Reasonable grounds for believing that a person should be arrested or searched.
probate • The process of proving and validating a will and settling all matters pertaining to an estate.
probate court • A state court of limited jurisdiction that conducts proceedings relating to the settlement of a deceased person's estate.
procedural law • Law that establishes the methods of enforcing the rights established by substantive law.
proceeds • Under Article 9 of the UCC, whatever is received when collateral is sold or otherwise disposed of, such as by exchange.
product liability • The legal liability of manufacturers, sellers, and lessors of goods to consumers, users, and bystanders for injuries or damage that are caused by the goods.
profit • In real property law, the right to enter onto and remove something of value from the property of another (for example, the right to enter onto another's land and remove sand and gravel).
promise • An assertion that something either will or will not happen in the future.
promisee • A person to whom a promise is made.
promisor • A person who makes a promise.
promissory estoppel • A doctrine that applies when a promisor makes a clear and definite promise on which the promisee justifiably relies. Such a promise is binding if justice will be better served by the enforcement of the promise.
promissory note • A written promise made by one person (the maker) to pay a fixed amount of money to another person (the payee or a subsequent holder) on demand or on a specified date.
property • Legally protected rights and interests in anything with an ascertainable value that is subject to ownership.
prospectus • A written document, required by securities laws, that describes the security being sold, the financial operations of the issuing corporation, and the investment or risk attaching to the security. It is designed to provide sufficient information to enable investors to evaluate the risk involved in purchasing the security.

protected class • A group of persons protected by specific laws because of the group's defining characteristics. Under laws prohibiting employment discrimination, these characteristics include race, color, religion, national origin, gender, age, and disability.
proximate cause • Legal cause; exists when the connection between an act and an injury is strong enough to justify imposing liability.
proxy • In corporate law, a written agreement between a stockholder and another party in which the stockholder authorizes the other party to vote the stockholder's shares in a certain manner.
puffery • A salesperson's often exaggerated claims concerning the quality of property offered for sale. Such claims involve opinions rather than facts and are not considered to be legally binding promises or warranties.
punitive damages • Monetary damages that may be awarded to a plaintiff to punish the defendant and deter similar conduct in the future.
purchase-money security interest (PMSI) • A security interest that arises when a seller or lender extends credit for part or all of the purchase price of goods purchased by a buyer.

Q

qualified indorsement • An indorsement on a negotiable instrument in which the indorser disclaims any contract liability on the instrument. The notation "without recourse" is commonly used to create a qualified indorsement.
quasi contract • A fictional contract imposed on the parties by a court in the interests of fairness and justice; usually imposed to avoid the unjust enrichment of one party at the expense of another.
question of fact • In a lawsuit, an issue that involves only disputed facts, and not what the law is on a given point. Questions of fact are decided by the jury in a jury trial (by the judge if there is no jury).
question of law • In a lawsuit, an issue involving the application or interpretation of a law. Only a judge, not a jury, can rule on questions of law.
quitclaim deed • A deed intended to pass any title, interest, or claim that the grantor may have in the property without warranting that such title is valid. A quitclaim deed offers the least amount of protection against defects in the title.
quorum • The number of members of a decision-making body that must be present before business may be transacted.
quota • A set limit on the amount of goods that can be imported.

R

ratification • The act of accepting and giving legal force to an obligation that previously was not enforceable.
reaffirmation agreement • An agreement between a debtor and a creditor in which the debtor voluntarily agrees to pay, or reaffirm, a debt dischargeable in bankruptcy. To be enforceable, the agreement must be made before the debtor is granted a discharge.
real property • Land and everything attached to it, such as trees and buildings.
reasonable person standard • The standard of behavior expected of a hypothetical "reasonable person"; the standard against which negligence is measured and that must be observed to avoid liability for negligence.
receiver • In a corporate dissolution, a court-appointed person who winds up corporate affairs and liquidates corporate assets.
record • According to the Uniform Electronic Transactions Act, information that is either inscribed on a tangible medium or stored in an electronic or other medium and is retrievable.
recording statutes • Statutes that allow deeds, mortgages, and other real property transactions to be recorded so as to provide notice to future purchasers or creditors of an existing claim on the property.
reformation • A court-ordered correction of a written contract so that it reflects the true intentions of the parties.
Regulation E • A set of rules issued by the Federal Reserve System's Board of Governors to protect users of elecronic fund transfer systems.
Regulation Z • A set of rules issued by the Federal Reserve Board of Governors to implement the provisions of the Truth-in-Lending Act.
release • A contract in which one party forfeits the right to pursue a legal claim against the other party.
remedy • The relief given to an innocent party to enforce a right or compensate for the violation of a right.
replevin • An action to recover identified goods in the hands of a party who is wrongfully withholding them from the other party. Under the UCC, this remedy is usually available only if the buyer or lessee is unable to cover.
reply • Procedurally, a plaintiff's response to a defendant's answer.
requirements contract • An agreement in which a buyer agrees to purchase and the seller agrees to sell all or up to a stated amount of what the buyer needs or requires.
resale price maintenance agreement • An agreement between a manufacturer and a retailer in which the manufacturer specifies what the retail prices of its products must be.
rescission • A remedy whereby a contract is canceled and the parties are returned to the positions they occupied before the contract was made; may be effected through the mutual consent of the parties, by the parties' conduct, or by court decree.
res ipsa loquitur • A doctrine under which negligence may be inferred simply because an event occurred, if it is the type of event that would not occur in the absence of negligence. Literally, the term means "the facts speak for themselves."
respondeat superior • Latin for "let the master respond." A doctrine under which a principal or an employer is held liable for the wrongful acts committed by agents or employees while acting within the course and scope of their agency or employment.
restitution • An equitable remedy under which a person is restored to his or her original position prior to loss or injury, or placed in the position he or she would have been in had the breach not occurred.
restrictive indorsement • Any indorsement on a negotiable instrument that requires the indorsee to comply with certain instructions regarding the funds involved. A restrictive indorsement does not prohibit the further negotiation of the instrument.
resulting trust • An implied trust arising from the conduct of the parties. A trust in which a party holds the actual legal title to another's property but only for that person's benefit.
retained earnings • The portion of a corporation's profits that has not been paid out as dividends to shareholders.
revocation • In contract law, the withdrawal of an offer by an offeror. Unless the offer is irrevocable, it can be revoked at any time prior to acceptance without liability.
right of contribution • The right of a co-surety who pays more than her or his proportionate share on a debtor's default to recover the excess paid from other co-sureties.
right of reimbursement • The legal right of a person to be restored, repaid, or indemnified for costs, expenses, or losses incurred or expended on behalf of another.
right of subrogation • The right of a person to stand in the place of (be substituted for) another, giving the substituted party the same legal rights that the original party had.
right-to-work law • A state law providing that employees may not be required to join a union as a condition of retaining employment.
risk • A prediction concerning potential loss based on known and unknown factors.
risk management • Planning that is undertaken to protect one's interest should some event threaten to undermine its security. In the context of insurance, risk management involves transferring certain risks from the insured to the insurance company.

robbery • The act of forcefully and unlawfully taking personal property of any value from another. Force or intimidation is usually necessary for an act of theft to be considered a robbery.
rulemaking • The process undertaken by an administrative agency when formally adopting a new regulation or amending an old one. Rulemaking involves notifying the public of a proposed rule or change and receiving and considering the public's comments.
rule of four • A rule of the United States Supreme Court under which the Court will not issue a writ of certiorari unless at least four justices approve of the decision to issue the writ.
rule of reason • A test by which a court balances the positive effects (such as economic efficiency) of an agreement against its potentially anticompetitive effects. In antitrust litigation, many practices are analyzed under the rule of reason.

S

sale • The passing of title to property from the seller to the buyer for a price.
sales contract • A contract for the sale of goods under which the ownership of goods is transferred from a seller to a buyer for a price.
scienter • Knowledge by the misrepresenting party that material facts have been falsely represented or omitted with an intent to deceive.
S corporation • A close business corporation that has met certain requirements set out in the Internal Revenue Code and thus qualifies for special income tax treatment. Essentially, an S corporation is taxed the same as a partnership, but its owners enjoy the privilege of limited liability.
search warrant • An order granted by a public authority, such as a judge, that authorizes law enforcement personnel to search particular premises or property.
seasonably • Within a specified time period or, if no period is specified, within a reasonable time.
secondary boycott • A union's refusal to work for, purchase from, or handle the products of a secondary employer, with whom the union has no dispute, in order to force that employer to stop doing business with the primary employer, with whom the union has a labor dispute.
secondary source of law • A publication that summarizes or interprets the law, such as a legal encyclopedia, a legal treatise, or an article in a law review.
SEC Rule 10b-5 • A rule of the Securities and Exchange Commission that makes it unlawful, in connection with the purchase or sale of any security, to make any untrue statement of a material fact or to omit a material fact if such omission causes the statement to be misleading.
secured party • A lender, seller, or any other person in whose favor there is a security interest, including a person to whom accounts or chattel paper have been sold.
secured transaction • Any transaction in which the payment of a debt is guaranteed, or secured, by personal property owned by the debtor or in which the debtor has a legal interest.
securities • Generally, stocks, bonds, notes, debentures, warrants, or other items that evidence an ownership interest in a corporation or a promise of repayment by a corporation.
security • Generally, a stock certificate, bond, note, debenture, warrant, or other document or record evidencing an ownership interest in a corporation or a promise of repayment of debt by a corporation.
security agreement • An agreement that creates or provides for a security interest between the debtor and a secured party.
security interest • Any interest in personal property or fixtures that secures payment or performance of an obligation.
self-defense • The legally recognized privilege to protect oneself or one's property against injury by another. The privilege of self-defense usually applies only to acts that are reasonably necessary to protect oneself, one's property, or another person.
self-incrimination • The giving of testimony that may subject the testifier to criminal prosecution. The Fifth Amendment to the U.S. Constitution protects against self-incrimination by providing that no person "shall be compelled in any criminal case to be a witness against himself."
seniority system • In regard to employment relationships, a system in which those who have worked longest for the employer are first in line for promotions, salary increases, and other benefits. They are also the last to be laid off if the workforce must be reduced.
service mark • A mark used in the sale or advertising of services to distinguish the services of one person from those of others. Titles, character names, and other distinctive features of radio and television programs may be registered as service marks.
sexual harassment • In the employment context, the demanding of sexual favors in return for job promotions or other benefits, or language or conduct that is so sexually offensive that it creates a hostile working environment.
share exchange • In a share exchange, some or all of the shares of one corporation are exchanged for some or all of the shares of another corporation, but both corporations continue to exist. Share exchanges are often used to create holding companies (companies that own part or all of other companies' stock).
shareholder's derivative suit • A suit brought by a shareholder to enforce a corporate cause of action against a third person.
shelter principle • The principle that the holder of a negotiable instrument who cannot qualify as a holder in due course (HDC), but who derives his or her title through an HDC, acquires the rights of an HDC.
shipment contract • A contract for the sale of goods in which the seller is required or authorized to ship the goods by carrier. The seller assumes liability for any losses or damage to the goods until they are delivered to the carrier.
short-form (parent-subsidiary) merger • A merger of companies in which one company (the parent corporation) owns at least 90 percent of the outstanding shares of each class of stock of the other corporation (the subsidiary corporation). The merger can be accomplished without the approval of the shareholders of either corporation.
short-swing profits • Profits earned by a purchase and sale, or sale and purchase, of the same security within a six-month period; under Section 16(b) of the 1934 Securities Exchange Act, must be returned to the corporation if earned by company insiders from transactions in the company's stock.
shrink-wrap agreement • An agreement whose terms are expressed in a document located inside a box in which goods (usually software) are packaged; sometimes called a shrink-wrap license.
slander • Defamation in oral form.
slander of quality (trade libel) • The publication of false information about another's product, alleging that it is not what its seller claims.
slander of title • The publication of a statement that denies or casts doubt on another's legal ownership of any property, causing financial loss to that property's owner.
small claims court • A special court in which parties may litigate small claims (such as $5,000 or less). Attorneys are not required in small claims courts and, in some states, are not allowed to represent the parties.
smart card • A card containing a microprocessor that permits storage of funds via security programming, can communicate with other computers, and does not require online authorization for fund transfers.
sociological school • A school of legal thought that views the law as a tool for promoting justice in society.
sole proprietorship • The simplest form of business organization, in which the owner is the business. The owner reports business income on his or her personal income tax return and is legally responsible for all debts and obligations incurred by the business.
sovereign immunity • A doctrine that immunizes foreign nations from the jurisdiction of U.S. courts when certain conditions are satisfied.

spam • Bulk e-mails, particularly of commercial advertising, sent in large quantities without the consent of the recipient.
special indorsement • An indorsement on an instrument that indicates the specific person to whom the indorser intends to make the instrument payable; that is, it names the indorsee.
special warranty deed • A deed in which the grantor warrants only that the grantor or seller held good title during his or her ownership of the property and does not warrant that there were no defects of title when the property was held by previous owners.
specific performance • An equitable remedy requiring exactly the performance that was specified in a contract; usually granted only when monetary damages would be an inadequate remedy and the subject matter of the contract is unique (for example, real property).
spendthrift trust • A trust created to protect the beneficiary from spending all the funds to which she or he is entitled. Only a certain portion of the total amount is given to the beneficiary at any one time, and most states prohibit creditors from attaching assets of the trust.
stale check • A check, other than a certified check, that is presented for payment more than six months after its date.
standing to sue • The requirement that an individual must have a sufficient stake in a controversy before he or she can bring a lawsuit. The plaintiff must demonstrate that he or she has been either injured or threatened with injury.
stare decisis • A common law doctrine under which judges are obligated to follow the precedents established in prior decisions.
Statute of Frauds • A state statute under which certain types of contracts must be in writing to be enforceable.
statute of limitations • A federal or state statute setting the maximum time period during which a certain action can be brought or certain rights enforced.
statutory law • The body of law enacted by legislative bodies (as opposed to constitutional law, administrative law, or case law).
stock • An equity (ownership) interest in a corporation, measured in units of shares.
stock buyback • The purchase of shares of a company's own stock by that company on the open market.
stock certificate • A certificate issued by a corporation evidencing the ownership of a specified number of shares in the corporation.
stock option • An agreement that grants the owner the option to buy a given number of shares of stock, usually within a set time period.
stock warrant • A certificate that grants the owner the option to buy a given number of shares of stock, usually within a set time period.
stop-payment order • An order by a bank customer to his or her bank not to pay or certify a certain check.
stored-value card • A card bearing a magnetic strip that holds magnetically encoded data, providing access to stored funds.
strict liability • Liability regardless of fault. In tort law, strict liability is imposed on those engaged in abnormally dangerous activities, on persons who keep dangerous animals, and on manufacturers or sellers that introduce into commerce goods that are unreasonably dangerous when in a defective condition.
strike • An action undertaken by unionized workers when collective bargaining fails; the workers leave their jobs, refuse to work, and (typically) picket the employer's workplace.
sublease • A lease executed by the lessee of real estate to a third person, conveying the same interest that the lessee enjoys but for a shorter term than that held by the lessee.
substantive law • Law that defines, describes, regulates, and creates legal rights and obligations.
summary jury trial (SJT) • A method of settling disputes, used in many federal courts, in which a trial is held, but the jury's verdict is not binding. The verdict acts only as a guide to both sides in reaching an agreement during the mandatory negotiations that immediately follow the summary jury trial.
summons • A document informing a defendant that a legal action has been commenced against her or him and that the defendant must appear in court on a certain date to answer the plaintiff's complaint.
supremacy clause • The requirement in Article VI of the U.S. Constitution that provides that the Constitution, laws, and treaties of the United States are "the supreme Law of the Land." Under this clause, state and local laws that directly conflict with federal law will be rendered invalid.
surety • A person, such as a cosigner on a note, who agrees to be primarily responsible for the debt of another.
suretyship • An express contract in which a third party to a debtor-creditor relationship (the surety) promises to be primarily responsible for the debtor's obligation.
symbolic speech • Nonverbal expressions of beliefs. Symbolic speech, which includes gestures, movements, and articles of clothing, is given substantial protection by the courts.
syndicate • A group of individuals or firms brought together for the purpose of financing a project that they would not or could not undertake independently; also called an investment group.

T

takeover • The acquisition of control over a corporation through the purchase of a substantial number of the voting shares of the corporation.
taking • The taking of private property by the government for public use. The government may not take private property for public use without "just compensation."
tangible employment action • A significant change in employment status, such as a change brought about by firing or failing to promote an employee; reassigning the employee to a position with significantly different responsibilities; or effecting a significant change in employment benefits.
tangible property • Property that has physical existence and can be distinguished by the senses of touch and sight. A car is tangible property; a patent right is intangible property.
target corporation • The corporation to be acquired in a corporate takeover; a corporation whose shareholders receive a tender offer.
tariff • A tax on imported goods.
tenancy at sufferance • A type of tenancy under which a tenant who, after rightfully being in possession of leased premises, continues (wrongfully) to occupy the property after the lease has terminated. The tenant has no rights to possess the property and occupies it only because the person entitled to evict the tenant has not done so.
tenancy at will • A type of tenancy that either party can terminate without notice; usually arises when a tenant who has been under a tenancy for years retains possession, with the landlord's consent, after the tenancy for years has terminated.
tenancy in common • Co-ownership of property in which each party owns an undivided interest that passes to her or his heirs at death.
tender • An unconditional offer to perform an obligation by a person who is ready, willing, and able to do so.
tender of delivery • Under the Uniform Commercial Code, a seller's or lessor's act of placing conforming goods at the disposal of the buyer or lessee and giving the buyer or lessee whatever notification is reasonably necessary to enable the buyer or lessee to take delivery.
tender offer • An offer made by one company directly to the shareholders of another (target) company to purchase their shares of stock; sometimes referred to as a takeover bid.
testamentary trust • A trust that is created by will and therefore does not take effect until the death of the testator.
testate • Having left a will at death.
testator • One who makes and executes a will.
third party beneficiary • One for whose benefit a promise is made in a contract but who is not a party to the contract.

tippee • A person who receives inside information.
tort • A civil wrong not arising from a breach of contract; a breach of a legal duty that proximately causes harm or injury to another.
tortfeasor • One who commits a tort.
Totten trust • A trust created when a person deposits funds in his or her own name as a trustee for another. It is a tentative trust, revocable at will until the depositor dies or completes the gift in his or her lifetime by some unequivocal act or declaration.
toxic tort • A civil wrong arising from exposure to a toxic substance, such as asbestos, radiation, or hazardous waste.
trade dress • The image and overall appearance of a product—for example, the distinctive decor, menu, layout, and style of service of a particular restaurant. Basically, trade dress is subject to the same protection as trademarks.
trademark • A distinctive mark, motto, device, or emblem that a manufacturer stamps, prints, or otherwise affixes to the goods it produces so that they may be identified on the market and their origins made known. Once a trademark is established (under the common law or through registration), the owner is entitled to its exclusive use.
trade name • A term that is used to indicate part or all of a business's name and that is directly related to the business's reputation and goodwill. Trade names are protected under the common law (and under trademark law, if the name is the same as the firm's trademarked product).
trade secret • Information or process that gives a business an advantage over competitors that do not know the information or process.
transfer warranties • Implied warranties, made by any person who transfers an instrument for consideration to subsequent transferees and holders who take the instrument in good faith, that (1) the transferor is entitled to enforce the instrument; (2) all signatures are authentic and authorized; (3) the instrument has not been altered; (4) the instrument is not subject to a defense or claim of any party that can be asserted against the transferor; and (5) the transferor has no knowledge of any insolvency proceedings against the maker, the acceptor, or the drawer of the instrument.
traveler's check • A check that is payable on demand, drawn on or payable through a financial institution (bank), and designated as a traveler's check.
treaty • In international law, a formal written agreement negotiated between two nations or among several nations. In the United States, all treaties must be approved by the Senate.
treble damages • Damages that, by statute, are three times the amount that the fact finder determines is owed.
trespass to land • The entry onto, above, or below the surface of land owned by another without the owner's permission or legal authorization.
trespass to personal property • The unlawful taking or harming of another's personal property; interference with another's right to the exclusive possession of his or her personal property.
Trojan horse • A computer program that appears to perform a legitimate function but in fact performs a malicious function that allows the sender to gain unauthorized access to the user's computer; named after the wooden horse that enabled the Greek forces to gain access to the city of Troy in the ancient story.
trust • An arrangement in which title to property is held by one person (a trustee) for the benefit of another (a beneficiary).
trust indorsement • An indorsement for the benefit of the indorser or a third person; also known as an agency indorsement. The indorsement results in legal title vesting in the original indorsee.
tying arrangement • An agreement between a buyer and a seller in which the buyer of a specific product or service becomes obligated to purchase additional products or services from the seller.

U

ultra vires • A Latin term meaning "beyond the powers"; in corporate law, acts of a corporation that are beyond its express and implied powers to undertake.
unconscionable (contract or clause) • A contract or clause that is void on the basis of public policy because one party, as a result of disproportionate bargaining power, is forced to accept terms that are unfairly burdensome and that unfairly benefit the dominating party.
underwriter • In insurance law, the insurer, or the one assuming a risk in return for the payment of a premium.
undisclosed principal • A principal whose identity is unknown by a third person, and the third person has no knowledge that the agent is acting for a principal at the time the agent and the third person form a contract.
unenforceable contract • A valid contract rendered unenforceable by some statute or law.
uniform law • A model law created by the National Conference of Commissioners on Uniform State Laws and/or the American Law Institute for the states to consider adopting. Each state has the option of adopting or rejecting all or part of a uniform law. If a state adopts the law, it becomes statutory law in that state.
unilateral contract • A contract that results when an offer can be accepted only by the offeree's performance.
union shop • A firm that requires all workers, once employed, to become union members within a specified period of time as a condition of their continued employment.
universal defense • A defense that is valid against all holders of a negotiable instrument, including holders in due course (HDCs) and holders with the rights of HDCs.
unreasonably dangerous product • In product liability law, a product that is defective to the point of threatening a consumer's health and safety. A product will be considered unreasonably dangerous if it is dangerous beyond the expectation of the ordinary consumer or if a less dangerous alternative was economically feasible for the manufacturer, but the manufacturer failed to produce it.
usage of trade • Any practice or method of dealing having such regularity of observance in a place, vocation, or trade as to justify an expectation that it will be observed with respect to the transaction in question.
U.S. trustee • A government official who performs certain administrative tasks that a bankruptcy judge would otherwise have to perform.
usury • Charging an illegal rate of interest.
utilitarianism • An approach to ethical reasoning that evaluates behavior in light of the consequences of that behavior for those who will be affected by it, rather than on the basis of any absolute ethical or moral values. In utilitarian reasoning, a "good" decision is one that results in the greatest good for the greatest number of people affected by the decision.

V

valid contract • A contract that results when the elements necessary for contract formation (agreement, consideration, legal purpose, and contractual capacity) are present.
venture capital • Capital (funds and other assets) provided by professional, outside investors (venture capitalists, usually groups of wealthy investors and securities firms) to start new business ventures.
venue • The geographic district in which a legal action is tried and from which the jury is selected.
vertically integrated firm • A firm that carries out two or more functional phases (manufacture, distribution, and retailing, for example) of the chain of production.
vertical merger • The acquisition by a company at one level in a marketing chain of a company at a higher or lower level in the chain (such as a company merging with one of its suppliers or retailers).
vertical restraint • Any restraint of trade created by agreements between firms at different levels in the manufacturing and distribution process.
vesting • The creation of an absolute or unconditional right or power.
vicarious liability • Legal responsibility placed on one person for the acts of another; indirect liability imposed on a supervisory party (such as an

employer) for the actions of a subordinate (such as an employee) because of the relationship between the two parties.

virus • A computer program that can replicate itself over a network, such as the Internet, and interfere with the normal use of a computer. A virus cannot exist as a separate entity and must attach itself to another program to move through a network.

vishing • A variation of phishing that involves some form of voice communication. The consumer receives either an e-mail or a phone call from someone claiming to be from a legitimate business and asking for personal information; instead of being asked to respond by e-mail as in phishing, the consumer is asked to call a phone number.

void contract • A contract having no legal force or binding effect.

voidable contract • A contract that may be legally avoided (canceled, or annulled) at the option of one or both of the parties.

voir dire • An Old French phrase meaning "to speak the truth." In legal language, the process in which the attorneys question prospective jurors to learn about their backgrounds, attitudes, biases, and other characteristics that may affect their ability to serve as impartial jurors.

W

warranty deed • A deed in which the grantor assures (warrants to) the grantee that the grantor has title to the property conveyed in the deed, that there are no encumbrances on the property other than what the grantor has represented, and that the grantee will enjoy quiet possession of the property; a deed that provides the greatest amount of protection for the grantee.

watered stock • Shares of stock issued by a corporation for which the corporation receives, as payment, less than the stated value of the shares.

wetlands • Water-saturated areas of land that are designated by a government agency (such as the Army Corps of Engineers or the Environmental Protection Agency) as protected areas that support wildlife and therefore cannot be filled in or dredged by private contractors or parties without a permit.

whistleblowing • An employee's disclosure to government authorities, upper-level managers, or the media that the employer is engaged in unsafe or illegal activities.

white-collar crime • Nonviolent crime committed by individuals or corporations to obtain a personal or business advantage.

will • An instrument directing what is to be done with the testator's property on his or her death, made by the testator and revocable during his or her lifetime. No interests in the testator's property pass until the testator dies.

will substitutes • Various documents that attempt to dispose of an estate in the same or similar manner as a will, such as trusts or life insurance plans.

winding up • The second of two stages in the termination of a partnership or corporation. Once the firm is dissolved, it continues to exist legally until the process of winding up all business affairs (collecting and distributing the firm's assets) is complete.

workers' compensation laws • State statutes establishing an administrative procedure for compensating workers for injuries that arise out of—or in the course of—their employment, regardless of fault.

working papers • The various documents used and developed by an accountant during an audit. Working papers include notes, computations, memoranda, copies, and other papers that make up the work product of an accountant's services to a client.

workout • An out-of-court agreement between a debtor and creditors in which the parties work out a payment plan or schedule under which the debtor's debts can be discharged.

worm • A computer program that can automatically replicate itself over a network such as the Internet and interfere with the normal use of a computer. A worm does not need to be attached to an existing file to move from one network to another.

writ of attachment • A court's order, issued prior to a trial to collect a debt, directing the sheriff or other public officer to seize nonexempt property of the debtor. If the creditor prevails at trial, the seized property can be sold to satisfy the judgment.

writ of *certiorari* • A writ from a higher court asking a lower court for the record of a case.

writ of execution • A court's order, issued after a judgment has been entered against a debtor, directing the sheriff to seize and sell any of the debtor's nonexempt real or personal property.

wrongful discharge • An employer's termination of an employee's employment in violation of the law.

Index

A

Ab initio (from the beginning), 462
Abatement, 934
Abstract, 75
Abuse of process, 100
Acceleration clause, 445–446
Acceptance(s)
  banker's, 440
  of bribe, 153
  contractual. *See* Contract(s), acceptance in; Lease contract(s), acceptance in; Sales contract(s), acceptance in
  of delivered goods, 398
    revocation of, 405
  of gift, 887, 889
  in negotiable instruments law, 440, 474
  online, 249–251
  partial, 398
  trade, 440, 457
Acceptor
  defined, 444, 457
  liability of, 456
Accession, acquisition of personal property by, 889–890
Accord
  defined, 267, 327
  satisfaction and
    contract discharge by, 327
    settlement of claim by, 267
Accountant(s)
  accountant-client relationship and, 874
  duty of, 207, 861–863
  liability of, 860–879
    criminal, 873
    under securities laws, 869–873
  working papers and, 868
Accounting
  agent's duty of, 588
  debtor's request for, 509–510
Act of state doctrine, 556–557
Action(s)
  affirmative, 656–657
  in *assumpsit,* 297
  in equity, 11, 13
  in law, 11, 13
Actual malice, 97
Actus reus (guilty act), 148
Adjudication, 7, 8
Administrative agencies, 5, 7–9. *See also* Administrative law; Government regulation(s)
  authority of, 9
  defined, 7
  parallel, 7
Administrative law, 7–9. *See also* Government regulation(s)
  dealing with, 17–18
  defined, 7
  finding, 22–23
Administrative Procedure Act (APA)(1946), 8, 9
Administrative process, 7–8
Administrator, 933
Admissions, exception to Statute of Frauds and, 301, 373–374
Adverse selection, 491
Advertisement(s), advertising
  bait-and-switch, 837
  as commercial speech, 41–42, 723
  contractual offers versus, 239
  counteradvertising and, 838
  deceptive, 836–838
  fax, 838–839
Affidavit, 71, 522, 531, 937
Age
  discrimination on basis of, 569, 638, 648–650, 843
  of majority, 269
Age Discrimination in Employment Act (ADEA)(1967), 569, 638, 648–650
Agency relationship(s), 580–605. *See also* Agent(s); Principal(s)
  bank-customer relationship as, 474–475
  defined, 580
  duties in, 586–589
  employer-employee, 581
  employer-independent contractor, 581–582
  exclusive, 589
  with foreign firm, 558
  formation of, 584–586
  liability in, 114, 592–598
  termination of, 598–600
Agent(s)
  agency termination by, 599
  authority of, 589–592
    agent's renunciation of, 599
    lacking, 458
    principal's revocation of, 599
  authorized and unauthorized acts of, 592–594
  bankruptcy of, agency termination and, 600
  corporate directors and, 754
  crimes of, 149–150, 594, 598, 726–727
  death or insanity of, agency termination and, 600
  defined, 580
  duties of, to principal, 586–588, 590
  e-, 594
  escrow, 918
  human, 594
  insurance, 925
  partner as, 689, 690
  principal's duties to, 588–589
  registered, 732–733
  signature of, 458
  torts of, 114, 594–598, 726–727
Agreement(s). *See also* Contract(s)
  agency formation by, 585
  to agree, 240–241
  bailment, 893–894
  bilateral, 555

contract discharge by, 326–327
contractual, 220, 236–261
creditors' composition, 523
defined, 236
distribution, 558
family settlement, 937
hot-cargo, 629
illegal, withdrawal from, 280
international, 555
lease. *See* Lease contract(s)
licensing, 248
multilateral, 555
mutual, agency termination and, 599
operating, 711–712, 714
partnering, 252
partnership, 685–686, 773
prenuptial (antenuptial), 299–300
price-fixing, 567, 815–816, 827
reaffirmation, 542
resale price maintenance, 817–818, 830
security, 497, 498
shareholder, 729
shareholder voting, 765
tie-in sales, 824
trade, 562, 570
Agricultural associations, exemption of, from antitrust laws, 828
Algorithm, 129n
Alien Tort Claims Act (ATCA)(1789), 568–569
Alienation, 314
Alteration(s)
on checks, 480–481
material, 316, 319, 370, 383–384, 461–462
Alternative dispute resolution (ADR), 78–83. *See also* Arbitration; Mediation; Negotiation(s)
defined, 78
in international contract disputes, 564–565
lawsuit versus, 84
American International Group (AIG), 198–199
American law
in global context, 566–569
sources of, 4–9
American Recovery and Reinvestment Act (ARRA)(2009), 199–200, 618n
Americans with Disabilities Act (ADA)(1990), 569, 622, 638, 650–655
Answer, 71
Antedating, 447
Anti-Counterfeiting Trade Agreement (ACTA)(proposed), 139
Anticybersquatting Consumer Protection Act (ACPA)(1999), 125–126
Antiplagiarism service, 187
Anti-Terrorism Act (ATA), 568–569
Antitrust law(s), 812–834
enforcement of, 826–827
exclusionary practices and, 823–824
exemptions from, 827, 828
extraterritorial effect of, 566–567, 827–828
foreign, application of, 828–829
in global context, 827–829
monopolization and, 818–822
per se violations of, 815–816, 817, 824, 828, 830
problems with, avoiding, 830
rule of reason and, 815, 817, 824
Appeals, 75–77
Appellant, 29
Appellate (reviewing) courts, 12, 23
appeals to, 75–77
federal, 68–69. *See also* United States Supreme Court
jurisdiction of, 61
state, 66, 67–68
Appellate review, 76–77
Appellee, 29
Application
for insurance, 928
for job, 653
Appropriate bargaining unit, 629
Appropriation, 97, 98–99
Arbitration, 249
automobile lemon laws and, 422
defined, 79
as form of ADR, 79–82
litigation versus, 565
mediation-, 83
nonbinding, 80
service providers of, 83
Arbitration Fairness Act (proposed), 82
Arbitrator, 79, 80
Army Corps of Engineers, 851
Arrest, 164
Arson, 151–152
Arthur Andersen, LLP, 204, 860
Articles
of consolidation, 741
of dissolution, 745
of incorporation, 732–733, 754, 761
of merger, 741
of organization, 708
of partnership, 685
Assault, 93
Assignment(s), 311–315, 332
of "all rights," 317
defined, 312
of lease, 918
rights not subject to, 312–314
of security interest, 508
transfer of negotiable instruments by, 314, 448
Assignor, assignee, 312, 313, 918
Assurance, right of, 396–397
Asymmetric cryptosystem, 251
Attachment
judicial lien and, 498n, 522
perfection upon, 502–504
secured transaction and, 498, 522
Attorney(s)
accused person's right to, 38, 161, 162–163
-at-law, 589n
attorney-client relationship and, 96n, 874
district (D.A.), 15, 146
duty of, 864
employer's right to, in immigration hearing, 624
-in-fact, 589n
malpractice and, 107, 864
Attribution, 255
Auctions, 239–240
Audit committee, 756, 798
Audits, auditors, 862, 875
Authentication, 498
Authority(ies)
actual, 589–590, 598, 690
of agent, 589–592
apparent, 591, 598, 599

binding, 10, 12
express, 589, 690
implied, 590, 690
of partner, 690
persuasive, 11, 12
Authorization card, 629
Automated teller machines (ATMs), 482, 487, 489
Award
arbitrator's, 80
jury, 75

B

Bailee
acknowledgment by, of buyer's or lessee's rights, 381, 392n
bailment for sole benefit of, 894, 897
bailor and, bailment for mutual benefit of, 894, 897
defined, 381, 892
duties of, 895–896
goods held by, 381
involuntary, finder as, 890n
liability of, 895
rights of, 894–895
Bailment(s), 892–899
defined, 892
elements of, 892–894
fitness for intended purpose of, 897
for hire (commercial), 894
involuntary (constructive), 893
ordinary, 894–897
special (extraordinary), 894, 897–899
voluntary, 893n
Bailor
bailee and, bailment for mutual benefit of, 894, 897
bailment for sole benefit of, 894
defined, 892
duties of, 897
Bank(s), 471–495
check collection process of
under Check 21, 484, 486
traditional, 483–487
collecting, 483
correspondent, 565–566
in crisis period, 491
customer of. *See* Bank customer(s)
defined, 471–472
depositary, 482, 483
depository, 483n
duty of
to accept deposits, 481–487
to honor checks, 475–481, 482
Export-Import, 559
intermediary, 483
liability of, 476–477, 479
negligence of, 479
online, 489–490
payor, 482, 483
stop-payment order and, 476–477
Bank customer(s)
death or incompetence of, 476n, 477
of different banks, check collection between, 484–486
liability of, 477–479, 480–481
negligence of, 477–479, 480–481
relationship of, with bank, 474–475
of same bank, check collection between, 483–484
Bank run, 491
Bank-owned life insurance (BOLI), 926
Bankruptcy, 528–548
automatic stay in, 534–535, 543, 546, 548
cram-down provision and, 545
discharge in, 328, 462, 540–542, 543, 545, 547, 548
estate in property of, 535
distribution of, 539–540
fraud in, 154
involuntary, 531, 533
ordinary, 530
petition in, 531, 543, 546, 548
preferences in, 538
relief in
order for, 533, 543, 544
types of, 529. *See also individual chapters of Bankruptcy Code*
straight, 530
substantial abuse presumption and, 532–533
trustee in, 532, 537–538
voluntary, 531–533
Bankruptcy Code (Bankruptcy Reform Act of 1978). *See also* Bankruptcy
Chapter 7 liquidation proceedings in, 529, 530–542, 543, 545, 546, 548
Chapter 9 adjustment of debts of a municipality in, 529
Chapter 11 reorganization in, 529, 532, 537n, 540n, 542–545, 546
Chapter 12 adjustment of debts by family farmers and family fisherman in, 529, 535n, 537n, 545, 547–548
Chapter 13 individuals' repayment plan in, 529, 530, 532n, 535n, 537, 545–547, 548
Bankruptcy Reform Act
of 1978. *See* Bankruptcy Code
of 2005 (Bankruptcy Abuse Prevention and Consumer Protection Act) (2005), 520, 529, 530, 531, 532, 533, 536, 543, 547–548, 549
Bankruptcy Reporter (Bankr.)(West), 25
Bargained-for exchange, 263
Barings Bank, 204
Baseball, professional, exemption of, from antitrust laws, 828
Basis of the bargain, 415
Battery, 93
Bearer, 447
Bearer instrument, 441
defined, 447
negotiating, 448–449
Behavior. *See also* Conduct
actionable, 95
predatory, 101
Beneficiary(ies)
creditor, 318
donee, 318
incidental, 318, 319–321
intended, 318–321
of public assistance, discrimination on basis of being, 843
third party, 317–321, 332
Bequest, 934
Berne Convention of 1886, 137
Beyond a reasonable doubt, 146, 164
Bill of lading, 361, 378, 381, 566
Bill of Rights. *See also individual amendments*
business and, 37–45
defined, 37
privacy rights and, 49–50
Binder, 928
Blogs, corporate, 787
Bona fide occupational qualification (BFOQ), 655
Bond(s)

issuing, 747
stocks versus, 739
types of, 738
Bond indenture, 738
Botnets (robot networks), 179–180
Boycott
group, 816
secondary, 629
Brady Handgun Violence Prevention Act (1993), 36n
Breach
of contract. *See* Contract(s), breach of; Sales contract(s), breach of
of duty
of care, 105–107
of loyalty, 590
of warranty. *See* Warranty(ies), breach of
Bribery
commercial, 153
of foreign officials, 153, 205–207, 562
of public officials, 153
Brief, 75
Burglary, 151
Business
agency relationships in. *See* Agency relationship(s)
Bill of Rights and, 37–45
cyber crimes in, 179–182
effects of bankruptcy law on, 549
international. *See* International business transactions; International contract(s)
legal environment and, 3–4
ongoing, sale of, covenants not to compete and, 274
searches and seizures in, 159–160, 723
single transaction in, laws affecting, 3
small
cooperative research by, exemption of, from antitrust laws, 828
law's role in, 4, 5
tort liability and, 114
wrongful interference with, 101–102
Business ethics, 194–198. *See also* Ethics
defined, 194
on global level, 205–207
importance of, 194
leadership in, importance of, 196–197
management's attitude regarding, 196–197
questions regarding, solutions to, 204–205
transgressions in, by financial institutions, 198–200
Business form(s)
business trust as, 716
cooperative as, 716–717
corporation as. *See* Corporation(s)
family limited liability partnership (FLLP) as, 697
franchise and, 320n, 558, 670–678, 679
joint stock company as, 716
joint venture as, 558–559, 715–716
limited liability company (LLC) as. *See* Limited liability company(ies)
limited liability limited partnership (LLLP) as, 701, 702
limited liability partnership as. *See* Limited liability partnership
limited partnership as. *See* Limited (special) partnership(s)
major, 668–714, 722–777
comparison of, 771–772
partnership as. *See* Partnership(s)
sole proprietorship as. *See* Sole proprietorships
special, 715–717
syndicate (investment group) as, 716
Business invitees, 106–107, 114
Business judgment rule, 757, 758–759
Business process patents, 131
Business trust, 716
Buyer(s). *See also* Purchaser(s)
breach by, 382, 399–402
of collateral, 508
insolvent, 401
insurable interest of, 382
issues to note, 385
as licensee, 248
merchant as, duties of, upon rejection of goods, 405
obligations of, 391, 397–398
in the ordinary course of business, 379–380, 504, 507, 508
remedies of, 402–406
Bystanders, strict liability and, 429

C

Cable Communications Act, 670
Cancellation. *See also* Rescission
of contract, 11, 794, 843
buyer's or lessee's right to, 399, 402
for insurance, 930
seller's or lessor's right to, 399
of offer, 222–223. *See also* Revocation
CAN-SPAM (Controlling the Assault of Non-Solicited Pornography and Marketing) Act (2003), 183
Capacity
contractual. *See* Contract(s), capacity in
testamentary, 934–935
Capital Markets Efficiency Act (1996), 780
Capper-Volstead Act (1922), 828
Care
due, 757
duty of
accountant's, 861–863
attorney's, 864
bailee's, 895
breach of, 105–107
corporate directors', 757–758
corporate officers', 757–758
defined, 105
extraordinary, 897
fiduciary's, 689–690, 712, 713
landowners and, 106–107
negligence and, 105–107
partner's, 689–690
product liability and, 423
professionals', 107
reasonable, 102
trustee's, 943
ordinary, 479
Carrier(s)
common, 897–898
substitution of, 393
Case(s). *See also* Lawsuit(s); Litigation
arbitrability of, 81–82
criminal, major steps in processing, 165
disposition of, by appellate court, 76, 77
of first impression, 11
following through state court system, 70–77
"no-asset," 539n
prima facie, 640, 647, 648, 654
sample, 29–31
titles and terminology of, 25, 29

Case law
common law doctrines and, 9
defined, 9
finding, 23–25
as primary source of law, 5
reading and understanding, 25, 29–31
Case Management/Electronic Case Files (CM/ECF), 77–78
Catalogues, contractual offers versus, 239
Categorical imperative, 201
Causation, 107–108, 109
Certificate(s)
of authority, 727
of deposit (CD), 439, 441–442, 443n
of incorporation, 733
of limited partnership, 698
stock, 766, 785
Certification mark, 123
C.&F. (cost and freight), 380
Chain-style business operation, as type of franchise, 671
Chancellor, 11
Chattel paper, 496
Chattels, 103, 884. *See also* Personal property
Check(s), 438, 439, 440–441, 471–474
altered, 480–481
cashier's, 441, 472–473
certified, 457, 474
clearance of, 486
collection process and
under Check 21, 484, 486
traditional, 483–487
defined, 440, 471
deposit of, availability schedule for, 481–483
dishonored, 475
drawn in blank, 464
electronic presentment of, 486–487
honoring of, 475–481, 482
overdrafts and, 475
payable to "Cash," 465
poorly filled-out, 480
postdated, 476
posting of, deferred, 485
signature on, forged, 477–480
stale, 476
stop-payment order and, 476–477
substitute, 484
teller's, 472–473
traveler's, 473–474
writing, 464–465
Check 21 (Check Clearing in the 21st Century Act)(2004), 481–482, 484, 486, 487n
Checks and balances system, 33, 58
Child Pornography Prevention Act (CPPA)(1996), 43
Child Protection and Toy Safety Act (1969), 842
Children. *See also* Infancy; Minor(s)
adopted, 938–939
child labor and, 610
grandchildren and, 939
illegitimate, 938–939
pornography and, 42–43
stepchildren and, 938–939
surviving, intestacy laws and, 938
Children's Internet Protection Act (CIPA)(2000), 42
Child's Online Protection Act (COPA)(1998), 42
Choice-of-language clause, 563
Choice-of-law clause, 564
C.I.F. (cost, insurance, and freight), 380
Circulars, contractual offers versus, 239
Circumstances, changed, agency termination and, 600
CISG (United Nations Convention on Contracts for the International Sale of Goods), 360, 382–384, 564
acceptance under, 383–384
revocation of, 407
offers under, 383
Statute of Frauds and, 302, 383
UCC compared with, 383–384, 556
Citation(s), 23
defined, 6
how to read, 26–28
parallel, 23, 25
Citizenship
corporate, 202–203
diversity of, 61
Civil law
criminal law versus, 15, 145–147
defined, 15, 145
Civil law system, 15, 16
Civil Rights Act
of 1866, 641
of 1964, Title VII of, 205, 569, 638, 639–648, 655, 656
remedies under, 647–648
Claim(s)
creditors', 535
to debtor's collateral, priority of, 506–508
international tort, 567–569
notice of, HDC status and, 455–456
proof of, 535
retaliation, 646, 648
settlement of, 267–268
Class, protected. *See* Protected classes
Class Action Fairness Act (CAFA)(2005), 92
Clayton Act (1914), 812, 822–826, 827, 828
Clean Air Act (1963), 848–849
Clean Water Act (CWA)(1972), 850–851
Clearinghouse, 486
Click-on agreements (click-on license)(click-wrap agreement), 249–250
Clients
accountant-client relationship and, 874
attorney-client relationship and, 96n, 874
common law liability to, 861–865
Closed shop, 628
Cloud computing, 135
COBRA (Consolidated Omnibus Budget Reconciliation Act)(1985), 618
C.O.D. (collect on delivery), 398
Code of Federal Regulations (C.F.R.), 23, 773
citation to, 27
Codicil, 936
Coinsurance clauses, 928–929
Collateral
buyers of, 508
of debtor, 497
debtor's rights in, 498
description of, in financing statement, 501
priority of claims to, 506–508, 509, 515
defined, 497
disposition of, 512–515
proceeds from, 504, 514
intangible, 499
redemption of, 514–515

release of, 508, 510
repossession of, "self-help," 510–511
retention of, by secured party, 512
tangible, 499
types of, and methods of perfection of security interest in, summarized, 500
Collective bargaining, 627, 630–631
Collective mark, 123
Color, discrimination on basis of, 569, 638, 639, 640–641, 843
Comity, principle of, 556, 565
Commerce clause, 33–37
Commercial activity, 557
Commercial impracticability, 329–331, 394–396
Commercial paper, 438. *See also* Negotiable instrument(s)
Commercial reasonableness, 367, 368, 390, 453, 513
Commercial unit, 398
Commission, act of, 148
Common law, 9–14
remedies against environmental pollution and, 846–847
Common law system, 16
Communication(s)
privileged, 96–97
stored, 620
Communications Decency Act (CDA)(1996), 42, 112–113, 291
Compelling state interest, 47
Compensation
bailee's right of, 895
just, 38, 914–915
principal's duty of, 588
tort plaintiff and, 93. *See also* Damages
workers'. *See* Workers' compensation
Compensation committee, 756, 798
Competition
covenant not to enter into, 265–266, 274–276
predatory behavior versus, 101
Compilations, 5
of facts, 132
Complaint, 70–71
Computer Crime and Security Survey, 180
Computer Fraud and Abuse Act (Counterfeit Access Device and Computer Fraud and Abuse Act)(CFAA)(1984), 186, 187, 590
Computer Software Copyright Act (1980), 134
Concentrated industry, 816
Condition(s)
concurrent, 323
defined, 321
offeror's assent and, 371
of performance, 321–323
precedent, 304–305, 322, 398
preexisting, 618
subsequent, 322
Conduct. *See also* Behavior
misrepresentation by, 292
of the parties, 223–224
Confederal form of government, 32–33
Confidentiality and privilege, 874
Confirmation, debtor's request for, 509–510
Confiscation, 556, 559
Confusion, 890
Consent, as defense, to assault or battery, 93
Consideration. *See* Contract(s), consideration in; Lease contract(s), consideration in; Sales contract(s), consideration in
Consolidation, 740, 741–742
Construction, rules of, 376
Consumer(s)
effects of bankruptcy law on, 549
financial data of, privacy and, 490
laws protecting. *See* Consumer law(s)
Consumer Credit Protection Act (CCPA)(1968), 487n, 523n, 843
Consumer goods, as collateral, 503–504, 512. *See also* Purchase-money security interest
Consumer law(s), 835–846
areas of, regulated by statutes, illustrated, 836
credit protection and, 842–846
deceptive advertising and, 836–838
defined, 835
health and safety protection and, 841–842
labeling and packaging and, 839–840
sales and, 840–841
telemarketing and, 838–839, 840
Consumer Leasing Act (CLA)(1988), 844
Consumer Price Index, 536n
Consumer Product Safety Act (1972), 842
Consumer Product Safety Commission (CPSC), 842
Consumer-debtor(s)
defined, 529
special bankruptcy treatment for, 529, 531, 533, 538
Contract(s), 218–355. *See also* Agreement(s); Contractual relationship
acceptance in, 220, 236, 326
communication of, 246
defined, 245
mode and timeliness of, 247–248
persons qualified for, 245
silence as, 246
unequivocal, 246
adhesion, 276
agent's liability and, 592–594
agreement in, 220, 236–261
alteration of, 327, 370, 383–384, 461–462
arbitration clause in, 80–82, 249, 273
assignment prohibited by, 314
bilateral, 221–222, 246n, 263
breach of
as defense to liability on negotiable instrument, 462
defined, 3, 337
material, 323, 325
minor, 325
professionals' liability and, 861
remedies for, 337–351, 408–409. *See also* Remedy(ies)
limitation of, 349–350
statute of limitations and, 327–328
cancellation of. *See* Cancellation of contract
capacity in, 220, 269–272
collateral, 296, 298–299
commercial, international. *See* International contract(s)
to commit a crime, 272
consideration in, 220, 262–268, 326
adequacy of, 263–264
defined, 262
lack of, 264–267
legal sufficiency of, 263–264
past, 265–266
construction, 339, 347n
contrary to public policy, 273–279
contrary to statute, 272–273
defined, 219
delegation prohibited by, 316
destination, 378, 381, 392

disaffirmance of, 269–270
discharge of, 311, 321–331
electronic. *See* E-contract(s)
elements of, 220–221
employment. *See* Employment contract(s)
enforceability of, 225, 305
 covenants not to compete and, 275–276
 defenses to, 221. *See also* Parol evidence rule; Statute of Frauds
enforceable, 226. *See also* Contract(s), valid
exclusive-dealing, 823–824
executed, 224–225, 270
executory, 224–225, 270, 326, 544
express, 223–224
form of, 221
formal, 223
formation of, 221–224
franchise, 674–676. *See also* Franchises
freedom from, 220
freedom of, 220, 263
function of, 219
implied (implied-in-fact), 223–224
incomplete, 304
indivisible, 280
informal (simple), 223
installment, 393–394
insurance. *See* Insurance, contract for
integrated, 305, 375
interpretation of, 227–230, 376
investment, 779–780
law governing
 major differences between general contract law and, 373
 overview of, 219–220
 relationship of, with sales contract law, illustrated, 362
 sources of, 219
legality of, 221, 272–280. *See also* Illegality
limitation-of-liability clauses in, 349–350
mirror image rule and, 244, 370
new, rescission and, 265
objective theory of, 220, 237
offer in, 220, 236, 326
 cancellation of, 222–223
 communication of, 241–242
 counteroffer and, 244, 370
 defined, 237
 irrevocable, 242–243, 245
 rejection of, 243–244
 requirements of, 237–242
 revocation of, 222–223, 242
 termination of, 242–245
option, 242–243
option-to-cancel clause in, 266–267
oral, 297. *See also* Statute of Frauds
output, 368
performance and, 224–225
for personal service. *See* Personal-service contracts
preincorporation, 708, 731
principal's liability and, 592–594
proposed, supervening illegality of, offer termination and, 245
quasi (implied in law), 225–227, 268, 348–349
ratification of. *See* Ratification
reformation and, 276, 292, 347–348
repudiation of, 396–397
 anticipatory, 325–326, 397
 retraction of, 399
requirements, 368
requirements of, 220–221, 326
rescission of, 11, 288, 289, 292, 794, 843
in restraint of trade. *See* Restraint(s) on trade
severable (divisible), 280
shipment, 378, 380–381, 392
within the Statute of Frauds, 296, 303. *See also* Statute of Frauds
types of, 221–225
unenforceable, 225, 226
unilateral, 221, 222, 246n, 263
valid, 225, 271–272
void, 225, 226, 271, 304
voidable, 225, 226, 271, 304, 589
voluntary consent on, 221, 287–296
Contract theory, exceptions to employment-at-will doctrine based on, 607
Contractor, nonperforming, avoidance of litigation by, 350–351
Contractual relationship
 bank-customer relationship as, 475
 wrongful interference with, 101–102
Contribution, right of, 527–528
Control(s)
 of bailed property, bailee's right to, 894
 de facto (actual), 770
 dominion and, 888–889
 employer's right to, 582, 583, 597
 export, 559
 import, 559–561
Controlled Substances Act (CSA)(1970), 36
Conversion, 103–104, 157, 344, 379n, 891
Conveyance, 909
Cooperation, duty of
 exception to perfect tender rule and, 396, 397
 principal's, 588–589
Cooperative, 716–717
Copyright Act (1976), 130–131, 132–134, 584
Copyright Term Extension Act (1998), 131n
Copyrights, 119, 127, 130–136, 138, 558, 584, 670
Corporate governance, 796–800
Corporate social responsibility, 201–203
Corporate-owned life insurance (COLI), 926–927
Corporation(s), 722–777
 alien, 727
 as artificial legal person, 46, 60n, 149, 161, 530n, 684, 723, 744, 753, 843
 assets of
  commingling of, with personal assets, 737
  liquidation of, 744n, 746
  purchase of, 743
 bylaws of, 732, 733, 754–755, 761
 classification of, 727–730
 close (closely held)(family)(privately held), 728–729, 737, 768
 compared with other major business forms, 771–772
 constitutional rights of, 723–724
 corporate governance and, 796–800
 criminal liability and, 149–150, 726–727
 de jure and *de facto*, 735
 defined, 723
 directors of. *See* Directors, corporate
 dividends of, 724, 767–768
 domestic, 727
 ethical questions regarding, solutions to, 204–205
 executives of
  bonuses for, 199–200
  role of, 757

financing of, 738–740, 746–747. *See also* Bond(s); Security(ies); Stock(s)
foreign, 727
formation of, 730–733
defects in, 735
incorporation of, 731–733
management of, 728, 754
nature of, 723–727
net profits of, 767
nonprofit (not-for-profit), 728
officers of. *See* Officers, corporate
owners of. *See* Shareholder(s)
parent, 741
as partner, 684
political speech and, 40–41, 723
powers of, 734
private, 727–728
professional, 730
profit maximization and, 195–196
public, 727–728
publicly held (public company), 727
reputation of, 206, 208
resolutions and, 763
retained earnings of, 724, 767
S, 702, 730
Section 12, 786, 791, 867
social responsibility and, 201–203
stakeholders and, 202
stock buybacks by, 198
subsidiary, 741
surplus of, 767
target, 743, 744
taxes and, 711, 724
termination of, 744–746
Corporations commissioner, 795
Cost-benefit analysis, 201
Costco Wholesale Corporation, Code of Ethics of, 197
Counterclaim, 71
Counteroffer, 244, 370
Court(s), 57–78
appellate. *See* Appellate courts
bankruptcy, 60, 68, 529
chancery, 11
criteria for determining whether worker is employee or independent contractor and, 582–583
cyber, 78
early English, 9–10, 11
citation to, 27
electronic filing and, 77–78
of equity, 11–13
federal. *See* Federal court system
Internet and, 77–78
king's *(curiae regis),* 9–10, 11
of law, 11–13
probate, 60, 67, 933
small claims, 66–67
state. *See* State court systems
trial. *See* Trial courts
Web sites of, 78
Covenant(s)
defined, 912
not to compete, 265–266, 274–276
not to sue, 267, 268
Cover, 403–404
Co-workers, harassment by, 646
Credit
consumer, 463
discrimination and, 843
laws protecting, 842–846
letters of, 223, 566, 567
line of, 746, 747
continuing, 505
price of, 281
reporting and, 543, 844–845
Credit Card Accountability Responsibility and Disclosure Act (2009), 843n
Credit Cardholder's Bill of Rights Act (2009), 281
Credit cards
consumer protection and, 842
crime involving, 179
price controls and, 281
TILA rule regarding, 844
unsolicited, 844
Creditor(s)
best interests of, 544
committee of, 544
composition agreements of, 523
laws assisting, 521–528
lien of, 521. *See also* Lien(s)
meeting and claims of, 535
preferred, 538
relationship of, with debtor, bank-customer relationship as, 474
rights and duties of, 508–510
secured. *See* Secured party(ies)
unsecured
bankruptcy property distribution and, 539–540
rules of priority among claims and, 506
Crime(s)
classification of, 156
computer, 172–173
contract to commit, 272
cyber. *See* Cyber crime(s)
organized, 154–155
persons accused of, constitutional protections for, 158–163. *See also individual protections*
property, 151–152
prosecution for, tort lawsuit for same act versus, 147, 148
public order, 152
types of, 150–156
violent, 150
white-collar, 152–154, 173–174, 726
Criminal law. *See also* Crime(s)
civil law versus, 15, 145–147
criminal process and, 164–166
defined, 15, 146
sentencing guidelines and, 164, 166, 726
Criminal liability, 147–150. *See also* Crime(s); Criminal law
corporate, 149–150, 726–727
defenses to, 156–158
Crops, sale of, 364, 906
Cross-collateralization, 505
Crown jewel, 744
Cruel and unusual punishment, 38, 161
Cumulative voting, 764–765
Cure, 381–382, 393, 405
Curiae regis (king's courts), 9–10, 11
Customer restrictions, 817
Cyber crime(s), 150, 172–192
in business world, 179–182
against community, 183–185

cost of, 179
defined, 173
fighting, 185–187
private efforts in, 186
juvenile, 180–181
against people and property, 173–179
prosecuting, 185–186
Cyberlaw, 15
Cybernotary, 251
Cybersquatting, 125–126
Cyberstalking, 177–179
Cyberterrorists, 181–182

D

Damages, 12, 157, 338–343
buyer's or lessee's right to recover, 404, 406
compensatory, 91, 107, 294, 338–339, 647–648
consequential (special), 338, 339–340, 403, 407–408
defined, 91
general, 91
incidental, 338, 400
injury requirement and, 107, 290, 295
liquidated, penalties versus, 343
mitigation of, 341–342
nominal, 338, 340
punitive (exemplary), 91–92, 107, 294, 295, 338, 340, 489, 533, 648, 845
seller's or lessor's right to recover, 400–401
special, 91, 96
in tort actions, 91–92
treble (triple), 130, 489, 827, 830
types of, 338–341
Danger(s)
commonly known, 431
"danger invites rescue" doctrine and, 110–111
notice of dangerous conditions and, 597
unreasonably dangerous products and, 425
Davis-Bacon Act (1931), 608–609
Dead peasant policies, 926
Deadly force, 156, 167
Death
of agent or principal, agency termination and, 600
of bank customer, 476n, 477
intestate, 932
of offeror or offeree, offer termination and, 245
of party to personal-service contract, 328
of principal or agent, agency termination and, 600
testate, 932
work-related, of employee, 615
Debit card (ATM card), 487
Debt(s)
collection of, 845–846
in dispute, 267
liquidated, 267
preexisting, 538
reaffirmation of, 535, 542
repurchasing (deleveraging), 802–803
unliquidated, 267
Debtor(s)
collateral of. *See* Collateral of debtor
consumer-. *See* Consumer-debtor(s)
creditors' meeting and, 535
default of, 497, 510–515
defined, 497
laws assisting, 528. *See also* Bankruptcy; Consumer law(s)
name of, in financing statement, 499–501
in possession (DIP), 544
property of, lien on, 538. *See also* Collateral of debtor
relationship of, with creditor, bank-customer relationship as, 474
rights and duties of, 508–510
Decisions, court, 5. *See also* Case law
Deeds, 911–913
Defamation, 42, 94–97, 112–113
Default of debtor, 497, 510–515
Defendant(s)
answer of, 71
criminal, constitutional protections for, 158–163. *See also individual protections*
defined, 11, 25, 29
service of process upon, 71
Defense(s)
affirmative, 71, 108
business necessity, 655
complete, 461
defined, 93
knowledgeable user, 432
notice of, HDC status and, 455–456
of others, 93
personal (limited), 462–463
of property, 93
self-, 93, 156
universal (real), 461–462
Defense activities, exemption of, from antitrust laws, 828
Defense Production Act (1950), 828
Delegation(s), 311, 312, 315–317, 332
defined, 315
duties not subject to, 315–317
Delegator, delagatee, 315
Deleveraging (repurchasing debt), 802–803
Delivery. *See also* Shipment
constructive, 888, 893
ex-ship (delivery from the carrying vessel), 380
of gift, 887–888
with movement of goods (carrier cases), 378, 380–381, 392
of nonconforming goods by seller or lessor, 369, 370, 404–406
passage of title and, 378
physical, 893
place of, 391–392
of possession, 893
seller's or lessor's right
to stop, 401
to withhold, 399–400
tender of, 378, 391
when seller or lessor refuses to make, 402–404
without movement of goods (noncarrier cases), 378, 381
Demand instruments, 439, 455, 476n
Deposit(s)
bank's duty to accept, 481–487
direct, 487
Deposited acceptance rule, 247
Deposition, 72
Design defects, 426–427
Destruction
of identified goods, exception to perfect tender rule and, 396
of subject matter. *See* Subject matter, destruction of
Devise, devisee, 934
Digital cash, 489, 490
Digital Millennium Copyright Act (1998), 134, 135, 182

Dilution, trademark, 121, 126–127
Directors, corporate, 723
- committees of, 756–757, 798
- corporate governance and, 797–798
- crimes of, 149–150, 726–727
- dissenting, 758
- duties of, 757–761
- failure of, to declare a dividend, 767–768
- inside versus outside, 755
- interlocking directorates and, 826
- liability of, 149–150, 726–727, 761
- meetings of, 755
- removal of, 754–755, 762
- rights of, 755–756
- role of, 753–757

Disability(ies)
- defined, 651–652
- discrimination on basis of, 569, 638, 650–655

Disaffirmance, 269–270
Discharge
- in bankruptcy, 328, 462, 540–542, 543, 545, 547, 548
- constructive, 644, 647
- of contract, 311, 321–331
- defined, 321
- wrongful, 608

Disclaimer
- audit and, 862
- of warranty, 420–421

Disclosure under SEC Rule 10b-5, 787–789
Discovery, 72–73, 74
- defined, 72
- electronic, 73, 74

Discrimination
- on basis of
  - age, 569, 638, 648–650, 843
  - color, 569, 638, 639, 640–641, 843
  - disability, 569, 638, 650–655
  - gender, 47, 74, 205, 569, 638, 639, 642–644, 843
  - marital status, 843
  - national origin, 569, 638, 639, 640–641, 843
  - pregnancy, 642
  - race, 74, 569, 638, 639, 640–641, 843
  - receiving public-assistance benefits, 843
  - religion, 569, 638, 639, 641–642, 843
- credit, 843
- employment. *See* Employment discrimination
- intentional (disparate-treatment), 639–640
- in jury selection, 74
- laws prohibiting, extraterritorial application of, 569
- price, 822–823
- reverse, 641
- unintentional (disparate-impact), 639, 640
- wage, 642, 643–644

Dishonor, of instruments, 455, 458, 475
Disparagement of property, 104
Disposition
- of collateral, 512–515
  - proceeds from, 504, 514
- testamentary, 932. *See also* Will(s)

Dissociation
- defined, 692, 713
- in limited (special) partnership, 700
- of member of LLC, 713–714
- of partner, 692–694, 713

Dissolution
- of corporation, 744, 745, 746, 768–769
  - defined, 694, 744, 745
- of limited (special) partnership, 700–701
- of LLC, 714
- of partnership, 694–695

Distributed network, 135
Distribution, under intestacy laws, 939
Distributorship, as type of franchise, 671
Do Not Call Registry, 839
Docket, 78
Document(s)
- e-, retention policies for, 773–774
- of title, 381, 899
  - defined, 378, 899n

Domain name(s)
- defined, 125
- second level (SLD), 125
- top level (TLD), 28, 125

Dominion, 888–889
Donor, donee, 887
Double jeopardy, 38, 160–161, 723
Drawee, 439, 440, 472
Drawer, 440
- defined, 439, 472
- liability of, 457
- signature of, forged, 477–480

Driver's Privacy Protection Act (1994), 50
Drugs
- consumer protection and, 841–842
- illegal, use of, 152
- prescription, in drinking water, 851–852
- substance abusers and, 653
- testing employees for, 621–622

Due diligence, 786, 869–870
Due process
- constitutional guarantee of, 38, 46–47, 91–92, 158, 160, 522, 723
- procedural, 46, 160
- substantive, 46–47

Dumping, 561
Duress
- defined, 157, 295
- extreme, as defense to liability on negotiable instrument, 462
- ordinary
  - contract illegal through, 280
  - as defense to criminal liability, 157
- voluntary consent and, 295–296

Duty(ies)
- absolute, 321
- antidumping, 561
- of care. *See* Care, duty of
- delegation of. *See* Delegation(s)
- ethics and, 200–201
- of loyalty. *See* Loyalty, duty of
- preexisting, 264–265

E

Early neutral case evaluation, 82
Easement, 909–910
Economic Espionage Act (1996), 137, 154
E-contract(s)
- agreement in, 248–252
- defined, 236
- dispute-settlement provisions in, 249

Eighth Amendment, 38, 158
Electronic Communications Privacy Act (ECPA)(1986), 50, 490, 620
Electronic fund transfer(s) (EFT), 487–489. *See also* Transfer(s), fund
  defined, 487
  systems for, types of, 487
  unauthorized, 488
Electronic Fund Transfer Act (EFTA)(1978), 487, 488–489
Eleventh Amendment, 650
E-mail (electronic mail)
  acceptance of offer via, 247
  contract creation and modification via, 609
  employee privacy and, 619, 632
  as enforceable contract, 306–307
  junk (spam), 182–183
  remailer and, 186
Emancipation of minor, 269
Embezzlement (defalcation), 152–153, 173, 344, 862
Eminent domain, 911, 914–915, 919
E-money, 489–490
Employee(s)
  confidential Web-based reporting systems available to, 197–198
  crimes of, 149–150
  with disability, reasonable accommodations for, 650, 652–653
  drug testing and, 621–622
  ethics training for, 197
  health of, 614–616
  immigration laws and, 623–627
  income security and, 616–619
  Internet policy and, 632
  key, 613
  layoffs and, 611–612
  lie-detector tests and, 621
  misconduct and, 656
  preemployment interviews and physical exams and, 622, 653
  privacy rights of, 619–622, 632
  religion of, reasonable accommodations for, 44, 642
  safety of. *See* Workplace, safety in
  seniority systems and, 656
  state, ADEA and, 650
  status as
    determining, 582–584, 601
    "works for hire" and, 584
  termination of, 608, 644, 647, 659. *See also* Employment at will
  torts of, 114
  work-related injury to, 108, 615–616
Employee Free Choice Act (proposed), 629n
Employee Polygraph Protection Act (1988), 621
Employee Retirement Income Security Act (ERISA)(1974), 617
Employer(s)
  liability of
    for employee's crimes, 149–150
    for employee's torts, 114
    for independent contractor's torts, 598
  reasonable accommodations by
    for employees' religion, 44, 642
    for employees with disabilities, 650, 652–653
    undue hardship versus, 642, 650, 653
  retaliation by, 646, 648
  tangible employment action and, 645
  using independent contractors, 601
Employer-employee relationships, 581
Employer-independent contractor relationships, 581–582
Employment
  discrimination in. *See* Employment discrimination
  employer-employee relationships and, 581
  foreign suppliers' practices and, 205
  I-9 verification and, 623–624
  immigration laws and, 623–627
  scope of, 114, 726
    respondeat superior and, 595–598, 726
  at will, 231, 606–608, 659
Employment contract(s)
  covenants not to compete in, 274–275
  creation and modification of, via e-mail, 609
  defined, 274
  implied, exception to employment-at-will doctrine based on, 231, 607
  mandatory arbitration clause in, 82
  unintended, avoiding, 231
Employment discrimination, 638–663
  association discrimination and, 654
  on basis of
    age, 569, 638, 648–650
    color, 569, 638, 639, 640–641
    disability, 569, 638, 650–655
    gender, 205, 569, 638, 639, 642–644. *See also* Sexual harassment
    national origin, 569, 638, 639, 640–641
    pregnancy, 642
    race, 569, 638, 639, 640–641
    religion, 569, 638, 639, 641–642
  defenses to, 655–656
  defined, 638
  employer-employee relationship and, 581
  laws prohibiting, extraterritorial application of, 569
  potential "Section 1981" claims of, 641
Enabling legislation, 7
Encryption, 186
Enforcement
  by administrative agencies, 7, 8, 18, 624
  of contract. *See* Contract(s), enforceability of
  of judgment, 77
Enron Corporation, 204, 860
Entrapment, 157–158
Entrepreneur, 668
Entrustment rule, 379–380
Environmental Protection Agency (EPA), 7, 847, 848–849, 850–851, 853–854, 855
Equal Credit Opportunity Act (ECOA)(1974), 843
Equal dignity rule, 584n, 589
Equal Employment Opportunity Commission (EEOC), 8, 17, 639, 642, 645, 651
  "four-fifths rule" devised by, 640
Equal Pay Act (1963), 642, 643
Equal protection clause, 46, 47–48, 656
Equitable principles and maxims, 12, 13
Equity
  action in, procedural differences between action at law and, 13
  courts of, 11–13
  defined, 11
  in home, 530
  merging of, with law, 11–12
  remedies in, 11–13, 337–338, 344–348
Error(s). *See also* Mistake(s)
  clerical (typographic), 305, 306, 843n
  UETA and, 255
Escrow account, 918
E-SIGN Act (Electronic Signatures in Global and National Commerce Act) (2000), 252, 253–254, 609
E-signatures, 251–252

Estate(s)
  dominant, 909
  leasehold, 915–916
    transferring rights to, 918
  life, 909, 943
  in property, 535
    distribution of, 539–540
  servient, 909
Estoppel
  agency formation by, 585–586
  apparent authority and, 591
  corporation by, 735–736
  defined, 268, 591, 735
  partnership by, 686–687
  promissory. *See* Promissory estoppel
Ethical reasoning, 200–203
Ethics
  accounting firm's liability when company held liable for securities violation and, 792–793
  administrative agency authority and, 9
  agent's breach of duty of loyalty and, 590
  business. *See* Business ethics
  business decision making and, 193–212
  business judgment rule and, 759
  codes of conduct and, 197
  companies taking out life insurance policies on rank-and-file employees and, 926–927
  contests and prizes and, 222
  Copyright Act versus bringing "idea submission" claims under state law and, 132
  defined, 194
  discrimination against transgender persons and, 643
  duty of care and, 106
  duty-based, 200–201
  eminent domain for private developments and, 915
  engagement ring ownership and, 887
  Expedited Funds Availability Act (EFAA), fraud and, 483
  fairness of enforcing shrink-wrap and click-wrap terms and, 250–251
  fiduciary duties of manager in manager-managed LLC and, 713
  fiduciary restrictions on trust instruments and, 451
  government regulation of pharmaceuticals in drinking water and, 851–852
  government rescue of debtors from foreclosure and, 524
  high costs of complying with Sarbanes-Oxley Act and, 869
  impossibility of performance and, 329
  information disclosed to prospective employees by employers and, 294
  Kantian, 200–201
  lawsuits against companies for aiding global terrorism and, 568–569
  leadership in, importance of, 196–197
  liability for defective products subject to government regulation and, 430
  liability of former partners after partnership dissolution and, 694–695
  more monopolies in the future and, 822
  offshore holding company to reduce taxes and, 725–726
  outcome-based, 201
  overtime pay for employee use of BlackBerrys after work and, 611
  private judges and, 66
  requirement that franchisors provide potential earning information and, 672
  specific performance and, 345
  time for seeking deficiency judgment and, 514
  transgressions in, by financial institutions, 198–200
  use of global financial crisis to escape contractual obligations and, 395–396
Event
  occurrence of, agency termination and, 599
    specific, gift *causa mortis* and, 889
Eviction, 917
Evidence
  after-acquired, 656
  e-, 73, 74
  extrinsic, 228
  parol (oral), 303, 443. *See also* Parol evidence rule
  preponderance of, 146
  prima facie, 862
Ex rel. (ex relatione), 66n, 838n
Examination(s)
  of bank statements, 478–479
  of goods, by buyer or lessee, 421
  of witness, 38, 75, 161
Excessive bail or fines, constitutional prohibition of, 38, 161
Exclusionary rule, 161–162
Exclusive bargaining representative, 630
Exculpatory clauses, 277–279, 349, 895
Execution, 511
Executive agencies, 7. *See also* Government regulation(s)
Executor, 933
Exemption(s)
  from antitrust laws, 827, 828
  in bankruptcy, 536
  homestead, 528, 530, 536
  overtime, 610–611
  from securities registration, 782–785
Expedited Funds Availability Act (EFAA)(1987), 481–483, 484
Export, exporting, 557–558, 559
  exemption of, from antitrust laws, 828
Export Administration Act (1979), 559
Export Trading Company Act (1982), 559, 828
Expression
  freedom of, 816. *See also* Speech, freedom of
  of opinion, 206, 238
Expropriation, 556, 559
Extension clause, 446

F

Fact(s)
  affirmations of, 415, 416
  causation in, 107
  honesty in, 453
  justifiable ignorance of, 279
  material, 787–789
    misrepresentation of, 99, 290–293
    mistake of, 288–290
  mistake of, 157, 288–290
  private, public disclosure of, 97–98
  statements of, 94–95, 99
Fair and Accurate Credit Transactions Act (FACT Act)(2003), 845
Fair Credit Reporting Act (FCRA)(1970), 543, 844–845
Fair Debt Collection Practices Act (FDCPA)(1977), 845–846
Fair Labor Standards Act (FLSA)(1938), 609–610, 643, 650
Fair Packaging and Labeling Act, 839
False imprisonment, 94
Family and Educational Rights and Privacy Act (1974), 50
Family and Medical Leave Act (FMLA)(1993), 608, 612–614, 650
Family fisherman, 548
Family limited liability partnership (FLLP), 697
Fannie Mae, 524
Farmer
  defined, 533n, 548n
  family, 548

F.A.S. (free alongside), 380
Featherbedding, 628
Federal Arbitration Act (FAA)(1925), 80–81, 273
Federal Aviation Administration, 655, 828
Federal Bureau of Investigation (FBI), 42, 48, 64, 173, 179, 180
Federal Communications Commission (FCC), 7, 42–43, 838, 839
Federal court system, 65, 68–70. *See also* Court(s)
  appellate (reviewing) courts of, 68–69. *See also* United States Supreme Court
  decisions of, 25
    citations to, 26–27
  illustrated, 65
  judges in, 66, 68
  jurisdiction of, 61
  trial (U.S. district) courts of, 60, 68, 69, 529
Federal Deposit Insurance Corporation (FDIC), 491
Federal Food, Drug and Cosmetic Act (FDCA)(1938), 841–842
Federal form of government, 34
Federal Hazardous Substances Act (1960), 842
Federal Housing Administration, 524
Federal Insecticide, Fungicide, and Rodenticide Act (FIFRA)(1947), 853
Federal Insurance Contributions Act (FICA), 616
Federal Register, 8, 839
Federal Reporter (F., F.2d, or F.3d)(West), 25
Federal Reserve System (Fed)
  Board of Governors of, 484
    defined, 486
    Regulation CC of, 481, 487
    Regulation E of, 488, 490
    Regulation Z of, 840, 843
  how checks are cleared by, 486
  price controls under, 281
  wire transfer network (Fedwire) of, 489
Federal Rules of Appellate Procedure, 12
Federal Rules of Civil Procedure, 72, 73, 773
Federal Savings and Loan Insurance Corporation (FSLIC), 491
Federal Supplement (F.Supp. or F.Supp.2d)(West), 25
Federal Trade Commission (FTC), 7, 9, 52, 819, 835
  antitrust laws enforced by, 826–827
  creation of, 7, 826
  deceptive advertising and, 836–838
  Do Not Call Registry and, 839
  Franchise Rule of, 671, 672, 673
  identity theft and, 845
  interlocking directorate threshold amounts and, 826
  limitations on HDC rights and, 463
  merger guidelines of, 825–826
  purchase of assets guidelines of, 743
  Rule 433 of, 463
  spamming and, 183
  telemarketing and, 839, 840
  telephone and mail-order sales and, 840–841
Federal Trade Commission Act (1914), 7, 463n, 812, 826
Federal Trademark Dilution Act (1995), 121
Federal Unemployment Tax Act (FUTA)(1935), 617
Federal Water Pollution Control Act (FWPCA)(1948), 850
Fee simple, 885, 907, 908
Felonies, 156
Fiduciary(ies)
  defined, 581
  at heart of agency law, 581
  indorsement restrictions and, 451
  undue influence and, 295
Fiduciary duty
  breach of, 758, 765–766, 790
  of corporate directors and officers, 712, 758
  of corporate insider, 790
  to disclose material facts, 293
  of insurance agent to insurer, 925
  of joint venturers, 715
  loyalty as, 587, 689–690, 712, 713
  of majority shareholders, 770–771
  of manager in manager-managed LLC, 712–713
  partner's, 689–690, 695
Fifth Amendment, 38, 46–47, 49–50, 158, 160–163, 619, 723–724, 914–915
Filing
  of appeal, 75–76
  electronic, 77–78
Financial institutions, ethical transgressions by, 198–200
Financial Services Modernization Act (Gramm-Leach-Bliley Act)(1999), 50, 52, 490
Financing statement
  amendment of, 509
  continuation statement and, 504
  defined, 497, 499
  filing of, 499–502
    improper, consequences of, 502
    place for, 501–502
  termination statement and, 510
First Amendment, 38, 39–45, 49–50, 68, 94, 95, 172, 206, 429, 565, 619, 631, 723, 816
First-in-time rule, 506–508
Fisheries, exemption of, from antitrust laws, 828
Fisheries Cooperative Marketing Act (1976), 828
Fixtures, 297, 496, 907
F.O.B. (free on board), 380
Food
  consumer protection and, 841–842
  labeling and packaging and, 839–840
  merchantable, 417–418
Food and Drug Administration (FDA), 5, 7, 17, 37, 430, 793, 839–840, 841–842, 847
Forbearance, 263, 264
Force, justifiable use of, 93, 156, 167
Force majeure clause, 564
Foreclosure
  lien, 521, 522, 895
  mortgage, 523–524
Foreclosure Prevention Act (2008), 524n
Foreign Corrupt Practices Act (FCPA)(1977), 153, 205–207, 562
Foreign exchange markets, 565, 570
Foreign Sovereign Immunities Act (FSIA)(1976), 557
Foreseeability
  of contingencies, 394–395
  of risk, 106–107, 114
  unforeseen difficulties and, 265
  of users of accountant's statements or reports, 867
Forfeiture, 154, 155, 184
Forgery(ies)
  on check, 477–480
  as defense against liability on negotiable instrument, 461
  defined, 152
  failing to detect, consequences of, 479
Forum shopping, 92, 95, 568–569
Forum-selection clauses, 249, 563–564
Fourteenth Amendment, 38, 46–48, 158, 522, 656
Fourth Amendment, 38, 49–50, 158–161, 615n, 619, 621
Franchisee, 670, 672, 679

Franchises, 320n, 558, 670–678, 679
Franchisor, 670, 672
Fraud, 99–100. *See also* Misrepresentation
  accountant's liability for, 864–865
  actual, 864
  auction, online, 174
  bankruptcy, 154
  constructive, 864
  contract illegal through, 280
  cyber, 173–174
  defined, 173
  elements of, 99, 290, 794, 864
  employment, 177
  in the execution, 461
  in the inducement (ordinary fraud), 463
  Internet, 841
  mail, 153
  offshore, 801
  online personals and, 291
  retail, online, 174
  "risk-free," 801
  securities, 166n, 800–802
  wire, 153
Fraudulent misrepresentation. *See* Fraud; Misrepresentation
Freddie Mac, 524
Freedom of Information Act (FOIA)(1966), 50, 64
Free-writing prospectus, 782
Fundamental right, 47, 97, 650
Future advances, 505

G

GAAP (generally accepted accounting principles), 861–862, 863, 869
GAAS (generally accepted auditing standards), 861–862, 863, 869
Gambling, 152, 154, 183–185, 272–273
Garnishment, garnishee, 523
Gender
  discrimination on basis of, 47, 74, 205, 569, 638, 639, 642–644, 843
  same-, harassment and, 646–647
General partnerships, 683, 685–695. *See also* Partnership(s)
  comparison of limited (special) partnership and, 698
  declining popularity of, 701–702
Genetic Information Nondiscrimination Act (GINA)(2008), 622
Genetic testing, 622
Genuineness of assent, 221. *See also* Contract(s), voluntary consent in
George S. May International Company, 204
Gift(s)
  acquisition of personal property by, 887–889
  causa mortis (deathbed gift), 889
  defined, 887
  to intended beneficiary, 318
  inter vivos, 889
  under will, types of, 934
Golden parachute, 744
Good faith
  in bankruptcy, 546
  collective bargaining and, 630–631
  defined, 453
  in franchising, 677–678
  insurance contracts and, 930–932
  sales contract modifications and, 371
  taking in, HDC status and, 453–454
  UCC and, 367, 368, 371, 390, 453
Goods. *See also* Product(s)
  acceptance of, 398
    revocation of, 405
  associated with real estate, 363–364
  buyer's or lessee's right to obtain, 402
  buyer's right
    to reject, 398, 404–405
    to replevy, 404
  conforming, 369, 378, 391, 392
  consumer. *See* Consumer goods
  counterfeit, 124, 139
  defined, 362–365
  delivery of. *See* Delivery
  dumping of, 561
  examination of, by buyer or lessee, 421
  existing, 377
  fungible, 377, 890, 894
  future, 377
  identification of, 377, 378
  identified. *See* Identified goods
  lessee's right
    to reject, 404–405
    to replevy, 404
  lessor's right to resell or dispose of, 400
  merchantable, 416–417
  obtaining, by false pretenses, 151
  in possession
    of bailee, 381
    of buyer, 401–402
    of lessee, 401–402
    of lessor, 399–401
    of seller, 381, 399–401
  seller's right to resell or dispose of, 400
  services combined with, 364–365
  shifting stock of, floating lien in, 506
  shipment of. *See* Delivery; Shipment
  specially manufactured, exception to Statute of Frauds and, 373
  stolen, receiving, 151
  in transit, 401
  unsolicited, 841
Government
  judiciary's role in, 57–58. *See also* Court(s)
  power(s) of
    concurrent, 37
    constitutional, 32–37
    limits on, 38–39
    separation of, 33
  regulation by. *See* Government regulation(s)
Government regulation(s), 17–18, 812–882
  antitrust. *See* Antitrust law(s)
  environmental, 835, 846–854, 855
  of franchises, 671–674
  of international business activities, 559–562
  as primary source of law, 5
  of securities. *See* Security(ies), regulation of
  of spam, 183
  by states. *See* State(s), regulation by
Grantor, grantee, 911
Greenmail, 744
Guarantee. *See* Warranty(ies)
Guaranty, guarantor, 299, 457, 525–528
Gun-Free School Zones Act (1990), 36n

H

Hackers, hacking, 176, 179–182, 801–802, 944
Hazardous waste disposal, 853–854, 855

Health
consumer protection and, 841–842
of employees, 614–616
Health insurance
COBRA and, 618
employer-sponsored, 618–619, 653–654
Medicare and, 616–617
Health Insurance Portability and Accountability Act (HIPAA)(1996), 50–51, 618–619
Heirs, collateral, 938
Herbicides, 853
Herfindahl-Hirschman Index (HHI), 825–826
Historical school, 14
Holder(s), 448
defined, 445
through an HDC, 456
Holder in due course (HDC), 452–456
defined, 448, 452
holder through, 456
rights of, federal limitations on, 463
status as, requirements for, 452–456
Holding (parent) company, 724–726
Horizontal market division, 816
Hostile-environment harassment, 644, 645, 647
claims under ADA and, 655

I

I-9 verifications, 623–624
I-551 Alien Registration Receipt ("green card"), 625
Identified goods, 378
destruction of, exception to perfect tender rule and, 396
place of delivery of, 391
Identity, appropriation of, 97, 98–99
Illegality
as defense to liability on negotiable instrument, 462, 463
effect of, 279–280
of performance, change in law and, 329
supervening, of proposed contract, 245
Immigration Act (1990), 623, 625–627
Immigration and Nationality Act (1952), 623n
Immigration Reform and Control Act (IRCA)(1986), 623–625
Immunity
from prosecution, 158
sovereign, 557, 650
Implication, easement or profit created by, 910
Implied warranty(ies), 416–419
of authority, 593
defined, 416
disclaimer of, 420–421
of fitness for a particular purpose, 419, 421, 897
of habitability, 912, 917–918
of merchantability, 416–418, 421, 897
overlapping warranties and, 419–420
prior dealings or trade custom and, 419
Important government objectives, 47–48
Impossibility
agency termination and, 600
objective, 328–329
of performance, 328–329, 331
subjective, 328
temporary, 329
Imposter, 459
In pari delicto, 279
Incapacity, mental. *See* Mental incompetence
Incompetence. *See* Mental incompetence
Incontestability clause, 929
Incorporators, 732, 733
Indemnification
corporate director's right to, 756
independent contractors and, 278–279
principal's duty of, 588
Independent contractor(s)
agency relationships and, 581–582. *See also* Agency relationship(s)
defined, 581
indemnification and, 278–279
insurance broker as, 925
torts of, 598
using, 601
Independent regulatory agencies, 7. *See also* Government regulation(s)
Indictment, 38
Individual retirement accounts (IRAs), 937
Indorsee
defined, 449
misspelled, 451
Indorsement(s), 449–451. *See also* Signature(s)
blank, 449, 465
for collection, 450
conditional, 450
defined, 449
for deposit, 450
forged, 480
qualified, 449–450
restrictive, 450–451
special, 449
transfer of order instrument and, 447
trust (agency), 450–451
unauthorized, special rules for, 459
unqualified, 450
"without recourse," 450, 456n
Indorser(s)
defined, 449
liability of, 457
qualified, 456n
unqualified, 457
Infancy, 269. *See also* Children; Minor(s)
Information
in criminal law, 164
digital, copyrights in, 134
inside, 154
material, 787–789
placing person in false light, publication of, 97
request for
in discovery, 72–73
by secured party or debtor, 508
Infringement
copyright, 81–82, 131, 133, 134, 136, 344, 415
patent, 130, 415, 560
trade dress, 124
trademark, 122, 124, 126, 127–128, 415
warranty of title and, 415
Inheritance, ownership of property transferred by, 913
Initial public offering (IPO), 746
via the Internet, 783
Injunction, 11, 34
Injury(ies)
fraudulent misrepresentation and, 99
to innocent party, 290, 295
legally recognizable, 107

as requirement for damages, 107
work-related, to employee, 108, 615–616
Innkeeper, liability of, 899
Insanity. *See* Mental incompetence
Insider trading, 154, 786–791
Insider Trading and Securities Fraud Enforcement Act (1988), 794
Insider Trading Sanctions Act (1984), 793n
Insiders, preferences to, 538
Insolvency
balance-sheet, 529n
of buyer, 401
defined, 340n, 379
equitable, 529n
of lessee, 401
of lessor, 379, 402
of seller, 379, 402
Inspection(s)
buyer's or lessee's refusal of, 421
right of
buyer's or lessee's, 398
corporate director's, 756
partner's, 688
shareholder's, 768
warrantless, 615n
Instrument(s)
defined, 439. *See also* Negotiable instrument(s)
face of, 228
Insurable interest, 382, 925–928
Insurance, 924–932
classifications of, 925, 926–927
contract for (insurance policy), 925, 928–932
defenses against payment under, 932
interpreting, 930
provisions and clauses in, 928–929
defined, 925
deposit, 491
exemption of, from antitrust laws, 828
health. *See* Health insurance
key-person, 926
liability, 756
life, 925–927
network intrusion, 944
policy and. *See* Insurance, contract for
premium for, 925
property, 927–928
terminology of, 925
unemployment, 617–618
Insurer, insured, 925
Intellectual property, 119–144. *See also specific forms of intellectual property*
defined, 119
forms of, summarized, 138
international protection for, 137–139
licensing of, 127–128, 320n, 558, 670
piracy of, online, 182
theft of, 173
Intent, intention
abandoned property and, 892
to associate, partnership and, 684
contractual offer and, 237–241
to deceive, 99, 290, 293–294
donative, 887
to exercise control, 893
monopolization and, 821
of owner, fixture and, 907
of parties, contract interpretation and, 229
signatures and, 369n, 443
statements of, 238
subjective, 237
testamentary, 935
third party beneficiaries and, 317
torts and. *See* Intentional tort(s)
Intentional infliction of emotional distress, 94
Intentional tort(s)
agent's, 597–598
defined, 92
against persons, 95–102
against property, 102–104
Interest(s)
conflict of, 760–761
protected, 91
rate of
judgment, 447
usury and, 272, 281
remainder, 943
security. *See* Security interest(s)
Interlocking directorates, 826
Intermediate scrutiny, 47–48
Internal Revenue Code, 730, 873
Internal Revenue Service (IRS), 176, 888
guidelines of, for determining whether worker is employee or independent contractor, 583–584, 601
information return filed with by partnership, 685
LLC taxation by, 707, 711
International business transactions, 557–559
global marketing and, 570
government regulation and, 559–562
making payment on, 565–566, 567
International contract(s), 382–384, 563–565
civil dispute resolution and, 564–565
clauses in, 563–564
sample (Starbucks), 563
International customs, 555
International Financial Reporting Standards (IFRS), 863
International law(s), 15
defined, 17, 554
in global economy, 554–574
sources of, 555–556
International organizations, 555–556
International principles and doctrines, 556–557
International Trade Commission, 560
Internet. *See also* World Wide Web
antiplagiarism service on, 187
banking on, 489–490
computer crime and, 172–173
consumer fraud on, 173–174
contracts formed on. *See* E-contract(s)
courts adapting to, 77–78
deceptive advertising on, 837–838
defamation on, 112–113
employee Internet policy and, 632
expansion of precedent and, 12
gambling on, 183–185
harassment via, 647
initial public offering (IPO) via, 783
international use and regulation of, 253
investment newsletters and forums on, 800–801
investment scams on, 800
jurisdiction and, 61–63

managing risk on, 944
obscene materials on, 42–43
public company information available on, 763
sales on
consumer protection and, 841
tax on, 363, 725
securities fraud via, 800–802
stock accounts on, hacking into, 801–802
trade secrets and, 137
trademark dilution and, 126–127
Internet Corporation for Assigned Names and Numbers (ICANN), 125
Internet Crime Complaint Center, 173, 174
Internet payment systems, 487
Internet service providers (ISPs), liability of, 112–113, 135, 183, 291
Internet Tax Freedom Act (1998), 725n
Interpretive rules, 8
Interrogatories, 72
Interstate Oil Compact (1935), 828
Intoxication, 271
Intrusion on person's affairs or seclusion, 97
Inventory
floating lien in, 505–506
future, 498
security interest in, 507–508
Investigation, by administrative agencies, 7, 8, 18
Investing in foreign nations, 559
Investment company, 784
Investor(s)
accredited, 784
protection of. *See* Security(ies), regulation of
Invitation to submit bids, 238
Involuntary servitude, 346
Issuer
defined, 867
well-known seasoned, 781, 782

J

Joint stock company, 716
Joint ventures, 558–559, 715–716
Judge(s)
administrative law (ALJ), 8, 18, 624, 780, 838
in federal court systems, 66
justice versus, 29
private, 66
in state court systems, 66
Judgment(s)
confession of, 688
default, 71
deficiency, 514, 524
enforcement of, 77
as a matter of law, 75
n.o.v. (notwithstanding the verdict), 75
on the pleadings, 71
summary, 71–72
Judicial review, 33n, 58, 59
Judiciary Act (1789), 59
Junior lienholder, 512
Junk Fax Protection Act (2005), 838n
Jurisdiction, 58–63
appellate, 61
concurrent, 61, 62
in cyberspace, 61–63
defined, 10, 58
exclusive, 61, 62
general (unlimited), 60, 66
international, 63
limited, 60, 66, 68
limited liability company and, 709–710
minimum contacts and, 59–60
offshore low-tax, 724–726
original, 59, 60–61, 68, 69
over corporations, 60
over persons *(in personam)*, 58–60
over property *(in rem)*, 58–60
over subject matter, 60
of Sherman Antitrust Act, 814
"sliding-scale" standard and, 62
of United States Supreme Court, 59, 69
Jurisprudence, 13
Jury(ies)
grand, 38, 164
instructions (charges) to, 75
prospective jurors for, challenges to, 74
selection of *(voir dire)*, 73–74
trial by, right to, 38, 73, 161
Justice, 29
Justiciable controversy, 64

L

Labor
child, 610
exemption of, from antitrust laws, 828
Labor Certification application, 626
Labor unions. *See* Unions
Labor-Management Relations Act (LMRA)(1947), 628
Labor-Management Reporting and Disclosure Act (LMRDA)(1959), 628–629
Land. *See also* Real property
defined, 906
interests in, contracts involving
breach of, 339
Statute of Frauds and, 296–297
trespass to, 102–103
Landlord, 916
Landlord-tenant relationships, 916–918
rights and duties in, 917–918
Landowner, duty of, 106–107
Lanham Act (1946), 121, 122, 125
Larceny, 151
Law(s). *See also* Statute(s)
action at, procedural differences between action in equity and, 13
administrative. *See* Administrative law; Government regulation(s)
affecting single business transaction, 3
American. *See* American law
areas of, business decision making affected by, 4
bankruptcy. *See* Bankruptcy; Bankruptcy Code
blue sky, 279, 795
case. *See* Case law
change in, illegal performance and, 329
classifications of, 14–17
"code," 16
constitutional, 5–6
consumer. *See* Consumer law(s)
contract. *See* Contract(s)
"cooling-off," 840
corporate, corporate governance and, 796–798
courts of, 11–13
defined, 2
disclosure, 488, 843

due process of. *See* Due process
duty-to-retreat, 167
environmental, 835, 846–854, 855
foreign, 39
governing franchising, 671–674
"gray areas" in, 194–195
immigration, 623–627
international. *See* International law(s)
intestacy, 932, 938–939
of Islam, 16, 67, 599
labeling and packaging, 839–840
labor, 627–629
lemon, 422
merging of, with equity, 11–12
misrepresentation of, 292
mistake of, 157
national, 15–16, 554
natural, 13–14
operation of. *See* Operation of law
other business school disciplines and, 3–4
plain-language, 227–228
procedural, 14–15
remedies at, 11–13, 337–338. *See also* Damages
right-to-work, 628
role of, in small business, 4, 5
sources of
primary, 4–5
secondary, 5
stand-your-ground, 167
statutory. *See* Statutory law
substantive, 14–15
tort. *See* Tort(s)
uniform, 6. *See also individual uniform laws*
wage and hour, 608–611
workers' compensation. *See* Workers' compensation
Lawsuit(s). *See also* Case(s); Litigation
alternative dispute resolution (ADR) versus, 84
basic judicial requirements for, 58–65
covenant not to bring, 267, 268
decision to bring, 84
derivative, shareholder's, 728n, 761, 769
standing to bring, 44, 64–65, 532
tort, criminal prosecution for same act versus, 147, 148
Lawyers' Edition of the Supreme Court Reports (L.Ed. or L.Ed.2d), 25
citation to, 26
Lease(s). *See also* Lease contract(s)
assignment of, 918
consumer, 366, 844
defined, 366
by nonowners, 378–380
Lease contract(s), 360–413. *See also* Contract(s); Uniform Commercial Code, Article 2 of
acceptance in, 369–371
communication of, 370
breach of
anticipatory, 398–399
remedies for, 408–409
of lessee, 402–406
of lessor, 399–402
limitation of, 407–408
risk of loss and, 381–382, 384–385
cancellation of
lessee's right to, 399, 402
lessor's right to, 399
consideration in, 371–372
defined, 366
formation of, 366–376
obligations under
of lessee, 391, 397–398
of lessor, 391–397
offer in, 366–369
terms of. *See* Term(s)
repudiation of, 396–397
anticipatory, 398–399
retraction of, 399
Statute of Frauds and, 372–374
Leased premises, use and maintenance of, 917
Legacy, legatee, 934
Legal encyclopedias, 5
Legal positivism, 14
Legal realism, 14
Legislative (substantive) rules, 7–8
Legitimate government interest, 48
Lessee
breach by, 382, 399–402
defined, 366
insolvent, 401
insurable interest of, 382
merchant as, duties of, upon rejection of goods, 405
obligations of, 391, 397–398
remedies of, 402–406
Lessor
breach by, 381–382, 402–406
defined, 366
goods reclaimed by, 401
insolvent, 379, 402
insurable interest of, 382
obligations of, 391–397
remedies of, 399–402
Levy, 511, 523
Lexis, 12
Liability(ies)
contingent, 457
joint, 691
joint and several, 691, 694–695, 827, 854
market-share, 428–429
primary, 456–457, 525
product. *See* Product liability
secondary, 457–458, 525
signature, 456–459
strict. *See* Strict liability
vicarious (indirect), 136n, 595, 597
warranty, 456n, 457n, 459–461, 897
without fault. *See* Strict liability
Libel, 95–96
Libel Terrorism Protection Act (proposed), 95
Libel tourism, 95
Library of Congress, 643
License, licensing
click-on (click-on agreement)(click-wrap agreement), 249–250
defined, 103, 910–911
of intellectual property, 127–128, 320n, 558, 670
revocation of, 103, 910
shrink-wrap (shrink-wrap agreement), 250–251
of software, 248
Licensee, 103, 127
Licensor, 127
Lien(s), 521–523

agricultural, 499n
artisan's, 103, 521–522, 895
bailee's, 895
on debtor's property, 538
defined, 415, 521
floating, 505–506
judicial, 498n, 521, 522–523
junior lienholder and, 512
mechanic's, 512, 521, 522
mortgage and, 523
possessory, 521–522, 895
statutory, 512, 521
warranty of title and, 415
Lilly Ledbetter Fair Pay Act (2009), 644
Limited liability company(ies) (LLC), 702, 706, 707–714, 730
choosing between LLP and, 717–718
compared with other major business forms, 771–772
defined, 706
management of, 712–713
nature of, 707–708
taxes and, 706, 707, 711, 718
Limited liability limited partnership (LLLP), 701, 702
Limited liability partnership (LLP), 683, 695–697, 702, 730
compared with other major business forms, 771–772
Limited (special) partnership(s), 683, 697–701, 702
compared with other major business forms, 771–772
comparison of general partnership and, 698
Lineal descendants, 938
Liquidation
Chapter 7, in bankruptcy, 529, 530–542, 543, 545, 546, 548
of corporation's assets, 744n, 746
defined, 529
Litigation. *See also* Case(s); Lawsuit(s)
arbitration versus, 565
avoiding, when contractor cannot perform, 350–351
defined, 70
frivolous or abusive, 100
workers' compensation versus, 615–616
Loan(s)
mortgage, 523–524
purchase-money, 463n
rescission of, 843n
Loss
of the bargain, 338
employment, 611
material, 392
risk of, 380–382, 384–385
Loyalty
defined, 759
duty of
agent's, 587, 590
breach of, 590
corporate directors', 759–760
corporate officers', 759–760
fiduciary's, 587, 689–690, 712, 713
joint venturers, 715
partner's, 689–690
trustee's, 943
Lucid interval, 272

M

Madrid Protocol, 137, 139
Magnuson-Moss Warranty Act (1975), 421–422
Mail
e-. *See* E-mail
sales through, 840–841
unsolicited merchandise sent by, 841
Mail Fraud Act (1990), 153
Mailbox rule, 247
Main purpose rule, 299, 526
Maker
act of, will revocation by, 936
defined, 441
liability of, 456
Malpractice, 74, 107, 864
Malware, 180
Management
customer relationship (CRM), 256–257
human resource (HRM), 658–659
top, attitude of, toward ethics, 196–197
total quality (TQM), 433
Manufacturing
abroad, 558–559
defects in products and, 426
or processing plant arrangement, as type of franchise, 671
Market concentration, 824–825
Marriage
engagement ring ownership and, 887
promises made in consideration of, 296, 299–300
status regarding, discrimination on basis of, 843
Mass layoff, 611–612
McCarran-Ferguson Act (1945), 828
Mediation
binding, 83
defined, 79
as form of ADR, 79
Medical Device Amendments (1976), 37, 430
Medicare, 616–617
Member of LLC, 707, 710, 712, 713
Mens rea (wrongful mental state), 148–149
Mental incapacity. *See* Mental incompetence
Mental incompetence
of agent or principal, agency termination and, 600
of bank customer, 477
contractual capacity and, 271–272
as defense
to criminal liability, 157
to liability on negotiable instrument, 462, 463
of offeror or offeree, offer termination and, 245
of party to personal-service contract, 328
of principal or agent, agency termination and, 600
Merchant(s)
both parties as, 370
as buyer, duties of, upon rejection of goods, 405
contracts between, special rules and, 301, 372
defined, 365–366
firm offer of, 369
as lessee, duties of, upon rejection of goods, 405
written confirmation between, 301
Mergers, 740–742, 824–826
Meta tags, 42, 126
Minerals, contract for sale of, 363–364
Minor(s). *See also* Children; Infancy
contractual capacity and, 269–271
defense to liability on negotiable instruments and, 462
as principal, 584n
Miranda rule, 161, 162–163
Mirror image rule, 244, 370

Misappropriation theory, 789, 790–791
Misdemeanors, 156
Misrepresentation
  by agent, 595
  fraudulent, 99, 290–295, 423. *See also* Fraud
  negligent, 99–100
  online personals and, 291
  product liability based on, 423
  reliance on, 99, 290, 294
  voluntary consent and, 290–295
Mistake(s). *See also* Error(s)
  bilateral (mutual), 288, 289–290
  as defense to criminal liability, 157
  unilateral, 288–289
  voluntary consent and, 288–290, 306
M'Naghten test, 157
Model Business Corporation Act (MBCA), 722
Money
  e-, 489–490
  fixed amount of, 444
  laundering of, 154–155, 185
  monetary systems and, 565–566
  right to receive, assignments and, 314
Monopolization, 818–821
  attempted, 818, 821–822
Monopoly, 813
Moral hazard, 491
Moral minimum, 194
Mortgage, 523–524
Mortgagee, mortgagor, 524
Motion(s)
  for directed verdict, 75
  to dismiss, 71
  for judgment
    as a matter of law, 75
    n.o.v. (notwithstanding the verdict), 75
    on the pleadings, 71
  for new trial, 75
  posttrial, 75
  pretrial, 71–72
  for summary judgment, 71–72
MP3, 134–136
Mutual fund, 784

N

Nation, 555
National Credit Union Shares Insurance Fund, 491
National Environmental Policy Act (NEPA)(1969), 847–848
National Information Infrastructure Protection Act (1996), 186
National Labor Relations Act (NLRA)(1935), 627–628, 631
National Labor Relations Board (NLRB), 17, 37, 629–630, 631
  creation of, 628
National origin
  discrimination on basis of, 569, 638, 639, 640–641, 843
  as suspect trait, 47
National Pollutant Discharge Elimination System (NPDES), 850
National Reporter System (West), 23, 24
National Securities Markets Improvement Act (1996), 780, 795
National Security Agency (NSA), 49
National White Collar Crime Center, 173
Necessaries, 270
Necessity
  as defense to criminal liability, 156
  easement or profit created by, 910
Negligence, 105–111
  of agent, 595–597
  comparative (fault), 109–110, 431
  contributory, 109
  criminal, 149
  defenses to, 108–110, 863
  defined, 105, 423
  elements of, 105
  gross, 91, 92, 107, 288–289, 689
  per se, 110
  product liability based on, 423, 430
  professionals' liability and, 861
  special doctrines and statutes regarding, 110–111
  strict liability and, 111–112, 846–847. *See also* Strict liability
  as unintentional tort, 92
  warehouse companies and, 899
Negotiable instrument(s), 438–495
  certificates of deposit (CD) as, 439, 441–442, 443n
  checks as. *See* Check(s)
  creation of, 223
  defined, 438
  dishonored, 455, 458, 475
  drafts as, 439
  incomplete, unauthorized completion of, 462
  liability on
    defenses to, 461–464
    discharge from, 463–464
    signature, 456–459
    warranty, 456n, 457n, 459–461
  negotiability of
    factors not affecting, 447–448
    requirements for, 442–448
  notes as. *See* Note(s); Promissory note
  overdue, HDC status and, 455
  signatures on, 443. *See also* Signature(s)
  transfer of
    by assignment, 314, 448
    by negotiation, 438, 448–449
    warranties and, 460
  types of, 439–442
    summarized, 439
  undated, 447
  use of, checklist for, 465
Negotiation(s)
  assisted, 82–83
  defined, 79, 448
  as form of ADR, 79
  preliminary, 238
  transfer of negotiable instruments by, 438, 448–449
New York Clearing House Interbank Payments Systems (CHIPS), 489
Ninth Amendment, 38, 49–50, 619
No Electronic Theft (NET) Act (1997), 134, 182
Nonconforming goods, 369, 370, 404–406
Nondeadly force, 156, 167
Nonemployees, harassment by, 646
Nonmerchant, one or both parties as, 370
Normal trade relations (NTR) status, 562
Norris-LaGuardia Act (1932), 627
Notarization, 255
Notary public, 590, 935n
Note(s), 441
  promissory, 439, 441
Notice(s)
  agent's duty of, 587

of assignment, 314–315
of claims or defenses, HDC status and, 455–456
constructive, 599
proper, 458
seasonable, 369
taking without, HDC status and, 454–456
timely, 401
Novation, 326–327, 708, 731
Nuclear Regulatory Commission (NRC), 847
Nuisance, 102, 846, 908, 917
Nutrition Labeling and Education Act (1990), 839–840

O

Obedience, agent's duty of, 587–588
Obligation(s)
of buyer, 391, 397–398
of lessee, 391, 397–398
of lessor, 391–397
primary, secondary obligation versus, 299
secondary, primary obligation versus, 299
of seller, 391–397
suspension of, 399
Obligor, obligee, 312, 313
Occupational Safety and Health Act (1970), 8, 614–615
Occupational Safety and Health Administration (OSHA), 8, 17, 614–615, 773
Ocean Dumping Act (Marine Protection, Research, and Sanctuaries Act) (1972), 852
Offer
of bribe, 153
contractual. *See* Contract(s), offer in; Lease contract(s), offer in; Sales contract(s), offer in
online, 248–249
settlement, 351
tender, 744
Offeree
counteroffer by, 244
death or incompetence of, offer termination and, 245
defined, 221, 237
rejection of offer by, 243–244
Offering circular, 673, 783
Offeror
assent of, 371
cancellation of offer by, 222–223
death or incompetence of, offer termination and, 245
defined, 221, 237
intent of, 237–241
revocation of offer by, 222–223, 242
Officers, corporate, 723
crimes of, 149–150, 726–727
duties of, 757–761
interests of, shareholders' interests and, 796
liability of, 149–150, 726–727, 761
role of, 757
torts of, 726–727
Oil marketing, exemption of, from antitrust laws, 828
Oil Pollution Act (1990), 852
Omission, act of, 148
Online contracts. *See* E-contract(s)
Online dispute resolution (ODR), 83
Operation of law
agency formation by, 586
agency termination by, 600
contract discharge by, 327–331
offer termination by, 244–245
will revocation by, 936–937
Opinion(s)
court decisions and, 29
from experts, 291–292
expression of, 206, 238
published, 12, 78
qualified, 862
statements of, 95, 99, 291, 415–416
types of, 29
unpublished, 12
Opportunity cost, 747
Order(s)
cease-and-desist, 628, 838
charging, 689
multiple product, 838
to pay, 439–441. *See also* Check(s)
unconditional, 443–444
for relief, 533, 543, 544
stop-payment, 476–477
unconditionality of, 444
Order instrument, 446–447
defined, 446
negotiating, 448
Ordinances, 6
Organized Crime Control Act (1970), 155
Outsiders, SEC Rule 10b-5 and, 789–791
Overdrafts, 475
Ownership
concurrent, 885–886
of property. *See* Personal property, ownership of; Property, ownership of; Real property, ownership interests in

P

PACER (Public Access to Court Electronic Records), 78
Pac-Man, 744
Parents, liability of, for minor's contract, 271
Parent-subsidiary merger, 742
Paris Convention of 1883, 137
Parol evidence rule, 287, 303–305
defined, 303
exceptions to, 304–305
UCC and, 304, 375–376
Partial performance
exception to perfect tender rule and, 395–396
exception to Statute of Frauds and, 300–301, 374
Participation, corporate director's right to, 755
Partner(s)
compensation of, 688
corporation as, 684
duties of, 689–691, 695
foreign, 687
general, 697
incoming, 691
interest of, in partnership, 688
liabilities of, 689–691, 693–695, 702
limited, 697
in limited (special) partnership, 697–701
in LLP, 695–697
rights of, 687–689
Partnership(s)
assets or profits of, accounting of, 688–689
basic concepts about, 683–685
compared with other major business forms, 771–772

defined, 684–685
duration, 686
entity versus aggregate theory of, 685
formation of, 685–687
general (ordinary). *See* General partnerships
joint ventures versus, 715–716
limited. *See* Limited (special) partnership(s)
management of, 687–688
operation of, 687–694
property of, 689
special. *See* Limited (special) partnership(s)
termination of, 694–695
trading, 690
Party(ies)
act of
agency termination and, 598–599
offer termination and, 242–244
agreement of
to conduct transactions electronically, 254–255
exception to perfect tender rule and, 393
conduct of, 223–224
potentially responsible (PRP), 854
secured. *See* Secured party(ies)
third. *See* Third party(ies)
Patents, 119, 127, 128–130, 131, 138, 558
Paycheck Fairness Act (2009), 643
Payee(s), 440
alternative or joint, 451
defined, 439
fictitious, 459
misspelled, 451
stacked, 451
Payment(s)
buyer's obligation to make, 397–398
at definite time, 444–446
on demand, 444–446
e-money, privacy and, 490
on international transactions, 565–566, 567
lease
lessee's obligation to make, 397–398
lessor's right to recover when due, 400
to order or to bearer, 446–447
promise to make. *See* Promise(s) to pay
Peer-to-peer (P2P) networking, 134–135
Penalty, 343
Pension Benefit Guaranty Corporation (PBGC), 617
Pension plans, 617
Pension Protection Act (2006), 617
Per se, 110
Perfect tender rule, 392–397
Perfection. *See* Security interest(s), perfection of
Performance
agent's duty of, 586–587
complete, 323, 346
contracts and, 224–225
course of, 229, 304, 366, 370, 375–376, 419
defined, 321
discharge of contract by, 323–326
partial. *See* Partial performance
to the satisfaction of a third party, 324–325
specific. *See* Specific performance
substantial, 323–324, 346
Performance obligations. *See* Obligation(s)
Person(s)
artificial legal, corporation as, 46, 60n, 149, 161, 530n, 684, 723, 744, 753, 843
natural, 723, 753, 843
Personal identification number (PIN), 487
Personal property, 884–904
bailed
bailee's duty to return, 897
bailee's right to use, 894
bailment of, 893. *See also* Bailment(s)
conversion and, 103–104, 157, 344, 379n, 891
defined, 102, 884
intangible, 362–363, 884, 893
ownership of, acquiring, 886–890
security interests in, 496–519
tangible, 362, 884, 893
trespass to, 103, 151, 157, 379n
Personal-service contracts
assignments and, 313
death or incapacity of party to, 328
delegations and, 315, 316
objective impossibility of performance and, 328
specific performance and, 346–347
Personalty, 103, 379n, 884. *See also* Personal property
Pesticides, 851, 853
Petitioner, 29
Petty offenses, 156
Phishing, 176–177
Physical presence, 725
Picketing, 628, 631
Piercing the corporate veil, 724, 736–737
Plain meaning rule, 227, 228
Plaintiff
complaint of, 70–71
defined, 11, 25, 29
Plant life, as real property, 906
Plea bargaining, 158
Pleadings, 70–71
Pledge, 503
Point-of-sale systems, 487
Poison pill, 744
Police powers, 36–37
Pollution, 846–847
air, 848–849
oil, 852
water, 849–852
Ponzi schemes, 801
Pornography, 42–43, 184
Portability, 442
Possession
acquisition of personal property by, 886–887
adverse, 887, 910, 913–914
bailee's right of, 894
debtor in (DIP), 544
delivery of, 893
peaceful, 510–511
perfection of security interest by, 503
Postal Reorganization Act (1970), 841
Postdating, 447, 476
Power(s)
of avoidance, 537
condemnation, 914–915
market, 814
monopoly, 814, 819
monopsony, 821

strong-arm, 537
Power of attorney, 589–590
defined, 589
durable, 590n
writing requirement and, 584n
Precedent, 10–11, 12
Predominant-factor test, 364
Preemption, 17, 37, 132, 430
Pregnancy, discrimination on basis of, 642
Pregnancy Discrimination Act (1978), 642
Preliminary prospectus, 782
Prescription, easement or profit created by, 910
Presentment
of checks, electronic, 486–487
defined, 445
proper, 457–458
warranties regarding, 460–461
Pretext (excuse), 640, 643, 649
Pretexting, 52
Pretrial conference, 73
Price(s)
buyout, 693, 714
discrimination and, 822–823
predatory bidding and, 821
predatory pricing and, 818, 821–822
purchase, seller's right to recover, 400
Price lists, contractual offers versus, 239
Principal(s)
agency termination by, 599
agent's duties to, 586–588, 590
bankruptcy of, agency termination and, 600
death or insanity of, agency termination and, 600
defined, 580
disclosure status of, 592–593
duties of, to agent, 588–589
liability of, 592–598
minor as, 584n
torts of, 594
Prior dealing (course of dealing), 229, 304, 366, 370, 375–376, 419
Privacy Act (1974), 50
Privacy right(s), 48–51
e-money and, 490
employee, 619–622, 632
invasion of, 97–98
protecting
Constitution and, 49–50, 97, 619
federal statutes, 50–51
Private equity capital, 739–740
Private Securities Litigation Reform Act (1995), 789, 872–873
Privilege, 96–97
confidentiality and, 874
Privity of contract, 311, 317, 318, 319, 423, 424, 865, 866
Probable cause, 94, 158–160
Proceeds from disposition of collateral, 504, 514
Process server, 71
Product(s). *See also* Goods
consumer, safety and, 842
defects in, 425–428
bailor's duty to reveal, 897
trademarks and, 124
unreasonably dangerous, 425
Product liability, 92, 414
defenses to, 430–432
defined, 423
misrepresentation and, 423
negligence and, 423, 430
strict, 111–112, 423–429
requirements for, 425
Product misuse, 431
Production, acquisition of personal property by, 887
Professionals. *See also* Accountant(s); Attorney(s)
duty of care of, 107
liability of, 860–879
Profit(s)
maximization of, 195–196
in real property law, 906, 909–910
short-swing, 791, 794
Promise(s)
absolute, 321
collateral, 296, 298–299
defined, 218
illusory, 266–267
to pay, 439. *See also* Certificate(s), of deposit; Note(s); Promissory note
unconditional, 443–444
to ship, 246n, 369
unconditionality of, 444
Promisor, promisee, 219
Promissory estoppel, 242. *See also* Detrimental reliance
defined, 268
exception to Statute of Frauds and, 301
requirements to establish, 268
Promissory note, 439, 441. *See also* Note(s)
Proof
burden of, 146, 164
of claim, 535
Property
abandoned, 891–892
after-acquired, 504–505
community, 535, 886
crimes involving, 151–152, 173–179
defense of, 93
defined, 884
disparagement of, 104
intangible, 362–363, 884, 893
intellectual. *See* Intellectual property
jurisdiction over (*in rem* jurisdiction), 58–60
lost, 890–891, 900
mislaid, 890
ownership of, 885–886
personal. *See* Personal property
real. *See* Real property
right of publicity as, 98–99
tangible, 362, 884, 893
Prosecution
of cyber crimes, 185–186
immunity from, 158
malicious, 100
Prospectus, 781, 782, 870n
Protect Act (Prosecutorial Remedies and Other Tools to end the Exploitation of Children Today)(2003), 43
Protected class(es)
defined, 638
employment discrimination against members of. *See* Employment discrimination, on basis of
illegal contracts and, 279
Protected expression, 132–133, 565. *See also* Copyright(s)
Proximate cause, 108, 109, 416n
Proxy, 762

Proxy materials, 762, 763
Public accounting firms, 867
Public Company Accounting Oversight Board, 798, 867
Public figures
 actual malice and, 97
 parodies of, 94
Public policy
 contracts contrary to, 273–279
 exceptions to employment-at-will doctrine based on, 608
 strict product liability and, 424
Publication
 defamation and, 95–96
 of information placing person in false light, 97
 of will, 936
Publicity, right of, 98–99
Public-key infrastructure, 251
Puffery, puffing (seller's talk), 99, 291, 416, 836
Purchase price, seller's right to recover, 400
Purchase-money security interest (PMSI)
 in consumer goods, 503–504, 506n
 defined, 503
 perfection of, 503–504, 506n, 507–508, 515
Purchaser(s). *See also* Buyer(s)
 bona fide, 537
 good faith, 379
Purdue Pharma, 195
Pure Food and Drugs Act (1906), 841
Purpose
 achievement of, agency termination and, 599
 frustration of, 331
 proper, 768

Q

Quality
 mistake of, 288
 slander of (trade libel), 104
Quality circles, 433
Quantum meruit, 349
Question(s)
 of fact, 68, 72
 federal, 61
 of law, 68, 72
Quid pro quo harassment, 644–645
Quo warranto proceeding, 735n
Quorum, 742, 755, 763–764
Quotas, 560, 570

R

Race
 BFOQ defense and, 655
 discrimination on basis of, 74, 569, 638, 639, 640–641, 843
 as suspect trait, 47
Ratification
 agency formation by, 585
 of contract, 225
  by minor, 270
  by principal, 592
 defined, 270, 585
 express, 270, 592
 implied, 270, 592
Rational basis test, 47, 48
Real estate. *See* Land; Real property
Real property, 905–923. *See also* Land
 defined, 102, 296, 884, 905
 goods associated with, 363–364
 nature of, 905–907
 ownership interests in, 907–911
  nonpossessory, 909–911
  transfer of, 911–915
 rights in, assignments and, 314
 sale of, contract(s) for, 326
  breach of, remedies for, 339
 "things attached" to, sale of, 364. *See also* Fixtures
Realty. *See* Land; Real property
Reasonable manner, 94, 369, 391
Reasonable person standard, 40, 93, 105–106, 220, 244, 267, 320, 324
Reasonably foreseeable users, liability to, 867
Rebuttal, 532
Receiver, 544, 746
Record(s)
 attribution and, 255
 defined, 252
 financial, privacy and, 490
 sending and receiving, 255–256
Redemption rights, 514–515
Reformation, 276, 292, 347–348
Refusal to deal, 821
Registration
 of domain name, 125
 of securities, 779, 781–782
 trademark, 121–122
Regulated industries, exemption of, from antitrust laws, 828
Reimbursement
 corporate director's right to, 756
 principal's duty of, 588
 right of, 527
Rejection
 of goods
  by buyer or lessee, 398, 404–405
  reason for, 405
 of offer, 243–244
Release, 691
 of collateral, 508, 510
 defined, 267
 from secured party, 508, 510
 settlement of claim and, 267–268
Relevant market, 819–820
Reliance
 detrimental, 242, 268, 319. *See also* Promissory estoppel
 justifiable, 99, 290, 294, 794
Religion
 accommodation of, 44
 discrimination on basis of, 569, 638, 639, 641–642, 843
 establishment clause and, 43–45
 ethical standards and, 200
 free exercise clause and, 43, 45
 freedom of, 38, 43–45
Remailer, 186
Remedy(ies)
 defined, 11, 337
 in equity, 11–13, 337–338, 344–348
 exclusive, 407
 judicial, 511
 at law, 11–13, 337–338. *See also* Damages
 limitation of, 349–350, 407–408
 prejudgment, 404, 522, 523
Rent, 918
Reorganization, bankruptcy. *See* Bankruptcy

Replevin, 404
Reply, 71
Reporters, reports, 23
Repossession, "self-help," 510–511
Res ipsa loquitur, 110
Resales of securities, 784–785
Rescission. *See also* Cancellation
of contract, 11, 288, 289, 292, 794, 843
contract discharge by, 326
defined, 265
of loan, 843n
mutual, 326, 344
new contract and, 265
restitution and, 344
unilateral, 344
Residuary, residuum, 934
Resource Conservation and Recovery Act (RCRA)(1976), 853–854
Respondeat superior, 595–598, 599, 726
Responsible corporate officer doctrine, 149–150
Restatement (Second) of Agency, 581n, 597
Restatement (Second) of Contracts, 223n, 249
Restatement (Second) of Torts, 425, 866
Restatement (Third) of Torts: Products Liability, 425–428
Restatements of the Law, 5. *See also individual restatements*
citation to, 27
defined, 223n
Restitution, 344
Restraint(s)
against alienation, 314
on trade. *See also* Antitrust law(s)
contracts as, 274–276
defined, 812
horizontal, 815–816
vertical, 815, 817–818
Revised Model Business Corporation Act (RMBCA), 722
Revised Uniform Limited Partnership Act (RULPA), 697
Revocation. *See also* Cancellation
of agent's authority, by principal, 599
of bankruptcy discharge, 542
of buyer's or lessee's acceptance of goods, 405
declaration of, 936
defined, 242
of license, 103, 910
of offer, 222–223, 242
of will, 936–937
RICO (Racketeer Influenced and Corrupt Organizations Act)(1970), 155, 869n
Right(s)
airspace, 906
appraisal, 742–743
assignment of. *See* Assignment(s)
of inspection. *See* Inspection(s), right of
preemptive, 766–767
principle of, 201
redemption, 514–515
subsurface, 906
survivorship, 885, 886, 937n
voidable, 537–538
Right to Financial Privacy Act (1978), 50, 490
Risk
assumption of, 108, 430
defined, 925
foreseeable, 106–107, 114
of loss, 380–382, 384–385
management of, 925, 944
obvious, 106
Rivers and Harbors Appropriations Act (1899), 849–850
Robbery, 150
Robinson-Patman Act (1936), 822–823
Rulemaking, 7–8, 18

S

Safe Drinking Water Act (1974), 851
Safety
consumer protection and, 841–842
in workplace. *See* Workplace, safety in
Sale(s)
consumer, 383
consumer protection and, 840–841
defined, 362
door-to-door, 244n, 840
mail-order, 840–841
by nonowners, 378–380
telephone, 840–841
Sales contract(s), 360–413. *See also* Contract(s); Uniform Commercial Code, Article 2 of
acceptance in, 246n, 369–371
communication of, 370
breach of
anticipatory, 398–399
as defense to liability on negotiable instrument, 462
defined, 3, 337
remedies for, 408–409
of buyer, 402–406
damages as, 314, 338–339. *See also* Damages
limitation of, 349, 407–408
of seller, 399–402
risk of loss and, 381–382, 384–385
cancellation of
buyer's right to, 399, 402
seller's right to, 399
consideration in, 371–372
lack or failure of, 462
defined, 362
formation of, 366–376
international. *See* International contract(s)
law governing
major differences between general contract law and, 373
relationship of, with general contract law, illustrated, 362
between merchants, special rules and, 301
mirror image rule and, 244n, 370
obligations under
of buyer, 391, 397–398
of seller, 391–397
offer in, 366–369
counteroffer and, 370
terms of. *See* Term(s)
ongoing, duration of, 368
performance and, 368
repudiation of, 396–397
anticipatory, 398–399
retraction of, 399
rescission of, 326
Statute of Frauds and, 296, 300, 301, 372–374
subsequently modified, 304
Sample court case, 29–31
Sarbanes-Oxley Act (2002), 166, 272, 726n, 778–779, 780, 793, 798–800, 860–861, 867–869, 873

key provisions of, 799, 868
Web-based reporting systems and, 197–198
Satisfaction
accord and
contract discharge by, 327
settlement of claim by, 267
defined, 267, 327
Schools of legal thought, 13–14
Scienter, 293–294, 792
Screening procedures, 622
Searches and seizures, unreasonable, constitutional prohibition of, 38, 49, 158–160, 615n, 621, 723
Second Amendment, 38–39
Secured party(ies)
bankruptcy property distribution and, 539
defined, 497
release from, 508, 510
remedies of, 510–515
rights and duties of, 508–510
rules of priority among claims and, 506
value given by, 498
Secured transaction(s). *See also* Secured party(ies); Security interest(s)
concept of, 497
defined, 496
terminology of, 497
Securities Act (truth-in-securities bill)(1933), 779–786, 787, 795, 800, 867, 869–870, 871, 873
Securities Act Amendments (1990), 780
Securities and Exchange Commission (SEC), 7
creation of, 780
EDGAR system of, 780, 781
expanding regulatory powers of, 780
global accounting rules adopted by, 863
major responsibilities of, 780
provisions of, relating to proxies and shareholder proposals, 762, 763
Public Company Accounting Oversight Board and, 798, 867
Regulation A of, 782–783
Regulation D of, 783–784
Rule 10b-5 of, 786–791
Section 16(b) compared with, 792
rules requiring attorney to report client's misconduct implemented by, 874
securities exchanges overseen by, 202n
securities law violations enforced by, 785–786, 793–794, 870
Securities Enforcement Remedies and Penny Stock Reform Act (1990), 780
Securities Exchange Act (1934), 780, 782, 786–795, 795, 867, 870–872, 873
Section 10(b) of, 786–791
Section 16(b) of, 791
Rule 10b-5 compared with, 792
Securities Litigation Uniform Standards Act (SLUSA)(1998), 789
Securities Offering Reform, 782n
Security(ies). *See also* Bond(s); Securities Act; Securities and Exchange Commission; Securities Exchange Act; Stock(s)
debt, 738. *See also* Bond(s)
defined, 738, 778, 779–781
equity, 738. *See also* Stock(s)
registration of, 779, 781–782
regulation of, 778–807
state, 279
restricted, 784–785
traded on exchanges, 202n
Security interest(s), 415
assignment of, 508
authentication and, 498
creating, 497–498
defined, 379, 497
in inventory, 507–508
perfection of, 498–504, 515
by attachment, 502–504
automatic, 503–504
defined, 498
effective time of, 504
by filing, 499–502, 515. *See also* Financing statement, filing of
methods of, types of collateral and, summarized, 500
by possession, 503
without filing, 502–504
in personal property, 496–519
priority of claims to debtor's collateral and, 506–508, 509, 515
scope of, 504–506
Self-incrimination, compulsory, constitutional prohibition of, 38, 158, 161, 162–163, 723–724
Seller(s)
breach by, 381–382, 402–406
goods held by, 381
goods reclaimed by, 401
insolvent, 379, 402
insurable interest of, 382
issues to note, 385
as licensor, 248
obligations of, 391–397
place of business of, 391
remedies of, 399–402
residence of, 391
Sentencing Reform Act (1984), 164
September 11, 2001 terrorist attacks, 48, 181, 928
Service mark, 123, 138, 140
Services, goods combined with, 364–365
Settlement(s)
of claims, 267–268
offer in, 351
Seventh Amendment, 38, 73
Sexual harassment, 205, 644–647, 648, 659
Share exchange, 741–742
Shareholder(s), 723
approval of, 742
duties of, 769–771
interests of, corporate officers' interests and, 796
liabilities of, 724, 736–737, 769–771
majority, 729, 764–765
meetings of, 762–763
minority, 729, 764–765, 770–771
powers of, 761–762
rights of, 742–743, 766–769
role of, 761–766
voting by, 742, 763–766
Sharia, 16, 67, 599
Sherman Antitrust Act (1890), 566–567, 812, 813–822, 824, 827–828, 830
Shipment, 246n, 369. *See also* Delivery
Short-form merger, 742, 743
Shrink-wrap agreement (shrink-wrap license), 250–251
Sight drafts, 440
Signature(s). *See also* Indorsement(s)
of agent, 458
defined, 369n, 443
digital, 251
digitized handwritten, 251
of drawer, forged, 477–480

electronic, 251–252
forged, 477–480
handwritten statement as, 443
merchant's firm offer and, 369
on negotiable instruments
forgery and, 477–480
liability for, 456–459
as requirement, 443
unauthorized, 458–459
on will, 935
Signature dynamics, 251
Silence
as acceptance, 246
misrepresentation by, 292–293
Sixth Amendment, 38, 158, 161–163
Slander, 95–96
Small Business Administration, 531
Small Business Administration Act (1958), 828
Smart cards, 489
Social hosts, 111
Social networks, cyberstalking on, 178–179
Social Security, 616
Social Security Act (OASDI)(1935), 616
Social Security Administration, 52, 616
Sociological school, 14
Software
antiplagiarism, 187
copyright protection for, 134
file-sharing, 134–136
filtering, 42, 619
malware and, 180
"sale" of, 248, 250–251
Sole proprietorships, 669–670
compared with other major business forms, 771–772
Spam (junk e-mail), 182–183
Specific performance, 300, 345–347
buyer's or lessee's right to obtain, 402–403
in construction contracts, 347n
defined, 11, 345
in land sale contracts, 339, 345–346
Speech
commercial, 41–42, 723
freedom of, 38, 39–43, 63, 68, 94, 206, 429, 619, 631, 723
obscene, 42–43
political, corporate, 40–41, 723
symbolic, 39–40
unprotected, 42–43. *See also* Defamation
Spouse, surviving, intestacy laws and, 938
Standing to sue, 44, 64–65, 532
Starbucks Coffee Company, 383, 563
Stare decisis, 10–11, 16
State(s)
administrative agencies of, 7
codes of, 22
constitution of, 5, 6, 48–49
courts of. *See* State court systems
foreign, 557
laws of, 6
governing e-signatures, 251–252
governing workers' compensation, 15, 108, 615–616. *See also* Workers' compensation
layoff notices required by, 612
prohibiting employment discrimination, 657–658
powers of, limits on, 38–39
regulation by, 7, 17–18
of environment, 847
of franchises, 673–674
police powers and, 36–37
of securities, 279, 795
of spam, 183
State court systems, 66–68. *See also* Court(s)
appellate courts of, 66, 67–68
decisions of, 23, 25
citations to, 26
following case through, 70–77
illustrated, 65
judges in, 66
supreme (highest) courts of, 23, 29, 58, 68, 77
trial courts of, 60–61, 66–67
Statement(s)
bank, examination of, 478–479
continuation, 504
environmental impact (EIS), 847–848
of fact, 94–95, 99
financial, 862–863
financing. *See* Financing statement
of intention, 238
of opinion, 95, 99, 291, 415–416
proxy, 791–792
registration, 781–782
termination, 510
of value, 415–416
Statistical sampling, 875
Statute(s). *See also* Law(s)
arbitration, 80–81
assignments prohibited by, 312–313
contracts contrary to, 272–273
dram shop, 111
estray, 891
federal, 6
of Frauds. *See* Statute of Frauds
Good Samaritan, 111
licensing, 273
of limitations. *See* Statute of limitations
long arm, 59–60
as primary source of law, 5
recording, 912–913
of repose, 430n
state. *See* State(s), laws of
workers' compensation. *See* Workers' compensation
Statute of Frauds, 287, 296–303, 365n
CISG and, 302, 383
contracts subject to, 296, 303, 348, 584n, 685
defined, 296
exceptions to, 300–301, 372–374
one-year rule and, 296, 297–298, 348n, 609, 893
UCC and, 296, 300, 301, 372–374
writing requirement and, 296–303
sufficiency of writing and, 302–303, 306, 372
Statute of limitations
contracts and, 327–328
as defense to criminal liability, 158
defined, 48, 71
product liability and, 430
for seeking deficiency judgment, 514
under UCC, 408
Statutory law
defined, 6

finding, 22–23
Stock(s), 738–739
bonds versus, 739
common, 738–739, 747
preferred, 738, 739, 747
purchase of, gaining control of corporation by, 743–744
types of, 740
watered, 770
Stock buybacks, 198
Stock options, 198, 796
Stop Counterfeiting in Manufactured Goods Act (SCMGA), 124
Stored communications, 620
Stored Communications Act (SCA), 620
Stored-value cards, 489
Strict liability
bystanders and, 429
common carriers and, 897–898
defined, 111
innkeepers and, 899
negligence and, 111–112, 846–847
product liability and. *See* Product liability, strict
requirements for, 425
Strict scrutiny, 47, 657
Strike, 631
Subject matter
destruction of
impossibility of performance and, 328
offer termination and, 245
jurisdiction over, 60
Sublease, 918
Subpoena, 773
Subrogation, right of, 527
Summons, 71
Superfund (Comprehensive Environmental Response, Compensation, and Liability Act)(CERCLA)(1980), 854, 855
Superseding cause, 109
Supervisors, harassment by, 645–646
Supremacy clause, 37
Supreme court
state (highest), 23, 29, 58, 68, 77
United States. *See* United States Supreme Court
Supreme Court Reporter (S.Ct.)(West), 25
citation to, 26
Suretyship, surety, 525–528
Suspect trait, 47
Syndicate (investment group), 716
Synthetic identity theft, 176

T

Takeover, corporate, 743–744
defenses to, terminology of, 744
defined, 743
Taking, 914–915
in good faith, HDC status and, 453–454
of private property, for public use, 38, 914–915, 919
for value, HDC status and, 452–453
without notice, HDC status and, 454–456
Tariffs, 560–561, 570
Tax, taxation
deleveraging (repurchasing debt) and, 802–803
double, 711, 724
export, 559
on imports, 560–561, 570
Medicare, 616–617
offshore low-tax jurisdictions and, 724–726
on online sales, 363, 725
pass-through entity and, 685, 696
Social Security, 581, 582, 584, 601, 616–617
tariffs and, 560–561, 570
unemployment, 582, 584, 601, 617
withholding, 581, 584, 601
Tax Reform Act (1976), 50
Technology(ies)
acceptance of offer and, 247
e-signature, 251
file-sharing, 134–136
maximum achievable control (MACT), 849
Telemarketing, 838–839, 840
Telemarketing and Consumer Fraud and Abuse Prevention Act (1994), 839
Telephone Consumer Protection Act (TCPA)(1991), 838–839
Telephone Records and Privacy Protection Act, 52
Tenancy. *See also* Tenant(s)
in common, 377, 885
fixed-term (tenancy for years), 915–916
joint, 885–886, 937n
periodic, 916
at sufferance, 916
at will, 916
Tenant(s). *See also* Tenancy
defined, 916
in partnership, 689n
Tender
defined, 323
of delivery, 378, 391
of performance, 323
self-, 744
Tender offer, 744
Tenth Amendment, 6, 38
Term(s)
additional, 370–371
consistent, 375
striking of, 371
ambiguous, 304
browse-wrap, 251
definiteness of, 241
definitions of, 380
generic, trademarks and, 123, 140
handwritten, 447
interpretation of contracts and, 229, 376
open, 367–369
open delivery, 368
open payment, 367
open price, 367
open quantity, 368–369
partnership for, 686
shrink-wrap agreements and, 250–251
Territorial restrictions, 817
Terrorism, 568–569
Testator, 933
Testing the waters, 783
Theft, 344
cyber, 175–177
identity, 175–176, 188, 845
of trade secrets, 137, 154
Third Amendment, 38, 49–50, 619
Third party(ies)
liability to
of accountants and other professionals, 865–867

of attorneys, 867
rights of, 311–321, 332
satisfaction of, performance to, 324–325
Thirteenth Amendment, 346
Time
for acceptance of offer, 247–248
of contract formation, 272, 317, 396, 420
for contract performance, 393
effective, of perfection of security interest, 504
for employee travel, 597
for examination of bank statements, 478–479
float, 484
lapse of
agency termination and, 598
offer termination and, 244–245
for proper presentment, 457–458
reasonable, 94, 242, 245, 370, 381, 391, 392n, 398, 405, 422, 484n, 598, 794n
for rejection of goods, 405
required for adverse possession, 913
for seeking deficiency judgment, 514
UETA and, 255–256
Time drafts, 440
Time instruments, 439, 455
Tippees, 790
Tipper/tippee theory, 789, 790
Title(s)
case, 25, 29
defined, 377, 885
document of. *See* Document(s) of title
good, 415
passage of, 378–380
slander of, 104
void, 378–379
voidable, 379
warranty of, 415
Tort(s), 90–118
business, 90, 101–102
classifications of, 92–104
cyber, 90, 112–113
defined, 90
intentional. *See* Intentional tort(s)
international claims in, 567–569
law of, basis of, 91–92
lawsuit for, criminal prosecution for same act versus, 147, 148
reform and, 92
Tort theory, exceptions to employment-at-will doctrine based on, 607–608
Tortfeasor, 92, 105
Toxic chemicals, 852–853
Toxic substances, 853
Toxic Substances Control Act (1976), 853
Trade
barriers to, minimizing, 562
restraints on. *See* Restraint(s) on trade
usage of, 229, 304, 366, 375–376, 419
Trade associations, 816
Trade dress, 124, 138
Trade libel (slander of quality), 104
Trade names, 124–125, 500–501, 670
Trade secrets, 127, 136–137, 138, 154, 558
Trademarks, 119, 120–128, 127–128, 138, 140, 320n, 558, 670
Trading with the Enemy Act (1917), 559
Transaction(s)
defined, 253
parties agree to conduct electronically, 254–255
Transfer(s)
fraudulent, 538
fund
commercial, 489
consumer, 488–489
electronic. *See* Electronic fund transfer(s)
unauthorized, 488
of shares, 728–729, 768
Transgender persons, 643
Treaties, 555
Trespass, 102–103, 151, 157, 379n
Trial(s)
by jury, right to, 38, 73, 161
mini-, 82–83
procedures at, 74–75
summary jury (SJT), 83
Trial courts, 23
federal (U.S. district), 60, 68, 69, 529
state, 60–61, 66–67
TRIPS (Trade-Related Aspects of Intellectual Property Rights) Agreement, 137–138
Trojan horse, 176
Troubled Asset Relief Program (TARP), 200
Trust(s), 940–943
beneficial interest in, as collateral, 498
business, 716
charitable, 941
constructive, 943
defined, 940
express, 940–941
implied, 941–942
living *(inter vivos)*, 937, 940–941
resulting, 941–942
spendthrift, 941
testamentary, 941
Totten, 941
Trustee(s)
bankruptcy, 532, 537–538
corporate directors and, 754
successor, 940
of trust, 940, 943
United States, 531, 532
Truth-in-Lending Act (TILA)(1968), 843–844
Truth-in-Lending Simplification and Reform Act (1980), 843n
Twenty-seventh Amendment, 37n
Twitter, tweeting (postings) by corporate bloggers, 787
Tying arrangement (tie-in sales agreement), 824
Typosquatting, 126

U

UCC. *See* Uniform Commercial Code
Ultra vires acts, 734, 745
Ultramares rule, 865–866
Unconscionability
defined, 276, 376
prima facie, 408
procedural, 276, 277
substantive, 276–277
under UCC, 276, 376, 408
warranty disclaimers and, 421
Underwriter, 925
Undue influence
contract illegal through, 280

voluntary consent and, 295
Unemployment compensation, 581
Uniform Arbitration Act, 80
Uniform Commercial Code (UCC), 219, 223, 360, 906
adoption of, 6, 361
Article 1 (General Provisions) of, 6n
Article 2 (Sales Contracts) of, 361. *See also* Sales contract(s)
E-SIGN Act and, 252
franchising under, 671
puffery and, 99n, 416
scope of, 362–366
UETA and, 253
warranties under, 99n, 414–422
Article 2A (Leases) of, 361
E-SIGN Act and, 252
scope of, 366
UETA and, 253
warranties under, 414–422, 897
Article 3 (Negotiable Instruments) of, 6n, 361, 438, 451, 471
Article 4 (Bank Deposits and Collections) of, 6n, 361, 438–439, 471
Article 4A (Funds Transfers) of, 361, 487
Article 5 (Letters of Credit) of, 6n, 361
Article 6 (Bulk Transfers) of, 361
Article 7 (Documents of Title) of, 6n, 361, 897, 899
Article 8 (Investment Securities) of, 6n, 795
Article 9 (Secured Transactions) of, 6n, 361, 496, 503, 510, 514, 520
CISG compared with, 383–384, 556
citation to, 27
commercial reasonableness under, 367, 368, 390, 453, 513
consideration under, 265n
creation of, 6
entrustment rule under, 379–380
fictitious payee rule of, 459
good faith and, 367, 368, 371, 390, 453
imposter rule of, 459
origins of, 361
parol evidence rule and, 304, 375–376
passage of title under, 378–380
penalties and, 343
perfect tender rule under, 392–397
periodic changes and updates to, 361
remedy(ies) for breach under
limitation of, 349, 407–408
rescission of contract under, 326
risk of loss under, 380–382, 384–385
rules of construction under, 376
signatures under, 369n
Statute of Frauds under, 296, 300, 301, 372–374
statute of limitations under, 408
unconscionability under, 276, 376, 408
waiver under, 267n
Uniform Electronic Transactions Act (UETA), 247, 251–256, 594, 609
Uniform Limited Liability Company Act (ULLCA), 707
Uniform Limited Partnership Act (ULPA), 697
Uniform Partnership Act (UPA), 684
Uniform Probate Code (UPC), 934
Uniform Residential Landlord and Tenant Act (URLTA), 917
Uniform resource locators (URLs), 28
Uniform Securities Act, 795
Uniform Trade Secrets Act, 137
Unintentional torts, 92, 105–111. *See also* Negligence
Union shop, 628
Unions, 627–631
collective bargaining and, 630–631
elections and, 629–630
labor laws and, 627–629
organization by, 629–630
strikes and, 631
United Nations
Commission of, on International Trade Law, 556
Convention of
on Contracts for the International Sale of Goods. *See* CISG
on the Recognition and Enforcement of Foreign Arbitral Awards (New York Convention), 564, 565
General Assembly of, 555
United States Bureau of the Census, 532
United States Citizenship and Immigration Services, 623
United States Code (U.S.C.), 22
citation to, 27
"gaps in," 529n
United States Code Annotated (U.S.C.A.)(West), 22
United States Constitution
amendments to. *See* Bill of Rights; *individual amendments*
bankruptcy provisions under, 549
brevity of, 32
commerce clause of, 33–37
compulsory self-incrimination prohibited by, 38, 158, 161, 162–163, 723–724
cruel and unusual punishment prohibited by, 38, 161
double jeopardy prohibited by, 38, 160–161, 723
due process clause of, 38, 46–47, 91–92, 158, 160, 522, 723
equal protection clause of, 46, 47–48, 656
establishment clause of, 43–45
excessive bail or fines prohibited by, 38, 161
export taxes prohibited by, 559
federal courts under, 58, 59, 61, 65, 68, 69
free exercise clause of, 43, 45
freedom of contract protected by, 220, 263
intellectual property protected by, 119
powers of government under, 32–37
as primary source of law, 5
privacy rights and, 49–50, 97, 619
privileges and immunities clause of, 724
protections guaranteed by, 158–163. *See also individual protections*
supremacy clause of, 37
as supreme law of the land, 6
takings clause of, 38, 914–915, 919
treaty ratification under, 555
unreasonable searches and seizures prohibited by, 38, 49, 158–160, 615n, 621, 723
United States Copyright Office, 131
United States Department of Agriculture (USDA), 839–840
United States Department of Defense, 180, 847
United States Department of Health and Human Services
Food and Drug Administration of, 7. *See also* Food and Drug Administration
Office for Civil Rights (OCR) in, 51
United States Department of Homeland Security
United States Citizenship and Immigration Services of, 623n
United States Immigration and Customs Enforcement (ICE) of, 623, 624–626
United States Department of the Interior, 847
United States Department of Justice (DOJ), 64, 172, 207
antitrust laws enforced by, 826–827
exporters certified by, 828
merger guidelines of, 825–826
purchase of assets guidelines of, 743
securities law violations enforced by, 785, 870

United States Department of Labor (DOL), 615, 617
  environmental matters regulated by, 847
  Labor Certification application reviewed by, 626
United States Department of Transportation, 653
United States Department of Veterans Affairs, 187
United States Immigration and Customs Enforcement (ICE), 623, 624–626
United States Patent and Trademark Office (USPTO), 121–122, 131
  Web site of, 128
United States Postal Service, 247, 490, 727, 840
United States Reports (U.S.), 25
  citation to, 26
United States Sentencing Commission, 164, 166, 726n
United States Statutes at Large, 22
United States Supreme Court, 10, 23
  appeals to, 69–70, 77
  foreign law and, 39
  jurisdiction of, 59, 69
  justice of, 29
  rule of four of, 70
  Web site of, 78
Unjust enrichment, 225–227, 344, 348
Unlawful Internet Gambling Enforcement Act (2006), 185
U.S. Safe Web Act (Undertaking Spam, Spyware, and Fraud Enforcement and Enforcers Beyond Borders Act)(2006), 183
USA Patriot Act (Uniting and Strengthening America by Providing Appropriate Tools Required to Intercept and Obstruct Terrorism Act) (2001), 48, 49
Usury, 272, 281
Utilitarianism, 201

V

Value(s)
  given by secured party, 498
  legal, 263
  mistake of, 288
  par, 770
  statement of, 415–416
  taking for, HDC status and, 452–453
Vegetation, as real property, 906
Venture capital, venture capitalists, 739–740
Venue, 63–64, 178–179
Verdict, 75, 146
Vertically integrated firms, 817
Vesting, 318–319, 617
Violence Against Women Act (1994), 36n
Virtual cash, 489
Virus, 180, 182
Visas, 625–627
Vishing, 177
Voice over Internet Protocol (VoIP) service, 177
Voting lists, 764

W

Wage(s)
  discrimination in, 642, 643–644
  garnishment of, 523
  hours and, 608–611
  minimum, 610
  overtime and, 610–611
Waiver, 267n, 762n
Walsh-Healey Act (1936), 609
War, agency termination and, 600
Warehouse companies, 899
Warehouse receipt, 361, 378, 381, 899
Warning(s)
  defects and, 427–428
  duty to provide, 106, 114
  video games and, 429
Warrant(s)
  general, 159
  inspections without, 615n
  search, 158–160, 615n
  stock, 767
Warranty(ies), 414–422
  breach of
    agent's unauthorized acts and, 593–594
    as defense to liability on negotiable instrument, 462
    recovery for, 460
  express, 415–416, 419–420, 422
  full, 422
  implied. *See* Implied warranty(ies)
  limited, 422
  Magnuson-Moss Warranty Act and, 421–422
  overlapping, 419–420
  presentment, 460–461
  of title, 415
  transfer, 460
  under UCC, 99n, 414–422
Water Quality Act (1987), 850
Webb-Pomerene Act (1918), 828
West Group, 22, 24, 25, 28
Westlaw©, 12, 25
  citation to, 28
Wetlands, 851
Whistleblower Protection Act (1989), 608
Whistleblowing, 608
White knight, 744
Will(s), 932–938
  defined, 932
  holographic (olographic), 935
  nuncupative (deathbed), 935
  ownership of property transferred by, 913
  partnership at, 686
  probate of, 937
  substitutes for, 937
  terminology of, 933–934
  valid, requirements for, 934–936
Winding up, 692–693, 694, 695, 746
Withdrawals, direct, 487
Witness(es)
  examination of, 38, 75, 161
  to will, 935
Worker Adjustment and Retraining Notification (WARN) Act (1988), 611–612
Workers' compensation
  employer-employee relationship and, 581
  future benefits from, assignment and, 313
  litigation versus, 615–616
  state laws governing, 15, 108, 615–616
Working papers, 868
Workouts, 544
Workplace
  electronic monitoring in, 619–621, 632
  safety in, 614–616
    employer-employee relationship and, 581
    principal's duty to provide, 589
"Works for hire," 584
World Wide Web (the Web)(WWW). *See also* Internet

defined, 28
risks related to, insurance for, 944
WorldCom, Inc., 860
Worm, 180
Writ(s)
of attachment, 522
of *certiorari,* 69–70
of execution, 522–523
of *mandamus,* 59
Writing
requirement(s) for
agency formation and, 584n, 589
agreement to form partnership and, 685
bailment agreement and, 893
confirmation between merchants and, 372
contract modification without consideration and, 371–372
guaranty contracts and, 526
LLC operating agreement and, 711–712
merchant's firm offer and, 369
negotiable instruments and, 442–443
power of attorney and, 584n, 589
rescission of sales contract and, 326
right of assurance and, 396
security interests and, 497, 498
Statute of Frauds and, 296–303
stop-payment order and, 476
transfers of realty and, 326
wills and, 935
sufficiency of, Statute of Frauds and, 302–303, 306, 372
Written memorandum, 302
Wrongful interference, 101–102

Y

Year Books, 10

Study Guide

Chapter 23:
Agency Relationships in Business

WHAT THIS CHAPTER IS ABOUT

This chapter covers agency relationships, including how they are formed and the duties involved. An ency relationship involves two parties: the principal and the agent. Agency relationships are essential to orporation, which can function and enter into contracts only through its agents.

CHAPTER OUTLINE

AGENCY RELATIONSHIPS

In an agency relationship, the parties agree that the agent will act on behalf and instead of the principal in negotiating and transacting business with third persons.

A. EMPLOYER-EMPLOYEE RELATIONSHIPS
Normally, all employees who deal with third parties are deemed to be agents. Statutes covering workers' compensation and so on apply only to employer-employee relationships.

B. EMPLOYER–INDEPENDENT CONTRACTOR RELATIONSHIPS
Those who hire independent contractors have no control over the details of their physical performance. Independent contractors can be agents.

C. DETERMINING EMPLOYEE STATUS
The greater an employer's control over the work, the more likely it is that the worker is an employee. Another key factor is whether the employer withholds taxes from payments to the worker and pays unemployment and Social Security taxes covering the worker.

I. HOW AGENCY RELATIONSHIPS ARE FORMED

Consideration is not required. A principal must have capacity to contract; anyone can be an agent. An agency can be created for any legal purpose.

A. AGENCY BY AGREEMENT
Normally, an agency must be based on an agreement that the agent will act for the principal. Such an agreement can be an express written contract, can be implied by conduct, or can be oral.

B. AGENCY BY RATIFICATION
A person who is not an agent (or who is an agent acting outside the scope of his or her authority) may make a contract on behalf of another (a principal). If the principal approves or affirms that contract by word or by action, an agency relationship is created by ratification.

C. AGENCY BY ESTOPPEL

1. Principal's Actions
When a principal causes a third person to believe that another person is his or her agent, and the third person deals with the supposed agent, the principal is estopped to deny the agency relationship.

2. **Third Party's Reasonable Belief**
The third person must prove that he or she reasonably believed that an agency relationsh existed and that the agent had authority—that an ordinary, prudent person familiar wi business practice and custom would have been justified in concluding that the agent h authority.

D. **AGENCY BY OPERATION OF LAW**
An agency relationship in the absence of a formal agreement may occur in family relationships in an emergency, if the agent's failure to act outside the scope of his or her authority would cau the principal substantial loss.

III. DUTIES OF AGENTS AND PRINCIPALS

The principal-agent relationship is fiduciary.

A. AGENT'S DUTIES TO THE PRINCIPAL

1. **Performance**
An agent must perform with reasonable diligence and skill.

2. **Notification**
An agent must notify the principal of all matters concerning the agency.

3. **Loyalty**
An agent must act solely for the benefit of the principal.

4. **Obedience**
An agent must follow all lawful instructions of the principal.

5. **Accounting**
An agent must keep and make available to the principal an account of everything receive and paid out on behalf of the principal.

B. PRINCIPAL'S DUTIES TO THE AGENT

1. **Compensation**
A principal must pay the agent for services rendered.

2. **Reimbursement and Indemnification**
A principal must (1) reimburse the agent for money paid at the principal's request or fo necessary expenses and (2) indemnify an agent for liability incurred because of authorize acts.

3. **Cooperation**
A principal must cooperate with his or her agent.

4. **Safe Working Conditions**
A principal must provide safe working conditions.

IV. AGENT'S AUTHORITY

A. ACTUAL AUTHORITY

1. **Express Authority**
Express authority may be oral or in writing. In most states, if a contract is or must be in writing, an agent's authority to enter into the contract must also be in writing.

2. **Power of Attorney**
A power of attorney can be special or general. An ordinary power terminates on th incapacity or death of the person giving it. A durable power is not affected by the principal' incapacity.

3. Implied Authority
Implied authority may be conferred by custom, can be inferred from the position an agent occupies, or is implied as reasonably necessary to carry out express authority.

B. APPARENT AUTHORITY
An agent has apparent authority when a principal, by word or action, causes a third party reasonably to believe that an agent has authority, though the agent has no authority. The principal may be estopped from denying it if the third party changes position in reliance.

C. RATIFICATION
A principal can ratify an unauthorized contract or act, if he or she is aware of all material facts. Ratification can be done expressly or impliedly (by accepting the benefits of a transaction). An entire transaction must be ratified; a principal cannot affirm only part.

LIABILITY IN AGENCY RELATIONSHIPS

A. LIABILITY FOR CONTRACTS
Who is liable to third parties for contracts formed by an agent?

1. If an Agent Acts within the Scope of His or Her Authority

a. Disclosed Principal
If a principal's identity is known to a third party when an agent makes a contract, the principal is liable. The agent is not liable.

b. Partially Disclosed Principal
If a principal's identity is not known to a third party when an agent makes a contract but the third party knows the agent is acting for a principal, the principal is liable. In most states, the agent is also liable.

c. Undisclosed Principal
If the principal's identity is not known to a third party when an agent makes a contract, the principal *and* the agent are liable. Exceptions—

1) The principal is expressly excluded as a party in the contract.
2) The contract is a negotiable instrument (check or note).
3) The performance of the agent is personal to the contract.

2. If the Agent Acts without Authority
The principal is not liable to a third party. The agent is liable (for breach of an implied warranty that the agent had authority), unless the third party knew the agent did not have authority.

3. If the Agent Is an E-agent
E-agents include semi-autonomous computer programs capable of executing specific tasks. Generally, a party who uses an e-agent is bound by the e-agent's acts. In some circumstances, the third party with whom the e-agent deals can avoid the transaction.

B. LIABILITY FOR TORTS AND CRIMES
An agent is liable to third parties for his or her torts and crimes. Is the principal also liable?

1. Principal's Tortious Conduct
A principal may be liable for harm resulting from the principal's negligence or recklessness (giving improper instructions; authorizing the use of improper materials or tools; establishing improper rules; or failing to prevent others' tortious conduct while they are on the principal's property or using the principal's equipment, materials, or tools).

2. Principal's Authorization of Agent's Tortious Conduct
A principal who authorizes an agent to commit a tortious act may be liable.

3. **Liability for Agent's Misrepresentation**
If a principal has given an agent authority to make statements and the agent makes fa claims, the principal is liable. If an agent appears to be acting within the scope of authority taking advantage of a third party, the principal who placed the agent in that position liable.

4. **Liability for Agent's Negligence**

a. **The Doctrine of *Respondeat Superior***
An employer is liable for harm caused (negligently or intentionally) to a third party by employee acting within the scope of employment, without regard to the fault of t employer.

b. **The Scope of Employment**
Factors for determining whether an act is within the scope of employment are—

1) the time, place, and purpose of the act.
2) whether the act was authorized by the employer.
3) whether the act is one commonly performed by employees on behalf of their employe
4) whether the employer's interest was advanced by the act.
5) whether the private interests of the employee were involved.
6) whether the employer furnished the means by which an injury was inflicted.
7) whether the employer had reason to know that the employee would do the act question.
8) whether the act involved the commission of a serious crime.

c. **Travel and Commuting**
The travel of those whose jobs require it is considered within the scope of employment f the duration of the trip, including the return. An employee going to and from work meals is usually considered outside the scope of employment.

d. **Notice of Dangerous Conditions**
An employer is charged with knowledge of dangerous conditions that concern t employment situation and that an employee discovers.

5. **Liability for Agent's Intentional Torts**
The doctrine of *respondeat superior* applies in these cases. Also, a principal is responsible f an agent's misrepresentation made within the scope of the agent's authority.

6. **Liability for Independent Contractor's Torts**
An employer is not liable for physical harm caused to a third person by an independe contractor's tort (except for hazardous activities, such as blasting operations, transportatic of volatile chemicals, and use of poisonous gases, in which strict liability is imposed).

7. **Liability for Agent's Crimes**
A principal is not liable for an agent's crime, unless the principal participated. In som states, a principal may be liable for an agent's violating, in the course and scope employment, such regulations as those governing sanitation, prices, weights, and the sale liquor.

VI. HOW AGENCY RELATIONSHIPS ARE TERMINATED

A. TERMINATION BY ACT OF THE PARTIES

1. **Lapse of Time**
An agency agreement may specify the time period during which the agency relationship wi exist. If so, the agency ends when that time expires. If no definite time is stated, an agenc continues for a reasonable time and can be terminated at will by either party.

2. **Purpose Achieved**
An agent can be employed to accomplish a particular objective. If so, the agency automatically ends when the objective is accomplished.

3. **Occurrence of a Specific Event**
An agency can be created to terminate on the occurrence of a certain event. If so, the agency automatically ends when the event occurs.

4. **Mutual Agreement**
Parties can cancel their agency by mutually agreeing to do so.

5. **Termination by One Party**
Both parties have the *power* to terminate an agency, but they may not have the *right* and may thus be liable for breach of contract. An agency coupled with an interest is created for the benefit of the agent, who acquires a beneficial interest in the subject matter, and thus it is not equitable to permit a principal to terminate it at will.

6. **Notice of Termination**
If the parties themselves terminate the agency, the principal must inform any third parties who know of the agency that it has ended. An agent's actual authority ends when the agent receives notice. An agent's apparent authority continues until the third person is notified (from any source).

B. TERMINATION BY OPERATION OF LAW

1. **Death or Insanity**
Death or insanity of either party automatically and immediately ends an agency. Knowledge of the death is not required.

2. **Impossibility**
When the specific subject matter of an agency is destroyed or lost, the agency terminates. When it is impossible for the agent to perform the agency lawfully because of a change in the law, the agency terminates.

3. **Changed Circumstances**
When an event occurs that has such an unusual effect on the subject matter of the agency that the agent can reasonably infer that the principal will not want the agency to continue, the agency terminates.

4. **Bankruptcy**
Bankruptcy of the principal or the agent usually terminates an agency. In some circumstances, as when the agent's financial status is irrelevant to the purpose of the agency, the agency relationship may continue.

5. **War**
When the principal's country and the agent's country are at war with each other, the agency is terminated.

TRUE-FALSE QUESTIONS

(Answers at the Back of the Book)

___ 1. Employees who deal with third parties are agents of their employers. T

___ 2. An agent owes his or her principal a duty to act in good faith. T

___ 3. An agent who fails to use reasonable diligence and skill in acting on behalf of his or her principal may be liable for breaching a duty of performance. T

T 4. A *disclosed* principal is liable to a third party for contracts made by the agent acting within t scope of authority.

F 5. A principal is not liable for harm caused to a third party by an agent acting in the scope employment.

T 6. An *undisclosed* principal is liable to a third party for contracts made by an agent acting witl the scope of authority.

F 7. Both parties to an agency have the right to terminate the agency at any time.

T 8. If a principal does not ratify an otherwise unauthorized contract, the principal is not bound.

F 9. An e-agent is a person.

F 10. When an agent enters into a contract on behalf of a principal, the principal must ratify tl contract to be bound.

FILL-IN QUESTIONS

(Answers at the Back of the Book)

An agent's use of reasonable diligence and skill is part of the agent's duty of ________________ (obedience/performance). Informing a principal of all material matters that come to the agent's attenti concerning the subject matter of the agency is an aspect of the agent's duty ________________ (accounting/notification). Acting solely for the benefit of the principal ar not in the interest of the agent or a third party is part of the agent's duty of ________________ (loyalty/performance). Following all lawful and clearly stated instructions of the principal is an aspect of tl agent's duty of ________________ (loyalty/obedience). If an agent is required to keep and make available t the principal a record of all property and money received and paid out on behalf of the principal, this is pa of the agent's duty of ________________ (accounting/notification).

MULTIPLE-CHOICE QUESTIONS

(Answers at the Back of the Book)

___ 1. Elman is an officer for Fizzy Frothy Corporation. When acting for Fizzy in ordinary busines situations, Elman is

a. an agent.
b. an agent and a principal.
c. a principal.
d. neither an agent nor a principal.

___ 2. Campbell is a salesperson for DownRiver Enterprises, Inc. In determining whether Campbell i DownRiver's employee or an independent contractor, the most important factor is

a. the degree of control that DownRiver exercises over Campbell.
b. the distinction between DownRiver's business and Campbell's occupation.
c. the length of the working relationship between DownRiver and Campbell.
d. the method of payment.

___ **3.** Estimable Finance Company hires Flotilda, who holds herself out as possessing special accounting skills, to act as its agent. As an agent, Flotilda must use the degree of skill or care expected of

a. an average, unskilled person.
b. a person having those special skills.
c. a reasonable person.
d. Estimable Company.

___ **4.** Gregg, a salesperson at Hubris Electronics store, tells Irma, a customer, "Buy your home theatre system here, and I'll set it up for less than what Hubris would charge." Irma buys the system, Gregg sets it up, and Irma pays Gregg, who keeps the money. Gregg has breached the duty of

a. loyalty.
b. notification.
c. obedience.
d. performance.

___ **5.** Java Company hires Keith to manage one of its kiosks. Although their employment agreement says nothing about Keith being able to hire employees to work in the kiosk, Keith has this authority. This is

a. apparent authority.
b. express authority.
c. imaginary authority.
d. implied authority.

___ **6.** Macro Company employs Nora as an agent. To terminate her authority, Macro must notify

a. Nora and third parties who know of the agency relationship.
b. only Nora.
c. only third parties who know of the agency relationship.
d. the public generally.

___ **7.** Midwest Mining, Inc., employs Nick as an agent. Nick enters into a contract with Oceana Resources Company within the scope of his authority but without disclosing that he is acting as Midwest's agent. Midwest does not perform. Oceana can recover from

a. Midwest only.
b. Midwest or Nick.
c. Nick only.
d. no one.

___ **8.** Questa Products Company requires its customers to pay by check. Ray, a Quality agent, tells customers that they can pay him with cash. Questa learns of Ray's collections, but takes no action to stop them. Ray steals some of the cash. Questa may be liable for the loss under the doctrine of

a. apparent authority. estoppel
b. express authority.
c. imaginary authority.
d. implied authority.

___ **9.** Swifty Delivery Company employs Taesha as a driver. While acting within the scope of employment, Taesha causes an accident in which Vaughn is injured. Vaughn can recover from

a. neither Swifty nor Taesha.
b. Swifty only.
c. Swifty or Taesha.
d. Taesha only.

____ **10.** Wendy contracts with Zip-It Investments, Inc., to act as Zip-It's agent in a fraudulent schem Wendy does not successfully complete the scheme. Zip-It can recover from Wendy for breach of

a. contract.
b. implied warranty.
c. performance.
d. none of the choices.

SHORT ESSAY QUESTIONS

1. What are the essential differences among the relationships of principal and agent, employer a employee, and employer and independent contractor? What factors indicate whether an individual is employee or an independent contractor?

2. In what situations is a principal liable for an agent's torts?

GAMEPOINTS

(Answers at the Back of the Book)

From the throne room in your base station on Alpha Centauri—in the video game "Galactic Empire"—yo dispatch your loyal, obedient minions to use their diligence and skill to loot the universe on your behalf a return with the treasure for its accounting and their compensation. Applying the agency principles outline in this chapter, answer the following questions.

1. One minion, Delilah, does not return with gems and gold, but brings back three contracts. Acting withi the scope of her authority, she contracted with Evon, who knew your identity at the time; Felipe, who kne that Delilah was acting on behalf of someone but not whom; and Giorgio, who did not know that Delilah wa acting on anyone's behalf. For which contracts, if any, are you liable? For which contracts, if any, is Delila liable?

2. A different minion, Hotspur, steals the treasure chest of a giant Cyclops from an asteroid orbiting distant star. Launching quickly to escape from the celestial body, Hotspur's space pod negligently bang into the Cyclops, who is injured. If the Cyclops files a suit against you, can there be a recovery for th injury?

Chapter 24:
Employment, Immigration, and Labor Law

WHAT THIS CHAPTER IS ABOUT

This chapter outlines the most significant laws regulating employment relationships. Other nificant laws regulating the workplace—those prohibiting employment discrimination—are dealt with in apter 25.

CHAPTER OUTLINE

EMPLOYMENT AT WILL

A. APPLICATION OF THE EMPLOYMENT-AT-WILL DOCTRINE
Under this doctrine, either the employer or the employee may terminate an employment relationship at any time and for any reason (unless a contract or the law provides to the contrary).

B. EXCEPTIONS TO THE EMPLOYMENT-AT-WILL DOCTRINE

1. **Exceptions Based on Contract Theory**
Some courts have held that an implied contract exists between an employer and an employee (if, for example, a personnel manual states that no employee will be fired without good cause). A few states have held all employment contracts contain an implied covenant of good faith.

2. **Exceptions Based on Tort Theory**
Discharge may give rise to a tort action (based on fraud, for example) for wrongful discharge.

3. **Exceptions Based on Public Policy**
An employer may not fire a worker for reasons that violate a public policy of the jurisdiction (for example, for refusing to violate the law). This policy must be expressed clearly in statutory law. Some state and federal statutes protect whistleblowers from retaliation. The False Claims Reform Act of 1986 gives a whistleblower 15 to 25 percent of proceeds recovered from fraud.

C. WRONGFUL DISCHARGE
An employer cannot fire an employee in violation of an employment contract or a federal or state statute. If so, the employee may bring an action for wrongful discharge.

I. WAGE AND HOUR LAWS

Davis-Bacon Act of 1931 requires "prevailing wages" for employees of some government contractors. Walsh-Healey Act of 1936 requires minimum wage and overtime for employees of some government contractors. Fair Labor Standards Act of 1938 (FLSA) covers all employees and regulates—

A. CHILD LABOR
Children under fourteen can deliver newspapers, work for their parents, and work in entertainment and agriculture. Children fourteen and older cannot work in hazardous occupations.

B. OVERTIME

Employees who work more than forty hours per week must be paid no less than one and a h times their regular pay for all hours over forty. Executives, administrative employe professional employees, outside salespersons, and computer employees are exempt if their p exceeds a certain amount, their duties do not include certain types of work, and they meet otl requirements.

C. MINIMUM WAGE

A specified amount (periodically revised) must be paid to employees in covered industries. Wag include the reasonable cost to furnish employees with board, lodging, and other facilities.

III. LAYOFFS

Restructuring an operation or downsizing a workforce means a layoff.

A. THE WORKER ADJUSTMENT AND RETRAINING NOTIFICATION (WARN) ACT OF 1988

Employers with at least one hundred full-time workers must provide sixty-days' notice bef imposing a mass layoff or closing a plant that employs more than fifty full-time workers. This to give the workers time to look for new jobs and state agencies time to provide retraining a other resources.

1. Mass Layoff

This is a reduction in force that, during any thirty-day period, results in an employme loss of at least 33 percent of the full-time employees at a single job site and at least fi employees, or at least five hundred full-time employees. An employment loss is a layoff th exceeds six months or a reduction in hours of more than 50 percent in each month of a six-month period.

2. Criticisms and Compliance Issues

Some argue that the WARN Act protects too few employees and covers too few businesse Employers can avoid giving notice by staggering layoffs over many months or many j sites.

3. Remedies for WARN Act Violations

These include fines of up to $500 per day. Employees can recover up to sixty-days' ba pay and job benefits, plus attorneys' fees. Discrimination claims are possible (see Chapt 25).

B. STATE LAWS MAY ALSO REQUIRE LAYOFF NOTICES

Many states have similar or stricter notice requirements that cover more employers ar employees.

IV. FAMILY AND MEDICAL LEAVE ACT (FMLA) OF 1993

Employers with fifty or more employees must provide them with up to twelve weeks of family medical leave during any twelve-month period, continue health-care coverage during the leave, ar guarantee employment in the same, or a comparable, position when the employee returns to work.

V. WORKER HEALTH AND SAFETY

A. THE OCCUPATIONAL SAFETY AND HEALTH ACT OF 1970

This act provides for workplace safety standards, with record-keeping, reporting, notice, an inspection requirements. The Occupational Safety and Health Administration (OSH administers the act. Penalties are limited, but an employer may also be prosecuted under stat law.

B. STATE WORKERS' COMPENSATION LAWS

State laws establish procedure for compensating workers injured on the job.

1. No State Covers All Employees

Often excluded are domestic workers, agricultural workers, temporary employees, an employees of common carriers.

2. **Requirements for Recovery**
There must be an employment relationship, and the injury must be accidental and occur on the job or in the course of employment.

3. **Filing a Claim**
An employee must notify the employer of an injury (usually within thirty days), and file a claim with a state agency within a certain period (sixty days to two years) from the time the injury is first noticed.

4. **Acceptance of Workers' Compensation Benefits Bars Suits**
An employee's acceptance of benefits bars the employee from suing for injuries caused by the employer's negligence.

I. INCOME SECURITY

A. SOCIAL SECURITY
The Social Security Act of 1935 provides for payments to persons who are retired, widowed, disabled, etc. Employers and employees must contribute under the Federal Insurance Contributions Act (FICA).

B. MEDICARE
A health insurance program administered by the Social Security Administration for people sixty-five years of age and older and for some under sixty-five who are disabled.

C. PRIVATE PENSION PLANS
The Employee Retirement Income Security Act (ERISA) of 1974 empowers the Labor Management Services Administration of the U.S. Department of Labor to oversee operators of private pension funds. The Pension Benefit Guaranty Corporation (PBGC) pays benefits to participants if their plans cannot.

1. **Vesting**
Generally, employee contributions to pension plans vest immediately; employee rights to employer contributions vest after five years.

2. **Investing**
Pension-fund managers must be cautious in investing and refrain from investing more than 10 percent of the fund in securities of the employer.

D. UNEMPLOYMENT INSURANCE
The Federal Unemployment Tax Act of 1935 created a state system that provides unemployment compensation to eligible individuals.

E. COBRA
The Consolidated Omnibus Budget Reconciliation Act (COBRA) of 1985 prohibits the elimination of a worker's medical, optical, or dental insurance coverage on the voluntary or involuntary termination or reduction in hours of the worker's employment.

1. **Procedures**
Except for those fired for gross misconduct, a worker can decide whether to continue coverage. Coverage must be continued for up to eighteen months (twenty-nine, if the worker is disabled).

2. **Payment**
A worker who opts to continue coverage must pay a premium plus an administrative fee. Penalties for violations include up to 10 percent of the annual cost of the group plan or $500,000, whichever is less.

F. EMPLOYER-SPONSORED GROUP HEALTH PLANS
Under the Health Insurance Portability and Accountability Act (HIPAA), employers who provide health insurance cannot exclude persons with certain preexisting conditions and are restricted in their collection and use of employees' health information.

VII. EMPLOYEE PRIVACY RIGHTS

A right to privacy has been inferred from constitutional guarantees provided by the First, Thir Fourth, Fifth, and Ninth Amendments to the Constitution. Tort law, state constitutions, and sor federal and state statutes also provide some privacy rights.

A. ELECTRONIC MONITORING IN THE WORKPLACE

1. Employee Privacy Rights under Constitutional and Tort Law

Privacy rights are protected at common law (invasion of privacy) and under the U. Constitution and state constitutions.

2. The Electronic Communications Privacy Act (ECPA) of 1986

Electronic monitoring may violate this act, which prohibits the intentional interception of ar wire or electronic communication or the intentional disclosure or use of the informati obtained by the interception. A "business-extension exception" permits employers to monit employee phone conversations in the ordinary course of business (though not to monit employees' personal communications).

3. Factors Considered by the Courts in Employee Privacy Cases

The courts generally weigh an employer's interests against an employee's reasonable expe tation of privacy, which may depend on whether the employee knows of the monitoring.

4. Stored Communications

Intentional, unauthorized access to stored electronic communications is prohibited.

B. OTHER TYPES OF MONITORING

1. Lie-Detector Tests

Under the Employee Polygraph Protection Act of 1988, most employers cannot, among oth things, require, request, or suggest that employees or applicants take lie-detector test except when investigating theft, including theft of trade secrets.

2. Drug Testing

a. Protection for the Privacy Rights of Private Employees

Some state constitutions may prohibit private employers from testing for drugs. Stat statutes may restrict drug testing by private employers. Other sources of protectio include collective bargaining agreements and tort actions for invasion of privacy (se Chapter 4).

b. Protection for Government Employees

Constitutional limitations (the Fourth Amendment) apply. Drug tests have been uphel when there was a reasonable basis for suspecting employees of using drugs, or when dru use could threaten public safety.

3. Genetic Testing

Employers cannot use the results of genetic tests of employees and applicants to mak decisions about hiring, firing, placement, or promotion under the Genetic Informatio Nondiscrimination Act of 2008.

4. Screening Procedures

A key factor in determining whether preemployment screening tests violate privacy rights i whether there is a connection between the questions and the job for which an applicant i applying.

VIII. IMMIGRATION LAW

Federal law sets standards for legal immigration, including preferences for persons with certai skills, and imposes sanctions on employers who hire illegal immigrants.

A. IMMIGRATION REFORM AND CONTROL ACT (IRCA) OF 1986

It is illegal to hire, recruit, or refer for a fee for work in the United States a person who is not authorized to work here.

1. I-9 Employment Verification

The U.S. Citizenship and Immigration Services (CIS) supplies Form I-9, Employment Eligibility Verification, which an employer must complete within three days of each employee's hiring (and retain for three years). The employer must verify an individual's identity and eligibility to work.

2. Enforcement

U.S. Immigration and Customs Enforcement (ICE) officers conduct random audits and act on written complaints. A determination of a violation is subject to administrative review at an employer's request. Employers' defenses include good faith and substantial compliance with documentation requirements.

3. Penalties

Possibilities include civil fines of up to $11,000 for each unauthorized employee and criminal penalties of increased fines and imprisonment. An employer may also be barred from future government contracts.

B. IMMIGRATION ACT OF 1990

Persons who immigrate to the United States to work include those with special skills. To hire such individuals, an employer must petition the CIS. An immigrant employee's ability to stay in the United States and to switch jobs here is limited.

1. I-551 Alien Registration Receipts

An employer may hire a noncitizen who is (a) a lawful permanent resident (as proved by an I-551 Alien Registration Receipt, or "green card") or (b) has a temporary Employment Authorization Document.

2. How an Employer Can Obtain a "Green Card"

To obtain a "green card" for an immigrant, an employer must show that no American worker is qualified, willing, and able to take the job. The job must be advertised, and its qualifications must be a business necessity.

3. The H-1B Visa Program

A sponsoring employer may obtain a visa for a person to work in the United States for three to six years in a specialty occupation that requires highly specialized knowledge and a college degree.

4. Labor Certification

Before submitting an H-1B application, an employer must obtain a Labor Certification form from the U.S. Department of Labor. To obtain the form, the employer must agree to pay a competitive wage and attest that the hiring will not adversely affect other similarly employed workers. The form must be posted.

5. H-2, O, L, and E Visas

Temporary nonimmigrant visas are also available for agricultural seasonal workers, a company's managers and executives, certain investors and entrepreneurs, and performers, athletes, and other acclaimed individuals.

X. LABOR UNIONS

A. FEDERAL LABOR LAWS

1. Norris-LaGuardia Act

Enacted in 1932. Restricts federal courts' power to issue injunctions against unions engaged in peaceful strikes, picketing, and boycotts.

2. **National Labor Relations Act (NLRA) of 1935**
Established rights to bargain collectively and to strike, and—

a. **Unfair Employer Practices**
Prohibits interfering with union activities, discriminating against union employee refusing to bargain with union, other practices.

b. **National Labor Relations Board (NLRB)**
Created to oversee union elections, prevent employers from engaging in unfair practice investigate employers in response to employee charges of unfair labor practices, iss cease-and-desist orders.

c. **Workers Protected by the NLRA**
Protected employees include job applicants, including those paid by a union to unioni the employer's work force.

3. **Labor-Management Relations Act (LMRA) of 1947**
Prohibits unions from refusing to bargain with employers, engaging in certain types picketing, featherbedding, and other unfair practices. Preserves union shops, but allov states to pass right-to-work laws, which make it illegal to require union membership f employment.

4. **Labor-Management Reporting and Disclosure Act (LMRDA) of 1959**

a. **Union Business**
Requires elections of union officers under secret ballot; prohibits ex-convicts an Communists from holding union office; makes officials accountable for union propert allows members to participate in union meetings, nominate officers, vote in proceedings.

b. **Hot-Cargo Agreements**
Outlaws hot-cargo agreements (or secondary boycotts, in which employers agree not t handle, use, or deal in non-union goods of other employers).

B. **UNION ORGANIZATION**
If a majority of workers sign authorization cards and the employer refuses to recognize the unio unionizers can petition the NLRB for an election.

1. **Union Elections**
For an election to be held, there must be support for the union by at least 30 percent of th workers. NLRB ensures secret voting.

2. **Union Election Campaigns**
Employers may limit campaign activities (fairly) and may campaign against union.

C. **COLLECTIVE BARGAINING**
This is the process by which labor and management negotiate terms and conditions employment. Each side must bargain in good faith (be willing to meet and to consider the other' offers and proposals). Refusing to bargain in good faith without justification is an unfair labo practice.

D. **STRIKES**
A strike occurs when workers leave their jobs and refuse to work.

1. **The Right to Strike**
The NLRA guarantees this right, within limits. Strike activities, such as picketing, ar protected by the First Amendment. Nonworkers have a right to participate in picketing Workers can also refuse to cross a picket line of fellow workers who are engaged in a lawfu strike.

2. The Rights of Strikers after a Strike Ends
An employer may hire replacement workers. After an economic strike over working conditions, strikers have no right to return to their jobs, but must be given preference to any vacancies and retain their seniority rights. After an unfair labor practice strike, strikers must be given their jobs back.

TRUE-FALSE QUESTIONS

(Answers at the Back of the Book)

___ **1.** Drug testing by private employers is permitted.

___ **2.** There are no exceptions to the employment "at will" doctrine.

___ **3.** Employers are required to establish retirement plans for their employees.

___ **4.** Federal wage-hour laws cover all employers engaged in interstate commerce.

___ **5.** Whistleblower statutes protect employers from workers' disclosure of the employer's wrongdoing.

___ **6.** Under federal law, employers can monitor employees' personal communications.

___ **7.** Management serves as the representative of workers in bargaining with a union.

___ **8.** An employer must consider all job applicants—citizen and noncitizen—in deciding whom to hire.

___ **9.** Similarity of workers' jobs is a factor in determining which workers are to be represented by a union.

___ **10.** An immigrant employee's ability to stay in the United States and to switch jobs here is limited.

FILL-IN QUESTIONS

(Answers at the Back of the Book)

Under the employment-at-will doctrine, ________________ (either/neither) party may terminate an nployment relationship at any time and for any reason _______________ (unless/even if) a contract provides the contrary. An employee who is fired in violation of a federal or state statute _________ (may/may not) ring an action for wrongful discharge. ___________ (Some/No) courts have held that an implied contract xists between an employer and an employee. ________________ (All/A few states) have held that all nployment contracts contain an implied covenant of good faith. An employer ____________ (may/may not) re a worker for reasons that violate a public policy of the jurisdiction.

MULTIPLE-CHOICE QUESTIONS

(Answers at the Back of the Book)

___ **1.** Michelle, an employee of Neverquit Company, is covered by federal overtime provisions. These rules apply only after an employee has worked more than

a. eight hours in a day.
b. five days in a week.
c. forty hours in a week.
d. 160 hours in a month.

___ **2.** National Workers Union (NWU) represents the employees of Office Supplies Company, Inc. NW calls an economic strike, and Office hires replacement workers. After the strike, the replaceme workers

a. must be retained and the former strikers must be rehired.
b. must be terminated and the former strikers must be rehired.
c. must be terminated whether or not the former strikers are rehired.
d. may be retained or terminated whether or not the former strikers are rehired.

___ **3.** Reddy Power Corporation provides health insurance for its employees. When Reddy closes one its offices and terminates the employees, the employees

a. can collect "severance pay" equal to twelve weeks' of health insurance coverage.
b. can continue their heath insurance at Reddy's expense.
c. can continue their heath insurance at their expense.
d. lose their heath insurance immediately on termination of employment.

___ **4.** Reba works for Silo Storage Company as an at-will employee. This employment may be term nated at any time for any reason by

a. neither Reba nor Silo Storage.
b. Reba only.
c. Reba or Silo Storage.
d. Silo Storage only.

___ **5.** Millions Mining Company is a private employer that wants to test its employees for drug us This testing may

a. be limited or prohibited at the sole discretion of the employer.
b. be limited or prohibited under a state constitution, statute, or court decision.
c. not be permitted under any circumstances.
d. not be prohibited under any circumstances.

___ **6.** Mosul, Natomi, and Omar apply to work for Precision Engineering, Inc. These individuals' ident ties and eligibility to work must be verified by

a. the employer.
b. the individuals.
c. the individuals' country of origin.
d. the U.S. Citizenship and Immigration Services.

___ **7.** Delta Aircraft Company, a U.S. employer, may hire Ewan, a noncitizen, if Ewan is

a. a lawful permanent resident of the United States.
b. an unlawful but currently employed visitor to the United States.
c. an unlawful but only temporary and unemployed resident in the United States.
d. all of the choices.

___ **8.** Omega Oil Refining Corporation wants to hire Parfez, who has certain special skills to fill a tech nical position. To hire Parfez, Omega must petition

a. CIS.
b. OSHA.
c. ICE.
d. NLRB

_ **9.** During a union election campaign at Wayward Shipping Corporation, Wayward may not

a. designate where and when campaigning may occur.
b. prohibit all solicitation during work time.
c. promise to hire more workers if the union loses the election.
d. threaten employees with the loss of their jobs if the union wins the election.

_ **10.** Fruit Packaging Corporation provides health insurance for its 150 employees, including Gladys. When Gladys takes twelve weeks' leave to care for her child, she

a. can collect "leave pay" equal to twelve weeks' of health insurance coverage.
b. can continue her heath insurance at Fruit Packaging's expense.
c. can continue her heath insurance at her expense.
d. loses her heath insurance immediately on taking leave.

SHORT ESSAY QUESTIONS

What is the employment-at-will doctrine? What are its exceptions?

What are important federal laws concerning labor unions? What specifically does each law provide?

GAMEPOINTS

(Answers at the Back of the Book)

You are playing "Brain Drain," a video game that involves a quest through the unexplored realms of the agination, attempting to reach Level 14. It is difficult to advance from level to level because the obstacles at must be overcome and the objectives that must be attained are different, complex, and puzzling. For ur consecutive weeks, you play 45, 42, 39, and 31 hours. If this play were work, and you were a nonexempt nployee covered by the Fair Labor Standards Act, how many hours of overtime pay, if any, would you be ntitled to? What would be the rate?

In the video game, "Invasive Species," Earth is invaded by huge, insect-like aliens with superior telligence. Your avatar Derek works for Invasion Extermination Service, Inc. Following the service's rescribed procedures, Derek sprays the invaders with "Eradicate," a chemical supplied by the service. radicate effectively wipes out the invaders—one at a time with a short delay, which allows for plenty of ame action—but also injures your avatar. According to the principles set out in this chapter, is Derek igible for workers' compensation? Could Derek successfully sue his employer for negligence?

Chapter 25: Employment Discrimination

WHAT THIS CHAPTER IS ABOUT

The law restricts employers and unions from discriminating against workers on the basis of race, lor, religion, national origin, gender, age, or handicap. A class of persons defined by one or more of these iteria is known as a **protected class**. This chapter outlines these laws.

CHAPTER OUTLINE

TITLE VII OF THE CIVIL RIGHTS ACT OF 1964

Prohibits employment discrimination against employees, applicants, and union members on the basis of race, color, national origin, religion, and gender.

A. WHO IS SUBJECT TO TITLE VII?
Employers with fifteen or more employees, labor unions with fifteen or more members, labor unions that operate hiring halls, employment agencies, and federal, state, and local agencies.

B. PROCEDURES UNDER TITLE VII
(1) A victim files a claim with the Equal Employment Opportunity Commission (EEOC); (2) the EEOC investigates and seeks a voluntary settlement; (3) if no settlement is reached, the EEOC may sue the employer; (4) if the EEOC chooses not to sue, the victim may file a lawsuit.

C. INTENTIONAL AND UNINTENTIONAL DISCRIMINATION
Title VII prohibits both intentional and unintentional discrimination.

1. Disparate-Treatment Discrimination
This is intentional discrimination by an employer against an employee.

a. *Prima Facie* Case—Plaintiff's Side of the Case
A plaintiff must show (1) he or she is a member of a protected class, (2) he or she applied and was qualified for the job, (3) he or she was rejected by the employer, (4) the employer continued to seek applicants or filled the job with a person not in a protected class.

b. Defense—Employer's Side of the Case
An employer must articulate a legal reason for not hiring the plaintiff. To prevail, a plaintiff must show that this reason is a pretext and discriminatory intent motivated the decision.

2. Disparate-Impact Discrimination

a. Types of Disparate-Impact Discrimination
Disparate-impact discrimination results if, because of a requirement or hiring practice—

1) an employer's work force does not reflect the percentage of members of protected classes that characterizes qualified individuals in the local labor market, or

2) members of a protected class are excluded from an employer's work force at substantially higher rate than nonmembers (under EEOC's "four-fifths rule," selection

rate for protected class must be at least 80 percent of rate for group with the high rate).

b. ***Prima Facie* Case—Plaintiff's Side of the Case**
Plaintiff must show a connection between a requirement or practice and a disparity; evidence of discriminatory intent is needed.

D. DISCRIMINATION BASED ON RACE, COLOR, AND NATIONAL ORIGIN

Employers cannot effectively discriminate against employees on the basis of race, color, nation origin, or religion (absent a substantial, demonstrable relationship between the trait and the jo etc.).

1. Reverse Discrimination

Discrimination against majority individuals is reverse discrimination.

2. Potential Section 1981 Claims

This statute (42 U.S.C. Section 1981) protects against discrimination on the basis of race ethnicity in the formation or enforcement of contracts, including employment contracts, wi no limit on the amount of damages.

E. DISCRIMINATION BASED ON RELIGION

Title VII prohibits employers and unions from discriminating against persons because of the religions.

F. DISCRIMINATION BASED ON GENDER

Employers cannot discriminate against employees on the basis of gender (unless gender essential to a job, etc.). The Pregnancy Discrimination Act of 1978 amended Title VII: employe affected by pregnancy or related conditions must be treated the same as persons not so affect but similar in ability to work.

1. Equal Pay Act

The Equal Pay Act of 1963 prohibits gender-based discrimination in wages paid for equ work when a job requires equal skill, effort, and responsibility under similar conditions.

2. 2009 Equal Pay Legislation

The Paycheck Fairness Act of 2009 prohibits gender-based discrimination in assessing a employee's education, training, or experience. Under the Lily Ledbetter Fair Pay Act of 200 each time a person is paid discriminatory wages, benefits, or compensation, a cause of actio arises and the victim has 180 days to file a complaint.

G. CONSTRUCTIVE DISCHARGE

Constructive discharge occurs when an employer causes working conditions to be so intolerabl that a reasonable person in an employee's position would feel compelled to quit.

1. Proving Constructive Discharge

An employee must show that the employer caused the intolerable conditions, and knew, o had reason to know, of the intolerable conditions and failed to correct them within reasonable time.

2. Can Be Applied to Any Type of Title VII Discrimination

An employee can seek damages for loss of income, including back pay.

H. SEXUAL HARASSMENT

1. Forms of Harassment

(1) *Quid pro quo* harassment: when promotions, etc., are doled out on the basis of sexua favors; (2) hostile-environment harassment: when an employee is subjected to offensive sexua comments, etc.

2. Harassment by Supervisors, Co-Workers, or Nonemployees

a. When Is an Employer Liable?
If anyone (employee or nonemployee) harasses an employee, and the employer knew, or should have known, and failed to take immediate corrective action, the employer may be liable. To be liable for a supervisor's harassment, the supervisor must have taken a tangible employment action against the employee.

b. Employer's Defense
(1) Employer took "reasonable care to prevent and correct promptly any sexually harassing behavior," and (2) employee suing for harassment failed to follow employer's policies and procedures.

3. Same-Gender Harassment
Title VII protects persons who are harassed by members of the same gender.

I. ONLINE HARASSMENT
Employers may avoid liability if they take prompt remedial action. Privacy rights must be considered if the action includes electronic monitoring of employees.

J. REMEDIES UNDER TITLE VII
Reinstatement, back pay, retroactive promotions, and damages.

1. Damages
Compensatory damages are available only in cases of intentional discrimination. Punitive damages are available only if an employer acted with malice or reckless indifference

2. Limitations
Total damages are limited to specific amounts against specific employers (from $50,000 against those with 100 or fewer employees to $300,000 against those with more than 500 employees).

I. DISCRIMINATION BASED ON AGE

A. THE AGE DISCRIMINATION IN EMPLOYMENT ACT (ADEA) OF 1967
Prohibits employment discrimination on the basis of age (including mandatory retirement), by employers with twenty or more employees, against individuals forty years of age or older. Administered by the EEOC, but private causes of action are also possible.

B. PRINCIPLES ARE SIMILAR TO TITLE VII
Requires the establishment of a *prima facie* case: plaintiff must show that he or she was (1) forty or older, (2) qualified for a position, and (3) rejected in circumstances that infer discrimination. The employer must articulate a legal reason; the plaintiff may show it is a pretext.

C. STATE EMPLOYEES
Under the Eleventh Amendment to the Constitution, a state is immune from suits brought by private individuals in federal court unless the state consents to the suit. A state agency sued by a state employee for age discrimination may have the suit dismissed on this ground.

II. DISCRIMINATION BASED ON DISABILITY
Under the Americans with Disabilities Act (ADA) of 1990, an employer cannot refuse to hire a person who is qualified but disabled. Covered are all employers (except the states) with fifteen or more employees.

A. PROCEDURES AND REMEDIES UNDER THE ADA

1. Procedures
A plaintiff must show he or she (1) has a disability, (2) is otherwise qualified for a job and (3) was excluded solely because of the disability. A suit may be filed only after a claim is pursued through the EEOC (which may file a suit even if the employee agrees to arbitration).

2. Remedies

These include reinstatement, back pay, some compensatory and punitive damages (f intentional discrimination), and certain other relief. Repeat violators may be fined up $100,000.

B. WHAT IS A DISABILITY?

"(1) A physical or mental impairment that substantially limits one or more of the major life activ ties . . . ; (2) a record of such impairment; or (3) being regarded as having such an impairment Includes AIDS, morbid obesity, diabetes, etc., but not kleptomania and certain others.

C. REASONABLE ACCOMMODATION

For a person with a disability, an employer may have to make a reasonable accommodatio (more flexible working hours, new job assignment, different training materials procedures)—but not an accommodation that will cause *undue hardship* ("significant difficulty expense").

1. Job Applications and Preemployment Physical Exams

The application process must be accessible to those with disabilities. Employers cann require a disabled person to take a preemployment physical (unless all applicants dc Disqualification must be from problems that render a person unable to perform the job

2. Substance Abusers

The ADA protects addicts who have completed or are in supervised rehabilitation, an alcoholics to the extent of equal treatment.

3. Health-Insurance Plans

Workers with disabilities must be given equal access to insurance plans provided to oth workers. If a plan includes a disability-based distinction, an employer must show (1) limitin coverage keeps the plan financially sound, (2) coverage would otherwise be too expensive f many workers, or (3) the distinction is justified by the risk and costs.

4. Association Discrimination

An employer cannot take an adverse employment action based on the disability of a perso with whom an applicant or employee is known to have a relationship or association (disabled spouse, for example).

IV. DEFENSES TO EMPLOYMENT DISCRIMINATION

The first defense is to assert that the plaintiff did not prove discrimination. If discrimination i proved, an employer may attempt to justify it as—

A. BUSINESS NECESSITY

An employer may show that there is a legitimate connection between a job requirement tha discriminates and job performance.

B. BONA FIDE OCCUPATIONAL QUALIFICATION (BFOQ)

Another defense applies when discrimination against a protected class is essential to a job—tha is, when a particular trait is a BFOQ. Generally restricted to cases in which gender is essentia Race can never be a BFOQ.

C. SENIORITY SYSTEMS

An employer with a history of discrimination may have no members of protected classes o disabled workers in upper-level positions. If no present intent to discriminate is shown, an promotions, etc., are distributed according to a fair seniority system, the employer has a goo defense.

D. AFTER-ACQUIRED EVIDENCE OF EMPLOYEE MISCONDUCT

Evidence of an employee's prior misconduct acquired after a lawsuit is filed may limit damage but is not otherwise a defense.

AFFIRMATIVE ACTION

An affirmative action program attempts to make up for past discrimination by giving members of protected classes preferential treatment in hiring or promotion. Such a program cannot use quotas or preferences for unqualified persons, and once a program has succeeded, it must be changed or dropped. In schools, automatic preference on the basis of a protected characteristic violates the equal protection clause.

I. STATE STATUTES

Most states have statutes that prohibit the kinds of discrimination prohibited under federal legislation. State statutes also often protect individuals, such as homosexuals, who are not protected under Title VII.

TRUE-FALSE QUESTIONS

(Answers at the Back of the Book)

___ **1.** Once an affirmative action program has succeeded, it must be changed or dropped.

___ **2.** In a sexual harassment case, an employer cannot be held liable if an employee did the harassing.

___ **3.** In a sexual harassment case, an employer cannot be held liable if a nonemployee did the harassing.

___ **4.** Women affected by pregnancy must be treated for all job-related purposes the same as persons not so affected but similar in ability to work.

___ **5.** Employment discrimination against persons with a physical or mental impairment that substantially limits their everyday activities is prohibited.

___ **6.** Discrimination complaints under federal law must be filed with the Equal Opportunity Employment Commission.

___ **7.** If the Equal Employment Opportunity Commission decides not to investigate a claim, the victim has no other option.

___ **8.** All employers are subject to Title VII of the Civil Rights Act of 1964.

___ **9.** Disparate-treatment discrimination occurs when an employer intentionally discriminates against an employee.

___ **10.** Title VII prohibits employers and unions from discriminating against persons because of their religions.

FILL-IN QUESTIONS

(Answers at the Back of the Book)

The Equal Employment Opportunity Commission (EEOC) monitors compliance with the federal ntidiscrimination laws. The EEOC ________________ (can/cannot) sue organizations that violate these aws. A victim files a claim with the EEOC, which investigates and ________________ ________________ (must sue/may sue if a settlement between the parties is not reached). If the EEOC does ot sue, the victim may sue. On proof of discrimination, a victim may be awarded ________________ ________________ (reinstatement and back pay/reinstatement, back pay, and retroactive promotions).

MULTIPLE-CHOICE QUESTIONS

(Answers at the Back of the Book)

___ **1.** Curt, personnel director for Digital Products, Inc., prefers to hire Asian Americans, becau "they're smarter and work harder" than other minorities. This is prohibited by

a. the Age Discrimination in Employment Act of 1967.
b. the Americans with Disabilities Act of 1990.
c. Title VII of the Civil Rights Act of 1964.
d. none of the choices.

___ **2.** Greg and Holly work for Power Ready Services, Inc. (PRS), as electrical engineers. Greg is pa more than Holly because, according to PRS, he is a man with a family to support. This prohibited by

a. the Age Discrimination in Employment Act of 1967.
b. the Americans with Disabilities Act of 1990.
c. the Equal Pay Act of 1963.
d. none of the choices.

___ **3.** Under the Age Discrimination in Employment Act of 1967, Turnover Corporation is prohibite from

a. committing unintentional age discrimination.
b. forcing an employee to retire.
c. terminating an employee between the ages of sixty-five and seventy for cause.
d. terminating an employee as part of a rational business decision.

___ **4.** Neville, who is hearing impaired, applies for a position with Mold Casters Company. Neville i qualified but is refused the job and sues Mold Casters. To succeed under the Americans wit Disabilities Act, Neville must show that

a. Neville was willing to make a "reasonable accommodation" for Mold Casters.
b. Neville would not have to accept "significant additional costs" to work for Mold Casters.
c. Mold Casters refused to make a "reasonable accommodation" for Neville.
d. Mold Casters would not have to accept "significant additional costs" to hire Neville.

___ **5.** Insurance Sales, Inc., promotes employees on the basis of color. Employees with darker skin colo are passed over in favor of those with lighter skin color, regardless of their race. This i prohibited by

a. the Americans with Disabilities Act of 1990.
b. the Equal Pay Act of 1963.
c. Title VII of the Civil Rights Act of 1964.
d. none of the choices.

___ **6.** Mina is an employee of Widebody Trucking Corporation. Mina attempts to resolve a gender based discrimination claim with Widebody, whose representative denies the claim. Mina's nex best step is to

a. ask the Equal Opportunity Employment Commission whether a claim is justified.
b. file a lawsuit.
c. forget about the matter.
d. secretly sabotage company operations for revenge.

_ **7.** Dona applies to Estuary Management Corporation for an administrative assistant's job, which requires certain typing skills. Dona cannot type but tells Estuary that she is willing to learn. Estuary does not hire her, and she later sues. To successfully defend against the suit under Title VII, Estuary must show that

a. being a member of the majority is a BFOQ.
b. Dona was not willing to learn to type.
c. Estuary has a valid business necessity defense.
d. Estuary's work force reflects the same percentage of members of a protected class that characterizes qualified individuals in the local labor market.

_ **8.** Simplex Corporation terminates Tom, who sues on the basis of age discrimination. To succeed under the Age Discrimination in Employment Act, Tom must show that at the time of the discharge, he was

a. forty or older.
b. forty or younger.
c. replaced with someone forty or older.
d. replaced with someone forty or younger.

_ **9.** Heavy Equipment Company requires job applicants to pass certain physical tests. Only a few female applicants can pass the tests, but if they pass, they are hired. To successfully defend against a suit on this basis under Title VII, the employer must show that

a. any discrimination is not intentional.
b. being a male is a BFOQ.
c. passing the tests is a business necessity.
d. some men cannot pass the tests.

_ **10.** Dex and Erin work for Citycore Promotions Company. Dex is Erin's supervisor. During work, he touches her in ways that she perceives as sexually offensive. She resists the advances. He cuts her pay. Citycore is

a. liable, because Dex's conduct constituted sexual harassment.
b. liable, because Erin resisted Dex's advances.
c. not liable, because Dex's conduct was not job-related.
d. not liable, because Erin resisted Dex's advances.

SHORT ESSAY QUESTIONS

. Compare and contrast disparate-treatment discrimination and disparate-impact discrimination, and itle VII's response to each in the context of employment.

. What does the Americans with Disabilities Act require employers to do?

GAMEPOINTS

(Answers at the Back of the Book)

. You are playing the video game "Discrimination!" in which a player accrues points by correctly potting, reporting, and resolving instances of discrimination in various workplaces. In one scenario, set in a acking plant owned and operated by Savory Treats, Inc., a gourmet-food packaging and shipping firm, anner, the company's owner, tells Vera, its human resources director, not to hire Willis, a disabled pplicant. In Tanner's words, "we don't want to make changes to accommodate this guy—it'll give the other mployees ideas." Is this discrimination? Why or why not?

2. Sam works as a driver for Toxic Games Warehouse, a wholesale distributor and online retailer of vid games and accessories. Over a ten-year period, Sam repeatedly applies for—and is denied—a promotion the position of dispatcher. Sam meets the requirements for the job, which are a year's driving experien and a specific license. After one interview, Sam overhears the interviewer tell a co-worker that Sam, who white, didn't get the job because "whites are lazy." Is this employment discrimination? Explain.

CUMULATIVE HYPOTHETICAL PROBLEM FOR UNIT FOUR—INCLUDING CHAPTERS 23–25

(Answers at the Back of the Book)

Dot, Earl, Frank, Gail, Hal, Ira, Jane, Karen, Larry, and Mike work for International Sal Corporation (ISC).

___ **1.** Dot, who works in ISC's warehouse, is injured on the job. Dot may NOT collect worke compensation benefits if she

a. files a civil suit against a third party based on the injury.
b. intentionally caused her own injury.
c. was injured as a result of a co-worker's act.
d. worked for ISC for less than sixty days.

___ **2.** Earl retires from ISC at the age of sixty-five. Frank retires at sixty-seven. Because of disability, Gail, after fifteen years, is unable to continue working for ISC. Hal is discharged fro ISC as part of a reduction in force. All of the following benefits are part of Social Securi EXCEPT

a. Earl's government retirement payments.
b. Frank's Medicare payments.
c. Gail's government disability payments.
d. Hal's unemployment benefits.

___ **3.** Ira works for ISC as a sales representative at a salary of $3,000 per month, plus a 10 perce commission. As ISC's agent, Ira

a. cannot be dismissed during the six-month period without cause.
b. cannot enforce the agency unless it is in writing and signed by Delta.
c. is an agent coupled with an interest.
d. must act solely in Delta's interest in matters concerning Delta's business.

___ **4.** Four employees file suits against ISC, alleging discrimination. Title VII of the Civil Rights Act 1964 covers all of the following EXCEPT Jane's suit alleging discrimination on the basis of

a. age.
b. gender.
c. race.
d. religion.

___ **5.** Karen, an ISC manager, wants to institute a policy of mandatory retirement for all employees a age sixty-four. Larry, an ISC manager, wants to discharge Mike, who is age sixty-seven, fo cause. Under federal anti-discrimination law

a. Karen's and Larry's wishes can be granted.
b. neither Karen's and Larry's wishes can be granted.
c. only Karen's wish can be granted.
d. only Larry's wish can be granted.

QUESTIONS ON THE EXTENDED CASE STUDY FOR UNIT FOUR— *MEDIA GENERAL OPERATIONS, INC. V. NATIONAL LABOR RELATIONS BOARD*

(Answers at the Back of the Book)

_ **1.** Stan is an employee of Rubric Company. The Pipefitters Union represents Rubric's employees in collective bargaining negotiations over a new contract. In a memo to the employees, Phil, Rubric's chief financial officer, accuses the union of delaying tactics. Later, Stan tells Noreen, his supervisor, that Phil is "a stupid s * * * t" who needs to be "set straight." Noreen fires Stan for violating a Rubric rule against "threats." Stan files a suit against the employer. Under the holding in *Media General Operations, Inc. v. National Labor Relations Board*, the court will most likely conclude that

a. Stan's conduct undermined workplace discipline.
b. Stan's discharge was an unfair labor practice.
c. Stan's remark was not protected by the National Labor Relations Act.
d. Stan's suit stifled his employer's exercise of rights with its "threat" of liability.

_ **2.** In the facts of the previous question, according to the dissent's opinion in *Media General Operations, Inc. v. National Labor Relations Board*, the court should focus on whether

a. Stan's conduct was protected by the National Labor Relations Act.
b. Stan's discharge was an unfair labor practice.
c. Stan's remark undermined workplace discipline.
d. Stan's suit stifled his employer's exercise of rights with its "threat" of liability.

_ **3.** In the facts of the previous question, according to the court in the *Media General Operations, Inc. v. National Labor Relations Board* case, in determining whether a discharge for an employee's "outburst" in violation of a workplace rule violates the NLRA, significant factors include

a. the conduct that accompanies an employee's outburst.
b. the degree to which workplace outbursts would be stifled by threats of liability.
c. the nature of an employee's outburst.
d. the need for an employer to tolerate personal attacks.

Chapter 26:
Sole Proprietorships and Private Franchises

WHAT THIS CHAPTER IS ABOUT

This chapter briefly outlines the features of a sole proprietorship, the most common form of business, d discusses private franchises, which are widely used by entrepreneurs to seek profits.

CHAPTER OUTLINE

SOLE PROPRIETORSHIPS

This is the simplest form of business—the owner is the business.

A. ADVANTAGES OF THE SOLE PROPRIETORSHIP

These include that the proprietor takes all the profits; this organization is easier to start than others (few legal forms involved); the form has more flexibility (the proprietor is free to make all decisions); and the owner pays only personal income tax on profits.

B. DISADVANTAGES OF THE SOLE PROPRIETORSHIP

These include that the proprietor has all the risk (unlimited liability for all debts); there is limited opportunity to raise capital; and the business dissolves when the owner dies.

I. FRANCHISES

A franchise is any arrangement in which the owner of a trademark, a trade name, or a copyright has licensed others to use it in selling goods or services.

A. TYPES OF FRANCHISES

1. Distributorship

This is when a manufacturer licenses a dealer to sell its product (such as an automobile dealer). Often covers an exclusive territory.

2. Chain-Style Business Operation

This occurs when a franchise operates under a franchisor's trade name and is identified as a member of a group of dealers engaged in the franchisor's business (such as most fast-food chains). The franchisee must follow standardized or prescribed methods of operations, and may be obligated to obtain supplies exclusively from the franchisor.

3. Manufacturing or Processing-Plant Arrangement

This type exists when a franchisor transmits to the franchisee the essential ingredients or formula to make a product (such as Coca-Cola), which the franchisee makes and markets according to the franchisor's standards.

B. LAWS GOVERNING FRANCHISING

1. Federal Regulation of Franchising

a. **Automobile Dealers' Franchise Act of 1965**
The Automobile Dealers' Franchise Act protects dealership franchisees fr manufacturers' bad faith termination of their franchises.

b. **Petroleum Marketing Practices Act (PMPA) of 1979**
The PMPA prescribes the grounds and conditions under which a gasoline stati franchisor may terminate or decline to renew a franchise.

c. **Antitrust Laws**
These laws may apply if there is an anticompetitive agreement (see Chapter 32).

d. **Federal Trade Commission (FTC) Franchise Rule**
Franchisors must disclose material facts necessary to a prospective franchisee's maki an informed decision concerning a franchise. This must be in writing, and there must be meeting between the parties at least ten business days before an agreement is signed or payment made.

2. **State Regulation of Franchising**
State law is similar to federal law. State deceptive practices acts may apply, as may Artic 2 of the Uniform Commercial Code.

III. THE FRANCHISE CONTRACT

A franchise relationship is created by a contract between the franchisor and the franchisee.

A. PAYMENT FOR THE FRANCHISE

A franchisee pays (1) a fee for the franchise license, (2) fees for products bought from or throug the franchisor, (3) a percentage of sales, and (4) a percentage of advertising and administrati costs.

B. BUSINESS PREMISES

The agreement may specify whether the premises for the business are leased or purchased ar who is to supply equipment and furnishings.

C. LOCATION OF THE FRANCHISE

The franchisor determines the territory to be served and its exclusivity.

D. QUALITY CONTROL BY THE FRANCHISOR

A franchisor may specify standards of operation (such as quality standards) and personn training methods. Too much control may result in a franchisor's liability for torts of a franchisee employees.

E. PRICING ARRANGEMENTS

A franchisor may require a franchisee to buy certain supplies from the franchisor at a established price. A franchisor may also suggest retail prices for the goods that the franchise sells.

IV. TERMINATION OF THE FRANCHISE

Determined by the parties. Usually, termination must be "for cause" (such as breach of the agre ment, etc.) and notice must be given. A franchisee must be given reasonable time to wind up th business.

A. WRONGFUL TERMINATION

Important in determining whether termination is wrongful is whether it occurred in bad faith whether the contract's relevant provisions are unconscionable, and so on.

B. THE IMPORTANCE OF GOOD FAITH AND FAIR DEALING

Courts generally try to balance the rights of both parties and provide a remedy if the franchiso acted unfairly. If termination occurred in the normal course of business and reasonable notic was given, however, termination was not likely wrongful.

TRUE-FALSE QUESTIONS

(Answers at the Back of the Book)

_ 1. In a sole proprietorship, the owner and the business are entirely separate.

_ 2. In a sole proprietorship, the owner receives all of the profits.

_ 3. The income of a sole proprietorship is taxed to the owner as personal income.

_ 4. The death of the owner automatically dissolves a sole proprietorship.

_ 5. A court always determines the termination of a franchise.

_ 6. A franchise is an arrangement in which the owner of a trademark, a trade name, or a copyright has licensed others to use it in selling goods or services.

_ 7. A franchisee is not subject to the franchisor's control in the area of product quality.

_ 8. There is no state law covering franchises.

_ 9. There are no federal laws covering franchises.

_ 10. A franchisor may specify the standards of operation of the franchisee's business.

FILL-IN QUESTIONS

(Answers at the Back of the Book)

An automobile dealership is an example of a ______________________________ (chain-yle/distributorship/manufacturing) franchise. McDonald's is an example of a ______________ ______________ (chain-style/distributorship/manufacturing) franchise. Coca-Cola is an example of a ______________________ (chain-style/distributorship/manufacturing) franchise.

MULTIPLE-CHOICE QUESTIONS

(Answers at the Back of the Book)

_ 1. Rae owns Solo Enterprises, a sole proprietorship. Rae's liability for the obligations of the business is

a. limited by state statute.
b. limited to the amount of his original investment.
c. limited to the total amount of capital Ann invests in the business.
d. unlimited.

_ 2. Violet invests in a franchise with Whiz Gas Stations, Inc. Whiz requires Violet to buy Whiz products for every phase of the operation. Violet's best argument to challenge this requirement is that it violates

a. an implied covenant of good faith and fair dealing.
b. antitrust laws.
c. the Federal Trade Commission's Franchise Rule.
d. the U.S. Franchise Agency's Purchase and Sale Regulations.

___ **3.** Bing invests in a franchise with Copy Centers, Inc. The franchise agreement may require Bing pay a percentage of Copy Center's

a. administrative expenses only.
b. advertising expenses only.
c. administrative and advertising expenses.
d. neither administrative nor advertising expenses.

___ **4.** Dryden wants the exclusive right to sell Elan Corporation software in a specific area. If El agrees, it may require Dryden to pay

a. a fee for a license and a percentage of the receipts.
b. neither a fee for a license nor a percentage of the receipts.
c. only a fee for a license to sell the software.
d. only a percentage of the receipts from sales of the software.

___ **5.** Fridley buys a franchise from Global Services, Inc. In their agreement, Global may specify

a. neither the location of the business nor the territory to be served.
b. the location of the business and the territory to be served.
c. the location of the business only.
d. the territory to be served only.

___ **6.** Rhett buys a franchise from Sports Club Corporation. If their agreement is like most franchi agreements, it will allow Sports Club to terminate the franchise

a. for any reason only with notice.
b. for any reason without notice.
c. for cause only.
d. under no circumstances.

___ **7.** Salvador invests in a franchise with Thai Foods Corporation. With respect to the franchis Salvador may have legal protection under

a. federal and state law.
b. federal law only.
c. neither federal nor state law.
d. state law only.

___ **8.** Devonna, the owner of Evangelina Sales, a sole proprietorship, wants to increase the business capital without sacrificing control. This can be attained most successfully by

a. borrowing funds.
b. bringing in partners.
c. issuing stock.
d. selling the business.

___ **9.** Parry considers buying a franchise instead of developing and marketing his own products. franchise could involve the licensing to Parry of

a. a copyright, a trademark, or a trade name.
b. a copyright only.
c. a trademark or a trade name only.
d. none of the choices.

___ **10.** Lathrop Farm & Ranch Outfitters, Inc., grants a franchise to Mort. Mort is Lathrop's

a. agent.
b. franchisee.
c. franchisor.
d. principal.

SHORT ESSAY QUESTIONS

What do franchise agreements generally provide with respect to a franchisee's location and form of ing business?

How do franchise agreements generally delegate price and quality controls over the franchisee's siness?

GAMEPOINTS

(Answers at the Back of the Book)

You're playing "Solo," a video game in which the goal is to amass as much personal profit from the vestment of your time and money in your business enterprise as possible. At the start of the game, your siness is small—your avatar is your only "employee"—and you expect to make little or no profit for at ast a couple of "years." Your competitors include seemingly heartless corporate money mongers and celess government bureaucrats, whose only reason for existence appears to be to prevent your success. hich form of business organization are you most likely to choose at the start? Why? What are its sadvantages? How can you raise additional capital without losing control of your outfit?

"Burgers & Fries" is a video game in which you operate fast food franchise restaurants. You start with single, small outlet that grows with its success. You expand your operation with your profits, adding as any outlets as you can, balancing your franchisor's requirements, your customers' requests, your business sts, and your desire to increase your wealth. Your agreement with your franchisor includes sales quotas. ne agreement also states that your franchise can be terminated at any time for "cause." Would a failure to eet those quotas constitute "cause"? Explain.

Chapter 27:
All Forms of Partnership

WHAT THIS CHAPTER IS ABOUT

This chapter outlines the law of different types of partnerships. These include general partnerships, nited partnerships, limited liability partnerships, and limited liability limited partnerships. Agency inciples (see Chapter 23) apply to all partnerships.

CHAPTER OUTLINE

BASIC PARTNERSHIP CONCEPTS

A partnership arises from an agreement between two or more persons to carry on a business for profit.

A. AGENCY CONCEPTS AND PARTNERSHIP LAW
Agency principles (see Chapter 23) apply to all partnerships.

B. THE UNIFORM PARTNERSHIP ACT
The Uniform Partnership Act (UPA) governs partnerships.

C. DEFINITION OF PARTNERSHIP
A partnership is "an association of two or more persons to carry on as co-owners a business for profit" [UPA 101(6)]. The intent to associate is a key element.

D. WHEN DOES A PARTNERSHIP EXIST?
There are three essential elements:

1. A sharing of profits or losses.
2. A joint ownership of the business.
3. An equal right in the management of the business.

E. ENTITY VERSUS AGGREGATE THEORY OF PARTNERSHIPS
Under the UPA, a partnership is treated as an entity [UPA 201, 307(a). A partnership can own property as an entity, and sue and be sued in the firm name. For at least one purpose (federal income taxes), a partnership is regarded as an aggregate of individual partners.

I. PARTNERSHIP FORMATION

A partnership agreement generally states the intention to create a partnership, contribute capital, share profits and losses, and participate in management.

A. THE PARTNERSHIP AGREEMENT
The agreement can be oral, written, or implied by conduct. Some must be in writing under the Statute of Frauds (see Chapter 12). Partners can agree to any term that is not illegal or contrary to public policy.

B. DURATION OF THE PARTNERSHIP
A partnership for a term ends on a specific date or the completion of a particular project. Dissolution without consent of all partners before the end of the term is a breach of the agreement. If there is no fixed term, a partnership is at will, and any partner can dissolve the firm at any time.

C. PARTNERSHIP BY ESTOPPEL

When parties who are not partners hold themselves out as partners and make representatio that third persons rely on in dealing with them, liability is imposed. A partner who misrepresen a non-partner's status is also liable (and the non-partner's acts may bind the partnership).

III. PARTNERSHIP OPERATION, DISSOCIATION, AND TERMINATION

A. RIGHTS OF PARTNERS

1. Management Rights

a. In Ordinary Matters, the Majority Rules
All partners have equal rights to manage the firm [UPA 401(e)]. Each partner has o vote.

b. When Unanimous Consent Is Required
Unanimous consent is required to (1) alter the essential nature of the firm's business capital structure; (2) admit new partners or enter a new business; (3) assign property in a trust for the benefit of creditors; (4) dispose of the firm's goodwill; (5) confess judgme against the firm or submit firm claims to arbitration; (6) undertake any act that wou make conduct of partnership business impossible; or (7) amend partnership articles [UP 301(2), 401(j)].

2. Interest in the Partnership

Unless the partners agree otherwise, profits and losses are shared equally [UPA 401(b)].

3. Compensation

Doing partnership business is a partner's duty and not compensable. On the death of partner, a surviving partner is entitled to compensation to wind up partnership affairs [UP 401(h)].

4. Inspection of Books

A partner has a right to complete information concerning the conduct of partnership busine [UPA 403]. Partnership books must be kept at the principal business office.

5. Accounting of Partnership Assets or Profits

An accounting can be called for voluntarily or compelled by a court. Formal accounting o curs by right in connection with dissolution. A partner also has the right to bring an actio for an accounting during the term of the partnership and on its dissolution and winding u [UPA 405(b)].

6. Property Rights

Property acquired by a partnership is normally partnership property [UPA 203, 204]. partner can use this property only on the firm's behalf [UPA 401(g)]. A partner is not a c owner of this property and has no interest in it that can be transferred (although a partn can assign his or her right to a share of the profits) [UPA 501]. A partner's interest is subje to a judgment creditor's lien, attachable through a charging order [UPA 504].

B. DUTIES AND LIABILITIES OF PARTNERS

1. Fiduciary Duties

A partner owes the firm and its partners duties of loyalty and care [UPA 404]. A partne may pursue his or her own interests without automatically violating these duties.

a. Duty of Loyalty
A partner must account to the firm for "any property, profit, or benefit" in the conduct its business or from a use of its property, and refrain from dealing with the firm as a adverse party or competing with it.

b. Duty of Care
A partner must refrain from "grossly negligent or reckless conduct, intentional misconduct, or a knowing violation of law." But simple negligence and honest errors of business judgment do not create liability.

2. Authority of Partners
Each partner is an agent of the partnership in carrying out its usual business, unless designated otherwise.

a. The Scope of Implied Powers
Partners exercise all implied powers necessary and customary to carry on the business.

b. Authorized versus Unauthorized Actions
A partner cannot act purportedly on behalf of the partnership outside the scope of the business (by, for example, selling partnership assets without consent).

3. Liability of Partners

a. Joint Liability
In some states, partners are only jointly liable for partnership obligations, including contracts [UPA 306(a)]. This does not include debts arising from torts, and a creditor must sue all of the partners together (though each may be held liable individually).

b. Joint and Several Liability
In most states, partners are jointly and severally liable for all partnership obligations, including contracts, torts, and breaches of trust [UPA 306(a)] (though a creditor must first try to collect a partnership debt from the firm). A partner who commits a tort must reimburse the partnership for any damages it pays.

c. Liability of an Incoming Partner
A newly admitted partner is liable for partnership debts incurred before his or her admission only to the extent of his or her interest in the partnership [UPA 306(b)].

V. PARTNER'S DISSOCIATION

Dissociation occurs when a partner ceases to be associated in the carrying on of the partnership business. The partner can have his or her interest bought by the firm, which otherwise continues in business.

A. EVENTS CAUSING DISSOCIATION

Dissociation occurs when a partner give notices and withdraws, declares bankruptcy, assigns his or her interest, dies, becomes incompetent, or is expelled by the firm or by a court. Other events can be specified in the partnership agreement [UPA 601].

B. WRONGFUL DISSOCIATION

Dissociation is wrongful if it is in breach of the partnership agreement [UPA 602]. A partner who wrongfully dissociates is liable to the partnership and to the other partners for damages caused by the dissociation.

C. EFFECTS OF DISSOCIATION

1. The Partner
A partner's right to participate in the firm's business ends [UPA 603]. The duty of loyalty ends. The duty of care continues only with respect to events that occurred before dissociation, unless the partner participates in winding up the firm's business.

2. The Partnership
The partner's interest in the firm must be purchased according to the rules in UPA 701. To avoid liability for obligations under a theory of apparent authority, a partnership should notify its creditors of a partner's dissociation and file a statement of dissociation in the appropriate state office [UPA 704].

V. PARTNERSHIP TERMINATION

Caused by any change in the relations of the partners that shows unwillingness or inability to car on partnership business [UPA 801]. To continue the business, a partner can organize a n partnership.

A. DISSOLUTION

Dissolution terminates the right of the partnership to exist as a going concern, but the fi remains long enough to wind up its affairs.

1. Dissolution by Acts of the Partners

a. Agreement

The partnership agreement can state events that will dissolve the firm. Partners c agree to dissolve the partnership early.

b. Death, Incapacity, or Bankruptcy

A partnership for a definite term or undertaking can be dissolved within ninety days of partner's dissociation caused by death, incapacity, or bankruptcy, if a majority of t remaining partners agree [UPA 801(2)].

2. Dissolution by Operation of Law

A partnership is dissolved if an event occurs that makes it impossible to continue lawfully, though the partners can continue if they change the nature of the business [UPA 801(4)].

3. Dissolution by Judicial Decree

A court can dissolve a partnership for commercial impracticality, a partner's improper co duct, or other circumstances [UPA 801(5)].

B. WINDING UP

Involves collecting and preserving partnership assets, paying debts, and accounting to eac partner for the value of his or her interest. No new obligations can be created on behalf of t partnership.

1. Distribution of Assets

Priorities for a partnership's assets are (1) payment of debts, including those owed to partn and non-partner creditors, and (2) return of capital contributions and distribution of profits partners.

2. If the Partnership's Liabilities Are Greater Than Its Assets

The general partners bear the losses in the same proportion in which they shared the profits

VI. LIMITED LIABILITY PARTNERSHIPS

A limited liability partnership (LLP) enjoys the tax advantages of a partnership, while partne avoid personal liability for the wrongdoing of other partners.

A. FORMATION OF AN LLP

The appropriate form must be filed with a central state agency. The business's name mu include "Limited Liability Partnership" or "LLP." Annual reports must be filed with the stat [UPA 1001, 1002, 1003].

B. LIABILITY IN AN LLP

The UPA exempts partners in an LLP from personal liability for any partnership obligatio "whether arising in contract, tort, or otherwise" [UPA 306(c)].

1. Liability outside the State of Formation

Most states apply the law of the state in which the LLP was formed [UPA 1101].

2. Sharing Liability among Partner

A partner who commits a wrongful act is liable for the results, as is any other partner wh committed the act. Some states provide that each partner is liable only up to the proportion c his or her responsibility for the result.

C. FAMILY LIMITED LIABILITY PARTNERSHIPS
This is a limited liability partnership (LLP) in which most of the partners are related. All partners must be natural persons or persons acting in a fiduciary capacity for natural persons. Family-owned farms may benefit from this form.

I. LIMITED PARTNERSHIPS

Limited partnerships must include at least one general partner and one or more limited partners. General partners assume management responsibility and liability for all partnership debts.

A. FORMATION OF A LIMITED PARTNERSHIP
Formation of a limited partnership is a public, formal proceeding: there must be two or more partners (at least one of whom is a general partner), and a certificate of limited partnership must be signed and filed with a designated state official (typically the secretary of state).

B. LIABILITIES OF PARTNERS IN A LIMITED PARTNERSHIP
General partners assume liability for all partnership debts. A limited partner is liable only to the extent of any contribution that is promised to the firm or any part of a contribution that was withdrawn [RULPA 502]. But participating in management results in a limited partner's personal liability for partnership debt, if creditors knew of participation [RULPA 303].

C. RIGHTS AND DUTIES IN A LIMITED PARTNERSHIP
Limited partners have essentially the same rights as general partners—a right of access to the partnership books and other information regarding partnership business.

D. DISSOCIATION AND DISSOLUTION

1. General Partners—Dissolution
Retirement, death, or mental incompetence of a general partner dissolves the firm, unless continued by the other general partners [RULPA 801]. Illegality, expulsion, or bankruptcy of a general partner dissolves a firm.

2. Limited Partners—No Dissolution
Death or assignment of interest of a limited partner does not dissolve the firm [RULPA 702, 704, 705], nor does personal bankruptcy.

3. Court Decree—Dissolution
A limited partnership can be dissolved by court decree [RULPA 802].

4. Priority to Assets on Dissolution
(1) Creditors, including partners who are creditors; (2) partners and former partners receive unpaid distributions of partnership assets and, except as otherwise agreed, a return on their contributions and amounts proportionate to their share of distributions [RULPA 804].

E. LIMITED LIABILITY LIMITED PARTNERSHIPS
This form is similar to a limited partnership, except that the liability of all partners in a limited liability limited partnership (LLLP) is limited to the amount of their investment in the firm.

TRUE-FALSE QUESTIONS

(Answers at the Back of the Book)

__ 1. A partnership is an association of two or more persons to carry on, as co-owners, a business for profit.

__ 2. In most states, no partnership can exist unless a certificate of partnership is filed with a state.

__ 3. A general partner is not personally liable for partnership debts if its assets are insufficient to pay its creditors.

___ **4.** Unless the partnership agreement states otherwise, a general partner has one vote management matters.

___ **5.** A partnership is usually considered a legal entity apart from its owners.

___ **6.** Unless a partnership agreement specifies otherwise, profits are shared in the same ratio as ca tal contributions.

___ **7.** The death of a *limited* partner dissolves a limited partnership.

___ **8.** In a limited liability partnership, no partner is exempt from personal liability for partnersh obligations.

___ **9.** In a limited partnership, the liability of a *limited* partner is limited to the amount of capital he she invests in the partnership.

___ **10.** In a limited liability limited partnership, the liability of a *general* partner is limited to the amou of capital he or she invests in the partnership.

FILL-IN QUESTIONS

(Answers at the Back of the Book)

In most states, partners _______________ (are/are not) subject to joint and several liability on partne ship debts, contracts, and torts. This means that a third party may sue _________________ (one more/only all) of the partners on a partnership _______________________ (obligation/tort). If the third par does not sue all of the partners, the liability of those partners who are not sued ______________ (is/is nc extinguished. The third party's release of one partner __________________ (does not release/releases) t other partners.

MULTIPLE-CHOICE QUESTIONS

(Answers at the Back of the Book)

___ **1.** Cosmo holds himself out as a partner of Dayton Associates, a partnership, even though he has connection to the firm. Cosmo obtains a loan based on the misrepresentation. Cosmo's default the loan results in

a. Cosmo and Dayton's joint liability for the amount.
b. Cosmo's sole liability for the amount.
c. Delta's sole liability for the amount.
d. neither Cosmo's nor Dayton's liability.

___ **2.** Holly owns International Imports. She hires Jordan as a salesperson, agreeing to pay $10.00 pe hour, plus a commission of 10 percent of his sales. The term is one year. Holly and Jordan are

a. not partners, because Jay does not have an ownership interest or management rights in th business.
b. not partners, because the pay includes an hourly wage.
c. not partners, because the pay includes only a 10-percent commission.
d. partners for one year.

_ **3.** Kris is admitted to an existing partnership. A partnership debt incurred before the date of her admission comes due. Kris is

a. not liable for the debt.
b. only liable for the debt to the amount of her capital contribution.
c. personally liable only to the extent that the other partners do not pay the debt.
d. personally liable to the full extent of the debt.

_ **4.** Delilah is a partner in Estelinda Technical Group. Delilah's dissociation from the partnership will cause

a. the automatic termination of the firm's legal existence.
b. the immediate maturity of all partnership debts.
c. the partnership's buyout of Delilah's interest in the firm.
d. the temporary suspension of all partnership business.

_ **5.** Owen and Page are partners in Quality Investments, a partnership. Owen convinces Roy, a customer, to invest in a nonexistent gold mine. Owen absconds with Roy's money. If Roy sues Page, Roy will

a. lose, because partners are not jointly and severally liable.
b. lose, because only partnership assets are available to pay the judgment.
c. win, because partners are jointly and severally liable.
d. win, because partnership assets are available to pay the judgment.

_ **6.** Bobbi owns Bobbi's Salon, which owes back rent to Capital Properties, a landlord. Bobbi agrees to pay a percentage of her profit each month until the debt is paid. Capital Properties is

a. Bobbi's creditor and partner.
b. Bobbi's creditor only.
c. Bobbi's partner only.
d. neither Bobbi's creditor nor partner.

_ **7.** Mona is a limited partner in Destination Travel, a limited partnership. Mona is liable for the firm's debts

a. in no way.
b. in proportion to the total number of partners in the firm.
c. to the extent of his capital contribution.
d. to the full extent of the debts.

_ **8.** Jack and Kiley form J&K, a limited partnership. Jack is a general partner. Kiley is a limited partner. Dissolution of the firm would result from Kiley's

a. assignment of her interest in the firm to a third party only.
b. assignment of her interest, bankruptcy, or death.
c. bankruptcy or death only.
d. none of the choices.

_ **9.** Myra, Nico, and Odel are partners in Payroll Accounting Services (PAS). Myra quits the firm, with Nico and Odel's knowledge. Later, Nico and Odel sign a contract with a supplier. The contract is binding on

a. Nico and Odel only.
b. Nico, Odel, and PAS only.
c. PAS only.
d. no one.

___ **10.** Drs. Lucas and Miko are partners in a medical clinic, which is organized as a limited liabili partnership. Lucas manages the clinic. A court holds Miko liable in a malpractice suit. Lucas liable

a. in no way.
b. in proportion to the total number of partners in the firm.
c. to the extent of her capital contribution.
d. to the full extent of the liability.

SHORT ESSAY QUESTIONS

1. What are the rights held by partners in terms of management, interest in the partnershi compensation, inspection of books, accounting, and property rights?

2. How do the concepts of joint liability, and joint and several liability, relate to partnerships?

GAMEPOINTS

(Answers at the Back of the Book)

1. The video game "Phantasm" requires two or more players who confront malicious phenomena—ghost zombies, and so on—and combine their abilities to capture the bad guys for delivery to university researc centers. In the game, you orally agree with your partner to pursue this adventure for five years, with th profits to be split 60/40. If this were a real partnership, would the agreement be enforceable? Should th terms be in writing? Explain.

2. You are playing "Business Buddy," a video game in which the play consists of two or more players wh operate as partners to buy, sell, and trade commodities—oil, corn, swine, and other animals, vegetables, an minerals—in global markets. One of your "buddies" is your cousin Melvin. Your agreement states that on you have the authority to bind the partnership to contracts with others. Without your knowledge, howeve Melvin tells the Greater Asian Goatherds Association that he represents your firm and contracts to buy large herd of goats. What factor determines whether your partnership is bound to this contract? If th contract is binding on the firm, to what extent are you personally liable?

Chapter 28:
Limited Liability Companies and Special Business Forms

WHAT THIS CHAPTER IS ABOUT

This chapter sets out the law relating to a relatively new form of business organization: limited ›ility companies (LLCs). The chief features of this business form are limited liability and tax advantages. e chapter also looks at the features of other forms for doing business—joint ventures, business trusts, peratives, and so on.

CHAPTER OUTLINE

LIMITED LIABILITY COMPANIES

Limited liability companies (LLCs) are subject to state statutes, some of which are based on the Uniform Limited Liability Company Act (ULLCA) or its revised version (Re-ULLCA).

A. THE NATURE OF AN LLC

An LLC is a hybrid form of business enterprise that offers limited liability of a corporation with tax advantages of a partnership. LLCs are legal entities apart from their owners, who are called members. An LLC can sue or be sued, enter into contracts, and hold title to property [ULLCA 201]. Members have limited liability [ULLCA 303] and can bring a derivative action on the LLC's behalf.

B. LLC FORMATION

Articles of organization must be filed with the state. Certain information is required. The business's name must include and LLC designation.

C. JURISDICTIONAL REQUIREMENTS

An LLC is a citizen of every state of which its members are citizens.

D. ADVANTAGES OF THE LLC

1. Limited Liability

An LLC is a hybrid form of business enterprise that offers the limited liability of the corporation.

2. Taxation

An LLC offers the tax advantages of a partnership. LLCs with two or more members can elect to be taxed as either a partnership or a corporation. If no choice is made, an LLC is taxed as a partnership. One-member LLCs are taxed as sole proprietorships unless they elect to be taxed as corporations.

3. Management and Foreign Investors

An LLC has flexibility in terms of its management and operations (see below). Foreign investors may become LLC members.

E. DISADVANTAGES OF THE LLC

Because the LLC is a new form, little case law exists; until uniform statutes are adopted by m states, an LLC with multistate operations may face difficulties.

II. LLC OPERATION AND MANAGEMENT

A. THE LLC OPERATING AGREEMENT

Members decide how to operate the business. Provisions relate to management, division profits, transfer of membership, what events trigger dissolution, and so on. In the absence of agreement, LLC statutes govern.

1. A Writing Is Preferred

An operating agreement is not required in all states and if required may not need to be writing. But a written agreement protects members' interests if there is a dispute or if LLC statute is contrary to their intent.

2. Partnership Law May Apply

If there is no operating agreement or LLC statute, the principles of partnership law app This may give the members broad authority to bind the LLC.

B. MANAGEMENT OF AN LLC

In a member-managed LLC, all members participate in management [ULLCA 404(a)]. In manager-managed LLC, the members designate a group of persons (member or not) to mana the firm. These managers owe the fiduciary duties of loyalty and care to the LLC and in so states to its members [ULLCA 409(a), (h)].

C. OPERATING PROCEDURES

The LLC's operating agreement may also specify procedures for making decisions. If it does n choosing and removing managers is done by majority vote [ULLCA 404(b)(3)]. Details concerni meetings and voting rights may also be included in the agreement. IF not, in some states, ea member has one vote.

III. DISSOCIATION AND DISSOLUTION OF AN LLC

Dissociation occurs when a person ceases to be associated with the carrying on of a business. member of an LLC has the power, but may not have the right, to dissociate from the LLC. Eve that trigger dissociation under the ULLCA are the same as those listed in the Uniform Partners Act (see Chapter 26).

A. THE EFFECT OF DISSOCIATION

On dissociation, a member's right to participate in the firm's business ends. The duty of loya also ends, and the duty of care continues only with respect to events that occurred bef dissociation. The member's interest in the firm must be bought out according to the L agreement, or for its "fair" value.

B. DISSOLUTION

A dissociating member does not normally have the right to force the LLC to dissolve (althou the other members can dissolve it if they want and a court might order dissolution). dissolution, any member can participate in winding up. After liquidation of the assets, t proceeds are distributed first to creditors (who may include members), then to capi contributors, and finally to members according to the operating agreement or in equal shares.

IV. SPECIAL BUSINESS FORMS

A. JOINT VENTURES

A joint venture is an enterprise in which two or more persons combine their efforts or prope for a single transaction or project, or a related series of transactions or projects. Unl otherwise agreed, joint venturers share profits and losses equally.

1. **Similarities to Partnerships**
   The characteristics of a joint venture are similar to those of a partnership.

2. **Differences from Partnerships**
   Members in a joint venture have less implied and apparent authority than partners.

B. SYNDICATES
A group of individuals getting together to finance a particular project, such as the building of a shopping center or the purchase of a professional basketball franchise, is a syndicate. It may exist as a corporation or a partnership. In some cases, the members merely own property jointly and have no legally recognized business arrangement.

C. JOINT STOCK COMPANIES
Usually treated like a partnership (formed by agreement, members have personal liability, etc.), but members are not agents of one another, and has many characteristics of a corporation: (1) ownership by shares of stock, (2) managed by directors and officers, and (3) perpetual existence.

D. BUSINESS TRUSTS
A business trust is created by a written trust agreement. Legal ownership and management of the property of the business is in one or more trustees; profits are distributed to beneficiaries, who are not personally responsible for the debts of the trust. A business trust resembles a corporation.

E. COOPERATIVES
A cooperative is an association organized to provide an economic service without profit to its members (or shareholders).

1. **Incorporated Cooperative**
   Subject to state laws governing nonprofit corporations. Distributes profits to owners on the basis of their transactions with the cooperative rather than on the basis of the amount of capital they contributed.

2. **Unincorporated Cooperatives**
   Often treated like partnerships. The members have joint liability for the cooperative's acts.

TRUE-FALSE QUESTIONS

(Answers at the Back of the Book)

___ **1.** Forming a limited liability company does not require the filing of any documents in a state office.

___ **2.** A limited liability company is a citizen of every state of which its members are citizens.

___ **3.** A limited liability company does not offer the limited liability of a corporation.

___ **4.** In a limited liability company, members do not have to participate in its management.

___ **5.** Most limited liability company (LLC) statutes provide that unless the members agree otherwise, all profits of the LLC will be divided equally.

___ **6.** A syndicate may exist in the form of a corporation.

___ **7.** A joint venture is similar to a sole proprietorship.

___ **8.** A cooperative may take the form of a partnership or a corporation, but its distinguishing feature is that it is organized to provide an economic service without profit.

___ **9.** A joint stock company has many characteristics of a corporation.

___ **10.** A business trust resembles a partnership.

FILL-IN QUESTIONS

(Answers at the Back of the Book)

Unless the participants agree otherwise, all of the ____________ (members/limited partne of a ____________ (limited liability company/limited partnership) may participate in manageme without assuming liability for the obligations of the firm. In contrast, the ____________ (members/limited partners) of a ____________ (limited liability company/limited partnership) w participate in management may be personally liable for the debts of the firm.

MULTIPLE-CHOICE QUESTIONS

(Answers at the Back of the Book)

___ **1.** Ebsen and Flossy form Eb & Flo, LLC, a limited liability company (LLC), to contract for t installation of custom plumbing and piping. One advantage of an LLC is that it may be taxed as

a. a corporation.
b. a partnership.
c. a sole proprietorship.
d. a syndicate.

___ **2.** Lonny is a member of Magna Management, a limited liability company that manages commerci properties for their owners. Lonny is liable for the firm's debts

a. in proportion to the total number of members.
b. to the extent of his capital contribution.
c. to the extent that the other members do not pay the debts.
d. to the full extent of the debts.

___ **3.** Cal and Dyson form Elemeno Construction, a limited liability company, to design and mak prefabricated housing. They can participate in its management

a. only to the extent that they assume personal liability for the firm's debts.
b. only to the extent of the amount of their investment in the firm.
c. to any extent.
d. to no extent.

___ **4.** Rhianna and Stuart form Toons, LLC, a limited liability company (LLC), to market anim related merchandise. A disadvantage of an LLC is that

a. its income is double taxed.
b. its members are subject to personal liability for the firm's debts.
c. its members cannot participate in its management.
d. state laws concerning limited liability companies are not yet uniform.

___ **5.** Tropical Trade Corporation and US Outlet Stores, Inc., form a joint venture to import and se foreign-made clothing. A joint venture is

a. a corporate enterprise for a single undertaking of limited duration.
b. an association limited to no more than two persons in business for profit.
c. an association of persons engaged as co-owners in a single undertaking for profit.
d. an enterprise of numerous co-owners in a nonprofit undertaking.

_ **6.** Mole Corporation and Nano, Inc., form a joint venture to develop and market molecular-based computer chips. A joint venture is similar to

a. a corporation.
b. a partnership.
c. a sole proprietorship.
d. a syndicate.

_ **7.** Evan and Freebo form a syndicate to finance Grande Vista, a real estate project. A syndicate

a. is similar to a corporation.
b. is similar to a partnership.
c. is a hybrid of a corporation and a partnership.
d. may exist as a partnership or a corporation.

_ **8.** Leza and Mike form a joint stock company to manage investments. A joint stock company is a hybrid of

a. a corporation and a joint venture.
b. a corporation and a partnership.
c. a joint venture and a partnership.
d. a limited liability company and a sole proprietorship.

_ **9.** Coastline Railway, Inc., and Drinkwater Transport Corporation pool their assets to form a business trust. This is similar to

a. a corporation.
b. a joint venture.
c. a partnership.
d. a sole proprietorship.

_ **10.** Organic Farms, LLC, is a limited liability company. Its members hire outside managers to operate the LLC These managers owe Organic Farms

a. a duty of care only.
b. a duty of loyalty only.
c. fiduciary duties of care and loyalty.
d. neither a duty of care nor a duty loyalty.

SHORT ESSAY QUESTIONS

. What are the advantages of doing business as a limited liability company?

. What are the principal characteristics of a cooperative?

GAMEPOINTS

(Answers at the Back of the Book)

. In the video game "Hamster Hotel," your avatar is a hotelier who joins efforts with an investment rm—specialists in vacation destination funding—to design, build, outfit, and operate a resort with rooms nd activities modeled on pet-hamster paraphernalia and preoccupations. Features include human-scaled heels, water bottles, and pet toys. Which form of business organization outlined in this chapter are you and ne investment firm most likely to use to engage in this endeavor? How will the profits and losses be shared?

. You are playing "Team Up," a video game in which the play consists of choosing athletes for a fantasy ports team to compete with other teams for a championship title. Before selecting your team's players, you form the team's organization, Super Sport LLC. You are Super Sport's sole member. According to t principles discussed in this chapter, how would the firm's profits be taxed? Can a "non-member" manage t day-to-day business of the firm? If one of your players assaults a fan during a game, could you be held fu liable?

Chapter 29: Corporate Formation, Merger, and Termination

WHAT THIS CHAPTER IS ABOUT

This chapter covers corporate rights, powers, classifications, formation, and financing. Most rporations are formed under state law, and a majority of states follow some version of the Revised Model isiness Corporation Act (RMBCA). This chapter also covers corporate mergers, consolidations, purchase another firm's assets, and purchase of a controlling interest in another firm, as well as the termination of a rporation.

CHAPTER OUTLINE

CORPORATE NATURE AND CLASSIFICATION

A. CORPORATE PERSONNEL
Shareholders elect a board of directors, which is responsible for overall management and hires corporate officers to run daily operations. Shareholders normally are not liable for corporate obligations beyond the extent of their investments.

B. THE CONSTITUTIONAL RIGHTS OF CORPORATIONS
A corporation is recognized by the law as a "person" and, under the Bill of Rights, has the same rights as a natural person (see Chapter 2). Only officers and employees have the right against self-incrimination, however, and the privileges and immunities clause does not protect corporations.

C. THE LIMITED LIABILITY OF SHAREHOLDERS
The key feature of a corporation is the limit of its owners' liability, for corporate obligations, to the amounts of their investments in the firm. Of course, a lender may require otherwise or a court may "pierce the corporate veil" (see below).

D. CORPORATE EARNINGS AND TAXATION
Profits that are not distributed are retained earnings and can be invested for higher profits, which may cause the price of the stock to rise, benefiting shareholders.

1. Corporate Taxation
Corporate profits are taxed twice: as income to the corporation and, when distributed as dividends, as income to the shareholders.

2. Holding Companies
A holding company (or parent company) holds the shares of another company. Such firms are often established in offshore no-tax or low-tax jurisdictions. A corporation whose shares are held in a holding company may transfer cash and other investments to be taxed in that jurisdiction.

E. TORTS AND CRIMINAL ACTS
A corporation is liable for torts committed by its agents within the course and scope of employment. A corporation may be liable for crimes of its employees and agents if punishment for

the crimes can be applied to a corporation. Penalties may include fines of up to hundreds millions of dollars, depending on the offense, the amount of money involved, and the extent which company officers are implicated.

F. CLASSIFICATION OF CORPORATIONS

1. Domestic, Foreign, and Alien Corporations
A corporation is a *domestic* corporation in the state in which it incorporated, a *forei* corporation in other states, and an *alien* corporation in other countries. A foreign corporati normally must obtain a certificate of authority to do business in any state except its ho state.

2. Public and Private Corporations
A *public* corporation is formed by the government to meet a political or governmental purpo (the U.S. Postal Service, AMTRAK). A *private* corporation is created for private benefit a is owned by private persons.

3. Nonprofit Corporations
These are corporations formed without a profit-making purpose (private hospita educational institutions, charities, and religious organizations).

4. Close Corporations
A close corporation is exempt from most of the nonessential formalities of corporate operati (bylaws, annual meetings, etc. [RMBCA 7.32]). To qualify, a firm must have a limit number of shareholders, and restrict its issue and transfer of stock.

a. Management of a Close Corporation
Resembles that of a sole proprietorship or a partnership—one or a few shareholde usually hold the positions of directors and officers.

b. Transfer of Shares in Close Corporations
Often restricted by stipulating that shareholders offer their shares to the corporation other shareholders before offering them to outsiders.

c. Misappropriation of Close Corporation Funds
The remedy for minority shareholders on a majority shareholder's misappropriation company funds is to have their shares appraised and be paid their fair market value.

5. S Corporations

a. Qualification Requirements
Must be a domestic corporation; must not be a member of an affiliated group corporations; shareholders must be individuals, estates, or certain trusts; must have 10 or fewer shareholders; can have only one class of stock; no shareholder can be nonresident alien.

b. Benefits
Shareholders can use corporate losses to offset other income; only a single tax o corporate income is imposed at individual income tax rates at the shareholder level (eve if it is not distributed).

6. Professional Corporations
Generally subject to the law governing ordinary corporations.

a. Limited Liability
A shareholder in a professional corporation is protected from liability for torts (excep malpractice) committed by other members.

b. Unlimited Liability
A court might regard a professional corporation as a partnership, in which each partne may be liable for the malpractice of the others.

CORPORATE FORMATION AND POWERS

A. PROMOTIONAL ACTIVITIES

Promoters take the first steps in organizing a corporation: issue a prospectus (see Chapter 30) and secure the corporate charter (see below). Promoters are personally liable on preincorporation contracts until the corporation assumes the contract by novation (see Chapter 13).

B. INCORPORATION PROCEDURES

1. Selecting the State of Incorporation

Some states offer more advantageous tax or incorporation provisions.

2. Securing the Corporate Name

The name cannot be the same as, or deceptively similar to, the name of a corporation doing business in the state.

3. Preparing the Articles of Incorporation

The articles include basic information about the corporation and serve as a primary source of authority for its organization and functions.

a. Shares of the Corporation

The amount of stock authorized for issuance; its valuation; and other information as to equity, capital, and credit must be outlined.

b. Registered Office and Agent

Usually, the registered office is the principal office of the corporation; the agent is a person designated to receive legal documents on behalf of the corporation.

c. Incorporators

Incorporators (some states require only one) must sign the articles when they are submitted to the state; often this is their only duty, and they need have no other interest in the corporation.

d. Duration and Purpose

A corporation can have perpetual existence in most states. The intended business activities of the corporation must be specified. Stating a general corporate purpose is usually sufficient.

e. Internal Organization

Management structure can be described in bylaws later.

4. Filing the Articles with the State

The articles of incorporation are sent to the appropriate state official (usually the secretary of state). Many states issue a certificate of incorporation authorizing the corporation to conduct business.

5. First Organizational Meeting to Adopt Bylaws

The incorporators or the board; the business conducted depends on state law, the nature of the corporation's business, the provisions of the articles, and the wishes of the promoters. Adoption of the bylaws is the most important function of the first organizational meeting.

C. CORPORATE POWERS

Express powers are in (in order of priority) the U.S. Constitution, state constitution, state statutes, articles of incorporation, bylaws, and board resolutions.

1. Implied Powers

A corporation has the *implied* power to perform all acts reasonably appropriate and necessary to accomplish its purposes.

2. *Ultra Vires* Doctrine
Ultra vires acts are beyond the purposes stated in the articles. Most such acts have involv contracts (which generally are enforced [RMBCA 3.04]). Courts usually allow any leg action a firm takes to profit shareholders.

III. DEFECTS IN FORMATION AND CORPORATE STATUS

On the basis of improper incorporation, a person attempting to enforce a contract or bring a tort su against the corporation could seek to make the shareholders personally liable. If a corporation see to enforce a contract, the defaulting party who learns of a defect in incorporation may be able avoid liability.

A. *DE JURE* AND *DE FACTO* CORPORATIONS

1. *De Jure* Existence
Occurs if there is substantial compliance with all requirements for incorporation. In mo states, the certificate of incorporation is evidence that all requirements have been met, a neither the state nor a third party can attack the corporation's existence.

2. *De Facto* Existence
The existence of a corporation cannot be challenged by third persons (except the state) if (there is a statute under which the firm can be incorporated, (2) the parties made a good fai attempt to comply with it, and (3) the firm has attempted to do business as a corporation.

B. CORPORATION BY ESTOPPEL

If an association that is neither an actual corporation nor a *de facto* or *de jure* corporation hol itself out as being a corporation, it will be estopped from denying corporate status in a suit by third party.

C. PIERCING THE CORPORATE VEIL

A court may ignore the corporate structure (pierce the corporate veil), exposing the shareholde to personal liability, if—

1. A party is tricked or misled into dealing with the corporation rather than the individual.
2. The corporation is set up never to make a profit or always to be insolvent, or it is too thin capitalized.
3. Statutory corporate formalities are not followed.
4. Personal and corporate interests are commingled to the extent that the corporation has r separate identity.

IV. CORPORATE FINANCING

A. BONDS

Bonds are issued as evidence of funds that business firms borrow from investors. A lendir agreement called a bond indenture specifies the terms (maturity date, interest). A truste ensures that the terms are met.

B. STOCKS

The most important characteristics of stocks are (1) they need not be paid back, (2) stockholde receive dividends only when voted by the directors, (3) stockholders are the last investors to b paid on dissolution, and (4) stockholders vote for management and on major issues.

C. VENTURE CAPITAL AND PRIVATE EQUITY CAPITAL

Start-up businesses and high-risk enterprises may obtain venture capital financing (capital fro professional investors), as well as managerial or technical expertise, in exchange for a share ownership in the firm or control over its decisions. Private equity investors pool their funds t buy an existing corporation and reorganize or sell it.

V. MERGERS AND ACQUISITIONS

Whether a combination is a merger or a consolidation, the rights and liabilities of shareholders, th corporation, and its creditors are the same.

A. MERGER
A merger is the combination of two or more corporations, often by one absorbing the other. After a merger, only one of the corporations exists. The surviving corporation has all of its rights, assets, liabilities, and debts and those of the other corporation. The survivor's articles of incorporation are deemed amended to include changes stated in the articles of merger.

B. CONSOLIDATION
In a consolidation, two or more corporations combine so that each corporation ceases to exist and a new one emerges. The results of a consolidation are essentially the same as the results of a merger.

C. SHARE EXCHANGE
In a share exchange, some or all of the stock of a company are exchanged for some or all of the stock of another. A company that holds all of the shares of another is the other's parent corporation of which the wholly owned firm is a subsidiary corporation.

D. MERGER, CONSOLIDATION, AND SHARE EXCHANGE PROCEDURES
The basic steps are (1) each board approves the plan; (2) each firm's shareholders vote on the plan at a shareholders' meeting; (3) the plan is filed, usually with the secretary of state; and (4) the state issues a certificate of merger or consolidation.

E. SHORT-FORM MERGERS
A substantially owned subsidiary corporation can merge into its parent corporation without shareholder approval, if the parent owns at least 90 percent of the subsidiary's outstanding stock.

F. SHAREHOLDER APPROVAL
The board of directors and the shareholders must authorize actions taken on extraordinary matters (sale, lease, or exchange of all or substantially all corporate assets; amendment to the articles of incorporation; merger; consolidation; dissolution).

G. APPRAISAL RIGHTS
If provided by statute, a shareholder can dissent from a merger, consolidation, share exchange, sale of substantially all the corporate assets not in the ordinary course of business, and (in some states) amendments to the articles, and obtain payment of fair value for his or her stock.

H. PURCHASE OF ASSETS
A corporation that buys all or substantially all of the assets of another corporation does not need shareholder approval. The corporation whose assets are acquired must obtain approval of its board and shareholders (and see the antitrust guidelines in Chapter 32).

I. POTENTIAL LIABILITY IN PURCHASES OF ASSETS
An acquiring corporation is not responsible for the seller's liabilities, unless there is (1) an implied or express assumption, (2) a sale amounting to a merger or consolidation, (3) a buyer retaining the seller's personnel and continuing the business, or (4) a sale executed in fraud to avoid liability.

J. PURCHASE OF STOCK AND TENDER OFFERS
A purchase of a substantial number of the voting shares of a corporation's stock enables an acquiring corporation to gain control. The acquiring corporation can deal directly with shareholders. A tender offer is a public offer. The offer can turn on the receipt of a specified number of shares by a specified date. Generally higher than the stock's market price before the tender offer.

K. RESPONSES TO TENDER OFFERS
Among other tactics, a target may make a self-tender (offer to buy its own stock). A target may also sell its most desirable assets or take other defensive measures (such as a poison pill: give its shareholders the right to buy additional shares at low prices). A request for an injunction on the ground that a takeover will violate antitrust laws may also succeed.

VI. TERMINATION

A. VOLUNTARY DISSOLUTION

Shareholders can initiate dissolution by a unanimous vote or directors may propose dissolution the shareholders for a vote. The corporation files articles of dissolution with the secretary state. The corporation notifies its creditors and sets a date (at least 120 days following the date dissolution) by which all claims against the corporation must be received [RMBCA 14.06].

B. INVOLUNTARY DISSOLUTION

1. By the State

In an action brought by the secretary of state or the state attorney general, a corporati may be dissolved for—

- **a.** Failing to comply with corporate formalities or other statutory requirements.
- **b.** Incorporating through fraud or misrepresentation.
- **c.** Abusing corporate powers (*ultra vires* acts).

2. By a Shareholder

The articles of a close corporation may empower any shareholder to dissolve the corporati at will or on the occurrence of a certain event (such as the death of another shareholder).

3. By a Court

A court can dissolve a corporation when a board is deadlocked or for mismanagement.

C. WINDING UP

If dissolution is by voluntary action, the members of the board act as trustees of the assets, a wind up the affairs of the corporation for the benefit of corporate creditors and shareholders. dissolution is involuntary, the board does not wish to act as trustee, or shareholders or credito can show why the board should not act as trustee, a court will appoint a receiver to wind up t corporate affairs.

TRUE-FALSE QUESTIONS

(Answers at the Back of the Book)

____ 1. A shareholder can sue a corporation, and a corporation can sue a shareholder.

____ 2. S corporations cannot avoid federal taxes at the corporate level.

____ 3. In some states, a close corporation can operate without formal shareholders' or directo meetings.

____ 4. State corporate laws are entirely uniform.

____ 5. A corporation is liable for the torts of its officers committed within the course and scope employment.

____ 6. Appraisal rights are always available to shareholders.

____ 7. Shareholder approval is not required when a corporation sells all of its assets to anoth company.

____ 8. Dissolution of a corporation cannot occur without the unanimous approval of its shareholders.

____ 9. A corporation that buys the assets of another corporation always assumes the debts of the seller

____ 10. In a merger, the surviving corporation inherits all of the disappearing corporation's preexisti rights.

FILL-IN QUESTIONS

(Answers at the Back of the Book)

Those who, for themselves or others, take the preliminary steps in organizing a corporation are ________________ (promoters/incorporators). These persons enter into contracts with professionals, ose services are needed in planning the corporation, and are personally liable on these contracts, ________________ (unless/even if) the third party issues a release or the corporation assumes the con- ct. A person who applies to the state on behalf of the corporation to obtain its certificate of incorporation ________________________ (a promoter/an incorporator). This person ______________ (must/need not) ve any interest in the corporation.

MULTIPLE-CHOICE QUESTIONS

(Answers at the Back of the Book)

_ **1.** Blaine and Cory want to incorporate to buy, play, sell, and trade video games. The first step in the incorporation procedure is to

a. file the articles of incorporation.
b. hold the first organizational meeting.
c. obtain a corporate charter.
d. select a state in which to incorporate.

_ **2.** Metal Fasteners Company (MFC) is a corporation. MFC has the implied power to

a. amend the corporate charter.
b. declare dividends.
c. file a derivative suit.
d. perform all acts reasonably appropriate and necessary to accomplish its corporate purposes.

_ **3.** Daystar Company is a private, for-profit corporation that (1) was formed for the purpose of marketing business office software, (2) is owned by ten shareholders, (3) is subject to double taxation, and (4) has made no public offering of its shares. Daystar is

a. a close corporation.
b. a nonprofit corporation.
c. an S corporation.
d. a professional corporation.

_ **4.** Simplex Corporation substantially complies with all conditions precedent to incorporation. Simplex

a. is a corporation by estoppel.
b. has de facto existence.
c. has de jure existence.
d. none of the choices.

_ **5.** Koz is a shareholder of Little Biz Company, Inc. A court might "pierce the corporate veil" and hold Koz personally liable for Little's debts

a. if Koz's personal interests are commingled with Little's interests to the extent it has no separate identity.
b. if Little calls too many shareholders' meetings.
c. if Little is overcapitalized.
d. under no circumstances.

___ **6.** Precision Corporation and Quotient Company consolidate to form PQ, Inc. PQ assum Precision's and Quotient's

a. assets and liabilities.
b. assets only.
c. liabilities only.
d. neither assets nor liabilities.

___ **7.** Oldway, Inc., is unprofitable. In a suit against Oldway, a court might order dissolution if the fi does not

a. buy its stock from its shareholders.
b. declare a dividend.
c. make a profit this year.
d. pay its taxes.

___ **8.** Spice Corporation and Sugar, Inc., combine so that only Spice remains as the surviving corpor tion. This is

a. a consolidation.
b. a merger.
c. a purchase of assets.
d. a purchase of stock.

___ **9.** Chewy files a suit against Diners con Dinero Inc. While the suit is pending, Edible Ea Comp;any merges with Diners. Edible absorbs Diners. After the merger, liability in the suit res with

a. Chewy.
b. Diners.
c. Edible.
d. the court.

___ **10.** Vinny is a shareholder in Whirlygigs, Inc. Vinny could typically exercise appraisal rights Whirlygigs was involved in

a. a consolidation only.
b. a merger only.
c. a consolidation or a merger.
d. neither a consolidation nor a merger.

SHORT ESSAY QUESTIONS

1. What is the significance of the following as they relate to a company's articles of incorporation: (corporate name, (2) nature and purpose, (3) duration, (4) capital structure, (5) internal organization, (registered office and agent, and (7) incorporators?

2. Describe the procedure for a merger or a consolidation.

GAMEPOINTS

(Answers at the Back of the Book)

1. You are playing the video game "Captains of Industry" in which the objective is to attain a domina position in an industry without violating, or creating the appearance of violating, the law. To begin play, yo make a good faith effort to incorporate Platinum, Inc., without realizing that you have not followed all of th prescribed procedures. As the game continues, you contract in good faith with Silver Corporation o ıtinum's behalf. What type of entity is Platinum? Can Silver avoid its contract with Platinum on the basis the defect in incorporation? Discuss.

"Money2Burn" is a video game of finance in which each player's goal is to become the wealthiest person the world. You are the chief executive officer of Gold, Inc. The articles of incorporation state that Gold may gage in any activity for "any lawful purpose." On the firm's behalf, you enter into a contract to sell bstantially all of its assets to Diamond Holdings. Is this an *ultra vires* act? Can the sale proceed without ›re? If not, what "more" is required? If a Gold shareholder dissents, to what, if anything, is he or she titled? Explain.

Chapter 30:
Corporate Directors, Officers, and Shareholders

WHAT THIS CHAPTER IS ABOUT

This chapter outlines the rights and responsibilities of all participants—directors, officers, and share-lders—in a corporate enterprise. Also noted are the ways in which conflicts among these participants are solved.

CHAPTER OUTLINE

ROLE OF DIRECTORS AND OFFICERS

The board of directors governs a corporation. Officers handle daily business.

A. ELECTION OF DIRECTORS

1. **Number of Directors**
   This number is set in a corporation's articles or bylaws [RMBCA 8.01].

2. **How Directors Are Chosen**
   The first board (appointed by the incorporators or named in the articles) serves until the first shareholders' meeting. A majority vote of the shareholders (see below) elects subsequent directors.

3. **Removal of Directors**
   Shareholder action can remove a director for cause (or the board may have the power). In most states, a director cannot be removed without cause, unless shareholders have reserved the right.

B. COMPENSATION OF DIRECTORS

Nominal sums may be paid to directors, and there is a trend to provide more. Directors may set their own compensation [RMBCA 8.11]. A director who is also a corporate officer is an inside director. A director who does not hold a management position is an outside director.

C. BOARD OF DIRECTORS' MEETINGS

1. **Formal Minutes and Notice**
   A board conducts business by holding formal meetings with recorded minutes, in person or via the Web or phone conferencing. The dates for regular meetings are usually set in the articles and bylaws or by board resolution. No other notice is required. Special meetings require notice to all directors.

2. **Quorum Requirements and Voting**
   Quorum requirements vary. If the firm specifies none, in most states a quorum is a majority of the number of directors authorized in the articles or bylaws. Voting is one vote per director.

D. RIGHTS OF DIRECTORS

1. Participation and Inspection
A director has a right to participate in corporate business. A director must have access to corporate books and records to make decisions.

2. Compensation and Indemnification
Nominal sums may be paid to directors, and there is a trend to provide more. Most stat permit a corporation to indemnify a director for costs and fees in defending against corpora related lawsuits. Many firms buy insurance to cover indemnification.

E. COMMITTEES OF THE BOARD OF DIRECTORS

1. Executive Committee
Most states permit a board to elect an executive committee from among the directors handle management between board meetings. The committee is limited to ordinary busine matters.

2. Audit Committee
Selects, compensates, and oversees independent public accountants who audit the firm financial records under the Sarbanes-Oxley Act of 2002.

3. Nominating Committee
Chooses candidates on which shareholders vote for the board of directors [RMBCA 8.25].

4. Compensation Committee
Sets salaries and benefits for corporate executives and may determine directo compensation.

5. Litigation Committee
Decides whether to pursue litigation on behalf of the corporation.

F. CORPORATE OFFICERS AND EXECUTIVES
The board hires officers and other executive employees. Officers act as corporate agents (s Chapter 23). The rights of corporate officers and other high-level managers are defined l employment contracts. Normally, the board can remove officers at any time (but the corporati could be liable for breach of contract). Officers' duties are the same as those of directors.

II. DUTIES AND LIABILITIES OF DIRECTORS AND OFFICERS
Directors and officers are fiduciaries of the corporation.

A. DUTY OF CARE
Directors and officers must act in good faith, in what they consider to be the best interests of tl corporation, and with the care that an ordinarily prudent person would exercise in simil circumstances.

1. Duty to Make Informed and Reasonable Decisions
Directors must be informed on corporate matters and act in accord with their knowledge ar training. A director can rely on information furnished by competent officers, or other without being accused of acting in bad faith or failing to exercise due care [RMBCA 8.30].

2. Duty to Exercise Reasonable Supervision
Directors must exercise reasonable supervision when work is delegated to others.

3. Dissenting Directors
Directors must attend board meetings; if not, he or she should register a dissent to actio taken (to avoid liability for mismanagement).

B. THE BUSINESS JUDGMENT RULE
Honest mistakes of judgment and poor business decisions do not make directors and office liable to the firm for poor results. There can be no bad faith, fraud, or breach of fiduciary dutie

The decision must be within the director's managerial authority and the power of the corporation. The director or officer must—

1. Take reasonable steps to become informed.
2. Have a reasonable basis for a decision.
3. Have no personal conflict of interest with the corporation on the matter.

C. DUTY OF LOYALTY

Directors and officers cannot use corporate funds or confidential information for personal advantage. Specifically, they cannot—

1. Compete with the corporation.
2. Usurp a corporate opportunity.
3. Have an interest that conflicts with the interest of the corporation.
4. Engage in insider trading (see Chapter 31).
5. Authorize a corporate transaction that is detrimental to minority shareholders, or (6) sell control over the corporation.
6. Sell control over the corporation.

D. CONFLICTS OF INTEREST

1. Disclosure Requirements

Directors and officers must disclose fully any conflict of interest that might occur in a deal involving the corporation. A contract may be upheld if it was fair and reasonable to the firm when it was made, there was full disclosure of the interest of the officers or directors involved, and it was approved by a majority of disinterested directors or shareholders.

2. Corporations with Common Directors

Transactions between corporations with one or more directors on both boards must be conducted with great care to avoid legal conflicts of interest and violations of antitrust law.

E. LIABILITY OF DIRECTORS AND OFFICERS

Directors and officers are personally liable for their torts and crimes, and may be liable for those of subordinates (under the "responsible corporate officer" doctrine or the "pervasiveness of control" theory). The corporation is liable for such acts when committed within the scope of employment.

I. ROLE OF SHAREHOLDERS

A. SHAREHOLDERS' POWERS

Shareholders own the corporation, approve fundamental corporate changes, and elect and remove directors.

B. SHAREHOLDERS' MEETINGS

Regular meetings must occur annually; special meetings can be called to handle urgent matters.

1. Notice of Meeting Must Be in Writing in Advance

Notice must occur at least ten days and not more than sixty days before a meeting [RMBCA 7.05]. Notice of a special meeting must state the purpose.

2. Proxies

Rather than attend a meeting, shareholders normally authorize third parties to vote their shares. A proxy may be revocable and may have a time limit.

3. Proxy Materials and Shareholder Proposals

When a firm sends proxy materials to its shareholders, it must allow them to vote on pending policy proposals.

C. SHAREHOLDER VOTING

1. **Quorum Requirements**
At the meeting, a quorum must be present. A majority vote of the shares present is requir to pass resolutions. Fundamental changes require a higher percentage.

2. **Voting Techniques**
Each common shareholder has one vote per share. The articles can exclude or limit voti rights.

a. **Cumulative Voting**
The number of members of the board to be elected multiplied by the total number of voti shares is the number of votes a shareholder has and can be cast for one or mo nominees.

b. **Shareholder Voting Agreements**
A group of shareholders can agree to vote their shares together. A shareholder can vo by proxy. Any person can solicit proxies.

c. **Voting Trust**
Exists when legal title (recorded ownership on the corporate books) is transferred to trustee who is responsible for voting the shares. The shareholder retains all oth ownership rights.

IV. RIGHTS OF SHAREHOLDERS

A. STOCK CERTIFICATES
Notice of shareholder meetings, dividends, and corporate reports are distributed to owners list in the corporate books, not on the basis of possession of stock certificates (which most states not require).

B. PREEMPTIVE RIGHTS
Usually apply only to additional, newly issued stock sold for cash and must be exercised within specified time (usually thirty days). When new shares are issued, each shareholder is given *sto warrants* (transferable options to acquire a certain number of shares at a stated price).

C. DIVIDENDS
Dividends can be paid in cash, property, or stock. Once declared, a cash dividend is a corpora debt. Dividends are payable only from (1) retained earnings, (2) current net profits, or (3) ar surplus.

1. **Illegal Dividends**
A dividend paid when a corporation is insolvent is illegal and must be repaid. A dividend pa from an unauthorized account or causing a corporation to become insolvent may have to b repaid. In any case, the directors can be held personally liable.

2. **If the Directors Fail to Declare a Dividend**
Shareholders can ask a court to compel a declaration of a dividend, but to succeed th directors' conduct must be an abuse of discretion.

D. INSPECTION RIGHTS
Shareholders (or their attorney, accountant, or agent) can inspect and copy corporate books an records for a proper purpose, if the request is made in advance [RMBCA 16.02]. This right ca be denied to prevent harassment or to protect confidential corporate information.

E. TRANSFER OF SHARES
Any restrictions on transferability must be noted on the face of a stock certificate. Restriction must be reasonable—for example, a right of first refusal remains with the corporation or th shareholders for only a specified time or a reasonable time.

F. RIGHTS ON DISSOLUTION
Shareholders can petition a court to dissolve a firm if [RMBCA 14.30]—

1. The directors are deadlocked, shareholders are unable to break the deadlock, and there is or could be irreparable injury to the firm.
2. The acts of the directors or those in control of the corporation are illegal, oppressive, or fraudulent.
3. Corporate assets are being misapplied or wasted.
4. The shareholders are deadlocked in voting power and have failed, for a specified period (usually two annual meetings), to elect successors to directors.

G. THE SHAREHOLDER'S DERIVATIVE SUIT
If directors fail to sue in the corporate name to redress a wrong suffered by the firm, shareholders can do so (after complaining to the board). Any recovery normally goes into the corporate treasury.

DUTIES AND LIABILITIES OF SHAREHOLDERS

In most cases, if a corporation fails, shareholders lose only their investment. Exceptions include (see also Chapter 29) watered stock.

A. WATERED STOCK
In most cases, a shareholder who receives watered stock (stock sold by a corporation for less than par value) must pay the difference to the corporation. In some states, such shareholders may be liable to creditors of the corporation for unpaid corporate debts.

B. DUTIES OF MAJORITY SHAREHOLDERS
A single shareholder (or a few acting together) who owns enough shares to control the corporation owes a fiduciary duty to the minority shareholders and creditors when they sell their shares.

I. MAJOR BUSINESS FORMS COMPARED

The appropriate form for doing business depends on an enterprise's characteristics, tax status, and goals.

TRUE-FALSE QUESTIONS

(Answers at the Back of the Book)

__ 1. The business judgment rule immunizes officers from liability for poor decisions made in good faith.

__ 2. An officer is a fiduciary of a corporation.

__ 3. Preemptive rights entitle shareholders to bring a derivative suit against the corporation.

__ 4. Only certain funds are legally available for paying dividends.

__ 5. Damages recovered in a shareholder's derivative suit are paid to the shareholder who filed the suit.

__ 6. Generally, shareholders are not personally responsible for the debts of the corporation.

__ 7. Directors, but not officers, owe a duty of loyalty to the corporation.

__ 8. The business judgment rule makes a director liable for losses to the firm in most cases.

__ 9. Shareholders may vote to remove members of the board of directors.

__ 10. At a shareholders' meeting, a quorum must be present to vote on resolutions.

FILL-IN QUESTIONS

(Answers at the Back of the Book)

A stock certificate may be lost or destroyed, ______________________(and ownership is/b ownership is not) destroyed with it. A new certificate ____________ (can/cannot) be issued to replace o that has been lost or destroyed. Notice of meetings, dividends, and operational and financial reports are distributed according to the individual ______________________ ______________________ (in possession of the certificate/recorded as the owner in the corp ration's books).

MULTIPLE-CHOICE QUESTIONS

(Answers at the Back of the Book)

___ **1.** Joeli is a shareholder of Agro Implement Company. As a shareholder, Joeli does *not* have a rig to

a. compensation.
b. dividends.
c. inspect corporate books and records.
d. transfer shares.

___ **2.** Crabtree is a shareholder of Orchards & Vines, Inc. (O&V). When the directors fail to act redress a wrong suffered by O&V, Crabtree may file

a. a derivative suit.
b. a preemptive right suit.
c. a proxy suit.
d. a suit of first refusal.

___ **3.** The board of directors of Omega, Inc., announces a cash dividend. A cash dividend may not b paid from

a. accumulated surplus.
b. gross profits.
c. net profits.
d. retained earnings.

___ **4.** Dylan and Evette are officers of Fullfit Clothing Corporation. As officers, their rights are set o in

a. international agreements.
b. state corporation statutes.
c. the firm's certificate of authority.
d. the officers' employment contracts.

___ **5.** Federico is a director of Green Energy Corporation. As a director, Federico owes Green a duty o

a. care only.
b. loyalty only.
c. care and loyalty.
d. neither care nor loyalty.

_ **6.** Jeans & Sweats Corporation uses cumulative voting in its elections of directors. Kyla owns 3,000 shares. At an annual meeting at which three directors are to be elected, Kyla may cast for any one candidate

a. 1,000 votes.
b. 3,000 votes.
c. 9,000 votes.
d. 27,000 votes.

_ **7.** HomeBase Corporation invests in intrastate businesses. In HomeBase's state, as in most states, the minimum number of directors that must be present before its board can transact business is

a. all of the directors authorized in the articles.
b. a majority of the number authorized in the articles or bylaws.
c. any odd number.
d. one.

_ **8.** Nanobyte Company makes and sells computer chips. Like most corporations, Nanobyte's officers are hired by its

a. directors.
b. incorporators.
c. officers.
d. shareholders.

_ **9.** Robin is a director of Sherwood Management Company. Robin has a right to

a. compensation.
b. first refusal.
c. participation.
d. preemption.

_ **10.** Pam is a director of Quik Purchasing Corporation. Without informing Quik, Pam goes into business with Rapid Buys, Inc., to compete with Quik. This violates

a. the business judgment rule.
b. the duty of care.
c. the duty of loyalty.
d. none of the above.

SHORT ESSAY QUESTIONS

How do the duty of care and the duty of loyalty govern the conduct of directors and officers in a rporation?

What are the rights of the shareholders of a corporation?

GAMEPOINTS

(Answers at the Back of the Book)

In the video game "Corporate Cowboy," your task is to investigate complaints of wrongdoing on the part corporate directors and officers, decide whether there is a violation of the law, and deal with the rongdoers accordingly. Jane, a shareholder of Goodly Corporation, alleges that its directors decided to vest heavily in the firm's growth in negligent reliance on its officers' faulty financial reports. This caused

Goodly to borrow to meet its obligations, resulting in a drop in its stock price. Are the directors liable? W or why not?

2. You are playing the video game "Conflict of Interest" in which you accrue points by correctly spotti corporate misconduct, skillfully battling against it, and successfully righting the wrong. Your chief oppon is the game's avatar. Ellen, a shareholder of Finagle, Inc., asks you to help her right a wrong suffered by firm as a result of an act by Bernie, one of the firm's directors and officers. Can Ellen sue Bernie on Finagl behalf? If so, and Bernie is held liable, who recovers the damages? What defense is the game's avatar lik to assert on Bernie's behalf?

Chapter 31:
Investor Protection, Insider Trading, and Corporate Governance

WHAT THIS CHAPTER IS ABOUT

The general purpose of securities laws is to provide sufficient, accurate information to investors to able them to make informed buying and selling decisions about **securities**—documents or records idencing corporate ownership (stocks) or debts (bonds). This chapter provides an outline of federal :urities laws.

CHAPTER OUTLINE

THE SECURITIES AND EXCHANGE COMMISSION (SEC)

The SEC administers the federal securities laws and regulates the sale and purchase of securities.

A. THE SEC'S MAJOR RESPONSIBILITIES

1. Interpret federal securities laws and investigate violations.
2. Issue new rules and amend existing rules.
3. Oversee the inspection of securities firms, brokers, investment advisers, and ratings agencies.
4. Oversee private regulatory organizations in the securities, accounting, and auditing fields.
5. Coordinate U.S. securities regulation with federal, state, and foreign authorities.

B. THE SEC'S EXPANDING REGULATORY POWERS

The SEC's powers include the power to seek sanctions against those who violate foreign securities laws; to suspend trading if prices rise and fall in short periods of time; to exempt persons, securities, and transactions from securities law requirements; and to require more corporate disclosure.

I. SECURITIES ACT OF 1933

Requires all essential information concerning issuance (sales) of new securities to be disclosed to investors.

A. WHAT IS A SECURITY?

1. **Courts' Interpretation of the Securities Act**
Securities include investment contracts, which exist in any transaction in which a person (1) invests (2) in a common enterprise (3) reasonably expecting profits (4) derived *primarily* or *substantially* from others' managerial or entrepreneurial efforts.

2. **A Security Is an Investment**
Examples: stocks, bonds, investment contracts in condominiums, franchises, limited partnerships, and oil or gas or other mineral rights.

B. REGISTRATION STATEMENT

Before offering securities for sale, issuing corporations must (1) file a registration statement w the Securities and Exchange Commission (SEC) and (2) provide investors with a prospectus th describes the security being sold, the issuing corporation, and the investment or risk. The documents must be written in "plain English" and may be delivered online.

1. Contents of the Registration Statement

The statement must be filed electronically for posting on the SEC's electronic databa EDGAR (Electronic Data Gathering, Analysis, and Retrieval), and must describe—

- **a.** The security being offered and its relationship to the registrant's other securities.
- **b.** The registrant's properties and business, including a financial statement certified by independent public accountant.
- **c.** The registrant's management; its compensation and other benefits, including pensio and stock options, and any interests of directors or officers in material transactions wi the corporation.
- **d.** How the registrant intends to use the proceeds of the sale.
- **e.** Pending lawsuits.

2. Waiting Period

Securities cannot be sold until after the SEC reviews the statement for completeness, Duri this period, only certain types of offers are allowed. A preliminary prospectus may be issue often without stating a price. A free-writing prospectus (any type of offer that describes t issuer or the security) tells investors to obtain a prospectus at the SEC's Web site.

3. Posteffective Period

Investors who were issued a preliminary or free-writing prospectus must be provided with final prospectus before or at the time they buy the securities.

4. Restrictions Relaxed for Well-Known Seasoned Issuers

A well-known seasoned issuer is a firm that has issued at least $1 billion in securities in th previous three years or has at least $700 million of value of outstanding stock in the public hands. This issuer can offer securities for sale without waiting for SEC review and approv of the statement.

C. EXEMPT SECURITIES

Securities that can be sold (and resold) without being registered include—

1. Government-issued securities.
2. Bank and financial institution securities.
3. Short-term notes and drafts (maturity does not exceed nine months.)
4. Securities of nonprofit, educational, and charitable organizations.
5. Securities issued by common carriers (trucking companies and railroads).
6. Any insurance, endowment, or annuity contract issued by a state-regulated insuranc company.
7. Securities issued in a corporate reorganization in which one security is exchanged for anothe or in a bankruptcy proceeding.
8. Securities issued in stock dividends and stock splits.

D. EXEMPT TRANSACTIONS

Securities that can be sold without being registered include those sold in transactions tha consist of—

1. Small Offerings under Regulation A

An issuer's offer of up to $5 million in securities in any twelve-month period (including up t $1.5 million in nonissuer resales) is exempt. The issuer must file with the SEC a notice of th issue and an offering circular (also provided to investors before the sale). A company can "tes the waters" (determine potential interest) before preparing the circular.

2. Small Offerings under Regulation D
Offers that involve a small amount of money or are not made publicly.

a. Offerings Up to $1 Million
Noninvestment company offerings up to $1 million in a twelve-month period [Rule 504].

b. Offerings Up to $5 Million
Private, noninvestment company offerings up to $5 million in a twelve-month period if (1) no general solicitation or advertising is used; (2) the SEC is notified of the sales; (3) precaution is taken against nonexempt, unregistered resales; and (4) there are no more than thirty-five unaccredited investors. If the sale involves any unaccredited investors, all investors must be given material information about the company, its business, the securities [Rule 505].

c. Private Offerings in Unlimited Amounts
Essentially the same requirements as Rule 505, except (1) there is no limit on the amount of the offering and (2) the issuer must believe that each unaccredited investor has sufficient knowledge or experience to evaluate the investment [Rule 506].

3. Small Offerings to Accredited Investors Only
An offer up to $5 million is exempt if (1) no general solicitation or advertising is used; (2) the SEC is notified of the sales; (3) precaution is taken against nonexempt, unregistered resales; and (4) there are no unaccredited investors [Section 4(6)].

4. Resales—"Safe Harbors"
Most securities can be resold without registration. Resales of small offerings [Rule 505], private offerings [Rule 506], and offers to accredited investors only [Section 4(6)] are exempt from registration if—

a. The Securities Have Been Owned for Two Years or More
If seller is not an affiliate (in control with the issuer) [Rule 144].

b. The Securities Have Been Owned for at Least One Year
There must be adequate public information about the issuer, the securities must be sold in limited amounts in unsolicited brokers' transactions, and the SEC must be notified of the resale [Rule 144].

c. The Securities Are Sold Only to an Institutional Investor
The securities, on issue, must not have been of the same class as securities listed on a national securities exchange or a U.S. automated interdealer quotation system, and the seller on resale must take steps to tell the buyer they are exempt [Rule 144A].

E. VIOLATIONS OF THE 1933 ACT
If registration statement or prospectus contains material false statements or omissions, liable parties include anyone who signed the statement.

1. Penalties
Fines up to $10,000; imprisonment up to five years; injunction against selling securities; order to refund profits; damages in civil suits.

2. Defenses
Statement or omission was not material; plaintiff knew of misrepresentation and bought stock anyway; *due diligence.*

II. SECURITIES EXCHANGE ACT OF 1934
Regulates the markets in which securities are traded by requiring disclosure by Section 12 companies (corporations with securities on the exchanges and firms with assets in excess of $5 million and five hundred or more shareholders).

A. INSIDER TRADING—SECTION 10(b) AND SEC RULE 10b-5

Section 10(b) proscribes the use of "any manipulative or deceptive device or contrivance contravention of such rules and regulations as the [SEC] may prescribe." Rule 10b-5 prohib the commission of fraud in connection with the purchase or sale of any security (registered unregistered).

1. What Triggers Liability

Any material omission or misrepresentation of material facts in connection with the purcha or sale of any security.

2. What Does Not Trigger Liability

Under the Private Securities Litigation Reform Act of 1995, financial forecasts and oth forward-looking statements do not trigger liability if they include "meaningful cautiona statements identifying factors that could cause actual results to differ materially."

3. Who Can Be Liable

Those who take advantage of inside information when they know it is unavailable to t person with whom they are dealing.

a. Insiders

Officers, directors, majority shareholders, and persons having access to or receivi information of a nonpublic nature on which trading is based (accountants, attorneys).

b. Outsiders

1) Tipper/Tippee Theory

One who acquires inside information as a result of an insider's breach of fiducia duty to the firm whose shares are traded can be liable, if (1) there is a breach of du not to disclose the information, (2) the disclosure is for personal benefit, and (3) t tippee knows or should know of the breach and benefits from it.

2) Misappropriation Theory

One who wrongfully obtains inside information and trades on it to his or her gain ca be liable, if a duty to the lawful possessor of information was violated and harm another results.

B. INSIDER REPORTING AND TRADING—SECTION 16(b)

Officers, directors, and shareholders owning 10 percent of the securities registered under Sectio 12 are required to file reports with the SEC concerning their ownership and trading of th securities.

1. Corporation Is Entitled to All Profits

A firm can recapture *all* profits realized by an insider on *any* purchase and sale or sale an purchase of its stock in any six-month period.

2. Applicability of Section 16(b)

Applies to stock, warrants, options, securities convertible into stock.

C. PROXY STATEMENTS—SECTION 14(A)

Regulates the solicitation of proxies from shareholders of Section 12 companies. Whoever solicit a proxy must disclose, in the proxy statement, all of the pertinent facts.

D. VIOLATIONS OF THE 1934 ACT

1. Criminal Penalties

Maximum jail term is twenty-five years; fines up to $5 million for individuals and $2.5 millio for partnerships and corporations.

2. Civil Sanctions

a. **Insider Trading Sanctions Act of 1984**
SEC can bring suit in federal court against anyone violating or aiding in a violation of the 1934 act or SEC rules. Penalties include triple the profits gained or loss avoided by the guilty party.

b. **Insider Trading and Securities Fraud Enforcement Act of 1988**
Enlarged the class of persons subject to civil liability for insider-trading violations, increased criminal penalties, and gave the SEC authority to (1) reward persons providing information and (2) make rules to prevent insider trading.

c. **Corporations and Other Private Parties**
A corporation can sue under Section 16(b) to recover short-swing profits. A private party can sue under Section 10(b) and Rule 10b-5 to rescind a contract to buy or sell securities or to obtain damages to the extent of a violator's illegal profits.

'. STATE SECURITIES LAWS

A. Requirements Under State Securities Laws
All states regulate the offer and sale of securities within individual state borders. Exemptions from federal law are not exemptions from state laws, which have their own exemptions. Disclosure requirements and antifraud regulations are often patterned on federal provisions.

B. Concurrent Regulation
Under the National Market Securities Improvement Act of 1996, the SEC regulates most national securities activities. The Uniform Securities Act, issued by the National Conference of Commissioners on Uniform State Laws and adopted in nine states, is designed to coordinate state and federal securities regulation and enforcement efforts.

CORPORATE GOVERNANCE
Corporate governance is the system by which corporations are governed and controlled, according to the Organization of Economic Cooperation and Development. Effective governance requires more than compliance with the law.

A. The Need for Good Corporate Governance
Because corporate ownership is separated from corporate control, conflicts of interest can arise.

B. Attempts at Aligning the Interests of Officers with Those of Shareholders
Providing stock options to align the financial interests of shareholders and officers has proved to be an imperfect control device. Officers have manipulated circumstances to artificially inflate stock prices to keep the value of options high, or the options have been "repriced" to avoid losses when stock prices dropped. "Outside" directors are often the friends of corporate officers.

C. Corporate Governance and Corporate Law
Corporate oversight involves (1) the audited reporting of corporate financial progress so that managers can be evaluated and (2) legal protection for shareholders.

1. **The Practical Significance of Good Corporate Governance**
Firms with greater shareholder rights have higher profits, higher sales growth, higher firm value, and other economic advantages.

2. **Governance and Corporation Law**
Under the law, a corporation must have a board of directors elected by the shareholders. Thus, the key element of corporate structure is the board, which makes important decisions about the firm.

3. **The Board of Directors**
Directors, who must operate for the shareholders' benefit, are responsible for monitoring officers and can be sued for failing to do their jobs effectively.

4. **Importance of the Audit Committee**
An audit committee oversees the corporate accounting and financial reporting process including the internal controls designed to ensure that the reports are accurate.

5. **The Role of the Compensation Committee**
This committee determines the amount of compensation to be paid to the officers and responsible for assessing those officers' performance.

D. THE SARBANES=OXLEY ACT OF 2002
This act imposes strict disclosure requirements and harsh penalties for violations of securiti laws.

1. **Responsible Parties**
Chief corporate executives (CEOs and CFOs) are responsible for the accuracy a completeness of financial statements and reports filed with the SEC [Sections 302 and 90 Penalties for knowingly certifying a report or statement that does not meet statuto requirements include up to $1 million in fines and ten years imprisonment ($5 million a twenty years for "willful" certification). Altering or destroying documents is also subject fines and imprisonment.

2. **Public Company Accounting Oversight Board**
The SEC oversees this entity, which regulates and oversees public accounting firms (Chapt 35).

3. **Limitations on Private Actions**
A private action for securities fraud must be brought within two years of the discovery of t violation or five years after the violation, whichever is earlier [Section 804].

VI. ONLINE SECURITIES FRAUD

A. INVESTMENT SCAMS
There are infinite variations of investment scams, but most promise spectacular returns f small investments. Many are pyramid ("Ponzi") schemes, in which initial "investors" are pa with funds provided by later participants. Scams may be propagated via spam, fraudulent W pages, online newsletters and bulletin boards, chat rooms, blogs, and tweets.

B. ONLINE INVESTMENT NEWSLETTERS AND FORUMS
To inflate the price of a stock and profit from its sale, its holders may pay others to tout t stock online. Potential investors may be duped if the identities of those who pay for this servi are not disclosed when the law requires it. The same tactic may be employed in other onli venues such as forums, using any number of aliases to falsify interest in the stock.

C. PONZI SCHEMES
These schemes often claim to consist of risk-free or low-risk investments. They sometimes fo U.S. residents into investing in offshore companies.

D. HACKING INTO ONLINE STOCK ACCOUNTS
A criminal hacker may use keystroke-monitoring software on a public-use computer termin (such as in a library) to uncover another's private online brokerage account number an password. With this data, a hacker can use the account's funds to trade in, and inflate the pric of, stock that the hacker owns. This profit may be masked through an offshore or dumm corporation.

TRUE-FALSE QUESTIONS

(Answers at the Back of the Book)

___ 1. A security that does not qualify for an exemption must be registered before it is offered to th public.

_ **2.** Before a security can be sold to the public, prospective investors must be provided with a prospectus.

_ **3.** Stock splits are exempt from the registration requirements of the Securities Act of 1933, if no commission is paid.

_ **4.** Sales of securities may not occur until twenty days after registration.

_ **5.** Private offerings of securities in unlimited amounts that are not generally solicited or advertised must be registered before they can be sold.

_ **6.** A proxy statement must fully and accurately disclose all of the facts that are pertinent to the matter on which shareholders are being asked to vote.

_ **7.** All states have disclosure requirements and antifraud provisions that cover securities.

_ **8.** Intent is not a requirement for liability under Section 10(b) of the Securities Exchange Act of 1934.

_ **9.** No one who receives inside information as a result of another's breach of his or her fiduciary duty can be liable under SEC Rule 10b-5.

_ **10.** No security can be resold without registration.

FILL-IN QUESTIONS

(Answers at the Back of the Book)

The SEC can award "bounty" payments to persons providing information leading to the ____________________ (conviction/prosecution) of insider-trading violations. Civil penalties include ____________ (double/triple) the profits gained or the loss avoided. Criminal penalties include maximum l terms of _____________ (five/ ten) years. Individuals and corporations ___________ (may/may not) also subject to million dollar fines.

MULTIPLE-CHOICE QUESTIONS

(Answers at the Back of the Book)

_ **1.** Elmo, a director of Far East Development Company, learns that a Far East engineer has developed a new, improved product. Over the next six months, Elmo buys and sells Far East stock for a profit. Of Elmo's profit, Far East may recapture

a. all.
b. half.
c. 10 percent.
d. none.

_ **2.** Centro Brokerage Associates sells securities. The definition of a security does *not* include, as an element,

a. an investment.
b. a common enterprise.
c. a reasonable expectation of profits.
d. profits derived entirely from the efforts of the investor.

___ **3.** Superior, Inc., is a private, noninvestment company. In one year, Superior advertises a $300,(offering. Concerning registration, this offering is

a. exempt because of the low amount of the issue.
b. exempt because it was advertised.
c. exempt because the issuer is a private company.
d. not exempt.

___ **4.** Eyrie Games, Inc.'s registration statement must include

a. a description of the accounting firm that audits Eyrie.
b. a description of the security being offered for sale.
c. a financial forecast for Eyrie's next five years.
d. a marketing and management plan to ensure Eyrie's success.

___ **5.** Great Lakes Company is a private, noninvestment company. Last year, as part of a $250,0 advertised offering, Great Lakes sold stock to Jon, a private investor. Jon would now like to s the shares. Concerning registration, this resale is

a. exempt because of the low amount of the original issue.
b. exempt because the offering was advertised.
c. exempt because all resales are exempt.
d. not exempt.

___ **6.** Huron, Inc., makes a $6 million private offering to twenty accredited investors and less th thirty unaccredited investors. Huron advertises the offering and believes that the unaccredit investors are sophisticated enough to evaluate the investment. Huron gives material informati about itself, its business, and the securities to all investors. Concerning registration, this offeri is

a. exempt because of the low amount of the issue.
b. exempt because it was advertised.
c. exempt because the issuer believed the unaccredited investors were sophisticated enough evaluate the investment.
d. not exempt.

___ **7.** Frank, an officer of Gyra Gizmo, Inc., learns that Gyra has developed a new source of energ Frank tells Huey, an outsider. They each buy Gyra stock. When the development is announce the stock price increases, and they each immediately sell their stock. Subject to liability f insider trading

a. are Frank and Huey.
b. is Frank only.
c. is Huey only
d. is neither Frank nor Huey.

___ **8.** Dibble Dabble, Inc., is a noninvestment company. In one year, Dibble Dabble advertises tw $1.75 million offerings. Buying the issues are sixty accredited investors and twenty unaccredite investors. Dibble Dabble gives information about itself, its business, and the securities unaccredited investors only. Concerning registration, this offering is

a. exempt because of the low amount of the issue.
b. exempt because it was advertised.
c. exempt because the unaccredited investors were informed.
d. not exempt.

_ **9.** Natural Soy, Inc., wants to make an offering of securities to the public. The offer is not exempt from registration. Before Natural Soy sells these securities, it must provide *investors* with

a. a marketing and management plan.
b. a prospectus.
c. a registration statement.
d. samples of its products.

_ **10.** Ontario, Inc., in one year, advertises two $2.25 million offerings. Buying the stock are twelve accredited investors. Concerning registration, this offering is

a. exempt because of the low amount of the issue.
b. exempt because it was advertised.
c. exempt because only accredited investors bought stock.
d. not exempt.

SHORT ESSAY QUESTIONS

What is the process by which a company sells securities to the public?

How is insider trading regulated by Section 10(b), SEC Rule 10b-5, and Section 16(b)?

GAMEPOINTS

(Answers at the Back of the Book)

The video game "High End High" is set in the world of finance. Your avatar has the opportunity to ·est in a variety of enterprises in different scenarios, mostly involving exotic or cutting edge products or ·vices. In the game, NanoGene, Inc., advertises online that it will make a $4.5 million offering of stock on thin thirty days. The firm makes the offer and less than a week after the first sale notifies the Securities d Exchange Commission (SEC). All buyers—including you and fifty-two other unaccredited investors, as ·ll as more sophisticated individuals and institutions—are given material information about the company, business, its possible future, and its stock. You invest heavily in NanoGene, and the offering, which the m does not register, is sold out within six months. Did you invest in a company that will soon be leveled th sanctions by the SEC? Discuss.

Still playing "High End High," which you can lose only by losing everything, you decide that, unlike ·ur precipitous invest mention NanoGene, you will now act only on "material information." What formation do you think meets this qualification?

CUMULATIVE HYPOTHETICAL PROBLEM FOR UNIT FIVE—INCLUDING CHAPTERS 24–31

(Answers at the Back of the Book)

Fern, Gigi, and Ho are sole proprietors who decide to pool their resources to produce and maintain · Internet game site, "we-World."

_ **1.** Fern, Gigi, and Ho decide to form a partnership. They transfer their business assets and liabilities to the firm and start business on May 1, 2010. The parties execute a formal partnership agreement on July 1. The partnership began its existence

a. on May 1.
b. on July 1.
c. when each partner's individual creditors consented to the asset transfer.
d. when the parties initially decided to form a partnership.

___ **2.** After six months in operation, Fern, Gigi, and Ho decide to change the form of their partners to a limited partnership. To form a limited partnership, they must

a. accept limited liability for all of the partners.
b. create the firm according to specific statutory requirements.
c. designate one general partner to be a limited partner.
d. each make a capital contribution.

___ **3.** Fern, Gigi, and Ho's we-World is very successful. In March 2012, they decide to incorporate. T articles of incorporation must include all of the following except

a. the name of a registered agent.
b. the name of the corporation.
c. the names of the incorporators.
d. the names of the initial officers.

___ **4.** In January 2013, Fern, Gigi, and Ho decide to issue additional stock in we-World, Inc. T registration statement must include

a. a copy of the corporation's most recent proxy statement.
b. the names of prospective accredited investors.
c. the names of the current shareholders.
d. the principal purposes for which the proceeds from the offering will be used.

___ **5.** The issue of shares that we-World, Inc., plans to make qualifies under Rule 504 of Regulation D the Securities Act of 1933. Under this rule, we-World

a. may not make the offering through general advertising.
b. may sell the shares to an unlimited number of investors.
c. must offer the shares for sale for more than twelve months.
d. must provide all prospective investors with a prospectus.

QUESTIONS ON THE EXTENDED CASE STUDY FOR UNIT FIVE— *NOTZ V. EVERETT SMITH GROUP, LTD.*

(Answers at the Back of the Book)

___ **1.** Portly Associates, a financial investment firm, owns 85 percent of Quiescent Thermo Corporati (QTC). All of QTC's directors are officers or directors of Portly. QTC's chief business is t development and marketing of heat-resistant products, including plastics. When QTC has t opportunity to buy Otro Plastics, Inc., a competitor, QTC's board declines. Portly then buys Ot and in less than a year also buys QTC's plastics division. Based on the court's reasoning in *No v. Everett Smith Group, Ltd.*,, a minority QTC shareholder could bring

a. a direct claim against QTC's majority shareholder-directors.
b. a shareholder's derivative suit against Portly.
c. claims against Portly and QTC's shareholder-directors.
d. no claim against Portly or QTC's shareholder-directors.

___ **2.** In the facts of the previous question, under the dissent's position in *Notz v. Everett Smith Grou Ltd.*,, a minority QTC shareholder could bring

a. a direct claim against QTC's majority shareholder-directors.
b. a shareholder's derivative suit against Portly.
c. claims against Portly and QTC's shareholder-directors.
d. no claim against Portly or QTC's shareholder-directors.

_ **3.** The facts in the previous questions and in *Notz v. Everett Smith Group, Ltd.* underscore that controlling shareholder-directors

a. have a duty to act in the best interest of the corporation that controls them.
b. have an ethical duty that parallels their legal duty to act in the best interest of their corporation.
c. should always act in the best interest of the minority shareholders.
d. should always act in their own best interest.

Chapter 33: Consumer and Environmental Law

What This Chapter Is About

Federal and state laws protect consumers from unfair trade practices, unsafe products, criminatory or unreasonable credit requirements, and other problems related to consumer transactions. is chapter focuses on *federal* consumer law. This chapter also covers the law that relates to environmental tection.

Chapter Outline

CONSUMER LAW

A. DECEPTIVE ADVERTISING

The Federal Trade Commission Act of 1914 created the Federal Trade Commission (FTC) to prevent unfair and deceptive trade practices. Deceptive advertising is advertising that would mislead a consumer.

1. Advertising that Is Deceptive

Scientifically untrue claims; misleading half-truths; and bait-and-switch ads (if a seller refuses to show an advertised item, fails to have adequate quantities on hand, fails to promise to deliver within a reasonable time, or discourages employees from selling the item.) are deceptive.

2. Advertising that Is Not Deceptive

Puffing (vague generalities, obvious exaggeration) is not deceptive.

3. Online Deceptive Advertising

The same laws that apply to other forms of advertising apply to online ads. Under FTC guidelines—

a. Ads must be truthful and no misleading.
b. Any claims in an ad must be substantiated.
c. Ads cannot be unfair (likely to cause substantial, reasonably unavoidable consumer injury not outweighed by any benefit to the consumer or competition).

4. FTC Actions against Deceptive Advertising

The FTC sends a complaint to the advertiser, who may settle. If not, the FTC can, after a hearing, issue a cease-and-desist order, require counteradvertising, and seek restitution.

B. TELEMARKETING AND FAX ADVERTISING

1. Telephone Consumer Protection Act (TCPA) of 1991

The TCPA prohibits (1) phone solicitation using an automatic dialing system or a prerecorded voice and (2) transmission of ads via fax without the recipient's permission. For each violation, consumers can recover actual losses or $500, whichever is greater. If a defendant willfully or knowingly violated the act, a court can award treble damages.

2. Telemarketing and Consumer Fraud and Abuse Prevention Act of 1994
This act authorized FTC to set rules for telemarketing and bring actions against fraudule telemarketers. The FTC's Telemarketing Sales Rule of 1995 makes it illegal to misreprese information and requires disclosure. In 2003, the FTC set up a national Do Not Call Regist which prohibits telemarketers from calling consumers whose names are listed.

C. LABELING AND PACKAGING
Under the Fair Packaging and Labeling Act of 1966, labels identify: the product; net quantity contents; quantity of servings, if the number of servings is stated; manufacturer; and packag or distributor. More can be required (such as fat content).

D. SALES
Federal agencies that regulate sales include the FTC and the Federal Reserve Board Governors (Regulation Z governs credit provisions in sales contracts). All states have some fo of consumer protection laws.

1. Cooling-Off Laws
Some states allow a buyer to rescind a purchase within a certain time—the FTC has a thre day period. The FTC also requires a seller to notify a buyer of the right to cancel (if the sale in Spanish, notice must be in Spanish). Other state laws, including the Uniform Commerci Code's warranty sections, also apply.

2. Telephone and Mail-Order Sales
Consumers are partly protected by federal laws prohibiting mail fraud (see Chapter 6) a by state law that parallels federal law.

a. FTC "Mail or Telephone Order Merchandise Rule" of 1993
For goods bought via phone lines or through the mail, merchants must ship orders with the time promised in their ads, notify consumers when orders cannot be shipped on tim and issue a refund within a specified time if a consumer cancels an order.

b. Postal Reorganization Act of 1970
Unsolicited merchandise sent by mail may be retained, used, discarded, or disposed without obligation to the sender.

3. Online Sales
Consumers are protected online by the same laws that apply to other media.

E. HEALTH AND SAFETY

1. Foods and Drugs
The Federal Food, Drug, and Cosmetic Act (FFDCA) of 1938 sets food standards, levels additives, classifications of food and food ads; regulates medical devices. Drugs must shown to be effective and safe. Enforced by the Food and Drug Administration (FDA).

2. Consumer Product Safety
The Consumer Product Safety Act of 1972 includes a scheme for the regulation of consum products and safety by the Consumer Product Safety Commission (CPSC). The CPSC—

a. Sets standards for consumer products.
b. Bans the manufacture and sale of a product that is potentially hazardous to consumers.
c. Removes from the market any products imminently hazardous.
d. Requires manufacturers to report on any products already sold or intended for sale if th products have proved to be hazardous.
e. Administers other product safety legislation.

F. CREDIT PROTECTION

1. Truth-in-Lending Act (TILA)
The TILA, Title I of the Consumer Credit Protection Act (CCPA), was enacted in 1968, administered by the Federal Reserve Board, and requires the disclosure of credit terms.

a. Who Is Subject to the TILA?
The TILA covers creditors who, in the ordinary course of business, lend money or sell goods on credit to consumers, or arrange for credit for consumers.

b. What Does the TILA Require?
Under Regulation Z, in any transaction involving a sales contract in which payment is to be made in more than four installments, a lender must disclose all the credit terms clearly and conspicuously.

c. Equal Credit Opportunity Act of 1974
This act prohibits (1) denial of credit on the basis of race, religion, national origin, color, sex, marital status, age and (2) credit discrimination based on whether an individual receives certain forms of income.

d. Credit-Card Rules
Liability of a cardholder is $50 per card for unauthorized charges made before the issuer is notified the card is lost. An issuer cannot bill for unauthorized charges if a card was improperly issued. If a cardholder wishes to withhold payment for a faulty product, there are specific procedures to follow. Other rules—

1) Protect consumers from retroactive increases in interest rates on existing balances unless an account is sixty days delinquent.
2) Require forty-five days advance notice to consumers before changing credit terms.
3) Require monthly bills to be sent twenty-one days before their due date.
4) Limit interest-rate increases to specific situations.
5) Prohibit over-limit fees except in specific situations.
6) Require the application of payments for more than the minimum amount due to the highest-interest balances (such as cash advances).
7) Prevent computing finance charges based on the previous billing cycle.

e. Consumer Leasing Act of 1988
Those who lease consumer goods in the ordinary course of their business, if the goods are priced at $25,000 or less and the lease term exceeds four months, must disclose all material terms in writing.

2. Fair Credit Reporting Act (FCRA) of 1970

a. What Does the FCRA Provide?
Consumer credit-reporting agencies may issue credit reports only for certain purposes (extension of credit, etc.); a consumer denied credit, or charged more than others would be, on the basis of a report must be notified and told of the agency that issued the report.

b. Consumers Can Have Inaccurate Information Deleted
If a consumer learns that the report contains inaccurate information, the agency must delete it within a reasonable period of time.

3. Fair and Accurate Credit Transactions (FACT) Act
The FACT Act established a national "fraud alert" system so that consumers who suspect ID theft can place an alert on their credit files. Also—

a. Credit-Reporting Agencies' Responsibilities
Consumer credit-reporting agencies must provide consumers with free copies of their reports and stop reporting allegedly fraudulent information once a consumer shows that ID theft occurred.

b. Other Businesses' Responsibilities
Businesses must include shortened ("truncated") account numbers on credit card receipts and provide consumers with copies of records to help prove an account or transaction was fraudulent.

4. **Fair Debt Collection Practices Act (FDCPA)**
Enacted in 1977, the FDCPA applies only to debt-collection agencies that, usually for percentage of the amount owed, attempt to collect debts on behalf of someone else. The FT enforces the act.

a. **What Does the FDCPA Prohibit?**

1) Contact the debtor at the debtor's place of employment if the employer objects.
3) Contact third parties or family members about payment.
4) Use harassment, or false and misleading information.

b. **Remedies**
A debt collector may be liable for actual damages, plus additional damages not to exce $1,000 and attorneys' fees.

II. ENVIRONMENTAL LAW

A. COMMON LAW ACTIONS

1. **Nuisance**
Persons cannot use their property in a way that unreasonably interferes with others' righ to use or enjoy their own property. An injured party may be awarded damages or a injunction.

2. **Negligence and Strict Liability**
A business that fails to use reasonable care may be liable to a party whose injury wa foreseeable. Businesses that engage in ultrahazardous activities are strictly liable f whatever injuries the activities cause.

B. STATE AND LOCAL REGULATION
States regulate the environment through zoning or more direct regulation. Local governmen control some aspects through waste removal and disposal regulations, aesthetic ordinances, ar others. State and local agencies also implement federal environmental statutes and regulations.

C. FEDERAL REGULATION

1. **Environmental Regulatory Agencies**
The Environmental Protection Agency (EPA) coordinates federal environment responsibilities and administers most federal environmental policies and statutes. Citizer can sue to enforce the regulations.

2. **Environmental Impact Statements**
The National Environmental Policy Act (NEPA) of 1969 requires all federal agencies t consider environmental factors in making significant decisions.

a. **When Must an Environmental Impact Statement (EIS) Be Prepared?**
When a major federal action significantly affects the quality of the environment. An actio is *major* if it involves substantial commitment of resources. An action is *federal* if federal agency has the power to control it.

b. **What Must an EIS Analyze?**
(1) The impact on the environment that the action will have, (2) any adverse effects to th environment and alternative actions that might be taken, and (3) irreversible effects th action might generate.

c. **Can an Agency Decide Not to Issue an EIS?**
Yes, but it must issue a statement explaining why an EIS is unnecessary.

D. AIR POLLUTION
The Clean Air Act of 1963 (and amendments) is the basis for regulation.

1. **Mobile Sources of Pollution**
Regulations governing air pollution from automobiles and other mobile sources specify standards and time schedules. For example, under the 1990 amendments to the Clean Air Act—

   a. **New Automobiles' Exhaust**
   Manufacturers had to cut emission of nitrogen oxide by 60 percent and emission of other pollutants by 35 percent. Other sets of emission controls went into effect in 2004 and 2007.

   b. **Sport Utility Vehicles and Light Trucks**
   These vehicles are now subject to the same standards as cars.

   c. **Gasoline**
   Service stations must sell gasoline with higher oxygen content.

   d. **New Standards**
   The EPA attempts to update these standards when new scientific evidence is available.

2. **Stationary Sources of Pollution**
The EPA sets air quality standards for stationary sources (such as industrial plants), and the states formulate plans to achieve them. For example, under the 1990 amendments to the Clean Air Act, major new sources must use the *maximum achievable control technology (MACT)* to reduce emissions from the combustion of fossil fuels (coal and oil).

3. **Penalties**
Civil penalties of up to $25,000 per day, or an amount equal to a violator's economic benefits from noncompliance. Criminal fines are possible. Private citizens can sue violators.

E. WATER POLLUTION

1. **The Clean Water Act**
The Clean Water Act of 1972 amended the Federal Water Pollution Control Act (FWPCA) of 1948 to provide—

   a. **Goals**
   (1) Make waters safe for swimming, (2) protect fish and wildlife, (3) eliminate the discharge of pollutants into the water.

   b. **Limits on Discharges Based on *Best Available Technology***
   Time schedules (extended by amendment in 1977 and by the Water Quality Act of 1987) limit discharges of pollutants.

   c. **Permits**
   Municipal and industrial polluters must obtain National Pollutant Discharge Elimination System (NPDES) permits from the EPA before discharging wastes into navigable waters.

   d. **Penalties and Remedies**
   Civil penalties from $10,000 per day (up to $25,000 per violation) to $25,000 per day. Criminal penalties from fines of $2,500 per day to $1 million total and one to fifteen years' imprisonment. Injunctions, damages, and clean-up costs can be imposed.

2. **Wetlands**
The EPA defines wetlands to include "areas that are inundated or saturated by surface or ground water at a frequency and duration sufficient to support, and that under normal circumstances do support, a prevalence off vegetation typically adapted for lien in saturated soil conditions." Filling or dredging wetlands requires a permit from the Army Corps of Engineers.

3. Drinking Water
The Safe Drinking Water Act of 1974 requires the EPA to set maximum levels for pollutar in public water systems. Operators must come as close as possible to the standards using t best available technology.

4. Ocean Dumping
The Marine Protection, Research, and Sanctuaries Act of 1972 (Ocean Dumping A prohibits ocean dumping of radiological, chemical, and biological-warfare agents and hig level radioactive waste. Civil penalty: $50,000. Criminal penalties: fine ($50,000) imprisonment (up to a year).

5. Oil Pollution
The Oil Pollution Act of 1990 provides that an oil facility, shipper, or vessel owner or operat who discharges oil may be liable for clean-up costs, damages, and fines up to $25,000 p day.

F. TOXIC CHEMICALS

1. Pesticides and Herbicides
Federal Insecticide, Fungicide, and Rodenticide Act (FIFRA) of 1947—

a. Registration, Certification, and Use
Pesticides and herbicides must be (1) registered before they can be sold, (2) certified a used only for approved applications, and (3) used in limited quantities when applied food crops.

b. Labels
Labels must include directions for use of a pesticide or herbicide, warnings to prote human health and the environment, a statement of treatment in the case of poisoning, a a list of the ingredients.

c. Penalties
For registrants and producers: fine of up to $50,000, imprisonment up to one year. F commercial dealers: $25,000, one year. For farmers and other private users: $1,00 thirty days.

2. Toxic Substances
Under the Toxic Substances Control Act of 1976, for substances that potentially pose a imminent hazard or an unreasonable risk of injury to health or the environment, the EP may require special labeling, set production quotas, or limit or prohibit the use of substance.

G. HAZARDOUS WASTE DISPOSAL

1. Resource Conservation and Recovery Act (RCRA) of 1976
The EPA determines which forms of solid waste are hazardous, and sets requirements f disposal, storage, and treatment. Penalties include up to $25,000 (civil) per violation, $50,00 (criminal) per day, imprisonment up to two years (may be doubled for repeaters).

2. Superfund
The Comprehensive Environmental Response, Compensation, and Liability Act (CERCLA) 1980 regulates the clean up of leaking hazardous waste disposal sites. If a release or threatened release occurs, the EPA can clean up the site and recover the cost from—

a. Potentially Responsible Parties
(1) The person who generated the wastes disposed of at the site, (2) the person wh transported the wastes to the site, (3) the person who owned or operated the site at th time of the disposal, or (4) the current owner or operator.

b. Joint and Several Liability
One party can be charged with the entire cost (which that party may recover in a contribution action against others).

TRUE-FALSE QUESTIONS

(Answers at the Back of the Book)

_ **1.** Advertising will be deemed deceptive if a consumer would be misled by the advertising claim.

_ **2.** Labels must be accurate.

_ **3.** Under no circumstances can a consumer rescind a contract freely entered into.

_ **4.** The TILA applies to creditors who, in the ordinary course of business, lend money or sell goods on credit to consumers.

_ **5.** A consumer can include a note in his or her credit file to explain any misinformation in the file, but the misinformation cannot be deleted.

_ **6.** No common law doctrines apply against polluters today.

_ **7.** Local governments can control some aspects of the environment through zoning laws.

_ **8.** Under federal environmental laws, there is a single standard for all polluters and all pollutants.

_ **9.** The Toxic Substances Control Act of 1976 regulates the clean up of hazardous waste disposal sites.

_ **10.** If a release of hazardous waste occurs at a hazardous waste disposal site, the Environmental Protection Agency (EPA) can clean it up and recover the entire cost from a potentially responsible party.

FILL-IN QUESTIONS

(Answers at the Back of the Book)

The Truth-in-Lending Act contains provisions regarding credit cards. One provision limits the liability the cardholder to ________ ($50/$500) per card for unauthorized charges made ____________ (after/be-e) the credit card issuer is notified that the card has been lost. Another provision ____________ llows/prohibits) a credit card company ____________ (from billing/to bill) a consumer for any authorized charges ____________ (unless/if) the credit card was improperly issued by the company.

MULTIPLE-CHOICE QUESTIONS

(Answers at the Back of the Book)

_ **1.** Tasty Treat Company advertises that its cereal, "Fiber Rich," reduces cholesterol. After an investigation and a hearing, the FTC finds no evidence to support the claim. To correct the public's impression of Fiber Rich, the most appropriate action would be

a. a cease-and-desist order.
b. a civil fine.
c. a criminal fine.
d. counteradvertising.

___ **2.** Snarky Bling Corporation sells consumer products. Generally, the product labels must use wor as they are

a. normally used in the scientific community.
b. ordinarily understood by consumers.
c. reasonably approved by ABC's officers.
d. typically explained by the marketing department.

___ **3.** LuAnn receives an unsolicited credit card in the mail and tosses it on her desk. Without LuAnn permission, her roommate Celia uses the card to buy new clothes for $1,000. LuAnn is liable for

a. $1,000.
b. $500.
c. $50.
d. $0.

___ **4.** Ed takes out a student loan from First National Bank. After graduation, Ed goes to work, but does not make payments on the loan. The bank agrees with Great Collection Agency that if collects the debt, it can keep a percentage of the amount. To collect the debt, the agency ca contact

a. Ed at his place of employment, even if his employer objects.
b. Ed at unusual or inconvenient times.
c. Ed only to advise him of further action that the agency will take.
d. third parties, including Ed's parents.

___ **5.** The ordinary business of Homeowners Credit Company (HCC) is to lend money to consumer HCC must disclose all credit terms clearly and conspicuously in

a. all credit transactions.
b. any credit transaction in which payments are to be made in more than four installments.
c. any credit transaction in which payments are to be made in more than one installment.
d. no credit transactions.

___ **6.** The U.S. Department of the Interior's approval of coal mining operations in several weste states requires an environmental impact statement

a. because it affects the quality of the environment, is "federal," and is "major."
b. only because it affects the quality of the environment.
c. only because it is "federal."
d. only because it is "major."

___ **7.** Red Glow Power Plant burns fossil fuels. Under the Clean Air Act and EPA regulations, as major new source of possible pollution, to reduce emissions the plant must use

a. the best available technology (BAT).
b. the lowest common denominator (LCD).
c. the maximum achievable control technology (MACT).
d. the minimum allowable technology (MAT).

___ **8.** Auto Motors Corporation (AMC) does not manufacture its cars to comply with current EPA sta dards for automobile exhaust emissions. The EPA can order

a. AMC's lender to pay clean-up costs.
b. AMC to recall its cars and repair or replace the exhaust controls.
c. customers to fix their AMC cars at the customers' expense.
d. the export of the cars to any non-adjacent country.